GOOD NEWS!

What is this Good News of Christmas? It's the amazing news that . . .

- God loves you
- God has sent a Savior
- God will never leave his own
- God wants you to be with him forever

Would you like to know more about the God who loves you and who sent his Son to be your Savior? If you would, here are some simple ways that you can find out more.

First, we encourage you to visit your local church this Christmas season to hear more about the good news of Christmas.

Second, inside this special Bible you'll find two "Christmas Reflections" that you can read yourself or with your family on Christmas Eve and on Christmas Day (see pages vi and vii).

Third, try reading this Bible, where you'll find out more about the God who loves you and who sent his Son to save you. A good place to start is to look through the pages located in the front of this Bible. These include a reading guide on "Where to Find Help" (page ix), another on "What the New Testament Says About" (pages x–xii), and a Bible reading plan called "Getting Started: A 30-Day New Testament Reading Plan" (page xiv). And, read the pages at the end of this Bible, which tell more about "God's Plan to Save You" (pages 211–214).

May this season be for you a time of great joy, filled with the Good News of Christmas!

God bless you this Christmas!

THE
Holy Bible
NEW TESTAMENT

ESV®
ENGLISH STANDARD VERSION

CROSSWAY
WHEATON, ILLINOIS

RRD	18	17	16	15	14	13	12	11	10	09
11	10	9	8	7	6	5	4	3	2	

CONTENTS

THE NEW TESTAMENT

READINGS AND REFLECTIONS FOR CHRISTMAS EVE

She will bear a son,
and you shall call his name Jesus,
for he will save his people from their sins.
(Matthew 1:21)

There is a special blessing in the Christmas message that is frequently missed by many. The birth of Jesus is not simply an interesting fact of history, wholly unrelated to present-day life. Rather it has direct bearing on your life and mine. Here's why.

Something extraordinary happened before Jesus was born. First the angel Gabriel came from heaven and announced to Mary that she would bear a child and that the child would be "the Son of God" (Luke 1:35). Then, sometime later, an angel came to Joseph and told him that Mary's baby had been conceived by the Holy Spirit and that Joseph must "call his name Jesus, for he will save his people from their sins" (Matthew 1:21).

Have you ever thought that it was for you that the Savior was born? Did you realize that when God sent his Son into the world, he sent him to become your Savior? Listen to the words of the angel who first proclaimed the birth of Jesus: "I bring you good news of great joy that will be for all the people. For unto you is born this day in the city of David a Savior, who is Christ the Lord" (Luke 2:10–11).

Jesus Christ did not come to be the inspiration for sacred art. Nor to be the theme of Christmas songs. Nor to be a great moral teacher. No, Jesus came to be the Savior—he was born for me, he was born for you.

How did Jesus become our Savior? Bound inseparably with Jesus' birth is the fact of Jesus' death. He came to save, and to save he had to die—to die in our place as sinners, to pay the full penalty for our sin, to bear the divine wrath of God that each one of us deserves. Just as Jesus was born personally for you, so also Jesus died personally for you.

What an amazing, personal message of God's love and grace—a message that likewise calls for our personal response. The Savior who was born is God's gift to you—a gift that can only be received by faith, by believing that Jesus was actually born to be your Savior and that he died for your sins. And because he rose again, he conquered sin and death, and he offers you, and to all who will receive it, the gift of life and joy—here and now, and for all eternity, in the presence of Jesus forever.

Won't you receive the gift of God this Christmas?

—Dr. Willard M. Aldrich*

Special Christmas Eve Scripture Readings:
Matthew 1:18–25 (page 1) • Luke 1:26–38 (pages 44–45)

*Adapted from the tract *Christmas Blessings to You* by Dr. Willard M. Aldrich, especially for this special Christmas edition of the ESV® New Testament.

READINGS AND REFLECTIONS FOR CHRISTMAS DAY

Glory to God in the highest,
and on earth peace ...
(Luke 2:14)

No matter where you look today, peace seems to be in very short supply. Each day the headlines seem to tell of some new financial or political crisis that threatens to plunge the whole world into chaos. People everywhere, here and around the world, are seeking frantically for something—anything—that will give them hope and peace of mind and heart.

We need to hear again those familiar words of the Christmas angels, spoken so many centuries ago to a small band of Jewish shepherds: "Glory to God in the highest, and on earth peace ..." (Luke 2:14).

But are those words really true? Can God's peace become a reality in our lives and in our world? Or was the promise of the angels just a hollow, empty hope, unrealistic for life as it really is?

Yes, peace is possible—possible not because people have discovered some new scheme of formula for instant peace, but because God's Son, born two thousand years ago, has come into the world. It is possible because that same Son who entered the world on that first Christmas Day wants to enter our lives today. As the prophet Isaiah predicted some seven hundred years before Jesus' birth: "his name shall be called Wonderful Counselor, Mighty God, Everlasting Father, Prince of Peace" (Isaiah 9:6).

The miracle of Christmas is that we can be at peace with God! We can come into a personal relationship with him and be restored and renewed. We can be born again spiritually by the grace of God.

It has been almost two thousand years since the angels hovered over the countryside in Judea, declaring their Good News to the shepherds: "Glory to God in the highest, and on earth peace ..." (Luke 2:14). Sadly, so much of the world still knows very little peace.

But God's peace is real, and it becomes a reality whenever people turn to Christ as their Savior and follow him as their Lord. In the midst of the difficulties and crises of life we can know "the peace of God, which surpasses all understanding" (Philippians 4:7).

And someday the Christ who came so humbly at Christmas will come again in glory to establish his eternal kingdom—and our world will finally know the peace of God in the deepest sense, forevermore.

—Billy Graham*

Special Christmas Day Scripture Readings:
Matthew 2:1-12 (pages 1-2); Luke 2:1-20 (page 46)

*Adapted from the tract *Prince of Peace* by Billy Graham, especially for this special Christmas edition of the ESV® New Testament.

Where To Find Help
When You Are . . .

AFRAID
John 14:27; 2 Timothy 1:7; Hebrews 13:6;
1 John 4:18

ANGRY
Matthew 5:22-24; Romans 12:10-21;
Ephesians 4:26, 31-32; James 1:19-20

ANXIOUS / WORRIED
Matthew 6:25-34; Philippians 4:6-7;
Luke 12:22, 25, 31; 1 Peter 5:7

BEREAVED
John 11:25; 14:1-3; 1 Corinthians 15:55;
2 Corinthians 5:1; Philippians 1:21;
1 Thessalonians 4:13-18; 1 Peter 1:3-4

BITTER / RESENTFUL
Matthew 6:14-15; Romans 12:14, 17-19;
Ephesians 4:31-32; Hebrews 12:14-15;
1 Peter 2:23

DEPRESSED
Matthew 11:28-30; Romans 8:28;
Philippians 4:13

DISCOURAGED / DISAPPOINTED
Matthew 11:28-30; Romans 8:28;
2 Corinthians 4:8-9, 16-18; Galatians 6:9;
Philippians 1:6; 4:6-7, 19; 1 Thessalonians
3:3; Hebrews 10:35-36; 1 Peter 1:6-9

DISTRAUGHT / UPSET
Luke 18:1-8; Hebrews 12:3; 13:5; 1 Peter 5:7

DOUBTING
Matthew 8:26; John 6:37; Philippians 1:6;
2 Timothy 1:12; Hebrews 11:6; 12:2;
James 1:6, 8; 1 John 5:13

FAR FROM GOD
Luke 15:11-24; Revelation 2:4-5

HOPELESS
Romans 15:13; Colossians 1:3-5, 27;
2 Thessalonians 2:16-17; Hebrews 11:1

JEALOUS / ENVIOUS
1 Corinthians 3:3; Galatians 5:19-21, 26;
Hebrews 13:5; James 3:16; 5:9

IMPATIENT
Romans 5:3-5; 8:25; 12:12; Galatians 5:19-
21

LONELY
John 14:15-21; Acts 2:25-26; Hebrews
13:5-6

SAD
2 Corinthians 1:3-4; 2 Thessalonians 2:16-
17; Hebrews 4:15-16

SICK
Matthew 18:19; 2 Corinthians 12:7-9;
James 1:6; 5:13-16

SUFFERING
Matthew 5:10-12; John 15:18-20;
Romans 8:35-39; 2 Corinthians 12:10;
2 Timothy 3:12; James 1:12; 1 Peter 4:12-14;
Revelation 2:10

TEMPTED
Matthew 4:1-4, 11; 26:41; Luke 17:1;
1 Corinthians 10:12-13; 1 Timothy 6:9;
Hebrews 4:15; James 1:2-3, 12-15; 4:7

TROUBLED BY WRONG THOUGHTS
Philippians 4:8; Colossians 3:2

WEAK
Romans 5:6; 2 Corinthians 12:9-10;
Ephesians 3:16; Philippians 4:13

WITHHOLDING FORGIVENESS
Matthew 6:14-15; 18:21-22; Mark 11:25;
Luke 6:37-38; 11:4; 23:34; Ephesians 4:32

WHAT THE NEW TESTAMENT SAYS ABOUT . . .

ACCEPTANCE
John 6:37; Romans 12:3, 6; Ephesians 1:5; 3:20

ANGELS/DEMONS
Matthew 10:1; 28:18; 22:30; Mark 1:13; Luke 4:41; 7:21; 2 Corinthians 11:14; Ephesians 6:10-18; Hebrews 1:3-4; 13:2; 1 Peter 1:12; Revelation 12:11

CHURCH
Acts 2:41; Romans 8:17; 12:5; 1 Corinthians 1:2; Ephesians 5:25; Colossians 1:18; Hebrews 2:11-12; 10:24-25

COURAGE
Acts 4:13-31; Ephesians 6:10-18

COVENANT
Matthew 26:26-28; 2 Corinthians 3:5-6; Hebrews 8:6-7; 13; 9:15; 12:22, 24

DEATH
John 11:25; 14:1-3; 1 Corinthians 15:54; 2 Corinthians 5:1; Philippians 1:21; 3:20-21; 2 Timothy 1:10

DISCIPLESHIP
Matthew 10:24-25; 10:38-39, 42; 12:49; 28:19-20; John 8:31-32; 14:15

DIVORCE
Matthew 5:32; 19:3-6, 9; 1 Corinthians 7:10-13

DRINKING AND DRUGS
Luke 4:18-36; John 8:36; Romans 6:11-13; 1 Corinthians 6:9-11; 10:13; Ephesians 5:18

ETERNITY
John 3:16; 4:14; 10:27-28; Romans 6:23; 1Corinthians 15:54-55; Hebrews 13:8; Revelation 21:1, 3; 22:5

FAITH
Matthew 17:20; Mark 11:22-26; Romans 1:17; 5:1-2; 10:8-11, 17; Hebrews 11; 12:2; 1 Peter 1:6-9

FINANCIAL DIFFICULTIES
Matthew 6:33; Philippians 4:19; 1 Timothy 6:10; 1 John 5:14-15

FORGIVENESS
Matthew 6:14-15; 18:21-22; Luke 6:37-38; 11:4; 23:34; John 8:11; Ephesians 4:32; Colossians 1:13-14; 2:13; Hebrews 10:18; 1 John 1:9

GIVING
Matthew 6:3-4; 25:40; Luke 6:38; 2 Corinthians 9:6-12

GODLINESS
1 Timothy 4:7-8; 6:6; 6:11; 2 Timothy 3:12; 2 Peter 1:5-8

GOD'S LOVE
John 3:16; 15:13-16; Romans 5:8; 8:38-39; Ephesians 3:16-19; 5:1-2; Hebrews 12:6; 1 John 3:1; 4:9-18

GOD'S POWER
Mark 14:60-62; John 2:18-22; Romans 1:16; 1 Corinthians 6:14; Ephesians 3:20-21; Colossians 2:11-12; 2 Peter 1:3

GOD'S WILL
Matthew 6:10; 12:50; Mark 14:36; John 4:34; 6:38-40; 1 John 2:17; 5:14; Romans 12:2

GOD'S WORD
2 Timothy 3:16; Hebrews 4:12; 2 Peter 1:21

GRACE
John 1:14-18; Acts 15:11; Romans 5:1-2; 2 Corinthians 12:7-10; Ephesians 1:3-7; 2:4-9; Titus 2:11-13; Hebrews 4:15-16

GRATITUDE
1 Thessalonians 5:18; Colossians 3:17

HAPPINESS
Matthew 5:11-12; Luke 2:10-11; Philippians 4:4; 1 Peter 1:8-9

HEALING
Matthew 18:19; 2 Corinthians 12:7-9; James 1:6; 5:13-16

HEAVEN
1 Corinthians 15:55, 57; 2 Corinthians 5:6-8; Philippians 1:21-24; 1 John 3:2; Revelation 21

HELL
Matthew 5:22; 10:28; Mark 9:44;
Luke 16:23-24; 2 Thessalonians 1:8-9;
Hebrews 9:27; Revelation 20:10-15

HONESTY
Acts 24:16; Ephesians 4:25, 28;
1 Timothy 1:5; Titus 2:7

HONOR
John 12:26; Romans 12:17; 1 Peter 2:17

HOPE
Romans 15:13; Colossians 1:3-5, 27;
2 Thessalonians 2:16-17; Hebrews 11:1

HOSPITALITY
Romans 12:13; Hebrews 13:2; 1 Peter 4:9

IDENTITY
1 Corinthians 3:16; 2 Corinthians 5:17;
Galatians 4:6-7; Ephesians 2:19

IMMORALITY
John 8:11; 1 Corinthians 6:13-20;
1 Thessalonians 5:23; 1 John 1:9

JOY
Luke 15:7; John 15:11; Romans 5:11;
Galatians 5:22; Philippians 4:4

JUDGMENT
Matthew 12:36; John 5:24; Romans 8:1;
1 Corinthians 3:11-15; 2 Corinthians 5:10;
Hebrews 9:27; Revelation 20:12-13

JUSTIFICATION
Romans 3:24; 5:1; Galatians 2:16; 2:21;
3:11; 2 Corinthians 5:21

LOVE
Matthew 22:37-40; John 13:34-35; 14:21-
24; 15:13; Romans 12:9-10; 1 Corinthians
13;
1 John 3:14; 4:11-21; 5:2

MARRIAGE
Matthew 19:3-6; 1 Corinthians 7:2-5;
Ephesians 5:22-32; Hebrews 13:4;
1 Peter 3:1-7

MERCY
Matthew 5:7; Luke 6:36; 10:30-35;
Romans 9:15; Colossians 3:12; James 2:13

MONEY
Matthew 6:24; Luke 6:38; 12:15;
1 Thessalonians 4:11-12; 1 Timothy 6:7-9;
Hebrews 13:5

OCCULT
Galatians 5:19-21; 2 Timothy 3:1-15;
Revelation 21:8

PATIENCE
Romans 5:3-5; 8:25; 12:12; Galatians 5:19-
21; Philippians 4:11; Hebrews 10:35-36;
James 1:2-4; 5:7-8

PEACE
John 14:27; 16:33; Romans 5:1; 8:6; 14:17-
19; Philippians 4:6-7; Colossians 3:15

PERSECUTION / SUFFERING
Matthew 5:10-12; John 15:18-20;
Romans 8:35-39; 2 Corinthians 12:10;
2 Timothy 3:12; James 1:12; 1 Peter 4:12-
14; Revelation 2:10

PERSEVERANCE
Mark 13:13; 1 Corinthians 15:58; Galatians
6:9; Philippians 3:14; Colossians 1:23;
2 Thessalonians 3:13; 2 Timothy 4:7;
Hebrews 10:23; 12:1-2; James 1:25

PRAYER
Matthew 6:6-7; 7:7; 26:39; Mark 11:24; John
14:13-14; 15:7; Romans 8:26; Ephesians
3:12; 6:18; Philippians 4:6; 1 Thessalonians
5:17-18; 1 Timothy 2:8; Hebrews 4:16;
James 5:16

PRIDE
James 4:6; 1 Peter 5:5-7

PURITY
Matthew 5:8; 1 Corinthians 6:18;
Philippians 4:8; Colossians 3:5; 1 Timothy
4:12;
2 Timothy 2:22; Titus 1:15; Hebrews 13:4;
1 Peter 1:22

SALVATION
John 1:12; 3:3, 16; 14:6; Acts 2:21;
Romans 3:23; 6:23; 10:9, 13; Ephesians 2:8;
Hebrews 9:22

SATAN
Luke 10:18; 13:16; John 8:44; 2 Corinthians
4:4; 11:3; Ephesians 6:11-18; James 4:7-8;
1 Peter 5:8-9; Revelation 12:9-10

SEXUAL PERVERSION
Romans 1:27-32; 12:2; 1 Corinthians 6:9-11;
10:13; Ephesians 4:22-24; 5:3-5; Hebrews
13:4

SHARING FAITH
Matthew 28:19; Romans 10:15;
2 Timothy 4:2; 1 Peter 3:15

SIN
John 6:37; Acts 10:43; 13:38-39; Romans
6:12-14; Ephesians 1:7; Colossians 3:5;
James 1:14; 1 John 1:7-9

STRENGTH
Romans 5:6; 2 Corinthians 12:9-10;
Ephesians 3:16; 6:10; Philippians 4:13

TRUTH
John 4:24; 8:31-32; 14:6; 16:13; Ephesians
6:14; Philippians 4:8; 2 Timothy 2:15

UNITY
John 17:20-21; Acts 4:32; Romans 12:16;
14:19; 15:5-6; 1 Corinthians 1:10; Ephesians
4:4-6; Philippians 1:27; 1 Peter 3:8

VICTORY OVER SIN
Matthew 6:13; John 16:33; Romans 8:37;
1 John 4:4; 5:4

WORK
Acts 20:35; 1 Thessalonians 4:11-12;
2 Thessalonians 3:7-8

How To Read The
New Testament

Reading the New Testament is different from reading any other book. So it helps to have a few suggestions on how to get started. The most important thing is to open your heart and mind to understand that these are God's words to you. Believe that God's truth is contained in his book, and you'll discover that it has the power to transform your life.

Getting started is the most important step, and to help you get started we've provided a "30-Day Bible Reading Plan," as shown on page xiv. This plan provides a good way to get an overview of the New Testament by reading some of its best-loved key passages. When you are ready to read through the entire New Testament, turn to the "Six-Month New Testament Reading Plan" on page 215.

It is especially helpful to read the Scriptures daily and to ask God to show you his truth for your life as you read. Your prayer can be as simple as "Dear God, show me what your words mean and help me apply them to my life." As you seek to know God through reading his Word, his Holy Spirit will guide you in your reading. You may also find it helpful to write down what you discover. You'll be surprised by the insights that you've received.

The New Testament is a powerful book on its own, but it is really the second half of an even grander story that spans all of history. The Old and New Testaments together form the complete Holy Bible, and once you have absorbed the truth and teachings of the New Testament, it would be helpful and fitting for you to explore the Old Testament. This will give you the background on God's redemptive plan and shed light on everything that happens in the New Testament. For information on where to find a copy of the Bible, visit www.esv.org.

Lastly, it will be especially helpful to find other people and a church that love and read and teach the Bible—a place where you can find fellowship and discover the riches of God's Word together. So don't be afraid to get started. You are about to begin the most important adventure of your life!

Getting Started:
A 30-Day New Testament Reading Plan

If this is your first time exploring the New Testament and you're looking for suggestions on where to start, we offer this 30-day reading program to help you gain an overall understanding of what the New Testament is all about. In 30 days you will read some of the most important New Testament passages, and you will begin to see the big picture of what God has done.

Day 1	Luke 1–2	The Birth of Jesus
Day 2	John 1:1-18	Who Jesus Is
Day 3	Luke 4:14-44	Jesus Begins His Ministry
Day 4	Matthew 5–6	The Core of Jesus' Teaching
Day 5	John 3	God's Love for the World
Day 6	John 5	Jesus' Miracles and Authority
Day 7	John 11	Jesus' Power Over Death
Day 8	John 15	The Christian Life Defined
Day 9	John 17	Jesus' High Priestly Prayer
Day 10	Matthew 26–27	The Arrest and Crucifixion of Jesus
Day 11	John 20	The Resurrection of Jesus
Day 12	Luke 24	The Ascension of Jesus
Day 13	Acts 2	The Coming of the Holy Spirit
Day 14	Acts 9	The Conversion of Saul
Day 15	Acts 16	The Gospel Spreads to Europe
Day 16	Acts 26	Paul's Defense of the Christian Faith
Day 17	Romans 3	Justification by Faith Alone
Day 18	Romans 7–8	The Battle With Sin: Life in the Spirit
Day 19	1 Corinthians 13	The Way of Love
Day 20	1 Corinthians 15	The Power of the Resurrection
Day 21	Galatians 5	Freedom in Christ
Day 22	Ephesians 4:1-16	Unity in Christ
Day 23	Ephesians 6	The Whole Armor of God
Day 24	Philippians 1:18–2:18	Christ's Example
Day 25	Colossians 3:1-17	Putting on the New Self
Day 26	Hebrews 4:14–5:10	Jesus the Great High Priest
Day 27	James 1	Pure Religion
Day 28	1 Peter 1:13-25	Called to Be Holy
Day 29	1 John 4:7-21	God Is Love
Day 30	Revelation 21–22	The New Heaven and Earth

The
NEW TESTAMENT

INTRODUCTION

As you turn now to the Gospel of Matthew, keep in mind that a long period of time had passed—traditionally called the 400 years of silence—since the last words of the Old Testament had been written. Although the prophets were "silent," however, God was working as one world empire after another rose and fell. If you study the Old Testament prophecies of Daniel (2:24, 45; 7:1-28; 8:1-17; 11:1-35), you'll see that these historical events occurred precisely as God had said they would. During this period, the small nation of Israel languished under the control of the Persians, the Greeks, and Rome.

The New Testament begins with the birth of Jesus Christ. Four hundred years of prophetic silence is broken by John the Baptist's announcement that the promised Savior has come.

The 27 books of the New Testament were written by eight or nine authors. The first book of the New Testament, probably one of Paul's letters, was written about A.D. 50, and John's Revelation, probably the last book written, would be dated around A.D. 95. The focus of the New Testament is the person of Jesus Christ—his life and teachings, his death, burial, resurrection, and ascension into heaven—as well as the coming of the Holy Spirit and the establishment of God's church.

The New Testament was written in Greek. Greek was spoken throughout the Roman Empire, including Palestine, where Aramaic and Hebrew were also used. The original manuscripts of the New Testament have not been found, but more than 5,000 ancient manuscripts that range from whole Testaments to scraps of papyri containing as little as one verse provide an extraordinary library of manuscripts that far exceeds the existing fragments of any other ancient literature. A few New Testament fragments date back to within 25-50 years of the original writing.

The New Testament books may be divided into four major categories:

THE GOSPELS

The first four books—Matthew, Mark, Luke, and John—are called the Gospels. The word *gospel* means "good news." The Gospels cover a period from approximately 5 B.C. to A.D. 30 and contain the good news of the most significant story in all of history—the story of God's Son, Jesus Christ. The four Gospels present different aspects of what Jesus did and said. These books are not biographies and were not written merely to report the events of Jesus' life. Their primary purpose is to define Jesus' birth, teachings, death, burial, and resurrection in an authoritative manner. Each of the Gospels is written from a unique perspective and for a different audience, and thus each Gospel has distinctive features.

A HISTORY OF THE EARLY CHURCH

The book of Acts provides a transition between the Gospels and the epistles or letters of the apostles. Beginning with Christ's ascension into heaven, it resumes the story that was begun in the Gospel of Luke and provides a historical account of the coming of the Holy Spirit on the Day of Pentecost, the birth of the church, and the tremendous spread and growth of the church all the way to Rome despite fierce persecution. The focus of this book is upon the ministry of the Holy Spirit in carrying out the saving work of Jesus Christ in the world, with most of the attention on the ministries of Peter and Paul. The followers of Jesus Christ were empowered and directed by the Holy Spirit to take the good news of Christ's salvation throughout the world.

THE LETTERS

The following 21 books—Romans, 1–2 Corinthians, Galatians, Ephesians, Philippians, Colossians, 1–2 Thessalonians, 1–2 Timothy, Titus, Philemon, Hebrews, James, 1–2 Peter, 1-2-3 John, and Jude—are "epistles" or letters written to churches or individuals to tell about the person and work of Christ and how believers are to live their lives until he returns. The struggles and problems of various believers are addressed in these letters. The inspired answers to these problems, whether regarding doctrine or spiritual unity or questions on marriage, remain as valid and as practical today as when they were written 2,000 years ago.

THE BOOK OF PROPHECY

The final book of the Bible—Revelation—begins with the apostle John addressing the churches of his day and culminates with a glorious vision of Christ's future return to the earth. It was written as an encouragement to believers who were facing great danger, and its full relevance remains for today's believer. Although there are different interpretations of Revelation, Christians can know with absolute certainty that Christ will triumph over all the evil in the world and that they will share in the final victory with Jesus at the end of time.

MATTHEW

Introduction

The Gospel of Matthew presents Jesus as Israel's Messiah. The account alternates between Jesus' activities of healing and casting out demons, and major blocks of his teaching, including the Sermon on the Mount (chs. 5–7), the Parables of the Kingdom (ch. 13), and the Olivet Discourse (chs. 24–25). The Sermon on the Mount includes the Beatitudes (5:3-12) and the Lord's Prayer (6:5-15). The book closes with the Great Commission (28:18-20). A recurring theme is the conflict between Jesus and the religious leaders, culminating in his pronouncement of "seven woes" upon them (ch. 23). As do all four Gospel accounts, Matthew focuses on Christ's three-year ministry and his death and resurrection. Matthew probably wrote his Gospel in the 50s or 60s A.D.

The Genealogy of Jesus Christ

1 The book of the genealogy of Jesus Christ, the son of David, the son of Abraham.

²Abraham was the father of Isaac, and Isaac the father of Jacob, and Jacob the father of Judah and his brothers, ³and Judah the father of Perez and Zerah by Tamar, and Perez the father of Hezron, and Hezron the father of Ram,¹ ⁴and Ram the father of Amminadab, and Amminadab the father of Nahshon, and Nahshon the father of Salmon, ⁵and Salmon the father of Boaz by Rahab, and Boaz the father of Obed by Ruth, and Obed the father of Jesse, ⁶and Jesse the father of David the king.

And David was the father of Solomon by the wife of Uriah, ⁷and Solomon the father of Rehoboam, and Rehoboam the father of Abijah, and Abijah the father of Asaph,² ⁸and Asaph the father of Jehoshaphat, and Jehoshaphat the father of Joram, and Joram the father of Uzziah, ⁹and Uzziah the father of Jotham, and Jotham the father of Ahaz, and Ahaz the father of Hezekiah, ¹⁰and Hezekiah the father of Manasseh, and Manasseh the father of Amos,³ and Amos the father of Josiah, ¹¹and Josiah the father of Jechoniah and his brothers, at the time of the deportation to Babylon.

¹²And after the deportation to Babylon: Jechoniah was the father of Shealtiel,⁴ and Shealtiel the father of Zerubbabel, ¹³and Zerubbabel the father of Abiud, and Abiud the father of Eliakim, and Eliakim the father of Azor, ¹⁴and Azor the father of Zadok, and Zadok the father of Achim, and Achim the father of Eliud, ¹⁵and Eliud the father of Eleazar, and Eleazar the father of Matthan, and Matthan the father of Jacob, ¹⁶and Jacob the father of Joseph the husband of Mary, of whom Jesus was born, who is called Christ.

¹⁷So all the generations from Abraham to David were fourteen generations, and from David to the deportation to Babylon fourteen generations, and from the deportation to Babylon to the Christ fourteen generations.

The Birth of Jesus Christ

¹⁸Now the birth of Jesus Christ⁵ took place in this way. When his mother Mary had been betrothed⁶ to Joseph, before they came together she was found to be with child from the Holy Spirit. ¹⁹And her husband Joseph, being a just man and unwilling to put her to shame, resolved to divorce her quietly. ²⁰But as he considered these things, behold, an angel of the Lord appeared to him in a dream, saying, "Joseph, son of David, do not fear to take Mary as your wife, for that which is conceived in her is from the Holy Spirit. ²¹She will bear a son, and you shall call his name Jesus, for he will save his people from their sins." ²²All this took place to fulfill what the Lord had spoken by the prophet:

²³ ᵃ"Behold, the virgin shall conceive and bear a son,
and they shall call his name Immanuel"

(which means, God with us). ²⁴When Joseph woke from sleep, he did as the angel of the Lord commanded him: he took his wife, ²⁵but knew her not until she had given birth to a son. And he called his name Jesus.

The Visit of the Wise Men

2 Now after Jesus was born in Bethlehem of Judea in the days of Herod the king, behold, wise men⁷ from the east came to Jerusalem, ²saying, "Where is he who has been born king of the Jews? For we saw his star when it rose⁸ and have come to worship him." ³When Herod the king heard this, he was troubled, and all Jerusalem with him; ⁴and assembling all the chief priests and scribes of the people, he inquired of them where the Christ was to be born. ⁵They told him, "In Bethlehem of Judea, for so it is written by the prophet:

⁶ᵇ"'And you, O Bethlehem, in the land of Judah,
are by no means least among the rulers of Judah;

---

¹Greek *Aram*; also verse 4 ²*Asaph* is probably an alternate spelling for *Asa*; some manuscripts read *Asa*; also verse 8 ³*Amos* is probably an alternate spelling for *Amon*; some manuscripts read *Amon*; twice in this verse ⁴Greek *Salathiel*; twice in this verse ⁵Some manuscripts read *of the Christ* ⁶That is, legally pledged to be married ⁷Greek *magi*; also verses 7, 16 ⁸Or *in the east*; also verse 9 ᵃIsa. 7:14 ᵇMic. 5:2

for from you shall come a ruler
  who will shepherd my people Israel.'"

7Then Herod summoned the wise men secretly and ascertained from them what time the star had appeared. **8**And he sent them to Bethlehem, saying, "Go and search diligently for the child, and when you have found him, bring me word, that I too may come and worship him." **9**After listening to the king, they went on their way. And behold, the star that they had seen when it rose went before them until it came to rest over the place where the child was. **10**When they saw the star, they rejoiced exceedingly with great joy. **11**And going into the house they saw the child with Mary his mother, and they fell down and worshiped him. Then, opening their treasures, they offered him gifts, gold and frankincense and myrrh. **12**And being warned in a dream not to return to Herod, they departed to their own country by another way.

The Flight to Egypt

13Now when they had departed, behold, an angel of the Lord appeared to Joseph in a dream and said, "Rise, take the child and his mother, and flee to Egypt, and remain there until I tell you, for Herod is about to search for the child, to destroy him." **14**And he rose and took the child and his mother by night and departed to Egypt **15**and remained there until the death of Herod. This was to fulfill what the Lord had spoken by the prophet, *a*"Out of Egypt I called my son."

Herod Kills the Children

16Then Herod, when he saw that he had been tricked by the wise men, became furious, and he sent and killed all the male children in Bethlehem and in all that region who were two years old or under, according to the time that he had ascertained from the wise men. **17**Then was fulfilled what was spoken by the prophet Jeremiah:

18 *b*"A voice was heard in Ramah,
  weeping and loud lamentation,
Rachel weeping for her children;
  she refused to be comforted, because they
    are no more."

The Return to Nazareth

19But when Herod died, behold, an angel of the Lord appeared in a dream to Joseph in Egypt, **20**saying, "Rise, take the child and his mother and go to the land of Israel, for those who sought the child's life are dead." **21**And he rose and took the child and his mother and went to the land of Israel. **22**But when he heard that Archelaus was reigning over Judea in place of his father Herod, he was afraid to go there, and being warned in a dream he withdrew to the district of Galilee. **23**And he went and lived in a city called Naza-

reth, that what was spoken by the prophets might be fulfilled: "He shall be called a Nazarene."

John the Baptist Prepares the Way

3 *c*In those days John the Baptist came preaching in the wilderness of Judea, **2**"Repent, for the kingdom of heaven is at hand." **3**For this is he who was spoken of by the prophet Isaiah when he said,

d"The voice of one crying in the wilderness:
  'Prepare *1* the way of the Lord;
    make his paths straight.'"

4Now John wore a garment of camel's hair and a leather belt around his waist, and his food was locusts and wild honey. **5**Then Jerusalem and all Judea and all the region about the Jordan were going out to him, **6**and they were baptized by him in the river Jordan, confessing their sins.

7But when he saw many of the Pharisees and Sadducees coming to his baptism, he said to them, "You brood of vipers! Who warned you to flee from the wrath to come? **8**Bear fruit in keeping with repentance. **9**And do not presume to say to yourselves, 'We have Abraham as our father,' for I tell you, God is able from these stones to raise up children for Abraham. **10**Even now the axe is laid to the root of the trees. Every tree therefore that does not bear good fruit is cut down and thrown into the fire.

11"I baptize you with water for repentance, but he who is coming after me is mightier than I, whose sandals I am not worthy to carry. He will baptize you with the Holy Spirit and fire. **12**His winnowing fork is in his hand, and he will clear his threshing floor and gather his wheat into the barn, but the chaff he will burn with unquenchable fire."

The Baptism of Jesus

13*e*Then Jesus came from Galilee to the Jordan to John, to be baptized by him. **14**John would have prevented him, saying, "I need to be baptized by you, and do you come to me?" **15**But Jesus answered him, "Let it be so now, for thus it is fitting for us to fulfill all righteousness." Then he consented. **16**And when Jesus was baptized, immediately he went up from the water, and behold, the heavens were opened to him,*2* and he saw the Spirit of God descending like a dove and coming to rest on him; **17**and behold, a voice from heaven said, "This is my beloved Son,*3* with whom I am well pleased."

The Temptation of Jesus

4 *f*Then Jesus was led up by the Spirit into the wilderness to be tempted by the devil. **2**And after fasting forty days and forty nights, he was hungry. **3**And the tempter came and said to him, "If you are the Son of God, command these

---

1 Or crying: *Prepare in the wilderness* 2 Some manuscripts omit *to him* 3 Or *my Son, my* (or *the*) *Beloved* a Hos. 11:1 b Jer. 31:15 c For 3:1-12 see parallels Mark 1:2-8; Luke 3:1-17 d Isa. 40:3 e For 3:13-17 see parallels Mark 1:9-11; Luke 3:21, 22 f For 4:1-11 see parallels Mark 1:12, 13; Luke 4:1-13

stones to become loaves of bread." ⁴But he answered, "It is written,

> ᵃ"'Man shall not live by bread alone,
> but by every word that comes from the
> mouth of God.'"

⁵Then the devil took him to the holy city and set him on the pinnacle of the temple ⁶and said to him, "If you are the Son of God, throw yourself down, for it is written,

> ᵇ"'He will command his angels concerning you,'

and

> "'On their hands they will bear you up,
> lest you strike your foot against a stone.'"

⁷Jesus said to him, "Again it is written, ᶜ'You shall not put the Lord your God to the test.'" ⁸Again, the devil took him to a very high mountain and showed him all the kingdoms of the world and their glory. ⁹And he said to him, "All these I will give you, if you will fall down and worship me." ¹⁰Then Jesus said to him, "Be gone, Satan! For it is written,

> ᵈ"'You shall worship the Lord your God
> and him only shall you serve.'"

¹¹Then the devil left him, and behold, angels came and were ministering to him.

Jesus Begins His Ministry

¹²Now when he heard that John had been arrested, he withdrew into Galilee. ¹³And leaving Nazareth he went and lived in Capernaum by the sea, in the territory of Zebulun and Naphtali, ¹⁴so that what was spoken by the prophet Isaiah might be fulfilled:

¹⁵ ᵉ"The land of Zebulun and the land of Naphtali,
    the way of the sea, beyond the Jordan, Gali-
lee of the Gentiles—
¹⁶   the people dwelling in darkness
        have seen a great light,
    and for those dwelling in the region and
        shadow of death,
    on them a light has dawned."

¹⁷From that time Jesus began to preach, saying, "Repent, for the kingdom of heaven is at hand."

Jesus Calls the First Disciples

¹⁸ᶠWhile walking by the Sea of Galilee, he saw two brothers, Simon (who is called Peter) and Andrew his brother, casting a net into the sea, for they were fishermen. ¹⁹And he said to them, "Follow me, and I will make you fishers of men." ²⁰Immediately they left their nets and followed him. ²¹And going on from there he saw two other brothers, James the son of Zebedee and John his brother, in the boat with Zebedee their father, mending their nets, and he called them. ²²Immediately they left the boat and their father and followed him.

Jesus Ministers to Great Crowds

²³And he went throughout all Galilee, teaching in their synagogues and proclaiming the gospel of the kingdom and healing every disease and every affliction among the people. ²⁴So his fame spread throughout all Syria, and they brought him all the sick, those afflicted with various diseases and pains, those oppressed by demons, epileptics, and paralytics, and he healed them. ²⁵And great crowds followed him from Galilee and the Decapolis, and from Jerusalem and Judea, and from beyond the Jordan.

The Sermon on the Mount

5 Seeing the crowds, he went up on the mountain, and when he sat down, his disciples came to him.

The Beatitudes

²And he opened his mouth and taught them, saying:
³"Blessed are the poor in spirit, for theirs is the kingdom of heaven.
⁴"Blessed are those who mourn, for they shall be comforted.
⁵"Blessed are the meek, for they shall inherit the earth.
⁶"Blessed are those who hunger and thirst for righteousness, for they shall be satisfied.
⁷"Blessed are the merciful, for they shall receive mercy.
⁸"Blessed are the pure in heart, for they shall see God.
⁹"Blessed are the peacemakers, for they shall be called sons¹ of God.
¹⁰"Blessed are those who are persecuted for righteousness' sake, for theirs is the kingdom of heaven.
¹¹"Blessed are you when others revile you and persecute you and utter all kinds of evil against you falsely on my account. ¹²Rejoice and be glad, for your reward is great in heaven, for so they persecuted the prophets who were before you.

Salt and Light

¹³"You are the salt of the earth, but if salt has lost its taste, how shall its saltiness be restored? It is no longer good for anything except to be thrown out and trampled under people's feet. ¹⁴"You are the light of the world. A city set on a hill cannot be hidden. ¹⁵Nor do people light a lamp and put it under a basket, but on a stand, and it gives light to all in the house. ¹⁶In the same way, let your light shine before others, so that they may see your good works and give glory to your Father who is in heaven.

---

¹ Greek huioi; see preface ᵃDeut. 8:3 ᵇPs. 91:11, 12 ᶜDeut. 6:16 ᵈDeut. 6:13 ᵉIsa. 9:1, 2 ᶠFor 4:18-22 see parallel Mark 1:16-20

Christ Came to Fulfill the Law

¹⁷"Do not think that I have come to abolish the Law or the Prophets; I have not come to abolish them but to fulfill them. ¹⁸For truly, I say to you, until heaven and earth pass away, not an iota, not a dot, will pass from the Law until all is accomplished. ¹⁹Therefore whoever relaxes one of the least of these commandments and teaches others to do the same will be called least in the kingdom of heaven, but whoever does them and teaches them will be called great in the kingdom of heaven. ²⁰For I tell you, unless your righteousness exceeds that of the scribes and Pharisees, you will never enter the kingdom of heaven.

Anger

²¹"You have heard that it was said to those of old, ^a'You shall not murder; and whoever murders will be liable to judgment.' ²²But I say to you that everyone who is angry with his brother[1] will be liable to judgment; whoever insults[2] his brother will be liable to the council; and whoever says, 'You fool!' will be liable to the hell[3] of fire. ²³So if you are offering your gift at the altar and there remember that your brother has something against you, ²⁴leave your gift there before the altar and go. First be reconciled to your brother, and then come and offer your gift. ²⁵Come to terms quickly with your accuser while you are going with him to court, lest your accuser hand you over to the judge, and the judge to the guard, and you be put in prison. ²⁶Truly, I say to you, you will never get out until you have paid the last penny.[4]

Lust

²⁷"You have heard that it was said, ^b'You shall not commit adultery.' ²⁸But I say to you that everyone who looks at a woman with lustful intent has already committed adultery with her in his heart. ²⁹If your right eye causes you to sin, tear it out and throw it away. For it is better that you lose one of your members than that your whole body be thrown into hell. ³⁰And if your right hand causes you to sin, cut it off and throw it away. For it is better that you lose one of your members than that your whole body go into hell.

Divorce

³¹"It was also said, ^c'Whoever divorces his wife, let him give her a certificate of divorce.' ³²But I say to you that everyone who divorces his wife, except on the ground of sexual immorality, makes her commit adultery, and whoever marries a divorced woman commits adultery.

Oaths

³³"Again you have heard that it was said to those of old, 'You shall not swear falsely, but shall perform to the Lord what you have sworn.' ³⁴But I say to you, Do not take an oath at all, either by heaven, for it is the throne of God, ³⁵or by the earth, for it is his footstool, or by Jerusalem, for it is the city of the great King. ³⁶And do not take an oath by your head, for you cannot make one hair white or black. ³⁷Let what you say be simply 'Yes' or 'No'; anything more than this comes from evil.[5]

Retaliation

³⁸"You have heard that it was said, ^d'An eye for an eye and a tooth for a tooth.' ³⁹But I say to you, Do not resist the one who is evil. But ^eif anyone slaps you on the right cheek, turn to him the other also. ⁴⁰And if anyone would sue you and take your tunic,[6] let him have your cloak as well. ⁴¹And if anyone forces you to go one mile, go with him two miles. ⁴²Give to the one who begs from you, and do not refuse the one who would borrow from you.

Love Your Enemies

⁴³"You have heard that it was said, ^f'You shall love your neighbor and hate your enemy.' ⁴⁴But I say to you, Love your enemies and pray for those who persecute you, ⁴⁵so that you may be sons of your Father who is in heaven. For he makes his sun rise on the evil and on the good, and sends rain on the just and on the unjust. ⁴⁶For if you love those who love you, what reward do you have? Do not even the tax collectors do the same? ⁴⁷And if you greet only your brothers,[7] what more are you doing than others? Do not even the Gentiles do the same? ⁴⁸You therefore must be perfect, as your heavenly Father is perfect.

Giving to the Needy

6 "Beware of practicing your righteousness before other people in order to be seen by them, for then you will have no reward from your Father who is in heaven.

²"Thus, when you give to the needy, sound no trumpet before you, as the hypocrites do in the synagogues and in the streets, that they may be praised by others. Truly, I say to you, they have received their reward. ³But when you give to the needy, do not let your left hand know what your right hand is doing, ⁴so that your giving may be in secret. And your Father who sees in secret will reward you.

The Lord's Prayer

⁵"And when you pray, you must not be like the hypocrites. For they love to stand and pray in the synagogues and at the street corners, that they may be seen by others. Truly, I say to you, they

---

[1] Some manuscripts insert *without cause* [2] Greek *says Raca to* (a term of abuse) [3] Greek *Gehenna*; also verses 29, 30 [4] Greek *kodrantes*, Roman copper coin (Latin *quadrans*) worth about 1/64 of a *denarius* (which was a day's wage for a laborer) [5] Or *the evil one* [6] Greek *chiton*, a long garment worn under the cloak next to the skin [7] Or *brothers and sisters*. The plural Greek word *adelphoi* (translated "brothers") refers to siblings in a family. In New Testament usage, depending on the context, *adelphoi* may refer either to *brothers* or to *brothers and sisters*. ^aEx. 20:13; Deut. 5:17 ^bEx. 20:14; Deut. 5:18 ^cDeut. 24:1 ^dEx. 21:24; Lev. 24:20; Deut. 19:21 ^eFor 5:39-42 see parallel Luke 6:29, 30 ^fLev. 19:18

have received their reward. ⁶But when you pray, go into your room and shut the door and pray to your Father who is in secret. And your Father who sees in secret will reward you.

⁷"And when you pray, do not heap up empty phrases as the Gentiles do, for they think that they will be heard for their many words. ⁸Do not be like them, for your Father knows what you need before you ask him. ⁹Pray then like this:

"Our Father in heaven,
     hallowed be your name.¹
¹⁰ Your kingdom come,
     your will be done,²
      on earth as it is in heaven.
¹¹ Give us this day our daily bread,³
¹² and forgive us our debts,
     as we also have forgiven our debtors.
¹³ And lead us not into temptation,
     but deliver us from evil.⁴

¹⁴For if you forgive others their trespasses, your heavenly Father will also forgive you, ¹⁵but if you do not forgive others their trespasses, neither will your Father forgive your trespasses.

Fasting

¹⁶"And when you fast, do not look gloomy like the hypocrites, for they disfigure their faces that their fasting may be seen by others. Truly, I say to you, they have received their reward. ¹⁷But when you fast, anoint your head and wash your face, ¹⁸that your fasting may not be seen by others but by your Father who is in secret. And your Father who sees in secret will reward you.

Lay Up Treasures in Heaven

¹⁹"Do not lay up for yourselves treasures on earth, where moth and rust⁵ destroy and where thieves break in and steal, ²⁰but lay up for yourselves treasures in heaven, where neither moth nor rust destroys and where thieves do not break in and steal. ²¹For where your treasure is, there your heart will be also.

²²"The eye is the lamp of the body. So, if your eye is healthy, your whole body will be full of light, ²³but if your eye is bad, your whole body will be full of darkness. If then the light in you is darkness, how great is the darkness!

²⁴"No one can serve two masters, for either he will hate the one and love the other, or he will be devoted to the one and despise the other. You cannot serve God and money.⁶

Do Not Be Anxious

²⁵ᵃ"Therefore I tell you, do not be anxious about your life, what you will eat or what you will drink, nor about your body, what you will put on. Is not life more than food, and the body

more than clothing? ²⁶Look at the birds of the air: they neither sow nor reap nor gather into barns, and yet your heavenly Father feeds them. Are you not of more value than they? ²⁷And which of you by being anxious can add a single hour to his span of life?⁷ ²⁸And why are you anxious about clothing? Consider the lilies of the field, how they grow: they neither toil nor spin, ²⁹yet I tell you, even Solomon in all his glory was not arrayed like one of these. ³⁰But if God so clothes the grass of the field, which today is alive and tomorrow is thrown into the oven, will he not much more clothe you, O you of little faith? ³¹Therefore do not be anxious, saying, 'What shall we eat?' or 'What shall we drink?' or 'What shall we wear?' ³²For the Gentiles seek after all these things, and your heavenly Father knows that you need them all. ³³But seek first the kingdom of God and his righteousness, and all these things will be added to you.

³⁴"Therefore do not be anxious about tomorrow, for tomorrow will be anxious for itself. Sufficient for the day is its own trouble.

Judging Others

7 ᵇ"Judge not, that you be not judged. ²For with the judgment you pronounce you will be judged, and with the measure you use it will be measured to you. ³Why do you see the speck that is in your brother's eye, but do not notice the log that is in your own eye? ⁴Or how can you say to your brother, 'Let me take the speck out of your eye,' when there is the log in your own eye? ⁵You hypocrite, first take the log out of your own eye, and then you will see clearly to take the speck out of your brother's eye.

⁶"Do not give dogs what is holy, and do not throw your pearls before pigs, lest they trample them underfoot and turn to attack you.

Ask, and It Will Be Given

⁷ᶜ"Ask, and it will be given to you; seek, and you will find; knock, and it will be opened to you. ⁸For everyone who asks receives, and the one who seeks finds, and to the one who knocks it will be opened. ⁹Or which one of you, if his son asks him for bread, will give him a stone? ¹⁰Or if he asks for a fish, will give him a serpent? ¹¹If you then, who are evil, know how to give good gifts to your children, how much more will your Father who is in heaven give good things to those who ask him!

The Golden Rule

¹²"So whatever you wish that others would do to you, do also to them, for this is the Law and the Prophets.

¹³"Enter by the narrow gate. For the gate is

---

¹Or *Let your name be kept holy,* or *Let your name be treated with reverence* ²Or *Let your kingdom come, let your will be done* ³Or *our bread for tomorrow* ⁴Or *the evil one;* some manuscripts add *For yours is the kingdom and the power and the glory, forever. Amen* ⁵Or *worm;* also verse 20 ⁶Greek *mammon,* a Semitic word for money or possessions ⁷Or *a single cubit to his stature; a cubit was about 18 inches or 45 centimeters* ᵃFor 6:25-33 see parallel Luke 12:22-31 ᵇFor 7:1-5 see parallel Luke 6:37, 38, 41, 42 ᶜFor 7:7-11 see parallel Luke 11:9-13

6

wide and the way is easy[1] that leads to destruction, and those who enter by it are many. [14]For the gate is narrow and the way is hard that leads to life, and those who find it are few.

A Tree and Its Fruit

[15]"Beware of false prophets, who come to you in sheep's clothing but inwardly are ravenous wolves. [16]You will recognize them by their fruits. Are grapes gathered from thornbushes, or figs from thistles? [17]So, every healthy tree bears good fruit, but the diseased tree bears bad fruit. [18]A healthy tree cannot bear bad fruit, nor can a diseased tree bear good fruit. [19]Every tree that does not bear good fruit is cut down and thrown into the fire. [20]Thus you will recognize them by their fruits.

I Never Knew You

[21]"Not everyone who says to me, 'Lord, Lord,' will enter the kingdom of heaven, but the one who does the will of my Father who is in heaven. [22]On that day many will say to me, 'Lord, Lord, did we not prophesy in your name, and cast out demons in your name, and do many mighty works in your name?' [23]And then will I declare to them, 'I never knew you; depart from me, you workers of lawlessness.'

Build Your House on the Rock

[24a]"Everyone then who hears these words of mine and does them will be like a wise man who built his house on the rock. [25]And the rain fell, and the floods came, and the winds blew and beat on that house, but it did not fall, because it had been founded on the rock. [26]And everyone who hears these words of mine and does not do them will be like a foolish man who built his house on the sand. [27]And the rain fell, and the floods came, and the winds blew and beat against that house, and it fell, and great was the fall of it."

The Authority of Jesus

[28]And when Jesus finished these sayings, the crowds were astonished at his teaching, [29]for he was teaching them as one who had authority, and not as their scribes.

Jesus Cleanses a Leper

8 When he came down from the mountain, great crowds followed him. [2b]And behold, a leper[2] came to him and knelt before him, saying, "Lord, if you will, you can make me clean." [3]And Jesus[3] stretched out his hand and touched him, saying, "I will; be clean." And immediately his leprosy was cleansed. [4]And Jesus said to him, "See that you say nothing to anyone, but go, show yourself to the priest and offer the gift that Moses commanded, for a proof to them."

The Faith of a Centurion

[5c]When he entered Capernaum, a centurion came forward to him, appealing to him, [6]"Lord, my servant is lying paralyzed at home, suffering terribly." [7]And he said to him, "I will come and heal him." [8]But the centurion replied, "Lord, I am not worthy to have you come under my roof, but only say the word, and my servant will be healed. [9]For I too am a man under authority, with soldiers under me. And I say to one, 'Go,' and he goes, and to another, 'Come,' and he comes, and to my servant,[4] 'Do this,' and he does it." [10]When Jesus heard this, he marveled and said to those who followed him, "Truly, I tell you, with no one in Israel[5] have I found such faith. [11]I tell you, many will come from east and west and recline at table with Abraham, Isaac, and Jacob in the kingdom of heaven, [12]while the sons of the kingdom will be thrown into the outer darkness. In that place there will be weeping and gnashing of teeth." [13]And to the centurion Jesus said, "Go; let it be done for you as you have believed." And the servant was healed at that very moment.

Jesus Heals Many

[14d]And when Jesus entered Peter's house, he saw his mother-in-law lying sick with a fever. [15]He touched her hand, and the fever left her, and she rose and began to serve him. [16]That evening they brought to him many who were oppressed by demons, and he cast out the spirits with a word and healed all who were sick. [17]This was to fulfill what was spoken by the prophet Isaiah: [e]"He took our illnesses and bore our diseases."

The Cost of Following Jesus

[18]Now when Jesus saw a crowd around him, he gave orders to go over to the other side. [19f]And a scribe came up and said to him, "Teacher, I will follow you wherever you go." [20]And Jesus said to him, "Foxes have holes, and birds of the air have nests, but the Son of Man has nowhere to lay his head." [21]Another of the disciples said to him, "Lord, let me first go and bury my father." [22]And Jesus said to him, "Follow me, and leave the dead to bury their own dead."

Jesus Calms a Storm

[23g]And when he got into the boat, his disciples followed him. [24]And behold, there arose a great storm on the sea, so that the boat was being swamped by the waves; but he was asleep. [25]And they went and woke him, saying, "Save us, Lord; we are perishing." [26]And he said to them, "Why are you afraid, O you of little faith?" Then he

---

[1] Some manuscripts *For the way is wide and easy* [2] *Leprosy* was a term for several skin diseases; see Leviticus 13 [3] Greek *he* [4] Greek *bondservant* [5] Some manuscripts *not even in Israel* [a] For 7:24-27 see parallel Luke 6:47-49 [b] For 8:2-4 see parallels Mark 1:40-44; Luke 5:12-14 [c] For 8:5-13 see parallel Luke 7:1-10 [d] For 8:14-17 see parallels Mark 1:29-34; Luke 4:38-41 [e] Isa. 53:4 [f] For 8:19-22 see parallel Luke 9:57-62 [g] For 8:23-27 see parallels Mark 4:35-41; Luke 8:22-25

rose and rebuked the winds and the sea, and there was a great calm. ²⁷And the men marveled, saying, "What sort of man is this, that even winds and sea obey him?"

Jesus Heals Two Men with Demons

²⁸ᵃAnd when he came to the other side, to the country of the Gadarenes,¹ two demon-possessed² men met him, coming out of the tombs, so fierce that no one could pass that way. ²⁹And behold, they cried out, "What have you to do with us, O Son of God? Have you come here to torment us before the time?" ³⁰Now a herd of many pigs was feeding at some distance from them. ³¹And the demons begged him, saying, "If you cast us out, send us away into the herd of pigs." ³²And he said to them, "Go." So they came out and went into the pigs, and behold, the whole herd rushed down the steep bank into the sea and drowned in the waters. ³³The herdsmen fled, and going into the city they told everything, especially what had happened to the demon-possessed men. ³⁴And behold, all the city came out to meet Jesus, and when they saw him, they begged him to leave their region.

Jesus Heals a Paralytic

9 And getting into a boat he crossed over and came to his own city. ²ᵇAnd behold, some people brought to him a paralytic, lying on a bed. And when Jesus saw their faith, he said to the paralytic, "Take heart, my son; your sins are forgiven." ³And behold, some of the scribes said to themselves, "This man is blaspheming." ⁴But Jesus, knowing³ their thoughts, said, "Why do you think evil in your hearts? ⁵For which is easier, to say, 'Your sins are forgiven,' or to say, 'Rise and walk'? ⁶But that you may know that the Son of Man has authority on earth to forgive sins"— he then said to the paralytic—"Rise, pick up your bed and go home." ⁷And he rose and went home. ⁸When the crowds saw it, they were afraid, and they glorified God, who had given such authority to men.

Jesus Calls Matthew

⁹ᶜAs Jesus passed on from there, he saw a man called Matthew sitting at the tax booth, and he said to him, "Follow me." And he rose and followed him.

¹⁰And as Jesus⁴ reclined at table in the house, behold, many tax collectors and sinners came and were reclining with Jesus and his disciples. ¹¹And when the Pharisees saw this, they said to his disciples, "Why does your teacher eat with tax collectors and sinners?" ¹²But when he heard it, he said, "Those who are well have no need of a physician, but those who are sick. ¹³Go and learn what this means, ᵈ'I desire mercy, and not sacrifice.' For I came not to call the righteous, but sinners."

A Question About Fasting

¹⁴Then the disciples of John came to him, saying, "Why do we and the Pharisees fast,⁵ but your disciples do not fast?" ¹⁵And Jesus said to them, "Can the wedding guests mourn as long as the bridegroom is with them? The days will come when the bridegroom is taken away from them, and then they will fast. ¹⁶No one puts a piece of unshrunk cloth on an old garment, for the patch tears away from the garment, and a worse tear is made. ¹⁷Neither is new wine put into old wineskins. If it is, the skins burst and the wine is spilled and the skins are destroyed. But new wine is put into fresh wineskins, and so both are preserved."

A Girl Restored to Life and a Woman Healed

¹⁸ᵉWhile he was saying these things to them, behold, a ruler came in and knelt before him, saying, "My daughter has just died, but come and lay your hand on her, and she will live." ¹⁹And Jesus rose and followed him, with his disciples. ²⁰And behold, a woman who had suffered from a discharge of blood for twelve years came up behind him and touched the fringe of his garment, ²¹for she said to herself, "If I only touch his garment, I will be made well." ²²Jesus turned, and seeing her he said, "Take heart, daughter; your faith has made you well." And instantly⁶ the woman was made well. ²³And when Jesus came to the ruler's house and saw the flute players and the crowd making a commotion, ²⁴he said, "Go away, for the girl is not dead but sleeping." And they laughed at him. ²⁵But when the crowd had been put outside, he went in and took her by the hand, and the girl arose. ²⁶And the report of this went through all that district.

Jesus Heals Two Blind Men

²⁷And as Jesus passed on from there, two blind men followed him, crying aloud, "Have mercy on us, Son of David." ²⁸When he entered the house, the blind men came to him, and Jesus said to them, "Do you believe that I am able to do this?" They said to him, "Yes, Lord." ²⁹Then he touched their eyes, saying, "According to your faith be it done to you." ³⁰And their eyes were opened. And Jesus sternly warned them, "See that no one knows about it." ³¹But they went away and spread his fame through all that district.

Jesus Heals a Man Unable to Speak

³²As they were going away, behold, a demon-oppressed man who was mute was brought to him. ³³And when the demon had been cast out, the mute man spoke. And the crowds marveled,

¹ Some manuscripts *Gergesenes*; some *Gerasenes* ²Greek *daimonizomai*; also verse 33; elsewhere rendered *oppressed by demons* ³Some manuscripts *perceiving* ⁴Greek *he* ⁵Some manuscripts add *much, or often* ⁶Greek *from that hour* ª For 8:28-34 see parallels Mark 5:1-21; Luke 8:26-39 ᵇ For 9:2-8 see parallels Mark 2:1-12; Luke 5:17-26 ᶜ For 9:9-17 see parallels Mark 2:13-22; Luke 5:27-39 ᵈ Hos. 6:6 ᵉ For 9:18-26 see parallels Mark 5:21-43; Luke 8:40-56

saying, "Never was anything like this seen in Israel." [34]But the Pharisees said, "He casts out demons by the prince of demons."

The Harvest Is Plentiful, the Laborers Few

[35]And Jesus went throughout all the cities and villages, teaching in their synagogues and proclaiming the gospel of the kingdom and healing every disease and every affliction. [36]When he saw the crowds, he had compassion for them, because they were harassed and helpless, like sheep without a shepherd. [37]Then he said to his disciples, "The harvest is plentiful, but the laborers are few; [38]therefore pray earnestly to the Lord of the harvest to send out laborers into his harvest."

The Twelve Apostles

10 And he called to him his twelve disciples and gave them authority over unclean spirits, to cast them out, and to heal every disease and every affliction. [2a]The names of the twelve apostles are these: first, Simon, who is called Peter, and Andrew his brother; James the son of Zebedee, and John his brother; [3]Philip and Bartholomew; Thomas and Matthew the tax collector; James the son of Alphaeus, and Thaddaeus;[1] [4]Simon the Cananaean, and Judas Iscariot, who betrayed him.

Jesus Sends Out the Twelve Apostles

[5]These twelve Jesus sent out, instructing them, "Go nowhere among the Gentiles and enter no town of the Samaritans, [6]but go rather to the lost sheep of the house of Israel. [7]And proclaim as you go, saying, 'The kingdom of heaven is at hand.' [8]Heal the sick, raise the dead, cleanse lepers,[2] cast out demons. You received without paying; give without pay. [9b]Acquire no gold nor silver nor copper for your belts, [10]no bag for your journey, nor two tunics[3] nor sandals nor a staff, for the laborer deserves his food. [11]And whatever town or village you enter, find out who is worthy in it and stay there until you depart. [12]As you enter the house, greet it. [13]And if the house is worthy, let your peace come upon it, but if it is not worthy, let your peace return to you. [14]And if anyone will not receive you or listen to your words, shake off the dust from your feet when you leave that house or town. [15]Truly, I say to you, it will be more bearable on the day of judgment for the land of Sodom and Gomorrah than for that town.

Persecution Will Come

[16]"Behold, I am sending you out as sheep in the midst of wolves, so be wise as serpents and innocent as doves. [17]Beware of men, for they will deliver you over to courts and flog you in their synagogues, [18]and you will be dragged before governors and kings for my sake, to bear witness before them and the Gentiles. [19]When they deliver you over, do not be anxious how you are to speak or what you are to say, for what you are to say will be given to you in that hour. [20]For it is not you who speak, but the Spirit of your Father speaking through you. [21]Brother will deliver brother over to death, and the father his child, and children will rise against parents and have them put to death, [22]and you will be hated by all for my name's sake. But the one who endures to the end will be saved. [23]When they persecute you in one town, flee to the next, for truly, I say to you, you will not have gone through all the towns of Israel before the Son of Man comes.

[24]"A disciple is not above his teacher, nor a servant[4] above his master. [25]It is enough for the disciple to be like his teacher, and the servant like his master. If they have called the master of the house Beelzebul, how much more will they malign[5] those of his household.

Have No Fear

[26]"So have no fear of them, [c]for nothing is covered that will not be revealed, or hidden that will not be known. [27]What I tell you in the dark, say in the light, and what you hear whispered, proclaim on the housetops. [28]And do not fear those who kill the body but cannot kill the soul. Rather fear him who can destroy both soul and body in hell.[6] [29]Are not two sparrows sold for a penny?[7] And not one of them will fall to the ground apart from your Father. [30]But even the hairs of your head are all numbered. [31]Fear not, therefore; you are of more value than many sparrows. [32]So everyone who acknowledges me before men, I also will acknowledge before my Father who is in heaven, [33]but whoever denies me before men, I also will deny before my Father who is in heaven.

Not Peace, but a Sword

[34d]"Do not think that I have come to bring peace to the earth. I have not come to bring peace, but a sword. [35]For I have come to set a man against his father, and a daughter against her mother, and a daughter-in-law against her mother-in-law. [36]And a person's enemies will be those of his own household. [37]Whoever loves father or mother more than me is not worthy of me, and whoever loves son or daughter more than me is not worthy of me. [38]And whoever does not take his cross and follow me is not worthy of me. [39]Whoever finds his life will lose it, and whoever loses his life for my sake will find it.

---

[1] Some manuscripts *Lebbaeus*, or *Lebbaeus called Thaddaeus* [2] *Leprosy* was a term for several skin diseases; see Leviticus 13 [3] Greek *chiton*, a long garment worn under the cloak next to the skin [4] Greek *bondservant*; also verse 25 [5] Greek lacks *will they malign* [6] Greek *Gehenna* [7] Greek *assarion*, Roman copper coin (Latin *quadrans*) worth about 1/16 of a *denarius* (which was a day's wage for a laborer) [a] For 10:2-4 see parallels Mark 3:16-19; Luke 6:13-16 [b] For 10:9-15 see parallels Mark 6:8-11; Luke 9:3-5 [c] For 10:26-33 see parallel Luke 12:2-9 [d] For 10:34, 35 see parallel Luke 12:51-53

Rewards

40"Whoever receives you receives me, and whoever receives me receives him who sent me. **41**The one who receives a prophet because he is a prophet will receive a prophet's reward, and the one who receives a righteous person because he is a righteous person will receive a righteous person's reward. **42**And whoever gives one of these little ones even a cup of cold water because he is a disciple, truly, I say to you, he will by no means lose his reward."

Messengers from John the Baptist

11 When Jesus had finished instructing his twelve disciples, he went on from there to teach and preach in their cities.

2[a]Now when John heard in prison about the deeds of the Christ, he sent word by his disciples **3**and said to him, "Are you the one who is to come, or shall we look for another?" **4**And Jesus answered them, "Go and tell John what you hear and see: **5**the blind receive their sight and the lame walk, lepers[1] are cleansed and the deaf hear, and the dead are raised up, and the poor have good news preached to them. **6**And blessed is the one who is not offended by me."

7As they went away, Jesus began to speak to the crowds concerning John: "What did you go out into the wilderness to see? A reed shaken by the wind? **8**What then did you go out to see? A man[2] dressed in soft clothing? Behold, those who wear soft clothing are in kings' houses. **9**What then did you go out to see? A prophet? Yes, I tell you, and more than a prophet. **10**This is he of whom it is written,

> [b]"'Behold, I send my messenger before your face, who will prepare your way before you.'

11Truly, I say to you, among those born of women there has arisen no one greater than John the Baptist. Yet the one who is least in the kingdom of heaven is greater than he. **12**From the days of John the Baptist until now the kingdom of heaven has suffered violence,[4] and the violent take it by force. **13**For all the Prophets and the Law prophesied until John, **14**and if you are willing to accept it, he is Elijah who is to come. **15**He who has ears to hear,[5] let him hear.

16"But to what shall I compare this generation? It is like children sitting in the marketplaces and calling to their playmates,

17 "'We played the flute for you, and you did not dance;
> we sang a dirge, and you did not mourn.'

18For John came neither eating nor drinking, and they say, 'He has a demon.' **19**The Son of Man came eating and drinking, and they say, 'Look at him! A glutton and a drunkard, a friend of tax collectors and sinners!' Yet wisdom is justified by her deeds."[6]

Woe to Unrepentant Cities

20Then he began to denounce the cities where most of his mighty works had been done, because they did not repent. **21**"Woe to you, Chorazin! Woe to you, Bethsaida! For if the mighty works done in you had been done in Tyre and Sidon, they would have repented long ago in sackcloth and ashes. **22**But I tell you, it will be more bearable on the day of judgment for Tyre and Sidon than for you. **23**And you, Capernaum, will you be exalted to heaven? You will be brought down to Hades. For if the mighty works done in you had been done in Sodom, it would have remained until this day. **24**But I tell you that it will be more tolerable on the day of judgment for the land of Sodom than for you."

Come to Me, and I Will Give You Rest

25[d]At that time Jesus declared, "I thank you, Father, Lord of heaven and earth, that you have hidden these things from the wise and understanding and revealed them to little children; **26**yes, Father, for such was your gracious will.[7] **27**All things have been handed over to me by my Father, and no one knows the Son except the Father, and no one knows the Father except the Son and anyone to whom the Son chooses to reveal him. **28**Come to me, all who labor and are heavy laden, and I will give you rest. **29**Take my yoke upon you, and learn from me, for I am gentle and lowly in heart, and you will find rest for your souls. **30**For my yoke is easy, and my burden is light."

Jesus Is Lord of the Sabbath

12 At that time [e]Jesus went through the grainfields on the Sabbath. His disciples were hungry, and they began to pluck heads of grain and to eat. **2**But when the Pharisees saw it, they said to him, "Look, your disciples are doing what is not lawful to do on the Sabbath." **3**He said to them, "Have you not read what David did when he was hungry, and those who were with him: **4**how he entered the house of God and ate the bread of the Presence, which it was not lawful for him to eat nor for those who were with him, but only for the priests? **5**Or have you not read in the Law how on the Sabbath the priests in the temple profane the Sabbath and are guiltless? **6**I tell you, something greater than the temple is here. **7**And if you had known what this means, [f]'I desire mercy, and not sacrifice,' you would not have condemned the guiltless. **8**For the Son of Man is lord of the Sabbath."

---

[1] *Leprosy* was a term for several skin diseases; see Leviticus 13 [2] Or *Why then did you go out? To see a man . . .* [3] Some manuscripts *Why then did you go out? To see a prophet?* [4] Or *has been coming violently* [5] Some manuscripts omit *to hear* [6] Some manuscripts *children* (compare Luke 7:35) [7] Or *so it pleased you well* [a] For 11:2-19 see parallel Luke 7:18-35 [b] Mal. 3:1 [c] For 11:21-24 see parallel Luke 10:13-15 [d] For 11:25-27 see parallel Luke 10:21, 22 [e] For 12:1-8 see parallels Mark 2:23-28; Luke 6:1-5 [f] Hos. 6:6

A Man with a Withered Hand

⁹He went on from there and ᵃentered their synagogue. ¹⁰And a man was there with a withered hand. And they asked him, "Is it lawful to heal on the Sabbath?"—so that they might accuse him. ¹¹He said to them, "Which one of you who has a sheep, if it falls into a pit on the Sabbath, will not take hold of it and lift it out? ¹²Of how much more value is a man than a sheep! So it is lawful to do good on the Sabbath." ¹³Then he said to the man, "Stretch out your hand." And the man stretched it out, and it was restored, healthy like the other. ¹⁴But the Pharisees went out and conspired against him, how to destroy him.

God's Chosen Servant

¹⁵Jesus, aware of this, withdrew from there. And many followed him, and he healed them all ¹⁶and ordered them not to make him known. ¹⁷This was to fulfill what was spoken by the prophet Isaiah:

¹⁸ ᵇ"Behold, my servant whom I have chosen,
　　my beloved with whom my soul is well
　　　pleased.
　I will put my Spirit upon him,
　　and he will proclaim justice to the Gentiles.
¹⁹ 　He will not quarrel or cry aloud,
　　nor will anyone hear his voice in the streets;
²⁰ 　a bruised reed he will not break,
　　and a smoldering wick he will not quench,
　　until he brings justice to victory;
²¹ 　and in his name the Gentiles will hope."

Blasphemy Against the Holy Spirit

²²ᶜThen a demon-oppressed man who was blind and mute was brought to him, and he healed him, so that the man spoke and saw. ²³And all the people were amazed, and said, "Can this be the Son of David?" ²⁴But when the Pharisees heard it, they said, "It is only by Beelzebul, the prince of demons, that this man casts out demons." ²⁵Knowing their thoughts, ᵈhe said to them, "Every kingdom divided against itself is laid waste, and no city or house divided against itself will stand. ²⁶And if Satan casts out Satan, he is divided against himself. How then will his kingdom stand? ²⁷And if I cast out demons by Beelzebul, by whom do your sons cast them out? Therefore they will be your judges. ²⁸But if it is by the Spirit of God that I cast out demons, then the kingdom of God has come upon you. ²⁹Or how can someone enter a strong man's house and plunder his goods, unless he first binds the strong man? Then indeed he may plunder his house. ³⁰Whoever is not with me is against me, and whoever does not gather with me scatters.

³¹ᵉTherefore I tell you, every sin and blasphemy will be forgiven people, but the blasphemy against the Spirit will not be forgiven. ³²And whoever speaks a word against the Son of Man will be forgiven, but whoever speaks against the Holy Spirit will not be forgiven, either in this age or in the age to come.

A Tree Is Known by Its Fruit

³³"Either make the tree good and its fruit good, or make the tree bad and its fruit bad, for the tree is known by its fruit. ³⁴You brood of vipers! How can you speak good, when you are evil? For out of the abundance of the heart the mouth speaks. ³⁵The good person out of his good treasure brings forth good, and the evil person out of his evil treasure brings forth evil. ³⁶I tell you, on the day of judgment people will give account for every careless word they speak, ³⁷for by your words you will be justified, and by your words you will be condemned."

The Sign of Jonah

³⁸Then some of the scribes and Pharisees answered him, saying, "Teacher, we wish to see a sign from you." ³⁹But he answered them, ᶠ"An evil and adulterous generation seeks for a sign, but no sign will be given to it except the sign of the prophet Jonah. ⁴⁰For just as Jonah was three days and three nights in the belly of the great fish, so will the Son of Man be three days and three nights in the heart of the earth. ⁴¹The men of Nineveh will rise up at the judgment with this generation and condemn it, for they repented at the preaching of Jonah, and behold, something greater than Jonah is here. ⁴²The queen of the South will rise up at the judgment with this generation and condemn it, for she came from the ends of the earth to hear the wisdom of Solomon, and behold, something greater than Solomon is here.

Return of an Unclean Spirit

⁴³"When ᵍthe unclean spirit has gone out of a person, it passes through waterless places seeking rest, but finds none. ⁴⁴Then it says, 'I will return to my house from which I came.' And when it comes, it finds the house empty, swept, and put in order. ⁴⁵Then it goes and brings with it seven other spirits more evil than itself, and they enter and dwell there, and the last state of that person is worse than the first. So also will it be with this evil generation."

Jesus' Mother and Brothers

⁴⁶While he was still speaking to the people, behold, ʰhis mother and his brothers stood outside, asking to speak to him.ⁱ ⁴⁸But he replied to

---

¹ Some manuscripts insert verse 47: *Someone told him, "Your mother and your brothers are standing outside, asking to speak to you"* ᵃFor 12:9-14 see parallels Mark 3:1-6; Luke 6:6-11 ᵇIsa. 42:1-3 ᶜFor 12:22-24 see parallel Luke 11:14, 15 ᵈFor 12:25-29 see parallels Mark 3:23-27; Luke 11:17-22 ᵉFor 12:31, 32 see parallel Mark 3:28-30 ᶠFor 12:39-42 see parallel Luke 11:29-32 ᵍFor 12:43-45 see parallel Luke 11:24-26 ʰFor 12:46-50 see parallels Mark 3:31-35; Luke 8:19-21

the man who told him, "Who is my mother, and who are my brothers?" ⁴⁹And stretching out his hand toward his disciples, he said, "Here are my mother and my brothers! ⁵⁰For whoever does the will of my Father in heaven is my brother and sister and mother."

The Parable of the Sower

13 That same day Jesus went out of the house ᵃand sat beside the sea. ²And great crowds gathered about him, so that he got into a boat and sat down. And the whole crowd stood on the beach. ³And he told them many things in parables, saying: "A sower went out to sow. ⁴And as he sowed, some seeds fell along the path, and the birds came and devoured them. ⁵Other seeds fell on rocky ground, where they did not have much soil, and immediately they sprang up, since they had no depth of soil, ⁶but when the sun rose they were scorched. And since they had no root, they withered away. ⁷Other seeds fell among thorns, and the thorns grew up and choked them. ⁸Other seeds fell on good soil and produced grain, some a hundredfold, some sixty, some thirty. ⁹He who has ears,¹ let him hear."

The Purpose of the Parables

¹⁰Then the disciples came and said to him, "Why do you speak to them in parables?" ¹¹And he answered them, "To you it has been given to know the secrets of the kingdom of heaven, but to them it has not been given. ¹²For to the one who has, more will be given, and he will have an abundance, but from the one who has not, even what he has will be taken away. ¹³This is why I speak to them in parables, because seeing they do not see, and hearing they do not hear, nor do they understand. ¹⁴Indeed, in their case the prophecy of Isaiah is fulfilled that says:

ᵇ"'You will indeed hear but never understand,
  and you will indeed see but never perceive.
¹⁵ For this people's heart has grown dull,
  and with their ears they can barely hear,
  and their eyes they have closed,
  lest they should see with their eyes
  and hear with their ears
  and understand with their heart
  and turn, and I would heal them.'

¹⁶But blessed are your eyes, for they see, and your ears, for they hear. ¹⁷For truly, I say to you, many prophets and righteous people longed to see what you see, and did not see it, and to hear what you hear, and did not hear it.

The Parable of the Sower Explained

¹⁸ᶜ"Hear then the parable of the sower: ¹⁹When anyone hears the word of the kingdom and does not understand it, the evil one comes and

snatches away what has been sown in his heart. This is what was sown along the path. ²⁰As for what was sown on rocky ground, this is the one who hears the word and immediately receives it with joy, ²¹yet he has no root in himself, but endures for a while, and when tribulation or persecution arises on account of the word, immediately he falls away.² ²²As for what was sown among thorns, this is the one who hears the word, but the cares of the world and the deceitfulness of riches choke the word, and it proves unfruitful. ²³As for what was sown on good soil, this is the one who hears the word and understands it. He indeed bears fruit and yields, in one case a hundredfold, in another sixty, and in another thirty."

The Parable of the Weeds

²⁴He put another parable before them, saying, "The kingdom of heaven may be compared to a man who sowed good seed in his field, ²⁵but while his men were sleeping, his enemy came and sowed weeds³ among the wheat and went away. ²⁶So when the plants came up and bore grain, then the weeds appeared also. ²⁷And the servants⁴ of the master of the house came and said to him, 'Master, did you not sow good seed in your field? How then does it have weeds?' ²⁸He said to them, 'An enemy has done this.' So the servants said to him, 'Then do you want us to go and gather them?' ²⁹But he said, 'No, lest in gathering the weeds you root up the wheat along with them. ³⁰Let both grow together until the harvest, and at harvest time I will tell the reapers, Gather the weeds first and bind them in bundles to be burned, but gather the wheat into my barn.'"

The Mustard Seed and the Leaven

³¹He put another parable before them, saying, ᵈ"The kingdom of heaven is like a grain of mustard seed that a man took and sowed in his field. ³²It is the smallest of all seeds, but when it has grown it is larger than all the garden plants and becomes a tree, so that the birds of the air come and make nests in its branches."

³³He told them another parable. "The kingdom of heaven is like leaven that a woman took and hid in three measures of flour, till it was all leavened."

Prophecy and Parables

³⁴All these things Jesus said to the crowds in parables; indeed, he said nothing to them without a parable. ³⁵This was to fulfill what was spoken by the prophet:⁵

---

¹ Some manuscripts add here and in verse 43 *to hear* ² Or *stumbles* ³ Probably *darnel*, a wheat-like weed ⁴ Greek *bondservants*; also verse 28 ⁵ Some manuscripts *Isaiah the prophet* ᵃ For 13:1-15 see parallels Mark 4:1-12; Luke 8:4-10 ᵇ Isa. 6:9, 10 ᶜ For 13:18-23 see parallels Mark 4:13-20; Luke 8:11-15 ᵈ For 13:31, 32 see parallels Mark 4:30-32; Luke 13:18, 19

ª"I will open my mouth in parables;
I will utter what has been hidden since the foundation of the world."

The Parable of the Weeds Explained

36Then he left the crowds and went into the house. And his disciples came to him, saying, "Explain to us the parable of the weeds of the field." **37**He answered, "The one who sows the good seed is the Son of Man. **38**The field is the world, and the good seed is the sons of the kingdom. The weeds are the sons of the evil one, **39**and the enemy who sowed them is the devil. The harvest is the close of the age, and the reapers are angels. **40**Just as the weeds are gathered and burned with fire, so will it be at the close of the age. **41**The Son of Man will send his angels, and they will gather out of his kingdom all causes of sin and all law-breakers, **42**and throw them into the fiery furnace. In that place there will be weeping and gnashing of teeth. **43**Then the righteous will shine like the sun in the kingdom of their Father. He who has ears, let him hear.

The Parable of the Hidden Treasure

44"The kingdom of heaven is like treasure hidden in a field, which a man found and covered up. Then in his joy he goes and sells all that he has and buys that field.

The Parable of the Pearl of Great Value

45"Again, the kingdom of heaven is like a merchant in search of fine pearls, **46**who, on finding one pearl of great value, went and sold all that he had and bought it.

The Parable of the Net

47"Again, the kingdom of heaven is like a net that was thrown into the sea and gathered fish of every kind. **48**When it was full, men drew it ashore and sat down and sorted the good into containers but threw away the bad. **49**So it will be at the close of the age. The angels will come out and separate the evil from the righteous **50**and throw them into the fiery furnace. In that place there will be weeping and gnashing of teeth.

New and Old Treasures

51"Have you understood all these things?" They said to him, "Yes." **52**And he said to them, "Therefore every scribe who has been trained for the kingdom of heaven is like a master of a house, who brings out of his treasure what is new and what is old."

Jesus Rejected at Nazareth

53And when Jesus had finished these parables, he went away from there, **54**ᵇand coming to his hometown he taught them in their synagogue, so that they were astonished, and said, "Where did this man get this wisdom and these mighty works? **55**Is not this the carpenter's son? Is not his mother called Mary? And are not his brothers James and Joseph and Simon and Judas? **56**And are not all his sisters with us? Where then did this man get all these things?" **57**And they took offense at him. But Jesus said to them, "A prophet is not without honor except in his hometown and in his own household." **58**And he did not do many mighty works there, because of their unbelief.

The Death of John the Baptist

14 ᶜAt that time Herod the tetrarch heard about the fame of Jesus, **2**and he said to his servants, "This is John the Baptist. He has been raised from the dead; that is why these miraculous powers are at work in him." **3**For Herod had seized John and bound him and put him in prison for the sake of Herodias, his brother Philip's wife,¹ **4**because John had been saying to him, "It is not lawful for you to have her." **5**And though he wanted to put him to death, he feared the people, because they held him to be a prophet. **6**But when Herod's birthday came, the daughter of Herodias danced before the company and pleased Herod, **7**so that he promised with an oath to give her whatever she might ask. **8**Prompted by her mother, she said, "Give me the head of John the Baptist here on a platter." **9**And the king was sorry, but because of his oaths and his guests he commanded it to be given. **10**He sent and had John beheaded in the prison, **11**and his head was brought on a platter and given to the girl, and she brought it to her mother. **12**And his disciples came and took the body and buried it, and they went and told Jesus.

Jesus Feeds the Five Thousand

13Now when Jesus heard this, ᵈhe withdrew from there in a boat to a desolate place by himself. But when the crowds heard it, they followed him on foot from the towns. **14**When he went ashore he saw a great crowd, and he had compassion on them and healed their sick. **15**Now when it was evening, the disciples came to him and said, "This is a desolate place, and the day is now over; send the crowds away to go into the villages and buy food for themselves." **16**But Jesus said, "They need not go away; you give them something to eat." **17**They said to him, "We have only five loaves here and two fish." **18**And he said, "Bring them here to me." **19**Then he ordered the crowds to sit down on the grass, and taking the five loaves and the two fish, he looked up to heaven and said a blessing. Then he broke the loaves and gave them to the disciples, and the disciples gave them to the crowds. **20**And they all ate and were satisfied. And they took up twelve

---

¹ Some manuscripts *his brother's wife* ªPs. 78:2 ᵇFor 13:54-58 see parallel Mark 6:1-6 ᶜFor 14:1-12 see parallels Mark 6:14-29; Luke 9:7-9 ᵈFor 14:13-21 see parallels Mark 6:32-44; Luke 9:10-17; John 6:1-13

baskets full of the broken pieces left over. ²¹And those who ate were about five thousand men, besides women and children.

Jesus Walks on the Water

²²ᵃImmediately he made the disciples get into the boat and go before him to the other side, while he dismissed the crowds. ²³And after he had dismissed the crowds, he went up on the mountain by himself to pray. When evening came, he was there alone, ²⁴but the boat by this time was a long way¹ from the land,² beaten by the waves, for the wind was against them. ²⁵And in the fourth watch of the night he came to them, walking on the sea. ²⁶But when the disciples saw him walking on the sea, they were terrified, and said, "It is a ghost!" and they cried out in fear. ²⁷But immediately Jesus spoke to them, saying, "Take heart; it is I. Do not be afraid."

²⁸And Peter answered him, "Lord, if it is you, command me to come to you on the water." ²⁹He said, "Come." So Peter got out of the boat and walked on the water and came to Jesus. ³⁰But when he saw the wind,³ he was afraid, and beginning to sink he cried out, "Lord, save me." ³¹Jesus immediately reached out his hand and took hold of him, saying to him, "O you of little faith, why did you doubt?" ³²And when they got into the boat, the wind ceased. ³³And those in the boat worshiped him, saying, "Truly you are the Son of God."

Jesus Heals the Sick in Gennesaret

³⁴ᵇAnd when they had crossed over, they came to land at Gennesaret. ³⁵And when the men of that place recognized him, they sent around to all that region and brought to him all who were sick ³⁶and implored him that they might only touch the fringe of his garment. And as many as touched it were made well.

Traditions and Commandments

15 ᶜThen Pharisees and scribes came to Jesus from Jerusalem and said, ²"Why do your disciples break the tradition of the elders? For they do not wash their hands when they eat." ³He answered them, "And why do you break the commandment of God for the sake of your tradition? ⁴For God commanded, ᵈ'Honor your father and your mother,' and, ᵉ'Whoever reviles father or mother must surely die.' ⁵But you say, 'If anyone tells his father or his mother, "What you would have gained from me is given to God,"⁴ ⁶he need not honor his father.' So for the sake of your tradition you have made void the word⁵ of God. ⁷You hypocrites! Well did Isaiah prophesy of you, when he said:

⁸ ᶠ"'This people honors me with their lips,
    but their heart is far from me;
⁹   in vain do they worship me,
    teaching as doctrines the commandments
       of men.'"

What Defiles a Person

¹⁰And he called the people to him and said to them, "Hear and understand: ¹¹it is not what goes into the mouth that defiles a person, but what comes out of the mouth; this defiles a person." ¹²Then the disciples came and said to him, "Do you know that the Pharisees were offended when they heard this saying?" ¹³He answered, "Every plant that my heavenly Father has not planted will be rooted up. ¹⁴Let them alone; they are blind guides.⁶ And if the blind lead the blind, both will fall into a pit." ¹⁵But Peter said to him, "Explain the parable to us." ¹⁶And he said, "Are you also still without understanding? ¹⁷Do you not see that whatever goes into the mouth passes into the stomach and is expelled?⁷ ¹⁸But what comes out of the mouth proceeds from the heart, and this defiles a person. ¹⁹For out of the heart come evil thoughts, murder, adultery, sexual immorality, theft, false witness, slander. ²⁰These are what defile a person. But to eat with unwashed hands does not defile anyone."

The Faith of a Canaanite Woman

²¹ᵍAnd Jesus went away from there and withdrew to the district of Tyre and Sidon. ²²And behold, a Canaanite woman from that region came out and was crying, "Have mercy on me, O Lord, Son of David; my daughter is severely oppressed by a demon." ²³But he did not answer her a word. And his disciples came and begged him, saying, "Send her away, for she is crying out after us." ²⁴He answered, "I was sent only to the lost sheep of the house of Israel." ²⁵But she came and knelt before him, saying, "Lord, help me." ²⁶And he answered, "It is not right to take the children's bread and throw it to the dogs." ²⁷She said, "Yes, Lord, yet even the dogs eat the crumbs that fall from their masters' table." ²⁸Then Jesus answered her, "O woman, great is your faith! Be it done for you as you desire." And her daughter was healed instantly.⁸

Jesus Heals Many

²⁹Jesus went on from there and walked beside the Sea of Galilee. And he went up on the mountain and sat down there. ³⁰And great crowds came to him, bringing with them the lame, the blind, the crippled, the mute, and many others, and they put them at his feet, and he healed them, ³¹so that the crowd wondered, when they saw the mute speaking, the crippled healthy, the

---

¹ Greek *many stadia, a stadion* was about 607 feet or 185 meters ² Some manuscripts *was out on the sea* ³ Some manuscripts *strong wind* ⁴ Or *is an offering* ⁵ Some manuscripts *law* ⁶ Some manuscripts add *of the blind* ⁷ Greek *is expelled into the latrine* ⁸ Greek *from that hour* ᵃ For 14:22-33 see parallels Mark 6:45-52; John 6:16-21 ᵇ For 14:34-36 see parallel Mark 6:53-56 ᶜ For 15:1-20 see parallel Mark 7:1-23 ᵈ Ex. 20:12 ᵉ Ex. 21:17 ᶠ Isa. 29:13 ᵍ For 15:21-28 see parallel Mark 7:24-30

lame walking, and the blind seeing. And they glorified the God of Israel.

Jesus Feeds the Four Thousand

32 ᵃThen Jesus called his disciples to him and said, "I have compassion on the crowd because they have been with me now three days and have nothing to eat. And I am unwilling to send them away hungry, lest they faint on the way." 33And the disciples said to him, "Where are we to get enough bread in such a desolate place to feed so great a crowd?" 34And Jesus said to them, "How many loaves do you have?" They said, "Seven, and a few small fish." 35And directing the crowd to sit down on the ground, 36he took the seven loaves and the fish, and having given thanks he broke them and gave them to the disciples, and the disciples gave them to the crowds. 37And they all ate and were satisfied. And they took up seven baskets full of the broken pieces left over. 38Those who ate were four thousand men, besides women and children. 39And after sending away the crowds, he got into the boat and went to the region of Magadan.

The Pharisees and Sadducees Demand Signs

16 ᵇAnd the Pharisees and Sadducees came, and to test him they asked him to show them a sign from heaven. 2He answered them,[1] "When it is evening, you say, 'It will be fair weather, for the sky is red.' 3And in the morning, 'It will be stormy today, for the sky is red and threatening.' You know how to interpret the appearance of the sky, but you cannot interpret the signs of the times. 4An evil and adulterous generation seeks for a sign, but no sign will be given to it except the sign of Jonah." So he left them and departed.

The Leaven of the Pharisees and Sadducees

5When the disciples reached the other side, they had forgotten to bring any bread. 6Jesus said to them, "Watch and beware of the leaven of the Pharisees and Sadducees." 7And they began discussing it among themselves, saying, "We brought no bread." 8But Jesus, aware of this, said, "O you of little faith, why are you discussing among yourselves the fact that you have no bread? 9Do you not yet perceive? Do you not remember the five loaves for the five thousand, and how many baskets you gathered? 10Or the seven loaves for the four thousand, and how many baskets you gathered? 11How is it that you fail to understand that I did not speak about bread? Beware of the leaven of the Pharisees and Sadducees." 12Then they understood that he did

not tell them to beware of the leaven of bread, but of the teaching of the Pharisees and Sadducees.

Peter Confesses Jesus as the Christ

13 ᶜNow when Jesus came into the district of Caesarea Philippi, he asked his disciples, "Who do people say that the Son of Man is?" 14And they said, "Some say John the Baptist, others say Elijah, and others Jeremiah or one of the prophets." 15He said to them, "But who do you say that I am?" 16Simon Peter replied, "You are the Christ, the Son of the living God." 17And Jesus answered him, "Blessed are you, Simon Bar-Jonah! For flesh and blood has not revealed this to you, but my Father who is in heaven. 18And I tell you, you are Peter, and on this rock[2] I will build my church, and the gates of hell[3] shall not prevail against it. 19I will give you the keys of the kingdom of heaven, and whatever you bind on earth shall be bound in heaven, and whatever you loose on earth shall be loosed[4] in heaven." 20Then he strictly charged the disciples to tell no one that he was the Christ.

Jesus Foretells His Death and Resurrection

21 ᵈFrom that time Jesus began to show his disciples that he must go to Jerusalem and suffer many things from the elders and chief priests and scribes, and be killed, and on the third day be raised. 22And Peter took him aside and began to rebuke him, saying, "Far be it from you, Lord![5] This shall never happen to you." 23But he turned and said to Peter, "Get behind me, Satan! You are a hindrance[6] to me. For you are not setting your mind on the things of God, but on the things of man."

Take Up Your Cross and Follow Jesus

24Then Jesus told his disciples, "If anyone would come after me, let him deny himself and take up his cross and follow me. 25For whoever would save his life[7] will lose it, but whoever loses his life for my sake will find it. 26For what will it profit a man if he gains the whole world and forfeits his soul? Or what shall a man give in return for his soul? 27For the Son of Man is going to come with his angels in the glory of his Father, and then he will repay each person according to what he has done. 28Truly, I say to you, there are some standing here who will not taste death until they see the Son of Man coming in his kingdom."

The Transfiguration

17 ᵉAnd after six days Jesus took with him Peter and James, and John his brother, and led them up a high mountain by themselves.

---

1 Some manuscripts omit the following words to the end of verse 3   2 The Greek words for *Peter* and *rock* sound similar   3 Greek *the gates of Hades* 4 Or *shall have been bound . . . shall have been loosed*   5 Or "[May God be] *merciful to you, Lord!*"   6 Greek *stumbling block*   7 The same Greek word can mean either *soul* or *life*, depending on the context; twice in this verse and twice in verse 26   ª For 15:32-39 see parallel Mark 8:1-10   ᵇ For 16:1-12 see parallel Mark 8:11-21   ᶜ For 16:13-16 see parallels Mark 8:27-29; Luke 9:18-20   ᵈ For 16:21-28 see parallels Mark 8:31–9:1; Luke 9:22-27   ᵉ For 17:1-8 see parallels Mark 9:2-8; Luke 9:28-36

[2]And he was transfigured before them, and his face shone like the sun, and his clothes became white as light. [3]And behold, there appeared to them Moses and Elijah, talking with him. [4]And Peter said to Jesus, "Lord, it is good that we are here. If you wish, I will make three tents here, one for you and one for Moses and one for Elijah." [5]He was still speaking when, behold, a bright cloud overshadowed them, and a voice from the cloud said, "This is my beloved Son,[1] with whom I am well pleased; listen to him." [6]When the disciples heard this, they fell on their faces and were terrified. [7]But Jesus came and touched them, saying, "Rise, and have no fear." [8]And when they lifted up their eyes, they saw no one but Jesus only.

[9a]And as they were coming down the mountain, Jesus commanded them, "Tell no one the vision, until the Son of Man is raised from the dead." [10]And the disciples asked him, "Then why do the scribes say that first Elijah must come?" [11]He answered, "Elijah does come, and he will restore all things. [12]But I tell you that Elijah has already come, and they did not recognize him, but did to him whatever they pleased. So also the Son of Man will certainly suffer at their hands." [13]Then the disciples understood that he was speaking to them of John the Baptist.

Jesus Heals a Boy with a Demon

[14b]And when they came to the crowd, a man came up to him and, kneeling before him, [15]said, "Lord, have mercy on my son, for he is an epileptic and he suffers terribly. For often he falls into the fire, and often into the water. [16]And I brought him to your disciples, and they could not heal him." [17]And Jesus answered, "O faithless and twisted generation, how long am I to be with you? How long am I to bear with you? Bring him here to me." [18]And Jesus rebuked the demon,[2] and it[3] came out of him, and the boy was healed instantly.[4] [19]Then the disciples came to Jesus privately and said, "Why could we not cast it out?" [20]He said to them, "Because of your little faith. For truly, I say to you, if you have faith like a grain of mustard seed, you will say to this mountain, 'Move from here to there,' and it will move, and nothing will be impossible for you."[5]

Jesus Again Foretells Death, Resurrection

[22c]As they were gathering[6] in Galilee, Jesus said to them, "The Son of Man is about to be delivered into the hands of men, [23]and they will kill him, and he will be raised on the third day." And they were greatly distressed.

The Temple Tax

[24]When they came to Capernaum, the collectors of the two-drachma tax went up to Peter and said, "Does your teacher not pay the tax?" [25]He said, "Yes." And when he came into the house, Jesus spoke to him first, saying, "What do you think, Simon? From whom do kings of the earth take toll or tax? From their sons or from others?" [26]And when he said, "From others," Jesus said to him, "Then the sons are free. [27]However, not to give offense to them, go to the sea and cast a hook and take the first fish that comes up, and when you open its mouth you will find a shekel.[7] Take that and give it to them for me and for yourself."

Who Is the Greatest?

18 [d]At that time the disciples came to Jesus, saying, "Who is the greatest in the kingdom of heaven?" [2]And calling to him a child, he put him in the midst of them [3]and said, "Truly, I say to you, unless you turn and become like children, you will never enter the kingdom of heaven. [4]Whoever humbles himself like this child is the greatest in the kingdom of heaven.

[5]"Whoever receives one such child in my name receives me, [6]but whoever causes one of these little ones who believe in me to sin,[8] it would be better for him to have a great millstone fastened around his neck and to be drowned in the depth of the sea.

Temptations to Sin

[7]"Woe to the world for temptations to sin![9] For it is necessary that temptations come, but woe to the one by whom the temptation comes! [8]And if your hand or your foot causes you to sin, cut it off and throw it away. It is better for you to enter life crippled or lame than with two hands or two feet to be thrown into the eternal fire. [9]And if your eye causes you to sin, tear it out and throw it away. It is better for you to enter life with one eye than with two eyes to be thrown into the hell[10] of fire.

The Parable of the Lost Sheep

[10]"See that you do not despise one of these little ones. For I tell you that in heaven their angels always see the face of my Father who is in heaven.[11] [12]What do you think? If a man has a hundred sheep, and one of them has gone astray, does he not leave the ninety-nine on the mountains and go in search of the one that went astray? [13]And if he finds it, truly, I say to you, he rejoices over it more than over the ninety-nine that never went astray. [14]So it is not the will of my[12] Father who is in heaven that one of these little ones should perish.

---

[1] Or my Son, my (or the) Beloved [2] Greek it [3] Greek the demon [4] Greek from that hour [5] Some manuscripts insert verse 21: But this kind never comes out except by prayer and fasting [6] Some manuscripts remained [7] Greek stater, a silver coin worth four drachmas or approximately one shekel [8] Greek causes . . . to stumble; also verses 8, 9 [9] Greek stumbling blocks [10] Greek Gehenna [11] Some manuscripts add verse 11: For the Son of Man came to save the lost [12] Some manuscripts your [a] For 17:9-13 see parallel Mark 9:9-13 [b] For 17:14-19 see parallels Mark 9:14-28; Luke 9:37-42 [c] For 17:22, 23 see parallels Mark 9:30-32; Luke 9:43-45 [d] For 18:1-5 see parallels Mark 9:33-37; Luke 9:46-48

If Your Brother Sins Against You

¹⁵"If your brother sins against you, go and tell him his fault, between you and him alone. If he listens to you, you have gained your brother. ¹⁶But if he does not listen, take one or two others along with you, that every charge may be established by the evidence of two or three witnesses. ¹⁷If he refuses to listen to them, tell it to the church. And if he refuses to listen even to the church, let him be to you as a Gentile and a tax collector. ¹⁸Truly, I say to you, whatever you bind on earth shall be bound in heaven, and whatever you loose on earth shall be loosed¹ in heaven. ¹⁹Again I say to you, if two of you agree on earth about anything they ask, it will be done for them by my Father in heaven. ²⁰For where two or three are gathered in my name, there am I among them."

The Parable of the Unforgiving Servant

²¹Then Peter came up and said to him, "Lord, how often will my brother sin against me, and I forgive him? As many as seven times?" ²²Jesus said to him, "I do not say to you seven times, but seventy times seven.² ²³"Therefore the kingdom of heaven may be compared to a king who wished to settle accounts with his servants.³ ²⁴When he began to settle, one was brought to him who owed him ten thousand talents.⁴ ²⁵And since he could not pay, his master ordered him to be sold, with his wife and children and all that he had, and payment to be made. ²⁶So the servant⁵ fell on his knees, imploring him, 'Have patience with me, and I will pay you everything.' ²⁷And out of pity for him, the master of that servant released him and forgave him the debt. ²⁸But when that same servant went out, he found one of his fellow servants who owed him a hundred denarii,⁶ and seizing him, he began to choke him, saying, 'Pay what you owe.' ²⁹So his fellow servant fell down and pleaded with him, 'Have patience with me, and I will pay you.' ³⁰He refused and went and put him in prison until he should pay the debt. ³¹When his fellow servants saw what had taken place, they were greatly distressed, and they went and reported to their master all that had taken place. ³²Then his master summoned him and said to him, 'You wicked servant! I forgave you all that debt because you pleaded with me. ³³And should not you have had mercy on your fellow servant, as I had mercy on you?' ³⁴And in anger his master delivered him to the jailers,⁷ until he should pay all his debt. ³⁵So also my heavenly Father will do to every one of you, if you do not forgive your brother from your heart."

Teaching About Divorce

19 Now when Jesus had finished these sayings, he went away from Galilee and ᵃentered the region of Judea beyond the Jordan. ²And large crowds followed him, and he healed them there.

³And Pharisees came up to him and tested him by asking, "Is it lawful to divorce one's wife for any cause?" ⁴He answered, "Have you not read that he who created them from the beginning made them male and female, ⁵and said, ᵇ'Therefore a man shall leave his father and his mother and hold fast to his wife, and the two shall become one flesh'? ⁶So they are no longer two but one flesh. What therefore God has joined together, let not man separate." ⁷They said to him, "Why then did Moses command one to give a certificate of divorce and to send her away?" ⁸He said to them, "Because of your hardness of heart Moses allowed you to divorce your wives, but from the beginning it was not so. ⁹And I say to you: whoever divorces his wife, except for sexual immorality, and marries another, commits adultery."⁸

¹⁰The disciples said to him, "If such is the case of a man with his wife, it is better not to marry." ¹¹But he said to them, "Not everyone can receive this saying, but only those to whom it is given. ¹²For there are eunuchs who have been so from birth, and there are eunuchs who have been made eunuchs by men, and there are eunuchs who have made themselves eunuchs for the sake of the kingdom of heaven. Let the one who is able to receive this receive it."

Let the Children Come to Me

¹³ᶜThen children were brought to him that he might lay his hands on them and pray. The disciples rebuked the people, ¹⁴but Jesus said, "Let the little children come to me and do not hinder them, for to such belongs the kingdom of heaven." ¹⁵And he laid his hands on them and went away.

The Rich Young Man

¹⁶ᵈAnd behold, a man came up to him, saying, "Teacher, what good deed must I do to have eternal life?" ¹⁷And he said to him, "Why do you ask me about what is good? There is only one who is good. If you would enter life, keep the commandments." ¹⁸He said to him, "Which ones?" And Jesus said, ᵉ"You shall not murder, You shall not commit adultery, You shall not steal, You shall not bear false witness, ¹⁹Honor your father and mother, and, ᶠYou shall love your neighbor as yourself." ²⁰The young man said to him, "All these I have kept. What do I still lack?" ²¹Jesus

---

¹Or *shall have been bound . . . shall have been loosed* ²Or *seventy-seven times* ³Greek *bondservants*; also verses 28, 31 ⁴A *talent* was a monetary unit worth about twenty years' wages for a laborer ⁵Greek *bondservant*; also verses 27, 28, 29, 32, 33 ⁶A *denarius* was a day's wage for a laborer ⁷Greek *torturers* ⁸Some manuscripts add *and whoever marries a divorced woman commits adultery*; other manuscripts *except for sexual immorality, makes her commit adultery, and whoever marries a divorced woman commits adultery* ᵃFor 19:1-9 see parallel Mark 10:1-12 ᵇGen. 2:24 ᶜFor 19:13-15 see parallels Mark 10:13-16; Luke 18:15-17 ᵈFor 19:16-30 see parallels Mark 10:17-31; Luke 18:18-30 ᵉEx. 20:12-16; Deut. 5:16-20 ᶠLev. 19:18

said to him, "If you would be perfect, go, sell what you possess and give to the poor, and you will have treasure in heaven; and come, follow me." ²²When the young man heard this he went away sorrowful, for he had great possessions.

²³And Jesus said to his disciples, "Truly, I say to you, only with difficulty will a rich person enter the kingdom of heaven. ²⁴Again I tell you, it is easier for a camel to go through the eye of a needle than for a rich person to enter the kingdom of God." ²⁵When the disciples heard this, they were greatly astonished, saying, "Who then can be saved?" ²⁶But Jesus looked at them and said, "With man this is impossible, but with God all things are possible." ²⁷Then Peter said in reply, "See, we have left everything and followed you. What then will we have?" ²⁸Jesus said to them, "Truly, I say to you, in the new world,¹ when the Son of Man will sit on his glorious throne, you who have followed me will also sit on twelve thrones, judging the twelve tribes of Israel. ²⁹And everyone who has left houses or brothers or sisters or father or mother or children or lands, for my name's sake, will receive a hundredfold² and will inherit eternal life. ³⁰But many who are first will be last, and the last first.

Laborers in the Vineyard

20 "For the kingdom of heaven is like a master of a house who went out early in the morning to hire laborers for his vineyard. ²After agreeing with the laborers for a denarius³ a day, he sent them into his vineyard. ³And going out about the third hour he saw others standing idle in the marketplace, ⁴and to them he said, 'You go into the vineyard too, and whatever is right I will give you.' ⁵So they went. Going out again about the sixth hour and the ninth hour, he did the same. ⁶And about the eleventh hour he went out and found others standing. And he said to them, 'Why do you stand here idle all day?' ⁷They said to him, 'Because no one has hired us.' He said to them, 'You go into the vineyard too.' ⁸And when evening came, the owner of the vineyard said to his foreman, 'Call the laborers and pay them their wages, beginning with the last, up to the first.' ⁹And when those hired about the eleventh hour came, each of them received a denarius. ¹⁰Now when those hired first came, they thought they would receive more, but each of them also received a denarius. ¹¹And on receiving it they grumbled at the master of the house, ¹²saying, 'These last worked only one hour, and you have made them equal to us who have borne the burden of the day and the scorching heat.' ¹³But he replied to one of them, 'Friend, I am doing you no wrong. Did you not agree with me for a denarius? ¹⁴Take what belongs to you and go. I choose to give to this last worker as I give to you.

¹⁵Am I not allowed to do what I choose with what belongs to me? Or do you begrudge my generosity?'⁴ ¹⁶So the last will be first, and the first last."

Jesus Foretells His Death a Third Time

¹⁷ᵃAnd as Jesus was going up to Jerusalem, he took the twelve disciples aside, and on the way he said to them, ¹⁸"See, we are going up to Jerusalem. And the Son of Man will be delivered over to the chief priests and scribes, and they will condemn him to death ¹⁹and deliver him over to the Gentiles to be mocked and flogged and crucified, and he will be raised on the third day."

A Mother's Request

²⁰ᵇThen the mother of the sons of Zebedee came up to him with her sons, and kneeling before him she asked him for something. ²¹And he said to her, "What do you want?" She said to him, "Say that these two sons of mine are to sit, one at your right hand and one at your left, in your kingdom." ²²Jesus answered, "You do not know what you are asking. Are you able to drink the cup that I am to drink?" They said to him, "We are able." ²³He said to them, "You will drink my cup, but to sit at my right hand and at my left is not mine to grant, but it is for those for whom it has been prepared by my Father." ²⁴And when the ten heard it, they were indignant at the two brothers. ²⁵But Jesus called them to him and said, "You know that the rulers of the Gentiles lord it over them, and their great ones exercise authority over them. ²⁶It shall not be so among you. But whoever would be great among you must be your servant,⁵ ²⁷and whoever would be first among you must be your slave,⁶ ²⁸even as the Son of Man came not to be served but to serve, and to give his life as a ransom for many."

Jesus Heals Two Blind Men

²⁹ᶜAnd as they went out of Jericho, a great crowd followed him. ³⁰And behold, there were two blind men sitting by the roadside, and when they heard that Jesus was passing by, they cried out, "Lord,⁷ have mercy on us, Son of David!" ³¹The crowd rebuked them, telling them to be silent, but they cried out all the more, "Lord, have mercy on us, Son of David!" ³²And stopping, Jesus called them and said, "What do you want me to do for you?" ³³They said to him, "Lord, let our eyes be opened." ³⁴And Jesus in pity touched their eyes, and immediately they recovered their sight and followed him.

The Triumphal Entry

21 ᵈNow when they drew near to Jerusalem and came to Bethphage, to the Mount of Olives, then Jesus sent two disciples, ²saying to

¹Greek in the regeneration ²Some manuscripts manifold ³A denarius was a day's wage for a laborer ⁴Or is your eye bad because I am good? ⁵Greek diakonos ⁶Greek bondservant (doulos) ⁷Some manuscripts omit Lord ᵃFor 20:17-19 see parallels Mark 10:32-34; Luke 18:31-33 ᵇFor 20:20-28 see parallel Mark 10:35-45 ᶜFor 20:29-34 see parallels Mark 10:46-52; Luke 18:35-43 ᵈFor 21:1-9 see parallels Mark 11:1-10; Luke 19:28-38; John 12:12-15

them, "Go into the village in front of you, and immediately you will find a donkey tied, and a colt with her. Untie them and bring them to me. [3]If anyone says anything to you, you shall say, 'The Lord needs them,' and he will send them at once." [4]This took place to fulfill what was spoken by the prophet, saying,

[5] [a]"Say to the daughter of Zion,
  'Behold, your king is coming to you,
    humble, and mounted on a donkey,
    and[1] on a colt, the foal of a beast of burden.'"

[6]The disciples went and did as Jesus had directed them. [7]They brought the donkey and the colt and put on them their cloaks, and he sat on them. [8]Most of the crowd spread their cloaks on the road, and others cut branches from the trees and spread them on the road. [9]And the crowds that went before him and that followed him were shouting, "Hosanna to the Son of David! Blessed is he who comes in the name of the Lord! Hosanna in the highest!" [10]And when he entered Jerusalem, the whole city was stirred up, saying, "Who is this?" [11]And the crowds said, "This is the prophet Jesus, from Nazareth of Galilee."

Jesus Cleanses the Temple

[12] [b]And Jesus entered the temple[2] and drove out all who sold and bought in the temple, and he overturned the tables of the money-changers and the seats of those who sold pigeons. [13]He said to them, "It is written, [c]'My house shall be called a house of prayer,' but you make it a den of robbers."

[14]And the blind and the lame came to him in the temple, and he healed them. [15]But when the chief priests and the scribes saw the wonderful things that he did, and the children crying out in the temple, "Hosanna to the Son of David!" they were indignant, [16]and they said to him, "Do you hear what these are saying?" And Jesus said to them, "Yes; have you never read,

[d]"'Out of the mouth of infants and nursing babies
  you have prepared praise'?"

[17]And leaving them, he went out of the city to Bethany and lodged there.

Jesus Curses the Fig Tree

[18] [e]In the morning, as he was returning to the city, he became hungry. [19]And seeing a fig tree by the wayside, he went to it and found nothing on it but only leaves. And he said to it, "May no fruit ever come from you again!" And the fig tree withered at once. [20]When the disciples saw it, they marveled,

saying, "How did the fig tree wither at once?" [21]And Jesus answered them, "Truly, I say to you, if you have faith and do not doubt, you will not only do what has been done to the fig tree, but even if you say to this mountain, 'Be taken up and thrown into the sea,' it will happen. [22]And whatever you ask in prayer, you will receive, if you have faith."

The Authority of Jesus Challenged

[23] [f]And when he entered the temple, the chief priests and the elders of the people came up to him as he was teaching, and said, "By what authority are you doing these things, and who gave you this authority?" [24]Jesus answered them, "I also will ask you one question, and if you tell me the answer, then I also will tell you by what authority I do these things. [25]The baptism of John, from where did it come? From heaven or from man?" And they discussed it among themselves, saying, "If we say, 'From heaven,' he will say to us, 'Why then did you not believe him?' [26]But if we say, 'From man,' we are afraid of the crowd, for they all hold that John was a prophet." [27]So they answered Jesus, "We do not know." And he said to them, "Neither will I tell you by what authority I do these things.

The Parable of the Two Sons

[28]"What do you think? A man had two sons. And he went to the first and said, 'Son, go and work in the vineyard today.' [29]And he answered, 'I will not,' but afterward he changed his mind and went. [30]And he went to the other son and said the same. And he answered, 'I go, sir,' but did not go. [31]Which of the two did the will of his father?" They said, "The first." Jesus said to them, "Truly, I say to you, the tax collectors and the prostitutes go into the kingdom of God before you. [32]For John came to you in the way of righteousness, and you did not believe him, but the tax collectors and the prostitutes believed him. And even when you saw it, you did not afterward change your minds and believe him.

The Parable of the Tenants

[33] [g]"Hear another parable. There was a master of a house who planted a vineyard and put a fence around it and dug a winepress in it and built a tower and leased it to tenants, and went into another country. [34]When the season for fruit drew near, he sent his servants[3] to the tenants to get his fruit. [35]And the tenants took his servants and beat one, killed another, and stoned another. [36]Again he sent other servants, more than the first. And they did the same to them. [37]Finally he sent his son to them, saying, 'They will respect my son.' [38]But when the tenants saw the son, they said to themselves, 'This is the heir.

[1]Or even [2]Some manuscripts add of God [3]Greek bondservants; also verses 35, 36 [a]Zech. 9:9 [b]For 21:12-16 see parallels Mark 11:15-18; Luke 19:45-47 [c]Isa. 56:7 [d]Ps. 8:2 (Gk.) [e]For 21:18-22 see parallel Mark 11:12-14, 20-24 [f]For 21:23-27 see parallels Mark 11:27-33; Luke 20:1-8 [g]For 21:33-46 see parallels Mark 12:1-12; Luke 20:9-18

Come, let us kill him and have his inheritance.' [39]And they took him and threw him out of the vineyard and killed him. [40]When therefore the owner of the vineyard comes, what will he do to those tenants?" [41]They said to him, "He will put those wretches to a miserable death and let out the vineyard to other tenants who will give him the fruits in their seasons."

[42]Jesus said to them, "Have you never read in the Scriptures:

[a]"'The stone that the builders rejected
    has become the cornerstone;[1]
 this was the Lord's doing,
    and it is marvelous in our eyes'?

[43]Therefore I tell you, the kingdom of God will be taken away from you and given to a people producing its fruits. [44]And the one who falls on this stone will be broken to pieces; and when it falls on anyone, it will crush him."[2]

[45]When the chief priests and the Pharisees heard his parables, they perceived that he was speaking about them. [46]And although they were seeking to arrest him, they feared the crowds, because they held him to be a prophet.

The Parable of the Wedding Feast

22 And again Jesus spoke to them in parables, saying, [2]"The kingdom of heaven may be compared to a king who gave a wedding feast for his son, [3]and sent his servants[3] to call those who were invited to the wedding feast, but they would not come. [4]Again he sent other servants, saying, 'Tell those who are invited, See, I have prepared my dinner, my oxen and my fat calves have been slaughtered, and everything is ready. Come to the wedding feast.' [5]But they paid no attention and went off, one to his farm, another to his business, [6]while the rest seized his servants, treated them shamefully, and killed them. [7]The king was angry, and he sent his troops and destroyed those murderers and burned their city. [8]Then he said to his servants, 'The wedding feast is ready, but those invited were not worthy. [9]Go therefore to the main roads and invite to the wedding feast as many as you find.' [10]And those servants went out into the roads and gathered all whom they found, both bad and good. So the wedding hall was filled with guests.

[11]"But when the king came in to look at the guests, he saw there a man who had no wedding garment. [12]And he said to him, 'Friend, how did you get in here without a wedding garment?' And he was speechless. [13]Then the king said to the attendants, 'Bind him hand and foot and cast him into the outer darkness. In that place there will be weeping and gnashing of teeth.' [14]For many are called, but few are chosen."

Paying Taxes to Caesar

[15b]Then the Pharisees went and plotted how to entangle him in his words. [16]And they sent their disciples to him, along with the Herodians, saying, "Teacher, we know that you are true and teach the way of God truthfully, and you do not care about anyone's opinion, for you are not swayed by appearances.[4] [17]Tell us, then, what you think. Is it lawful to pay taxes to Caesar, or not?" [18]But Jesus, aware of their malice, said, "Why put me to the test, you hypocrites? [19]Show me the coin for the tax." And they brought him a denarius.[5] [20]And Jesus said to them, "Whose likeness and inscription is this?" [21]They said, "Caesar's." Then he said to them, "Therefore render to Caesar the things that are Caesar's, and to God the things that are God's." [22]When they heard it, they marveled. And they left him and went away.

Sadducees Ask About the Resurrection

[23]The same day Sadducees came to him, who say that there is no resurrection, and they asked him a question, [24]saying, "Teacher, Moses said, 'If a man dies having no children, his brother must marry the widow and raise up children for his brother.' [25]Now there were seven brothers among us. The first married and died, and having no children left his wife to his brother. [26]So too the second and third, down to the seventh. [27]After them all, the woman died. [28]In the resurrection, therefore, of the seven, whose wife will she be? For they all had her."

[29]But Jesus answered them, "You are wrong, because you know neither the Scriptures nor the power of God. [30]For in the resurrection they neither marry nor are given in marriage, but are like angels in heaven. [31]And as for the resurrection of the dead, have you not read what was said to you by God: [32]'I am the God of Abraham, and the God of Isaac, and the God of Jacob'? He is not God of the dead, but of the living." [33]And when the crowd heard it, they were astonished at his teaching.

The Great Commandment

[34d]But when the Pharisees heard that he had silenced the Sadducees, they gathered together. [35]And one of them, a lawyer, asked him a question to test him. [36]"Teacher, which is the great commandment in the Law?" [37]And he said to him, "You shall love the Lord your God with all your heart and with all your soul and with all your mind. [38]This is the great and first commandment. [39]And a second is like it: You shall love your neighbor as yourself. [40]On these two commandments depend all the Law and the Prophets."

---

[1] Greek *the head of the corner* [2] Some manuscripts omit verse 44 [3] Greek *bondservants*; also verses 4, 6, 8, 10 [4] Greek *for you do not look at people's faces* [5] A *denarius* was a day's wage for a laborer [a] Ps. 118:22, 23 [b] For 22:15-32 see parallels Mark 12:13-27; Luke 20:20-38 [c] Ex. 3:6 [d] For 22:34-40 see parallel Mark 12:28-33

Whose Son Is the Christ?

⁴¹*a*Now while the Pharisees were gathered together, Jesus asked them a question, ⁴²saying, "What do you think about the Christ? Whose son is he?" They said to him, "The son of David." ⁴³He said to them, "How is it then that David, in the Spirit, calls him Lord, saying,

⁴⁴*b*"'The Lord said to my Lord,
    Sit at my right hand,
        until I put your enemies under your feet'?

⁴⁵If then David calls him Lord, how is he his son?" ⁴⁶And no one was able to answer him a word, nor from that day did anyone dare to ask him any more questions.

Seven Woes to the Scribes and Pharisees

23 Then Jesus *c*said to the crowds and to his disciples, ²"The scribes and the Pharisees sit on Moses' seat, ³so practice and observe whatever they tell you—but not what they do. For they preach, but do not practice. ⁴They tie up heavy burdens, hard to bear,¹ and lay them on people's shoulders, but they themselves are not willing to move them with their finger. ⁵They do all their deeds to be seen by others. For they make their phylacteries broad and their fringes long, ⁶and they love the place of honor at feasts and the best seats in the synagogues ⁷and greetings in the marketplaces and being called rabbi² by others. ⁸But you are not to be called rabbi, for you have one teacher, and you are all brothers.³ ⁹And call no man your father on earth, for you have one Father, who is in heaven. ¹⁰Neither be called instructors, for you have one instructor, the Christ. ¹¹The greatest among you shall be your servant. ¹²Whoever exalts himself will be humbled, and whoever humbles himself will be exalted.

¹³"But woe to you, scribes and Pharisees, hypocrites! For you shut the kingdom of heaven in people's faces. For you neither enter yourselves nor allow those who would enter to go in.⁴ ¹⁵Woe to you, scribes and Pharisees, hypocrites! For you travel across sea and land to make a single proselyte, and when he becomes a proselyte, you make him twice as much a child of hell⁵ as yourselves.

¹⁶"Woe to you, blind guides, who say, 'If anyone swears by the temple, it is nothing, but if anyone swears by the gold of the temple, he is bound by his oath.' ¹⁷You blind fools! For which is greater, the gold or the temple that has made the gold sacred? ¹⁸And you say, 'If anyone swears by the altar, it is nothing, but if anyone swears by the gift that is on the altar, he is bound by his oath.' ¹⁹You blind men! For which is greater, the gift or the altar that makes the gift sacred? ²⁰So whoever swears by the altar swears by it and by everything on it. ²¹And whoever swears by the temple swears by it and by him who dwells in it. ²²And whoever swears by heaven swears by the throne of God and by him who sits upon it.

²³"Woe to you, scribes and Pharisees, hypocrites! For you tithe mint and dill and cumin, and have neglected the weightier matters of the law: justice and mercy and faithfulness. These you ought to have done, without neglecting the others. ²⁴You blind guides, straining out a gnat and swallowing a camel!

²⁵"Woe to you, scribes and Pharisees, hypocrites! For you clean the outside of the cup and the plate, but inside they are full of greed and self-indulgence. ²⁶You blind Pharisee! First clean the inside of the cup and the plate, that the outside also may be clean.

²⁷"Woe to you, scribes and Pharisees, hypocrites! For you are like whitewashed tombs, which outwardly appear beautiful, but within are full of dead people's bones and all uncleanness. ²⁸So you also outwardly appear righteous to others, but within you are full of hypocrisy and lawlessness.

²⁹"Woe to you, scribes and Pharisees, hypocrites! For you build the tombs of the prophets and decorate the monuments of the righteous, ³⁰saying, 'If we had lived in the days of our fathers, we would not have taken part with them in shedding the blood of the prophets.' ³¹Thus you witness against yourselves that you are sons of those who murdered the prophets. ³²Fill up, then, the measure of your fathers. ³³You serpents, you brood of vipers, how are you to escape being sentenced to hell? ³⁴Therefore I send you prophets and wise men and scribes, some of whom you will kill and crucify, and some you will flog in your synagogues and persecute from town to town, ³⁵so that on you may come all the righteous blood shed on earth, from the blood of innocent Abel to the blood of Zechariah the son of Barachiah,⁶ whom you murdered between the sanctuary and the altar. ³⁶Truly, I say to you, all these things will come upon this generation.

Lament over Jerusalem

³⁷*d*"O Jerusalem, Jerusalem, the city that kills the prophets and stones those who are sent to it! How often would I have gathered your children together as a hen gathers her brood under her wings, and you would not! ³⁸See, your house is left to you desolate. ³⁹For I tell you, you will not see me again, until you say, *e*'Blessed is he who comes in the name of the Lord.'"

¹ Some manuscripts omit *hard to bear* ² *Rabbi* means *my teacher*, or *my master*; also verse 8 ³ Or *brothers and sisters* ⁴ Some manuscripts add here (or after verse 12) verse 14: *Woe to you, scribes and Pharisees, hypocrites! For you devour widows' houses and for a pretense you make long prayers; therefore you will receive the greater condemnation* ⁵ Greek *Gehenna*; also verse 33 ⁶ Some manuscripts omit *the son of Barachiah* *a* For 22:41-45 see parallels Mark 12:35-37; Luke 20:41-44 *b* Ps. 110:1 *c* For 23:1, 2, 5-7 see parallels Mark 12:38-40; Luke 20:45, 46 *d* For 23:37-39 see parallel Luke 13:34, 35 *e* Ps. 118:26

Jesus Foretells Destruction of the Temple

24 ᵃJesus left the temple and was going away, when his disciples came to point out to him the buildings of the temple. ²But he answered them, "You see all these, do you not? Truly, I say to you, there will not be left here one stone upon another that will not be thrown down."

Signs of the Close of the Age

³As he sat on the Mount of Olives, the disciples came to him privately, saying, "Tell us, when will these things be, and what will be the sign of your coming and of the close of the age?" ⁴And Jesus answered them, "See that no one leads you astray. ⁵For many will come in my name, saying, 'I am the Christ,' and they will lead many astray. ⁶And you will hear of wars and rumors of wars. See that you are not alarmed, for this must take place, but the end is not yet. ⁷For nation will rise against nation, and kingdom against kingdom, and there will be famines and earthquakes in various places. ⁸All these are but the beginning of the birth pains.

⁹"Then they will deliver you up to tribulation and put you to death, and you will be hated by all nations for my name's sake. ¹⁰And then many will fall away¹ and betray one another and hate one another. ¹¹And many false prophets will arise and lead many astray. ¹²And because lawlessness will be increased, the love of many will grow cold. ¹³But the one who endures to the end will be saved. ¹⁴And this gospel of the kingdom will be proclaimed throughout the whole world as a testimony to all nations, and then the end will come.

The Abomination of Desolation

¹⁵"So when you see the abomination of desolation spoken of by the prophet Daniel, standing in the holy place (let the reader understand), ¹⁶then let those who are in Judea flee to the mountains. ¹⁷Let the one who is on the housetop not go down to take what is in his house, ¹⁸and let the one who is in the field not turn back to take his cloak. ¹⁹And alas for women who are pregnant and for those who are nursing infants in those days! ²⁰Pray that your flight may not be in winter or on a Sabbath. ²¹For then there will be great tribulation, such as has not been from the beginning of the world until now, no, and never will be. ²²And if those days had not been cut short, no human being would be saved. But for the sake of the elect those days will be cut short. ²³Then if anyone says to you, 'Look, here is the Christ!' or 'There he is!' do not believe it. ²⁴For false christs and false prophets will arise and perform great signs and wonders, so as to lead astray, if possible, even the elect. ²⁵See, I have told you beforehand. ²⁶So, if they

say to you, 'Look, he is in the wilderness,' do not go out. If they say, 'Look, he is in the inner rooms,' do not believe it. ²⁷For as the lightning comes from the east and shines as far as the west, so will be the coming of the Son of Man. ²⁸Wherever the corpse is, there the vultures will gather.

The Coming of the Son of Man

²⁹"Immediately after the tribulation of those days the sun will be darkened, and the moon will not give its light, and the stars will fall from heaven, and the powers of the heavens will be shaken. ³⁰Then will appear in heaven the sign of the Son of Man, and then all the tribes of the earth will mourn, and they will see the Son of Man coming on the clouds of heaven with power and great glory. ³¹And he will send out his angels with a loud trumpet call, and they will gather his elect from the four winds, from one end of heaven to the other.

The Lesson of the Fig Tree

³²"From the fig tree learn its lesson: as soon as its branch becomes tender and puts out its leaves, you know that summer is near. ³³So also, when you see all these things, you know that he is near, at the very gates. ³⁴Truly, I say to you, this generation will not pass away until all these things take place. ³⁵Heaven and earth will pass away, but my words will not pass away.

No One Knows That Day and Hour

³⁶"But concerning that day and hour no one knows, not even the angels of heaven, nor the Son,² but the Father only. ³⁷For as were the days of Noah, so will be the coming of the Son of Man. ³⁸For as in those days before the flood they were eating and drinking, marrying and giving in marriage, until the day when Noah entered the ark, ³⁹and they were unaware until the flood came and swept them all away, so will be the coming of the Son of Man. ⁴⁰Then two men will be in the field; one will be taken and one left. ⁴¹Two women will be grinding at the mill; one will be taken and one left. ⁴²Therefore, stay awake, for you do not know on what day your Lord is coming. ⁴³But know this, that if the master of the house had known in what part of the night the thief was coming, he would have stayed awake and would not have let his house be broken into. ⁴⁴Therefore you also must be ready, for the Son of Man is coming at an hour you do not expect.

⁴⁵"Who then is the faithful and wise servant,³ whom his master has set over his household, to give them their food at the proper time? ⁴⁶Blessed is that servant whom his master will find so doing when he comes. ⁴⁷Truly, I say to you, he will set him over all his possessions. ⁴⁸But if that wicked servant says to himself, 'My master is

¹ Or *stumble* ² Some manuscripts omit *nor the Son* ³ Greek *bondservant*; also verses 46, 48, 50 ᵃ For 24:1-51 see parallels Mark 13:1-37; Luke 21:5-36

delayed,' [49] and begins to beat his fellow servants[1] and eats and drinks with drunkards, [50] the master of that servant will come on a day when he does not expect him and at an hour he does not know [51] and will cut him in pieces and put him with the hypocrites. In that place there will be weeping and gnashing of teeth.

The Parable of the Ten Virgins

25 "Then the kingdom of heaven will be like ten virgins who took their lamps[2] and went to meet the bridegroom.[3] [2] Five of them were foolish, and five were wise. [3] For when the foolish took their lamps, they took no oil with them, [4] but the wise took flasks of oil with their lamps. [5] As the bridegroom was delayed, they all became drowsy and slept. [6] But at midnight there was a cry, 'Here is the bridegroom! Come out to meet him.' [7] Then all those virgins rose and trimmed their lamps. [8] And the foolish said to the wise, 'Give us some of your oil, for our lamps are going out.' [9] But the wise answered, saying, 'Since there will not be enough for us and for you, go rather to the dealers and buy for yourselves.' [10] And while they were going to buy, the bridegroom came, and those who were ready went in with him to the marriage feast, and the door was shut. [11] Afterward the other virgins came also, saying, 'Lord, lord, open to us.' [12] But he answered, 'Truly, I say to you, I do not know you.' [13] Watch therefore, for you know neither the day nor the hour.

The Parable of the Talents

[14] "For it will be like a man going on a journey, who called his servants[4] and entrusted to them his property. [15] To one he gave five talents,[5] to another two, to another one, to each according to his ability. Then he went away. [16] He who had received the five talents went at once and traded with them, and he made five talents more. [17] So also he who had the two talents made two talents more. [18] But he who had received the one talent went and dug in the ground and hid his master's money. [19] Now after a long time the master of those servants came and settled accounts with them. [20] And he who had received the five talents came forward, bringing five talents more, saying, 'Master, you delivered to me five talents; here I have made five talents more.' [21] His master said to him, 'Well done, good and faithful servant.[6] You have been faithful over a little; I will set you over much. Enter into the joy of your master.' [22] And he also who had the two talents came forward, saying, 'Master, you delivered to me two talents; here I have made two talents more.' [23] His master said to him, 'Well done, good and faithful servant. You have been faithful over a little; I will set you over much. Enter into the joy of your master.' [24] He also who

had received the one talent came forward, saying, 'Master, I knew you to be a hard man, reaping where you did not sow, and gathering where you scattered no seed, [25] so I was afraid, and I went and hid your talent in the ground. Here you have what is yours.' [26] But his master answered him, 'You wicked and slothful servant! You knew that I reap where I have not sown and gather where I scattered no seed? [27] Then you ought to have invested my money with the bankers, and at my coming I should have received what was my own with interest. [28] So take the talent from him and give it to him who has the ten talents. [29] For to everyone who has will more be given, and he will have an abundance. But from the one who has not, even what he has will be taken away. [30] And cast the worthless servant into the outer darkness. In that place there will be weeping and gnashing of teeth.'

The Final Judgment

[31] "When the Son of Man comes in his glory, and all the angels with him, then he will sit on his glorious throne. [32] Before him will be gathered all the nations, and he will separate people one from another as a shepherd separates the sheep from the goats. [33] And he will place the sheep on his right, but the goats on the left. [34] Then the King will say to those on his right, 'Come, you who are blessed by my Father, inherit the kingdom prepared for you from the foundation of the world. [35] For I was hungry and you gave me food, I was thirsty and you gave me drink, I was a stranger and you welcomed me, [36] I was naked and you clothed me, I was sick and you visited me, I was in prison and you came to me.' [37] Then the righteous will answer him, saying, 'Lord, when did we see you hungry and feed you, or thirsty and give you drink? [38] And when did we see you a stranger and welcome you, or naked and clothe you? [39] And when did we see you sick or in prison and visit you?' [40] And the King will answer them, 'Truly, I say to you, as you did it to one of the least of these my brothers,[7] you did it to me.'

[41] "Then he will say to those on his left, 'Depart from me, you cursed, into the eternal fire prepared for the devil and his angels. [42] For I was hungry and you gave me no food, I was thirsty and you gave me no drink, [43] I was a stranger and you did not welcome me, naked and you did not clothe me, sick and in prison and you did not visit me.' [44] Then they also will answer, saying, 'Lord, when did we see you hungry or thirsty or a stranger or naked or sick or in prison, and did not minister to you?' [45] Then he will answer them, saying, 'Truly, I say to you, as you did not do it to one of the least of these, you did not do it to me.' [46] And these will go away into eternal punishment, but the righteous into eternal life."

---

[1] Greek *bondservants* [2] Or *torches* [3] Some manuscripts add *and the bride* [4] Greek *bondservants*; also verse 19 [5] A *talent* was a monetary unit worth about twenty years' wages for a laborer [6] Greek *bondservant*; also verses 23, 26, 30 [7] Or *brothers and sisters*

The Plot to Kill Jesus

26 When Jesus had finished all these sayings, he said to his disciples, [2]*a*"You know that after two days the Passover is coming, and the Son of Man will be delivered up to be crucified."

[3]Then the chief priests and the elders of the people gathered in the palace of the high priest, whose name was Caiaphas, [4]and plotted together in order to arrest Jesus by stealth and kill him. [5]But they said, "Not during the feast, lest there be an uproar among the people."

Jesus Anointed at Bethany

[6]*b*Now when Jesus was at Bethany in the house of Simon the leper,[1] [7]a woman came up to him with an alabaster flask of very expensive ointment, and she poured it on his head as he reclined at table. [8]And when the disciples saw it, they were indignant, saying, "Why this waste? [9]For this could have been sold for a large sum and given to the poor." [10]But Jesus, aware of this, said to them, "Why do you trouble the woman? For she has done a beautiful thing to me. [11]For you always have the poor with you, but you will not always have me. [12]In pouring this ointment on my body, she has done it to prepare me for burial. [13]Truly, I say to you, wherever this gospel is proclaimed in the whole world, what she has done will also be told in memory of her."

Judas to Betray Jesus

[14]*c*Then one of the twelve, whose name was Judas Iscariot, went to the chief priests [15]and said, "What will you give me if I deliver him over to you?" And they paid him thirty pieces of silver. [16]And from that moment he sought an opportunity to betray him.

The Passover with the Disciples

[17]*d*Now on the first day of Unleavened Bread the disciples came to Jesus, saying, "Where will you have us prepare for you to eat the Passover?" [18]He said, "Go into the city to a certain man and say to him, 'The Teacher says, My time is at hand. I will keep the Passover at your house with my disciples.'" [19]And the disciples did as Jesus had directed them, and they prepared the Passover.

[20]*e*When it was evening, he reclined at table with the twelve.[2] [21]And as they were eating, he said, "Truly, I say to you, one of you will betray me." [22]And they were very sorrowful and began to say to him one after another, "Is it I, Lord?" [23]He answered, "He who has dipped his hand in the dish with me will betray me. [24]The Son of Man goes as it is written of him, but woe to that man by whom the Son of Man is betrayed! It would have been better for that man if he had not been born." [25]Judas, who would betray him, answered, "Is it I, Rabbi?" He said to him, "You have said so."

Institution of the Lord's Supper

[26]*f*Now as they were eating, Jesus took bread, and after blessing it broke it and gave it to the disciples, and said, "Take, eat; this is my body." [27]And he took a cup, and when he had given thanks he gave it to them, saying, "Drink of it, all of you, [28]for this is my blood of the[3] covenant, which is poured out for many for the forgiveness of sins. [29]I tell you I will not drink again of this fruit of the vine until that day when I drink it new with you in my Father's kingdom."

Jesus Foretells Peter's Denial

[30]*g*And when they had sung a hymn, they went out to the Mount of Olives. [31]Then Jesus said to them, "You will all fall away because of me this night. For it is written, 'I will *h*strike the shepherd, and the sheep of the flock will be scattered.' [32]But after I am raised up, I will go before you to Galilee." [33]Peter answered him, "Though they all fall away because of you, I will never fall away." [34]Jesus said to him, "Truly, I tell you, this very night, before the rooster crows, you will deny me three times." [35]Peter said to him, "Even if I must die with you, I will not deny you!" And all the disciples said the same.

Jesus Prays in Gethsemane

[36]*i*Then Jesus went with them to a place called Gethsemane, and he said to his disciples, "Sit here, while I go over there and pray." [37]And taking with him Peter and the two sons of Zebedee, he began to be sorrowful and troubled. [38]Then he said to them, "My soul is very sorrowful, even to death; remain here, and watch[4] with me." [39]And going a little farther he fell on his face and prayed, saying, "My Father, if it be possible, let this cup pass from me; nevertheless, not as I will, but as you will." [40]And he came to the disciples and found them sleeping. And he said to Peter, "So, could you not watch with me one hour? [41]Watch and pray that you may not enter into temptation. The spirit indeed is willing, but the flesh is weak." [42]Again, for the second time, he went away and prayed, "My Father, if this cannot pass unless I drink it, your will be done." [43]And again he came and found them sleeping, for their eyes were heavy. [44]So, leaving them again, he went away and prayed for the third time, saying the same words again. [45]Then he came to the disciples and said to them, "Sleep and take your rest later on.[5] See, the hour is at hand, and the Son of Man is

---

[1]*Leprosy* was a term for several skin diseases; see Leviticus 13 [2]Some manuscripts add *disciples* [3]Some manuscripts insert *new* [4]Or *keep awake; also verses 40, 41* [5]Or *Are you still sleeping and taking your rest?* *a*For 26:2-5 see parallels Mark 14:1, 2; Luke 22:1, 2 *b*For 26:6-13 see parallels Mark 14:3-9; John 12:1-8 *c*For 26:14-16 see parallels Mark 14:10, 11; Luke 22:3-6 *d*For 26:17-19 see parallels Mark 14:12-16; Luke 22:7-13 *e*For 26:20-24 see parallel Mark 14:17-21 *f*For 26:26-29 see parallels Mark 14:22-25; Luke 22:18-20 *g*For 26:30-35 see parallel Mark 14:26-31 *h*Zech. 13:7 *i*For 26:36-46 see parallels Mark 14:32-42; Luke 22:39-46

betrayed into the hands of sinners. **46**Rise, let us be going; see, my betrayer is at hand."

Betrayal and Arrest of Jesus

47*a*While he was still speaking, Judas came, one of the twelve, and with him a great crowd with swords and clubs, from the chief priests and the elders of the people. **48**Now the betrayer had given them a sign, saying, "The one I will kiss is the man; seize him." **49**And he came up to Jesus at once and said, "Greetings, Rabbi!" And he kissed him. **50**Jesus said to him, "Friend, do what you came to do."*1* Then they came up and laid hands on Jesus and seized him. **51**And behold, one of those who were with Jesus stretched out his hand and drew his sword and struck the servant*2* of the high priest and cut off his ear. **52**Then Jesus said to him, "Put your sword back into its place. For all who take the sword will perish by the sword. **53**Do you think that I cannot appeal to my Father, and he will at once send me more than twelve legions of angels? **54**But how then should the Scriptures be fulfilled, that it must be so?" **55**At that hour Jesus said to the crowds, "Have you come out as against a robber, with swords and clubs to capture me? Day after day I sat in the temple teaching, and you did not seize me. **56**But all this has taken place that the Scriptures of the prophets might be fulfilled." Then all the disciples left him and fled.

Jesus Before Caiaphas and the Council

57Then *b*those who had seized Jesus led him to Caiaphas the high priest, where the scribes and the elders had gathered. **58**And Peter was following him at a distance, as far as the courtyard of the high priest, and going inside he sat with the guards to see the end. **59**Now the chief priests and the whole Council*3* were seeking false testimony against Jesus that they might put him to death, **60**but they found none, though many false witnesses came forward. At last two came forward **61**and said, "This man said, 'I am able to destroy the temple of God, and to rebuild it in three days.'" **62**And the high priest stood up and said, "Have you no answer to make? What is it that these men testify against you?"*4* **63**But Jesus remained silent. And the high priest said to him, "I adjure you by the living God, tell us if you are the Christ, the Son of God." **64**Jesus said to him, "You have said so. But I tell you, from now on you will see the Son of Man seated at the right hand of Power and coming on the clouds of heaven." **65**Then the high priest tore his robes and said, "He has uttered blasphemy. What further witnesses do we need? You have now heard his blasphemy. **66**What is your judgment?" They answered, "He deserves death." **67**Then they spit in his face and struck him. And some slapped him, **68**saying, "Prophesy to us, you Christ! Who is it that struck you?"

Peter Denies Jesus

69*c*Now Peter was sitting outside in the courtyard. And a servant girl came up to him and said, "You also were with Jesus the Galilean." **70**But he denied it before them all, saying, "I do not know what you mean." **71**And when he went out to the entrance, another servant girl saw him, and she said to the bystanders, "This man was with Jesus of Nazareth." **72**And again he denied it with an oath: "I do not know the man." **73**After a little while the bystanders came up and said to Peter, "Certainly you too are one of them, for your accent betrays you." **74**Then he began to invoke a curse on himself and to swear, "I do not know the man." And immediately the rooster crowed. **75**And Peter remembered the saying of Jesus, "Before the rooster crows, you will deny me three times." And he went out and wept bitterly.

Jesus Delivered to Pilate

27 When morning came, all the chief priests and the elders of the people took counsel against Jesus to put him to death. **2**And they bound him and led him away and delivered him over to Pilate the governor.

Judas Hangs Himself

3Then when Judas, his betrayer, saw that Jesus*5* was condemned, he changed his mind and brought back the thirty pieces of silver to the chief priests and the elders, **4**saying, "I have sinned by betraying innocent blood." They said, "What is that to us? See to it yourself." **5**And throwing down the pieces of silver into the temple, he departed, and he went and hanged himself. **6**But the chief priests, taking the pieces of silver, said, "It is not lawful to put them into the treasury, since it is blood money." **7**So they took counsel and bought with them the potter's field as a burial place for strangers. **8**Therefore that field has been called the Field of Blood to this day. **9**Then was fulfilled what had been spoken by the prophet Jeremiah, saying, *d*"And they took the thirty pieces of silver, the price of him on whom a price had been set by some of the sons of Israel, **10**and they gave them for the potter's field, as the Lord directed me."

Jesus Before Pilate

11*e*Now Jesus stood before the governor, and the governor asked him, "Are you the King of the Jews?" Jesus said, "You have said so." **12**But when he was accused by the chief priests and elders, he gave no answer. **13**Then Pilate said to him, "Do you not hear how many things they testify against you?" **14**But he gave him no answer, not

*1*Or *Friend, why are you here?* *2*Greek *bondservant* *3*Greek *Sanhedrin* *4*Or *Have you no answer to what these men testify against you?* *5*Greek *he* *a*For 26:47-56 see parallels Mark 14:43-50; Luke 22:47-53; John 18:3-11 *b*For 26:57-68 see parallel Mark 14:53-65 *c*For 26:69-75 see parallels Mark 14:66-72; Luke 22:55-62; John 18:16-18, 25-27 *d*Zech. 11:13 *e*For 27:11-14 see parallels Mark 15:1-5; Luke 23:1-3; John 18:28-38 even to a single charge, so that the governor was greatly amazed.

The Crowd Chooses Barabbas

¹⁵ᵃNow at the feast the governor was accustomed to release for the crowd any one prisoner whom they wanted. ¹⁶And they had then a notorious prisoner called Barabbas. ¹⁷So when they had gathered, Pilate said to them, "Whom do you want me to release for you: Barabbas, or Jesus who is called Christ?" ¹⁸For he knew that it was out of envy that they had delivered him up. ¹⁹Besides, while he was sitting on the judgment seat, his wife sent word to him, "Have nothing to do with that righteous man, for I have suffered much because of him today in a dream." ²⁰Now the chief priests and the elders persuaded the crowd to ask for Barabbas and destroy Jesus. ²¹The governor again said to them, "Which of the two do you want me to release for you?" And they said, "Barabbas." ²²Pilate said to them, "Then what shall I do with Jesus who is called Christ?" They all said, "Let him be crucified!" ²³And he said, "Why, what evil has he done?" But they shouted all the more, "Let him be crucified!"

Pilate Delivers Jesus to Be Crucified

²⁴So when Pilate saw that he was gaining nothing, but rather that a riot was beginning, he took water and washed his hands before the crowd, saying, "I am innocent of this man's blood;¹ see to it yourselves." ²⁵And all the people answered, "His blood be on us and on our children!" ²⁶Then he released for them Barabbas, and having scourged² Jesus, delivered him to be crucified.

Jesus Is Mocked

²⁷ᵇThen the soldiers of the governor took Jesus into the governor's headquarters,³ and they gathered the whole battalion⁴ before him. ²⁸And they stripped him and put a scarlet robe on him, ²⁹and twisting together a crown of thorns, they put it on his head and put a reed in his right hand. And kneeling before him, they mocked him, saying, "Hail, King of the Jews!" ³⁰And they spit on him and took the reed and struck him on the head. ³¹And when they had mocked him, they stripped him of the robe and put his own clothes on him and led him away to crucify him.

The Crucifixion

³²As they went out, they found a man of Cyrene, Simon by name. They compelled this man to carry his cross. ³³ᶜAnd when they came to a place called Golgotha (which means Place of a Skull), ³⁴they offered him wine to drink, mixed with gall, but when he tasted it, he would not

drink it. ³⁵And when they had crucified him, they divided his garments among them by casting lots. ³⁶Then they sat down and kept watch over him there. ³⁷And over his head they put the charge against him, which read, "This is Jesus, the King of the Jews." ³⁸Then two robbers were crucified with him, one on the right and one on the left. ³⁹And those who passed by derided him, wagging their heads ⁴⁰and saying, "You who would destroy the temple and rebuild it in three days, save yourself! If you are the Son of God, come down from the cross." ⁴¹So also the chief priests, with the scribes and elders, mocked him, saying, ⁴²"He saved others; he cannot save himself. He is the King of Israel; let him come down now from the cross, and we will believe in him. ⁴³He trusts in God; let God deliver him now, if he desires him. For he said, 'I am the Son of God.'" ⁴⁴And the robbers who were crucified with him also reviled him in the same way.

The Death of Jesus

⁴⁵Now from the sixth hour⁵ there was darkness over all the land⁶ until the ninth hour.⁷ ⁴⁶And about the ninth hour Jesus cried out with a loud voice, saying, ᵈ"Eli, Eli, lema sabachthani?" that is, "My God, my God, why have you forsaken me?" ⁴⁷And some of the bystanders, hearing it, said, "This man is calling Elijah." ⁴⁸And one of them at once ran and took a sponge, filled it with sour wine, and put it on a reed and gave it to him to drink. ⁴⁹But the others said, "Wait, let us see whether Elijah will come to save him." ⁵⁰And Jesus cried out again with a loud voice and yielded up his spirit.

⁵¹And behold, the curtain of the temple was torn in two, from top to bottom. And the earth shook, and the rocks were split. ⁵²The tombs also were opened. And many bodies of the saints who had fallen asleep were raised, ⁵³and coming out of the tombs after his resurrection they went into the holy city and appeared to many. ⁵⁴ᵉWhen the centurion and those who were with him, keeping watch over Jesus, saw the earthquake and what took place, they were filled with awe and said, "Truly this was the Son⁸ of God!"

⁵⁵There were also many women there, looking on from a distance, who had followed Jesus from Galilee, ministering to him, ⁵⁶among whom were Mary Magdalene and Mary the mother of James and Joseph and the mother of the sons of Zebedee.

Jesus Is Buried

⁵⁷ᶠWhen it was evening, there came a rich man from Arimathea, named Joseph, who also was a disciple of Jesus. ⁵⁸He went to Pilate and

---

¹ Some manuscripts *this righteous blood*, or *this righteous man's blood* ² A Roman judicial penalty, consisting of a severe beating with a multi-lashed whip containing imbedded pieces of bone and metal ³ Greek *the praetorium* ⁴ Greek *cohort*; a tenth of a Roman legion, usually about 600 men ⁵ That is, noon ⁶ Or *earth* ⁷ That is, 3 P.M. ⁸ Or *a son* ᵃ For 27:15-26 see parallels Mark 15:6-15; Luke 23:18-25; John 18:39, 40; 19:16 ᵇ For 27:27-31 see parallels Mark 15:16-20; John 19:2, 3 ᶜ For 27:33-51 see parallels Mark 15:22-38; Luke 23:32-38, 44-46; John 19:17-19, 23, 24, 28-30 ᵈ Ps. 22:1 ᵉ For 27:54-56 see parallels Mark 15:39-41; Luke 23:47, 49 ᶠ For 27:57-61 see parallels Mark 15:42-47; Luke 23:50-56; John 19:38-42

asked for the body of Jesus. Then Pilate ordered it to be given to him. [59]And Joseph took the body and wrapped it in a clean linen shroud [60]and laid it in his own new tomb, which he had cut in the rock. And he rolled a great stone to the entrance of the tomb and went away. [61]Mary Magdalene and the other Mary were there, sitting opposite the tomb.

The Guard at the Tomb

[62]The next day, that is, after the day of Preparation, the chief priests and the Pharisees gathered before Pilate [63]and said, "Sir, we remember how that impostor said, while he was still alive, 'After three days I will rise.' [64]Therefore order the tomb to be made secure until the third day, lest his disciples go and steal him away and tell the people, 'He has risen from the dead,' and the last fraud will be worse than the first." [65]Pilate said to them, "You have a guard[1] of soldiers. Go, make it as secure as you can." [66]So they went and made the tomb secure by sealing the stone and setting a guard.

The Resurrection

28 [a]Now after the Sabbath, toward the dawn of the first day of the week, Mary Magdalene and the other Mary went to see the tomb. [2]And behold, there was a great earthquake, for an angel of the Lord descended from heaven and came and rolled back the stone and sat on it. [3]His appearance was like lightning, and his clothing white as snow. [4]And for fear of him the guards trembled and became like dead men. [5]But the angel said to the women, "Do not be afraid, for I know that you seek Jesus who was crucified. [6]He is not here, for he has risen, as he said. Come, see the place where he[2] lay. [7]Then go

quickly and tell his disciples that he has risen from the dead, and behold, he is going before you to Galilee; there you will see him. See, I have told you." [8]So they departed quickly from the tomb with fear and great joy, and ran to tell his disciples. [9]And behold, Jesus met them and said, "Greetings!" And they came up and took hold of his feet and worshiped him. [10]Then Jesus said to them, "Do not be afraid; go and tell my brothers to go to Galilee, and there they will see me."

The Report of the Guard

[11]While they were going, behold, some of the guard went into the city and told the chief priests all that had taken place. [12]And when they had assembled with the elders and taken counsel, they gave a sufficient sum of money to the soldiers [13]and said, "Tell people, 'His disciples came by night and stole him away while we were asleep.' [14]And if this comes to the governor's ears, we will satisfy him and keep you out of trouble." [15]So they took the money and did as they were directed. And this story has been spread among the Jews to this day.

The Great Commission

[16]Now the eleven disciples went to Galilee, to the mountain to which Jesus had directed them. [17]And when they saw him they worshiped him, but some doubted. [18]And Jesus came and said to them, "All authority in heaven and on earth has been given to me. [19]Go therefore and make disciples of all nations, baptizing them in[3] the name of the Father and of the Son and of the Holy Spirit, [20]teaching them to observe all that I have commanded you. And behold, I am with you always, to the end of the age."

MARK

Introduction

The Gospel of Mark emphasizes that Jesus is the Christ, the Son of God. Jesus announced the Kingdom of God, healed the sick, and died as a ransom for sinners. In addition to Jesus, Mark features three main groups of people: the disciples, the crowds, and the religious leaders, none of whom understood Jesus. When the time came for Jesus to go to the cross, the religious leaders arrested him, the disciples abandoned him, and the crowds jeered him. Only when he died alone on the cross did a Roman centurion recognize that he was the Son of God. Though the book is anonymous, tradition identifies John Mark (Acts 12:12) as the author. He may have based his Gospel on Peter's preaching, writing sometime in the 50s or 60s A.D.

John the Baptist Prepares the Way

1 The beginning of the gospel of Jesus Christ, the Son of God.[1]

[2] [a]As it is written in Isaiah the prophet,[2]

[b]"Behold, I send my messenger before your face,
    who will prepare your way,
[3] [c]the voice of one crying in the wilderness:
    'Prepare[3] the way of the Lord,
    make his paths straight,'"

[4]John appeared, baptizing in the wilderness and proclaiming a baptism of repentance for the forgiveness of sins. [5]And all the country of Judea and all Jerusalem were going out to him and were being baptized by him in the river Jordan, confessing their sins. [6]Now John was clothed with camel's hair and wore a leather belt around his waist and ate locusts and wild honey. [7]And he preached, saying, "After me comes he who is mightier than I, the strap of whose sandals I am not worthy to stoop down and untie. [8]I have baptized you with water, but he will baptize you with the Holy Spirit."

The Baptism of Jesus

[9][d]In those days Jesus came from Nazareth of Galilee and was baptized by John in the Jordan. [10]And when he came up out of the water, immediately he saw the heavens being torn open and the Spirit descending on him like a dove. [11]And a voice came from heaven, "You are my beloved Son;[4] with you I am well pleased."

The Temptation of Jesus

[12]The Spirit immediately drove him out into the wilderness. [13]And he was in the wilderness forty days, being tempted by Satan. And he was with the wild animals, and the angels were ministering to him.

Jesus Begins His Ministry

[14]Now after John was arrested, Jesus came into Galilee, proclaiming the gospel of God, [15]and saying, "The time is fulfilled, and the kingdom of God is at hand; repent and believe in the gospel."

Jesus Calls the First Disciples

[16][e]Passing alongside the Sea of Galilee, he saw Simon and Andrew the brother of Simon casting a net into the sea, for they were fishermen. [17]And Jesus said to them, "Follow me, and I will make you become fishers of men." [18]And immediately they left their nets and followed him. [19]And going on a little farther, he saw James the son of Zebedee and John his brother, who were in their boat mending the nets. [20]And immediately he called them, and they left their father Zebedee in the boat with the hired servants and followed him.

Jesus Heals a Man with an Unclean Spirit

[21][f]And they went into Capernaum, and immediately on the Sabbath he entered the synagogue and was teaching. [22]And they were astonished at his teaching, for he taught them as one who had authority, and not as the scribes. [23]And immediately there was in their synagogue a man with an unclean spirit. And he cried out, [24]"What have you to do with us, Jesus of Nazareth? Have you come to destroy us? I know who you are—the Holy One of God." [25]But Jesus rebuked him, saying, "Be silent, and come out of him!" [26]And the unclean spirit, convulsing him and crying out with a loud voice, came out of him. [27]And they were all amazed, so that they questioned among themselves, saying, "What is this? A new teaching with authority! He commands even the unclean spirits, and they obey him." [28]And at once his fame spread everywhere throughout all the surrounding region of Galilee.

Jesus Heals Many

[29][g]And immediately he[5] left the synagogue and entered the house of Simon and Andrew, with James and John. [30]Now Simon's mother-in-

---

[1] Some manuscripts omit the Son of God [2] Some manuscripts in the prophets [3] Or crying: Prepare in the wilderness [4] Or my Son, my (or the) Beloved [5] Some manuscripts they [a] For 1:2-8 see parallels Matt. 3:1-12; Luke 3:2-17 [b] Mal. 3:1 [c] Isa. 40:3 [d] For 1:9-11 see parallels Matt. 3:13-17; Luke 3:21, 22 [e] For 1:16-20 see parallel Matt. 4:18-22 [f] For 1:21-28 see parallel Luke 4:31-37 [g] For 1:29-34 see parallels Matt. 8:14-16; Luke 4:38-41

law lay ill with a fever, and immediately they told him about her. [31]And he came and took her by the hand and lifted her up, and the fever left her, and she began to serve them.

[32]That evening at sundown they brought to him all who were sick or oppressed by demons. [33]And the whole city was gathered together at the door. [34]And he healed many who were sick with various diseases, and cast out many demons. And he would not permit the demons to speak, because they knew him.

Jesus Preaches in Galilee

[35a]And rising very early in the morning, while it was still dark, he departed and went out to a desolate place, and there he prayed. [36]And Simon and those who were with him searched for him, [37]and they found him and said to him, "Everyone is looking for you." [38]And he said to them, "Let us go on to the next towns, that I may preach there also, for that is why I came out." [39]And he went throughout all Galilee, preaching in their synagogues and casting out demons.

Jesus Cleanses a Leper

[40b]And a leper[1] came to him, imploring him, and kneeling said to him, "If you will, you can make me clean." [41]Moved with pity, he stretched out his hand and touched him and said to him, "I will; be clean." [42]And immediately the leprosy left him, and he was made clean. [43]And Jesus[2] sternly charged him and sent him away at once, [44]and said to him, "See that you say nothing to anyone, but go, show yourself to the priest and offer for your cleansing what Moses commanded, for a proof to them." [45]But he went out and began to talk freely about it, and to spread the news, so that Jesus could no longer openly enter a town, but was out in desolate places, and people were coming to him from every quarter.

Jesus Heals a Paralytic

2 And when he returned to Capernaum after some days, it was reported that he was at home. [2]And many were gathered together, so that there was no more room, not even at the door. And he was preaching the word to them. [3c]And they came, bringing to him a paralytic carried by four men. [4]And when they could not get near him because of the crowd, they removed the roof above him, and when they had made an opening, they let down the bed on which the paralytic lay. [5]And when Jesus saw their faith, he said to the paralytic, "Son, your sins are forgiven." [6]Now some of the scribes were sitting there, questioning in their hearts, [7]"Why does this man speak like that? He is blaspheming! Who can forgive sins but God alone?" [8]And immediately Jesus, perceiving in his spirit that they thus questioned within themselves, said to them, "Why do you question these things in your hearts? [9]Which is easier, to say to the paralytic, 'Your sins are forgiven,' or to say, 'Rise, take up your bed and walk'? [10]But that you may know that the Son of Man has authority on earth to forgive sins"—he said to the paralytic— [11]"I say to you, rise, pick up your bed, and go home." [12]And he rose and immediately picked up his bed and went out before them all, so that they were all amazed and glorified God, saying, "We never saw anything like this!"

Jesus Calls Levi

[13]He went out again beside the sea, and all the crowd was coming to him, and he was teaching them. [14d]And as he passed by, he saw Levi the son of Alphaeus sitting at the tax booth, and he said to him, "Follow me." And he rose and followed him.

[15]And as he reclined at table in his house, many tax collectors and sinners were reclining with Jesus and his disciples, for there were many who followed him. [16]And the scribes of[3] the Pharisees, when they saw that he was eating with sinners and tax collectors, said to his disciples, "Why does he eat[4] with tax collectors and sinners?" [17]And when Jesus heard it, he said to them, "Those who are well have no need of a physician, but those who are sick. I came not to call the righteous, but sinners."

A Question About Fasting

[18]Now John's disciples and the Pharisees were fasting. And people came and said to him, "Why do John's disciples and the disciples of the Pharisees fast, but your disciples do not fast?" [19]And Jesus said to them, "Can the wedding guests fast while the bridegroom is with them? As long as they have the bridegroom with them, they cannot fast. [20]The days will come when the bridegroom is taken away from them, and then they will fast in that day. [21]No one sews a piece of unshrunk cloth on an old garment. If he does, the patch tears away from it, the new from the old, and a worse tear is made. [22]And no one puts new wine into old wineskins. If he does, the wine will burst the skins—and the wine is destroyed, and so are the skins. But new wine is for fresh wineskins."[5]

Jesus Is Lord of the Sabbath

[23e]One Sabbath he was going through the grainfields, and as they made their way, his disciples began to pluck heads of grain. [24]And the Pharisees were saying to him, "Look, why are they doing what is not lawful on the Sabbath?" [25]And he said to them, "Have you never read what David did, when he was in need and was

---

[1] *Leprosy* was a term for several skin diseases; see Leviticus 13 [2] Greek *he*; also verse 45 [3] Some manuscripts *and* [4] Some manuscripts add *and drink* [5] Some manuscripts omit *But new wine is for fresh wineskins* [a] For 1:35-38 see parallel Luke 4:42, 43 [b] For 1:40-44 see parallels Matt. 8:2-4; Luke 5:12-14 [c] For 2:3-12 see parallels Matt. 9:2-8; Luke 5:17-26 [d] For 2:14-22 see parallels Matt. 9:9-17; Luke 5:27-39 [e] For 2:23-28 see parallels Matt. 12:1-8; Luke 6:1-5

hungry, he and those who were with him: [26]how he entered the house of God, in the time of Abiathar the high priest, and ate the bread of the Presence, which it is not lawful for any but the priests to eat, and also gave it to those who were with him?" [27]And he said to them, "The Sabbath was made for man, not man for the Sabbath. [28]So the Son of Man is lord even of the Sabbath."

A Man with a Withered Hand

3 [a]Again he entered the synagogue, and a man was there with a withered hand. [2]And they watched Jesus,[1] to see whether he would heal him on the Sabbath, so that they might accuse him. [3]And he said to the man with the withered hand, "Come here." [4]And he said to them, "Is it lawful on the Sabbath to do good or to do harm, to save life or to kill?" But they were silent. [5]And he looked around at them with anger, grieved at their hardness of heart, and said to the man, "Stretch out your hand." He stretched it out, and his hand was restored. [6]The Pharisees went out and immediately held counsel with the Herodians against him, how to destroy him.

A Great Crowd Follows Jesus

[7]Jesus withdrew with his disciples to the sea, and a great crowd followed, from Galilee and Judea [8]and Jerusalem and Idumea and from beyond the Jordan and from around Tyre and Sidon. When the great crowd heard all that he was doing, they came to him. [9]And he told his disciples to have a boat ready for him because of the crowd, lest they crush him, [10]for he had healed many, so that all who had diseases pressed around him to touch him. [11]And whenever the unclean spirits saw him, they fell down before him and cried out, "You are the Son of God." [12]And he strictly ordered them not to make him known.

The Twelve Apostles

[13]And he went up on the mountain and called to him those whom he desired, and they came to him. [14]And he appointed twelve (whom he also named apostles) so that they might be with him and he might send them out to preach [15]and have authority to cast out demons. [16]He appointed the twelve: [b]Simon (to whom he gave the name Peter); [17]James the son of Zebedee and John the brother of James (to whom he gave the name Boanerges, that is, Sons of Thunder); [18]Andrew, and Philip, and Bartholomew, and Matthew, and Thomas, and James the son of Alphaeus, and Thaddaeus, and Simon the Cananaean, [19]and Judas Iscariot, who betrayed him.

[20]Then he went home, and the crowd gathered again, so that they could not even eat. [21]And when his family heard it, they went out to seize him, for they were saying, "He is out of his mind."

Blasphemy Against the Holy Spirit

[22]And the scribes who came down from Jerusalem were saying, "He is possessed by Beelzebul," and "by the prince of demons he casts out the demons." [23c]And he called them to him and said to them in parables, "How can Satan cast out Satan? [24]If a kingdom is divided against itself, that kingdom cannot stand. [25]And if a house is divided against itself, that house will not be able to stand. [26]And if Satan has risen up against himself and is divided, he cannot stand, but is coming to an end. [27]But no one can enter a strong man's house and plunder his goods, unless he first binds the strong man. Then indeed he may plunder his house.

[28d]"Truly, I say to you, all sins will be forgiven the children of man, and whatever blasphemies they utter, [29]but whoever blasphemes against the Holy Spirit never has forgiveness, but is guilty of an eternal sin"— [30]for they were saying, "He has an unclean spirit."

Jesus' Mother and Brothers

[31e]And his mother and his brothers came, and standing outside they sent to him and called him. [32]And a crowd was sitting around him, and they said to him, "Your mother and your brothers[2] are outside, seeking you." [33]And he answered them, "Who are my mother and my brothers?" [34]And looking about at those who sat around him, he said, "Here are my mother and my brothers! [35]For whoever does the will of God, he is my brother and sister and mother."

The Parable of the Sower

4 Again [f]he began to teach beside the sea. And a very large crowd gathered about him, so that he got into a boat and sat in it on the sea, and the whole crowd was beside the sea on the land. [2]And he was teaching them many things in parables, and in his teaching he said to them: [3]"Listen! A sower went out to sow. [4]And as he sowed, some seed fell along the path, and the birds came and devoured it. [5]Other seed fell on rocky ground, where it did not have much soil, and immediately it sprang up, since it had no depth of soil. [6]And when the sun rose, it was scorched, and since it had no root, it withered away. [7]Other seed fell among thorns, and the thorns grew up and choked it, and it yielded no grain. [8]And other seeds fell into good soil and produced grain, growing up and increasing and yielding thirtyfold and sixtyfold and a hundredfold." [9]And he said, "He who has ears to hear, let him hear."

[1]Greek *him* [2]Other early manuscripts add *and your sisters* [a]For 3:1-6 see parallels Matt. 12:9-14; Luke 6:6-11 [b]For 3:16-19 see parallels Matt. 10:2-4; Luke 6:13-16 [c]For 3:23-27 see parallels Matt. 12:25-29; Luke 11:17-22 [d]For 3:28-30 see parallel Matt. 12:31, 32 [e]For 3:31-35 see parallels Matt. 12:46-50; Luke 8:19-21 [f]For 4:1-12 see parallels Matt. 13:1-15; Luke 8:4-10

The Purpose of the Parables

[10]And when he was alone, those around him with the twelve asked him about the parables. [11]And he said to them, "To you has been given the secret of the kingdom of God, but for those outside everything is in parables, [12]so that

"they may indeed see but not perceive,
    and may indeed hear but not understand,
lest they should turn and be forgiven."

[13a]And he said to them, "Do you not understand this parable? How then will you understand all the parables? [14]The sower sows the word. [15]And these are the ones along the path, where the word is sown: when they hear, Satan immediately comes and takes away the word that is sown in them. [16]And these are the ones sown on rocky ground: the ones who, when they hear the word, immediately receive it with joy. [17]And they have no root in themselves, but endure for a while; then, when tribulation or persecution arises on account of the word, immediately they fall away.[1] [18]And others are the ones sown among thorns. They are those who hear the word, [19]but the cares of the world and the deceitfulness of riches and the desires for other things enter in and choke the word, and it proves unfruitful. [20]But those that were sown on the good soil are the ones who hear the word and accept it and bear fruit, thirtyfold and sixtyfold and a hundredfold."

A Lamp Under a Basket

[21b]And he said to them, "Is a lamp brought in to be put under a basket, or under a bed, and not on a stand? [22]For nothing is hidden except to be made manifest; nor is anything secret except to come to light. [23]If anyone has ears to hear, let him hear." [24]And he said to them, "Pay attention to what you hear: with the measure you use, it will be measured to you, and still more will be added to you. [25]For to the one who has, more will be given, and from the one who has not, even what he has will be taken away."

The Parable of the Seed Growing

[26]And he said, "The kingdom of God is as if a man should scatter seed on the ground. [27]He sleeps and rises night and day, and the seed sprouts and grows; he knows not how. [28]The earth produces by itself, first the blade, then the ear, then the full grain in the ear. [29]But when the grain is ripe, at once he puts in the sickle, because the harvest has come."

The Parable of the Mustard Seed

[30c]And he said, "With what can we compare the kingdom of God, or what parable shall we use for it? [31]It is like a grain of mustard seed, which, when sown on the ground, is the smallest of all the seeds on earth, [32]yet when it is sown it grows up and becomes larger than all the garden plants and puts out large branches, so that the birds of the air can make nests in its shade."

[33]With many such parables he spoke the word to them, as they were able to hear it. [34]He did not speak to them without a parable, but privately to his own disciples he explained everything.

Jesus Calms a Storm

[35d]On that day, when evening had come, he said to them, "Let us go across to the other side." [36]And leaving the crowd, they took him with them in the boat, just as he was. And other boats were with him. [37]And a great windstorm arose, and the waves were breaking into the boat, so that the boat was already filling. [38]But he was in the stern, asleep on the cushion. And they woke him and said to him, "Teacher, do you not care that we are perishing?" [39]And he awoke and rebuked the wind and said to the sea, "Peace! Be still!" And the wind ceased, and there was a great calm. [40]He said to them, "Why are you so afraid? Have you still no faith?" [41]And they were filled with great fear and said to one another, "Who then is this, that even the wind and the sea obey him?"

Jesus Heals a Man with a Demon

5 [1]They came to the other side of the sea, to the country of the Gerasenes.[2] [2]And when Jesus[3] had stepped out of the boat, immediately there met him out of the tombs a man with an unclean spirit. [3]He lived among the tombs. And no one could bind him anymore, not even with a chain, [4]for he had often been bound with shackles and chains, but he wrenched the chains apart, and he broke the shackles in pieces. No one had the strength to subdue him. [5]Night and day among the tombs and on the mountains he was always crying out and cutting himself with stones. [6]And when he saw Jesus from afar, he ran and fell down before him. [7]And crying out with a loud voice, he said, "What have you to do with me, Jesus, Son of the Most High God? I adjure you by God, do not torment me." [8]For he was saying to him, "Come out of the man, you unclean spirit!" [9]And Jesus asked him, "What is your name?" He replied, "My name is Legion, for we are many." [10]And he begged him earnestly not to send them out of the country. [11]Now a great herd of pigs was feeding there on the hillside, [12]and they begged him, saying, "Send us to the pigs; let us enter them." [13]So he gave them permission. And the unclean spirits came out, and entered the pigs, and the herd, numbering

---

[1]Or *stumble* [2]Some manuscripts *Gergesenes*; some *Gadarenes* [3]Greek *he*; also verse 9 [a]For 4:13-20 see parallels Matt. 13:18-23; Luke 8:11-15 [b]For 4:21-25 see parallel Luke 8:16-18 [c]For 4:30-32 see parallels Matt. 13:31, 32; Luke 13:18, 19 [d]For 4:35-41 see parallels Matt. 8:18, 23-27; Luke 8:22-25 [e]For 5:1-20 see parallels Matt. 8:28-34; Luke 8:26-39

about two thousand, rushed down the steep bank into the sea and were drowned in the sea. [14]The herdsmen fled and told it in the city and in the country. And people came to see what it was that had happened. [15]And they came to Jesus and saw the demon-possessed[1] man, the one who had had the legion, sitting there, clothed and in his right mind, and they were afraid. [16]And those who had seen it described to them what had happened to the demon-possessed man and to the pigs. [17]And they began to beg Jesus[2] to depart from their region. [18]As he was getting into the boat, the man who had been possessed with demons begged him that he might be with him. [19]And he did not permit him but said to him, "Go home to your friends and tell them how much the Lord has done for you, and how he has had mercy on you." [20]And he went away and began to proclaim in the Decapolis how much Jesus had done for him, and everyone marveled.

Jesus Heals a Woman and Jairus's Daughter

[21]And when Jesus had crossed again in the boat to the other side, a great crowd gathered about him, and he was beside the sea. [22][a]Then came one of the rulers of the synagogue, Jairus by name, and seeing him, he fell at his feet [23]and implored him earnestly, saying, "My little daughter is at the point of death. Come and lay your hands on her, so that she may be made well and live." [24]And he went with him.

And a great crowd followed him and thronged about him. [25]And there was a woman who had had a discharge of blood for twelve years, [26]and who had suffered much under many physicians, and had spent all that she had, and was no better but rather grew worse. [27]She had heard the reports about Jesus and came up behind him in the crowd and touched his garment. [28]For she said, "If I touch even his garments, I will be made well." [29]And immediately the flow of blood dried up, and she felt in her body that she was healed of her disease. [30]And Jesus, perceiving in himself that power had gone out from him, immediately turned about in the crowd and said, "Who touched my garments?" [31]And his disciples said to him, "You see the crowd pressing around you, and yet you say, 'Who touched me?'" [32]And he looked around to see who had done it. [33]But the woman, knowing what had happened to her, came in fear and trembling and fell down before him and told him the whole truth. [34]And he said to her, "Daughter, your faith has made you well; go in peace, and be healed of your disease."

[35]While he was still speaking, there came from the ruler's house some who said, "Your daughter is dead. Why trouble the Teacher any further?" [36]But overhearing[3] what they said,

Jesus said to the ruler of the synagogue, "Do not fear, only believe." [37]And he allowed no one to follow him except Peter and James and John the brother of James. [38]They came to the house of the ruler of the synagogue, and Jesus[4] saw a commotion, people weeping and wailing loudly. [39]And when he had entered, he said to them, "Why are you making a commotion and weeping? The child is not dead but sleeping." [40]And they laughed at him. But he put them all outside and took the child's father and mother and those who were with him and went in where the child was. [41]Taking her by the hand he said to her, "Talitha cumi," which means, "Little girl, I say to you, arise." [42]And immediately the girl got up and began walking (for she was twelve years of age), and they were immediately overcome with amazement. [43]And he strictly charged them that no one should know this, and told them to give her something to eat.

Jesus Rejected at Nazareth

6 [b]He went away from there and came to his hometown, and his disciples followed him. [2]And on the Sabbath he began to teach in the synagogue, and many who heard him were astonished, saying, "Where did this man get these things? What is the wisdom given to him? How are such mighty works done by his hands? [3]Is not this the carpenter, the son of Mary and brother of James and Joses and Judas and Simon? And are not his sisters here with us?" And they took offense at him. [4]And Jesus said to them, "A prophet is not without honor, except in his hometown and among his relatives and in his own household." [5]And he could do no mighty work there, except that he laid his hands on a few sick people and healed them. [6]And he marveled because of their unbelief.

And he went about among the villages teaching.

Jesus Sends Out the Twelve Apostles

[7][c]And he called the twelve and began to send them out two by two, and gave them authority over the unclean spirits. [8]He charged them to take nothing for their journey except a staff—no bread, no bag, no money in their belts— [9]but to wear sandals and not put on two tunics.[5] [10]And he said to them, "Whenever you enter a house, stay there until you depart from there. [11]And if any place will not receive you and they will not listen to you, when you leave, shake off the dust that is on your feet as a testimony against them." [12]So they went out and proclaimed that people should repent. [13]And they cast out many demons and anointed with oil many who were sick and healed them.

---

[1]Greek *daimonizomai*; also verses 16, 18; elsewhere rendered *oppressed by demons* [2]Greek *him* [3]Or *ignoring*; some manuscripts *hearing* [4]Greek *he* [5]Greek *chiton*, a long garment worn under the cloak next to the skin [a]For 5:22-43 see parallels Matt. 9:18-26; Luke 8:40-56 [b]For 6:1-6 see parallel Matt. 13:54-58 [c]For 6:7-11 see parallels Matt. 10:1, 5, 9-14; Luke 9:1, 3-5

The Death of John the Baptist

[14]ªKing Herod heard of it, for Jesus'[1] name had become known. Some[2] said, "John the Baptist[3] has been raised from the dead. That is why these miraculous powers are at work in him." [15]But others said, "He is Elijah." And others said, "He is a prophet, like one of the prophets of old." [16]But when Herod heard of it, he said, "John, whom I beheaded, has been raised." [17]For it was Herod who had sent and seized John and bound him in prison for the sake of Herodias, his brother Philip's wife, because he had married her. [18]For John had been saying to Herod, "It is not lawful for you to have your brother's wife." [19]And Herodias had a grudge against him and wanted to put him to death. But she could not, [20]for Herod feared John, knowing that he was a righteous and holy man, and he kept him safe. When he heard him, he was greatly perplexed, and yet he heard him gladly.

[21]But an opportunity came when Herod on his birthday gave a banquet for his nobles and military commanders and the leading men of Galilee. [22]For when Herodias's daughter came in and danced, she pleased Herod and his guests. And the king said to the girl, "Ask me for whatever you wish, and I will give it to you." [23]And he vowed to her, "Whatever you ask me, I will give you, up to half of my kingdom." [24]And she went out and said to her mother, "For what should I ask?" And she said, "The head of John the Baptist." [25]And she came in immediately with haste to the king and asked, saying, "I want you to give me at once the head of John the Baptist on a platter." [26]And the king was exceedingly sorry, but because of his oaths and his guests he did not want to break his word to her. [27]And immediately the king sent an executioner with orders to bring John's[4] head. He went and beheaded him in the prison [28]and brought his head on a platter and gave it to the girl, and the girl gave it to her mother. [29]When his disciples heard of it, they came and took his body and laid it in a tomb.

Jesus Feeds the Five Thousand

[30]The apostles returned to Jesus and told him all that they had done and taught. [31]And he said to them, "Come away by yourselves to a desolate place and rest a while." For many were coming and going, and they had no leisure even to eat. [32]ᵇAnd they went away in the boat to a desolate place by themselves. [33]Now many saw them going and recognized them, and they ran there on foot from all the towns and got there ahead of them. [34]When he went ashore he saw a great crowd, and he had compassion on them, because they were like sheep without a shepherd. And he began to teach them many things. [35]And when it grew late, his disciples came to him and said, "This is a desolate place, and the hour is now late. [36]Send them away to go into the surrounding countryside and villages and buy themselves something to eat." [37]But he answered them, "You give them something to eat." And they said to him, "Shall we go and buy two hundred denarii[5] worth of bread and give it to them to eat?" [38]And he said to them, "How many loaves do you have? Go and see." And when they had found out, they said, "Five, and two fish." [39]Then he commanded them all to sit down in groups on the green grass. [40]So they sat down in groups, by hundreds and by fifties. [41]And taking the five loaves and the two fish he looked up to heaven and said a blessing and broke the loaves and gave them to the disciples to set before the people. And he divided the two fish among them all. [42]And they all ate and were satisfied. [43]And they took up twelve baskets full of broken pieces and of the fish. [44]And those who ate the loaves were five thousand men.

Jesus Walks on the Water

[45]ᶜImmediately he made his disciples get into the boat and go before him to the other side, to Bethsaida, while he dismissed the crowd. [46]And after he had taken leave of them, he went up on the mountain to pray. [47]And when evening came, the boat was out on the sea, and he was alone on the land. [48]And he saw that they were making headway painfully, for the wind was against them. And about the fourth watch of the night[6] he came to them, walking on the sea. He meant to pass by them, [49]but when they saw him walking on the sea they thought it was a ghost, and cried out, [50]for they all saw him and were terrified. But immediately he spoke to them and said, "Take heart; it is I. Do not be afraid." [51]And he got into the boat with them, and the wind ceased. And they were utterly astounded, [52]for they did not understand about the loaves, but their hearts were hardened.

Jesus Heals the Sick in Gennesaret

[53]ᵈWhen they had crossed over, they came to land at Gennesaret and moored to the shore. [54]And when they got out of the boat, the people immediately recognized him [55]and ran about the whole region and began to bring the sick people on their beds to wherever they heard he was. [56]And wherever he came, in villages, cities, or countryside, they laid the sick in the marketplaces and implored him that they might touch even the fringe of his garment. And as many as touched it were made well.

[1]Greek *his* [2]Some manuscripts *He* [3]Greek *baptizer*; also verse 24 [4]Greek *his* [5]A *denarius* was a day's wage for a laborer [6]That is, between 3 A.M. and 6 A.M. ªFor 6:14-29 see parallels Matt. 14:1-12; Luke 9:7-9 ᵇFor 6:32-44 see parallels Matt. 14:13-21; Luke 9:10-17; John 6:1-13 ᶜFor 6:45-52 see parallels Matt. 14:22-33; John 6:16-21 ᵈFor 6:53-56 see parallel Matt. 14:34-36

Traditions and Commandments

7 ªNow when the Pharisees gathered to him, with some of the scribes who had come from Jerusalem, ²they saw that some of his disciples ate with hands that were defiled, that is, unwashed. ³(For the Pharisees and all the Jews do not eat unless they wash¹ their hands, holding to the tradition of the elders, ⁴and when they come from the marketplace, they do not eat unless they wash.² And there are many other traditions that they observe, such as the washing of cups and pots and copper vessels and dining couches.³) ⁵And the Pharisees and the scribes asked him, "Why do your disciples not walk according to the tradition of the elders, but eat with defiled hands?" ⁶And he said to them, "Well did Isaiah prophesy of you hypocrites, as it is written,

ᵇ"'This people honors me with their lips,
     but their heart is far from me;
⁷ in vain do they worship me,
     teaching as doctrines the commandments
       of men.'

⁸You leave the commandment of God and hold to the tradition of men."

⁹And he said to them, "You have a fine way of rejecting the commandment of God in order to establish your tradition! ¹⁰For Moses said, ᶜ'Honor your father and your mother'; and, ᵈ'Whoever reviles father or mother must surely die.' ¹¹But you say, 'If a man tells his father or his mother, "Whatever you would have gained from me is Corban"' (that is, given to God)ᵈ— ¹²then you no longer permit him to do anything for his father or mother, ¹³thus making void the word of God by your tradition that you have handed down. And many such things you do."

What Defiles a Person

¹⁴And he called the people to him again and said to them, "Hear me, all of you, and understand: ¹⁵There is nothing outside a person that by going into him can defile him, but the things that come out of a person are what defile him."⁵ ¹⁷And when he had entered the house and left the people, his disciples asked him about the parable. ¹⁸And he said to them, "Then are you also without understanding? Do you not see that whatever goes into a person from outside cannot defile him, ¹⁹since it enters not his heart but his stomach, and is expelled?"⁶ (Thus he declared all foods clean.) ²⁰And he said, "What comes out of a person is what defiles him. ²¹For from within, out of the heart of man, come evil thoughts, sexual immorality, theft, murder, adultery, ²²coveting, wickedness, deceit, sensuality, envy, slander,

pride, foolishness. ²³All these evil things come from within, and they defile a person."

The Syrophoenician Woman's Faith

²⁴And from there he arose and went away to the region of Tyre and Sidon.⁷ And he entered a house and did not want anyone to know, yet he could not be hidden. ²⁵But immediately a woman whose little daughter had an unclean spirit heard of him and came and fell down at his feet. ²⁶Now the woman was a Gentile, a Syrophoenician by birth. And she begged him to cast the demon out of her daughter. ²⁷And he said to her, "Let the children be fed first, for it is not right to take the children's bread and throw it to the dogs." ²⁸But she answered him, "Yes, Lord; yet even the dogs under the table eat the children's crumbs." ²⁹And he said to her, "For this statement you may go your way; the demon has left your daughter." ³⁰And she went home and found the child lying in bed and the demon gone.

Jesus Heals a Deaf Man

³¹Then he returned from the region of Tyre and went through Sidon to the Sea of Galilee, in the region of the Decapolis. ³²And they brought to him a man who was deaf and had a speech impediment, and they begged him to lay his hand on him. ³³And taking him aside from the crowd privately, he put his fingers into his ears, and after spitting touched his tongue. ³⁴And looking up to heaven, he sighed and said to him, "Ephphatha," that is, "Be opened." ³⁵And his ears were opened, his tongue was released, and he spoke plainly. ³⁶And Jesusᵍ charged them to tell no one. But the more he charged them, the more zealously they proclaimed it. ³⁷And they were astonished beyond measure, saying, "He has done all things well. He even makes the deaf hear and the mute speak."

Jesus Feeds the Four Thousand

8 ᵉIn those days, when again a great crowd had gathered, and they had nothing to eat, he called his disciples to him and said to them, ²"I have compassion on the crowd, because they have been with me now three days and have nothing to eat. ³And if I send them away hungry to their homes, they will faint on the way. And some of them have come from far away." ⁴And his disciples answered him, "How can one feed these people with bread here in this desolate place?" ⁵And he asked them, "How many loaves do you have?" They said, "Seven." ⁶And he directed the crowd to sit down on the ground. And he took the seven loaves, and having given thanks, he broke them and gave them to his disciples to set before the people; and they set them

¹ Greek *unless they wash with a fist*, probably indicating a kind of ceremonial washing ² Greek *unless they baptize*; some manuscripts *unless they purify themselves* ³ Some manuscripts omit *and dining couches* ⁴ Or *an offering* ⁵ Some manuscripts add verse 16: *If anyone has ears to hear, let him hear* ⁶ Greek *goes out into the latrine* ⁷ Some manuscripts omit *and Sidon* ⁸ Greek *he* ª For 7:1-30 see parallel Matt. 15:1-28 ᵇ Isa. 29:13 ᶜ Ex. 20:12 ᵈ Ex. 21:17 ᵉ For 8:1-10 see parallel Matt. 15:32-39

before the crowd. [7]And they had a few small fish. And having blessed them, he said that these also should be set before them. [8]And they ate and were satisfied. And they took up the broken pieces left over, seven baskets full. [9]And there were about four thousand people. And he sent them away. [10]And immediately he got into the boat with his disciples and went to the district of Dalmanutha.[1]

The Pharisees Demand a Sign

[11][a]The Pharisees came and began to argue with him, seeking from him a sign from heaven to test him. [12]And he sighed deeply in his spirit and said, "Why does this generation seek a sign? Truly, I say to you, no sign will be given to this generation." [13]And he left them, got into the boat again, and went to the other side.

The Leaven of the Pharisees and Herod

[14]Now they had forgotten to bring bread, and they had only one loaf with them in the boat. [15]And he cautioned them, saying, "Watch out; beware of the leaven of the Pharisees and the leaven of Herod."[2] [16]And they began discussing with one another the fact that they had no bread. [17]And Jesus, aware of this, said to them, "Why are you discussing the fact that you have no bread? Do you not yet perceive or understand? Are your hearts hardened? [18]Having eyes do you not see, and having ears do you not hear? And do you not remember? [19]When I broke the five loaves for the five thousand, how many baskets full of broken pieces did you take up?" They said to him, "Twelve." [20]"And the seven for the four thousand, how many baskets full of broken pieces did you take up?" And they said to him, "Seven." [21]And he said to them, "Do you not yet understand?"

Jesus Heals a Blind Man at Bethsaida

[22]And they came to Bethsaida. And some people brought to him a blind man and begged him to touch him. [23]And he took the blind man by the hand and led him out of the village, and when he had spit on his eyes and laid his hands on him, he asked him, "Do you see anything?" [24]And he looked up and said, "I see men, but they look like trees, walking." [25]Then Jesus[3] laid his hands on his eyes again; and he opened his eyes, his sight was restored, and he saw everything clearly. [26]And he sent him to his home, saying, "Do not even enter the village."

Peter Confesses Jesus as the Christ

[27][b]And Jesus went on with his disciples to the villages of Caesarea Philippi. And on the way he asked his disciples, "Who do people say that I am?" [28]And they told him, "John the Baptist; and

others say, Elijah; and others, one of the prophets." [29]And he asked them, "But who do you say that I am?" Peter answered him, "You are the Christ." [30]And he strictly charged them to tell no one about him.

Jesus Foretells His Death and Resurrection

[31][c]And he began to teach them that the Son of Man must suffer many things and be rejected by the elders and the chief priests and the scribes and be killed, and after three days rise again. [32]And he said this plainly. And Peter took him aside and began to rebuke him. [33]But turning and seeing his disciples, he rebuked Peter and said, "Get behind me, Satan! For you are not setting your mind on the things of God, but on the things of man."

[34]And calling the crowd to him with his disciples, he said to them, "If anyone would come after me, let him deny himself and take up his cross and follow me. [35]For whoever would save his life[4] will lose it, but whoever loses his life for my sake and the gospel's will save it. [36]For what does it profit a man to gain the whole world and forfeit his soul? [37]For what can a man give in return for his soul? [38]For whoever is ashamed of me and of my words in this adulterous and sinful generation, of him will the Son of Man also be ashamed when he comes in the glory of his Father with the holy angels."

9 And he said to them, "Truly, I say to you, there are some standing here who will not taste death until they see the kingdom of God after it has come with power."

The Transfiguration

[2][d]And after six days Jesus took with him Peter and James and John, and led them up a high mountain by themselves. And he was transfigured before them, [3]and his clothes became radiant, intensely white, as no one[5] on earth could bleach them. [4]And there appeared to them Elijah with Moses, and they were talking with Jesus. [5]And Peter said to Jesus, "Rabbi,[6] it is good that we are here. Let us make three tents, one for you and one for Moses and one for Elijah." [6]For he did not know what to say, for they were terrified. [7]And a cloud overshadowed them, and a voice came out of the cloud, "This is my beloved Son;[7] listen to him." [8]And suddenly, looking around, they no longer saw anyone with them but Jesus only.

[9][e]And as they were coming down the mountain, he charged them to tell no one what they had seen, until the Son of Man had risen from the dead. [10]So they kept the matter to themselves, questioning what this rising from the dead might mean. [11]And they asked him, "Why do the scribes say that first Elijah must come?" [12]And

---

[1] Some manuscripts *Magadan*, or *Magdala* [2] Some manuscripts *the Herodians* [3] Greek *he* [4] The same Greek word can mean either *soul* or *life*, depending on the context; twice in this verse and once in verse 36 and once in verse 37 [5] Greek *no cloth refiner* [6] *Rabbi* means *my teacher*, or *my master* [7] Or *my Son, my* (or *the) Beloved* [a] For 8:11-21 see parallel Matt. 16:1-12 [b] For 8:27-29 see parallels Matt. 16:13-16; Luke 9:18-20 [c] For 8:31–9:1 see parallels Matt. 16:21-28; Luke 9:22-27 [d] For 9:2-8 see parallels Matt. 17:1-8; Luke 9:28-36 [e] For 9:9-13 see parallel Matt. 17:9-13

he said to them, "Elijah does come first to restore all things. And how is it written of the Son of Man that he should suffer many things and be treated with contempt? ¹³But I tell you that Elijah has come, and they did to him whatever they pleased, as it is written of him."

Jesus Heals a Boy with an Unclean Spirit

¹⁴ᵃAnd when they came to the disciples, they saw a great crowd around them, and scribes arguing with them. ¹⁵And immediately all the crowd, when they saw him, were greatly amazed and ran up to him and greeted him. ¹⁶And he asked them, "What are you arguing about with them?" ¹⁷And someone from the crowd answered him, "Teacher, I brought my son to you, for he has a spirit that makes him mute. ¹⁸And whenever it seizes him, it throws him down, and he foams and grinds his teeth and becomes rigid. So I asked your disciples to cast it out, and they were not able." ¹⁹And he answered them, "O faithless generation, how long am I to be with you? How long am I to bear with you? Bring him to me." ²⁰And they brought the boy to him. And when the spirit saw him, immediately it convulsed the boy, and he fell on the ground and rolled about, foaming at the mouth. ²¹And Jesus asked his father, "How long has this been happening to him?" And he said, "From childhood. ²²And it has often cast him into fire and into water, to destroy him. But if you can do anything, have compassion on us and help us." ²³And Jesus said to him, "'If you can'! All things are possible for one who believes." ²⁴Immediately the father of the child cried out¹ and said, "I believe; help my unbelief!" ²⁵And when Jesus saw that a crowd came running together, he rebuked the unclean spirit, saying to it, "You mute and deaf spirit, I command you, come out of him and never enter him again." ²⁶And after crying out and convulsing him terribly, it came out, and the boy was like a corpse, so that most of them said, "He is dead." ²⁷But Jesus took him by the hand and lifted him up, and he arose. ²⁸And when he had entered the house, his disciples asked him privately, "Why could we not cast it out?" ²⁹And he said to them, "This kind cannot be driven out by anything but prayer."²

Jesus Again Foretells Death, Resurrection

³⁰ᵇThey went on from there and passed through Galilee. And he did not want anyone to know, ³¹for he was teaching his disciples, saying to them, "The Son of Man is going to be delivered into the hands of men, and they will kill him. And when he is killed, after three days he will rise." ³²But they did not understand the saying, and were afraid to ask him.

Who Is the Greatest?

³³And they came to Capernaum. And when he was in the house ᶜhe asked them, "What were you discussing on the way?" ³⁴But they kept silent, for on the way they had argued with one another about who was the greatest. ³⁵And he sat down and called the twelve. And he said to them, "If anyone would be first, he must be last of all and servant of all." ³⁶And he took a child and put him in the midst of them, and taking him in his arms, he said to them, ³⁷"Whoever receives one such child in my name receives me, and whoever receives me, receives not me but him who sent me."

Anyone Not Against Us Is for Us

³⁸ᵈJohn said to him, "Teacher, we saw someone casting out demons in your name,³ and we tried to stop him, because he was not following us." ³⁹But Jesus said, "Do not stop him, for no one who does a mighty work in my name will be able soon afterward to speak evil of me. ⁴⁰For the one who is not against us is for us. ⁴¹For truly, I say to you, whoever gives you a cup of water to drink because you belong to Christ will by no means lose his reward.

Temptations to Sin

⁴²"Whoever causes one of these little ones who believe in me to sin,⁴ it would be better for him if a great millstone were hung around his neck and he were thrown into the sea. ⁴³And if your hand causes you to sin, cut it off. It is better for you to enter life crippled than with two hands to go to hell,⁵ to the unquenchable fire.⁶ ⁴⁵And if your foot causes you to sin, cut it off. It is better for you to enter life lame than with two feet to be thrown into hell. ⁴⁷And if your eye causes you to sin, tear it out. It is better for you to enter the kingdom of God with one eye than with two eyes to be thrown into hell, ⁴⁸'where their worm does not die and the fire is not quenched.' ⁴⁹For everyone will be salted with fire.⁷ ⁵⁰Salt is good, but if the salt has lost its saltiness, how will you make it salty again? Have salt in yourselves, and be at peace with one another."

Teaching About Divorce

10 ᵉAnd he left there and went to the region of Judea and beyond the Jordan, and crowds gathered to him again. And again, as was his custom, he taught them.

²And Pharisees came up and in order to test him asked, "Is it lawful for a man to divorce his wife?" ³He answered them, "What did Moses command you?" ⁴They said, "Moses allowed a man to write a certificate of divorce and to send her away." ⁵And Jesus said to them, "Because of

---

¹Some manuscripts add *with tears* ²Some manuscripts add *and fasting* ³Some manuscripts add *who does not follow us* ⁴Greek *to stumble*; also verses 43, 45, 47 ⁵Greek *Gehenna*; also verse 47 ⁶Some manuscripts add verses 44 and 46 (which are identical with verse 48) ⁷Some manuscripts add *and every sacrifice will be salted with salt* ᵃFor 9:14-28 see parallels Matt. 17:14-19; Luke 9:37-42 ᵇFor 9:30-32 see parallels Matt. 17:22, 23; Luke 9:43-45 ᶜFor 9:33-37 see parallels Matt. 18:1-5; Luke 9:46-48 ᵈFor 9:38-40 see parallel Luke 9:49, 50 ᵉFor 10:1-12 see parallel Matt. 19:1-9

your hardness of heart he wrote you this commandment. [6]But from the beginning of creation, 'God made them ᵃmale and female.' [7]ᵇTherefore a man shall leave his father and mother and hold fast to his wife,[1] [8]and the two shall become one flesh.' So they are no longer two but one flesh. [9]What therefore God has joined together, let not man separate."

[10]And in the house the disciples asked him again about this matter. [11]And he said to them, "Whoever divorces his wife and marries another commits adultery against her, [12]and if she divorces her husband and marries another, she commits adultery."

Let the Children Come to Me

[13]ᶜAnd they were bringing children to him that he might touch them, and the disciples rebuked them. [14]But when Jesus saw it, he was indignant and said to them, "Let the children come to me; do not hinder them, for to such belongs the kingdom of God. [15]Truly, I say to you, whoever does not receive the kingdom of God like a child shall not enter it." [16]And he took them in his arms and blessed them, laying his hands on them.

The Rich Young Man

[17]ᵈAnd as he was setting out on his journey, a man ran up and knelt before him and asked him, "Good Teacher, what must I do to inherit eternal life?" [18]And Jesus said to him, "Why do you call me good? No one is good except God alone. [19]You know the commandments: ᵉ'Do not murder, Do not commit adultery, Do not steal, Do not bear false witness, Do not defraud, Honor your father and mother.'" [20]And he said to him, "Teacher, all these I have kept from my youth." [21]And Jesus, looking at him, loved him, and said to him, "You lack one thing: go, sell all that you have and give to the poor, and you will have treasure in heaven; and come, follow me." [22]Disheartened by the saying, he went away sorrowful, for he had great possessions.

[23]And Jesus looked around and said to his disciples, "How difficult it will be for those who have wealth to enter the kingdom of God!" [24]And the disciples were amazed at his words. But Jesus said to them again, "Children, how difficult it is[2] to enter the kingdom of God! [25]It is easier for a camel to go through the eye of a needle than for a rich person to enter the kingdom of God." [26]And they were exceedingly astonished, and said to him,[3] "Then who can be saved?" [27]Jesus looked at them and said, "With man it is impossible, but not with God. For all things are possible with God." [28]Peter began to say to him, "See, we have left everything and followed you." [29]Jesus said,

"Truly, I say to you, there is no one who has left house or brothers or sisters or mother or father or children or lands, for my sake and for the gospel, [30]who will not receive a hundredfold now in this time, houses and brothers and sisters and mothers and children and lands, with persecutions, and in the age to come eternal life. [31]But many who are first will be last, and the last first."

Jesus Foretells His Death a Third Time

[32]ᶠAnd they were on the road, going up to Jerusalem, and Jesus was walking ahead of them. And they were amazed, and those who followed were afraid. And taking the twelve again, he began to tell them what was to happen to him, [33]saying, "See, we are going up to Jerusalem, and the Son of Man will be delivered over to the chief priests and the scribes, and they will condemn him to death and deliver him over to the Gentiles. [34]And they will mock him and spit on him, and flog him and kill him. And after three days he will rise."

The Request of James and John

[35]ᵍAnd James and John, the sons of Zebedee, came up to him and said to him, "Teacher, we want you to do for us whatever we ask of you." [36]And he said to them, "What do you want me to do for you?" [37]And they said to him, "Grant us to sit, one at your right hand and one at your left, in your glory." [38]Jesus said to them, "You do not know what you are asking. Are you able to drink the cup that I drink, or to be baptized with the baptism with which I am baptized?" [39]And they said to him, "We are able." And Jesus said to them, "The cup that I drink you will drink, and with the baptism with which I am baptized, you will be baptized, [40]but to sit at my right hand or at my left is not mine to grant, but it is for those for whom it has been prepared." [41]And when the ten heard it, they began to be indignant at James and John. [42]And Jesus called them to him and said to them, "You know that those who are considered rulers of the Gentiles lord it over them, and their great ones exercise authority over them. [43]But it shall not be so among you. But whoever would be great among you must be your servant,[4] [44]and whoever would be first among you must be slave[5] of all. [45]For even the Son of Man came not to be served but to serve, and to give his life as a ransom for many."

Jesus Heals Blind Bartimaeus

[46]ʰAnd they came to Jericho. And as he was leaving Jericho with his disciples and a great crowd, Bartimaeus, a blind beggar, the son of Timaeus, was sitting by the roadside. [47]And when he heard that it was Jesus of Nazareth, he

[1] Some manuscripts omit *and hold fast to his wife* [2] Some manuscripts add *for those who trust in riches* [3] Some manuscripts *to one another* [4] Greek *diakonos* [5] Greek *bondservant (doulos)* ᵃGen. 1:27; 5:2 ᵇGen. 2:24 ᶜFor 10:13-16 see parallels Matt. 19:13-15; Luke 18:15-17 ᵈFor 10:17-31 see parallels Matt. 19:16-30; Luke 18:18-30 ᵉEx. 20:12-16; Deut. 5:16-20 ᶠFor 10:32-34 see parallels Matt. 20:17-19; Luke 18:31-33 ᵍFor 10:35-45 see parallel Matt. 20:20-28 ʰFor 10:46-52 see parallels Matt. 20:29-34; Luke 18:35-43

began to cry out and say, "Jesus, Son of David, have mercy on me!" [48]And many rebuked him, telling him to be silent. But he cried out all the more, "Son of David, have mercy on me!" [49]And Jesus stopped and said, "Call him." And they called the blind man, saying to him, "Take heart. Get up; he is calling you." [50]And throwing off his cloak, he sprang up and came to Jesus. [51]And Jesus said to him, "What do you want me to do for you?" And the blind man said to him, "Rabbi, let me recover my sight." [52]And Jesus said to him, "Go your way; your faith has made you well." And immediately he recovered his sight and followed him on the way.

The Triumphal Entry

11 [a]Now when they drew near to Jerusalem, to Bethphage and Bethany, at the Mount of Olives, Jesus[1] sent two of his disciples [2]and said to them, "Go into the village in front of you, and immediately as you enter it you will find a colt tied, on which no one has ever sat. Untie it and bring it. [3]If anyone says to you, 'Why are you doing this?' say, 'The Lord has need of it and will send it back here immediately.'" [4]And they went away and found a colt tied at a door outside in the street, and they untied it. [5]And some of those standing there said to them, "What are you doing, untying the colt?" [6]And they told them what Jesus had said, and they let them go. [7]And they brought the colt to Jesus and threw their cloaks on it, and he sat on it. [8]And many spread their cloaks on the road, and others spread leafy branches that they had cut from the fields. [9]And those who went before and those who followed were shouting, "Hosanna! Blessed is he who comes in the name of the Lord! [10]Blessed is the coming kingdom of our father David! Hosanna in the highest!"

[11]And he entered Jerusalem and went into the temple. And when he had looked around at everything, as it was already late, he went out to Bethany with the twelve.

Jesus Curses the Fig Tree

[12]On the following day, when they came from Bethany, he was hungry. [13]And seeing in the distance a fig tree in leaf, he went to see if he could find anything on it. When he came to it, he found nothing but leaves, for it was not the season for figs. [14]And he said to it, "May no one ever eat fruit from you again." And his disciples heard it.

Jesus Cleanses the Temple

[15b]And they came to Jerusalem. And he entered the temple and began to drive out those who sold and those who bought in the temple, and he overturned the tables of the money-changers and the seats of those who sold pigeons. [16]And he would not allow anyone to carry anything through the temple. [17]And he was teaching and saying to them, "Is it not written, 'My house shall be called a house of prayer for all the nations'? But you have made it a den of robbers." [18]And the chief priests and the scribes heard it and were seeking a way to destroy him, for they feared him, because all the crowd was astonished at his teaching. [19]And when evening came they[2] went out of the city.

The Lesson from the Withered Fig Tree

[20d]As they passed by in the morning, they saw the fig tree withered away to its roots. [21]And Peter remembered and said to him, "Rabbi, look! The fig tree that you cursed has withered." [22]And Jesus answered them, "Have faith in God. [23]Truly, I say to you, whoever says to this mountain, 'Be taken up and thrown into the sea,' and does not doubt in his heart, but believes that what he says will come to pass, it will be done for him. [24]Therefore I tell you, whatever you ask in prayer, believe that you have received[3] it, and it will be yours. [25]And whenever you stand praying, forgive, if you have anything against anyone, so that your Father also who is in heaven may forgive you your trespasses."[4]

The Authority of Jesus Challenged

[27e]And they came again to Jerusalem. And as he was walking in the temple, the chief priests and the scribes and the elders came to him, [28]and they said to him, "By what authority are you doing these things, or who gave you this authority to do them?" [29]Jesus said to them, "I will ask you one question; answer me, and I will tell you by what authority I do these things. [30]Was the baptism of John from heaven or from man? Answer me." [31]And they discussed it with one another, saying, "If we say, 'From heaven,' he will say, 'Why then did you not believe him?' [32]But shall we say, 'From man'?"—they were afraid of the people, for they all held that John really was a prophet. [33]So they answered Jesus, "We do not know." And Jesus said to them, "Neither will I tell you by what authority I do these things."

The Parable of the Tenants

12 [f]And he began to speak to them in parables. "A man planted a vineyard and put a fence around it and dug a pit for the winepress and built a tower, and leased it to tenants and went into another country. [2]When the season came, he sent a servant[5] to the tenants to get from them some of the fruit of the vineyard. [3]And they took him and beat him and sent him away empty-handed. [4]Again he sent to them

---

[1] Greek *he* [2] Some manuscripts *he* [3] Some manuscripts *are receiving* [4] Some manuscripts add verse 26: *But if you do not forgive, neither will your Father who is in heaven forgive your trespasses* [5] Greek *bondservant*; also verse 4 [a] For 11:1-10 see parallels Matt. 21:1-9; Luke 19:28-38; John 12:12-15 [b] For 11:15-18 see parallels Matt. 21:12-16; Luke 19:45-47 [c] Isa. 56:7 [d] For 11:20-24 see parallel Matt. 21:19-22 [e] For 11:27-33 see parallels Matt. 21:23-27; Luke 20:1-8 [f] For 12:1-12 see parallels Matt. 21:33-46; Luke 20:9-18

another servant, and they struck him on the head and treated him shamefully. [5]And he sent another, and him they killed. And so with many others: some they beat, and some they killed. [6]He had still one other, a beloved son. Finally he sent him to them, saying, 'They will respect my son.' [7]But those tenants said to one another, 'This is the heir. Come, let us kill him, and the inheritance will be ours.' [8]And they took him and killed him and threw him out of the vineyard. [9]What will the owner of the vineyard do? He will come and destroy the tenants and give the vineyard to others. [10]Have you not read this Scripture:

[a]"'The stone that the builders rejected
    has become the cornerstone;[1]
[11] this was the Lord's doing,
    and it is marvelous in our eyes'?"

[12]And they were seeking to arrest him but feared the people, for they perceived that he had told the parable against them. So they left him and went away.

Paying Taxes to Caesar

[13][b]And they sent to him some of the Pharisees and some of the Herodians, to trap him in his talk. [14]And they came and said to him, "Teacher, we know that you are true and do not care about anyone's opinion. For you are not swayed by appearances,[2] but truly teach the way of God. Is it lawful to pay taxes to Caesar, or not? Should we pay them, or should we not?" [15]But, knowing their hypocrisy, he said to them, "Why put me to the test? Bring me a denarius[3] and let me look at it." [16]And they brought one. And he said to them, "Whose likeness and inscription is this?" They said to him, "Caesar's." [17]Jesus said to them, "Render to Caesar the things that are Caesar's, and to God the things that are God's." And they marveled at him.

The Sadducees Ask About the Resurrection

[18]And Sadducees came to him, who say that there is no resurrection. And they asked him a question, saying, [19]"Teacher, Moses wrote for us that if a man's brother dies and leaves a wife, but leaves no child, the man[4] must take the widow and raise up offspring for his brother. [20]There were seven brothers; the first took a wife, and when he died left no offspring. [21]And the second took her, and died, leaving no offspring. And the third likewise. [22]And the seven left no offspring. Last of all the woman also died. [23]In the resurrection, when they rise again, whose wife will she be? For the seven had her as wife."

[24]Jesus said to them, "Is this not the reason you are wrong, because you know neither the Scriptures nor the power of God? [25]For when they

rise from the dead, they neither marry nor are given in marriage, but are like angels in heaven. [26]And as for the dead being raised, have you not read in the book of Moses, in the passage about the bush, how God spoke to him, saying, [c]'I am the God of Abraham, and the God of Isaac, and the God of Jacob'? [27]He is not God of the dead, but of the living. You are quite wrong."

The Great Commandment

[28][d]And one of the scribes came up and heard them disputing with one another, and seeing that he answered them well, asked him, "Which commandment is the most important of all?" [29]Jesus answered, "The most important is, [e]'Hear, O Israel: The Lord our God, the Lord is one. [30]And you shall love the Lord your God with all your heart and with all your soul and with all your mind and with all your strength.' [31]The second is this: [f]'You shall love your neighbor as yourself.' There is no other commandment greater than these." [32]And the scribe said to him, "You are right, Teacher. You have truly said that he is one, and there is no other besides him. [33]And to love him with all the heart and with all the understanding and with all the strength, and to love one's neighbor as oneself, is much more than all whole burnt offerings and sacrifices." [34]And when Jesus saw that he answered wisely, he said to him, "You are not far from the kingdom of God." And after that no one dared to ask him any more questions.

Whose Son Is the Christ?

[35][g]And as Jesus taught in the temple, he said, "How can the scribes say that the Christ is the son of David? [36]David himself, in the Holy Spirit, declared,

[h]"'The Lord said to my Lord,
    Sit at my right hand,
        until I put your enemies under your feet.'

[37]David himself calls him Lord. So how is he his son?" And the great throng heard him gladly.

Beware of the Scribes

[38][i]And in his teaching he said, "Beware of the scribes, who like to walk around in long robes and like greetings in the marketplaces [39]and have the best seats in the synagogues and the places of honor at feasts, [40]who devour widows' houses and for a pretense make long prayers. They will receive the greater condemnation."

The Widow's Offering

[41][j]And he sat down opposite the treasury and watched the people putting money into the offering box. Many rich people put in large sums. [42]And a poor widow came and put in two small

---

[1] Greek *the head of the corner* [2] Greek *you do not look at people's faces* [3] A denarius was a day's wage for a laborer [4] Greek *his brother* [a] Ps. 118:22, 23 [b] For 12:13-27 see parallels Matt. 22:15-32; Luke 20:20-38 [c] Ex. 3:6 [d] For 12:28-34 see parallel Matt. 22:34-40, 46 [e] Deut. 6:4, 5 [f] Lev. 19:18 [g] For 12:35-37 see parallels Matt. 22:41-45; Luke 20:41-44 [h] Ps. 110:1 [i] For 12:38-40 see parallels Matt. 23:1, 2, 5-7; Luke 20:45, 46 [j] For 12:41-44 see parallel Luke 21:1-4

copper coins, which make a penny.[1] [43]And he called his disciples to him and said to them, "Truly, I say to you, this poor widow has put in more than all those who are contributing to the offering box. [44]For they all contributed out of their abundance, but she out of her poverty has put in everything she had, all she had to live on."

Jesus Foretells Destruction of the Temple

13 [a]And as he came out of the temple, one of his disciples said to him, "Look, Teacher, what wonderful stones and what wonderful buildings!" [2]And Jesus said to him, "Do you see these great buildings? There will not be left here one stone upon another that will not be thrown down."

Signs of the Close of the Age

[3]And as he sat on the Mount of Olives opposite the temple, Peter and James and John and Andrew asked him privately, [4]"Tell us, when will these things be, and what will be the sign when all these things are about to be accomplished?" [5]And Jesus began to say to them, "See that no one leads you astray. [6]Many will come in my name, saying, 'I am he!' and they will lead many astray. [7]And when you hear of wars and rumors of wars, do not be alarmed. This must take place, but the end is not yet. [8]For nation will rise against nation, and kingdom against kingdom. There will be earthquakes in various places; there will be famines. These are but the beginning of the birth pains.

[9]"But be on your guard. For they will deliver you over to councils, and you will be beaten in synagogues, and you will stand before governors and kings for my sake, to bear witness before them. [10]And the gospel must first be proclaimed to all nations. [11]And when they bring you to trial and deliver you over, do not be anxious beforehand what you are to say, but say whatever is given you in that hour, for it is not you who speak, but the Holy Spirit. [12]And brother will deliver brother over to death, and the father his child, and children will rise against parents and have them put to death. [13]And you will be hated by all for my name's sake. But the one who endures to the end will be saved.

The Abomination of Desolation

[14]"But when you see the abomination of desolation standing where he ought not to be (let the reader understand), then let those who are in Judea flee to the mountains. [15]Let the one who is on the housetop not go down, nor enter his house, to take anything out, [16]and let the one who is in the field not turn back to take his cloak. [17]And alas for women who are pregnant and for those who are nursing infants in those

days! [18]Pray that it may not happen in winter. [19]For in those days there will be such tribulation as has not been from the beginning of the creation that God created until now, and never will be. [20]And if the Lord had not cut short the days, no human being would be saved. But for the sake of the elect, whom he chose, he shortened the days. [21]And then if anyone says to you, 'Look, here is the Christ!' or 'Look, there he is!' do not believe it. [22]For false christs and false prophets will arise and perform signs and wonders, to lead astray, if possible, the elect. [23]But be on guard; I have told you all things beforehand.

The Coming of the Son of Man

[24]"But in those days, after that tribulation, the sun will be darkened, and the moon will not give its light, [25]and the stars will be falling from heaven, and the powers in the heavens will be shaken. [26]And then they will see the Son of Man coming in clouds with great power and glory. [27]And then he will send out the angels and gather his elect from the four winds, from the ends of the earth to the ends of heaven.

The Lesson of the Fig Tree

[28]"From the fig tree learn its lesson: as soon as its branch becomes tender and puts out its leaves, you know that summer is near. [29]So also, when you see these things taking place, you know that he is near, at the very gates. [30]Truly, I say to you, this generation will not pass away until all these things take place. [31]Heaven and earth will pass away, but my words will not pass away.

No One Knows That Day or Hour

[32]"But concerning that day or that hour, no one knows, not even the angels in heaven, nor the Son, but only the Father. [33]Be on guard, keep awake.[2] For you do not know when the time will come. [34]It is like a man going on a journey, when he leaves home and puts his servants[3] in charge, each with his work, and commands the doorkeeper to stay awake. [35]Therefore stay awake—for you do not know when the master of the house will come, in the evening, or at midnight, or when the rooster crows,[4] or in the morning— [36]lest he come suddenly and find you asleep. [37]And what I say to you I say to all: Stay awake."

The Plot to Kill Jesus

14 [b]It was now two days before the Passover and the Feast of Unleavened Bread. And the chief priests and the scribes were seeking how to arrest him by stealth and kill him, [2]for they said, "Not during the feast, lest there be an uproar from the people."

[1]Greek two lepta, which make a kodrantes; a kodrantes (Latin quadrans) was a Roman copper coin worth about 1/64 of a denarius (which was a day's wage for a laborer) [2]Some manuscripts add and pray [3]Greek bondservants [4]That is, the third watch of the night, between midnight and 3 A.M.
[a]For 13:1-37 see parallels Matt. 24:1-51; Luke 21:5-36 [b]For 14:1, 2 see parallels Matt. 26:2-5; Luke 22:1, 2

Jesus Anointed at Bethany

3ᵃAnd while he was at Bethany in the house of Simon the leper,[1] as he was reclining at table, a woman came with an alabaster flask of ointment of pure nard, very costly, and she broke the flask and poured it over his head. **4**There were some who said to themselves indignantly, "Why was the ointment wasted like that? **5**For this ointment could have been sold for more than three hundred denarii[2] and given to the poor." And they scolded her. **6**But Jesus said, "Leave her alone. Why do you trouble her? She has done a beautiful thing to me. **7**For you always have the poor with you, and whenever you want, you can do good for them. But you will not always have me. **8**She has done what she could; she has anointed my body beforehand for burial. **9**And truly, I say to you, wherever the gospel is proclaimed in the whole world, what she has done will be told in memory of her."

Judas to Betray Jesus

10ᵇThen Judas Iscariot, who was one of the twelve, went to the chief priests in order to betray him to them. **11**And when they heard it, they were glad and promised to give him money. And he sought an opportunity to betray him.

The Passover with the Disciples

12ᶜAnd on the first day of Unleavened Bread, when they sacrificed the Passover lamb, his disciples said to him, "Where will you have us go and prepare for you to eat the Passover?" **13**And he sent two of his disciples and said to them, "Go into the city, and a man carrying a jar of water will meet you. Follow him, **14**and wherever he enters, say to the master of the house, 'The Teacher says, Where is my guest room, where I may eat the Passover with my disciples?' **15**And he will show you a large upper room furnished and ready; there prepare for us." **16**And the disciples set out and went to the city and found it just as he had told them, and they prepared the Passover.

17ᵈAnd when it was evening, he came with the twelve. **18**And as they were reclining at table and eating, Jesus said, "Truly, I say to you, one of you will betray me, one who is eating with me." **19**They began to be sorrowful and to say to him one after another, "Is it I?" **20**He said to them, "It is one of the twelve, one who is dipping bread into the dish with me. **21**For the Son of Man goes as it is written of him, but woe to that man by whom the Son of Man is betrayed! It would have been better for that man if he had not been born."

Institution of the Lord's Supper

22ᵉAnd as they were eating, he took bread, and after blessing it broke it and gave it to them, and said, "Take; this is my body." **23**And he took a cup, and when he had given thanks he gave it to them, and they all drank of it. **24**And he said to them, "This is my blood of the[3] covenant, which is poured out for many. **25**Truly, I say to you, I will not drink again of the fruit of the vine until that day when I drink it new in the kingdom of God."

Jesus Foretells Peter's Denial

26ᶠAnd when they had sung a hymn, they went out to the Mount of Olives. **27**And Jesus said to them, "You will all fall away, for it is written, 'I will ᵍstrike the shepherd, and the sheep will be scattered.' **28**But after I am raised up, I will go before you to Galilee." **29**Peter said to him, "Even though they all fall away, I will not." **30**And Jesus said to him, "Truly, I tell you, this very night, before the rooster crows twice, you will deny me three times." **31**But he said emphatically, "If I must die with you, I will not deny you." And they all said the same.

Jesus Prays in Gethsemane

32ʰAnd they went to a place called Gethsemane. And he said to his disciples, "Sit here while I pray." **33**And he took with him Peter and James and John, and began to be greatly distressed and troubled. **34**And he said to them, "My soul is very sorrowful, even to death. Remain here and watch."[4] **35**And going a little farther, he fell on the ground and prayed that, if it were possible, the hour might pass from him. **36**And he said, "Abba, Father, all things are possible for you. Remove this cup from me. Yet not what I will, but what you will." **37**And he came and found them sleeping, and he said to Peter, "Simon, are you asleep? Could you not watch one hour? **38**Watch and pray that you may not enter into temptation. The spirit indeed is willing, but the flesh is weak." **39**And again he went away and prayed, saying the same words. **40**And again he came and found them sleeping, for their eyes were very heavy, and they did not know what to answer him. **41**And he came the third time and said to them, "Are you still sleeping and taking your rest? It is enough; the hour has come. The Son of Man is betrayed into the hands of sinners. **42**Rise, let us be going; see, my betrayer is at hand."

Betrayal and Arrest of Jesus

43ⁱAnd immediately, while he was still speaking, Judas came, one of the twelve, and with him a crowd with swords and clubs, from the chief

---

[1] *Leprosy* was a term for several skin diseases; see Leviticus 13 [2] A *denarius* was a day's wage for a laborer [3] Some manuscripts insert *new* [4] Or *keep awake*; also verses 37, 38 ᵃFor 14:3-9 see parallels Matt. 26:6-13; John 12:1-8 ᵇFor 14:10, 11 see parallels Matt. 26:14-16; Luke 22:3-6 ᶜFor 14:12-16 see parallels Matt. 26:17-19; Luke 22:7-13 ᵈFor 14:17-21 see parallel Matt. 26:20-24 ᵉFor 14:22-25 see parallels Matt. 26:26-29; Luke 22:18-20 ᶠFor 14:26-31 see parallel Matt. 26:30-35 ᵍZech. 13:7 ʰFor 14:32-42 see parallels Matt. 26:36-46; Luke 22:39-46 ⁱFor 14:43-50 see parallels Matt. 26:47-56; Luke 22:47-53; John 18:3-11

priests and the scribes and the elders. [44]Now the betrayer had given them a sign, saying, "The one I will kiss is the man. Seize him and lead him away under guard." [45]And when he came, he went up to him at once and said, "Rabbi!" And he kissed him. [46]And they laid hands on him and seized him. [47]But one of those who stood by drew his sword and struck the servant[1] of the high priest and cut off his ear. [48]And Jesus said to them, "Have you come out as against a robber, with swords and clubs to capture me? [49]Day after day I was with you in the temple teaching, and you did not seize me. But let the Scriptures be fulfilled." [50]And they all left him and fled.

A Young Man Flees

[51]And a young man followed him, with nothing but a linen cloth about his body. And they seized him, [52]but he left the linen cloth and ran away naked.

Jesus Before the Council

[53][a]And they led Jesus to the high priest. And all the chief priests and the elders and the scribes came together. [54]And Peter had followed him at a distance, right into the courtyard of the high priest. And he was sitting with the guards and warming himself at the fire. [55]Now the chief priests and the whole Council[2] were seeking testimony against Jesus to put him to death, but they found none. [56]For many bore false witness against him, but their testimony did not agree. [57]And some stood up and bore false witness against him, saying, [58]"We heard him say, 'I will destroy this temple that is made with hands, and in three days I will build another, not made with hands.'" [59]Yet even about this their testimony did not agree. [60]And the high priest stood up in the midst and asked Jesus, "Have you no answer to make? What is it that these men testify against you?"[3] [61]But he remained silent and made no answer. Again the high priest asked him, "Are you the Christ, the Son of the Blessed?" [62]And Jesus said, "I am, and you will see the Son of Man seated at the right hand of Power, and coming with the clouds of heaven." [63]And the high priest tore his garments and said, "What further witnesses do we need? [64]You have heard his blasphemy. What is your decision?" And they all condemned him as deserving death. [65]And some began to spit on him and to cover his face and to strike him, saying to him, "Prophesy!" And the guards received him with blows.

Peter Denies Jesus

[66][b]And as Peter was below in the courtyard, one of the servant girls of the high priest came, [67]and seeing Peter warming himself, she looked at him and said, "You also were with the Nazarene, Jesus." [68]But he denied it, saying, "I neither know nor understand what you mean." And he went out into the gateway[4] and the rooster crowed.[5] [69]And the servant girl saw him and began again to say to the bystanders, "This man is one of them." [70]But again he denied it. And after a little while the bystanders again said to Peter, "Certainly you are one of them, for you are a Galilean." [71]But he began to invoke a curse on himself and to swear, "I do not know this man of whom you speak." [72]And immediately the rooster crowed a second time. And Peter remembered how Jesus had said to him, "Before the rooster crows twice, you will deny me three times." And he broke down and wept.[6]

Jesus Delivered to Pilate

15 And as soon as it was morning, the chief priests held a consultation with the elders and scribes and the whole Council. And they bound Jesus and led him away and delivered him over to Pilate. [2][c]And Pilate asked him, "Are you the King of the Jews?" And he answered him, "You have said so." [3]And the chief priests accused him of many things. [4]And Pilate again asked him, "Have you no answer to make? See how many charges they bring against you." [5]But Jesus made no further answer, so that Pilate was amazed.

Pilate Delivers Jesus to Be Crucified

[6][d]Now at the feast he used to release for them one prisoner for whom they asked. [7]And among the rebels in prison, who had committed murder in the insurrection, there was a man called Barabbas. [8]And the crowd came up and began to ask Pilate to do as he usually did for them. [9]And he answered them, saying, "Do you want me to release for you the King of the Jews?" [10]For he perceived that it was out of envy that the chief priests had delivered him up. [11]But the chief priests stirred up the crowd to have him release for them Barabbas instead. [12]And Pilate again said to them, "Then what shall I do with the man you call the King of the Jews?" [13]And they cried out again, "Crucify him." [14]And Pilate said to them, "Why, what evil has he done?" But they shouted all the more, "Crucify him." [15]So Pilate, wishing to satisfy the crowd, released for them Barabbas, and having scourged[7] Jesus, he delivered him to be crucified.

Jesus Is Mocked

[16][e]And the soldiers led him away inside the palace (that is, the governor's headquarters),[8] and they called together the whole battalion.[9] [17]And they clothed him in a purple cloak, and

[1] Greek bondservant [2] Greek Sanhedrin [3] Or Have you no answer to what these men testify against you? [4] Or forecourt [5] Some manuscripts omit and the rooster crowed [6] Or And when he had thought about it, he wept [7] A Roman judicial penalty, consisting of a severe beating with a multi-lashed whip containing imbedded pieces of bone and metal [8] Greek the praetorium [9] Greek cohort; a tenth of a Roman legion, usually about 600 men [a] For 14:53-65 see parallel Matt. 26:57-68 [b] For 14:66-72 see parallels Matt. 26:69-75; Luke 22:55-62; John 18:16-18, 25-27 [c] For 15:2-5 see parallels Matt. 27:11-14; Luke 23:1-3; John 18:28-38 [d] For 15:6-15 see parallels Matt. 27:15-26; Luke 23:18-25; John 18:39, 40; 19:16 [e] For 15:16-20 see parallels Matt. 27:27-31; John 19:2, 3

twisting together a crown of thorns, they put it on him. [18]And they began to salute him, "Hail, King of the Jews!" [19]And they were striking his head with a reed and spitting on him and kneeling down in homage to him. [20]And when they had mocked him, they stripped him of the purple cloak and put his own clothes on him. And they led him out to crucify him.

The Crucifixion

[21]And they compelled a passerby, Simon of Cyrene, who was coming in from the country, the father of Alexander and Rufus, to carry his cross. [22a]And they brought him to the place called Golgotha (which means Place of a Skull). [23]And they offered him wine mixed with myrrh, but he did not take it. [24]And they crucified him and divided his garments among them, casting lots for them, to decide what each should take. [25]And it was the third hour[1] when they crucified him. [26]And the inscription of the charge against him read, "The King of the Jews." [27]And with him they crucified two robbers, one on his right and one on his left.[2] [29]And those who passed by derided him, wagging their heads and saying, "Aha! You who would destroy the temple and rebuild it in three days, [30]save yourself, and come down from the cross!" [31]So also the chief priests with the scribes mocked him to one another, saying, "He saved others; he cannot save himself. [32]Let the Christ, the King of Israel, come down now from the cross that we may see and believe." Those who were crucified with him also reviled him.

The Death of Jesus

[33]And when the sixth hour[3] had come, there was darkness over the whole land until the ninth hour.[4] [34]And at the ninth hour Jesus cried with a loud voice, [b]"Eloi, Eloi, lema sabachthani?" which means, "My God, my God, why have you forsaken me?" [35]And some of the bystanders hearing it said, "Behold, he is calling Elijah." [36]And someone ran and filled a sponge with sour wine, put it on a reed and gave it to him to drink, saying, "Wait, let us see whether Elijah will come to take him down." [37]And Jesus uttered a loud cry and breathed his last. [38]And the curtain of the temple was torn in two, from top to bottom. [39c]And when the centurion, who stood facing him, saw that in this way he[5] breathed his last, he said, "Truly this man was the Son[6] of God!"

[40]There were also women looking on from a distance, among whom were Mary Magdalene, and Mary the mother of James the younger and of Joses, and Salome. [41]When he was in Galilee,

they followed him and ministered to him, and there were also many other women who came up with him to Jerusalem.

Jesus Is Buried

[42d]And when evening had come, since it was the day of Preparation, that is, the day before the Sabbath, [43]Joseph of Arimathea, a respected member of the Council, who was also himself looking for the kingdom of God, took courage and went to Pilate and asked for the body of Jesus. [44]Pilate was surprised to hear that he should have already died.[7] And summoning the centurion, he asked him whether he was already dead. [45]And when he learned from the centurion that he was dead, he granted the corpse to Joseph. [46]And Joseph[8] bought a linen shroud, and taking him down, wrapped him in the linen shroud and laid him in a tomb that had been cut out of the rock. And he rolled a stone against the entrance of the tomb. [47]Mary Magdalene and Mary the mother of Joses saw where he was laid.

The Resurrection

16 [e]When the Sabbath was past, Mary Magdalene and Mary the mother of James and Salome bought spices, so that they might go and anoint him. [2]And very early on the first day of the week, when the sun had risen, they went to the tomb. [3]And they were saying to one another, "Who will roll away the stone for us from the entrance of the tomb?" [4]And looking up, they saw that the stone had been rolled back—it was very large. [5]And entering the tomb, they saw a young man sitting on the right side, dressed in a white robe, and they were alarmed. [6]And he said to them, "Do not be alarmed. You seek Jesus of Nazareth, who was crucified. He has risen; he is not here. See the place where they laid him. [7]But go, tell his disciples and Peter that he is going before you to Galilee. There you will see him, just as he told you." [8]And they went out and fled from the tomb, for trembling and astonishment had seized them, and they said nothing to anyone, for they were afraid.

[Some of the earliest manuscripts
do not include 16:9-20.][9]

Jesus Appears to Mary Magdalene

[9][[Now when he rose early on the first day of the week, he appeared first to Mary Magdalene, from whom he had cast out seven demons. [10]She went and told those who had been with him, as they mourned and wept. [11]But when they heard

[1] That is, 9 A.M. [2] Some manuscripts insert verse 28: And the Scripture was fulfilled that says, "He was numbered with the transgressors" [3] That is, noon [4] That is, 3 P.M. [5] Some manuscripts insert cried out and [6] Or a son [7] Or Pilate wondered whether he had already died [8] Greek he [9] Some manuscripts end the book with 16:8; others include verses 9-20 immediately after verse 8. A few manuscripts insert additional material after verse 14; one Latin manuscript adds after verse 8 the following: But they reported briefly to Peter and those with him all that they had been told. And after this, Jesus himself sent out by means of them, from east to west, the sacred and imperishable proclamation of eternal salvation. Other manuscripts include this same wording after verse 8, then continue with verses 9-20 [a] For 15:22-38 see parallels Matt. 27:33-51; Luke 23:32-38, 44-46; John 19:17-19, 23, 24, 28-30 [b] Ps. 22:1 [c] For 15:39-41 see parallels Matt. 27:54-56; Luke 23:47, 49 [d] For 15:42-47 see parallels Matt. 27:57-61; John 19:38-42 [e] For 16:1-8 see parallels Matt. 28:1-8; Luke 24:1-10; John 20:1

that he was alive and had been seen by her, they would not believe it.

Jesus Appears to Two Disciples

[12]After these things he appeared in another form to two of them, as they were walking into the country. [13]And they went back and told the rest, but they did not believe them.

The Great Commission

[14]Afterward he appeared to the eleven themselves as they were reclining at table, and he rebuked them for their unbelief and hardness of heart, because they had not believed those who saw him after he had risen. [15]And he said to them, "Go into all the world and proclaim the gospel to the whole creation. [16]Whoever believes and is baptized will be saved, but whoever does not believe will be condemned. [17]And these signs will accompany those who believe: in my name they will cast out demons; they will speak in new tongues; [18]they will pick up serpents with their hands; and if they drink any deadly poison, it will not hurt them; they will lay their hands on the sick, and they will recover."

[19]So then the Lord Jesus, after he had spoken to them, was taken up into heaven and sat down at the right hand of God. [20]And they went out and preached everywhere, while the Lord worked with them and confirmed the message by accompanying signs.]]

LUKE

Introduction

The Gospel of Luke is in the form of a letter to a man named Theophilus. Luke wrote after having carefully investigated all the facts about Christ (1:1-4). Luke documents Christ's life from before his birth through his ministry, death, and resurrection. Jesus carried out his ministry in the power of the Holy Spirit, announcing the good news of salvation. He showed numerous times his compassion for the poor and the outcast. He fulfilled prophecy and carried out his purpose: to seek and save the lost. Luke gives the fullest account of Christ's birth, and only Luke records the parables of the Good Samaritan and the Prodigal Son. Luke, a physician and a colleague of Paul, probably wrote this account in the early 60s A.D. He also wrote Acts.

Dedication to Theophilus

1 Inasmuch as many have undertaken to compile a narrative of the things that have been accomplished among us, ²just as those who from the beginning were eyewitnesses and ministers of the word have delivered them to us, ³it seemed good to me also, having followed all things closely for some time past, to write an orderly account for you, most excellent Theophilus, ⁴that you may have certainty concerning the things you have been taught.

Birth of John the Baptist Foretold

⁵In the days of Herod, king of Judea, there was a priest named Zechariah,¹ of the division of Abijah. And he had a wife from the daughters of Aaron, and her name was Elizabeth. ⁶And they were both righteous before God, walking blamelessly in all the commandments and statutes of the Lord. ⁷But they had no child, because Elizabeth was barren, and both were advanced in years.

⁸Now while he was serving as priest before God when his division was on duty, ⁹according to the custom of the priesthood, he was chosen by lot to enter the temple of the Lord and burn incense. ¹⁰And the whole multitude of the people were praying outside at the hour of incense. ¹¹And there appeared to him an angel of the Lord standing on the right side of the altar of incense. ¹²And Zechariah was troubled when he saw him, and fear fell upon him. ¹³But the angel said to him, "Do not be afraid, Zechariah, for your prayer has been heard, and your wife Elizabeth will bear you a son, and you shall call his name John. ¹⁴And you will have joy and gladness, and many will rejoice at his birth, ¹⁵for he will be great before the Lord. And he must not drink wine or strong drink, and he will be filled with the Holy Spirit, even from his mother's womb. ¹⁶And he will turn many of the children of Israel to the Lord their God, ¹⁷and he will go before him in the spirit and power of Elijah, to turn the hearts of the fathers to the children, and the disobedient to the wisdom of the just, to make ready for the Lord a people prepared."

¹⁸And Zechariah said to the angel, "How shall I know this? For I am an old man, and my wife is advanced in years." ¹⁹And the angel answered him, "I am Gabriel. I stand in the presence of God, and I was sent to speak to you and to bring you this good news. ²⁰And behold, you will be silent and unable to speak until the day that these things take place, because you did not believe my words, which will be fulfilled in their time." ²¹And the people were waiting for Zechariah, and they were wondering at his delay in the temple. ²²And when he came out, he was unable to speak to them, and they realized that he had seen a vision in the temple. And he kept making signs to them and remained mute. ²³And when his time of service was ended, he went to his home.

²⁴After these days his wife Elizabeth conceived, and for five months she kept herself hidden, saying, ²⁵"Thus the Lord has done for me in the days when he looked on me, to take away my reproach among people."

Birth of Jesus Foretold

²⁶In the sixth month the angel Gabriel was sent from God to a city of Galilee named Nazareth, ²⁷to a virgin betrothed² to a man whose name was Joseph, of the house of David. And the virgin's name was Mary. ²⁸And he came to her and said, "Greetings, O favored one, the Lord is with you!"³ ²⁹But she was greatly troubled at the saying, and tried to discern what sort of greeting this might be. ³⁰And the angel said to her, "Do not be afraid, Mary, for you have found favor with God. ³¹And behold, you will conceive in your womb and bear a son, and you shall call his name Jesus. ³²He will be great and will be called the Son of the Most High. And the Lord God will give to him the throne of his father David, ³³and he will reign over the house of Jacob forever, and of his kingdom there will be no end."

---

¹ Greek Zacharias ² That is, legally pledged to be married ³ Some manuscripts add *Blessed are you among women!*

³⁴And Mary said to the angel, "How will this be, since I am a virgin?"[1]

³⁵And the angel answered her, "The Holy Spirit will come upon you, and the power of the Most High will overshadow you; therefore the child to be born[2] will be called holy—the Son of God. ³⁶And behold, your relative Elizabeth in her old age has also conceived a son, and this is the sixth month with her who was called barren. ³⁷For nothing will be impossible with God." ³⁸And Mary said, "Behold, I am the servant[3] of the Lord; let it be to me according to your word." And the angel departed from her.

Mary Visits Elizabeth

³⁹In those days Mary arose and went with haste into the hill country, to a town in Judah, ⁴⁰and she entered the house of Zechariah and greeted Elizabeth. ⁴¹And when Elizabeth heard the greeting of Mary, the baby leaped in her womb. And Elizabeth was filled with the Holy Spirit, ⁴²and she exclaimed with a loud cry, "Blessed are you among women, and blessed is the fruit of your womb! ⁴³And why is this granted to me that the mother of my Lord should come to me? ⁴⁴For behold, when the sound of your greeting came to my ears, the baby in my womb leaped for joy. ⁴⁵And blessed is she who believed that there would be[4] a fulfillment of what was spoken to her from the Lord."

Mary's Song of Praise: The Magnificat

⁴⁶And Mary said,

"My soul magnifies the Lord,
⁴⁷ and my spirit rejoices in God my Savior,
⁴⁸ for he has looked on the humble estate of his servant.
    For behold, from now on all generations will call me blessed;
⁴⁹ for he who is mighty has done great things for me,
    and holy is his name.
⁵⁰ And his mercy is for those who fear him from generation to generation.
⁵¹ He has shown strength with his arm; he has scattered the proud in the thoughts of their hearts;
⁵² he has brought down the mighty from their thrones and exalted those of humble estate;
⁵³ he has filled the hungry with good things, and the rich he has sent away empty.
⁵⁴ He has helped his servant Israel, in remembrance of his mercy,
⁵⁵ as he spoke to our fathers, to Abraham and to his offspring forever."

⁵⁶And Mary remained with her about three months and returned to her home.

The Birth of John the Baptist

⁵⁷Now the time came for Elizabeth to give birth, and she bore a son. ⁵⁸And her neighbors and relatives heard that the Lord had shown great mercy to her, and they rejoiced with her. ⁵⁹And on the eighth day they came to circumcise the child. And they would have called him Zechariah after his father, ⁶⁰but his mother answered, "No; he shall be called John." ⁶¹And they said to her, "None of your relatives is called by this name." ⁶²And they made signs to his father, inquiring what he wanted him to be called. ⁶³And he asked for a writing tablet and wrote, "His name is John." And they all wondered. ⁶⁴And immediately his mouth was opened and his tongue loosed, and he spoke, blessing God. ⁶⁵And fear came on all their neighbors. And all these things were talked about through all the hill country of Judea, ⁶⁶and all who heard them laid them up in their hearts, saying, "What then will this child be?" For the hand of the Lord was with him.

Zechariah's Prophecy

⁶⁷And his father Zechariah was filled with the Holy Spirit and prophesied, saying,

⁶⁸ "Blessed be the Lord God of Israel, for he has visited and redeemed his people
⁶⁹ and has raised up a horn of salvation for us in the house of his servant David,
⁷⁰ as he spoke by the mouth of his holy prophets from of old,
⁷¹ that we should be saved from our enemies and from the hand of all who hate us;
⁷² to show the mercy promised to our fathers and to remember his holy covenant,
⁷³ the oath that he swore to our father Abraham, to grant us
⁷⁴ that we, being delivered from the hand of our enemies, might serve him without fear,
⁷⁵ in holiness and righteousness before him all our days.
⁷⁶ And you, child, will be called the prophet of the Most High; for you will go before the Lord to prepare his ways,
⁷⁷ to give knowledge of salvation to his people in the forgiveness of their sins,
⁷⁸ because of the tender mercy of our God, whereby the sunrise shall visit us[5] from on high
⁷⁹ to give light to those who sit in darkness and in the shadow of death, to guide our feet into the way of peace."

⁸⁰And the child grew and became strong in spirit, and he was in the wilderness until the day of his public appearance to Israel.

---

[1] Greek since I do not know a man [2] Some manuscripts add of you [3] Greek bondservant; also verse 48 [4] Or believed, for there will be [5] Or when the sunrise shall dawn upon us; some manuscripts since the sunrise has visited us

The Birth of Jesus Christ

2 In those days a decree went out from Caesar Augustus that all the world should be registered. [2]This was the first registration when[1] Quirinius was governor of Syria. [3]And all went to be registered, each to his own town. [4]And Joseph also went up from Galilee, from the town of Nazareth, to Judea, to the city of David, which is called Bethlehem, because he was of the house and lineage of David, [5]to be registered with Mary, his betrothed,[2] who was with child. [6]And while they were there, the time came for her to give birth. [7]And she gave birth to her firstborn son and wrapped him in swaddling cloths and laid him in a manger, because there was no place for them in the inn.

The Shepherds and the Angels

[8]And in the same region there were shepherds out in the field, keeping watch over their flock by night. [9]And an angel of the Lord appeared to them, and the glory of the Lord shone around them, and they were filled with fear. [10]And the angel said to them, "Fear not, for behold, I bring you good news of great joy that will be for all the people. [11]For unto you is born this day in the city of David a Savior, who is Christ the Lord. [12]And this will be a sign for you: you will find a baby wrapped in swaddling cloths and lying in a manger." [13]And suddenly there was with the angel a multitude of the heavenly host praising God and saying,

[14] "Glory to God in the highest,
    and on earth peace among those with
        whom he is pleased!"[3]

[15]When the angels went away from them into heaven, the shepherds said to one another, "Let us go over to Bethlehem and see this thing that has happened, which the Lord has made known to us." [16]And they went with haste and found Mary and Joseph, and the baby lying in a manger. [17]And when they saw it, they made known the saying that had been told them concerning this child. [18]And all who heard it wondered at what the shepherds told them. [19]But Mary treasured up all these things, pondering them in her heart. [20]And the shepherds returned, glorifying and praising God for all they had heard and seen, as it had been told them.

[21]And at the end of eight days, when he was circumcised, he was called Jesus, the name given by the angel before he was conceived in the womb.

Jesus Presented at the Temple

[22]And when the time came for their purification according to the Law of Moses, they brought him up to Jerusalem to present him to the Lord [23](as it is written in the Law of the Lord, [a]"Every male who first opens the womb shall be called holy to the Lord") [24]and to offer a sacrifice according to what is said in the Law of the Lord, [b]"a pair of turtledoves, or two young pigeons." [25]Now there was a man in Jerusalem, whose name was Simeon, and this man was righteous and devout, waiting for the consolation of Israel, and the Holy Spirit was upon him. [26]And it had been revealed to him by the Holy Spirit that he would not see death before he had seen the Lord's Christ. [27]And he came in the Spirit into the temple, and when the parents brought in the child Jesus, to do for him according to the custom of the Law, [28]he took him up in his arms and blessed God and said,

[29] "Lord, now you are letting your servant[4] depart
        in peace,
    according to your word;
[30]   for my eyes have seen your salvation
[31]   that you have prepared in the presence of
            all peoples,
[32]   a light for revelation to the Gentiles,
        and for glory to your people Israel."

[33]And his father and his mother marveled at what was said about him. [34]And Simeon blessed them and said to Mary his mother, "Behold, this child is appointed for the fall and rising of many in Israel, and for a sign that is opposed [35](and a sword will pierce through your own soul also), so that thoughts from many hearts may be revealed."

[36]And there was a prophetess, Anna, the daughter of Phanuel, of the tribe of Asher. She was advanced in years, having lived with her husband seven years from when she was a virgin, [37]and then as a widow until she was eighty-four.[5] She did not depart from the temple, worshiping with fasting and prayer night and day. [38]And coming up at that very hour she began to give thanks to God and to speak of him to all who were waiting for the redemption of Jerusalem.

The Return to Nazareth

[39]And when they had performed everything according to the Law of the Lord, they returned into Galilee, to their own town of Nazareth. [40]And the child grew and became strong, filled with wisdom. And the favor of God was upon him.

The Boy Jesus in the Temple

[41]Now his parents went to Jerusalem every year at the Feast of the Passover. [42]And when he was twelve years old, they went up according to custom. [43]And when the feast was ended, as they were returning, the boy Jesus stayed behind in Jerusalem. His parents did not know it, [44]but sup-

[1] Or This was the registration before [2] That is, one legally pledged to be married [3] Some manuscripts peace, good will among men [4] Greek bondservant [5] Or as a widow for eighty-four years [a] Ex. 13:2, 12 [b] Lev. 12:8

posing him to be in the group they went a day's journey, but then they began to search for him among their relatives and acquaintances, ⁴⁵and when they did not find him, they returned to Jerusalem, searching for him. ⁴⁶After three days they found him in the temple, sitting among the teachers, listening to them and asking them questions. ⁴⁷And all who heard him were amazed at his understanding and his answers. ⁴⁸And when his parents¹ saw him, they were astonished. And his mother said to him, "Son, why have you treated us so? Behold, your father and I have been searching for you in great distress." ⁴⁹And he said to them, "Why were you looking for me? Did you not know that I must be in my Father's house?"² ⁵⁰And they did not understand the saying that he spoke to them. ⁵¹And he went down with them and came to Nazareth and was submissive to them. And his mother treasured up all these things in her heart.

⁵²And Jesus increased in wisdom and in stature³ and in favor with God and man.

John the Baptist Prepares the Way

3 In the fifteenth year of the reign of Tiberius Caesar, Pontius Pilate being governor of Judea, and Herod being tetrarch of Galilee, and his brother Philip tetrarch of the region of Ituraea and Trachonitis, and Lysanias tetrarch of Abilene, ²during the high priesthood of Annas and Caiaphas, ᵃthe word of God came to John the son of Zechariah in the wilderness. ³And he went into all the region around the Jordan, proclaiming a baptism of repentance for the forgiveness of sins. ⁴As it is written in the book of the words of Isaiah the prophet,

ᵇ"The voice of one crying in the wilderness:
  'Prepare the way of the Lord,⁴
    make his paths straight.
⁵ Every valley shall be filled,
    and every mountain and hill shall be made low,
  and the crooked shall become straight,
    and the rough places shall become level ways,
⁶ and all flesh shall see the salvation of God.'"

⁷He said therefore to the crowds that came out to be baptized by him, "You brood of vipers! Who warned you to flee from the wrath to come? ⁸Bear fruits in keeping with repentance. And do not begin to say to yourselves, 'We have Abraham as our father.' For I tell you, God is able from these stones to raise up children for Abraham. ⁹Even now the axe is laid to the root of the trees. Every tree therefore that does not bear good fruit is cut down and thrown into the fire."

¹⁰And the crowds asked him, "What then shall we do?" ¹¹And he answered them, "Whoever has

two tunics⁵ is to share with him who has none, and whoever has food is to do likewise." ¹²Tax collectors also came to be baptized and said to him, "Teacher, what shall we do?" ¹³And he said to them, "Collect no more than you are authorized to do." ¹⁴Soldiers also asked him, "And we, what shall we do?" And he said to them, "Do not extort money from anyone by threats or by false accusation, and be content with your wages."

¹⁵As the people were in expectation, and all were questioning in their hearts concerning John, whether he might be the Christ, ¹⁶John answered them all, saying, "I baptize you with water, but he who is mightier than I is coming, the strap of whose sandals I am not worthy to untie. He will baptize you with the Holy Spirit and with fire. ¹⁷His winnowing fork is in his hand, to clear his threshing floor and to gather the wheat into his barn, but the chaff he will burn with unquenchable fire."

¹⁸So with many other exhortations he preached good news to the people. ¹⁹But Herod the tetrarch, who had been reproved by him for Herodias, his brother's wife, and for all the evil things that Herod had done, ²⁰added this to them all, that he locked up John in prison.

²¹Now when all the people were baptized, and when ᶜJesus also had been baptized and was praying, the heavens were opened, ²²and the Holy Spirit descended on him in bodily form, like a dove; and a voice came from heaven, "You are my beloved Son;⁶ with you I am well pleased."⁷

The Genealogy of Jesus Christ

²³Jesus, when he began his ministry, was about thirty years of age, being the son (as was supposed) of Joseph, the son of Heli, ²⁴the son of Matthat, the son of Levi, the son of Melchi, the son of Jannai, the son of Joseph, ²⁵the son of Mattathias, the son of Amos, the son of Nahum, the son of Esli, the son of Naggai, ²⁶the son of Maath, the son of Mattathias, the son of Semein, the son of Josech, the son of Joda, ²⁷the son of Joanan, the son of Rhesa, the son of Zerubbabel, the son of Shealtiel,⁸ the son of Neri, ²⁸the son of Melchi, the son of Addi, the son of Cosam, the son of Elmadam, the son of Er, ²⁹the son of Joshua, the son of Eliezer, the son of Jorim, the son of Matthat, the son of Levi, ³⁰the son of Simeon, the son of Judah, the son of Joseph, the son of Jonam, the son of Eliakim, ³¹the son of Melea, the son of Menna, the son of Mattatha, the son of Nathan, the son of David, ³²the son of Jesse, the son of Obed, the son of Boaz, the son of Sala, the son of Nahshon, ³³the son of Amminadab, the son of Admin, the son of Arni, the son of Hezron, the son of Perez, the son of Judah, ³⁴the son of Jacob, the son of Isaac, the son of Abraham, the son of Terah, the son of Nahor,

¹ Greek *they* ² Or *about my Father's business* ³ Or *years* ⁴ Or *crying, Prepare in the wilderness the way of the Lord* ⁵ Greek *chiton*, a long garment worn under the cloak next to the skin ⁶ Or *my Son, my (or the) Beloved* ⁷ Some manuscripts *beloved Son; today I have begotten you* ⁸ Greek *Salathiel*
ᵃ For 3:2-17 see parallels Matt. 3:1-12; Mark 1:2-8 ᵇ Isa. 40:3-5 ᶜ For 3:21, 22 see parallels Matt. 3:13-17; Mark 1:9-11

[35]the son of Serug, the son of Reu, the son of Peleg, the son of Eber, the son of Shelah, [36]the son of Cainan, the son of Arphaxad, the son of Shem, the son of Noah, the son of Lamech, [37]the son of Methuselah, the son of Enoch, the son of Jared, the son of Mahalaleel, the son of Cainan, [38]the son of Enos, the son of Seth, the son of Adam, the son of God.

The Temptation of Jesus

4 [a]And Jesus, full of the Holy Spirit, returned from the Jordan and was led by the Spirit in the wilderness [2]for forty days, being tempted by the devil. And he ate nothing during those days. And when they were ended, he was hungry. [3]The devil said to him, "If you are the Son of God, command this stone to become bread." [4]And Jesus answered him, "It is written, [b]'Man shall not live by bread alone.'" [5]And the devil took him up and showed him all the kingdoms of the world in a moment of time, [6]and said to him, "To you I will give all this authority and their glory, for it has been delivered to me, and I give it to whom I will. [7]If you, then, will worship me, it will all be yours." [8]And Jesus answered him, "It is written,

[c]"'You shall worship the Lord your God,
    and him only shall you serve.'"

[9]And he took him to Jerusalem and set him on the pinnacle of the temple and said to him, "If you are the Son of God, throw yourself down from here, [10]for it is written,

[d]"'He will command his angels concerning you,
    to guard you,'

[11]and

[e]"'On their hands they will bear you up,
    lest you strike your foot against a stone.'"

[12]And Jesus answered him, "It is said, [f]'You shall not put the Lord your God to the test.'" [13]And when the devil had ended every temptation, he departed from him until an opportune time.

Jesus Begins His Ministry

[14]And Jesus returned in the power of the Spirit to Galilee, and a report about him went out through all the surrounding country. [15]And he taught in their synagogues, being glorified by all.

Jesus Rejected at Nazareth

[16]And he came to Nazareth, where he had been brought up. And as was his custom, he went to the synagogue on the Sabbath day, and he stood up to read. [17]And the scroll of the prophet Isaiah was given to him. He unrolled the scroll and found the place where it was written,

[18] [g]"The Spirit of the Lord is upon me,
    because he has anointed me
    to proclaim good news to the poor.
He has sent me to proclaim liberty to the captives
    and recovering of sight to the blind,
    to set at liberty those who are oppressed,
[19]   to proclaim the year of the Lord's favor."

[20]And he rolled up the scroll and gave it back to the attendant and sat down. And the eyes of all in the synagogue were fixed on him. [21]And he began to say to them, "Today this Scripture has been fulfilled in your hearing." [22]And all spoke well of him and marveled at the gracious words that were coming from his mouth. And they said, "Is not this Joseph's son?" [23]And he said to them, "Doubtless you will quote to me this proverb, 'Physician, heal yourself.' What we have heard you did at Capernaum, do here in your hometown as well." [24]And he said, "Truly, I say to you, no prophet is acceptable in his hometown. [25]But in truth, I tell you, there were many widows in Israel in the days of Elijah, when the heavens were shut up three years and six months, and a great famine came over all the land, [26]and Elijah was sent to none of them but only to Zarephath, in the land of Sidon, to a woman who was a widow. [27]And there were many lepers[1] in Israel in the time of the prophet Elisha, and none of them was cleansed, but only Naaman the Syrian." [28]When they heard these things, all in the synagogue were filled with wrath. [29]And they rose up and drove him out of the town and brought him to the brow of the hill on which their town was built, so that they could throw him down the cliff. [30]But passing through their midst, he went away.

Jesus Heals a Man with an Unclean Demon

[31][h]And he went down to Capernaum, a city of Galilee. And he was teaching them on the Sabbath, [32]and they were astonished at his teaching, for his word possessed authority. [33]And in the synagogue there was a man who had the spirit of an unclean demon, and he cried out with a loud voice, [34]"Ha![2] What have you to do with us, Jesus of Nazareth? Have you come to destroy us? I know who you are—the Holy One of God." [35]But Jesus rebuked him, saying, "Be silent and come out of him!" And when the demon had thrown him down in their midst, he came out of him, having done him no harm. [36]And they were all amazed and said to one another, "What is this word? For with authority and power he commands the unclean spirits, and they come out!" [37]And reports about him went out into every place in the surrounding region.

---

[1]*Leprosy* was a term for several skin diseases; see Leviticus 13 [2]Or *Leave us alone* [a]For 4:1-13 see parallels Matt. 4:1-11; Mark 1:12, 13 [b]Deut. 8:3 [c]Deut. 6:13 [d]Ps. 91:11 [e]Ps. 91:12 [f]Deut. 6:16 [g]Isa. 61:1, 2 [h]For 4:31-37 see parallel Mark 1:21-28

Jesus Heals Many

[38]ᵃAnd he arose and left the synagogue and entered Simon's house. Now Simon's mother-in-law was ill with a high fever, and they appealed to him on her behalf. [39]And he stood over her and rebuked the fever, and it left her, and immediately she rose and began to serve them.

[40]Now when the sun was setting, all those who had any who were sick with various diseases brought them to him, and he laid his hands on every one of them and healed them. [41]And demons also came out of many, crying, "You are the Son of God!" But he rebuked them and would not allow them to speak, because they knew that he was the Christ.

Jesus Preaches in Synagogues

[42]ᵇAnd when it was day, he departed and went into a desolate place. And the people sought him and came to him, and would have kept him from leaving them, [43]but he said to them, "I must preach the good news of the kingdom of God to the other towns as well; for I was sent for this purpose." [44]And he was preaching in the synagogues of Judea.¹

Jesus Calls the First Disciples

5 On one occasion, while the crowd was pressing in on him to hear the word of God, he was standing by the lake of Gennesaret, ²and he saw two boats by the lake, but the fishermen had gone out of them and were washing their nets. ³Getting into one of the boats, which was Simon's, he asked him to put out a little from the land. And he sat down and taught the people from the boat. ⁴And when he had finished speaking, he said to Simon, "Put out into the deep and let down your nets for a catch." ⁵And Simon answered, "Master, we toiled all night and took nothing! But at your word I will let down the nets." ⁶And when they had done this, they enclosed a large number of fish, and their nets were breaking. ⁷They signaled to their partners in the other boat to come and help them. And they came and filled both the boats, so that they began to sink. ⁸But when Simon Peter saw it, he fell down at Jesus' knees, saying, "Depart from me, for I am a sinful man, O Lord." ⁹For he and all who were with him were astonished at the catch of fish that they had taken, ¹⁰and so also were James and John, sons of Zebedee, who were partners with Simon. And Jesus said to Simon, "Do not be afraid; from now on you will be catching men." ¹¹And when they had brought their boats to land, they left everything and followed him.

Jesus Cleanses a Leper

[12]While he was in one of the cities, ᶜthere came a man full of leprosy.² And when he saw Jesus, he fell on his face and begged him, "Lord, if you will, you can make me clean." [13]And Jesus³ stretched out his hand and touched him, saying, "I will; be clean." And immediately the leprosy left him. [14]And he charged him to tell no one, but "go and show yourself to the priest, and make an offering for your cleansing, as Moses commanded, for a proof to them." [15]But now even more the report about him went abroad, and great crowds gathered to hear him and to be healed of their infirmities. [16]But he would withdraw to desolate places and pray.

Jesus Heals a Paralytic

[17]On one of those days, as he was teaching, Pharisees and teachers of the law were sitting there, who had come from every village of Galilee and Judea and from Jerusalem. And the power of the Lord was with him to heal.⁴ [18]ᵈAnd behold, some men were bringing on a bed a man who was paralyzed, and they were seeking to bring him in and lay him before Jesus, [19]but finding no way to bring him in, because of the crowd, they went up on the roof and let him down with his bed through the tiles into the midst before Jesus. [20]And when he saw their faith, he said, "Man, your sins are forgiven you." [21]And the scribes and the Pharisees began to question, saying, "Who is this who speaks blasphemies? Who can forgive sins but God alone?" [22]When Jesus perceived their thoughts, he answered them, "Why do you question in your hearts? [23]Which is easier, to say, 'Your sins are forgiven you,' or to say, 'Rise and walk'? [24]But that you may know that the Son of Man has authority on earth to forgive sins"—he said to the man who was paralyzed—"I say to you, rise, pick up your bed and go home." [25]And immediately he rose up before them and picked up what he had been lying on and went home, glorifying God. [26]And amazement seized them all, and they glorified God and were filled with awe, saying, "We have seen extraordinary things today."

Jesus Calls Levi

[27]ᵉAfter this he went out and saw a tax collector named Levi, sitting at the tax booth. And he said to him, "Follow me." [28]And leaving everything, he rose and followed him.

[29]And Levi made him a great feast in his house, and there was a large company of tax collectors and others reclining at table with them. [30]And the Pharisees and their scribes grumbled at his disciples, saying, "Why do you eat and drink with tax collectors and sinners?" [31]And Jesus answered them, "Those who are well have no need of a physician, but those who

¹Some manuscripts Galilee ²Leprosy was a term for several skin diseases; see Leviticus 13 ³Greek he ⁴Some manuscripts was present to heal them ᵃFor 4:38-41 see parallels Matt. 8:14-17; Mark 1:29-34 ᵇFor 4:42, 43 see parallel Mark 1:35-38 ᶜFor 5:12-14 see parallels Matt. 8:2-4; Mark 1:40-44 ᵈFor 5:18-26 see parallels Matt. 9:2-8; Mark 2:1-12 ᵉFor 5:27-38 see parallels Matt. 9:9-17; Mark 2:13-22

are sick. ³²I have not come to call the righteous but sinners to repentance."

A Question About Fasting

³³And they said to him, "The disciples of John fast often and offer prayers, and so do the disciples of the Pharisees, but yours eat and drink." ³⁴And Jesus said to them, "Can you make wedding guests fast while the bridegroom is with them? ³⁵The days will come when the bridegroom is taken away from them, and then they will fast in those days." ³⁶He also told them a parable: "No one tears a piece from a new garment and puts it on an old garment. If he does, he will tear the new, and the piece from the new will not match the old. ³⁷And no one puts new wine into old wineskins. If he does, the new wine will burst the skins and it will be spilled, and the skins will be destroyed. ³⁸But new wine must be put into fresh wineskins. ³⁹And no one after drinking old wine desires new, for he says, 'The old is good.'"¹

Jesus Is Lord of the Sabbath

6 ᵃOn a Sabbath,² while he was going through the grainfields, his disciples plucked and ate some heads of grain, rubbing them in their hands. ²But some of the Pharisees said, "Why are you doing what is not lawful to do on the Sabbath?" ³And Jesus answered them, "Have you not read what David did when he was hungry, he and those who were with him: ⁴how he entered the house of God and took and ate the bread of the Presence, which is not lawful for any but the priests to eat, and also gave it to those with him?" ⁵And he said to them, "The Son of Man is lord of the Sabbath."

A Man with a Withered Hand

⁶On another Sabbath, ᵇhe entered the synagogue and was teaching, and a man was there whose right hand was withered. ⁷And the scribes and the Pharisees watched him, to see whether he would heal on the Sabbath, so that they might find a reason to accuse him. ⁸But he knew their thoughts, and he said to the man with the withered hand, "Come and stand here." And he rose and stood there. ⁹And Jesus said to them, "I ask you, is it lawful on the Sabbath to do good or to do harm, to save life or to destroy it?" ¹⁰And after looking around at them all he said to him, "Stretch out your hand." And he did so, and his hand was restored. ¹¹But they were filled with fury and discussed with one another what they might do to Jesus.

The Twelve Apostles

¹²In these days he went out to the mountain to pray, and all night he continued in prayer to God. ¹³And when day came, he called his disciples ᶜand chose from them twelve, whom he named apostles: ¹⁴Simon, whom he named Peter, and Andrew his brother, and James and John, and Philip, and Bartholomew, ¹⁵and Matthew, and Thomas, and James the son of Alphaeus, and Simon who was called the Zealot, ¹⁶and Judas the son of James, and Judas Iscariot, who became a traitor.

Jesus Ministers to a Great Multitude

¹⁷And he came down with them and stood on a level place, with a great crowd of his disciples and a great multitude of people from all Judea and Jerusalem and the seacoast of Tyre and Sidon, ¹⁸who came to hear him and to be healed of their diseases. And those who were troubled with unclean spirits were cured. ¹⁹And all the crowd sought to touch him, for power came out from him and healed them all.

The Beatitudes

²⁰And he lifted up his eyes on his disciples, and said:

"Blessed are you who are poor, for yours is the kingdom of God.

²¹"Blessed are you who are hungry now, for you shall be satisfied.

"Blessed are you who weep now, for you shall laugh.

²²"Blessed are you when people hate you and when they exclude you and revile you and spurn your name as evil, on account of the Son of Man! ²³Rejoice in that day, and leap for joy, for behold, your reward is great in heaven; for so their fathers did to the prophets.

Jesus Pronounces Woes

²⁴"But woe to you who are rich, for you have received your consolation.

²⁵"Woe to you who are full now, for you shall be hungry.

"Woe to you who laugh now, for you shall mourn and weep.

²⁶"Woe to you, when all people speak well of you, for so their fathers did to the false prophets.

Love Your Enemies

²⁷"But I say to you who hear, Love your enemies, do good to those who hate you, ²⁸bless those who curse you, pray for those who abuse you. ²⁹ᵈTo one who strikes you on the cheek, offer the other also, and from one who takes away your cloak do not withhold your tunic³ either. ³⁰Give to everyone who begs from you, and from one who takes away your goods do not demand them back. ³¹And as you wish that others would do to you, do so to them. ³²"If you love those who love you, what benefit

---

¹ Some manuscripts better ² Some manuscripts On the second first Sabbath (that is, on the second Sabbath after the first) ³ Greek chiton, a long garment worn under the cloak next to the skin ᵃFor 6:1-5 see parallels Matt. 12:1-8; Mark 2:23-28 ᵇFor 6:6-11 see parallels Matt. 12:9-14; Mark 3:1-6 ᶜFor 6:13-16 see parallels Matt. 10:2-4; Mark 3:16-19 ᵈFor 6:29, 30 see parallel Matt. 5:39-42

is that to you? For even sinners love those who love them. ³³And if you do good to those who do good to you, what benefit is that to you? For even sinners do the same. ³⁴And if you lend to those from whom you expect to receive, what credit is that to you? Even sinners lend to sinners, to get back the same amount. ³⁵But love your enemies, and do good, and lend, expecting nothing in return, and your reward will be great, and you will be sons of the Most High, for he is kind to the ungrateful and the evil. ³⁶Be merciful, even as your Father is merciful.

Judging Others

³⁷ᵃ"Judge not, and you will not be judged; condemn not, and you will not be condemned; forgive, and you will be forgiven; ³⁸give, and it will be given to you. Good measure, pressed down, shaken together, running over, will be put into your lap. For with the measure you use it will be measured back to you."

³⁹He also told them a parable: "Can a blind man lead a blind man? Will they not both fall into a pit? ⁴⁰A disciple is not above his teacher, but everyone when he is fully trained will be like his teacher. ⁴¹Why do you see the speck that is in your brother's eye, but do not notice the log that is in your own eye? ⁴²How can you say to your brother, 'Brother, let me take out the speck that is in your eye,' when you yourself do not see the log that is in your own eye? You hypocrite, first take the log out of your own eye, and then you will see clearly to take out the speck that is in your brother's eye.

A Tree and Its Fruit

⁴³"For ᵇno good tree bears bad fruit, nor again does a bad tree bear good fruit, ⁴⁴for each tree is known by its own fruit. For figs are not gathered from thornbushes, nor are grapes picked from a bramble bush. ⁴⁵The good person out of the good treasure of his heart produces good, and the evil person out of his evil treasure produces evil, for out of the abundance of the heart his mouth speaks.

Build Your House on the Rock

⁴⁶"Why do you call me 'Lord, Lord,' and not do what I tell you? ⁴⁷ᶜEveryone who comes to me and hears my words and does them, I will show you what he is like: ⁴⁸he is like a man building a house, who dug deep and laid the foundation on the rock. And when a flood arose, the stream broke against that house and could not shake it, because it had been well built.¹ ⁴⁹But the one who hears and does not do them is like a man who built a house on the ground without a foundation. When the stream broke against it, imme-

diately it fell, and the ruin of that house was great."

Jesus Heals a Centurion's Servant

7 After he had finished all his sayings in the hearing of the people, ᵈhe entered Capernaum. ²Now a centurion had a servant² who was sick and at the point of death, who was highly valued by him. ³When the centurion³ heard about Jesus, he sent to him elders of the Jews, asking him to come and heal his servant. ⁴And when they came to Jesus, they pleaded with him earnestly, saying, "He is worthy to have you do this for him, ⁵for he loves our nation, and he is the one who built us our synagogue." ⁶And Jesus went with them. When he was not far from the house, the centurion sent friends, saying to him, "Lord, do not trouble yourself, for I am not worthy to have you come under my roof. ⁷Therefore I did not presume to come to you. But say the word, and let my servant be healed. ⁸For I too am a man set under authority, with soldiers under me: and I say to one, 'Go,' and he goes; and to another, 'Come,' and he comes; and to my servant, 'Do this,' and he does it." ⁹When Jesus heard these things, he marveled at him, and turning to the crowd that followed him, said, "I tell you, not even in Israel have I found such faith." ¹⁰And when those who had been sent returned to the house, they found the servant well.

Jesus Raises a Widow's Son

¹¹Soon afterward⁴ he went to a town called Nain, and his disciples and a great crowd went with him. ¹²As he drew near to the gate of the town, behold, a man who had died was being carried out, the only son of his mother, and she was a widow, and a considerable crowd from the town was with her. ¹³And when the Lord saw her, he had compassion on her and said to her, "Do not weep." ¹⁴Then he came up and touched the bier, and the bearers stood still. And he said, "Young man, I say to you, arise." ¹⁵And the dead man sat up and began to speak, and Jesus⁵ gave him to his mother. ¹⁶Fear seized them all, and they glorified God, saying, "A great prophet has arisen among us!" and "God has visited his people!" ¹⁷And this report about him spread through the whole of Judea and all the surrounding country.

Messengers from John the Baptist

¹⁸ᵉThe disciples of John reported all these things to him. And John, ¹⁹calling two of his disciples to him, sent them to the Lord, saying, "Are you the one who is to come, or shall we look for another?" ²⁰And when the men had come to him, they said, "John the Baptist has sent us to

---

¹ Some manuscripts *founded upon the rock* ² Greek *bondservant*; also verses 3, 8, 10 ³ Greek *he* ⁴ Some manuscripts *The next day* ⁵ Greek *he* ᵃFor 6:37, 38, 41, 42 see parallel Matt. 7:1-5 ᵇFor 6:43, 44 see parallel Matt. 7:16, 20 ᶜFor 6:47-49 see parallel Matt. 7:24-27 ᵈFor 7:1-10 see parallel Matt. 8:5-13 ᵉFor 7:18-35 see parallel Matt. 11:2-19

you, saying, 'Are you the one who is to come, or shall we look for another?'" ²¹In that hour he healed many people of diseases and plagues and evil spirits, and on many who were blind he bestowed sight. ²²And he answered them, "Go and tell John what you have seen and heard: the blind receive their sight, the lame walk, lepers¹ are cleansed, and the deaf hear, the dead are raised up, the poor have good news preached to them. ²³And blessed is the one who is not offended by me."

²⁴When John's messengers had gone, Jesus² began to speak to the crowds concerning John: "What did you go out into the wilderness to see? A reed shaken by the wind? ²⁵What then did you go out to see? A man dressed in soft clothing? Behold, those who are dressed in splendid clothing and live in luxury are in kings' courts. ²⁶What then did you go out to see? A prophet? Yes, I tell you, and more than a prophet. ²⁷This is he of whom it is written,

ᵃ"'Behold, I send my messenger before your face,
who will prepare your way before you.'

²⁸I tell you, among those born of women none is greater than John. Yet the one who is least in the kingdom of God is greater than he." ²⁹(When all the people heard this, and the tax collectors too, they declared God just,³ having been baptized with the baptism of John, ³⁰but the Pharisees and the lawyers rejected the purpose of God for themselves, not having been baptized by him.)

³¹"To what then shall I compare the people of this generation, and what are they like? ³²They are like children sitting in the marketplace and calling to one another,

"'We played the flute for you, and you did not dance;
we sang a dirge, and you did not weep.'

³³For John the Baptist has come eating no bread and drinking no wine, and you say, 'He has a demon.' ³⁴The Son of Man has come eating and drinking, and you say, 'Look at him! A glutton and a drunkard, a friend of tax collectors and sinners!' ³⁵Yet wisdom is justified by all her children."

A Sinful Woman Forgiven

³⁶One of the Pharisees asked him to eat with him, and he went into the Pharisee's house and took his place at the table. ³⁷And behold, a woman of the city, who was a sinner, when she learned that he was reclining at table in the Pharisee's house, brought an alabaster flask of ointment, ³⁸and standing behind him at his feet, weeping, she began to wet his feet with her tears and wiped them with the hair of her head and kissed his feet and anointed them with the oint-

ment. ³⁹Now when the Pharisee who had invited him saw this, he said to himself, "If this man were a prophet, he would have known who and what sort of woman this is who is touching him, for she is a sinner." ⁴⁰And Jesus answering said to him, "Simon, I have something to say to you." And he answered, "Say it, Teacher."

⁴¹"A certain moneylender had two debtors. One owed five hundred denarii, and the other fifty. ⁴²When they could not pay, he cancelled the debt of both. Now which of them will love him more?" ⁴³Simon answered, "The one, I suppose, for whom he cancelled the larger debt." And he said to him, "You have judged rightly." ⁴⁴Then turning toward the woman he said to Simon, "Do you see this woman? I entered your house; you gave me no water for my feet, but she has wet my feet with her tears and wiped them with her hair. ⁴⁵You gave me no kiss, but from the time I came in she has not ceased to kiss my feet. ⁴⁶You did not anoint my head with oil, but she has anointed my feet with ointment. ⁴⁷Therefore I tell you, her sins, which are many, are forgiven—for she loved much. But he who is forgiven little, loves little." ⁴⁸And he said to her, "Your sins are forgiven." ⁴⁹Then those who were at table with him began to say among⁴ themselves, "Who is this, who even forgives sins?" ⁵⁰And he said to the woman, "Your faith has saved you; go in peace."

Women Accompanying Jesus

8 Soon afterward he went on through cities and villages, proclaiming and bringing the good news of the kingdom of God. And the twelve were with him, ²and also some women who had been healed of evil spirits and infirmities: Mary, called Magdalene, from whom seven demons had gone out, ³and Joanna, the wife of Chuza, Herod's household manager, and Susanna, and many others, who provided for them⁵ out of their means.

The Parable of the Sower

⁴ᵇAnd when a great crowd was gathering and people from town after town came to him, he said in a parable: ⁵"A sower went out to sow his seed. And as he sowed, some fell along the path and was trampled underfoot, and the birds of the air devoured it. ⁶And some fell on the rock, and as it grew up, it withered away, because it had no moisture. ⁷And some fell among thorns, and the thorns grew up with it and choked it. ⁸And some fell into good soil and grew and yielded a hundredfold." As he said these things, he called out, "He who has ears to hear, let him hear."

The Purpose of the Parables

⁹And when his disciples asked him what this parable meant, ¹⁰he said, "To you it has been

---

¹ Leprosy was a term for several skin diseases; see Leviticus 13 ² Greek he ³ Greek they justified God ⁴ Or to ⁵ Some manuscripts him ᵃ Mal. 3:1 ᵇ For 8:4-10 see parallels Matt. 13:1-15; Mark 4:1-12

given to know the secrets of the kingdom of God, but for others they are in parables, so [a]that 'seeing they may not see, and hearing they may not understand.' [b]Now the parable is this: The seed is the word of God. [12]The ones along the path are those who have heard; then the devil comes and takes away the word from their hearts, so that they may not believe and be saved. [13]And the ones on the rock are those who, when they hear the word, receive it with joy. But these have no root; they believe for a while, and in time of testing fall away. [14]And as for what fell among the thorns, they are those who hear, but as they go on their way they are choked by the cares and riches and pleasures of life, and their fruit does not mature. [15]As for that in the good soil, they are those who, hearing the word, hold it fast in an honest and good heart, and bear fruit with patience.

A Lamp Under a Jar

[16c]"No one after lighting a lamp covers it with a jar or puts it under a bed, but puts it on a stand, so that those who enter may see the light. [17]For nothing is hidden that will not be made manifest, nor is anything secret that will not be known and come to light. [18]Take care then how you hear, for to the one who has, more will be given, and from the one who has not, even what he thinks that he has will be taken away."

Jesus' Mother and Brothers

[19d]Then his mother and his brothers came to him, but they could not reach him because of the crowd. [20]And he was told, "Your mother and your brothers are standing outside, desiring to see you." [21]But he answered them, "My mother and my brothers are those who hear the word of God and do it."

Jesus Calms a Storm

[22e]One day he got into a boat with his disciples, and he said to them, "Let us go across to the other side of the lake." So they set out, [23]and as they sailed he fell asleep. And a windstorm came down on the lake, and they were filling with water and were in danger. [24]And they went and woke him, saying, "Master, Master, we are perishing!" And he awoke and rebuked the wind and the raging waves, and they ceased, and there was a calm. [25]He said to them, "Where is your faith?" And they were afraid, and they marveled, saying to one another, "Who then is this, that he commands even winds and water, and they obey him?"

Jesus Heals a Man with a Demon

[26f]Then they sailed to the country of the Gerasenes,[1] which is opposite Galilee. [27]When Jesus[2]

had stepped out on land, there met him a man from the city who had demons. For a long time he had worn no clothes, and he had not lived in a house but among the tombs. [28]When he saw Jesus, he cried out and fell down before him and said with a loud voice, "What have you to do with me, Jesus, Son of the Most High God? I beg you, do not torment me." [29]For he had commanded the unclean spirit to come out of the man. (For many a time it had seized him. He was kept under guard and bound with chains and shackles, but he would break the bonds and be driven by the demon into the desert.) [30]Jesus then asked him, "What is your name?" And he said, "Legion," for many demons had entered him. [31]And they begged him not to command them to depart into the abyss. [32]Now a large herd of pigs was feeding there on the hillside, and they begged him to let them enter these. So he gave them permission. [33]Then the demons came out of the man and entered the pigs, and the herd rushed down the steep bank into the lake and were drowned.

[34]When the herdsmen saw what had happened, they fled and told it in the city and in the country. [35]Then people went out to see what had happened, and they came to Jesus and found the man from whom the demons had gone, sitting at the feet of Jesus, clothed and in his right mind, and they were afraid. [36]And those who had seen it told them how the demon-possessed[3] man had been healed. [37]Then all the people of the surrounding country of the Gerasenes asked him to depart from them, for they were seized with great fear. So he got into the boat and returned. [38]The man from whom the demons had gone begged that he might be with him, but Jesus sent him away, saying, [39]"Return to your home, and declare how much God has done for you." And he went away, proclaiming throughout the whole city how much Jesus had done for him.

Jesus Heals a Woman and Jairus's Daughter

[40]Now when Jesus returned, the crowd welcomed him, for they were all waiting for him. [41g]And there came a man named Jairus, who was a ruler of the synagogue. And falling at Jesus' feet, he implored him to come to his house, [42]for he had an only daughter, about twelve years of age, and she was dying.

As Jesus went, the people pressed around him. [43]And there was a woman who had had a discharge of blood for twelve years, and though she had spent all her living on physicians,[4] she could not be healed by anyone. [44]She came up behind him and touched the fringe of his garment, and immediately her discharge of blood

---

[1] Some manuscripts *Gadarenes*; others *Gergesenes*; also verse 37   [2] Greek *he*; also verses 38, 42   [3] Greek *daimonizomai*; elsewhere rendered *oppressed by demons*   [4] Some manuscripts omit *and though she had spent all her living on physicians*,   [a] Isa. 6:9, 10   [b] For 8:11-15 see parallels Matt. 13:18-23; Mark 4:13-20   [c] For 8:16-18 see parallel Mark 4:21-25   [d] For 8:19-21 see parallels Matt. 12:46-50; Mark 3:31-35   [e] For 8:22-25 see parallels Matt. 8:23-27; Mark 4:35-41   [f] For 8:26-39 see parallels Matt. 8:28-34; Mark 5:1-20   [g] For 8:41-56 see parallels Matt. 9:18-26; Mark 5:21-43

ceased. **45**And Jesus said, "Who was it that touched me?" When all denied it, Peter*¹* said, "Master, the crowds surround you and are pressing in on you!" **46**But Jesus said, "Someone touched me, for I perceive that power has gone out from me." **47**And when the woman saw that she was not hidden, she came trembling, and falling down before him declared in the presence of all the people why she had touched him, and how she had been immediately healed. **48**And he said to her, "Daughter, your faith has made you well; go in peace."

49While he was still speaking, someone from the ruler's house came and said, "Your daughter is dead; do not trouble the Teacher any more." **50**But Jesus on hearing this answered him, "Do not fear; only believe, and she will be well." **51**And when he came to the house, he allowed no one to enter with him, except Peter and John and James, and the father and mother of the child. **52**And all were weeping and mourning for her, but he said, "Do not weep, for she is not dead but sleeping." **53**And they laughed at him, knowing that she was dead. **54**But taking her by the hand he called, saying, "Child, arise." **55**And her spirit returned, and she got up at once. And he directed that something should be given her to eat. **56**And her parents were amazed, but he charged them to tell no one what had happened.

Jesus Sends Out the Twelve Apostles

9 And he called the twelve together and gave them power and authority over all demons and to cure diseases, **²**and he sent them out to proclaim the kingdom of God and to heal. ³*ᵃ*And he said to them, "Take nothing for your journey, no staff, nor bag, nor bread, nor money; and do not have two tunics.*²* **4**And whatever house you enter, stay there, and from there depart. **5**And wherever they do not receive you, when you leave that town shake off the dust from your feet as a testimony against them." **6**And they departed and went through the villages, preaching the gospel and healing everywhere.

Herod Is Perplexed by Jesus

*⁷ᵇ*Now Herod the tetrarch heard about all that was happening, and he was perplexed, because it was said by some that John had been raised from the dead, **8**by some that Elijah had appeared, and by others that one of the prophets of old had risen. **9**Herod said, "John I beheaded, but who is this about whom I hear such things?" And he sought to see him.

Jesus Feeds the Five Thousand

10On their return the apostles told him all that they had done. *ᶜ*And he took them and withdrew apart to a town called Bethsaida. **11**When the crowds learned it, they followed him, and he welcomed them and spoke to them of the kingdom of God and cured those who had need of healing. **12**Now the day began to wear away, and the twelve came and said to him, "Send the crowd away to go into the surrounding villages and countryside to find lodging and get provisions, for we are here in a desolate place." **13**But he said to them, "You give them something to eat." They said, "We have no more than five loaves and two fish—unless we are to go and buy food for all these people." **14**For there were about five thousand men. And he said to his disciples, "Have them sit down in groups of about fifty each." **15**And they did so, and had them all sit down. **16**And taking the five loaves and the two fish, he looked up to heaven and said a blessing over them. Then he broke the loaves and gave them to the disciples to set before the crowd. **17**And they all ate and were satisfied. And what was left over was picked up, twelve baskets of broken pieces.

Peter Confesses Jesus as the Christ

18*ᵈ*Now it happened that as he was praying alone, the disciples were with him. And he asked them, "Who do the crowds say that I am?" **19**And they answered, "John the Baptist. But others say, Elijah, and others, that one of the prophets of old has risen." **20**Then he said to them, "But who do you say that I am?" And Peter answered, "The Christ of God."

Jesus Foretells His Death

21And he strictly charged and commanded them to tell this to no one, **22***ᵉ*saying, "The Son of Man must suffer many things and be rejected by the elders and chief priests and scribes, and be killed, and on the third day be raised."

Take Up Your Cross and Follow Jesus

23And he said to all, "If anyone would come after me, let him deny himself and take up his cross daily and follow me. **24**For whoever would save his life will lose it, but whoever loses his life for my sake will save it. **25**For what does it profit a man if he gains the whole world and loses or forfeits himself? **26**For whoever is ashamed of me and of my words, of him will the Son of Man be ashamed when he comes in his glory and the glory of the Father and of the holy angels. **27**But I tell you truly, there are some standing here who will not taste death until they see the kingdom of God."

The Transfiguration

28Now about eight days after these sayings he took with him Peter and John and James and went up on the mountain to pray. **29**And as he

---

¹ Some manuscripts add *and those who were with him* *²* Greek *chiton,* a long garment worn under the cloak next to the skin *ᵃ* For 9:3-5 see parallels Matt. 10:9-15; Mark 6:8-11 *ᵇ* For 9:7-9 see parallels Matt. 14:1-12; Mark 6:14-29 *ᶜ* For 9:10-17 see parallels Matt. 14:13-21; Mark 6:32-44; John 6:1-13 *ᵈ* For 9:18-20 see parallels Matt. 16:13-16; Mark 8:27-29 *ᵉ* For 9:22-27 see parallels Matt. 16:21-28; Mark 8:31–9:1

was praying, the appearance of his face was altered, and his clothing became dazzling white. [30]And behold, two men were talking with him, Moses and Elijah, [31]who appeared in glory and spoke of his departure,[1] which he was about to accomplish at Jerusalem. [32]Now Peter and those who were with him were heavy with sleep, but when they became fully awake they saw his glory and the two men who stood with him. [33]And as the men were parting from him, Peter said to Jesus, "Master, it is good that we are here. Let us make three tents, one for you and one for Moses and one for Elijah"—not knowing what he said. [34]As he was saying these things, a cloud came and overshadowed them, and they were afraid as they entered the cloud. [35]And a voice came out of the cloud, saying, "This is my Son, my Chosen One;[2] listen to him!" [36]And when the voice had spoken, Jesus was found alone. And they kept silent and told no one in those days anything of what they had seen.

Jesus Heals a Boy with an Unclean Spirit

[37]On the next day, when they had come down from the mountain, a great crowd met him. [38]And behold, a man from the crowd cried out, "Teacher, I beg you to look at my son, for he is my only child. [39]And behold, a spirit seizes him, and he suddenly cries out. It convulses him so that he foams at the mouth, and shatters him, and will hardly leave him. [40]And I begged your disciples to cast it out, but they could not." [41]Jesus answered, "O faithless and twisted generation, how long am I to be with you and bear with you? Bring your son here." [42]While he was coming, the demon threw him to the ground and convulsed him. But Jesus rebuked the unclean spirit and healed the boy, and gave him back to his father. [43]And all were astonished at the majesty of God.

Jesus Again Foretells His Death

But while they were all marveling at everything he was doing, Jesus[3] said to his disciples, [44]"Let these words sink into your ears: The Son of Man is about to be delivered into the hands of men." [45]But they did not understand this saying, and it was concealed from them, so that they might not perceive it. And they were afraid to ask him about this saying.

Who Is the Greatest?

[46]An argument arose among them as to which of them was the greatest. [47]But Jesus, knowing the reasoning of their hearts, took a child and put him by his side [48]and said to them, "Whoever receives this child in my name receives me, and whoever receives me receives him who sent me. For he who is least among you all is the one who is great."

Anyone Not Against Us Is For Us

[49]John answered, "Master, we saw someone casting out demons in your name, and we tried to stop him, because he does not follow with us." [50]But Jesus said to him, "Do not stop him, for the one who is not against you is for you."

A Samaritan Village Rejects Jesus

[51]When the days drew near for him to be taken up, he set his face to go to Jerusalem. [52]And he sent messengers ahead of him, who went and entered a village of the Samaritans, to make preparations for him. [53]But the people did not receive him, because his face was set toward Jerusalem. [54]And when his disciples James and John saw it, they said, "Lord, do you want us to tell fire to come down from heaven and consume them?"[4] [55]But he turned and rebuked them.[5] [56]And they went on to another village.

The Cost of Following Jesus

[57a]As they were going along the road, someone said to him, "I will follow you wherever you go." [58]And Jesus said to him, "Foxes have holes, and birds of the air have nests, but the Son of Man has nowhere to lay his head." [59]To another he said, "Follow me." But he said, "Lord, let me first go and bury my father." [60]And Jesus[6] said to him, "Leave the dead to bury their own dead. But as for you, go and proclaim the kingdom of God." [61]Yet another said, "I will follow you, Lord, but let me first say farewell to those at my home." [62]Jesus said to him, "No one who puts his hand to the plow and looks back is fit for the kingdom of God."

Jesus Sends Out the Seventy-Two

10 After this the Lord appointed seventy-two[7] others and sent them on ahead of him, two by two, into every town and place where he himself was about to go. [2]And he said to them, "The harvest is plentiful, but the laborers are few. Therefore pray earnestly to the Lord of the harvest to send out laborers into his harvest. [3]Go your way; behold, I am sending you out as lambs in the midst of wolves. [4]Carry no moneybag, no knapsack, no sandals, and greet no one on the road. [5]Whatever house you enter, first say, 'Peace be to this house!' [6]And if a son of peace is there, your peace will rest upon him. But if not, it will return to you. [7]And remain in the same house, eating and drinking what they provide, for the laborer deserves his wages. Do not go from house to house. [8]Whenever you enter a town and they receive you, eat what is set before you. [9]Heal the sick in it and say to them, 'The

---

[1]Greek exodus [2]Some manuscripts my Beloved [3]Greek he [4]Some manuscripts add as Elijah did [5]Some manuscripts add and he said, "You do not know what manner of spirit you are of; for the Son of Man came not to destroy people's lives but to save them" [6]Greek he [7]Some manuscripts seventy; also verse 17 [a]For 9:57-62 see parallel Matt. 8:19-22

kingdom of God has come near to you.' [10]But whenever you enter a town and they do not receive you, go into its streets and say, [11]'Even the dust of your town that clings to our feet we wipe off against you. Nevertheless know this, that the kingdom of God has come near.' [12a]I tell you, it will be more bearable on that day for Sodom than for that town.

Woe to Unrepentant Cities

[13]"Woe to you, Chorazin! Woe to you, Bethsaida! For if the mighty works done in you had been done in Tyre and Sidon, they would have repented long ago, sitting in sackcloth and ashes. [14]But it will be more bearable in the judgment for Tyre and Sidon than for you. [15]And you, Capernaum, will you be exalted to heaven? You shall be brought down to Hades.

[16]"The one who hears you hears me, and the one who rejects you rejects me, and the one who rejects me rejects him who sent me."

The Return of the Seventy-Two

[17]The seventy-two returned with joy, saying, "Lord, even the demons are subject to us in your name!" [18]And he said to them, "I saw Satan fall like lightning from heaven. [19]Behold, I have given you authority to tread on serpents and scorpions, and over all the power of the enemy, and nothing shall hurt you. [20]Nevertheless, do not rejoice in this, that the spirits are subject to you, but rejoice that your names are written in heaven."

Jesus Rejoices in the Father's Will

[21b]In that same hour he rejoiced in the Holy Spirit and said, "I thank you, Father, Lord of heaven and earth, that you have hidden these things from the wise and understanding and revealed them to little children; yes, Father, for such was your gracious will.[1] [22]All things have been handed over to me by my Father, and no one knows who the Son is except the Father, or who the Father is except the Son and anyone to whom the Son chooses to reveal him."

[23]Then turning to the disciples he said privately, "Blessed are the eyes that see what you see! [24]For I tell you that many prophets and kings desired to see what you see, and did not see it, and to hear what you hear, and did not hear it."

The Parable of the Good Samaritan

[25]And behold, a lawyer stood up to put him to the test, saying, "Teacher, what shall I do to inherit eternal life?" [26]He said to him, "What is written in the Law? How do you read it?" [27]And he answered, c"You shall love the Lord your God with all your heart and with all your soul and with all your strength and with all your mind, and dyour neighbor as yourself." [28]And he said to

him, "You have answered correctly; do this, and you will live."

[29]But he, desiring to justify himself, said to Jesus, "And who is my neighbor?" [30]Jesus replied, "A man was going down from Jerusalem to Jericho, and he fell among robbers, who stripped him and beat him and departed, leaving him half dead. [31]Now by chance a priest was going down that road, and when he saw him he passed by on the other side. [32]So likewise a Levite, when he came to the place and saw him, passed by on the other side. [33]But a Samaritan, as he journeyed, came to where he was, and when he saw him, he had compassion. [34]He went to him and bound up his wounds, pouring on oil and wine. Then he set him on his own animal and brought him to an inn and took care of him. [35]And the next day he took out two denarii[2] and gave them to the innkeeper, saying, 'Take care of him, and whatever more you spend, I will repay you when I come back.' [36]Which of these three, do you think, proved to be a neighbor to the man who fell among the robbers?" [37]He said, "The one who showed him mercy." And Jesus said to him, "You go, and do likewise."

Martha and Mary

[38]Now as they went on their way, Jesus[3] entered a village. And a woman named Martha welcomed him into her house. [39]And she had a sister called Mary, who sat at the Lord's feet and listened to his teaching. [40]But Martha was distracted with much serving. And she went up to him and said, "Lord, do you not care that my sister has left me to serve alone? Tell her then to help me." [41]But the Lord answered her, "Martha, Martha, you are anxious and troubled about many things, [42]but one thing is necessary.[4] Mary has chosen the good portion, which will not be taken away from her."

The Lord's Prayer

11 Now Jesus[5] was praying in a certain place, and when he finished, one of his disciples said to him, "Lord, teach us to pray, as John taught his disciples." [2]And he said to them, "When you pray, say:

> "Father, hallowed be your name.
> Your kingdom come.
> [3] Give us each day our daily bread,[6]
> [4] and forgive us our sins,
>   for we ourselves forgive everyone who is
>   indebted to us.
>   And lead us not into temptation."

[5]And he said to them, "Which of you who has a friend will go to him at midnight and say to him, 'Friend, lend me three loaves, [6]for a friend of mine has arrived on a journey, and I have

[1]Or for so it pleased you well [2]A denarius was a day's wage for a laborer [3]Greek he [4]Some manuscripts few things are necessary, or only one [5]Greek he [6]Or our bread for tomorrow aFor 10:13-15 see parallel Matt. 11:21-24 bFor 10:21, 22 see parallel Matt. 11:25-27 cDeut. 6:5 dLev. 19:18

nothing to set before him'; ⁷and he will answer from within, 'Do not bother me; the door is now shut, and my children are with me in bed. I cannot get up and give you anything'? ⁸I tell you, though he will not get up and give him anything because he is his friend, yet because of his impudence*ʲ* he will rise and give him whatever he needs. ⁹And I tell you, *ᵃ*ask, and it will be given to you; seek, and you will find; knock, and it will be opened to you. ¹⁰For everyone who asks receives, and the one who seeks finds, and to the one who knocks it will be opened. ¹¹What father among you, if his son asks for*²* a fish give him a serpent; ¹²or if he asks for an egg, will give him a scorpion? ¹³If you then, who are evil, know how to give good gifts to your children, how much more will the heavenly Father give the Holy Spirit to those who ask him!"

Jesus and Beelzebul

¹⁴*ᵇ*Now he was casting out a demon that was mute. When the demon had gone out, the mute man spoke, and the people marveled. ¹⁵But some of them said, "He casts out demons by Beelzebul, the prince of demons," ¹⁶while others, to test him, kept seeking from him a sign from heaven. ¹⁷*ᶜ*But he, knowing their thoughts, said to them, "Every kingdom divided against itself is laid waste, and a divided household falls. ¹⁸And if Satan also is divided against himself, how will his kingdom stand? For you say that I cast out demons by Beelzebul. ¹⁹And if I cast out demons by Beelzebul, by whom do your sons cast them out? Therefore they will be your judges. ²⁰But if it is by the finger of God that I cast out demons, then the kingdom of God has come upon you. ²¹When a strong man, fully armed, guards his own palace, his goods are safe; ²²but when one stronger than he attacks him and overcomes him, he takes away his armor in which he trusted and divides his spoil. ²³Whoever is not with me is against me, and whoever does not gather with me scatters.

Return of an Unclean Spirit

²⁴*ᵈ*"When the unclean spirit has gone out of a person, it passes through waterless places seeking rest, and finding none it says, 'I will return to my house from which I came.' ²⁵And when it comes, it finds the house swept and put in order. ²⁶Then it goes and brings seven other spirits more evil than itself, and they enter and dwell there. And the last state of that person is worse than the first."

True Blessedness

²⁷As he said these things, a woman in the crowd raised her voice and said to him, "Blessed is the womb that bore you, and the breasts at which you nursed!" ²⁸But he said, "Blessed rather are those who hear the word of God and keep it!"

The Sign of Jonah

²⁹When the crowds were increasing, he began to say, *ᵉ*"This generation is an evil generation. It seeks for a sign, but no sign will be given to it except the sign of Jonah. ³⁰For as Jonah became a sign to the people of Nineveh, so will the Son of Man be to this generation. ³¹The queen of the South will rise up at the judgment with the men of this generation and condemn them, for she came from the ends of the earth to hear the wisdom of Solomon, and behold, something greater than Solomon is here. ³²The men of Nineveh will rise up at the judgment with this generation and condemn it, for they repented at the preaching of Jonah, and behold, something greater than Jonah is here.

The Light in You

³³"No one after lighting a lamp puts it in a cellar or under a basket, but on a stand, so that those who enter may see the light. ³⁴Your eye is the lamp of your body. When your eye is healthy, your whole body is full of light, but when it is bad, your body is full of darkness. ³⁵Therefore be careful lest the light in you be darkness. ³⁶If then your whole body is full of light, having no part dark, it will be wholly bright, as when a lamp with its rays gives you light."

Woes to the Pharisees and Lawyers

³⁷While Jesus*³* was speaking, a Pharisee asked him to dine with him, so he went in and reclined at table. ³⁸The Pharisee was astonished to see that he did not first wash before dinner. ³⁹And the Lord said to him, "Now you Pharisees cleanse the outside of the cup and of the dish, but inside you are full of greed and wickedness. ⁴⁰You fools! Did not he who made the outside make the inside also? ⁴¹But give as alms those things that are within, and behold, everything is clean for you.

⁴²"But woe to you Pharisees! For you tithe mint and rue and every herb, and neglect justice and the love of God. These you ought to have done, without neglecting the others. ⁴³Woe to you Pharisees! For you love the best seat in the synagogues and greetings in the marketplaces. ⁴⁴Woe to you! For you are like unmarked graves, and people walk over them without knowing it."

⁴⁵One of the lawyers answered him, "Teacher, in saying these things you insult us also." ⁴⁶And he said, "Woe to you lawyers also! For you load people with burdens hard to bear, and you yourselves do not touch the burdens with one of your fingers. ⁴⁷Woe to you! For you build the

---

¹ Or *persistence* ² Some manuscripts insert *bread, will give him a stone; or if he asks for* ³ Greek *he* ᵃ For 11:9-13 see parallel Matt. 7:7-11 ᵇ For 11:14, 15 see parallel Matt. 12:22-24 ᶜ For 11:17-22 see parallels Matt. 12:25-29; Mark 3:23-27 ᵈ For 11:24-26 see parallel Matt. 12:43-45 ᵉ For 11:29-32 see parallel Matt. 12:39-42

tombs of the prophets whom your fathers killed. [48]So you are witnesses and you consent to the deeds of your fathers, for they killed them, and you build their tombs. [49]Therefore also the Wisdom of God said, 'I will send them prophets and apostles, some of whom they will kill and persecute,' [50]so that the blood of all the prophets, shed from the foundation of the world, may be charged against this generation, [51]from the blood of Abel to the blood of Zechariah, who perished between the altar and the sanctuary. Yes, I tell you, it will be required of this generation. [52]Woe to you lawyers! For you have taken away the key of knowledge. You did not enter yourselves, and you hindered those who were entering."

[53]As he went away from there, the scribes and the Pharisees began to press him hard and to provoke him to speak about many things, [54]lying in wait for him, to catch him in something he might say.

Beware of the Leaven of the Pharisees

12 In the meantime, when so many thousands of the people had gathered together that they were trampling one another, he began to say to his disciples first, "Beware of the leaven of the Pharisees, which is hypocrisy. [2a]Nothing is covered up that will not be revealed, or hidden that will not be known. [3]Therefore whatever you have said in the dark shall be heard in the light, and what you have whispered in private rooms shall be proclaimed on the housetops.

Have No Fear

[4]"I tell you, my friends, do not fear those who kill the body, and after that have nothing more that they can do. [5]But I will warn you whom to fear: fear him who, after he has killed, has authority to cast into hell.[1] Yes, I tell you, fear him! [6]Are not five sparrows sold for two pennies?[2] And not one of them is forgotten before God. [7]Why, even the hairs of your head are all numbered. Fear not; you are of more value than many sparrows.

Acknowledge Christ Before Men

[8]"And I tell you, everyone who acknowledges me before men, the Son of Man also will acknowledge before the angels of God, [9]but the one who denies me before men will be denied before the angels of God. [10]And everyone who speaks a word against the Son of Man will be forgiven, but the one who blasphemes against the Holy Spirit will not be forgiven. [11]And when they bring you before the synagogues and the rulers and the authorities, do not be anxious about how you should defend yourself

or what you should say, [12]for the Holy Spirit will teach you in that very hour what you ought to say."

The Parable of the Rich Fool

[13]Someone in the crowd said to him, "Teacher, tell my brother to divide the inheritance with me." [14]But he said to him, "Man, who made me a judge or arbitrator over you?" [15]And he said to them, "Take care, and be on your guard against all covetousness, for one's life does not consist in the abundance of his possessions." [16]And he told them a parable, saying, "The land of a rich man produced plentifully, [17]and he thought to himself, 'What shall I do, for I have nowhere to store my crops?' [18]And he said, 'I will do this: I will tear down my barns and build larger ones, and there I will store all my grain and my goods. [19]And I will say to my soul, Soul, you have ample goods laid up for many years; relax, eat, drink, be merry.' [20]But God said to him, 'Fool! This night your soul is required of you, and the things you have prepared, whose will they be?' [21]So is the one who lays up treasure for himself and is not rich toward God."

Do Not Be Anxious

[22]And he said to his disciples, [b]"Therefore I tell you, do not be anxious about your life, what you will eat, nor about your body, what you will put on. [23]For life is more than food, and the body more than clothing. [24]Consider the ravens: they neither sow nor reap, they have neither storehouse nor barn, and yet God feeds them. Of how much more value are you than the birds! [25]And which of you by being anxious can add a single hour to his span of life?[3] [26]If then you are not able to do as small a thing as that, why are you anxious about the rest? [27]Consider the lilies, how they grow: they neither toil nor spin,[4] yet I tell you, even Solomon in all his glory was not arrayed like one of these. [28]But if God so clothes the grass, which is alive in the field today, and tomorrow is thrown into the oven, how much more will he clothe you, O you of little faith! [29]And do not seek what you are to eat and what you are to drink, nor be worried. [30]For all the nations of the world seek after these things, and your Father knows that you need them. [31]Instead, seek his[5] kingdom, and these things will be added to you.

[32]"Fear not, little flock, for it is your Father's good pleasure to give you the kingdom. [33]Sell your possessions, and give to the needy. Provide yourselves with moneybags that do not grow old, with a treasure in the heavens that does not fail, where no thief approaches and no moth destroys. [34]For where your treasure is, there will your heart be also.

---

[1]Greek *Gehenna* [2]Greek *two assaria; an assarion* was a Roman copper coin worth about 1/16 of a *denarius* (which was a day's wage for a laborer) [3]Or *a single cubit to his stature;* a *cubit* was about 18 inches or 45 centimeters [4]Some manuscripts *Consider the lilies; they neither spin nor weave* [5]Some manuscripts *God's* [a]For 12:2-9 see parallel Matt. 10:26-33 [b]For 12:22-31 see parallel Matt. 6:25-33

You Must Be Ready

[35] "Stay dressed for action[1] and keep your lamps burning, [36] and be like men who are waiting for their master to come home from the wedding feast, so that they may open the door to him at once when he comes and knocks. [37] Blessed are those servants[2] whom the master finds awake when he comes. Truly, I say to you, he will dress himself for service and have them recline at table, and he will come and serve them. [38] If he comes in the second watch, or in the third, and finds them awake, blessed are those servants! [39] But know this, that if the master of the house had known at what hour the thief was coming, he[3] would not have left his house to be broken into. [40] You also must be ready, for the Son of Man is coming at an hour you do not expect."

[41] Peter said, "Lord, are you telling this parable for us or for all?" [42] And the Lord said, "Who then is the faithful and wise manager, whom his master will set over his household, to give them their portion of food at the proper time? [43] Blessed is that servant[4] whom his master will find so doing when he comes. [44] Truly, I say to you, he will set him over all his possessions. [45] But if that servant says to himself, 'My master is delayed in coming,' and begins to beat the male and female servants, and to eat and drink and get drunk, [46] the master of that servant will come on a day when he does not expect him and at an hour he does not know, and will cut him in pieces and put him with the unfaithful. [47] And that servant who knew his master's will but did not get ready or act according to his will, will receive a severe beating. [48] But the one who did not know, and did what deserved a beating, will receive a light beating. Everyone to whom much was given, of him much will be required, and from him to whom they entrusted much, they will demand the more.

Not Peace, but Division

[49] "I came to cast fire on the earth, and would that it were already kindled! [50] I have a baptism to be baptized with, and how great is my distress until it is accomplished! [51a] Do you think that I have come to give peace on earth? No, I tell you, but rather division. [52] For from now on in one house there will be five divided, three against two and two against three. [53] They will be divided, father against son and son against father, mother against daughter and daughter against mother, mother-in-law against her daughter-in-law and daughter-in-law against mother-in-law."

Interpreting the Time

[54] He also said to the crowds, "When you see a cloud rising in the west, you say at once, 'A shower is coming.' And so it happens. [55] And when you see the south wind blowing, you say, 'There will be scorching heat,' and it happens. [56] You hypocrites! You know how to interpret the appearance of earth and sky, but why do you not know how to interpret the present time?

Settle with Your Accuser

[57] "And why do you not judge for yourselves what is right? [58] As you go with your accuser before the magistrate, make an effort to settle with him on the way, lest he drag you to the judge, and the judge hand you over to the officer, and the officer put you in prison. [59] I tell you, you will never get out until you have paid the very last penny."[5]

Repent or Perish

13 There were some present at that very time who told him about the Galileans whose blood Pilate had mingled with their sacrifices. [2] And he answered them, "Do you think that these Galileans were worse sinners than all the other Galileans, because they suffered in this way? [3] No, I tell you; but unless you repent, you will all likewise perish. [4] Or those eighteen on whom the tower in Siloam fell and killed them: do you think that they were worse offenders than all the others who lived in Jerusalem? [5] No, I tell you; but unless you repent, you will all likewise perish."

The Parable of the Barren Fig Tree

[6] And he told this parable: "A man had a fig tree planted in his vineyard, and he came seeking fruit on it and found none. [7] And he said to the vinedresser, 'Look, for three years now I have come seeking fruit on this fig tree, and I find none. Cut it down. Why should it use up the ground?' [8] And he answered him, 'Sir, let it alone this year also, until I dig around it and put on manure. [9] Then if it should bear fruit next year, well and good; but if not, you can cut it down.'"

A Woman with a Disabling Spirit

[10] Now he was teaching in one of the synagogues on the Sabbath. [11] And there was a woman who had had a disabling spirit for eighteen years. She was bent over and could not fully straighten herself. [12] When Jesus saw her, he called her over and said to her, "Woman, you are freed from your disability." [13] And he laid his hands on her, and immediately she was made straight, and she glorified God. [14] But the ruler of the synagogue, indignant because Jesus had healed on the Sabbath, said to the people, "There are six days in which work ought to be done. Come on those days and be healed, and not on the Sabbath day." [15] Then the Lord answered him, "You hypocrites! Does not each of you on the Sabbath untie his ox or his donkey from the

---

[1] Greek *Let your loins stay girded;* compare Exodus 12:11   [2] Greek *bondservants*   [3] Some manuscripts add *would have stayed awake and*   [4] Greek *bondservant;* also verses 45, 46, 47   [5] Greek *lepton,* a Jewish bronze or copper coin worth about 1/128 of a *denarius* (which was a day's wage for a laborer)   [a] For 12:51-53 see parallel Matt. 10:34, 35

manger and lead it away to water it? [16]And ought not this woman, a daughter of Abraham whom Satan bound for eighteen years, be loosed from this bond on the Sabbath day?" [17]As he said these things, all his adversaries were put to shame, and all the people rejoiced at all the glorious things that were done by him.

The Mustard Seed and the Leaven

[18a]He said therefore, "What is the kingdom of God like? And to what shall I compare it? [19]It is like a grain of mustard seed that a man took and sowed in his garden, and it grew and became a tree, and the birds of the air made nests in its branches."

[20]And again he said, "To what shall I compare the kingdom of God? [21]It is like leaven that a woman took and hid in three measures of flour, until it was all leavened."

The Narrow Door

[22]He went on his way through towns and villages, teaching and journeying toward Jerusalem. [23]And someone said to him, "Lord, will those who are saved be few?" And he said to them, [24]"Strive to enter through the narrow door. For many, I tell you, will seek to enter and will not be able. [25]When once the master of the house has risen and shut the door, and you begin to stand outside and to knock at the door, saying, 'Lord, open to us,' then he will answer you, 'I do not know where you come from.' [26]Then you will begin to say, 'We ate and drank in your presence, and you taught in our streets.' [27]But he will say, 'I tell you, I do not know where you come from. Depart from me, all you workers of evil!' [28]In that place there will be weeping and gnashing of teeth, when you see Abraham and Isaac and Jacob and all the prophets in the kingdom of God but you yourselves cast out. [29]And people will come from east and west, and from north and south, and recline at table in the kingdom of God. [30]And behold, some are last who will be first, and some are first who will be last."

Lament over Jerusalem

[31]At that very hour some Pharisees came and said to him, "Get away from here, for Herod wants to kill you." [32]And he said to them, "Go and tell that fox, 'Behold, I cast out demons and perform cures today and tomorrow, and the third day I finish my course. [33]Nevertheless, I must go on my way today and tomorrow and the day following, for it cannot be that a prophet should perish away from Jerusalem.' [34b]O Jerusalem, Jerusalem, the city that kills the prophets and stones those who are sent to it! How often would I have gathered your children together as a hen gathers her brood under her wings, and

you would not! [35]Behold, your house is forsaken. And I tell you, you will not see me until you say, [c]'Blessed is he who comes in the name of the Lord!'"

Healing of a Man on the Sabbath

14 One Sabbath, when he went to dine at the house of a ruler of the Pharisees, they were watching him carefully. [2]And behold, there was a man before him who had dropsy. [3]And Jesus responded to the lawyers and Pharisees, saying, "Is it lawful to heal on the Sabbath, or not?" [4]But they remained silent. Then he took him and healed him and sent him away. [5]And he said to them, "Which of you, having a son[1] or an ox that has fallen into a well on a Sabbath day, will not immediately pull him out?" [6]And they could not reply to these things.

The Parable of the Wedding Feast

[7]Now he told a parable to those who were invited, when he noticed how they chose the places of honor, saying to them, [8]"When you are invited by someone to a wedding feast, do not sit down in a place of honor, lest someone more distinguished than you be invited by him, [9]and he who invited you both will come and say to you, 'Give your place to this person,' and then you will begin with shame to take the lowest place. [10]But when you are invited, go and sit in the lowest place, so that when your host comes he may say to you, 'Friend, move up higher.' Then you will be honored in the presence of all who sit at table with you. [11]For everyone who exalts himself will be humbled, and he who humbles himself will be exalted."

The Parable of the Great Banquet

[12]He said also to the man who had invited him, "When you give a dinner or a banquet, do not invite your friends or your brothers[2] or your relatives or rich neighbors, lest they also invite you in return and you be repaid. [13]But when you give a feast, invite the poor, the crippled, the lame, the blind, [14]and you will be blessed, because they cannot repay you. For you will be repaid at the resurrection of the just."

[15]When one of those who reclined at table with him heard these things, he said to him, "Blessed is everyone who will eat bread in the kingdom of God!" [16]But he said to him, "A man once gave a great banquet and invited many. [17]And at the time for the banquet he sent his servant[3] to say to those who had been invited, 'Come, for everything is now ready.' [18]But they all alike began to make excuses. The first said to him, 'I have bought a field, and I must go out and see it. Please have me excused.' [19]And another said, 'I have bought five yoke of oxen,

---

[1] Some manuscripts *a donkey* [2] Or *your brothers and sisters*. The plural Greek word *adelphoi* (translated "brothers") refers to siblings in a family. In New Testament usage, depending on the context, *adelphoi* may refer either to *brothers* or to *brothers and sisters* [3] Greek *bondservant*; also verses 21, 22, 23 [a] For 13:18, 19 see parallels Matt. 13:31, 32; Mark 4:30-32 [b] For 13:34, 35 see parallel Matt. 25:37-39 [c] Ps. 118:26

and I go to examine them. Please have me excused.' [20] And another said, 'I have married a wife, and therefore I cannot come.' [21] So the servant came and reported these things to his master. Then the master of the house became angry and said to his servant, 'Go out quickly to the streets and lanes of the city, and bring in the poor and crippled and blind and lame.' [22] And the servant said, 'Sir, what you commanded has been done, and still there is room.' [23] And the master said to the servant, 'Go out to the highways and hedges and compel people to come in, that my house may be filled. [24] For I tell you,[1] none of those men who were invited shall taste my banquet.'"

The Cost of Discipleship

[25] Now great crowds accompanied him, and he turned and said to them, [26] "If anyone comes to me and does not hate his own father and mother and wife and children and brothers and sisters, yes, and even his own life, he cannot be my disciple. [27] Whoever does not bear his own cross and come after me cannot be my disciple. [28] For which of you, desiring to build a tower, does not first sit down and count the cost, whether he has enough to complete it? [29] Otherwise, when he has laid a foundation and is not able to finish, all who see it begin to mock him, [30] saying, 'This man began to build and was not able to finish.' [31] Or what king, going out to encounter another king in war, will not sit down first and deliberate whether he is able with ten thousand to meet him who comes against him with twenty thousand? [32] And if not, while the other is yet a great way off, he sends a delegation and asks for terms of peace. [33] So therefore, any one of you who does not renounce all that he has cannot be my disciple.

Salt Without Taste Is Worthless

[34] "Salt is good, but if salt has lost its taste, how shall its saltiness be restored? [35] It is of no use either for the soil or for the manure pile. It is thrown away. He who has ears to hear, let him hear."

The Parable of the Lost Sheep

15 Now the tax collectors and sinners were all drawing near to hear him. [2] And the Pharisees and the scribes grumbled, saying, "This man receives sinners and eats with them."

[3] So he told them this parable: [4] "What man of you, having a hundred sheep, if he has lost one of them, does not leave the ninety-nine in the open country, and go after the one that is lost, until he finds it? [5] And when he has found it, he lays it on his shoulders, rejoicing. [6] And when he comes home, he calls together his friends and his neighbors, saying to them, 'Rejoice with me,

for I have found my sheep that was lost.' [7] Just so, I tell you, there will be more joy in heaven over one sinner who repents than over ninety-nine righteous persons who need no repentance.

The Parable of the Lost Coin

[8] "Or what woman, having ten silver coins,[2] if she loses one coin, does not light a lamp and sweep the house and seek diligently until she finds it? [9] And when she has found it, she calls together her friends and neighbors, saying, 'Rejoice with me, for I have found the coin that I had lost.' [10] Just so, I tell you, there is joy before the angels of God over one sinner who repents."

The Parable of the Prodigal Son

[11] And he said, "There was a man who had two sons. [12] And the younger of them said to his father, 'Father, give me the share of property that is coming to me.' And he divided his property between them. [13] Not many days later, the younger son gathered all he had and took a journey into a far country, and there he squandered his property in reckless living. [14] And when he had spent everything, a severe famine arose in that country, and he began to be in need. [15] So he went and hired himself out to[3] one of the citizens of that country, who sent him into his fields to feed pigs. [16] And he was longing to be fed with the pods that the pigs ate, and no one gave him anything.

[17] "But when he came to himself, he said, 'How many of my father's hired servants have more than enough bread, but I perish here with hunger! [18] I will arise and go to my father, and I will say to him, "Father, I have sinned against heaven and before you. [19] I am no longer worthy to be called your son. Treat me as one of your hired servants."' [20] And he arose and came to his father. But while he was still a long way off, his father saw him and felt compassion, and ran and embraced him and kissed him. [21] And the son said to him, 'Father, I have sinned against heaven and before you. I am no longer worthy to be called your son.'[4] [22] But the father said to his servants,[5] 'Bring quickly the best robe, and put it on him, and put a ring on his hand, and shoes on his feet. [23] And bring the fattened calf and kill it, and let us eat and celebrate. [24] For this my son was dead, and is alive again; he was lost, and is found.' And they began to celebrate.

[25] "Now his older son was in the field, and as he came and drew near to the house, he heard music and dancing. [26] And he called one of the servants and asked what these things meant. [27] And he said to him, 'Your brother has come, and your father has killed the fattened calf, because he has received him back safe and sound.' [28] But he was angry and refused to go in. His father came out and entreated him, [29] but he answered his father, 'Look, these many years I

---

[1] The Greek word for *you* here is plural   [2] Greek *ten drachmas*; a *drachma* was a Greek coin approximately equal in value to a Roman *denarius*, worth about a day's wage for a laborer   [3] Greek *joined himself to*   [4] Some manuscripts add *treat me as one of your hired servants*   [5] Greek *bondservants*

have served you, and I never disobeyed your command, yet you never gave me a young goat, that I might celebrate with my friends. ³⁰But when this son of yours came, who has devoured your property with prostitutes, you killed the fattened calf for him!' ³¹And he said to him, 'Son, you are always with me, and all that is mine is yours. ³²It was fitting to celebrate and be glad, for this your brother was dead, and is alive; he was lost, and is found.'"

The Parable of the Dishonest Manager

16 He also said to the disciples, "There was a rich man who had a manager, and charges were brought to him that this man was wasting his possessions. ²And he called him and said to him, 'What is this that I hear about you? Turn in the account of your management, for you can no longer be manager.' ³And the manager said to himself, 'What shall I do, since my master is taking the management away from me? I am not strong enough to dig, and I am ashamed to beg. ⁴I have decided what to do, so that when I am removed from management, people may receive me into their houses.' ⁵So, summoning his master's debtors one by one, he said to the first, 'How much do you owe my master?' ⁶He said, 'A hundred measures¹ of oil.' He said to him, 'Take your bill, and sit down quickly and write fifty.' ⁷Then he said to another, 'And how much do you owe?' He said, 'A hundred measures² of wheat.' He said to him, 'Take your bill, and write eighty.' ⁸The master commended the dishonest manager for his shrewdness. For the sons of this world³ are more shrewd in dealing with their own generation than the sons of light. ⁹And I tell you, make friends for yourselves by means of unrighteous wealth,⁴ so that when it fails they may receive you into the eternal dwellings.

¹⁰"One who is faithful in a very little is also faithful in much, and one who is dishonest in a very little is also dishonest in much. ¹¹If then you have not been faithful in the unrighteous wealth, who will entrust to you the true riches? ¹²And if you have not been faithful in that which is another's, who will give you that which is your own? ¹³No servant can serve two masters, for either he will hate the one and love the other, or he will be devoted to the one and despise the other. You cannot serve God and money."

The Law and the Kingdom of God

¹⁴The Pharisees, who were lovers of money, heard all these things, and they ridiculed him. ¹⁵And he said to them, "You are those who justify yourselves before men, but God knows your hearts. For what is exalted among men is an abomination in the sight of God.

¹⁶"The Law and the Prophets were until John; since then the good news of the kingdom of God is preached, and everyone forces his way into it.⁵ ¹⁷But it is easier for heaven and earth to pass away than for one dot of the Law to become void.

Divorce and Remarriage

¹⁸"Everyone who divorces his wife and marries another commits adultery, and he who marries a woman divorced from her husband commits adultery.

The Rich Man and Lazarus

¹⁹"There was a rich man who was clothed in purple and fine linen and who feasted sumptuously every day. ²⁰And at his gate was laid a poor man named Lazarus, covered with sores, ²¹who desired to be fed with what fell from the rich man's table. Moreover, even the dogs came and licked his sores. ²²The poor man died and was carried by the angels to Abraham's side.⁶ The rich man also died and was buried, ²³and in Hades, being in torment, he lifted up his eyes and saw Abraham far off and Lazarus at his side. ²⁴And he called out, 'Father Abraham, have mercy on me, and send Lazarus to dip the end of his finger in water and cool my tongue, for I am in anguish in this flame.' ²⁵But Abraham said, 'Child, remember that you in your lifetime received your good things, and Lazarus in like manner bad things; but now he is comforted here, and you are in anguish. ²⁶And besides all this, between us and you a great chasm has been fixed, in order that those who would pass from here to you may not be able, and none may cross from there to us.' ²⁷And he said, 'Then I beg you, father, to send him to my father's house— ²⁸for I have five brothers⁷—so that he may warn them, lest they also come into this place of torment.' ²⁹But Abraham said, 'They have Moses and the Prophets; let them hear them.' ³⁰And he said, 'No, father Abraham, but if someone goes to them from the dead, they will repent.' ³¹He said to him, 'If they do not hear Moses and the Prophets, neither will they be convinced if someone should rise from the dead.'"

Temptations to Sin

17 And he said to his disciples, "Temptations to sin⁸ are sure to come, but woe to the one through whom they come! ²It would be better for him if a millstone were hung around his neck and he were cast into the sea than that he should cause one of these little ones to sin.⁹ ³Pay attention to yourselves! If your brother sins, rebuke him, and if he repents, forgive him, ⁴and if he sins against you seven times in the day, and turns to you seven times, saying, 'I repent,' you must forgive him."

¹ About 875 gallons ²Between 1,000 and 1,200 bushels ³Greek age ⁴Greek mammon, a Semitic word for money or possessions; also verse 11; rendered money in verse 13 ⁵Or everyone is forcefully urged into it ⁶Greek bosom; also verse 23 ⁷Or brothers and sisters ⁸Greek Stumbling blocks ⁹Greek stumble

Increase Our Faith

[5]The apostles said to the Lord, "Increase our faith!" [6]And the Lord said, "If you had faith like a grain of mustard seed, you could say to this mulberry tree, 'Be uprooted and planted in the sea,' and it would obey you.

Unworthy Servants

[7]"Will any one of you who has a servant[1] plowing or keeping sheep say to him when he has come in from the field, 'Come at once and recline at table'? [8]Will he not rather say to him, 'Prepare supper for me, and dress properly,[2] and serve me while I eat and drink, and afterward you will eat and drink'? [9]Does he thank the servant because he did what was commanded? [10]So you also, when you have done all that you were commanded, say, 'We are unworthy servants;[3] we have only done what was our duty.'"

Jesus Cleanses Ten Lepers

[11]On the way to Jerusalem he was passing along between Samaria and Galilee. [12]And as he entered a village, he was met by ten lepers,[4] who stood at a distance [13]and lifted up their voices, saying, "Jesus, Master, have mercy on us." [14]When he saw them he said to them, "Go and show yourselves to the priests." And as they went they were cleansed. [15]Then one of them, when he saw that he was healed, turned back, praising God with a loud voice; [16]and he fell on his face at Jesus' feet, giving him thanks. Now he was a Samaritan. [17]Then Jesus answered, "Were not ten cleansed? Where are the nine? [18]Was no one found to return and give praise to God except this foreigner?" [19]And he said to him, "Rise and go your way; your faith has made you well."[5]

The Coming of the Kingdom

[20]Being asked by the Pharisees when the kingdom of God would come, he answered them, "The kingdom of God is not coming with signs to be observed, [21]nor will they say, 'Look, here it is!' or 'There!' for behold, the kingdom of God is in the midst of you."[6] [22]And he said to the disciples, "The days are coming when you will desire to see one of the days of the Son of Man, and you will not see it. [23]And they will say to you, 'Look, there!' or 'Look, here!' Do not go out or follow them. [24]For as the lightning flashes and lights up the sky from one side to the other, so will the Son of Man be in his day.[7] [25]But first he must suffer many things and be rejected by this generation. [26]Just as it was in the days of Noah, so will it be in the days of the Son of Man. [27]They were eating and drinking and marrying and being given in marriage, until the day when Noah entered the ark, and the flood came and destroyed them all. [28]Likewise,

just as it was in the days of Lot—they were eating and drinking, buying and selling, planting and building, [29]but on the day when Lot went out from Sodom, fire and sulfur rained from heaven and destroyed them all— [30]so will it be on the day when the Son of Man is revealed. [31]On that day, let the one who is on the housetop, with his goods in the house, not come down to take them away, and likewise let the one who is in the field not turn back. [32]Remember Lot's wife. [33]Whoever seeks to preserve his life will lose it, but whoever loses his life will keep it. [34]I tell you, in that night there will be two in one bed. One will be taken and the other left. [35]There will be two women grinding together. One will be taken and the other left."[8] [37]And they said to him, "Where, Lord?" He said to them, "Where the corpse[9] is, there the vultures[10] will gather."

The Parable of the Persistent Widow

18 And he told them a parable to the effect that they ought always to pray and not lose heart. [2]He said, "In a certain city there was a judge who neither feared God nor respected man. [3]And there was a widow in that city who kept coming to him and saying, 'Give me justice against my adversary.' [4]For a while he refused, but afterward he said to himself, 'Though I neither fear God nor respect man, [5]yet because this widow keeps bothering me, I will give her justice, so that she will not beat me down by her continual coming.'" [6]And the Lord said, "Hear what the unrighteous judge says. [7]And will not God give justice to his elect, who cry to him day and night? Will he delay long over them? [8]I tell you, he will give justice to them speedily. Nevertheless, when the Son of Man comes, will he find faith on earth?"

The Pharisee and the Tax Collector

[9]He also told this parable to some who trusted in themselves that they were righteous, and treated others with contempt: [10]"Two men went up into the temple to pray, one a Pharisee and the other a tax collector. [11]The Pharisee, standing by himself, prayed[11] thus: 'God, I thank you that I am not like other men, extortioners, unjust, adulterers, or even like this tax collector. [12]I fast twice a week; I give tithes of all that I get.' [13]But the tax collector, standing far off, would not even lift up his eyes to heaven, but beat his breast, saying, 'God, be merciful to me, a sinner!' [14]I tell you, this man went down to his house justified, rather than the other. For everyone who exalts himself will be humbled, but the one who humbles himself will be exalted."

Let the Children Come to Me

[15a]Now they were bringing even infants to him that he might touch them. And when the

---

[1]Greek *bondservant*; also verse 9 [2]Greek *gird yourself* [3]Greek *bondservants* [4]*Leprosy* was a term for several skin diseases; see Leviticus 13 [5]Or *has saved you* [6]Or *within you, or within your grasp* [7]Some manuscripts omit *in his day* [8]Some manuscripts add verse 36: *Two men will be in the field; one will be taken and the other left* [9]Greek *body* [10]Or *eagles* [11]Or *standing, prayed to himself* [a]For 18:15-17 see parallels Matt. 19:13-15; Mark 10:13-16

disciples saw it, they rebuked them. **16**But Jesus called them to him, saying, "Let the children come to me, and do not hinder them, for to such belongs the kingdom of God. **17**Truly, I say to you, whoever does not receive the kingdom of God like a child shall not enter it."

The Rich Ruler

18ᵃAnd a ruler asked him, "Good Teacher, what must I do to inherit eternal life?" **19**And Jesus said to him, "Why do you call me good? No one is good except God alone. **20**You know the commandments: ᵇ'Do not commit adultery, Do not murder, Do not steal, Do not bear false witness, Honor your father and mother.'" **21**And he said, "All these I have kept from my youth." **22**When Jesus heard this, he said to him, "One thing you still lack. Sell all that you have and distribute to the poor, and you will have treasure in heaven; and come, follow me." **23**But when he heard these things, he became very sad, for he was extremely rich. **24**Jesus, seeing that he had become sad, said, "How difficult it is for those who have wealth to enter the kingdom of God! **25**For it is easier for a camel to go through the eye of a needle than for a rich person to enter the kingdom of God." **26**Those who heard it said, "Then who can be saved?" **27**But he said, "What is impossible with men is possible with God." **28**And Peter said, "See, we have left our homes and followed you." **29**And he said to them, "Truly, I say to you, there is no one who has left house or wife or brothers¹ or parents or children, for the sake of the kingdom of God, **30**who will not receive many times more in this time, and in the age to come eternal life."

Jesus Foretells His Death a Third Time

31ᶜAnd taking the twelve, he said to them, "See, we are going up to Jerusalem, and everything that is written about the Son of Man by the prophets will be accomplished. **32**For he will be delivered over to the Gentiles and will be mocked and shamefully treated and spit upon. **33**And after flogging him, they will kill him, and on the third day he will rise." **34**But they understood none of these things. This saying was hidden from them, and they did not grasp what was said.

Jesus Heals a Blind Beggar

35ᵈAs he drew near to Jericho, a blind man was sitting by the roadside begging. **36**And hearing a crowd going by, he inquired what this meant. **37**They told him, "Jesus of Nazareth is passing by." **38**And he cried out, "Jesus, Son of David, have mercy on me!" **39**And those who were in front rebuked him, telling him to be silent. But he cried out all the more, "Son of David, have mercy on me!" **40**And Jesus stopped and commanded him to be brought to him. And when he came near, he asked him, **41**"What do you want me to do for you?" He said, "Lord, let me recover my sight." **42**And Jesus said to him, "Recover your sight; your faith has made you well." **43**And immediately he recovered his sight and followed him, glorifying God. And all the people, when they saw it, gave praise to God.

Jesus and Zacchaeus

19 He entered Jericho and was passing through. **2**And there was a man named Zacchaeus. He was a chief tax collector and was rich. **3**And he was seeking to see who Jesus was, but on account of the crowd he could not, because he was small of stature. **4**So he ran on ahead and climbed up into a sycamore tree to see him, for he was about to pass that way. **5**And when Jesus came to the place, he looked up and said to him, "Zacchaeus, hurry and come down, for I must stay at your house today." **6**So he hurried and came down and received him joyfully. **7**And when they saw it, they all grumbled, "He has gone in to be the guest of a man who is a sinner." **8**And Zacchaeus stood and said to the Lord, "Behold, Lord, the half of my goods I give to the poor. And if I have defrauded anyone of anything, I restore it fourfold." **9**And Jesus said to him, "Today salvation has come to this house, since he also is a son of Abraham. **10**For the Son of Man came to seek and to save the lost."

The Parable of the Ten Minas

11As they heard these things, he proceeded to tell a parable, because he was near to Jerusalem, and because they supposed that the kingdom of God was to appear immediately. **12**He said therefore, "A nobleman went into a far country to receive for himself a kingdom and then return. **13**Calling ten of his servants,² he gave them ten minas,³ and said to them, 'Engage in business until I come.' **14**But his citizens hated him and sent a delegation after him, saying, 'We do not want this man to reign over us.' **15**When he returned, having received the kingdom, he ordered these servants to whom he had given the money to be called to him, that he might know what they had gained by doing business. **16**The first came before him, saying, 'Lord, your mina has made ten minas more.' **17**And he said to him, 'Well done, good servant!⁴ Because you have been faithful in a very little, you shall have authority over ten cities.' **18**And the second came, saying, 'Lord, your mina has made five minas.' **19**And he said to him, 'And you are to be over five cities.' **20**Then another came, saying, 'Lord, here is your mina, which I kept laid away in a handkerchief; **21**for I was afraid of you, because you are

---

¹Or *wife or brothers and sisters* ²Greek *bondservants*; also verse 15 ³A *mina* was about three months' wages for a laborer ⁴Greek *bondservant*; also verse 22 ᵃFor 18:18-30 see parallels Matt. 19:16-30; Mark 10:17-31 ᵇEx. 20:12-16; Deut. 5:16-20 ᶜFor 18:31-33 see parallels Matt. 20:17-19; Mark 10:32-34 ᵈFor 18:35-43 see parallels Matt. 20:29-34; Mark 10:46-52

a severe man. You take what you did not deposit, and reap what you did not sow.' ²²He said to him, 'I will condemn you with your own words, you wicked servant! You knew that I was a severe man, taking what I did not deposit and reaping what I did not sow? ²³Why then did you not put my money in the bank, and at my coming I might have collected it with interest?' ²⁴And he said to those who stood by, 'Take the mina from him, and give it to the one who has the ten minas.' ²⁵And they said to him, 'Lord, he has ten minas!' ²⁶'I tell you that to everyone who has, more will be given, but from the one who has not, even what he has will be taken away. ²⁷But as for these enemies of mine, who did not want me to reign over them, bring them here and slaughter them before me.'"

The Triumphal Entry

²⁸And when he had said these things, he went on ahead, going up to Jerusalem. ^{29a}When he drew near to Bethphage and Bethany, at the mount that is called Olivet, he sent two of the disciples, ³⁰saying, "Go into the village in front of you, where on entering you will find a colt tied, on which no one has ever yet sat. Untie it and bring it here. ³¹If anyone asks you, 'Why are you untying it?' you shall say this: 'The Lord has need of it.'" ³²So those who were sent went away and found it just as he had told them. ³³And as they were untying the colt, its owners said to them, "Why are you untying the colt?" ³⁴And they said, "The Lord has need of it." ³⁵And they brought it to Jesus, and throwing their cloaks on the colt, they set Jesus on it. ³⁶And as he rode along, they spread their cloaks on the road. ³⁷As he was drawing near—already on the way down the Mount of Olives—the whole multitude of his disciples began to rejoice and praise God with a loud voice for all the mighty works that they had seen, ³⁸saying, "Blessed is the King who comes in the name of the Lord! Peace in heaven and glory in the highest!" ³⁹And some of the Pharisees in the crowd said to him, "Teacher, rebuke your disciples." ⁴⁰He answered, "I tell you, if these were silent, the very stones would cry out."

Jesus Weeps over Jerusalem

⁴¹And when he drew near and saw the city, he wept over it, ⁴²saying, "Would that you, even you, had known on this day the things that make for peace! But now they are hidden from your eyes. ⁴³For the days will come upon you, when your enemies will set up a barricade around you and surround you and hem you in on every side ⁴⁴and tear you down to the ground, you and your children within you. And they will not leave one stone upon another in you, because you did not know the time of your visitation."

Jesus Cleanses the Temple

^{45b}And he entered the temple and began to drive out those who sold, ⁴⁶saying to them, "It is written, ^c'My house shall be a house of prayer,' but you have made it a den of robbers."

⁴⁷And he was teaching daily in the temple. The chief priests and the scribes and the principal men of the people were seeking to destroy him, ⁴⁸but they did not find anything they could do, for all the people were hanging on his words.

The Authority of Jesus Challenged

20 ^dOne day, as Jesus¹ was teaching the people in the temple and preaching the gospel, the chief priests and the scribes with the elders came up ²and said to him, "Tell us by what authority you do these things, or who it is that gave you this authority." ³He answered them, "I also will ask you a question. Now tell me, ⁴was the baptism of John from heaven or from man?" ⁵And they discussed it with one another, saying, "If we say, 'From heaven,' he will say, 'Why did you not believe him?' ⁶But if we say, 'From man,' all the people will stone us to death, for they are convinced that John was a prophet." ⁷So they answered that they did not know where it came from. ⁸And Jesus said to them, "Neither will I tell you by what authority I do these things."

The Parable of the Wicked Tenants

^{9e}And he began to tell the people this parable: "A man planted a vineyard and let it out to tenants and went into another country for a long while. ¹⁰When the time came, he sent a servant² to the tenants, so that they would give him some of the fruit of the vineyard. But the tenants beat him and sent him away empty-handed. ¹¹And he sent another servant. But they also beat and treated him shamefully, and sent him away empty-handed. ¹²And he sent yet a third. This one also they wounded and cast out. ¹³Then the owner of the vineyard said, 'What shall I do? I will send my beloved son; perhaps they will respect him.' ¹⁴But when the tenants saw him, they said to themselves, 'This is the heir. Let us kill him, so that the inheritance may be ours.' ¹⁵And they threw him out of the vineyard and killed him. What then will the owner of the vineyard do to them? ¹⁶He will come and destroy those tenants and give the vineyard to others." When they heard this, they said, "Surely not!" ¹⁷But he looked directly at them and said, "What then is this that is written:

^f"'The stone that the builders rejected
    has become the cornerstone'?³

¹⁸Everyone who falls on that stone will be broken

¹Greek *he* ²Greek *bondservant; also verse 11* ³Greek *the head of the corner* ^aFor 19:29-38 see parallels Matt. 21:1-9; Mark 11:1-10; John 12:12-15 ^bFor 19:45-47 see parallels Matt. 21:12-16; Mark 11:15-18 ^cIsa. 56:7 ^dFor 20:1-8 see parallels Matt. 21:23-27; Mark 11:27-33 ^eFor 20:9-18 see parallels Matt. 21:33-46; Mark 12:1-12 ^fPs. 118:22

to pieces, and when it falls on anyone, it will crush him."

Paying Taxes to Caesar

[19]The scribes and the chief priests sought to lay hands on him at that very hour, for they perceived that he had told this parable against them, but they feared the people. [20a]So they watched him and sent spies, who pretended to be sincere, that they might catch him in something he said, so as to deliver him up to the authority and jurisdiction of the governor. [21]So they asked him, "Teacher, we know that you speak and teach rightly, and show no partiality,[1] but truly teach the way of God. [22]Is it lawful for us to give tribute to Caesar, or not?" [23]But he perceived their craftiness, and said to them, [24]"Show me a denarius.[2] Whose likeness and inscription does it have?" They said, "Caesar's." [25]He said to them, "Then render to Caesar the things that are Caesar's, and to God the things that are God's." [26]And they were not able in the presence of the people to catch him in what he said, but marveling at his answer they became silent.

Sadducees Ask About the Resurrection

[27]There came to him some Sadducees, those who deny that there is a resurrection, [28]and they asked him a question, saying, "Teacher, Moses wrote for us that if a man's brother dies, having a wife but no children, the man[3] must take the widow and raise up offspring for his brother. [29]Now there were seven brothers. The first took a wife, and died without children. [30]And the second [31]and the third took her, and likewise all seven left no children and died. [32]Afterward the woman also died. [33]In the resurrection, therefore, whose wife will the woman be? For the seven had her as wife."

[34]And Jesus said to them, "The sons of this age marry and are given in marriage, [35]but those who are considered worthy to attain to that age and to the resurrection from the dead neither marry nor are given in marriage, [36]for they cannot die anymore, because they are equal to angels and are sons of God, being sons[4] of the resurrection. [37]But that the dead are raised, even Moses showed, in the passage about the bush, where he calls the Lord the God of Abraham and the God of Isaac and the God of Jacob. [38]Now he is not God of the dead, but of the living, for all live to him." [39]Then some of the scribes answered, "Teacher, you have spoken well." [40]For they no longer dared to ask him any question.

Whose Son Is the Christ?

[41b]But he said to them, "How can they say that the Christ is David's son? [42]For David himself says in the Book of Psalms,

[c]"'The Lord said to my Lord,
    Sit at my right hand,
[43]   until I make your enemies your foot-
        stool.'

[44]David thus calls him Lord, so how is he his son?"

Beware of the Scribes

[45d]And in the hearing of all the people he said to his disciples, [46]"Beware of the scribes, who like to walk around in long robes, and love greetings in the marketplaces and the best seats in the synagogues and the places of honor at feasts, [47]who devour widows' houses and for a pretense make long prayers. They will receive the greater condemnation."

The Widow's Offering

21 [e]Jesus[5] looked up and saw the rich putting their gifts into the offering box, [2]and he saw a poor widow put in two small copper coins.[6] [3]And he said, "Truly, I tell you, this poor widow has put in more than all of them. [4]For they all contributed out of their abundance, but she out of her poverty put in all she had to live on."

Jesus Foretells Destruction of the Temple

[5f]And while some were speaking of the temple, how it was adorned with noble stones and offerings, he said, [6]"As for these things that you see, the days will come when there will not be left here one stone upon another that will not be thrown down." [7]And they asked him, "Teacher, when will these things be, and what will be the sign when these things are about to take place?" [8]And he said, "See that you are not led astray. For many will come in my name, saying, 'I am he!' and, 'The time is at hand!' Do not go after them. [9]And when you hear of wars and tumults, do not be terrified, for these things must first take place, but the end will not be at once."

Jesus Foretells Wars and Persecution

[10]Then he said to them, "Nation will rise against nation, and kingdom against kingdom. [11]There will be great earthquakes, and in various places famines and pestilences. And there will be terrors and great signs from heaven. [12]But before all this they will lay their hands on you and persecute you, delivering you up to the synagogues and prisons, and you will be brought before kings and governors for my name's sake. [13]This will be your opportunity to bear witness. [14]Settle it therefore in your minds not to meditate beforehand how to answer, [15]for I will give you a mouth and wisdom, which none of your adversaries will be able to withstand or contradict.

---

[1] Greek *and do not receive a face* [2] A *denarius* was a day's wage for a laborer [3] Greek *his brother* [4] Greek *huioi;* see preface [5] Greek *He* [6] Greek *two lepta;* a *lepton* was a Jewish bronze or copper coin worth about 1/128 of a *denarius* (which was a day's wage for a laborer) [a] For 20:20-38 see parallels Matt. 22:15-32; Mark 12:13-27 [b] For 20:41-44 see parallels Matt. 22:41-45; Mark 12:35-37 [c] Ps. 110:1 [d] For 20:45, 46 see parallels Matt. 23:1, 2, 5-7; Mark 12:38-40 [e] For 21:1-4 see parallel Mark 12:41-44 [f] For 21:5-36 see parallels Matt. 24:1-51; Mark 13:1-37

¹⁶You will be delivered up even by parents and brothers¹ and relatives and friends, and some of you they will put to death. ¹⁷You will be hated by all for my name's sake. ¹⁸But not a hair of your head will perish. ¹⁹By your endurance you will gain your lives.

Jesus Foretells Destruction of Jerusalem

²⁰"But when you see Jerusalem surrounded by armies, then know that its desolation has come near. ²¹Then let those who are in Judea flee to the mountains, and let those who are inside the city depart, and let not those who are out in the country enter it, ²²for these are days of vengeance, to fulfill all that is written. ²³Alas for women who are pregnant and for those who are nursing infants in those days! For there will be great distress upon the earth and wrath against this people. ²⁴They will fall by the edge of the sword and be led captive among all nations, and Jerusalem will be trampled underfoot by the Gentiles, until the times of the Gentiles are fulfilled.

The Coming of the Son of Man

²⁵"And there will be signs in sun and moon and stars, and on the earth distress of nations in perplexity because of the roaring of the sea and the waves, ²⁶people fainting with fear and with foreboding of what is coming on the world. For the powers of the heavens will be shaken. ²⁷And then they will see the Son of Man coming in a cloud with power and great glory. ²⁸Now when these things begin to take place, straighten up and raise your heads, because your redemption is drawing near."

The Lesson of the Fig Tree

²⁹And he told them a parable: "Look at the fig tree, and all the trees. ³⁰As soon as they come out in leaf, you see for yourselves and know that the summer is already near. ³¹So also, when you see these things taking place, you know that the kingdom of God is near. ³²Truly, I say to you, this generation will not pass away until all has taken place. ³³Heaven and earth will pass away, but my words will not pass away.

Watch Yourselves

³⁴"But watch yourselves lest your hearts be weighed down with dissipation and drunkenness and cares of this life, and that day come upon you suddenly like a trap. ³⁵For it will come upon all who dwell on the face of the whole earth. ³⁶But stay awake at all times, praying that you may have strength to escape all these things that are going to take place, and to stand before the Son of Man."

³⁷And every day he was teaching in the temple, but at night he went out and lodged on the mount called Olivet. ³⁸And early in the morning all the people came to him in the temple to hear him.

The Plot to Kill Jesus

22 Now the Feast of Unleavened Bread drew near, which is called the Passover. ²And the chief priests and the scribes were seeking how to put him to death, for they feared the people.

Judas to Betray Jesus

³ᵃThen Satan entered into Judas called Iscariot, who was of the number of the twelve. ⁴He went away and conferred with the chief priests and officers how he might betray him to them. ⁵And they were glad, and agreed to give him money. ⁶So he consented and sought an opportunity to betray him to them in the absence of a crowd.

The Passover with the Disciples

⁷ᵇThen came the day of Unleavened Bread, on which the Passover lamb had to be sacrificed. ⁸So Jesus² sent Peter and John, saying, "Go and prepare the Passover for us, that we may eat it." ⁹They said to him, "Where will you have us prepare it?" ¹⁰He said to them, "Behold, when you have entered the city, a man carrying a jar of water will meet you. Follow him into the house that he enters ¹¹and tell the master of the house, 'The Teacher says to you, Where is the guest room, where I may eat the Passover with my disciples?' ¹²And he will show you a large upper room furnished; prepare it there." ¹³And they went and found it just as he had told them, and they prepared the Passover.

Institution of the Lord's Supper

¹⁴And when the hour came, he reclined at table, and the apostles with him. ¹⁵And he said to them, "I have earnestly desired to eat this Passover with you before I suffer. ¹⁶For I tell you I will not eat it³ until it is fulfilled in the kingdom of God." ¹⁷And he took a cup, and when he had given thanks he said, "Take this, and divide it among yourselves. ¹⁸For I tell you that from now on I will not drink of the fruit of the vine until the kingdom of God comes." ¹⁹ᶜAnd he took bread, and when he had given thanks, he broke it and gave it to them, saying, "This is my body, which is given for you. Do this in remembrance of me." ²⁰And likewise the cup after they had eaten, saying, "This cup that is poured out for you is the new covenant in my blood.⁴ ²¹But behold, the hand of him who betrays me is with me on the table. ²²For the Son of Man goes as it has been determined, but woe to that man by whom he is betrayed!" ²³And they began to ques-

---

¹ Or *parents and brothers and sisters* ² Greek *he* ³ Some manuscripts *never eat it again* ⁴ Some manuscripts omit, in whole or in part, verses 19b-20 (*which is given . . . in my blood*) ᵃ For 22:3-6 see parallels Matt. 26:14-16; Mark 14:10, 11 ᵇ For 22:7-13 see parallels Matt. 26:17-19; Mark 14:12-16 ᶜ For 22:19, 20 see parallels Matt. 26:26-28; Mark 14:22-24 ᵈ For 22:21-23 see parallels Matt. 26:21-24; Mark 14:18-21

tion one another, which of them it could be who was going to do this.

Who Is the Greatest?

[24] A dispute also arose among them, as to which of them was to be regarded as the greatest. [25] And he said to them, "The kings of the Gentiles exercise lordship over them, and those in authority over them are called benefactors. [26] But not so with you. Rather, let the greatest among you become as the youngest, and the leader as one who serves. [27] For who is the greater, one who reclines at table or one who serves? Is it not the one who reclines at table? But I am among you as the one who serves.

[28] "You are those who have stayed with me in my trials, [29] and I assign to you, as my Father assigned to me, a kingdom, [30] that you may eat and drink at my table in my kingdom and sit on thrones judging the twelve tribes of Israel.

Jesus Foretells Peter's Denial

[31] "Simon, Simon, behold, Satan demanded to have you,[1] that he might sift you like wheat, [32] but I have prayed for you that your faith may not fail. And when you have turned again, strengthen your brothers." [33] Peter[2] said to him, "Lord, I am ready to go with you both to prison and to death." [34] Jesus[3] said, "I tell you, Peter, the rooster will not crow this day, until you deny three times that you know me."

Scripture Must Be Fulfilled in Jesus

[35] And he said to them, "When I sent you out with no moneybag or knapsack or sandals, did you lack anything?" They said, "Nothing." [36] He said to them, "But now let the one who has a moneybag take it, and likewise a knapsack. And let the one who has no sword sell his cloak and buy one. [37] For I tell you that this Scripture must be fulfilled in me: a'And he was numbered with the transgressors.' For what is written about me has its fulfillment." [38] And they said, "Look, Lord, here are two swords." And he said to them, "It is enough."

Jesus Prays on the Mount of Olives

[39] And he came out and went, as was his custom, to the Mount of Olives, and the disciples followed him. [40]b And when he came to the place, he said to them, "Pray that you may not enter into temptation." [41] And he withdrew from them about a stone's throw, and knelt down and prayed, [42] saying, "Father, if you are willing, remove this cup from me. Nevertheless, not my will, but yours, be done." [43] And there appeared to him an angel from heaven, strengthening him. [44] And being in an agony he prayed more earnestly; and his sweat became like great drops of blood falling down to the ground.[4] [45] And when he rose from prayer, he came to the disciples and found them sleeping for sorrow, [46] and he said to them, "Why are you sleeping? Rise and pray that you may not enter into temptation."

Betrayal and Arrest of Jesus

[47]c While he was still speaking, there came a crowd, and the man called Judas, one of the twelve, was leading them. He drew near to Jesus to kiss him, [48] but Jesus said to him, "Judas, would you betray the Son of Man with a kiss?" [49] And when those who were around him saw what would follow, they said, "Lord, shall we strike with the sword?" [50] And one of them struck the servant[5] of the high priest and cut off his right ear. [51] But Jesus said, "No more of this!" And he touched his ear and healed him. [52] Then Jesus said to the chief priests and officers of the temple and elders, who had come out against him, "Have you come out as against a robber, with swords and clubs? [53] When I was with you day after day in the temple, you did not lay hands on me. But this is your hour, and the power of darkness."

Peter Denies Jesus

[54] Then they seized him and led him away, bringing him into the high priest's house, and Peter was following at a distance. [55]d And when they had kindled a fire in the middle of the courtyard and sat down together, Peter sat down among them. [56] Then a servant girl, seeing him as he sat in the light and looking closely at him, said, "This man also was with him." [57] But he denied it, saying, "Woman, I do not know him." [58] And a little later someone else saw him and said, "You also are one of them." But Peter said, "Man, I am not." [59] And after an interval of about an hour still another insisted, saying, "Certainly this man also was with him, for he too is a Galilean." [60] But Peter said, "Man, I do not know what you are talking about." And immediately, while he was still speaking, the rooster crowed. [61] And the Lord turned and looked at Peter. And Peter remembered the saying of the Lord, how he had said to him, "Before the rooster crows today, you will deny me three times." [62] And he went out and wept bitterly.

Jesus Is Mocked

[63] Now the men who were holding Jesus in custody were mocking him as they beat him. [64] They also blindfolded him and kept asking him, "Prophesy! Who is it that struck you?" [65] And they said many other things against him, blaspheming him.

Jesus Before the Council

[66] When day came, the assembly of the elders of the people gathered together, both chief

[1] The Greek word for *you* (twice in this verse) is plural; in verse 32, all four instances are singular [2] Greek *He* [3] Greek *He* [4] Some manuscripts omit verses 43 and 44 [5] Greek *bondservant* a Isa. 53:12 b For 22:40-46 see parallels Matt. 26:36-46; Mark 14:32-42 c For 22:47-53 see parallels Matt. 26:47-56; Mark 14:43-50; John 18:3-11 d For 22:55-62 see parallels Matt. 26:69-75; Mark 14:66-72; John 18:16-18, 25-27

priests and scribes. And they led him away to their council, and they said, [67]"If you are the Christ, tell us." But he said to them, "If I tell you, you will not believe, [68]and if I ask you, you will not answer. [69]But from now on the Son of Man shall be seated at the right hand of the power of God." [70]So they all said, "Are you the Son of God, then?" And he said to them, "You say that I am." [71]Then they said, "What further testimony do we need? We have heard it ourselves from his own lips."

Jesus Before Pilate

23 Then the whole company of them arose and brought him before Pilate. [2]And they began to accuse him, saying, "We found this man misleading our nation and forbidding us to give tribute to Caesar, and saying that he himself is Christ, a king." [3]And Pilate asked him, "Are you the King of the Jews?" And he answered him, "You have said so." [4]Then Pilate said to the chief priests and the crowds, "I find no guilt in this man." [5]But they were urgent, saying, "He stirs up the people, teaching throughout all Judea, from Galilee even to this place."

Jesus Before Herod

[6]When Pilate heard this, he asked whether the man was a Galilean. [7]And when he learned that he belonged to Herod's jurisdiction, he sent him over to Herod, who was himself in Jerusalem at that time. [8]When Herod saw Jesus, he was very glad, for he had long desired to see him, because he had heard about him, and he was hoping to see some sign done by him. [9]So he questioned him at some length, but he made no answer. [10]The chief priests and the scribes stood by, vehemently accusing him. [11]And Herod with his soldiers treated him with contempt and mocked him. Then, arraying him in splendid clothing, he sent him back to Pilate. [12]And Herod and Pilate became friends with each other that very day, for before this they had been at enmity with each other.

[13]Pilate then called together the chief priests and the rulers and the people, [14]and said to them, "You brought me this man as one who was misleading the people. And after examining him before you, behold, I did not find this man guilty of any of your charges against him. [15]Neither did Herod, for he sent him back to us. Look, nothing deserving death has been done by him. [16]I will therefore punish and release him."[1]

Pilate Delivers Jesus to Be Crucified

[18a]But they all cried out together, "Away with this man, and release to us Barabbas"— [19]a man who had been thrown into prison for an insurrection started in the city and for murder. [20]Pilate addressed them once more, desiring to release Jesus, [21]but they kept shouting, "Crucify, crucify him!" [22]A third time he said to them, "Why, what evil has he done? I have found in him no guilt deserving death. I will therefore punish and release him." [23]But they were urgent, demanding with loud cries that he should be crucified. And their voices prevailed. [24]So Pilate decided that their demand should be granted. [25]He released the man who had been thrown into prison for insurrection and murder, for whom they asked, but he delivered Jesus over to their will.

The Crucifixion

[26]And as they led him away, they seized one Simon of Cyrene, who was coming in from the country, and laid on him the cross, to carry it behind Jesus. [27]And there followed him a great multitude of the people and of women who were mourning and lamenting for him. [28]But turning to them Jesus said, "Daughters of Jerusalem, do not weep for me, but weep for yourselves and for your children. [29]For behold, the days are coming when they will say, 'Blessed are the barren and the wombs that never bore and the breasts that never nursed!' [30]Then they will begin to say to the mountains, 'Fall on us,' and to the hills, 'Cover us.' [31]For if they do these things when the wood is green, what will happen when it is dry?"

[32]Two others, who were criminals, were led away to be put to death with him. [33]And when they came to the place that is called The Skull, there they crucified him, and the criminals, one on his right and one on his left. [34]And Jesus said, "Father, forgive them, for they know not what they do."[2] And they cast lots to divide his garments. [35]And the people stood by, watching, but the rulers scoffed at him, saying, "He saved others; let him save himself, if he is the Christ of God, his Chosen One!" [36]The soldiers also mocked him, coming up and offering him sour wine [37]and saying, "If you are the King of the Jews, save yourself!" [38]There was also an inscription over him,[3] "This is the King of the Jews."

[39]One of the criminals who were hanged railed at him,[4] saying, "Are you not the Christ? Save yourself and us!" [40]But the other rebuked him, saying, "Do you not fear God, since you are under the same sentence of condemnation? [41]And we indeed justly, for we are receiving the due reward of our deeds; but this man has done nothing wrong." [42]And he said, "Jesus, remember me when you come into your kingdom." [43]And he said to him, "Truly, I say to you, today you will be with me in Paradise."

The Death of Jesus

[44]It was now about the sixth hour,[5] and there was darkness over the whole land until the

---

[1] Here, or after verse 19, some manuscripts add verse 17: *Now he was obliged to release one man to them at the festival* [2] Some manuscripts omit the sentence *And Jesus . . . what they do* [3] Some manuscripts add *in letters of Greek and Latin and Hebrew* [4] Or *blasphemed him* [5] That is, noon [a] For 23:18-25 see parallels Matt. 27:15-26; Mark 15:6-15; John 18:39, 40; 19:16

ninth hour,[1] [45]while the sun's light failed. And the curtain of the temple was torn in two. [46]Then Jesus, calling out with a loud voice, said, "Father, into your hands I commit my spirit!" And having said this he breathed his last. [47]Now when the centurion saw what had taken place, he praised God, saying, "Certainly this man was innocent!" [48]And all the crowds that had assembled for this spectacle, when they saw what had taken place, returned home beating their breasts. [49]And all his acquaintances and the women who had followed him from Galilee stood at a distance watching these things.

Jesus Is Buried

[50a]Now there was a man named Joseph, from the Jewish town of Arimathea. He was a member of the council, a good and righteous man, [51]who had not consented to their decision and action; and he was looking for the kingdom of God. [52]This man went to Pilate and asked for the body of Jesus. [53]Then he took it down and wrapped it in a linen shroud and laid him in a tomb cut in stone, where no one had ever yet been laid. [54]It was the day of Preparation, and the Sabbath was beginning.[2] [55]The women who had come with him from Galilee followed and saw the tomb and how his body was laid. [56]Then they returned and prepared spices and ointments.

On the Sabbath they rested according to the commandment.

The Resurrection

24 [b]But on the first day of the week, at early dawn, they went to the tomb, taking the spices they had prepared. [2]And they found the stone rolled away from the tomb, [3]but when they went in they did not find the body of the Lord Jesus. [4]While they were perplexed about this, behold, two men stood by them in dazzling apparel. [5]And as they were frightened and bowed their faces to the ground, the men said to them, "Why do you seek the living among the dead? [6]He is not here, but has risen. Remember how he told you, while he was still in Galilee, [7]that the Son of Man must be delivered into the hands of sinful men and be crucified and on the third day rise." [8]And they remembered his words, [9]and returning from the tomb they told all these things to the eleven and to all the rest. [10]Now it was Mary Magdalene and Joanna and Mary the mother of James and the other women with them who told these things to the apostles, [11]but these words seemed to them an idle tale, and they did not believe them. [12]But Peter rose and ran to the tomb; stooping and looking in, he saw the linen cloths by themselves; and he went home marveling at what had happened.

On the Road to Emmaus

[13]That very day two of them were going to a village named Emmaus, about seven miles[3] from Jerusalem, [14]and they were talking with each other about all these things that had happened. [15]While they were talking and discussing together, Jesus himself drew near and went with them. [16]But their eyes were kept from recognizing him. [17]And he said to them, "What is this conversation that you are holding with each other as you walk?" And they stood still, looking sad. [18]Then one of them, named Cleopas, answered him, "Are you the only visitor to Jerusalem who does not know the things that have happened there in these days?" [19]And he said to them, "What things?" And they said to him, "Concerning Jesus of Nazareth, a man who was a prophet mighty in deed and word before God and all the people, [20]and how our chief priests and rulers delivered him up to be condemned to death, and crucified him. [21]But we had hoped that he was the one to redeem Israel. Yes, and besides all this, it is now the third day since these things happened. [22]Moreover, some women of our company amazed us. They were at the tomb early in the morning, [23]and when they did not find his body, they came back saying that they had even seen a vision of angels, who said that he was alive. [24]Some of those who were with us went to the tomb and found it just as the women had said, but him they did not see." [25]And he said to them, "O foolish ones, and slow of heart to believe all that the prophets have spoken! [26]Was it not necessary that the Christ should suffer these things and enter into his glory?" [27]And beginning with Moses and all the Prophets, he interpreted to them in all the Scriptures the things concerning himself.

[28]So they drew near to the village to which they were going. He acted as if he were going farther, [29]but they urged him strongly, saying, "Stay with us, for it is toward evening and the day is now far spent." So he went in to stay with them. [30]When he was at table with them, he took the bread and blessed and broke it and gave it to them. [31]And their eyes were opened, and they recognized him. And he vanished from their sight. [32]They said to each other, "Did not our hearts burn within us while he talked to us on the road, while he opened to us the Scriptures?" [33]And they rose that same hour and returned to Jerusalem. And they found the eleven and those who were with them gathered together, [34]saying, "The Lord has risen indeed, and has appeared to Simon!" [35]Then they told what had happened on the road, and how he was known to them in the breaking of the bread.

---

[1] That is, 3 P.M. [2] Greek *was dawning* [3] Greek *sixty stadia*; a *stadion* was about 607 feet or 185 meters [a]For 23:50-56 see parallels Matt. 27:57-61; Mark 15:42-47; John 19:38-42 [b]For 24:1-10 see parallels Matt. 28:1-8; Mark 16:1-8; John 20:1

Jesus Appears to His Disciples

36As they were talking about these things, Jesus himself stood among them, and said to them, "Peace to you!" **37**But they were startled and frightened and thought they saw a spirit. **38**And he said to them, "Why are you troubled, and why do doubts arise in your hearts? **39**See my hands and my feet, that it is I myself. Touch me, and see. For a spirit does not have flesh and bones as you see that I have." **40**And when he had said this, he showed them his hands and his feet. **41**And while they still disbelieved for joy and were marveling, he said to them, "Have you anything here to eat?" **42**They gave him a piece of broiled fish,[1] **43**and he took it and ate before them.

44Then he said to them, "These are my words that I spoke to you while I was still with you, that everything written about me in the Law of Moses

and the Prophets and the Psalms must be fulfilled." **45**Then he opened their minds to understand the Scriptures, **46**and said to them, "Thus it is written, that the Christ should suffer and on the third day rise from the dead, **47**and that repentance and forgiveness of sins should be proclaimed in his name to all nations, beginning from Jerusalem. **48**You are witnesses of these things. **49**And behold, I am sending the promise of my Father upon you. But stay in the city until you are clothed with power from on high."

The Ascension

50Then he led them out as far as Bethany, and lifting up his hands he blessed them. **51**While he blessed them, he parted from them and was carried up into heaven. **52**And they worshiped him and returned to Jerusalem with great joy, **53**and were continually in the temple blessing God.

---

[1] Some manuscripts add *and some honeycomb*

JOHN

Introduction

The Gospel of John was written to persuade people to believe in Jesus (20:30-31). The opening verses declare that Jesus is God, stressing his unique relationship with God the Father. The book focuses on seven of Jesus' signs (miracles), to show his divinity. Jesus called people to believe in him, promising eternal life. He proved he could give life by raising Lazarus (ch. 11) and by his own death and resurrection. John features Christ's seven "I am" statements, his encounters with Nicodemus and the Samaritan woman, his Upper Room teachings and washing of the disciples' feet (chs. 13–16), and his high priestly prayer (ch. 17). It includes the most well-known summary of the gospel (3:16). The author was probably the apostle John, writing about A.D. 85.

The Word Became Flesh

1 In the beginning was the Word, and the Word was with God, and the Word was God. ²He was in the beginning with God. ³All things were made through him, and without him was not any thing made that was made. ⁴In him was life,¹ and the life was the light of men. ⁵The light shines in the darkness, and the darkness has not overcome it.

⁶There was a man sent from God, whose name was John. ⁷He came as a witness, to bear witness about the light, that all might believe through him. ⁸He was not the light, but came to bear witness about the light.

⁹The true light, which enlightens everyone, was coming into the world. ¹⁰He was in the world, and the world was made through him, yet the world did not know him. ¹¹He came to his own,² and his own people³ did not receive him. ¹²But to all who did receive him, who believed in his name, he gave the right to become children of God, ¹³who were born, not of blood nor of the will of the flesh nor of the will of man, but of God.

¹⁴And the Word became flesh and dwelt among us, and we have seen his glory, glory as of the only Son from the Father, full of grace and truth. ¹⁵(John bore witness about him, and cried out, "This was he of whom I said, 'He who comes after me ranks before me, because he was before me.'") ¹⁶And from his fullness we have all received, grace upon grace. ¹⁷For the law was given through Moses; grace and truth came through Jesus Christ. ¹⁸No one has ever seen God; the only God,⁴ who is at the Father's side,⁵ he has made him known.

The Testimony of John the Baptist

¹⁹And this is the testimony of John, when the Jews sent priests and Levites from Jerusalem to ask him, "Who are you?" ²⁰He confessed, and did not deny, but confessed, "I am not the Christ." ²¹And they asked him, "What then? Are you Elijah?" He said, "I am not." "Are you the Prophet?" And he answered, "No." ²²So they said to him, "Who are you? We need to give an answer to those who sent us. What do you say about yourself?" ²³He said, "I am ªthe voice of one crying out in the wilderness, 'Make straight⁶ the way of the Lord,' as the prophet Isaiah said."

²⁴(Now they had been sent from the Pharisees.) ²⁵They asked him, "Then why are you baptizing, if you are neither the Christ, nor Elijah, nor the Prophet?" ²⁶John answered them, "I baptize with water, but among you stands one you do not know, ²⁷even he who comes after me, the strap of whose sandal I am not worthy to untie." ²⁸These things took place in Bethany across the Jordan, where John was baptizing.

Behold, the Lamb of God

²⁹The next day he saw Jesus coming toward him, and said, "Behold, the Lamb of God, who takes away the sin of the world! ³⁰This is he of whom I said, 'After me comes a man who ranks before me, because he was before me.' ³¹I myself did not know him, but for this purpose I came baptizing with water, that he might be revealed to Israel." ³²And John bore witness: "I saw the Spirit descend from heaven like a dove, and it remained on him. ³³I myself did not know him, but he who sent me to baptize with water said to me, 'He on whom you see the Spirit descend and remain, this is he who baptizes with the Holy Spirit.' ³⁴And I have seen and have borne witness that this is the Son of God."

Jesus Calls the First Disciples

³⁵The next day again John was standing with two of his disciples, ³⁶and he looked at Jesus as he walked by and said, "Behold, the Lamb of God!" ³⁷The two disciples heard him say this, and they followed Jesus. ³⁸Jesus turned and saw them following and said to them, "What are you seeking?" And they said to him, "Rabbi" (which means Teacher), "where are you staying?" ³⁹He said to them, "Come and you will see." So they

---

¹ Or *was not any thing made. That which has been made was life in him* ² Greek *to his own things;* that is, to his own domain, or to his own people ³ *People* is implied in Greek ⁴ Or *the only One, who is God;* some manuscripts *the only Son* ⁵ Greek *in the bosom of the Father* ⁶ Or *crying out, 'In the wilderness make straight* ª Isa. 40:3

came and saw where he was staying, and they stayed with him that day, for it was about the tenth hour.[1] [40]One of the two who heard John speak and followed Jesus[2] was Andrew, Simon Peter's brother. [41]He first found his own brother Simon and said to him, "We have found the Messiah" (which means Christ). [42]He brought him to Jesus. Jesus looked at him and said, "So you are Simon the son of John? You shall be called Cephas" (which means Peter[3]).

Jesus Calls Philip and Nathanael

[43]The next day Jesus decided to go to Galilee. He found Philip and said to him, "Follow me." [44]Now Philip was from Bethsaida, the city of Andrew and Peter. [45]Philip found Nathanael and said to him, "We have found him of whom Moses in the Law and also the prophets wrote, Jesus of Nazareth, the son of Joseph." [46]Nathanael said to him, "Can anything good come out of Nazareth?" Philip said to him, "Come and see." [47]Jesus saw Nathanael coming toward him and said of him, "Behold, an Israelite indeed, in whom there is no deceit!" [48]Nathanael said to him, "How do you know me?" Jesus answered him, "Before Philip called you, when you were under the fig tree, I saw you." [49]Nathanael answered him, "Rabbi, you are the Son of God! You are the King of Israel!" [50]Jesus answered him, "Because I said to you, 'I saw you under the fig tree,' do you believe? You will see greater things than these." [51]And he said to him, "Truly, truly, I say to you,[4] you will see heaven opened, and the angels of God ascending and descending on the Son of Man."

The Wedding at Cana

2 On the third day there was a wedding at Cana in Galilee, and the mother of Jesus was there. [2]Jesus also was invited to the wedding with his disciples. [3]When the wine ran out, the mother of Jesus said to him, "They have no wine." [4]And Jesus said to her, "Woman, what does this have to do with me? My hour has not yet come." [5]His mother said to the servants, "Do whatever he tells you."

[6]Now there were six stone water jars there for the Jewish rites of purification, each holding twenty or thirty gallons.[5] [7]Jesus said to the servants, "Fill the jars with water." And they filled them up to the brim. [8]And he said to them, "Now draw some out and take it to the master of the feast." So they took it. [9]When the master of the feast tasted the water now become wine, and did not know where it came from (though the servants who had drawn the water knew), the master of the feast called the bridegroom [10]and said to him, "Everyone serves the good wine first, and

when people have drunk freely, then the poor wine. But you have kept the good wine until now." [11]This, the first of his signs, Jesus did at Cana in Galilee, and manifested his glory. And his disciples believed in him.

[12]After this he went down to Capernaum, with his mother and his brothers[6] and his disciples, and they stayed there for a few days.

Jesus Cleanses the Temple

[13]The Passover of the Jews was at hand, and Jesus went up to Jerusalem. [14]In the temple he found those who were selling oxen and sheep and pigeons, and the money-changers sitting there. [15]And making a whip of cords, he drove them all out of the temple, with the sheep and oxen. And he poured out the coins of the money-changers and overturned their tables. [16]And he told those who sold the pigeons, "Take these things away; do not make my Father's house a house of trade." [17]His disciples remembered that it was written, a"Zeal for your house will consume me." [18]So the Jews said to him, "What sign do you show us for doing these things?" [19]Jesus answered them, "Destroy this temple, and in three days I will raise it up." [20]The Jews then said, "It has taken forty-six years to build this temple, and will you raise it up in three days?" [21]But he was speaking about the temple of his body. [22]When therefore he was raised from the dead, his disciples remembered that he had said this, and they believed the Scripture and the word that Jesus had spoken.

Jesus Knows What Is in Man

[23]Now when he was in Jerusalem at the Passover Feast, many believed in his name when they saw the signs that he was doing. [24]But Jesus on his part did not entrust himself to them, because he knew all people [25]and needed no one to bear witness about man, for he himself knew what was in man.

You Must Be Born Again

3 Now there was a man of the Pharisees named Nicodemus, a ruler of the Jews. [2]This man came to Jesus[7] by night and said to him, "Rabbi, we know that you are a teacher come from God, for no one can do these signs that you do unless God is with him." [3]Jesus answered him, "Truly, truly, I say to you, unless one is born again[8] he cannot see the kingdom of God." [4]Nicodemus said to him, "How can a man be born when he is old? Can he enter a second time into his mother's womb and be born?" [5]Jesus answered, "Truly, truly, I say to you, unless one is born of water and the Spirit, he cannot enter the

---

[1] That is, about 4 P.M. [2] Greek him [3] Cephas and Peter are from the word for rock in Aramaic and Greek, respectively [4] The Greek for you is plural; twice in this verse [5] Greek two or three measures (metrētas); a metrētēs was about 10 gallons or 35 liters [6] Or brothers and sisters. The plural Greek word adelphoi (translated "brothers") refers to siblings in a family. In New Testament usage, depending on the context, adelphoi may refer either to brothers or to brothers and sisters [7] Greek him [8] Or from above; the Greek is purposely ambiguous and can mean both again and from above; also verse 7 a Ps. 69:9

kingdom of God. [6]That which is born of the flesh is flesh, and that which is born of the Spirit is spirit.[1] [7]Do not marvel that I said to you, 'You[2] must be born again.' [8]The wind[3] blows where it wishes, and you hear its sound, but you do not know where it comes from or where it goes. So it is with everyone who is born of the Spirit."

[9]Nicodemus said to him, "How can these things be?" [10]Jesus answered him, "Are you the teacher of Israel and yet you do not understand these things? [11]Truly, truly, I say to you, we speak of what we know, and bear witness to what we have seen, but you[4] do not receive our testimony. [12]If I have told you earthly things and you do not believe, how can you believe if I tell you heavenly things? [13]No one has ascended into heaven except he who descended from heaven, the Son of Man.[5] [14]And as Moses lifted up the serpent in the wilderness, so must the Son of Man be lifted up, [15]that whoever believes in him may have eternal life.[6]

For God So Loved the World

[16]"For God so loved the world,[7] that he gave his only Son, that whoever believes in him should not perish but have eternal life. [17]For God did not send his Son into the world to condemn the world, but in order that the world might be saved through him. [18]Whoever believes in him is not condemned, but whoever does not believe is condemned already, because he has not believed in the name of the only Son of God. [19]And this is the judgment: the light has come into the world, and people loved the darkness rather than the light because their works were evil. [20]For everyone who does wicked things hates the light and does not come to the light, lest his works should be exposed. [21]But whoever does what is true comes to the light, so that it may be clearly seen that his works have been carried out in God."

John the Baptist Exalts Christ

[22]After this Jesus and his disciples went into the Judean countryside, and he remained there with them and was baptizing. [23]John also was baptizing at Aenon near Salim, because water was plentiful there, and people were coming and being baptized [24](for John had not yet been put in prison).

[25]Now a discussion arose between some of John's disciples and a Jew over purification. [26]And they came to John and said to him, "Rabbi, he who was with you across the Jordan, to whom you bore witness—look, he is baptizing, and all are going to him." [27]John answered, "A person cannot receive even one thing unless it is given him from heaven. [28]You yourselves bear me witness, that I said, 'I am not the Christ, but I have been sent before him.' [29]The one who has the bride is the bridegroom. The friend of the bridegroom, who stands and hears him, rejoices greatly at the bridegroom's voice. Therefore this joy of mine is now complete. [30]He must increase, but I must decrease."[8]

[31]He who comes from above is above all. He who is of the earth belongs to the earth and speaks in an earthly way. He who comes from heaven is above all. [32]He bears witness to what he has seen and heard, yet no one receives his testimony. [33]Whoever receives his testimony sets his seal to this, that God is true. [34]For he whom God has sent utters the words of God, for he gives the Spirit without measure. [35]The Father loves the Son and has given all things into his hand. [36]Whoever believes in the Son has eternal life; whoever does not obey the Son shall not see life, but the wrath of God remains on him.

Jesus and the Woman of Samaria

4 Now when Jesus learned that the Pharisees had heard that Jesus was making and baptizing more disciples than John [2](although Jesus himself did not baptize, but only his disciples), [3]he left Judea and departed again for Galilee. [4]And he had to pass through Samaria. [5]So he came to a town of Samaria called Sychar, near the field that Jacob had given to his son Joseph. [6]Jacob's well was there; so Jesus, wearied as he was from his journey, was sitting beside the well. It was about the sixth hour.[9]

[7]A woman from Samaria came to draw water. Jesus said to her, "Give me a drink." [8](For his disciples had gone away into the city to buy food.) [9]The Samaritan woman said to him, "How is it that you, a Jew, ask for a drink from me, a woman of Samaria?" (For Jews have no dealings with Samaritans.) [10]Jesus answered her, "If you knew the gift of God, and who it is that is saying to you, 'Give me a drink,' you would have asked him, and he would have given you living water." [11]The woman said to him, "Sir, you have nothing to draw water with, and the well is deep. Where do you get that living water? [12]Are you greater than our father Jacob? He gave us the well and drank from it himself, as did his sons and his livestock." [13]Jesus said to her, "Everyone who drinks of this water will be thirsty again, [14]but whoever drinks of the water that I will give him will never be thirsty again.[10] The water that I will give him will become in him a spring of water welling up to eternal life." [15]The woman said to him, "Sir, give me this water, so that I will not be thirsty or have to come here to draw water."

[16]Jesus said to her, "Go, call your husband, and come here." [17]The woman answered him, "I have no husband." Jesus said to her, "You are right in saying, 'I have no husband'; [18]for you have had five husbands, and the one you now have is not

---

[1] The same Greek word means both *wind* and *spirit* [2] The Greek for *you* is plural here [3] The same Greek word means both *wind* and *spirit* [4] The Greek for *you* is plural here; also four times in verse 12 [5] Some manuscripts add *who is in heaven* [6] Some interpreters hold that the quotation ends at verse 15 [7] Or *For this is how God loved the world* [8] Some interpreters hold that the quotation continues through verse 36 [9] That is, about noon [10] Greek *forever*

your husband. What you have said is true." [19]The woman said to him, "Sir, I perceive that you are a prophet. [20]Our fathers worshiped on this mountain, but you say that in Jerusalem is the place where people ought to worship." [21]Jesus said to her, "Woman, believe me, the hour is coming when neither on this mountain nor in Jerusalem will you worship the Father. [22]You worship what you do not know; we worship what we know, for salvation is from the Jews. [23]But the hour is coming, and is now here, when the true worshipers will worship the Father in spirit and truth, for the Father is seeking such people to worship him. [24]God is spirit, and those who worship him must worship in spirit and truth." [25]The woman said to him, "I know that Messiah is coming (he who is called Christ). When he comes, he will tell us all things." [26]Jesus said to her, "I who speak to you am he."

[27]Just then his disciples came back. They marveled that he was talking with a woman, but no one said, "What do you seek?" or, "Why are you talking with her?" [28]So the woman left her water jar and went away into town and said to the people, [29]"Come, see a man who told me all that I ever did. Can this be the Christ?" [30]They went out of the town and were coming to him.

[31]Meanwhile the disciples were urging him, saying, "Rabbi, eat." [32]But he said to them, "I have food to eat that you do not know about." [33]So the disciples said to one another, "Has anyone brought him something to eat?" [34]Jesus said to them, "My food is to do the will of him who sent me and to accomplish his work. [35]Do you not say, 'There are yet four months, then comes the harvest'? Look, I tell you, lift up your eyes, and see that the fields are white for harvest. [36]Already the one who reaps is receiving wages and gathering fruit for eternal life, so that sower and reaper may rejoice together. [37]For here the saying holds true, 'One sows and another reaps.' [38]I sent you to reap that for which you did not labor. Others have labored, and you have entered into their labor."

[39]Many Samaritans from that town believed in him because of the woman's testimony, "He told me all that I ever did." [40]So when the Samaritans came to him, they asked him to stay with them, and he stayed there two days. [41]And many more believed because of his word. [42]They said to the woman, "It is no longer because of what you said that we believe, for we have heard for ourselves, and we know that this is indeed the Savior of the world."

[43]After the two days he departed for Galilee. [44](For Jesus himself had testified that a prophet has no honor in his own hometown.) [45]So when he came to Galilee, the Galileans welcomed him, having seen all that he had done in Jerusalem at the feast. For they too had gone to the feast.

Jesus Heals an Official's Son

[46]So he came again to Cana in Galilee, where he had made the water wine. And at Capernaum there was an official whose son was ill. [47]When this man heard that Jesus had come from Judea to Galilee, he went to him and asked him to come down and heal his son, for he was at the point of death. [48]So Jesus said to him, "Unless you see signs and wonders you will not believe." [49]The official said to him, "Sir, come down before my child dies." [50]Jesus said to him, "Go; your son will live." The man believed the word that Jesus spoke to him and went on his way. [51]As he was going down, his servants[1] met him and told him that his son was recovering. [52]So he asked them the hour when he began to get better, and they said to him, "Yesterday at the seventh hour[2] the fever left him." [53]The father knew that was the hour when Jesus had said to him, "Your son will live." And he himself believed, and all his household. [54]This was now the second sign that Jesus did when he had come from Judea to Galilee.

The Healing at the Pool on the Sabbath

5 After this there was a feast of the Jews, and Jesus went up to Jerusalem.

[2]Now there is in Jerusalem by the Sheep Gate a pool, in Aramaic[3] called Bethesda,[4] which has five roofed colonnades. [3]In these lay a multitude of invalids—blind, lame, and paralyzed.[5] [5]One man was there who had been an invalid for thirty-eight years. [6]When Jesus saw him lying there and knew that he had already been there a long time, he said to him, "Do you want to be healed?" [7]The sick man answered him, "Sir, I have no one to put me into the pool when the water is stirred up, and while I am going another steps down before me." [8]Jesus said to him, "Get up, take up your bed, and walk." [9]And at once the man was healed, and he took up his bed and walked.

Now that day was the Sabbath. [10]So the Jews said to the man who had been healed, "It is the Sabbath, and it is not lawful for you to take up your bed." [11]But he answered them, "The man who healed me, that man said to me, 'Take up your bed, and walk.'" [12]They asked him, "Who is the man who said to you, 'Take up your bed and walk'?" [13]Now the man who had been healed did not know who it was, for Jesus had withdrawn, as there was a crowd in the place. [14]Afterward Jesus found him in the temple and said to him, "See, you are well! Sin no more, that nothing worse may happen to you." [15]The man went away and told the Jews that it was Jesus who had healed him. [16]And this was why the Jews were persecuting Jesus, because he was doing these things on the Sabbath. [17]But Jesus

---

[1] Greek *bondservants* [2] That is, at 1 P.M. [3] Or *Hebrew* [4] Some manuscripts *Bethsaida* [5] Some manuscripts insert, wholly or in part, *waiting for the moving of the water;* [4]*for an angel of the Lord went down at certain seasons into the pool, and stirred the water; whoever stepped in first after the stirring of the water was healed of whatever disease he had*

answered them, "My Father is working until now, and I am working."

Jesus Is Equal with God

[18]This was why the Jews were seeking all the more to kill him, because not only was he breaking the Sabbath, but he was even calling God his own Father, making himself equal with God.

The Authority of the Son

[19]So Jesus said to them, "Truly, truly, I say to you, the Son can do nothing of his own accord, but only what he sees the Father doing. For whatever the Father[1] does, that the Son does likewise. [20]For the Father loves the Son and shows him all that he himself is doing. And greater works than these will he show him, so that you may marvel. [21]For as the Father raises the dead and gives them life, so also the Son gives life to whom he will. [22]The Father judges no one, but has given all judgment to the Son, [23]that all may honor the Son, just as they honor the Father. Whoever does not honor the Son does not honor the Father who sent him. [24]Truly, truly, I say to you, whoever hears my word and believes him who sent me has eternal life. He does not come into judgment, but has passed from death to life.

[25]"Truly, truly, I say to you, an hour is coming, and is now here, when the dead will hear the voice of the Son of God, and those who hear will live. [26]For as the Father has life in himself, so he has granted the Son also to have life in himself. [27]And he has given him authority to execute judgment, because he is the Son of Man. [28]Do not marvel at this, for an hour is coming when all who are in the tombs will hear his voice [29]and come out, those who have done good to the resurrection of life, and those who have done evil to the resurrection of judgment.

Witnesses to Jesus

[30]"I can do nothing on my own. As I hear, I judge, and my judgment is just, because I seek not my own will but the will of him who sent me. [31]If I alone bear witness about myself, my testimony is not deemed true. [32]There is another who bears witness about me, and I know that the testimony that he bears about me is true. [33]You sent to John, and he has borne witness to the truth. [34]Not that the testimony that I receive is from man, but I say these things so that you may be saved. [35]He was a burning and shining lamp, and you were willing to rejoice for a while in his light. [36]But the testimony that I have is greater than that of John. For the works that the Father has given me to accomplish, the very works that I am doing, bear witness about me that the Father has sent me. [37]And the Father who sent me has himself borne witness about me. His voice you have never heard, his form you have

never seen, [38]and you do not have his word abiding in you, for you do not believe the one whom he has sent. [39]You search the Scriptures because you think that in them you have eternal life; and it is they that bear witness about me, [40]yet you refuse to come to me that you may have life. [41]I do not receive glory from people. [42]But I know that you do not have the love of God within you. [43]I have come in my Father's name, and you do not receive me. If another comes in his own name, you will receive him. [44]How can you believe, when you receive glory from one another and do not seek the glory that comes from the only God? [45]Do not think that I will accuse you to the Father. There is one who accuses you: Moses, on whom you have set your hope. [46]For if you believed Moses, you would believe me; for he wrote of me. [47]But if you do not believe his writings, how will you believe my words?"

Jesus Feeds the Five Thousand

6 After this [a]Jesus went away to the other side of the Sea of Galilee, which is the Sea of Tiberias. [2]And a large crowd was following him, because they saw the signs that he was doing on the sick. [3]Jesus went up on the mountain, and there he sat down with his disciples. [4]Now the Passover, the feast of the Jews, was at hand. [5]Lifting up his eyes, then, and seeing that a large crowd was coming toward him, Jesus said to Philip, "Where are we to buy bread, so that these people may eat?" [6]He said this to test him, for he himself knew what he would do. [7]Philip answered him, "Two hundred denarii[2] would not buy enough bread for each of them to get a little." [8]One of his disciples, Andrew, Simon Peter's brother, said to him, [9]"There is a boy here who has five barley loaves and two fish, but what are they for so many?" [10]Jesus said, "Have the people sit down." Now there was much grass in the place. So the men sat down, about five thousand in number. [11]Jesus then took the loaves, and when he had given thanks, he distributed them to those who were seated. So also the fish, as much as they wanted. [12]And when they had eaten their fill, he told his disciples, "Gather up the leftover fragments, that nothing may be lost." [13]So they gathered them up and filled twelve baskets with fragments from the five barley loaves left by those who had eaten. [14]When the people saw the sign that he had done, they said, "This is indeed the Prophet who is to come into the world!"

[15]Perceiving then that they were about to come and take him by force to make him king, Jesus [b]withdrew again to the mountain by himself.

Jesus Walks on Water

[16]When evening came, his disciples went down to the sea, [17]got into a boat, and started

---

[1] Greek he   [2] A *denarius* was a day's wage for a laborer   [a] For 6:1-13 see parallels Matt. 14:13-21; Mark 6:32-44; Luke 9:10-17   [b] For 6:15-21 see parallels Matt. 14:22-33; Mark 6:45-52

across the sea to Capernaum. It was now dark, and Jesus had not yet come to them. [18]The sea became rough because a strong wind was blowing. [19]When they had rowed about three or four miles,[1] they saw Jesus walking on the sea and coming near the boat, and they were frightened. [20]But he said to them, "It is I; do not be afraid." [21]Then they were glad to take him into the boat, and immediately the boat was at the land to which they were going.

I Am the Bread of Life

[22]On the next day the crowd that remained on the other side of the sea saw that there had been only one boat there, and that Jesus had not entered the boat with his disciples, but that his disciples had gone away alone. [23]Other boats from Tiberias came near the place where they had eaten the bread after the Lord had given thanks. [24]So when the crowd saw that Jesus was not there, nor his disciples, they themselves got into the boats and went to Capernaum, seeking Jesus.

[25]When they found him on the other side of the sea, they said to him, "Rabbi, when did you come here?" [26]Jesus answered them, "Truly, truly, I say to you, you are seeking me, not because you saw signs, but because you ate your fill of the loaves. [27]Do not labor for the food that perishes, but for the food that endures to eternal life, which the Son of Man will give to you. For on him God the Father has set his seal." [28]Then they said to him, "What must we do, to be doing the works of God?" [29]Jesus answered them, "This is the work of God, that you believe in him whom he has sent." [30]So they said to him, "Then what sign do you do, that we may see and believe you? What work do you perform? [31]Our fathers ate the manna in the wilderness; as it is written, *a*'He gave them bread from heaven to eat.'" [32]Jesus then said to them, "Truly, truly, I say to you, it was not Moses who gave you the bread from heaven, but my Father gives you the true bread from heaven. [33]For the bread of God is he who comes down from heaven and gives life to the world." [34]They said to him, "Sir, give us this bread always."

[35]Jesus said to them, "I am the bread of life; whoever comes to me shall not hunger, and whoever believes in me shall never thirst. [36]But I said to you that you have seen me and yet do not believe. [37]All that the Father gives me will come to me, and whoever comes to me I will never cast out. [38]For I have come down from heaven, not to do my own will but the will of him who sent me. [39]And this is the will of him who sent me, that I should lose nothing of all that he has given me, but raise it up on the last day. [40]For this is the will of my Father, that everyone who looks on the Son and believes in him should have eternal life, and I will raise him up on the last day."

[41]So the Jews grumbled about him, because he said, "I am the bread that came down from heaven." [42]They said, "Is not this Jesus, the son of Joseph, whose father and mother we know? How does he now say, 'I have come down from heaven'?" [43]Jesus answered them, "Do not grumble among yourselves. [44]No one can come to me unless the Father who sent me draws him. And I will raise him up on the last day. [45]It is written in the Prophets, *b*'And they will all be taught by God.' Everyone who has heard and learned from the Father comes to me— [46]not that anyone has seen the Father except he who is from God; he has seen the Father. [47]Truly, truly, I say to you, whoever believes has eternal life. [48]I am the bread of life. [49]Your fathers ate the manna in the wilderness, and they died. [50]This is the bread that comes down from heaven, so that one may eat of it and not die. [51]I am the living bread that came down from heaven. If anyone eats of this bread, he will live forever. And the bread that I will give for the life of the world is my flesh."

[52]The Jews then disputed among themselves, saying, "How can this man give us his flesh to eat?" [53]So Jesus said to them, "Truly, truly, I say to you, unless you eat the flesh of the Son of Man and drink his blood, you have no life in you. [54]Whoever feeds on my flesh and drinks my blood has eternal life, and I will raise him up on the last day. [55]For my flesh is true food, and my blood is true drink. [56]Whoever feeds on my flesh and drinks my blood abides in me, and I in him. [57]As the living Father sent me, and I live because of the Father, so whoever feeds on me, he also will live because of me. [58]This is the bread that came down from heaven, not like the bread[2] the fathers ate and died. Whoever feeds on this bread will live forever." [59]Jesus[3] said these things in the synagogue, as he taught at Capernaum.

The Words of Eternal Life

[60]When many of his disciples heard it, they said, "This is a hard saying; who can listen to it?" [61]But Jesus, knowing in himself that his disciples were grumbling about this, said to them, "Do you take offense at this? [62]Then what if you were to see the Son of Man ascending to where he was before? [63]It is the Spirit who gives life; the flesh is no help at all. The words that I have spoken to you are spirit and life. [64]But there are some of you who do not believe." (For Jesus knew from the beginning who those were who did not believe, and who it was who would betray him.) [65]And he said, "This is why I told you that no one can come to me unless it is granted him by the Father."

[66]After this many of his disciples turned back and no longer walked with him. [67]So Jesus said to the Twelve, "Do you want to go away as well?"

---

[1] Greek *twenty-five or thirty stadia; a stadion* was about 607 feet or 185 meters　[2] Greek lacks *the bread*　[3] Greek *He*　*a* Neh. 9:15　*b* Isa. 54:13

⁶⁸Simon Peter answered him, "Lord, to whom shall we go? You have the words of eternal life, ⁶⁹and we have believed, and have come to know, that you are the Holy One of God." ⁷⁰Jesus answered them, "Did I not choose you, the Twelve? And yet one of you is a devil." ⁷¹He spoke of Judas the son of Simon Iscariot, for he, one of the Twelve, was going to betray him.

Jesus at the Feast of Booths

7 After this Jesus went about in Galilee. He would not go about in Judea, because the Jews¹ were seeking to kill him. ²Now the Jews' Feast of Booths was at hand. ³So his brothers² said to him, "Leave here and go to Judea, that your disciples also may see the works you are doing. ⁴For no one works in secret if he seeks to be known openly. If you do these things, show yourself to the world." ⁵For not even his brothers believed in him. ⁶Jesus said to them, "My time has not yet come, but your time is always here. ⁷The world cannot hate you, but it hates me because I testify about it that its works are evil. ⁸You go up to the feast. I am not³ going up to this feast, for my time has not yet fully come." ⁹After saying this, he remained in Galilee.

¹⁰But after his brothers had gone up to the feast, then he also went up, not publicly but in private. ¹¹The Jews were looking for him at the feast, and saying, "Where is he?" ¹²And there was much muttering about him among the people. While some said, "He is a good man," others said, "No, he is leading the people astray." ¹³Yet for fear of the Jews no one spoke openly of him.

¹⁴About the middle of the feast Jesus went up into the temple and began teaching. ¹⁵The Jews therefore marveled, saying, "How is it that this man has learning,⁴ when he has never studied?" ¹⁶So Jesus answered them, "My teaching is not mine, but his who sent me. ¹⁷If anyone's will is to do God's⁵ will, he will know whether the teaching is from God or whether I am speaking on my own authority. ¹⁸The one who speaks on his own authority seeks his own glory; but the one who seeks the glory of him who sent him is true, and in him there is no falsehood. ¹⁹Has not Moses given you the law? Yet none of you keeps the law. Why do you seek to kill me?" ²⁰The crowd answered, "You have a demon! Who is seeking to kill you?" ²¹Jesus answered them, "I did one work, and you all marvel at it. ²²Moses gave you circumcision (not that it is from Moses, but from the fathers), and you circumcise a man on the Sabbath. ²³If on the Sabbath a man receives circumcision, so that the law of Moses may not be broken, are you angry with me because on the Sabbath I made a man's whole body well? ²⁴Do not judge by appearances, but judge with right judgment."

Can This Be the Christ?

²⁵Some of the people of Jerusalem therefore said, "Is not this the man whom they seek to kill? ²⁶And here he is, speaking openly, and they say nothing to him! Can it be that the authorities really know that this is the Christ? ²⁷But we know where this man comes from, and when the Christ appears, no one will know where he comes from." ²⁸So Jesus proclaimed, as he taught in the temple, "You know me, and you know where I come from? But I have not come of my own accord. He who sent me is true, and him you do not know. ²⁹I know him, for I come from him, and he sent me." ³⁰So they were seeking to arrest him, but no one laid a hand on him, because his hour had not yet come. ³¹Yet many of the people believed in him. They said, "When the Christ appears, will he do more signs than this man has done?"

Officers Sent to Arrest Jesus

³²The Pharisees heard the crowd muttering these things about him, and the chief priests and Pharisees sent officers to arrest him. ³³Jesus then said, "I will be with you a little longer, and then I am going to him who sent me. ³⁴You will seek me and you will not find me. Where I am you cannot come." ³⁵The Jews said to one another, "Where does this man intend to go that we will not find him? Does he intend to go to the Dispersion among the Greeks and teach the Greeks? ³⁶What does he mean by saying, 'You will seek me and you will not find me,' and, 'Where I am you cannot come'?"

Rivers of Living Water

³⁷On the last day of the feast, the great day, Jesus stood up and cried out, "If anyone thirsts, let him come to me and drink. ³⁸Whoever believes in me, as⁶ the Scripture has said, 'Out of his heart will flow rivers of living water.'" ³⁹Now this he said about the Spirit, whom those who believed in him were to receive, for as yet the Spirit had not been given, because Jesus was not yet glorified.

Division Among the People

⁴⁰When they heard these words, some of the people said, "This really is the Prophet." ⁴¹Others said, "This is the Christ." But some said, "Is the Christ to come from Galilee? ⁴²Has not the Scripture said that the Christ comes from the offspring of David, and comes from Bethlehem, the village where David was?" ⁴³So there was a division among the people over him. ⁴⁴Some of them wanted to arrest him, but no one laid hands on him.

⁴⁵The officers then came to the chief priests and Pharisees, who said to them, "Why did you not bring him?" ⁴⁶The officers answered, "No

¹Or Judeans ²Or brothers and sisters; also verses 5, 10 ³Some manuscripts add yet ⁴Or this man knows his letters ⁵Greek his ⁶Or let him come to me, and let him who believes in me drink. As

one ever spoke like this man!" ⁴⁷The Pharisees answered them, "Have you also been deceived? ⁴⁸Have any of the authorities or the Pharisees believed in him? ⁴⁹But this crowd that does not know the law is accursed." ⁵⁰Nicodemus, who had gone to him before, and who was one of them, said to them, ⁵¹"Does our law judge a man without first giving him a hearing and learning what he does?" ⁵²They replied, "Are you from Galilee too? Search and see that no prophet arises from Galilee."

[THE EARLIEST MANUSCRIPTS DO NOT INCLUDE 7.53–8.11.]¹

The Woman Caught in Adultery

8 ⁵³[[They went each to his own house, ¹but Jesus went to the Mount of Olives. ²Early in the morning he came again to the temple. All the people came to him, and he sat down and taught them. ³The scribes and the Pharisees brought a woman who had been caught in adultery, and placing her in the midst ⁴they said to him, "Teacher, this woman has been caught in the act of adultery. ⁵Now in the Law Moses commanded us to stone such women. So what do you say?" ⁶This they said to test him, that they might have some charge to bring against him. Jesus bent down and wrote with his finger on the ground. ⁷And as they continued to ask him, he stood up and said to them, "Let him who is without sin among you be the first to throw a stone at her." ⁸And once more he bent down and wrote on the ground. ⁹But when they heard it, they went away one by one, beginning with the older ones, and Jesus was left alone with the woman standing before him. ¹⁰Jesus stood up and said to her, "Woman, where are they? Has no one condemned you?" ¹¹She said, "No one, Lord." And Jesus said, "Neither do I condemn you; go, and from now on sin no more."]]

I Am the Light of the World

¹²Again Jesus spoke to them, saying, "I am the light of the world. Whoever follows me will not walk in darkness, but will have the light of life." ¹³So the Pharisees said to him, "You are bearing witness about yourself; your testimony is not true." ¹⁴Jesus answered, "Even if I do bear witness about myself, my testimony is true, for I know where I came from and where I am going, but you do not know where I come from or where I am going. ¹⁵You judge according to the flesh; I judge no one. ¹⁶Yet even if I do judge, my judgment is true, for it is not I alone who judge, but I and the Father² who sent me. ¹⁷In your Law it is written that the testimony of two people is true. ¹⁸I am the one who bears witness about myself, and the Father who sent me bears witness about me." ¹⁹They said to him therefore, "Where is your Father?" Jesus answered, "You

know neither me nor my Father. If you knew me, you would know my Father also." ²⁰These words he spoke in the treasury, as he taught in the temple; but no one arrested him, because his hour had not yet come.

²¹So he said to them again, "I am going away, and you will seek me, and you will die in your sin. Where I am going, you cannot come." ²²So the Jews said, "Will he kill himself, since he says, 'Where I am going, you cannot come'?" ²³He said to them, "You are from below; I am from above. You are of this world; I am not of this world. ²⁴I told you that you would die in your sins, for unless you believe that I am he you will die in your sins." ²⁵So they said to him, "Who are you?" Jesus said to them, "Just what I have been telling you from the beginning. ²⁶I have much to say about you and much to judge, but he who sent me is true, and I declare to the world what I have heard from him." ²⁷They did not understand that he had been speaking to them about the Father. ²⁸So Jesus said to them, "When you have lifted up the Son of Man, then you will know that I am he, and that I do nothing on my own authority, but speak just as the Father taught me. ²⁹And he who sent me is with me. He has not left me alone, for I always do the things that are pleasing to him." ³⁰As he was saying these things, many believed in him.

The Truth Will Set You Free

³¹So Jesus said to the Jews who had believed in him, "If you abide in my word, you are truly my disciples, ³²and you will know the truth, and the truth will set you free." ³³They answered him, "We are offspring of Abraham and have never been enslaved to anyone. How is it that you say, 'You will become free'?"

³⁴Jesus answered them, "Truly, truly, I say to you, everyone who commits sin is a slave³ to sin. ³⁵The slave does not remain in the house forever; the son remains forever. ³⁶So if the Son sets you free, you will be free indeed. ³⁷I know that you are offspring of Abraham; yet you seek to kill me because my word finds no place in you. ³⁸I speak of what I have seen with my Father, and you do what you have heard from your father."

You Are of Your Father the Devil

³⁹They answered him, "Abraham is our father." Jesus said to them, "If you were Abraham's children, you would be doing the works Abraham did, ⁴⁰but now you seek to kill me, a man who has told you the truth that I heard from God. This is not what Abraham did. ⁴¹You are doing the works your father did." They said to him, "We were not born of sexual immorality. We have one Father—even God." ⁴²Jesus said to them, "If God were your Father, you would love me, for I came from God and I am here. I came

¹ Some manuscripts do not include 7:53–8:11; others add the passage here or after 7:36 or after 21:25 or after Luke 21:38, with variations in the text
² Some manuscripts he ³ Greek bondservant; also verse 35

not of my own accord, but he sent me. [43]Why do you not understand what I say? It is because you cannot bear to hear my word. [44]You are of your father the devil, and your will is to do your father's desires. He was a murderer from the beginning, and has nothing to do with the truth, because there is no truth in him. When he lies, he speaks out of his own character, for he is a liar and the father of lies. [45]But because I tell the truth, you do not believe me. [46]Which one of you convicts me of sin? If I tell the truth, why do you not believe me? [47]Whoever is of God hears the words of God. The reason why you do not hear them is that you are not of God."

Before Abraham Was, I Am

[48]The Jews answered him, "Are we not right in saying that you are a Samaritan and have a demon?" [49]Jesus answered, "I do not have a demon, but I honor my Father, and you dishonor me. [50]Yet I do not seek my own glory; there is One who seeks it, and he is the judge. [51]Truly, truly, I say to you, if anyone keeps my word, he will never see death." [52]The Jews said to him, "Now we know that you have a demon! Abraham died, as did the prophets, yet you say, 'If anyone keeps my word, he will never taste death.' [53]Are you greater than our father Abraham, who died? And the prophets died! Who do you make yourself out to be?" [54]Jesus answered, "If I glorify myself, my glory is nothing. It is my Father who glorifies me, of whom you say, 'He is our God.'[1] [55]But you have not known him. I know him. If I were to say that I do not know him, I would be a liar like you, but I do know him and I keep his word. [56]Your father Abraham rejoiced that he would see my day. He saw it and was glad." [57]So the Jews said to him, "You are not yet fifty years old, and have you seen Abraham?"[2] [58]Jesus said to them, "Truly, truly, I say to you, before Abraham was, I am." [59]So they picked up stones to throw at him, but Jesus hid himself and went out of the temple.

Jesus Heals a Man Born Blind

9 As he passed by, he saw a man blind from birth. [2]And his disciples asked him, "Rabbi, who sinned, this man or his parents, that he was born blind?" [3]Jesus answered, "It was not that this man sinned, or his parents, but that the works of God might be displayed in him. [4]We must work the works of him who sent me while it is day; night is coming, when no one can work. [5]As long as I am in the world, I am the light of the world." [6]Having said these things, he spat on the ground and made mud with the saliva. Then he anointed the man's eyes with the mud [7]and said to him, "Go, wash in the pool of Siloam" (which means Sent). So he went and washed and came back seeing.

[8]The neighbors and those who had seen him before as a beggar were saying, "Is this not the man who used to sit and beg?" [9]Some said, "It is he." Others said, "No, but he is like him." He kept saying, "I am the man." [10]So they said to him, "Then how were your eyes opened?" [11]He answered, "The man called Jesus made mud and anointed my eyes and said to me, 'Go to Siloam and wash.' So I went and washed and received my sight." [12]They said to him, "Where is he?" He said, "I do not know."

[13]They brought to the Pharisees the man who had formerly been blind. [14]Now it was a Sabbath day when Jesus made the mud and opened his eyes. [15]So the Pharisees again asked him how he had received his sight. And he said to them, "He put mud on my eyes, and I washed, and I see." [16]Some of the Pharisees said, "This man is not from God, for he does not keep the Sabbath." But others said, "How can a man who is a sinner do such signs?" And there was a division among them. [17]So they said again to the blind man, "What do you say about him, since he has opened your eyes?" He said, "He is a prophet."

[18]The Jews did not believe that he had been blind and had received his sight, until they called the parents of the man who had received his sight [19]and asked them, "Is this your son, who you say was born blind? How then does he now see?" [20]His parents answered, "We know that this is our son and that he was born blind. [21]But how he now sees we do not know, nor do we know who opened his eyes. Ask him; he is of age. He will speak for himself." [22](His parents said these things because they feared the Jews, for the Jews had already agreed that if anyone should confess Jesus[3] to be Christ, he was to be put out of the synagogue.) [23]Therefore his parents said, "He is of age; ask him."

[24]So for the second time they called the man who had been blind and said to him, "Give glory to God. We know that this man is a sinner." [25]He answered, "Whether he is a sinner I do not know. One thing I do know, that though I was blind, now I see." [26]They said to him, "What did he do to you? How did he open your eyes?" [27]He answered them, "I have told you already, and you would not listen. Why do you want to hear it again? Do you also want to become his disciples?" [28]And they reviled him, saying, "You are his disciple, but we are disciples of Moses. [29]We know that God has spoken to Moses, but as for this man, we do not know where he comes from." [30]The man answered, "Why, this is an amazing thing! You do not know where he comes from, and yet he opened my eyes. [31]We know that God does not listen to sinners, but if anyone is a worshiper of God and does his will, God listens to him. [32]Never since the world began has it been heard that anyone opened the eyes of

---

[1] Some manuscripts your God [2] Some manuscripts has Abraham seen you? [3] Greek him

a man born blind. [33]If this man were not from God, he could do nothing." [34]They answered him, "You were born in utter sin, and would you teach us?" And they cast him out.

[35]Jesus heard that they had cast him out, and having found him he said, "Do you believe in the Son of Man?"[1] [36]He answered, "And who is he, sir, that I may believe in him?" [37]Jesus said to him, "You have seen him, and it is he who is speaking to you." [38]He said, "Lord, I believe," and he worshiped him. [39]Jesus said, "For judgment I came into this world, that those who do not see may see, and those who see may become blind." [40]Some of the Pharisees near him heard these things, and said to him, "Are we also blind?" [41]Jesus said to them, "If you were blind, you would have no guilt;[2] but now that you say, 'We see,' your guilt remains.

I Am the Good Shepherd

10 "Truly, truly, I say to you, he who does not enter the sheepfold by the door but climbs in by another way, that man is a thief and a robber. [2]But he who enters by the door is the shepherd of the sheep. [3]To him the gatekeeper opens. The sheep hear his voice, and he calls his own sheep by name and leads them out. [4]When he has brought out all his own, he goes before them, and the sheep follow him, for they know his voice. [5]A stranger they will not follow, but they will flee from him, for they do not know the voice of strangers." [6]This figure of speech Jesus used with them, but they did not understand what he was saying to them.

[7]So Jesus again said to them, "Truly, truly, I say to you, I am the door of the sheep. [8]All who came before me are thieves and robbers, but the sheep did not listen to them. [9]I am the door. If anyone enters by me, he will be saved and will go in and out and find pasture. [10]The thief comes only to steal and kill and destroy. I came that they may have life and have it abundantly. [11]I am the good shepherd. The good shepherd lays down his life for the sheep. [12]He who is a hired hand and not a shepherd, who does not own the sheep, sees the wolf coming and leaves the sheep and flees, and the wolf snatches them and scatters them. [13]He flees because he is a hired hand and cares nothing for the sheep. [14]I am the good shepherd. I know my own and my own know me, [15]just as the Father knows me and I know the Father; and I lay down my life for the sheep. [16]And I have other sheep that are not of this fold. I must bring them also, and they will listen to my voice. So there will be one flock, one shepherd. [17]For this reason the Father loves me, because I lay down my life that I may take it up again. [18]No one takes it from me, but I lay it down of my own accord. I have authority to lay it down, and I have authority to take it up again. This charge I have received from my Father."

[19]There was again a division among the Jews because of these words. [20]Many of them said, "He has a demon, and is insane; why listen to him?" [21]Others said, "These are not the words of one who is oppressed by a demon. Can a demon open the eyes of the blind?"

I and the Father Are One

[22]At that time the Feast of Dedication took place at Jerusalem. It was winter, [23]and Jesus was walking in the temple, in the colonnade of Solomon. [24]So the Jews gathered around him and said to him, "How long will you keep us in suspense? If you are the Christ, tell us plainly." [25]Jesus answered them, "I told you, and you do not believe. The works that I do in my Father's name bear witness about me, [26]but you do not believe because you are not part of my flock. [27]My sheep hear my voice, and I know them, and they follow me. [28]I give them eternal life, and they will never perish, and no one will snatch them out of my hand. [29]My Father, who has given them to me,[3] is greater than all, and no one is able to snatch them out of the Father's hand. [30]I and the Father are one."

[31]The Jews picked up stones again to stone him. [32]Jesus answered them, "I have shown you many good works from the Father; for which of them are you going to stone me?" [33]The Jews answered him, "It is not for a good work that we are going to stone you but for blasphemy, because you, being a man, make yourself God." [34]Jesus answered them, "Is it not written in your Law, [a]'I said, you are gods'? [35]If he called them gods to whom the word of God came—and Scripture cannot be broken— [36]do you say of him whom the Father consecrated and sent into the world, 'You are blaspheming,' because I said, 'I am the Son of God'? [37]If I am not doing the works of my Father, then do not believe me; [38]but if I do them, even though you do not believe me, believe the works, that you may know and understand that the Father is in me and I am in the Father." [39]Again they sought to arrest him, but he escaped from their hands.

[40]He went away again across the Jordan to the place where John had been baptizing at first, and there he remained. [41]And many came to him. And they said, "John did no sign, but everything that John said about this man was true." [42]And many believed in him there.

The Death of Lazarus

11 Now a certain man was ill, Lazarus of Bethany, the village of Mary and her sister Martha. [2]It was Mary who anointed the Lord with ointment and wiped his feet with her hair, whose brother Lazarus was ill. [3]So the sisters sent

---

[1] Some manuscripts *the Son of God* [2] Greek *you would not have sin* [3] Some manuscripts *What my Father has given me* [a] Ps. 82:6

to him, saying, "Lord, he whom you love is ill." [4]But when Jesus heard it he said, "This illness does not lead to death. It is for the glory of God, so that the Son of God may be glorified through it."

[5]Now Jesus loved Martha and her sister and Lazarus. [6]So, when he heard that Lazarus[1] was ill, he stayed two days longer in the place where he was. [7]Then after this he said to the disciples, "Let us go to Judea again." [8]The disciples said to him, "Rabbi, the Jews were just now seeking to stone you, and are you going there again?" [9]Jesus answered, "Are there not twelve hours in the day? If anyone walks in the day, he does not stumble, because he sees the light of this world. [10]But if anyone walks in the night, he stumbles, because the light is not in him." [11]After saying these things, he said to them, "Our friend Lazarus has fallen asleep, but I go to awaken him." [12]The disciples said to him, "Lord, if he has fallen asleep, he will recover." [13]Now Jesus had spoken of his death, but they thought that he meant taking rest in sleep. [14]Then Jesus told them plainly, "Lazarus has died, [15]and for your sake I am glad that I was not there, so that you may believe. But let us go to him." [16]So Thomas, called the Twin,[2] said to his fellow disciples, "Let us also go, that we may die with him."

I Am the Resurrection and the Life

[17]Now when Jesus came, he found that Lazarus had already been in the tomb four days. [18]Bethany was near Jerusalem, about two miles[3] off, [19]and many of the Jews had come to Martha and Mary to console them concerning their brother. [20]So when Martha heard that Jesus was coming, she went and met him, but Mary remained seated in the house. [21]Martha said to Jesus, "Lord, if you had been here, my brother would not have died. [22]But even now I know that whatever you ask from God, God will give you." [23]Jesus said to her, "Your brother will rise again." [24]Martha said to him, "I know that he will rise again in the resurrection on the last day." [25]Jesus said to her, "I am the resurrection and the life.[4] Whoever believes in me, though he die, yet shall he live, [26]and everyone who lives and believes in me shall never die. Do you believe this?" [27]She said to him, "Yes, Lord; I believe that you are the Christ, the Son of God, who is coming into the world."

Jesus Weeps

[28]When she had said this, she went and called her sister Mary, saying in private, "The Teacher is here and is calling for you." [29]And when she heard it, she rose quickly and went to him. [30]Now Jesus had not yet come into the village, but was still in the place where Martha had met him. [31]When the Jews who were with her in the house, consoling her, saw Mary rise quickly and go out, they followed her, supposing that she was going to the tomb to weep there. [32]Now when Mary came to where Jesus was and saw him, she fell at his feet, saying to him, "Lord, if you had been here, my brother would not have died." [33]When Jesus saw her weeping, and the Jews who had come with her also weeping, he was deeply moved in his spirit and greatly troubled. [34]And he said, "Where have you laid him?" They said to him, "Lord, come and see." [35]Jesus wept. [36]So the Jews said, "See how he loved him!" [37]But some of them said, "Could not he who opened the eyes of the blind man also have kept this man from dying?"

Jesus Raises Lazarus

[38]Then Jesus, deeply moved again, came to the tomb. It was a cave, and a stone lay against it. [39]Jesus said, "Take away the stone." Martha, the sister of the dead man, said to him, "Lord, by this time there will be an odor, for he has been dead four days." [40]Jesus said to her, "Did I not tell you that if you believed you would see the glory of God?" [41]So they took away the stone. And Jesus lifted up his eyes and said, "Father, I thank you that you have heard me. [42]I knew that you always hear me, but I said this on account of the people standing around, that they may believe that you sent me." [43]When he had said these things, he cried out with a loud voice, "Lazarus, come out." [44]The man who had died came out, his hands and feet bound with linen strips, and his face wrapped with a cloth. Jesus said to them, "Unbind him, and let him go."

The Plot to Kill Jesus

[45]Many of the Jews therefore, who had come with Mary and had seen what he did, believed in him, [46]but some of them went to the Pharisees and told them what Jesus had done. [47]So the chief priests and the Pharisees gathered the Council and said, "What are we to do? For this man performs many signs. [48]If we let him go on like this, everyone will believe in him, and the Romans will come and take away both our place and our nation." [49]But one of them, Caiaphas, who was high priest that year, said to them, "You know nothing at all. [50]Nor do you understand that it is better for you that one man should die for the people, not that the whole nation should perish." [51]He did not say this of his own accord, but being high priest that year he prophesied that Jesus would die for the nation, [52]and not for the nation only, but also to gather into one the children of God who are scattered abroad. [53]So from that day on they made plans to put him to death.

[54]Jesus therefore no longer walked openly among the Jews, but went from there to the region near the wilderness, to a town called Ephraim, and there he stayed with the disciples.

---

[1]Greek he; also verse 17 [2]Greek Didymus [3]Greek fifteen stadia; a stadion was about 607 feet or 185 meters [4]Some manuscripts omit and the life

[55]Now the Passover of the Jews was at hand, and many went up from the country to Jerusalem before the Passover to purify themselves. [56]They were looking for[1] Jesus and saying to one another as they stood in the temple, "What do you think? That he will not come to the feast at all?" [57]Now the chief priests and the Pharisees had given orders that if anyone knew where he was, he should let them know, so that they might arrest him.

Mary Anoints Jesus at Bethany

12 Six days before the Passover, Jesus therefore came to Bethany, where Lazarus was, whom Jesus had raised from the dead. [2]So they gave a dinner for him there. Martha served, and Lazarus was one of those reclining with him at table. [3]Mary therefore took a pound[2] of expensive ointment made from pure nard, and anointed the feet of Jesus and wiped his feet with her hair. The house was filled with the fragrance of the perfume. [4]But Judas Iscariot, one of his disciples (he who was about to betray him), said, [5]"Why was this ointment not sold for three hundred denarii[3] and given to the poor?" [6]He said this, not because he cared about the poor, but because he was a thief, and having charge of the moneybag he used to help himself to what was put into it. [7]Jesus said, "Leave her alone, so that she may keep it[4] for the day of my burial. [8]For the poor you always have with you, but you do not always have me."

The Plot to Kill Lazarus

[9]When the large crowd of the Jews learned that Jesus[5] was there, they came, not only on account of him but also to see Lazarus, whom he had raised from the dead. [10]So the chief priests made plans to put Lazarus to death as well, [11]because on account of him many of the Jews were going away and believing in Jesus.

The Triumphal Entry

[12]The next day [a]the large crowd that had come to the feast heard that Jesus was coming to Jerusalem. [13]So they took branches of palm trees and went out to meet him, crying out, "Hosanna! Blessed is he who comes in the name of the Lord, even the King of Israel!" [14]And Jesus found a young donkey and sat on it, just as it is written,

[15] [b]"Fear not, daughter of Zion;
    behold, your king is coming,
        sitting on a donkey's colt!"

[16]His disciples did not understand these things at first, but when Jesus was glorified, then they remembered that these things had been written about him and had been done to him. [17]The crowd that had been with him when he called Lazarus out of the tomb and raised him from the dead continued to bear witness. [18]The reason why the crowd went to meet him was that they heard he had done this sign. [19]So the Pharisees said to one another, "You see that you are gaining nothing. Look, the world has gone after him."

Some Greeks Seek Jesus

[20]Now among those who went up to worship at the feast were some Greeks. [21]So these came to Philip, who was from Bethsaida in Galilee, and asked him, "Sir, we wish to see Jesus." [22]Philip went and told Andrew; Andrew and Philip went and told Jesus. [23]And Jesus answered them, "The hour has come for the Son of Man to be glorified. [24]Truly, truly, I say to you, unless a grain of wheat falls into the earth and dies, it remains alone; but if it dies, it bears much fruit. [25]Whoever loves his life loses it, and whoever hates his life in this world will keep it for eternal life. [26]If anyone serves me, he must follow me; and where I am, there will my servant be also. If anyone serves me, the Father will honor him.

The Son of Man Must Be Lifted Up

[27]"Now is my soul troubled. And what shall I say? 'Father, save me from this hour'? But for this purpose I have come to this hour. [28]Father, glorify your name." Then a voice came from heaven: "I have glorified it, and I will glorify it again." [29]The crowd that stood there and heard it said that it had thundered. Others said, "An angel has spoken to him." [30]Jesus answered, "This voice has come for your sake, not mine. [31]Now is the judgment of this world; now will the ruler of this world be cast out. [32]And I, when I am lifted up from the earth, will draw all people to myself." [33]He said this to show by what kind of death he was going to die. [34]So the crowd answered him, "We have heard from the Law that the Christ remains forever. How can you say that the Son of Man must be lifted up? Who is this Son of Man?" [35]So Jesus said to them, "The light is among you for a little while longer. Walk while you have the light, lest darkness overtake you. The one who walks in the darkness does not know where he is going. [36]While you have the light, believe in the light, that you may become sons of light."

The Unbelief of the People

When Jesus had said these things, he departed and hid himself from them. [37]Though he had done so many signs before them, they still did not believe in him, [38]so that the word spoken by the prophet Isaiah might be fulfilled:

[c]"Lord, who has believed what he heard from
        us,
    and to whom has the arm of the Lord been
        revealed?"

---

[1] Greek were seeking for [2] Greek litra; a litra (or Roman pound) was equal to about 11 1/2 ounces or 327 grams [3] A denarius was a day's wage for a laborer [4] Or Leave her alone; she intended to keep it [5] Greek he [a] For 12:12-15 see parallels Matt. 21:4-9; Mark 11:7-10; Luke 19:35-38 [b] Zech. 9:9 [c] Isa. 53:1

[39] Therefore they could not believe. For again Isaiah said,

[40] a "He has blinded their eyes
    and hardened their heart,
    lest they see with their eyes,
    and understand with their heart, and turn,
    and I would heal them."

[41] Isaiah said these things because he saw his glory and spoke of him. [42] Nevertheless, many even of the authorities believed in him, but for fear of the Pharisees they did not confess it, so that they would not be put out of the synagogue; [43] for they loved the glory that comes from man more than the glory that comes from God.

Jesus Came to Save the World

[44] And Jesus cried out and said, "Whoever believes in me, believes not in me but in him who sent me. [45] And whoever sees me sees him who sent me. [46] I have come into the world as light, so that whoever believes in me may not remain in darkness. [47] If anyone hears my words and does not keep them, I do not judge him; for I did not come to judge the world but to save the world. [48] The one who rejects me and does not receive my words has a judge; the word that I have spoken will judge him on the last day. [49] For I have not spoken on my own authority, but the Father who sent me has himself given me a commandment—what to say and what to speak. [50] And I know that his commandment is eternal life. What I say, therefore, I say as the Father has told me."

Jesus Washes the Disciples' Feet

13 Now before the Feast of the Passover, when Jesus knew that his hour had come to depart out of this world to the Father, having loved his own who were in the world, he loved them to the end. [2] During supper, when the devil had already put it into the heart of Judas Iscariot, Simon's son, to betray him, [3] Jesus, knowing that the Father had given all things into his hands, and that he had come from God and was going back to God, [4] rose from supper. He laid aside his outer garments, and taking a towel, tied it around his waist. [5] Then he poured water into a basin and began to wash the disciples' feet and to wipe them with the towel that was wrapped around him. [6] He came to Simon Peter, who said to him, "Lord, do you wash my feet?" [7] Jesus answered him, "What I am doing you do not understand now, but afterward you will understand." [8] Peter said to him, "You shall never wash my feet." Jesus answered him, "If I do not wash you, you have no share with me." [9] Simon Peter said to him, "Lord, not my feet only but also my hands and my head!" [10] Jesus said to him, "The one who has bathed does not need to wash, except for his feet,[1] but is completely clean. And you[2] are clean, but not every one of you." [11] For he knew who was to betray him; that was why he said, "Not all of you are clean."

[12] When he had washed their feet and put on his outer garments and resumed his place, he said to them, "Do you understand what I have done to you? [13] You call me Teacher and Lord, and you are right, for so I am. [14] If I then, your Lord and Teacher, have washed your feet, you also ought to wash one another's feet. [15] For I have given you an example, that you also should do just as I have done to you. [16] Truly, truly, I say to you, a servant[3] is not greater than his master, nor is a messenger greater than the one who sent him. [17] If you know these things, blessed are you if you do them. [18] I am not speaking of all of you; I know whom I have chosen. But the Scripture will be fulfilled,[4] b "He who ate my bread has lifted his heel against me." [19] I am telling you this now, before it takes place, that when it does take place you may believe that I am he. [20] Truly, truly, I say to you, whoever receives the one I send receives me, and whoever receives me receives the one who sent me."

One of You Will Betray Me

[21] After saying these things, Jesus was troubled in his spirit, and testified, "Truly, truly, I say to you, one of you will betray me." [22] The disciples looked at one another, uncertain of whom he spoke. [23] One of his disciples, whom Jesus loved, was reclining at table close to Jesus,[5] [24] so Simon Peter motioned to him to ask Jesus[6] of whom he was speaking. [25] So that disciple, leaning back against Jesus, said to him, "Lord, who is it?" [26] Jesus answered, "It is he to whom I will give this morsel of bread when I have dipped it." So when he had dipped the morsel, he gave it to Judas, the son of Simon Iscariot. [27] Then after he had taken the morsel, Satan entered into him. Jesus said to him, "What you are going to do, do quickly." [28] Now no one at the table knew why he said this to him. [29] Some thought that, because Judas had the moneybag, Jesus was telling him, "Buy what we need for the feast," or that he should give something to the poor. [30] So, after receiving the morsel of bread, he immediately went out. And it was night.

A New Commandment

[31] When he had gone out, Jesus said, "Now is the Son of Man glorified, and God is glorified in him. [32] If God is glorified in him, God will also glorify him in himself, and glorify him at once. [33] Little children, yet a little while I am with you. You will seek me, and just as I said to the Jews, so now I also say to you, 'Where I am going you cannot come.' [34] A new commandment I give to you, that you love one another: just as I have

---

[1] Some manuscripts omit except for his feet [2] The Greek words for you in this verse are plural [3] Greek bondservant [4] Greek But in order that the Scripture may be fulfilled [5] Greek in the bosom of Jesus [6] Greek lacks Jesus a Isa. 6:10 b Ps. 41:9

loved you, you also are to love one another. [35]By this all people will know that you are my disciples, if you have love for one another."

Jesus Foretells Peter's Denial

[36]Simon Peter said to him, "Lord, where are you going?" Jesus answered him, "Where I am going you cannot follow me now, but you will follow afterward." [37]Peter said to him, "Lord, why can I not follow you now? I will lay down my life for you." [38]Jesus answered, "Will you lay down your life for me? Truly, truly, I say to you, the rooster will not crow till you have denied me three times.

I Am the Way, and the Truth, and the Life

14 "Let not your hearts be troubled. Believe in God;[1] believe also in me. [2]In my Father's house are many rooms. If it were not so, would I have told you that I go to prepare a place for you?[2] [3]And if I go and prepare a place for you, I will come again and will take you to myself, that where I am you may be also. [4]And you know the way to where I am going."[3] [5]Thomas said to him, "Lord, we do not know where you are going. How can we know the way?" [6]Jesus said to him, "I am the way, and the truth, and the life. No one comes to the Father except through me. [7]If you had known me, you would have known my Father also.[4] From now on you do know him and have seen him."

[8]Philip said to him, "Lord, show us the Father, and it is enough for us." [9]Jesus said to him, "Have I been with you so long, and you still do not know me, Philip? Whoever has seen me has seen the Father. How can you say, 'Show us the Father'? [10]Do you not believe that I am in the Father and the Father is in me? The words that I say to you I do not speak on my own authority, but the Father who dwells in me does his works. [11]Believe me that I am in the Father and the Father is in me, or else believe on account of the works themselves.

[12]"Truly, truly, I say to you, whoever believes in me will also do the works that I do; and greater works than these will he do, because I am going to the Father. [13]Whatever you ask in my name, this I will do, that the Father may be glorified in the Son. [14]If you ask me[5] anything in my name, I will do it.

Jesus Promises the Holy Spirit

[15]"If you love me, you will keep my commandments. [16]And I will ask the Father, and he will give you another Helper,[6] to be with you forever, [17]even the Spirit of truth, whom the world cannot receive, because it neither sees him nor knows him. You know him, for he dwells with you and will be in you.

[18]"I will not leave you as orphans; I will come to you. [19]Yet a little while and the world will see me no more, but you will see me. Because I live, you also will live. [20]In that day you will know that I am in my Father, and you in me, and I in you. [21]Whoever has my commandments and keeps them, he it is who loves me. And he who loves me will be loved by my Father, and I will love him and manifest myself to him." [22]Judas (not Iscariot) said to him, "Lord, how is it that you will manifest yourself to us, and not to the world?" [23]Jesus answered him, "If anyone loves me, he will keep my word, and my Father will love him, and we will come to him and make our home with him. [24]Whoever does not love me does not keep my words. And the word that you hear is not mine but the Father's who sent me.

[25]"These things I have spoken to you while I am still with you. [26]But the Helper, the Holy Spirit, whom the Father will send in my name, he will teach you all things and bring to your remembrance all that I have said to you. [27]Peace I leave with you; my peace I give to you. Not as the world gives do I give to you. Let not your hearts be troubled, neither let them be afraid. [28]You heard me say to you, 'I am going away, and I will come to you.' If you loved me, you would have rejoiced, because I am going to the Father, for the Father is greater than I. [29]And now I have told you before it takes place, so that when it does take place you may believe. [30]I will no longer talk much with you, for the ruler of this world is coming. He has no claim on me, [31]but I do as the Father has commanded me, so that the world may know that I love the Father. Rise, let us go from here.

I Am the True Vine

15 "I am the true vine, and my Father is the vinedresser. [2]Every branch in me that does not bear fruit he takes away, and every branch that does bear fruit he prunes, that it may bear more fruit. [3]Already you are clean because of the word that I have spoken to you. [4]Abide in me, and I in you. As the branch cannot bear fruit by itself, unless it abides in the vine, neither can you, unless you abide in me. [5]I am the vine; you are the branches. Whoever abides in me and I in him, he it is that bears much fruit, for apart from me you can do nothing. [6]If anyone does not abide in me he is thrown away like a branch and withers; and the branches are gathered, thrown into the fire, and burned. [7]If you abide in me, and my words abide in you, ask whatever you wish, and it will be done for you. [8]By this my Father is glorified, that you bear much fruit and so prove to be my disciples. [9]As the Father has loved me, so have I loved you. Abide in my love. [10]If you keep my

---

[1] Or You believe in God [2] Or In my Father's house are many rooms; if it were not so, I would have told you; for I go to prepare a place for you [3] Some manuscripts Where I am going you know, and the way you know [4] Or If you know me, you will know my Father also, or If you have known me, you will know my Father also [5] Some manuscripts omit me [6] Or Advocate, or Counselor; also 14:26; 15:26; 16:7

commandments, you will abide in my love, just as I have kept my Father's commandments and abide in his love. [11] These things I have spoken to you, that my joy may be in you, and that your joy may be full.

[12] "This is my commandment, that you love one another as I have loved you. [13] Greater love has no one than this, that someone lay down his life for his friends. [14] You are my friends if you do what I command you. [15] No longer do I call you servants,[1] for the servant[2] does not know what his master is doing; but I have called you friends, for all that I have heard from my Father I have made known to you. [16] You did not choose me, but I chose you and appointed you that you should go and bear fruit and that your fruit should abide, so that whatever you ask the Father in my name, he may give it to you. [17] These things I command you, so that you will love one another.

The Hatred of the World

[18] "If the world hates you, know that it has hated me before it hated you. [19] If you were of the world, the world would love you as its own; but because you are not of the world, but I chose you out of the world, therefore the world hates you. [20] Remember the word that I said to you: 'A servant is not greater than his master.' If they persecuted me, they will also persecute you. If they kept my word, they will also keep yours. [21] But all these things they will do to you on account of my name, because they do not know him who sent me. [22] If I had not come and spoken to them, they would not have been guilty of sin,[3] but now they have no excuse for their sin. [23] Whoever hates me hates my Father also. [24] If I had not done among them the works that no one else did, they would not be guilty of sin, but now they have seen and hated both me and my Father. [25] But the word that is written in their Law must be fulfilled: *a* 'They hated me without a cause.'

[26] "But when the Helper comes, whom I will send to you from the Father, the Spirit of truth, who proceeds from the Father, he will bear witness about me. [27] And you also will bear witness, because you have been with me from the beginning.

16 "I have said all these things to you to keep you from falling away. [2] They will put you out of the synagogues. Indeed, the hour is coming when whoever kills you will think he is offering service to God. [3] And they will do these things because they have not known the Father, nor me. [4] But I have said these things to you, that when their hour comes you may remember that I told them to you.

The Work of the Holy Spirit

"I did not say these things to you from the beginning, because I was with you. [5] But now I am going to him who sent me, and none of you asks me, 'Where are you going?' [6] But because I have said these things to you, sorrow has filled your heart. [7] Nevertheless, I tell you the truth: it is to your advantage that I go away, for if I do not go away, the Helper will not come to you. But if I go, I will send him to you. [8] And when he comes, he will convict the world concerning sin and righteousness and judgment: [9] concerning sin, because they do not believe in me; [10] concerning righteousness, because I go to the Father, and you will see me no longer; [11] concerning judgment, because the ruler of this world is judged.

[12] "I still have many things to say to you, but you cannot bear them now. [13] When the Spirit of truth comes, he will guide you into all the truth, for he will not speak on his own authority, but whatever he hears he will speak, and he will declare to you the things that are to come. [14] He will glorify me, for he will take what is mine and declare it to you. [15] All that the Father has is mine; therefore I said that he will take what is mine and declare it to you.

Your Sorrow Will Turn into Joy

[16] "A little while, and you will see me no longer; and again a little while, and you will see me." [17] So some of his disciples said to one another, "What is this that he says to us, 'A little while, and you will not see me, and again a little while, and you will see me'; and, 'because I am going to the Father'?" [18] So they were saying, "What does he mean by 'a little while'? We do not know what he is talking about." [19] Jesus knew that they wanted to ask him, so he said to them, "Is this what you are asking yourselves, what I meant by saying, 'A little while and you will not see me, and again a little while and you will see me'? [20] Truly, truly, I say to you, you will weep and lament, but the world will rejoice. You will be sorrowful, but your sorrow will turn into joy. [21] When a woman is giving birth, she has sorrow because her hour has come, but when she has delivered the baby, she no longer remembers the anguish, for joy that a human being has been born into the world. [22] So also you have sorrow now, but I will see you again, and your hearts will rejoice, and no one will take your joy from you. [23] In that day you will ask nothing of me. Truly, truly, I say to you, whatever you ask of the Father in my name, he will give it to you. [24] Until now you have asked nothing in my name. Ask, and you will receive, that your joy may be full.

I Have Overcome the World

[25] "I have said these things to you in figures of speech. The hour is coming when I will no longer speak to you in figures of speech but will tell you plainly about the Father. [26] In that day you will ask in my name, and I do not say to you

---

[1] Greek *bondservants* [2] Greek *bondservant*; also verse 20 [3] Greek *they would not have sin*; also verse 24 *a* Ps. 35:19 or 69:4

that I will ask the Father on your behalf; [27] for the Father himself loves you, because you have loved me and have believed that I came from God.[1] [28] I came from the Father and have come into the world, and now I am leaving the world and going to the Father."

[29] His disciples said, "Ah, now you are speaking plainly and not using figurative speech! [30] Now we know that you know all things and do not need anyone to question you; this is why we believe that you came from God." [31] Jesus answered them, "Do you now believe? [32] Behold, the hour is coming, indeed it has come, when you will be scattered, each to his own home, and will leave me alone. Yet I am not alone, for the Father is with me. [33] I have said these things to you, that in me you may have peace. In the world you will have tribulation. But take heart; I have overcome the world."

The High Priestly Prayer

17 When Jesus had spoken these words, he lifted up his eyes to heaven, and said, "Father, the hour has come; glorify your Son that the Son may glorify you, [2] since you have given him authority over all flesh, to give eternal life to all whom you have given him. [3] And this is eternal life, that they know you the only true God, and Jesus Christ whom you have sent. [4] I glorified you on earth, having accomplished the work that you gave me to do. [5] And now, Father, glorify me in your own presence with the glory that I had with you before the world existed.

[6] "I have manifested your name to the people whom you gave me out of the world. Yours they were, and you gave them to me, and they have kept your word. [7] Now they know that everything that you have given me is from you. [8] For I have given them the words that you gave me, and they have received them and have come to know in truth that I came from you; and they have believed that you sent me. [9] I am praying for them. I am not praying for the world but for those whom you have given me, for they are yours. [10] All mine are yours, and yours are mine, and I am glorified in them. [11] And I am no longer in the world, but they are in the world, and I am coming to you. Holy Father, keep them in your name, which you have given me, that they may be one, even as we are one. [12] While I was with them, I kept them in your name, which you have given me. I have guarded them, and not one of them has been lost except the son of destruction, that the Scripture might be fulfilled. [13] But now I am coming to you, and these things I speak in the world, that they may have my joy fulfilled in themselves. [14] I have given them your word, and the world has hated them because they are not

of the world, just as I am not of the world. [15] I do not ask that you take them out of the world, but that you keep them from the evil one.[2] [16] They are not of the world, just as I am not of the world. [17] Sanctify them[3] in the truth; your word is truth. [18] As you sent me into the world, so I have sent them into the world. [19] And for their sake I consecrate myself,[4] that they also may be sanctified[5] in truth.

[20] "I do not ask for these only, but also for those who will believe in me through their word, [21] that they may all be one, just as you, Father, are in me, and I in you, that they also may be in us, so that the world may believe that you have sent me. [22] The glory that you have given me I have given to them, that they may be one even as we are one, [23] I in them and you in me, that they may become perfectly one, so that the world may know that you sent me and loved them even as you loved me. [24] Father, I desire that they also, whom you have given me, may be with me where I am, to see my glory that you have given me because you loved me before the foundation of the world. [25] O righteous Father, even though the world does not know you, I know you, and these know that you have sent me. [26] I made known to them your name, and I will continue to make it known, that the love with which you have loved me may be in them, and I in them."

Betrayal and Arrest of Jesus

18 When Jesus had spoken these words, he went out with his disciples across the Kidron Valley, where there was a garden, which he and his disciples entered. [2] Now Judas, who betrayed him, also knew the place, for Jesus often met there with his disciples. [3ᵃ] So Judas, having procured a band of soldiers and some officers from the chief priests and the Pharisees, went there with lanterns and torches and weapons. [4] Then Jesus, knowing all that would happen to him, came forward and said to them, "Whom do you seek?" [5] They answered him, "Jesus of Nazareth." Jesus said to them, "I am he."[6] Judas, who betrayed him, was standing with them. [6] When Jesus[7] said to them, "I am he," they drew back and fell to the ground. [7] So he asked them again, "Whom do you seek?" And they said, "Jesus of Nazareth." [8] Jesus answered, "I told you that I am he. So, if you seek me, let these men go." [9] This was to fulfill the word that he had spoken: "Of those whom you gave me I have lost not one." [10] Then Simon Peter, having a sword, drew it and struck the high priest's servant[8] and cut off his right ear. (The servant's name was Malchus.) [11] So Jesus said to Peter, "Put your sword into its sheath; shall I not drink the cup that the Father has given me?"

---

[1] Some manuscripts *from the Father* [2] Or *from evil* [3] Greek *Set them apart* (for holy service to God) [4] Or *I sanctify myself; or I set myself apart* (for holy service to God) [5] Greek *may be set apart* (for holy service to God) [6] Greek *I am*; also verses 6, 8 [7] Greek *he* [8] Greek *bondservant*; twice in this verse
[a] For 18:3-11 see parallels Matt. 26:47-56; Mark 14:43-50; Luke 22:47-53

Jesus Faces Annas and Caiaphas

[12] So the band of soldiers and their captain and the officers of the Jews arrested Jesus and bound him. [13] First they led him to Annas, for he was the father-in-law of Caiaphas, who was high priest that year. [14] It was Caiaphas who had advised the Jews that it would be expedient that one man should die for the people.

Peter Denies Jesus

[15] Simon Peter followed Jesus, and so did another disciple. Since that disciple was known to the high priest, he entered with Jesus into the court of the high priest, [16a] but Peter stood outside at the door. So the other disciple, who was known to the high priest, went out and spoke to the servant girl who kept watch at the door, and brought Peter in. [17] The servant girl at the door said to Peter, "You also are not one of this man's disciples, are you?" He said, "I am not." [18] Now the servants[1] and officers had made a charcoal fire, because it was cold, and they were standing and warming themselves. Peter also was with them, standing and warming himself.

The High Priest Questions Jesus

[19] The high priest then questioned Jesus about his disciples and his teaching. [20] Jesus answered him, "I have spoken openly to the world. I have always taught in synagogues and in the temple, where all Jews come together. I have said nothing in secret. [21] Why do you ask me? Ask those who have heard me what I said to them; they know what I said." [22] When he had said these things, one of the officers standing by struck Jesus with his hand, saying, "Is that how you answer the high priest?" [23] Jesus answered him, "If what I said is wrong, bear witness about the wrong; but if what I said is right, why do you strike me?" [24] Annas then sent him bound to Caiaphas the high priest.

Peter Denies Jesus Again

[25b] Now Simon Peter was standing and warming himself. So they said to him, "You also are not one of his disciples, are you?" He denied it and said, "I am not." [26] One of the servants of the high priest, a relative of the man whose ear Peter had cut off, asked, "Did I not see you in the garden with him?" [27] Peter again denied it, and at once a rooster crowed.

Jesus Before Pilate

[28] Then they led Jesus from the house of Caiaphas to the governor's headquarters.[2] It was early morning. They themselves did not enter the governor's headquarters, so that they would not be defiled, but could eat the Passover. [29c] So Pilate went outside to them and said, "What accusa-tion do you bring against this man?" [30] They answered him, "If this man were not doing evil, we would not have delivered him over to you." [31] Pilate said to them, "Take him yourselves and judge him by your own law." The Jews said to him, "It is not lawful for us to put anyone to death." [32] This was to fulfill the word that Jesus had spoken to show by what kind of death he was going to die.

My Kingdom Is Not of This World

[33] So Pilate entered his headquarters again and called Jesus and said to him, "Are you the King of the Jews?" [34] Jesus answered, "Do you say this of your own accord, or did others say it to you about me?" [35] Pilate answered, "Am I a Jew? Your own nation and the chief priests have delivered you over to me. What have you done?" [36] Jesus answered, "My kingdom is not of this world. If my kingdom were of this world, my servants would have been fighting, that I might not be delivered over to the Jews. But my kingdom is not from the world." [37] Then Pilate said to him, "So you are a king?" Jesus answered, "You say that I am a king. For this purpose I was born and for this purpose I have come into the world—to bear witness to the truth. Everyone who is of the truth listens to my voice." [38] Pilate said to him, "What is truth?"

After he had said this, he went back outside to the Jews and told them, "I find no guilt in him. [39d] But you have a custom that I should release one man for you at the Passover. So do you want me to release to you the King of the Jews?" [40] They cried out again, "Not this man, but Barabbas!" Now Barabbas was a robber.[3]

Jesus Delivered to Be Crucified

19 Then Pilate took Jesus and flogged him. [2] And the soldiers twisted together a crown of thorns and put it on his head and arrayed him in a purple robe. [3] They came up to him, saying, "Hail, King of the Jews!" and struck him with their hands. [4] Pilate went out again and said to them, "See, I am bringing him out to you that you may know that I find no guilt in him." [5] So Jesus came out, wearing the crown of thorns and the purple robe. Pilate said to them, "Behold the man!" [6] When the chief priests and the officers saw him, they cried out, "Crucify him, crucify him!" Pilate said to them, "Take him yourselves and crucify him, for I find no guilt in him." [7] The Jews answered him, "We have a law, and according to that law he ought to die because he has made himself the Son of God." [8] When Pilate heard this statement, he was even more afraid. [9] He entered his headquarters again and said to Jesus, "Where are you from?" But Jesus gave him no answer. [10] So Pilate said to him, "You will not

---

[1] Greek bondservants; also verse 26 [2] Greek the praetorium [3] Or an insurrectionist [a] For 18:16-18 see parallels Matt. 26:69, 70; Mark 14:66-68; Luke 22:55-57 [b] For 18:25-27 see parallels Matt. 26:71-75; Mark 14:69-72; Luke 22:58-62 [c] For 18:29-38 see parallels Matt. 27:11-14; Mark 15:1-5; Luke 23:1-3 [d] For 18:39, 40 see parallels Matt. 27:15-18, 20-23; Mark 15:6-14; Luke 23:18-23

speak to me? Do you not know that I have authority to release you and authority to crucify you?" [11]Jesus answered him, "You would have no authority over me at all unless it had been given you from above. Therefore he who delivered me over to you has the greater sin."

[12]From then on Pilate sought to release him, but the Jews cried out, "If you release this man, you are not Caesar's friend. Everyone who makes himself a king opposes Caesar." [13]So when Pilate heard these words, he brought Jesus out and sat down on the judgment seat at a place called The Stone Pavement, and in Aramaic[1] Gabbatha. [14]Now it was the day of Preparation of the Passover. It was about the sixth hour.[2] He said to the Jews, "Behold your King!" [15]They cried out, "Away with him, away with him, crucify him!" Pilate said to them, "Shall I crucify your King?" The chief priests answered, "We have no king but Caesar." [16]So he delivered him over to them to be crucified.

The Crucifixion

So they took Jesus, [17]and he went out, bearing his own cross, to the place called The Place of a Skull, which in Aramaic is called Golgotha. [18]There they crucified him, and with him two others, one on either side, and Jesus between them. [19]Pilate also wrote an inscription and put it on the cross. It read, "Jesus of Nazareth, the King of the Jews." [20]Many of the Jews read this inscription, for the place where Jesus was crucified was near the city, and it was written in Aramaic, in Latin, and in Greek. [21]So the chief priests of the Jews said to Pilate, "Do not write, 'The King of the Jews,' but rather, 'This man said, I am King of the Jews.'" [22]Pilate answered, "What I have written I have written."

[23]When the soldiers had crucified Jesus, they took his garments and divided them into four parts, one part for each soldier; also his tunic.[3] But the tunic was seamless, woven in one piece from top to bottom, [24]so they said to one another, "Let us not tear it, but cast lots for it to see whose it shall be." This was to fulfill the Scripture which says,

[a]"They divided my garments among them,
    and for my clothing they cast lots."

So the soldiers did these things, [25]but standing by the cross of Jesus were his mother and his mother's sister, Mary the wife of Clopas, and Mary Magdalene. [26]When Jesus saw his mother and the disciple whom he loved standing nearby, he said to his mother, "Woman, behold, your son!" [27]Then he said to the disciple, "Behold, your mother!" And from that hour the disciple took her to his own home.

The Death of Jesus

[28]After this, Jesus, knowing that all was now finished, said (to fulfill the Scripture), "I thirst." [29]A jar full of sour wine stood there, so they put a sponge full of the sour wine on a hyssop branch and held it to his mouth. [30]When Jesus had received the sour wine, he said, "It is finished," and he bowed his head and gave up his spirit.

Jesus' Side Is Pierced

[31]Since it was the day of Preparation, and so that the bodies would not remain on the cross on the Sabbath (for that Sabbath was a high day), the Jews asked Pilate that their legs might be broken and that they might be taken away. [32]So the soldiers came and broke the legs of the first, and of the other who had been crucified with him. [33]But when they came to Jesus and saw that he was already dead, they did not break his legs. [34]But one of the soldiers pierced his side with a spear, and at once there came out blood and water. [35]He who saw it has borne witness—his testimony is true, and he knows that he is telling the truth—that you also may believe. [36]For these things took place that the Scripture might be fulfilled: [b]"Not one of his bones will be broken." [37]And again another Scripture says, [c]"They will look on him whom they have pierced."

Jesus Is Buried

[38][d]After these things Joseph of Arimathea, who was a disciple of Jesus, but secretly for fear of the Jews, asked Pilate that he might take away the body of Jesus, and Pilate gave him permission. So he came and took away his body. [39]Nicodemus also, who earlier had come to Jesus[4] by night, came bringing a mixture of myrrh and aloes, about seventy-five pounds[5] in weight. [40]So they took the body of Jesus and bound it in linen cloths with the spices, as is the burial custom of the Jews. [41]Now in the place where he was crucified there was a garden, and in the garden a new tomb in which no one had yet been laid. [42]So because of the Jewish day of Preparation, since the tomb was close at hand, they laid Jesus there.

The Resurrection

20 Now on the first day of the week Mary Magdalene came to the tomb early, while it was still dark, and saw that the stone had been taken away from the tomb. [2]So she ran and went to Simon Peter and the other disciple, the one whom Jesus loved, and said to them, "They have taken the Lord out of the tomb, and we do not know where they have laid him." [3]So Peter went out with the other disciple, and they were going toward the tomb. [4]Both of them were running

---

[1] Or *Hebrew;* also verses 17, 20 [2] That is, about noon [3] Greek *chiton,* a long garment worn under the cloak next to the skin [4] Greek *him* [5] Greek *one hundred litras;* a *litra* (or Roman pound) was equal to about 11 1/2 ounces or 327 grams [a] Ps. 22:18 [b] Ex. 12:46; Num. 9:12 [c] Zech. 12:10 [d] For 19:38-42 see parallels Matt. 27:57-61; Mark 15:42-47; Luke 23:50-56

together, but the other disciple outran Peter and reached the tomb first. [5]And stooping to look in, he saw the linen cloths lying there, but he did not go in. [6]Then Simon Peter came, following him, and went into the tomb. He saw the linen cloths lying there, [7]and the face cloth, which had been on Jesus'[1] head, not lying with the linen cloths but folded up in a place by itself. [8]Then the other disciple, who had reached the tomb first, also went in, and he saw and believed; [9]for as yet they did not understand the Scripture, that he must rise from the dead. [10]Then the disciples went back to their homes.

Jesus Appears to Mary Magdalene

[11]But Mary stood weeping outside the tomb, and as she wept she stooped to look into the tomb. [12]And she saw two angels in white, sitting where the body of Jesus had lain, one at the head and one at the feet. [13]They said to her, "Woman, why are you weeping?" She said to them, "They have taken away my Lord, and I do not know where they have laid him." [14]Having said this, she turned around and saw Jesus standing, but she did not know that it was Jesus. [15]Jesus said to her, "Woman, why are you weeping? Whom are you seeking?" Supposing him to be the gardener, she said to him, "Sir, if you have carried him away, tell me where you have laid him, and I will take him away." [16]Jesus said to her, "Mary." She turned and said to him in Aramaic,[2] "Rabboni!" (which means Teacher). [17]Jesus said to her, "Do not cling to me, for I have not yet ascended to the Father; but go to my brothers and say to them, 'I am ascending to my Father and your Father, to my God and your God.'" [18]Mary Magdalene went and announced to the disciples, "I have seen the Lord"—and that he had said these things to her.

Jesus Appears to the Disciples

[19]On the evening of that day, the first day of the week, the doors being locked where the disciples were for fear of the Jews, Jesus came and stood among them and said to them, "Peace be with you." [20]When he had said this, he showed them his hands and his side. Then the disciples were glad when they saw the Lord. [21]Jesus said to them again, "Peace be with you. As the Father has sent me, even so I am sending you." [22]And when he had said this, he breathed on them and said to them, "Receive the Holy Spirit. [23]If you forgive the sins of any, they are forgiven them; if you withhold forgiveness from any, it is withheld."

Jesus and Thomas

[24]Now Thomas, one of the Twelve, called the Twin,[3] was not with them when Jesus came. [25]So the other disciples told him, "We have seen the Lord." But he said to them, "Unless I see in his hands the mark of the nails, and place my finger into the mark of the nails, and place my hand into his side, I will never believe."

[26]Eight days later, his disciples were inside again, and Thomas was with them. Although the doors were locked, Jesus came and stood among them and said, "Peace be with you." [27]Then he said to Thomas, "Put your finger here, and see my hands; and put out your hand, and place it in my side. Do not disbelieve, but believe." [28]Thomas answered him, "My Lord and my God!" [29]Jesus said to him, "Have you believed because you have seen me? Blessed are those who have not seen and yet have believed."

The Purpose of This Book

[30]Now Jesus did many other signs in the presence of the disciples, which are not written in this book; [31]but these are written so that you may believe that Jesus is the Christ, the Son of God, and that by believing you may have life in his name.

Jesus Appears to Seven Disciples

21 After this Jesus revealed himself again to the disciples by the Sea of Tiberias, and he revealed himself in this way. [2]Simon Peter, Thomas (called the Twin), Nathanael of Cana in Galilee, the sons of Zebedee, and two others of his disciples were together. [3]Simon Peter said to them, "I am going fishing." They said to him, "We will go with you." They went out and got into the boat, but that night they caught nothing.

[4]Just as day was breaking, Jesus stood on the shore; yet the disciples did not know that it was Jesus. [5]Jesus said to them, "Children, do you have any fish?" They answered him, "No." [6]He said to them, "Cast the net on the right side of the boat, and you will find some." So they cast it, and now they were not able to haul it in, because of the quantity of fish. [7]That disciple whom Jesus loved therefore said to Peter, "It is the Lord!" When Simon Peter heard that it was the Lord, he put on his outer garment, for he was stripped for work, and threw himself into the sea. [8]The other disciples came in the boat, dragging the net full of fish, for they were not far from the land, but about a hundred yards[4] off.

[9]When they got out on land, they saw a charcoal fire in place, with fish laid out on it, and bread. [10]Jesus said to them, "Bring some of the fish that you have just caught." [11]So Simon Peter went aboard and hauled the net ashore, full of large fish, 153 of them. And although there were so many, the net was not torn. [12]Jesus said to them, "Come and have breakfast." Now none of the disciples dared ask him, "Who are you?" They knew it was the Lord. [13]Jesus came and took the bread and gave it to them, and so with the fish. [14]This was now the third time that Jesus

---

[1] Greek his [2] Or Hebrew [3] Greek Didymus [4] Greek two hundred cubits; a cubit was about 18 inches or 45 centimeters

was revealed to the disciples after he was raised from the dead.

Jesus and Peter

¹⁵When they had finished breakfast, Jesus said to Simon Peter, "Simon, son of John, do you love me more than these?" He said to him, "Yes, Lord; you know that I love you." He said to him, "Feed my lambs." ¹⁶He said to him a second time, "Simon, son of John, do you love me?" He said to him, "Yes, Lord; you know that I love you." He said to him, "Tend my sheep." ¹⁷He said to him the third time, "Simon, son of John, do you love me?" Peter was grieved because he said to him the third time, "Do you love me?" and he said to him, "Lord, you know everything; you know that I love you." Jesus said to him, "Feed my sheep. ¹⁸Truly, truly, I say to you, when you were young, you used to dress yourself and walk wherever you wanted, but when you are old, you will stretch out your hands, and another will dress you and carry you where you do not want to go." ¹⁹(This he said to show by what kind of death he

was to glorify God.) And after saying this he said to him, "Follow me."

Jesus and the Beloved Apostle

²⁰Peter turned and saw the disciple whom Jesus loved following them, the one who had been reclining at table close to him and had said, "Lord, who is it that is going to betray you?" ²¹When Peter saw him, he said to Jesus, "Lord, what about this man?" ²²Jesus said to him, "If it is my will that he remain until I come, what is that to you? You follow me!" ²³So the saying spread abroad among the brothers[1] that this disciple was not to die; yet Jesus did not say to him that he was not to die, but, "If it is my will that he remain until I come, what is that to you?"

²⁴This is the disciple who is bearing witness about these things, and who has written these things, and we know that his testimony is true.

²⁵Now there are also many other things that Jesus did. Were every one of them to be written, I suppose that the world itself could not contain the books that would be written.

---

[1] Or brothers and sisters

ACTS

Introduction

Acts picks up where Luke's Gospel leaves off, recording the early progress of the gospel as Jesus' disciples took it from Jerusalem throughout Judea, Samaria, and the rest of the Mediterranean world. The story begins with Christ's ascension and the events of Pentecost. As Gentiles begin responding to the gospel, the focus shifts to Paul and his missionary journeys. Acts forms a bridge between the four Gospels and the rest of the New Testament, showing how the apostles carried on Christ's work and providing a historical background for Romans through Revelation. The Acts of the Apostles is the second of two New Testament books written by Luke. Like his Gospel, Acts was a letter to Luke's friend Theophilus, written sometime in A.D. 62–64.

The Promise of the Holy Spirit

1 In the first book, O Theophilus, I have dealt with all that Jesus began to do and teach, ²until the day when he was taken up, after he had given commands through the Holy Spirit to the apostles whom he had chosen. ³He presented himself alive to them after his suffering by many proofs, appearing to them during forty days and speaking about the kingdom of God.

⁴And while staying¹ with them he ordered them not to depart from Jerusalem, but to wait for the promise of the Father, which, he said, "you heard from me; ⁵for John baptized with water, but you will be baptized with² the Holy Spirit not many days from now."

The Ascension

⁶So when they had come together, they asked him, "Lord, will you at this time restore the kingdom to Israel?" ⁷He said to them, "It is not for you to know times or seasons that the Father has fixed by his own authority. ⁸But you will receive power when the Holy Spirit has come upon you, and you will be my witnesses in Jerusalem and in all Judea and Samaria, and to the end of the earth." ⁹And when he had said these things, as they were looking on, he was lifted up, and a cloud took him out of their sight. ¹⁰And while they were gazing into heaven as he went, behold, two men stood by them in white robes, ¹¹and said, "Men of Galilee, why do you stand looking into heaven? This Jesus, who was taken up from you into heaven, will come in the same way as you saw him go into heaven."

Matthias Chosen to Replace Judas

¹²Then they returned to Jerusalem from the mount called Olivet, which is near Jerusalem, a Sabbath day's journey away. ¹³And when they had entered, they went up to the upper room, where they were staying, Peter and John and James and Andrew, Philip and Thomas, Bartholomew and Matthew, James the son of Alphaeus and Simon the Zealot and Judas the son of James. ¹⁴All these with one accord were devoting themselves to prayer, together with the women and Mary the mother of Jesus, and his brothers.³

¹⁵In those days Peter stood up among the brothers (the company of persons was in all about 120) and said, ¹⁶"Brothers, the Scripture had to be fulfilled, which the Holy Spirit spoke beforehand by the mouth of David concerning Judas, who became a guide to those who arrested Jesus. ¹⁷For he was numbered among us and was allotted his share in this ministry." ¹⁸(Now this man acquired a field with the reward of his wickedness, and falling headlong⁴ he burst open in the middle and all his bowels gushed out. ¹⁹And it became known to all the inhabitants of Jerusalem, so that the field was called in their own language Akeldama, that is, Field of Blood.) ²⁰"For it is written in the Book of Psalms,

> ᵃ"'May his camp become desolate,
>   and let there be no one to dwell in it';

and

> ᵇ"'Let another take his office.'

²¹So one of the men who have accompanied us during all the time that the Lord Jesus went in and out among us, ²²beginning from the baptism of John until the day when he was taken up from us—one of these men must become with us a witness to his resurrection." ²³And they put forward two, Joseph called Barsabbas, who was also called Justus, and Matthias. ²⁴And they prayed and said, "You, Lord, who know the hearts of all, show which one of these two you have chosen ²⁵to take the place in this ministry and apostleship from which Judas turned aside to go to his own place." ²⁶And they cast lots for them, and the lot fell on Matthias, and he was numbered with the eleven apostles.

---

¹ Or eating ² Or in ³ Or brothers and sisters. The plural Greek word adelphoi (translated "brothers") refers to siblings in a family. In New Testament usage, depending on the context, adelphoi may refer either to men or to both men and women who are siblings (brothers and sisters) in God's family, the church; also verse 15 ⁴ Or swelling up ᵃPs. 69:25 ᵇPs. 109:8

The Coming of the Holy Spirit

2 When the day of Pentecost arrived, they were all together in one place. ²And suddenly there came from heaven a sound like a mighty rushing wind, and it filled the entire house where they were sitting. ³And divided tongues as of fire appeared to them and rested[1] on each one of them. ⁴And they were all filled with the Holy Spirit and began to speak in other tongues as the Spirit gave them utterance.

⁵Now there were dwelling in Jerusalem Jews, devout men from every nation under heaven. ⁶And at this sound the multitude came together, and they were bewildered, because each one was hearing them speak in his own language. ⁷And they were amazed and astonished, saying, "Are not all these who are speaking Galileans? ⁸And how is it that we hear, each of us in his own native language? ⁹Parthians and Medes and Elamites and residents of Mesopotamia, Judea and Cappadocia, Pontus and Asia, ¹⁰Phrygia and Pamphylia, Egypt and the parts of Libya belonging to Cyrene, and visitors from Rome, ¹¹both Jews and proselytes, Cretans and Arabians—we hear them telling in our own tongues the mighty works of God." ¹²And all were amazed and perplexed, saying to one another, "What does this mean?" ¹³But others mocking said, "They are filled with new wine."

Peter's Sermon at Pentecost

¹⁴But Peter, standing with the eleven, lifted up his voice and addressed them: "Men of Judea and all who dwell in Jerusalem, let this be known to you, and give ear to my words. ¹⁵For these people are not drunk, as you suppose, since it is only the third hour of the day.[2] ¹⁶But this is what was uttered through the prophet Joel:

¹⁷ᵃ"'And in the last days it shall be, God declares,
　　that I will pour out my Spirit on all flesh,
　　and your sons and your daughters shall
　　　prophesy,
　　and your young men shall see visions,
　　and your old men shall dream dreams;
¹⁸　even on my male servants[3] and female servants
　　in those days I will pour out my Spirit, and
　　　they shall prophesy.
¹⁹　And I will show wonders in the heavens
　　　above
　　and signs on the earth below,
　　　blood, and fire, and vapor of smoke;
²⁰　the sun shall be turned to darkness
　　and the moon to blood,
　　before the day of the Lord comes, the great
　　　and magnificent day.
²¹　And it shall come to pass that everyone who
　　　calls upon the name of the Lord shall
　　　be saved.'

²²"Men of Israel, hear these words: Jesus of Nazareth, a man attested to you by God with mighty works and wonders and signs that God did through him in your midst, as you yourselves know— ²³this Jesus, delivered up according to the definite plan and foreknowledge of God, you crucified and killed by the hands of lawless men. ²⁴God raised him up, loosing the pangs of death, because it was not possible for him to be held by it. ²⁵For David says concerning him,

ᵇ"'I saw the Lord always before me,
　　for he is at my right hand that I may not be
　　　shaken;
²⁶　therefore my heart was glad, and my tongue
　　　rejoiced;
　　my flesh also will dwell in hope.
²⁷　For you will not abandon my soul to Hades,
　　or let your Holy One see corruption.
²⁸　You have made known to me the paths of life;
　　you will make me full of gladness with your
　　　presence.'

²⁹"Brothers, I may say to you with confidence about the patriarch David that he both died and was buried, and his tomb is with us to this day. ³⁰Being therefore a prophet, and knowing that God had sworn with an oath to him that he would set one of his descendants on his throne, ³¹he foresaw and spoke about the resurrection of the Christ, that he was not abandoned to Hades, nor did his flesh see corruption. ³²This Jesus God raised up, and of that we all are witnesses. ³³Being therefore exalted at the right hand of God, and having received from the Father the promise of the Holy Spirit, he has poured out this that you yourselves are seeing and hearing. ³⁴For David did not ascend into the heavens, but he himself says,

ᶜ"'The Lord said to my Lord,
　　Sit at my right hand,
³⁵　until I make your enemies your footstool.'

³⁶Let all the house of Israel therefore know for certain that God has made him both Lord and Christ, this Jesus whom you crucified."

³⁷Now when they heard this they were cut to the heart, and said to Peter and the rest of the apostles, "Brothers, what shall we do?" ³⁸And Peter said to them, "Repent and be baptized every one of you in the name of Jesus Christ for the forgiveness of your sins, and you will receive the gift of the Holy Spirit. ³⁹For the promise is for you and for your children and for all who are far off, everyone whom the Lord our God calls to himself." ⁴⁰And with many other words he bore witness and continued to exhort them, saying, "Save yourselves from this crooked generation." ⁴¹So those who received his word were baptized,

---

¹ Or And tongues as of fire appeared to them, distributed among them, and rested ² That is, 9 A.M. ³ Greek bondservants; twice in this verse ª Joel 2:28-32 ᵇ Ps. 16:8-11 ᶜ Ps. 110:1

and there were added that day about three thousand souls.

The Fellowship of the Believers

[42]And they devoted themselves to the apostles' teaching and the fellowship, to the breaking of bread and the prayers. [43]And awe[1] came upon every soul, and many wonders and signs were being done through the apostles. [44]And all who believed were together and had all things in common. [45]And they were selling their possessions and belongings and distributing the proceeds to all, as any had need. [46]And day by day, attending the temple together and breaking bread in their homes, they received their food with glad and generous hearts, [47]praising God and having favor with all the people. And the Lord added to their number day by day those who were being saved.

The Lame Beggar Healed

3 Now Peter and John were going up to the temple at the hour of prayer, the ninth hour.[2] [2]And a man lame from birth was being carried, whom they laid daily at the gate of the temple that is called the Beautiful Gate to ask alms of those entering the temple. [3]Seeing Peter and John about to go into the temple, he asked to receive alms. [4]And Peter directed his gaze at him, as did John, and said, "Look at us." [5]And he fixed his attention on them, expecting to receive something from them. [6]But Peter said, "I have no silver and gold, but what I do have I give to you. In the name of Jesus Christ of Nazareth, rise up and walk!" [7]And he took him by the right hand and raised him up, and immediately his feet and ankles were made strong. [8]And leaping up he stood and began to walk, and entered the temple with them, walking and leaping and praising God. [9]And all the people saw him walking and praising God, [10]and recognized him as the one who sat at the Beautiful Gate of the temple, asking for alms. And they were filled with wonder and amazement at what had happened to him.

Peter Speaks in Solomon's Portico

[11]While he clung to Peter and John, all the people, utterly astounded, ran together to them in the portico called Solomon's. [12]And when Peter saw it he addressed the people: "Men of Israel, why do you wonder at this, or why do you stare at us, as though by our own power or piety we have made him walk? [13]The God of Abraham, the God of Isaac, and the God of Jacob, the God of our fathers, glorified his servant[3] Jesus, whom you delivered over and denied in the presence of Pilate, when he had decided to release him. [14]But you denied the Holy and Righteous One, and asked for a murderer to be granted to you, [15]and you killed the Author of life, whom God raised from the dead. To this we are witnesses. [16]And his name—by faith in his name—has made this man strong whom you see and know, and the faith that is through Jesus[4] has given the man this perfect health in the presence of you all.

[17]"And now, brothers, I know that you acted in ignorance, as did also your rulers. [18]But what God foretold by the mouth of all the prophets, that his Christ would suffer, he thus fulfilled. [19]Repent therefore, and turn again, that your sins may be blotted out, [20]that times of refreshing may come from the presence of the Lord, and that he may send the Christ appointed for you, Jesus, [21]whom heaven must receive until the time for restoring all the things about which God spoke by the mouth of his holy prophets long ago. [22]Moses said, 'The Lord God will raise up for you [a]a prophet like me from your brothers. You shall listen to him in whatever he tells you. [23]And it shall be that every soul who does not listen to that prophet shall be destroyed from the people.' [24]And all the prophets who have spoken, from Samuel and those who came after him, also proclaimed these days. [25]You are the sons of the prophets and of the covenant that God made with your fathers, saying to Abraham, [b]'And in your offspring shall all the families of the earth be blessed.' [26]God, having raised up his servant, sent him to you first, to bless you by turning every one of you from your wickedness."

Peter and John Before the Council

4 And as they were speaking to the people, the priests and the captain of the temple and the Sadducees came upon them, [2]greatly annoyed because they were teaching the people and proclaiming in Jesus the resurrection from the dead. [3]And they arrested them and put them in custody until the next day, for it was already evening. [4]But many of those who had heard the word believed, and the number of the men came to about five thousand.

[5]On the next day their rulers and elders and scribes gathered together in Jerusalem, [6]with Annas the high priest and Caiaphas and John and Alexander, and all who were of the high-priestly family. [7]And when they had set them in the midst, they inquired, "By what power or by what name did you do this?" [8]Then Peter, filled with the Holy Spirit, said to them, "Rulers of the people and elders, [9]if we are being examined today concerning a good deed done to a crippled man, by what means this man has been healed, [10]let it be known to all of you and to all the people of Israel that by the name of Jesus Christ of Nazareth, whom you crucified, whom God raised from the dead—by him this man is standing before you well. [11]This Jesus[5] is the stone that was rejected by you, the builders, which has become the cornerstone.[6] [12]And there is salva-

---

[1] Or fear [2] That is, 3 P.M. [3] Or child; also verse 26 [4] Greek him [5] Greek This one [6] Greek the head of the corner [a] Deut. 18:15, 18, 19 [b] Gen. 22:18

tion in no one else, for there is no other name under heaven given among men by which we must be saved."

¹³Now when they saw the boldness of Peter and John, and perceived that they were uneducated, common men, they were astonished. And they recognized that they had been with Jesus. ¹⁴But seeing the man who was healed standing beside them, they had nothing to say in opposition. ¹⁵But when they had commanded them to leave the council, they conferred with one another, ¹⁶saying, "What shall we do with these men? For that a notable sign has been performed through them is evident to all the inhabitants of Jerusalem, and we cannot deny it. ¹⁷But in order that it may spread no further among the people, let us warn them to speak no more to anyone in this name." ¹⁸So they called them and charged them not to speak or teach at all in the name of Jesus. ¹⁹But Peter and John answered them, "Whether it is right in the sight of God to listen to you rather than to God, you must judge, ²⁰for we cannot but speak of what we have seen and heard." ²¹And when they had further threatened them, they let them go, finding no way to punish them, because of the people, for all were praising God for what had happened. ²²For the man on whom this sign of healing was performed was more than forty years old.

The Believers Pray for Boldness

²³When they were released, they went to their friends and reported what the chief priests and the elders had said to them. ²⁴And when they heard it, they lifted their voices together to God and said, "Sovereign Lord, who made the heaven and the earth and the sea and everything in them, ²⁵who through the mouth of our father David, your servant,¹ said by the Holy Spirit,

ᵃ"'Why did the Gentiles rage,
    and the peoples plot in vain?
²⁶ The kings of the earth set themselves,
    and the rulers were gathered together,
    against the Lord and against his
      Anointed'²—

²⁷for truly in this city there were gathered together against your holy servant Jesus, whom you anointed, both Herod and Pontius Pilate, along with the Gentiles and the peoples of Israel, ²⁸to do whatever your hand and your plan had predestined to take place. ²⁹And now, Lord, look upon their threats and grant to your servants³ to continue to speak your word with all boldness, ³⁰while you stretch out your hand to heal, and signs and wonders are performed through the name of your holy servant Jesus." ³¹And when they had prayed, the place in which they were gathered together was shaken, and they were all filled with the Holy Spirit and continued to speak the word of God with boldness.

They Had Everything in Common

³²Now the full number of those who believed were of one heart and soul, and no one said that any of the things that belonged to him was his own, but they had everything in common. ³³And with great power the apostles were giving their testimony to the resurrection of the Lord Jesus, and great grace was upon them all. ³⁴There was not a needy person among them, for as many as were owners of lands or houses sold them and brought the proceeds of what was sold ³⁵and laid it at the apostles' feet, and it was distributed to each as any had need. ³⁶Thus Joseph, who was also called by the apostles Barnabas (which means son of encouragement), a Levite, a native of Cyprus, ³⁷sold a field that belonged to him and brought the money and laid it at the apostles' feet.

Ananias and Sapphira

5 But a man named Ananias, with his wife Sapphira, sold a piece of property, ²and with his wife's knowledge he kept back for himself some of the proceeds and brought only a part of it and laid it at the apostles' feet. ³But Peter said, "Ananias, why has Satan filled your heart to lie to the Holy Spirit and to keep back for yourself part of the proceeds of the land? ⁴While it remained unsold, did it not remain your own? And after it was sold, was it not at your disposal? Why is it that you have contrived this deed in your heart? You have not lied to men but to God." ⁵When Ananias heard these words, he fell down and breathed his last. And great fear came upon all who heard of it. ⁶The young men rose and wrapped him up and carried him out and buried him.

⁷After an interval of about three hours his wife came in, not knowing what had happened. ⁸And Peter said to her, "Tell me whether you⁴ sold the land for so much." And she said, "Yes, for so much." ⁹But Peter said to her, "How is it that you have agreed together to test the Spirit of the Lord? Behold, the feet of those who have buried your husband are at the door, and they will carry you out." ¹⁰Immediately she fell down at his feet and breathed her last. When the young men came in they found her dead, and they carried her out and buried her beside her husband. ¹¹And great fear came upon the whole church and upon all who heard of these things.

Many Signs and Wonders Done

¹²Now many signs and wonders were regularly done among the people by the hands of the apostles. And they were all together in Solomon's Portico. ¹³None of the rest dared join them, but the people held them in high esteem. ¹⁴And more

---

¹ Or *child*; also verses 27, 30   ² Or *Christ*   ³ Greek *bondservants*   ⁴ The Greek for *you* is plural here   ᵃ Ps. 2:1, 2

than ever believers were added to the Lord, multitudes of both men and women, [15]so that they even carried out the sick into the streets and laid them on cots and mats, that as Peter came by at least his shadow might fall on some of them. [16]The people also gathered from the towns around Jerusalem, bringing the sick and those afflicted with unclean spirits, and they were all healed.

The Apostles Arrested and Freed

[17]But the high priest rose up, and all who were with him (that is, the party of the Sadducees), and filled with jealousy [18]they arrested the apostles and put them in the public prison. [19]But during the night an angel of the Lord opened the prison doors and brought them out, and said, [20]"Go and stand in the temple and speak to the people all the words of this Life." [21]And when they heard this, they entered the temple at daybreak and began to teach.

Now when the high priest came, and those who were with him, they called together the council and all the senate of the people of Israel and sent to the prison to have them brought. [22]But when the officers came, they did not find them in the prison, so they returned and reported, [23]"We found the prison securely locked and the guards standing at the doors, but when we opened them we found no one inside." [24]Now when the captain of the temple and the chief priests heard these words, they were greatly perplexed about them, wondering what this would come to. [25]And someone came and told them, "Look! The men whom you put in prison are standing in the temple and teaching the people." [26]Then the captain with the officers went and brought them, but not by force, for they were afraid of being stoned by the people.

[27]And when they had brought them, they set them before the council. And the high priest questioned them, [28]saying, "We strictly charged you not to teach in this name, yet here you have filled Jerusalem with your teaching, and you intend to bring this man's blood upon us." [29]But Peter and the apostles answered, "We must obey God rather than men. [30]The God of our fathers raised Jesus, whom you killed by hanging him on a tree. [31]God exalted him at his right hand as Leader and Savior, to give repentance to Israel and forgiveness of sins. [32]And we are witnesses to these things, and so is the Holy Spirit, whom God has given to those who obey him."

[33]When they heard this, they were enraged and wanted to kill them. [34]But a Pharisee in the council named Gamaliel, a teacher of the law held in honor by all the people, stood up and gave orders to put the men outside for a little while. [35]And he said to them, "Men of Israel, take care what you are about to do with these men. [36]For

before these days Theudas rose up, claiming to be somebody, and a number of men, about four hundred, joined him. He was killed, and all who followed him were dispersed and came to nothing. [37]After him Judas the Galilean rose up in the days of the census and drew away some of the people after him. He too perished, and all who followed him were scattered. [38]So in the present case I tell you, keep away from these men and let them alone, for if this plan or this undertaking is of man, it will fail; [39]but if it is of God, you will not be able to overthrow them. You might even be found opposing God!" So they took his advice, [40]and when they had called in the apostles, they beat them and charged them not to speak in the name of Jesus, and let them go. [41]Then they left the presence of the council, rejoicing that they were counted worthy to suffer dishonor for the name. [42]And every day, in the temple and from house to house, they did not cease teaching and preaching Jesus as the Christ.

Seven Chosen to Serve

6 Now in these days when the disciples were increasing in number, a complaint by the Hellenists[1] arose against the Hebrews because their widows were being neglected in the daily distribution. [2]And the twelve summoned the full number of the disciples and said, "It is not right that we should give up preaching the word of God to serve tables. [3]Therefore, brothers,[2] pick out from among you seven men of good repute, full of the Spirit and of wisdom, whom we will appoint to this duty. [4]But we will devote ourselves to prayer and to the ministry of the word." [5]And what they said pleased the whole gathering, and they chose Stephen, a man full of faith and of the Holy Spirit, and Philip, and Prochorus, and Nicanor, and Timon, and Parmenas, and Nicolaus, a proselyte of Antioch. [6]These they set before the apostles, and they prayed and laid their hands on them.

[7]And the word of God continued to increase, and the number of the disciples multiplied greatly in Jerusalem, and a great many of the priests became obedient to the faith.

Stephen Is Seized

[8]And Stephen, full of grace and power, was doing great wonders and signs among the people. [9]Then some of those who belonged to the synagogue of the Freedmen (as it was called), and of the Cyrenians, and of the Alexandrians, and of those from Cilicia and Asia, rose up and disputed with Stephen. [10]But they could not withstand the wisdom and the Spirit with which he was speaking. [11]Then they secretly instigated men who said, "We have heard him speak blasphemous words against Moses and God." [12]And they stirred up the people and the elders and the

scribes, and they came upon him and seized him and brought him before the council, [13]and they set up false witnesses who said, "This man never ceases to speak words against this holy place and the law, [14]for we have heard him say that this Jesus of Nazareth will destroy this place and will change the customs that Moses delivered to us." [15]And gazing at him, all who sat in the council saw that his face was like the face of an angel.

Stephen's Speech

7 And the high priest said, "Are these things so?" [2]And Stephen said:

"Brothers and fathers, hear me. The God of glory appeared to our father Abraham when he was in Mesopotamia, before he lived in Haran, [3]and said to him, [a]'Go out from your land and from your kindred and go into the land that I will show you.' [4]Then he went out from the land of the Chaldeans and lived in Haran. And after his father died, God removed him from there into this land in which you are now living. [5]Yet he gave him no inheritance in it, not even a foot's length, but promised to give it to him as a possession and to his offspring after him, though he had no child. [6]And God spoke to this effect—that [b]his offspring would be sojourners in a land belonging to others, who would enslave them and afflict them four hundred years. [7]'But I will judge the nation that they serve,' said God, 'and after that they shall come out and worship me in this place.' [8]And he gave him the covenant of circumcision. And so Abraham became the father of Isaac, and circumcised him on the eighth day, and Isaac became the father of Jacob, and Jacob of the twelve patriarchs.

[9]"And the patriarchs, jealous of Joseph, sold him into Egypt; but God was with him [10]and rescued him out of all his afflictions and gave him favor and wisdom before Pharaoh, king of Egypt, who made him ruler over Egypt and over all his household. [11]Now there came a famine throughout all Egypt and Canaan, and great affliction, and our fathers could find no food. [12]But when Jacob heard that there was grain in Egypt, he sent out our fathers on their first visit. [13]And on the second visit Joseph made himself known to his brothers, and Joseph's family became known to Pharaoh. [14]And Joseph sent and summoned Jacob his father and all his kindred, seventy-five persons in all. [15]And Jacob went down into Egypt, and he died, he and our fathers, [16]and they were carried back to Shechem and laid in the tomb that Abraham had bought for a sum of silver from the sons of Hamor in Shechem.

[17]"But as the time of the promise drew near, which God had granted to Abraham, the people increased and multiplied in Egypt [18]until there arose over Egypt another king who did not know

Joseph. [19]He dealt shrewdly with our race and forced our fathers to expose their infants, so that they would not be kept alive. [20]At this time Moses was born; and he was beautiful in God's sight. And he was brought up for three months in his father's house, [21]and when he was exposed, Pharaoh's daughter adopted him and brought him up as her own son. [22]And Moses was instructed in all the wisdom of the Egyptians, and he was mighty in his words and deeds.

[23]"When he was forty years old, it came into his heart to visit his brothers, the children of Israel. [24]And seeing one of them being wronged, he defended the oppressed man and avenged him by striking down the Egyptian. [25]He supposed that his brothers would understand that God was giving them salvation by his hand, but they did not understand. [26]And on the following day he appeared to them as they were quarreling and tried to reconcile them, saying, 'Men, you are brothers. Why do you wrong each other?' [27]But the man who was wronging his neighbor thrust him aside, saying, 'Who made you a ruler and a judge over us? [28]Do you want to kill me as you killed the Egyptian yesterday?' [29]At this retort Moses fled and became an exile in the land of Midian, where he became the father of two sons.

[30]"Now when forty years had passed, an angel appeared to him in the wilderness of Mount Sinai, in a flame of fire in a bush. [31]When Moses saw it, he was amazed at the sight, and as he drew near to look, there came the voice of the Lord: [32c]'I am the God of your fathers, the God of Abraham and of Isaac and of Jacob.' And Moses trembled and did not dare to look. [33]Then the Lord said to him, 'Take off the sandals from your feet, for the place where you are standing is holy ground. [34]I have surely seen the affliction of my people who are in Egypt, and have heard their groaning, and I have come down to deliver them. And now come, I will send you to Egypt.'

[35]"This Moses, whom they rejected, saying, 'Who made you a ruler and a judge?'—this man God sent as both ruler and redeemer by the hand of the angel who appeared to him in the bush. [36]This man led them out, performing wonders and signs in Egypt and at the Red Sea and in the wilderness for forty years. [37]This is the Moses who said to the Israelites, 'God will raise up for you [d]a prophet like me from your brothers.' [38]This is the one who was in the congregation in the wilderness with the angel who spoke to him at Mount Sinai, and with our fathers. He received living oracles to give to us. [39]Our fathers refused to obey him, but thrust him aside, and in their hearts they turned to Egypt, [40]saying to Aaron, [e]'Make for us gods who will go before us. As for this Moses who led us out from the land of Egypt, we do not know what has become of him.'

[a]Gen. 12:1 [b]Gen. 15:13, 14 [c]Ex. 3:6 [d]Deut. 18:15 [e]Ex. 32:1, 23

⁴¹And they made a calf in those days, and offered a sacrifice to the idol and were rejoicing in the works of their hands. ⁴²But God turned away and gave them over to worship the host of heaven, as it is written in the book of the prophets:

ᵃ"'Did you bring to me slain beasts and sacrifices,
    during the forty years in the wilderness,
    O house of Israel?
⁴³ You took up the tent of Moloch
    and the star of your god Rephan,
    the images that you made to worship;
and I will send you into exile beyond Babylon.'

⁴⁴"Our fathers had the tent of witness in the wilderness, just as he who spoke to Moses directed him to make it, according to the pattern that he had seen. ⁴⁵Our fathers in turn brought it in with Joshua when they dispossessed the nations that God drove out before our fathers. So it was until the days of David, ⁴⁶who found favor in the sight of God and asked to find a dwelling place for the God of Jacob.¹ ⁴⁷But it was Solomon who built a house for him. ⁴⁸Yet the Most High does not dwell in houses made by hands, as the prophet says,

⁴⁹ᵇ"'Heaven is my throne,
    and the earth is my footstool.
What kind of house will you build for me,
    says the Lord,
    or what is the place of my rest?
⁵⁰ Did not my hand make all these things?'

⁵¹"You stiff-necked people, uncircumcised in heart and ears, you always resist the Holy Spirit. As your fathers did, so do you. ⁵²Which of the prophets did your fathers not persecute? And they killed those who announced beforehand the coming of the Righteous One, whom you have now betrayed and murdered, ⁵³you who received the law as delivered by angels and did not keep it."

The Stoning of Stephen

⁵⁴Now when they heard these things they were enraged, and they ground their teeth at him. ⁵⁵But he, full of the Holy Spirit, gazed into heaven and saw the glory of God, and Jesus standing at the right hand of God. ⁵⁶And he said, "Behold, I see the heavens opened, and the Son of Man standing at the right hand of God." ⁵⁷But they cried out with a loud voice and stopped their ears and rushed together² at him. ⁵⁸Then they cast him out of the city and stoned him. And the witnesses laid down their garments at the feet of a young man named Saul. ⁵⁹And as they were stoning Stephen, he called out, "Lord Jesus, receive my spirit." ⁶⁰And falling to his knees he cried out with a loud voice, "Lord, do not hold this sin against them." And when he had said this, he fell asleep.

Saul Ravages the Church

8 And Saul approved of his execution.
And there arose on that day a great persecution against the church in Jerusalem, and they were all scattered throughout the regions of Judea and Samaria, except the apostles. ²Devout men buried Stephen and made great lamentation over him. ³But Saul was ravaging the church, and entering house after house, he dragged off men and women and committed them to prison.

Philip Proclaims Christ in Samaria

⁴Now those who were scattered went about preaching the word. ⁵Philip went down to the city³ of Samaria and proclaimed to them the Christ. ⁶And the crowds with one accord paid attention to what was being said by Philip when they heard him and saw the signs that he did. ⁷For unclean spirits, crying out with a loud voice, came out of many who had them, and many who were paralyzed or lame were healed. ⁸So there was much joy in that city.

Simon the Magician Believes

⁹But there was a man named Simon, who had previously practiced magic in the city and amazed the people of Samaria, saying that he himself was somebody great. ¹⁰They all paid attention to him, from the least to the greatest, saying, "This man is the power of God that is called Great." ¹¹And they paid attention to him because for a long time he had amazed them with his magic. ¹²But when they believed Philip as he preached good news about the kingdom of God and the name of Jesus Christ, they were baptized, both men and women. ¹³Even Simon himself believed, and after being baptized he continued with Philip. And seeing signs and great miracles⁴ performed, he was amazed.

¹⁴Now when the apostles at Jerusalem heard that Samaria had received the word of God, they sent to them Peter and John, ¹⁵who came down and prayed for them that they might receive the Holy Spirit, ¹⁶for he had not yet fallen on any of them, but they had only been baptized in the name of the Lord Jesus. ¹⁷Then they laid their hands on them and they received the Holy Spirit. ¹⁸Now when Simon saw that the Spirit was given through the laying on of the apostles' hands, he offered them money, ¹⁹saying, "Give me this power also, so that anyone on whom I lay my hands may receive the Holy Spirit." ²⁰But Peter said to him, "May your silver perish with you, because you thought you could obtain the gift of God with money! ²¹You have neither part nor lot in this matter, for your heart is not right before God. ²²Repent, therefore, of this wickedness of yours, and pray to the Lord that, if possible, the

---

¹ Some manuscripts *for the house of Jacob* ² Or *rushed with one mind* ³ Some manuscripts *a city* ⁴ Greek *works of power* ᵃ Amos 5:25-27 ᵇ Isa. 66:1, 2

intent of your heart may be forgiven you. ²³For I see that you are in the gall¹ of bitterness and in the bond of iniquity." ²⁴And Simon answered, "Pray for me to the Lord, that nothing of what you have said may come upon me."

²⁵Now when they had testified and spoken the word of the Lord, they returned to Jerusalem, preaching the gospel to many villages of the Samaritans.

Philip and the Ethiopian Eunuch

²⁶Now an angel of the Lord said to Philip, "Rise and go toward the south² to the road that goes down from Jerusalem to Gaza." This is a desert place. ²⁷And he rose and went. And there was an Ethiopian, a eunuch, a court official of Candace, queen of the Ethiopians, who was in charge of all her treasure. He had come to Jerusalem to worship ²⁸and was returning, seated in his chariot, and he was reading the prophet Isaiah. ²⁹And the Spirit said to Philip, "Go over and join this chariot." ³⁰So Philip ran to him and heard him reading Isaiah the prophet and asked, "Do you understand what you are reading?" ³¹And he said, "How can I, unless someone guides me?" And he invited Philip to come up and sit with him. ³²Now the passage of the Scripture that he was reading was this:

ᵃ"Like a sheep he was led to the slaughter
    and like a lamb before its shearer is silent,
    so he opens not his mouth.
³³   In his humiliation justice was denied him.
    Who can describe his generation?
    For his life is taken away from the earth."

³⁴And the eunuch said to Philip, "About whom, I ask you, does the prophet say this, about himself or about someone else?" ³⁵Then Philip opened his mouth, and beginning with this Scripture he told him the good news about Jesus. ³⁶And as they were going along the road they came to some water, and the eunuch said, "See, here is water! What prevents me from being baptized?"³ ³⁸And he commanded the chariot to stop, and they both went down into the water, Philip and the eunuch, and he baptized him. ³⁹And when they came up out of the water, the Spirit of the Lord carried Philip away, and the eunuch saw him no more, and went on his way rejoicing. ⁴⁰But Philip found himself at Azotus, and as he passed through he preached the gospel to all the towns until he came to Caesarea.

The Conversion of Saul

9 But Saul, still breathing threats and murder against the disciples of the Lord, went to the high priest ²and asked him for letters to the synagogues at Damascus, so that if he found any belonging to the Way, men or women, he might bring them bound to Jerusalem. ³Now as he went on his way, he approached Damascus, and suddenly a light from heaven flashed around him. ⁴And falling to the ground he heard a voice saying to him, "Saul, Saul, why are you persecuting me?" ⁵And he said, "Who are you, Lord?" And he said, "I am Jesus, whom you are persecuting. ⁶But rise and enter the city, and you will be told what you are to do." ⁷The men who were traveling with him stood speechless, hearing the voice but seeing no one. ⁸Saul rose from the ground, and although his eyes were opened, he saw nothing. So they led him by the hand and brought him into Damascus. ⁹And for three days he was without sight, and neither ate nor drank.

¹⁰Now there was a disciple at Damascus named Ananias. The Lord said to him in a vision, "Ananias." And he said, "Here I am, Lord." ¹¹And the Lord said to him, "Rise and go to the street called Straight, and at the house of Judas look for a man of Tarsus named Saul, for behold, he is praying, ¹²and he has seen in a vision a man named Ananias come in and lay his hands on him so that he might regain his sight." ¹³But Ananias answered, "Lord, I have heard from many about this man, how much evil he has done to your saints at Jerusalem. ¹⁴And here he has authority from the chief priests to bind all who call on your name." ¹⁵But the Lord said to him, "Go, for he is a chosen instrument of mine to carry my name before the Gentiles and kings and the children of Israel. ¹⁶For I will show him how much he must suffer for the sake of my name." ¹⁷So Ananias departed and entered the house. And laying his hands on him he said, "Brother Saul, the Lord Jesus who appeared to you on the road by which you came has sent me so that you may regain your sight and be filled with the Holy Spirit." ¹⁸And immediately something like scales fell from his eyes, and he regained his sight. Then he rose and was baptized; ¹⁹and taking food, he was strengthened.

Saul Proclaims Jesus in Synagogues

For some days he was with the disciples at Damascus. ²⁰And immediately he proclaimed Jesus in the synagogues, saying, "He is the Son of God." ²¹And all who heard him were amazed and said, "Is not this the man who made havoc in Jerusalem of those who called upon this name? And has he not come here for this purpose, to bring them bound before the chief priests?" ²²But Saul increased all the more in strength, and confounded the Jews who lived in Damascus by proving that Jesus was the Christ.

Saul Escapes from Damascus

²³When many days had passed, the Jews plotted to kill him, ²⁴but their plot became known to

¹ That is, a bitter fluid secreted by the liver; bile   ² Or *go at about noon*   ³ Some manuscripts add all or most of verse 37: *And Philip said, "If you believe with all your heart, you may." And he replied, "I believe that Jesus Christ is the Son of God."*   ᵃ Isa. 53:7, 8

Saul. They were watching the gates day and night in order to kill him, ²⁵but his disciples took him by night and let him down through an opening in the wall,¹ lowering him in a basket.

Saul in Jerusalem

²⁶And when he had come to Jerusalem, he attempted to join the disciples. And they were all afraid of him, for they did not believe that he was a disciple. ²⁷But Barnabas took him and brought him to the apostles and declared to them how on the road he had seen the Lord, who spoke to him, and how at Damascus he had preached boldly in the name of Jesus. ²⁸So he went in and out among them at Jerusalem, preaching boldly in the name of the Lord. ²⁹And he spoke and disputed against the Hellenists.² But they were seeking to kill him. ³⁰And when the brothers learned this, they brought him down to Caesarea and sent him off to Tarsus.

³¹So the church throughout all Judea and Galilee and Samaria had peace and was being built up. And walking in the fear of the Lord and in the comfort of the Holy Spirit, it multiplied.

The Healing of Aeneas

³²Now as Peter went here and there among them all, he came down also to the saints who lived at Lydda. ³³There he found a man named Aeneas, bedridden for eight years, who was paralyzed. ³⁴And Peter said to him, "Aeneas, Jesus Christ heals you; rise and make your bed." And immediately he rose. ³⁵And all the residents of Lydda and Sharon saw him, and they turned to the Lord.

Dorcas Restored to Life

³⁶Now there was in Joppa a disciple named Tabitha, which, translated, means Dorcas.³ She was full of good works and acts of charity. ³⁷In those days she became ill and died, and when they had washed her, they laid her in an upper room. ³⁸Since Lydda was near Joppa, the disciples, hearing that Peter was there, sent two men to him, urging him, "Please come to us without delay." ³⁹So Peter rose and went with them. And when he arrived, they took him to the upper room. All the widows stood beside him weeping and showing tunics⁴ and other garments that Dorcas made while she was with them. ⁴⁰But Peter put them all outside, and knelt down and prayed; and turning to the body he said, "Tabitha, arise." And she opened her eyes, and when she saw Peter she sat up. ⁴¹And he gave her his hand and raised her up. Then calling the saints and widows, he presented her alive. ⁴²And it became known throughout all Joppa, and many believed in the Lord. ⁴³And he stayed in Joppa for many days with one Simon, a tanner.

Peter and Cornelius

10 At Caesarea there was a man named Cornelius, a centurion of what was known as the Italian Cohort, ²a devout man who feared God with all his household, gave alms generously to the people, and prayed continually to God. ³About the ninth hour of the day⁵ he saw clearly in a vision an angel of God come in and say to him, "Cornelius." ⁴And he stared at him in terror and said, "What is it, Lord?" And he said to him, "Your prayers and your alms have ascended as a memorial before God. ⁵And now send men to Joppa and bring one Simon who is called Peter. ⁶He is lodging with one Simon, a tanner, whose house is by the sea." ⁷When the angel who spoke to him had departed, he called two of his servants and a devout soldier from among those who attended him, ⁸and having related everything to them, he sent them to Joppa.

Peter's Vision

⁹The next day, as they were on their journey and approaching the city, Peter went up on the housetop about the sixth hour⁶ to pray. ¹⁰And he became hungry and wanted something to eat, but while they were preparing it, he fell into a trance ¹¹and saw the heavens opened and something like a great sheet descending, being let down by its four corners upon the earth. ¹²In it were all kinds of animals and reptiles and birds of the air. ¹³And there came a voice to him: "Rise, Peter; kill and eat." ¹⁴But Peter said, "By no means, Lord; for I have never eaten anything that is common or unclean." ¹⁵And the voice came to him again a second time, "What God has made clean, do not call common." ¹⁶This happened three times, and the thing was taken up at once to heaven.

¹⁷Now while Peter was inwardly perplexed as to what the vision that he had seen might mean, behold, the men who were sent by Cornelius, having made inquiry for Simon's house, stood at the gate ¹⁸and called out to ask whether Simon who was called Peter was lodging there. ¹⁹And while Peter was pondering the vision, the Spirit said to him, "Behold, three men are looking for you. ²⁰Rise and go down and accompany them without hesitation, for I have sent them." ²¹And Peter went down to the men and said, "I am the one you are looking for. What is the reason for your coming?" ²²And they said, "Cornelius, a centurion, an upright and God-fearing man, who is well spoken of by the whole Jewish nation, was directed by a holy angel to send for you to come to his house and to hear what you have to say." ²³So he invited them in to be his guests.

The next day he rose and went away with them, and some of the brothers from Joppa

---

¹Greek through the wall ²That is, Greek-speaking Jews ³The Aramaic name Tabitha and the Greek name Dorcas both mean gazelle ⁴Greek chiton, a long garment worn under the cloak next to the skin ⁵That is, 3 P.M. ⁶That is, noon

accompanied him. [24]And on the following day they entered Caesarea. Cornelius was expecting them and had called together his relatives and close friends. [25]When Peter entered, Cornelius met him and fell down at his feet and worshiped him. [26]But Peter lifted him up, saying, "Stand up; I too am a man." [27]And as he talked with him, he went in and found many persons gathered. [28]And he said to them, "You yourselves know how unlawful it is for a Jew to associate with or to visit anyone of another nation, but God has shown me that I should not call any person common or unclean. [29]So when I was sent for, I came without objection. I ask then why you sent for me."

[30]And Cornelius said, "Four days ago, about this hour, I was praying in my house at the ninth hour,[1] and behold, a man stood before me in bright clothing [31]and said, 'Cornelius, your prayer has been heard and your alms have been remembered before God. [32]Send therefore to Joppa and ask for Simon who is called Peter. He is lodging in the house of Simon, a tanner, by the sea.' [33]So I sent for you at once, and you have been kind enough to come. Now therefore we are all here in the presence of God to hear all that you have been commanded by the Lord."

Gentiles Hear the Good News

[34]So Peter opened his mouth and said: "Truly I understand that God shows no partiality, [35]but in every nation anyone who fears him and does what is right is acceptable to him. [36]As for the word that he sent to Israel, preaching good news of peace through Jesus Christ (he is Lord of all), [37]you yourselves know what happened throughout all Judea, beginning from Galilee after the baptism that John proclaimed: [38]how God anointed Jesus of Nazareth with the Holy Spirit and with power. He went about doing good and healing all who were oppressed by the devil, for God was with him. [39]And we are witnesses of all that he did both in the country of the Jews and in Jerusalem. They put him to death by hanging him on a tree, [40]but God raised him on the third day and made him to appear, [41]not to all the people but to us who had been chosen by God as witnesses, who ate and drank with him after he rose from the dead. [42]And he commanded us to preach to the people and to testify that he is the one appointed by God to be judge of the living and the dead. [43]To him all the prophets bear witness that everyone who believes in him receives forgiveness of sins through his name."

The Holy Spirit Falls on the Gentiles

[44]While Peter was still saying these things, the Holy Spirit fell on all who heard the word. [45]And the believers from among the circumcised who had come with Peter were amazed, because the gift of the Holy Spirit was poured out even on the Gentiles. [46]For they were hearing them speaking in tongues and extolling God. Then Peter declared, [47]"Can anyone withhold water for baptizing these people, who have received the Holy Spirit just as we have?" [48]And he commanded them to be baptized in the name of Jesus Christ. Then they asked him to remain for some days.

Peter Reports to the Church

11 Now the apostles and the brothers[2] who were throughout Judea heard that the Gentiles also had received the word of God. [2]So when Peter went up to Jerusalem, the circumcision party criticized him, saying, [3]"You went to uncircumcised men and ate with them." [4]But Peter began and explained it to them in order: [5]"I was in the city of Joppa praying, and in a trance I saw a vision, something like a great sheet descending, being let down from heaven by its four corners, and it came down to me. [6]Looking at it closely, I observed animals and beasts of prey and reptiles and birds of the air. [7]And I heard a voice saying to me, 'Rise, Peter; kill and eat.' [8]But I said, 'By no means, Lord; for nothing common or unclean has ever entered my mouth.' [9]But the voice answered a second time from heaven, 'What God has made clean, do not call common.' [10]This happened three times, and all was drawn up again into heaven. [11]And behold, at that very moment three men arrived at the house in which we were, sent to me from Caesarea. [12]And the Spirit told me to go with them, making no distinction. These six brothers also accompanied me, and we entered the man's house. [13]And he told us how he had seen the angel stand in his house and say, 'Send to Joppa and bring Simon who is called Peter; [14]he will declare to you a message by which you will be saved, you and all your household.' [15]As I began to speak, the Holy Spirit fell on them just as on us at the beginning. [16]And I remembered the word of the Lord, how he said, 'John baptized with water, but you will be baptized with the Holy Spirit.' [17]If then God gave the same gift to them as he gave to us when we believed in the Lord Jesus Christ, who was I that I could stand in God's way?" [18]When they heard these things they fell silent. And they glorified God, saying, "Then to the Gentiles also God has granted repentance that leads to life."

The Church in Antioch

[19]Now those who were scattered because of the persecution that arose over Stephen traveled as far as Phoenicia and Cyprus and Antioch, speaking the word to no one except Jews. [20]But there were some of them, men of Cyprus and Cyrene, who on coming to Antioch spoke to the Hellenists[3] also, preaching the Lord Jesus. [21]And

---

[1] That is, 3 P.M. [2] Or brothers and sisters [3] Or Greeks (that is, Greek-speaking non-Jews)

the hand of the Lord was with them, and a great number who believed turned to the Lord. ²²The report of this came to the ears of the church in Jerusalem, and they sent Barnabas to Antioch. ²³When he came and saw the grace of God, he was glad, and he exhorted them all to remain faithful to the Lord with steadfast purpose, ²⁴for he was a good man, full of the Holy Spirit and of faith. And a great many people were added to the Lord. ²⁵So Barnabas went to Tarsus to look for Saul, ²⁶and when he had found him, he brought him to Antioch. For a whole year they met with the church and taught a great many people. And in Antioch the disciples were first called Christians.

²⁷Now in these days prophets came down from Jerusalem to Antioch. ²⁸And one of them named Agabus stood up and foretold by the Spirit that there would be a great famine over all the world (this took place in the days of Claudius). ²⁹So the disciples determined, everyone according to his ability, to send relief to the brothers¹ living in Judea. ³⁰And they did so, sending it to the elders by the hand of Barnabas and Saul.

James Killed and Peter Imprisoned

12 About that time Herod the king laid violent hands on some who belonged to the church. ²He killed James the brother of John with the sword, ³and when he saw that it pleased the Jews, he proceeded to arrest Peter also. This was during the days of Unleavened Bread. ⁴And when he had seized him, he put him in prison, delivering him over to four squads of soldiers to guard him, intending after the Passover to bring him out to the people. ⁵So Peter was kept in prison, but earnest prayer for him was made to God by the church.

Peter Is Rescued

⁶Now when Herod was about to bring him out, on that very night, Peter was sleeping between two soldiers, bound with two chains, and sentries before the door were guarding the prison. ⁷And behold, an angel of the Lord stood next to him, and a light shone in the cell. He struck Peter on the side and woke him, saying, "Get up quickly." And the chains fell off his hands. ⁸And the angel said to him, "Dress yourself and put on your sandals." And he did so. And he said to him, "Wrap your cloak around you and follow me." ⁹And he went out and followed him. He did not know that what was being done by the angel was real, but thought he was seeing a vision. ¹⁰When they had passed the first and the second guard, they came to the iron gate leading into the city. It opened for them of its own accord, and they went out and went along one street, and immediately the angel left him. ¹¹When Peter came to himself, he said,

"Now I am sure that the Lord has sent his angel and rescued me from the hand of Herod and from all that the Jewish people were expecting." ¹²When he realized this, he went to the house of Mary, the mother of John whose other name was Mark, where many were gathered together and were praying. ¹³And when he knocked at the door of the gateway, a servant girl named Rhoda came to answer. ¹⁴Recognizing Peter's voice, in her joy she did not open the gate but ran in and reported that Peter was standing at the gate. ¹⁵They said to her, "You are out of your mind." But she kept insisting that it was so, and they kept saying, "It is his angel!" ¹⁶But Peter continued knocking, and when they opened, they saw him and were amazed. ¹⁷But motioning to them with his hand to be silent, he described to them how the Lord had brought him out of the prison. And he said, "Tell these things to James and to the brothers."² Then he departed and went to another place.

¹⁸Now when day came, there was no little disturbance among the soldiers over what had become of Peter. ¹⁹And after Herod searched for him and did not find him, he examined the sentries and ordered that they should be put to death. Then he went down from Judea to Caesarea and spent time there.

The Death of Herod

²⁰Now Herod was angry with the people of Tyre and Sidon, and they came to him with one accord, and having persuaded Blastus, the king's chamberlain, they asked for peace, because their country depended on the king's country for food. ²¹On an appointed day Herod put on his royal robes, took his seat upon the throne, and delivered an oration to them. ²²And the people were shouting, "The voice of a god, and not of a man!" ²³Immediately an angel of the Lord struck him down, because he did not give God the glory, and he was eaten by worms and breathed his last.

²⁴But the word of God increased and multiplied.

²⁵And Barnabas and Saul returned from³ Jerusalem when they had completed their service, bringing with them John, whose other name was Mark.

Barnabas and Saul Sent Off

13 Now there were in the church at Antioch prophets and teachers, Barnabas, Simeon who was called Niger,⁴ Lucius of Cyrene, Manaen a member of the court of Herod the tetrarch, and Saul. ²While they were worshiping the Lord and fasting, the Holy Spirit said, "Set apart for me Barnabas and Saul for the work to which I have called them." ³Then after fasting and praying they laid their hands on them and sent them off.

---

¹Or brothers and sisters ²Or brothers and sisters ³Some manuscripts to ⁴Niger is a Latin word meaning black, or dark

Barnabas and Saul on Cyprus

⁴So, being sent out by the Holy Spirit, they went down to Seleucia, and from there they sailed to Cyprus. ⁵When they arrived at Salamis, they proclaimed the word of God in the synagogues of the Jews. And they had John to assist them. ⁶When they had gone through the whole island as far as Paphos, they came upon a certain magician, a Jewish false prophet named Bar-Jesus. ⁷He was with the proconsul, Sergius Paulus, a man of intelligence, who summoned Barnabas and Saul and sought to hear the word of God. ⁸But Elymas the magician (for that is the meaning of his name) opposed them, seeking to turn the proconsul away from the faith. ⁹But Saul, who was also called Paul, filled with the Holy Spirit, looked intently at him ¹⁰and said, "You son of the devil, you enemy of all righteousness, full of all deceit and villainy, will you not stop making crooked the straight paths of the Lord? ¹¹And now, behold, the hand of the Lord is upon you, and you will be blind and unable to see the sun for a time." Immediately mist and darkness fell upon him, and he went about seeking people to lead him by the hand. ¹²Then the proconsul believed, when he saw what had occurred, for he was astonished at the teaching of the Lord.

Paul and Barnabas at Antioch in Pisidia

¹³Now Paul and his companions set sail from Paphos and came to Perga in Pamphylia. And John left them and returned to Jerusalem, ¹⁴but they went on from Perga and came to Antioch in Pisidia. And on the Sabbath day they went into the synagogue and sat down. ¹⁵After the reading from the Law and the Prophets, the rulers of the synagogue sent a message to them, saying, "Brothers, if you have any word of encouragement for the people, say it." ¹⁶So Paul stood up, and motioning with his hand said:

"Men of Israel and you who fear God, listen. ¹⁷The God of this people Israel chose our fathers and made the people great during their stay in the land of Egypt, and with uplifted arm he led them out of it. ¹⁸And for about forty years he put up with[1] them in the wilderness. ¹⁹And after destroying seven nations in the land of Canaan, he gave them their land as an inheritance. ²⁰All this took about 450 years. And after that he gave them judges until Samuel the prophet. ²¹Then they asked for a king, and God gave them Saul the son of Kish, a man of the tribe of Benjamin, for forty years. ²²And when he had removed him, he raised up David to be their king, of whom he testified and said, ᵃ'I have found in David the son of Jesse ᵇa man after my heart, who will do all my will.' ²³Of this man's offspring God has brought to Israel a Savior, Jesus, as he promised.

²⁴Before his coming, John had proclaimed a baptism of repentance to all the people of Israel. ²⁵And as John was finishing his course, he said, 'What do you suppose that I am? I am not he. No, but behold, after me one is coming, the sandals of whose feet I am not worthy to untie.'

²⁶"Brothers, sons of the family of Abraham, and those among you who fear God, to us has been sent the message of this salvation. ²⁷For those who live in Jerusalem and their rulers, because they did not recognize him nor understand the utterances of the prophets, which are read every Sabbath, fulfilled them by condemning him. ²⁸And though they found in him no guilt worthy of death, they asked Pilate to have him executed. ²⁹And when they had carried out all that was written of him, they took him down from the tree and laid him in a tomb. ³⁰But God raised him from the dead, ³¹and for many days he appeared to those who had come up with him from Galilee to Jerusalem, who are now his witnesses to the people. ³²And we bring you the good news that what God promised to the fathers, ³³this he has fulfilled to us their children by raising Jesus, as also it is written in the second Psalm,

ᶜ"'You are my Son,
  today I have begotten you.'

³⁴And as for the fact that he raised him from the dead, no more to return to corruption, he has spoken in this way,

"'I will give you ᵈthe holy and sure blessings of
  David.'

³⁵Therefore he says also in another psalm,

ᵉ"'You will not let your Holy One see corruption.'

³⁶For David, after he had served the purpose of God in his own generation, fell asleep and was laid with his fathers and saw corruption, ³⁷but he whom God raised up did not see corruption. ³⁸Let it be known to you therefore, brothers, that through this man forgiveness of sins is proclaimed to you, ³⁹and by him everyone who believes is freed[2] from everything from which you could not be freed by the law of Moses. ⁴⁰Beware, therefore, lest what is said in the Prophets should come about:

⁴¹ᶠ"'Look, you scoffers,
  be astounded and perish;
for I am doing a work in your days,
  a work that you will not believe, even if one
    tells it to you.'"

⁴²As they went out, the people begged that these things might be told them the next Sabbath. ⁴³And after the meeting of the synagogue

¹ Some manuscripts *he carried* (compare Deuteronomy 1:31) ² Greek *justified*; twice in this verse ᵃ Ps. 89:20 ᵇ 1 Sam. 13:14 ᶜ Ps. 2:7 ᵈ Isa. 55:3 ᵉ Ps. 16:10 ᶠ Hab. 1:5

broke up, many Jews and devout converts to Judaism followed Paul and Barnabas, who, as they spoke with them, urged them to continue in the grace of God.

⁴⁴The next Sabbath almost the whole city gathered to hear the word of the Lord. ⁴⁵But when the Jews saw the crowds, they were filled with jealousy and began to contradict what was spoken by Paul, reviling him. ⁴⁶And Paul and Barnabas spoke out boldly, saying, "It was necessary that the word of God be spoken first to you. Since you thrust it aside and judge yourselves unworthy of eternal life, behold, we are turning to the Gentiles. ⁴⁷For so the Lord has commanded us, saying,

ᵃ"'I have made you a light for the Gentiles,
  that you may bring salvation to the ends of
    the earth.'"

⁴⁸And when the Gentiles heard this, they began rejoicing and glorifying the word of the Lord, and as many as were appointed to eternal life believed. ⁴⁹And the word of the Lord was spreading throughout the whole region. ⁵⁰But the Jews incited the devout women of high standing and the leading men of the city, stirred up persecution against Paul and Barnabas, and drove them out of their district. ⁵¹But they shook off the dust from their feet against them and went to Iconium. ⁵²And the disciples were filled with joy and with the Holy Spirit.

Paul and Barnabas at Iconium

14 Now at Iconium they entered together into the Jewish synagogue and spoke in such a way that a great number of both Jews and Greeks believed. ²But the unbelieving Jews stirred up the Gentiles and poisoned their minds against the brothers.¹ ³So they remained for a long time, speaking boldly for the Lord, who bore witness to the word of his grace, granting signs and wonders to be done by their hands. ⁴But the people of the city were divided; some sided with the Jews and some with the apostles. ⁵When an attempt was made by both Gentiles and Jews, with their rulers, to mistreat them and to stone them, ⁶they learned of it and fled to Lystra and Derbe, cities of Lycaonia, and to the surrounding country, ⁷and there they continued to preach the gospel.

Paul and Barnabas at Lystra

⁸Now at Lystra there was a man sitting who could not use his feet. He was crippled from birth and had never walked. ⁹He listened to Paul speaking. And Paul, looking intently at him and seeing that he had faith to be made well,² ¹⁰said in a loud voice, "Stand upright on your feet." And he sprang up and began walking. ¹¹And when the crowds saw what Paul had done, they

lifted up their voices, saying in Lycaonian, "The gods have come down to us in the likeness of men!" ¹²Barnabas they called Zeus, and Paul, Hermes, because he was the chief speaker. ¹³And the priest of Zeus, whose temple was at the entrance to the city, brought oxen and garlands to the gates and wanted to offer sacrifice with the crowds. ¹⁴But when the apostles Barnabas and Paul heard of it, they tore their garments and rushed out into the crowd, crying out, ¹⁵"Men, why are you doing these things? We also are men, of like nature with you, and we bring you good news, that you should turn from these vain things to a living God, who made the heaven and the earth and the sea and all that is in them. ¹⁶In past generations he allowed all the nations to walk in their own ways. ¹⁷Yet he did not leave himself without witness, for he did good by giving you rains from heaven and fruitful seasons, satisfying your hearts with food and gladness." ¹⁸Even with these words they scarcely restrained the people from offering sacrifice to them.

Paul Stoned at Lystra

¹⁹But Jews came from Antioch and Iconium, and having persuaded the crowds, they stoned Paul and dragged him out of the city, supposing that he was dead. ²⁰But when the disciples gathered about him, he rose up and entered the city, and on the next day he went on with Barnabas to Derbe. ²¹When they had preached the gospel to that city and had made many disciples, they returned to Lystra and to Iconium and to Antioch, ²²strengthening the souls of the disciples, encouraging them to continue in the faith, and saying that through many tribulations we must enter the kingdom of God. ²³And when they had appointed elders for them in every church, with prayer and fasting they committed them to the Lord in whom they had believed.

Paul and Barnabas Return to Antioch in Syria

²⁴Then they passed through Pisidia and came to Pamphylia. ²⁵And when they had spoken the word in Perga, they went down to Attalia, ²⁶and from there they sailed to Antioch, where they had been commended to the grace of God for the work that they had fulfilled. ²⁷And when they arrived and gathered the church together, they declared all that God had done with them, and how he had opened a door of faith to the Gentiles. ²⁸And they remained no little time with the disciples.

The Jerusalem Council

15 But some men came down from Judea and were teaching the brothers, "Unless you are circumcised according to the custom of Moses, you cannot be saved." ²And after Paul

---

¹Or brothers and sisters ²Or be saved ᵃIsa. 49:6

and Barnabas had no small dissension and debate with them, Paul and Barnabas and some of the others were appointed to go up to Jerusalem to the apostles and the elders about this question. [3]So, being sent on their way by the church, they passed through both Phoenicia and Samaria, describing in detail the conversion of the Gentiles, and brought great joy to all the brothers.[1] [4]When they came to Jerusalem, they were welcomed by the church and the apostles and the elders, and they declared all that God had done with them. [5]But some believers who belonged to the party of the Pharisees rose up and said, "It is necessary to circumcise them and to order them to keep the law of Moses."

[6]The apostles and the elders were gathered together to consider this matter. [7]And after there had been much debate, Peter stood up and said to them, "Brothers, you know that in the early days God made a choice among you, that by my mouth the Gentiles should hear the word of the gospel and believe. [8]And God, who knows the heart, bore witness to them, by giving them the Holy Spirit just as he did to us, [9]and he made no distinction between us and them, having cleansed their hearts by faith. [10]Now, therefore, why are you putting God to the test by placing a yoke on the neck of the disciples that neither our fathers nor we have been able to bear? [11]But we believe that we will be saved through the grace of the Lord Jesus, just as they will."

[12]And all the assembly fell silent, and they listened to Barnabas and Paul as they related what signs and wonders God had done through them among the Gentiles. [13]After they finished speaking, James replied, "Brothers, listen to me. [14]Simeon has related how God first visited the Gentiles, to take from them a people for his name. [15]And with this the words of the prophets agree, just as it is written,

[16a]"'After this I will return,
 and I will rebuild the tent of David that has
  fallen;
 I will rebuild its ruins,
  and I will restore it,
[17] that the remnant[2] of mankind may seek the
  Lord,
 and all the Gentiles who are called by my
  name,
 says the Lord, who makes these things
[18]known from of old.'

[19]Therefore my judgment is that we should not trouble those of the Gentiles who turn to God, [20]but should write to them to abstain from the things polluted by idols, and from sexual immorality, and from what has been strangled, and from blood. [21]For from ancient generations Moses

has had in every city those who proclaim him, for he is read every Sabbath in the synagogues."

The Council's Letter to Gentile Believers

[22]Then it seemed good to the apostles and the elders, with the whole church, to choose men from among them and send them to Antioch with Paul and Barnabas. They sent Judas called Barsabbas, and Silas, leading men among the brothers, [23]with the following letter: "The brothers, both the apostles and the elders, to the brothers[3] who are of the Gentiles in Antioch and Syria and Cilicia, greetings. [24]Since we have heard that some persons have gone out from us and troubled you[4] with words, unsettling your minds, although we gave them no instructions, [25]it has seemed good to us, having come to one accord, to choose men and send them to you with our beloved Barnabas and Paul, [26]men who have risked their lives for the sake of our Lord Jesus Christ. [27]We have therefore sent Judas and Silas, who themselves will tell you the same things by word of mouth. [28]For it has seemed good to the Holy Spirit and to us to lay on you no greater burden than these requirements: [29]that you abstain from what has been sacrificed to idols, and from blood, and from what has been strangled, and from sexual immorality. If you keep yourselves from these, you will do well. Farewell."

[30]So when they were sent off, they went down to Antioch, and having gathered the congregation together, they delivered the letter. [31]And when they had read it, they rejoiced because of its encouragement. [32]And Judas and Silas, who were themselves prophets, encouraged and strengthened the brothers with many words. [33]And after they had spent some time, they were sent off in peace by the brothers to those who had sent them.[5] [35]But Paul and Barnabas remained in Antioch, teaching and preaching the word of the Lord, with many others also.

Paul and Barnabas Separate

[36]And after some days Paul said to Barnabas, "Let us return and visit the brothers in every city where we proclaimed the word of the Lord, and see how they are." [37]Now Barnabas wanted to take with them John called Mark. [38]But Paul thought best not to take with them one who had withdrawn from them in Pamphylia and had not gone with them to the work. [39]And there arose a sharp disagreement, so that they separated from each other. Barnabas took Mark with him and sailed away to Cyprus, [40]but Paul chose Silas and departed, having been commended by the brothers to the grace of the Lord. [41]And he went through Syria and Cilicia, strengthening the churches.

Timothy Joins Paul and Silas

16 Paul[1] came also to Derbe and to Lystra. A disciple was there, named Timothy, the son of a Jewish woman who was a believer, but his father was a Greek. [2]He was well spoken of by the brothers[2] at Lystra and Iconium. [3]Paul wanted Timothy to accompany him, and he took him and circumcised him because of the Jews who were in those places, for they all knew that his father was a Greek. [4]As they went on their way through the cities, they delivered to them for observance the decisions that had been reached by the apostles and elders who were in Jerusalem. [5]So the churches were strengthened in the faith, and they increased in numbers daily.

The Macedonian Call

[6]And they went through the region of Phrygia and Galatia, having been forbidden by the Holy Spirit to speak the word in Asia. [7]And when they had come up to Mysia, they attempted to go into Bithynia, but the Spirit of Jesus did not allow them. [8]So, passing by Mysia, they went down to Troas. [9]And a vision appeared to Paul in the night: a man of Macedonia was standing there, urging him and saying, "Come over to Macedonia and help us." [10]And when Paul[3] had seen the vision, immediately we sought to go on into Macedonia, concluding that God had called us to preach the gospel to them.

The Conversion of Lydia

[11]So, setting sail from Troas, we made a direct voyage to Samothrace, and the following day to Neapolis, [12]and from there to Philippi, which is a leading city of the[4] district of Macedonia and a Roman colony. We remained in this city some days. [13]And on the Sabbath day we went outside the gate to the riverside, where we supposed there was a place of prayer, and we sat down and spoke to the women who had come together. [14]One who heard us was a woman named Lydia, from the city of Thyatira, a seller of purple goods, who was a worshiper of God. The Lord opened her heart to pay attention to what was said by Paul. [15]And after she was baptized, and her household as well, she urged us, saying, "If you have judged me to be faithful to the Lord, come to my house and stay." And she prevailed upon us.

Paul and Silas in Prison

[16]As we were going to the place of prayer, we were met by a slave girl who had a spirit of divination and brought her owners much gain by fortune-telling. [17]She followed Paul and us, crying out, "These men are servants[5] of the Most High God, who proclaim to you the way of salvation." [18]And this she kept doing for many days. Paul, having become greatly annoyed, turned and said to the spirit, "I command you in the name of Jesus Christ to come out of her." And it came out that very hour.

[19]But when her owners saw that their hope of gain was gone, they seized Paul and Silas and dragged them into the marketplace before the rulers. [20]And when they had brought them to the magistrates, they said, "These men are Jews, and they are disturbing our city. [21]They advocate customs that are not lawful for us as Romans to accept or practice." [22]The crowd joined in attacking them, and the magistrates tore the garments off them and gave orders to beat them with rods. [23]And when they had inflicted many blows upon them, they threw them into prison, ordering the jailer to keep them safely. [24]Having received this order, he put them into the inner prison and fastened their feet in the stocks.

The Philippian Jailer Converted

[25]About midnight Paul and Silas were praying and singing hymns to God, and the prisoners were listening to them, [26]and suddenly there was a great earthquake, so that the foundations of the prison were shaken. And immediately all the doors were opened, and everyone's bonds were unfastened. [27]When the jailer woke and saw that the prison doors were open, he drew his sword and was about to kill himself, supposing that the prisoners had escaped. [28]But Paul cried with a loud voice, "Do not harm yourself, for we are all here." [29]And the jailer[6] called for lights and rushed in, and trembling with fear he fell down before Paul and Silas. [30]Then he brought them out and said, "Sirs, what must I do to be saved?" [31]And they said, "Believe in the Lord Jesus, and you will be saved, you and your household." [32]And they spoke the word of the Lord to him and to all who were in his house. [33]And he took them the same hour of the night and washed their wounds; and he was baptized at once, he and all his family. [34]Then he brought them up into his house and set food before them. And he rejoiced along with his entire household that he had believed in God.

[35]But when it was day, the magistrates sent the police, saying, "Let those men go." [36]And the jailer reported these words to Paul, saying, "The magistrates have sent to let you go. Therefore come out now and go in peace." [37]But Paul said to them, "They have beaten us publicly, uncondemned, men who are Roman citizens, and have thrown us into prison; and do they now throw us out secretly? No! Let them come themselves and take us out." [38]The police reported these words to the magistrates, and they were afraid when they heard that they were Roman citizens. [39]So they came and apologized to them. And they took them out and asked them to leave the city. [40]So they went out

---

[1]Greek *He* [2]Or *brothers and sisters;* also verse 40 [3]Greek *he* [4]Or *that* [5]Greek *bondservants* [6]Greek *he*

of the prison and visited Lydia. And when they had seen the brothers, they encouraged them and departed.

Paul and Silas in Thessalonica

17 Now when they had passed through Amphipolis and Apollonia, they came to Thessalonica, where there was a synagogue of the Jews. [2] And Paul went in, as was his custom, and on three Sabbath days he reasoned with them from the Scriptures, [3] explaining and proving that it was necessary for the Christ to suffer and to rise from the dead, and saying, "This Jesus, whom I proclaim to you, is the Christ." [4] And some of them were persuaded and joined Paul and Silas, as did a great many of the devout Greeks and not a few of the leading women. [5] But the Jews were jealous, and taking some wicked men of the rabble, they formed a mob, set the city in an uproar, and attacked the house of Jason, seeking to bring them out to the crowd. [6] And when they could not find them, they dragged Jason and some of the brothers before the city authorities, shouting, "These men who have turned the world upside down have come here also, [7] and Jason has received them, and they are all acting against the decrees of Caesar, saying that there is another king, Jesus." [8] And the people and the city authorities were disturbed when they heard these things. [9] And when they had taken money as security from Jason and the rest, they let them go.

Paul and Silas in Berea

[10] The brothers[1] immediately sent Paul and Silas away by night to Berea, and when they arrived they went into the Jewish synagogue. [11] Now these Jews were more noble than those in Thessalonica; they received the word with all eagerness, examining the Scriptures daily to see if these things were so. [12] Many of them therefore believed, with not a few Greek women of high standing as well as men. [13] But when the Jews from Thessalonica learned that the word of God was proclaimed by Paul at Berea also, they came there too, agitating and stirring up the crowds. [14] Then the brothers immediately sent Paul off on his way to the sea, but Silas and Timothy remained there. [15] Those who conducted Paul brought him as far as Athens, and after receiving a command for Silas and Timothy to come to him as soon as possible, they departed.

Paul in Athens

[16] Now while Paul was waiting for them at Athens, his spirit was provoked within him as he saw that the city was full of idols. [17] So he reasoned in the synagogue with the Jews and the devout persons, and in the marketplace every day with those who happened to be there. [18] Some of the Epicurean and Stoic philosophers also conversed with him. And some said, "What does this babbler wish to say?" Others said, "He seems to be a preacher of foreign divinities"—because he was preaching Jesus and the resurrection. [19] And they took him and brought him to the Areopagus, saying, "May we know what this new teaching is that you are presenting? [20] For you bring some strange things to our ears. We wish to know therefore what these things mean." [21] Now all the Athenians and the foreigners who lived there would spend their time in nothing except telling or hearing something new.

Paul Addresses the Areopagus

[22] So Paul, standing in the midst of the Areopagus, said: "Men of Athens, I perceive that in every way you are very religious. [23] For as I passed along and observed the objects of your worship, I found also an altar with this inscription, 'To the unknown god.' What therefore you worship as unknown, this I proclaim to you. [24] The God who made the world and everything in it, being Lord of heaven and earth, does not live in temples made by man,[2] [25] nor is he served by human hands, as though he needed anything, since he himself gives to all mankind life and breath and everything. [26] And he made from one man every nation of mankind to live on all the face of the earth, having determined allotted periods and the boundaries of their dwelling place, [27] that they should seek God, in the hope that they might feel their way toward him and find him. Yet he is actually not far from each one of us, [28] for

"'In him we live and move and have our being';[3]

as even some of your own poets have said,

"'For we are indeed his offspring.'[4]

[29] Being then God's offspring, we ought not to think that the divine being is like gold or silver or stone, an image formed by the art and imagination of man. [30] The times of ignorance God overlooked, but now he commands all people everywhere to repent, [31] because he has fixed a day on which he will judge the world in righteousness by a man whom he has appointed; and of this he has given assurance to all by raising him from the dead."

[32] Now when they heard of the resurrection of the dead, some mocked. But others said, "We will hear you again about this." [33] So Paul went out from their midst. [34] But some men joined him and believed, among whom also were Dionysius the Areopagite and a woman named Damaris and others with them.

---

[1] Or brothers and sisters; also verse 14 [2] Greek made by hands [3] Probably from Epimenides of Crete [4] From Aratus's poem "Phainomena"

Paul in Corinth

18 After this Paul[1] left Athens and went to Corinth. [2]And he found a Jew named Aquila, a native of Pontus, recently come from Italy with his wife Priscilla, because Claudius had commanded all the Jews to leave Rome. And he went to see them, [3]and because he was of the same trade he stayed with them and worked, for they were tentmakers by trade. [4]And he reasoned in the synagogue every Sabbath, and tried to persuade Jews and Greeks.

[5]When Silas and Timothy arrived from Macedonia, Paul was occupied with the word, testifying to the Jews that the Christ was Jesus. [6]And when they opposed and reviled him, he shook out his garments and said to them, "Your blood be on your own heads! I am innocent. From now on I will go to the Gentiles." [7]And he left there and went to the house of a man named Titius Justus, a worshiper of God. His house was next door to the synagogue. [8]Crispus, the ruler of the synagogue, believed in the Lord, together with his entire household. And many of the Corinthians hearing Paul believed and were baptized. [9]And the Lord said to Paul one night in a vision, "Do not be afraid, but go on speaking and do not be silent, [10]for I am with you, and no one will attack you to harm you, for I have many in this city who are my people." [11]And he stayed a year and six months, teaching the word of God among them.

[12]But when Gallio was proconsul of Achaia, the Jews made a united attack on Paul and brought him before the tribunal, [13]saying, "This man is persuading people to worship God contrary to the law." [14]But when Paul was about to open his mouth, Gallio said to the Jews, "If it were a matter of wrongdoing or vicious crime, O Jews, I would have reason to accept your complaint. [15]But since it is a matter of questions about words and names and your own law, see to it yourselves. I refuse to be a judge of these things." [16]And he drove them from the tribunal. [17]And they all seized Sosthenes, the ruler of the synagogue, and beat him in front of the tribunal. But Gallio paid no attention to any of this.

Paul Returns to Antioch

[18]After this, Paul stayed many days longer and then took leave of the brothers[2] and set sail for Syria, and with him Priscilla and Aquila. At Cenchreae he had cut his hair, for he was under a vow. [19]And they came to Ephesus, and he left them there, but he himself went into the synagogue and reasoned with the Jews. [20]When they asked him to stay for a longer period, he declined. [21]But on taking leave of them he said, "I will return to you if God wills," and he set sail from Ephesus.

[22]When he had landed at Caesarea, he went up and greeted the church, and then went down to Antioch. [23]After spending some time there, he departed and went from one place to the next through the region of Galatia and Phrygia, strengthening all the disciples.

Apollos Speaks Boldly in Ephesus

[24]Now a Jew named Apollos, a native of Alexandria, came to Ephesus. He was an eloquent man, competent in the Scriptures. [25]He had been instructed in the way of the Lord. And being fervent in spirit,[3] he spoke and taught accurately the things concerning Jesus, though he knew only the baptism of John. [26]He began to speak boldly in the synagogue, but when Priscilla and Aquila heard him, they took him and explained to him the way of God more accurately. [27]And when he wished to cross to Achaia, the brothers encouraged him and wrote to the disciples to welcome him. When he arrived, he greatly helped those who through grace had believed, [28]for he powerfully refuted the Jews in public, showing by the Scriptures that the Christ was Jesus.

Paul in Ephesus

19 And it happened that while Apollos was at Corinth, Paul passed through the inland[4] country and came to Ephesus. There he found some disciples. [2]And he said to them, "Did you receive the Holy Spirit when you believed?" And they said, "No, we have not even heard that there is a Holy Spirit." [3]And he said, "Into what then were you baptized?" They said, "Into John's baptism." [4]And Paul said, "John baptized with the baptism of repentance, telling the people to believe in the one who was to come after him, that is, Jesus." [5]On hearing this, they were baptized in[5] the name of the Lord Jesus. [6]And when Paul had laid his hands on them, the Holy Spirit came on them, and they began speaking in tongues and prophesying. [7]There were about twelve men in all.

[8]And he entered the synagogue and for three months spoke boldly, reasoning and persuading them about the kingdom of God. [9]But when some became stubborn and continued in unbelief, speaking evil of the Way before the congregation, he withdrew from them and took the disciples with him, reasoning daily in the hall of Tyrannus.[6] [10]This continued for two years, so that all the residents of Asia heard the word of the Lord, both Jews and Greeks.

The Sons of Sceva

[11]And God was doing extraordinary miracles by the hands of Paul, [12]so that even handkerchiefs or aprons that had touched his skin were carried away to the sick, and their diseases left them and the evil spirits came out of them.

---

[1] Greek *he* [2] Or *brothers and sisters*; also verse 27 [3] Or *in the Spirit* [4] Greek *upper* (that is, highland) [5] Or *into* [6] Some manuscripts add *from the fifth hour to the tenth* (that is, from 11 A.M. to 4 P.M.)

¹³Then some of the itinerant Jewish exorcists undertook to invoke the name of the Lord Jesus over those who had evil spirits, saying, "I adjure you by the Jesus whom Paul proclaims." ¹⁴Seven sons of a Jewish high priest named Sceva were doing this. ¹⁵But the evil spirit answered them, "Jesus I know, and Paul I recognize, but who are you?" ¹⁶And the man in whom was the evil spirit leaped on them, mastered all¹ of them and overpowered them, so that they fled out of that house naked and wounded. ¹⁷And this became known to all the residents of Ephesus, both Jews and Greeks. And fear fell upon them all, and the name of the Lord Jesus was extolled. ¹⁸Also many of those who were now believers came, confessing and divulging their practices. ¹⁹And a number of those who had practiced magic arts brought their books together and burned them in the sight of all. And they counted the value of them and found it came to fifty thousand pieces of silver. ²⁰So the word of the Lord continued to increase and prevail mightily.

A Riot at Ephesus

²¹Now after these events Paul resolved in the Spirit to pass through Macedonia and Achaia and go to Jerusalem, saying, "After I have been there, I must also see Rome." ²²And having sent into Macedonia two of his helpers, Timothy and Erastus, he himself stayed in Asia for a while.

²³About that time there arose no little disturbance concerning the Way. ²⁴For a man named Demetrius, a silversmith, who made silver shrines of Artemis, brought no little business to the craftsmen. ²⁵These he gathered together, with the workmen in similar trades, and said, "Men, you know that from this business we have our wealth. ²⁶And you see and hear that not only in Ephesus but in almost all of Asia this Paul has persuaded and turned away a great many people, saying that gods made with hands are not gods. ²⁷And there is danger not only that this trade of ours may come into disrepute but also that the temple of the great goddess Artemis may be counted as nothing, and that she may even be deposed from her magnificence, she whom all Asia and the world worship."

²⁸When they heard this they were enraged and were crying out, "Great is Artemis of the Ephesians!" ²⁹So the city was filled with the confusion, and they rushed together into the theater, dragging with them Gaius and Aristarchus, Macedonians who were Paul's companions in travel. ³⁰But when Paul wished to go in among the crowd, the disciples would not let him. ³¹And even some of the Asiarchs,² who were friends of his, sent to him and were urging him not to venture into the theater. ³²Now some cried out one thing, some another, for the assembly was in confusion, and most of them did not know why they had come together. ³³Some of the crowd prompted Alexander, whom the Jews had put forward. And Alexander, motioning with his hand, wanted to make a defense to the crowd. ³⁴But when they recognized that he was a Jew, for about two hours they all cried out with one voice, "Great is Artemis of the Ephesians!"

³⁵And when the town clerk had quieted the crowd, he said, "Men of Ephesus, who is there who does not know that the city of the Ephesians is temple keeper of the great Artemis, and of the sacred stone that fell from the sky?³ ³⁶Seeing then that these things cannot be denied, you ought to be quiet and do nothing rash. ³⁷For you have brought these men here who are neither sacrilegious nor blasphemers of our goddess. ³⁸If therefore Demetrius and the craftsmen with him have a complaint against anyone, the courts are open, and there are proconsuls. Let them bring charges against one another. ³⁹But if you seek anything further,⁴ it shall be settled in the regular assembly. ⁴⁰For we really are in danger of being charged with rioting today, since there is no cause that we can give to justify this commotion." ⁴¹And when he had said these things, he dismissed the assembly.

Paul in Macedonia and Greece

20 After the uproar ceased, Paul sent for the disciples, and after encouraging them, he said farewell and departed for Macedonia. ²When he had gone through those regions and had given them much encouragement, he came to Greece. ³There he spent three months, and when a plot was made against him by the Jews as he was about to set sail for Syria, he decided to return through Macedonia. ⁴Sopater the Berean, son of Pyrrhus, accompanied him; and of the Thessalonians, Aristarchus and Secundus; and Gaius of Derbe, and Timothy; and the Asians, Tychicus and Trophimus. ⁵These went on ahead and were waiting for us at Troas, ⁶but we sailed away from Philippi after the days of Unleavened Bread, and in five days we came to them at Troas, where we stayed for seven days.

Eutychus Raised from the Dead

⁷On the first day of the week, when we were gathered together to break bread, Paul talked with them, intending to depart on the next day, and he prolonged his speech until midnight. ⁸There were many lamps in the upper room where we were gathered. ⁹And a young man named Eutychus, sitting at the window, sank into a deep sleep as Paul talked still longer. And being overcome by sleep, he fell down from the third story and was taken up dead. ¹⁰But Paul went down and bent over him, and taking him in his arms, said, "Do not be alarmed, for his life is in him." ¹¹And when Paul had gone up and

---

¹Or *both* ²That is, high-ranking officers of the province of Asia ³The meaning of the Greek is uncertain ⁴Some manuscripts *seek about other matters*

had broken bread and eaten, he conversed with them a long while, until daybreak, and so departed. [12]And they took the youth away alive, and were not a little comforted.

[13]But going ahead to the ship, we set sail for Assos, intending to take Paul aboard there, for so he had arranged, intending himself to go by land. [14]And when he met us at Assos, we took him on board and went to Mitylene. [15]And sailing from there we came the following day opposite Chios; the next day we touched at Samos; and[1] the day after that we went to Miletus. [16]For Paul had decided to sail past Ephesus, so that he might not have to spend time in Asia, for he was hastening to be at Jerusalem, if possible, on the day of Pentecost.

Paul Speaks to the Ephesian Elders

[17]Now from Miletus he sent to Ephesus and called the elders of the church to come to him. [18]And when they came to him, he said to them:

"You yourselves know how I lived among you the whole time from the first day that I set foot in Asia, [19]serving the Lord with all humility and with tears and with trials that happened to me through the plots of the Jews; [20]how I did not shrink from declaring to you anything that was profitable, and teaching you in public and from house to house, [21]testifying both to Jews and to Greeks of repentance toward God and of faith in our Lord Jesus Christ. [22]And now, behold, I am going to Jerusalem, constrained by[2] the Spirit, not knowing what will happen to me there, [23]except that the Holy Spirit testifies to me in every city that imprisonment and afflictions await me. [24]But I do not account my life of any value nor as precious to myself, if only I may finish my course and the ministry that I received from the Lord Jesus, to testify to the gospel of the grace of God. [25]And now, behold, I know that none of you among whom I have gone about proclaiming the kingdom will see my face again. [26]Therefore I testify to you this day that I am innocent of the blood of all of you, [27]for I did not shrink from declaring to you the whole counsel of God. [28]Pay careful attention to yourselves and to all the flock, in which the Holy Spirit has made you overseers, to care for the church of God,[3] which he obtained with his own blood.[4] [29]I know that after my departure fierce wolves will come in among you, not sparing the flock; [30]and from among your own selves will arise men speaking twisted things, to draw away the disciples after them. [31]Therefore be alert, remembering that for three years I did not cease night or day to admonish everyone with tears. [32]And now I commend you to God and to the word of his grace, which is able to build you up and to give you the inheritance among all those who are sanctified. [33]I coveted no one's silver or gold

or apparel. [34]You yourselves know that these hands ministered to my necessities and to those who were with me. [35]In all things I have shown you that by working hard in this way we must help the weak and remember the words of the Lord Jesus, how he himself said, 'It is more blessed to give than to receive.'"

[36]And when he had said these things, he knelt down and prayed with them all. [37]And there was much weeping on the part of all; they embraced Paul and kissed him, [38]being sorrowful most of all because of the word he had spoken, that they would not see his face again. And they accompanied him to the ship.

Paul Goes to Jerusalem

21 And when we had parted from them and set sail, we came by a straight course to Cos, and the next day to Rhodes, and from there to Patara.[5] [2]And having found a ship crossing to Phoenicia, we went aboard and set sail. [3]When we had come in sight of Cyprus, leaving it on the left we sailed to Syria and landed at Tyre, for there the ship was to unload its cargo. [4]And having sought out the disciples, we stayed there for seven days. And through the Spirit they were telling Paul not to go on to Jerusalem. [5]When our days there were ended, we departed and went on our journey, and they all, with wives and children, accompanied us until we were outside the city. And kneeling down on the beach, we prayed [6]and said farewell to one another. Then we went on board the ship, and they returned home.

[7]When we had finished the voyage from Tyre, we arrived at Ptolemais, and we greeted the brothers[6] and stayed with them for one day. [8]On the next day we departed and came to Caesarea, and we entered the house of Philip the evangelist, who was one of the seven, and stayed with him. [9]He had four unmarried daughters, who prophesied. [10]While we were staying for many days, a prophet named Agabus came down from Judea. [11]And coming to us, he took Paul's belt and bound his own feet and hands and said, "Thus says the Holy Spirit, 'This is how the Jews at Jerusalem will bind the man who owns this belt and deliver him into the hands of the Gentiles.'" [12]When we heard this, we and the people there urged him not to go up to Jerusalem. [13]Then Paul answered, "What are you doing, weeping and breaking my heart? For I am ready not only to be imprisoned but even to die in Jerusalem for the name of the Lord Jesus." [14]And since he would not be persuaded, we ceased and said, "Let the will of the Lord be done."

[15]After these days we got ready and went up to Jerusalem. [16]And some of the disciples from Caesarea went with us, bringing us to the house of Mnason of Cyprus, an early disciple, with whom we should lodge.

---

[1] Some manuscripts add *after remaining at Trogyllium* [2] Or *bound in* [3] Some manuscripts *of the Lord* [4] Or *with the blood of his Own* [5] Some manuscripts add *and Myra* [6] Or *brothers and sisters*; also verse 17

Paul Visits James

17When we had come to Jerusalem, the brothers received us gladly. **18**On the following day Paul went in with us to James, and all the elders were present. **19**After greeting them, he related one by one the things that God had done among the Gentiles through his ministry. **20**And when they heard it, they glorified God. And they said to him, "You see, brother, how many thousands there are among the Jews of those who have believed. They are all zealous for the law, **21**and they have been told about you that you teach all the Jews who are among the Gentiles to forsake Moses, telling them not to circumcise their children or walk according to our customs. **22**What then is to be done? They will certainly hear that you have come. **23**Do therefore what we tell you. We have four men who are under a vow; **24**take these men and purify yourself along with them and pay their expenses, so that they may shave their heads. Thus all will know that there is nothing in what they have been told about you, but that you yourself also live in observance of the law. **25**But as for the Gentiles who have believed, we have sent a letter with our judgment that they should abstain from what has been sacrificed to idols, and from blood, and from what has been strangled,[1] and from sexual immorality." **26**Then Paul took the men, and the next day he purified himself along with them and went into the temple, giving notice when the days of purification would be fulfilled and the offering presented for each one of them.

Paul Arrested in the Temple

27When the seven days were almost completed, the Jews from Asia, seeing him in the temple, stirred up the whole crowd and laid hands on him, **28**crying out, "Men of Israel, help! This is the man who is teaching everyone everywhere against the people and the law and this place. Moreover, he even brought Greeks into the temple and has defiled this holy place." **29**For they had previously seen Trophimus the Ephesian with him in the city, and they supposed that Paul had brought him into the temple. **30**Then all the city was stirred up, and the people ran together. They seized Paul and dragged him out of the temple, and at once the gates were shut. **31**And as they were seeking to kill him, word came to the tribune of the cohort that all Jerusalem was in confusion. **32**He at once took soldiers and centurions and ran down to them. And when they saw the tribune and the soldiers, they stopped beating Paul. **33**Then the tribune came up and arrested him and ordered him to be bound with two chains. He inquired who he was and what he had done. **34**Some in the crowd were shouting one thing, some another. And as

he could not learn the facts because of the uproar, he ordered him to be brought into the barracks. **35**And when he came to the steps, he was actually carried by the soldiers because of the violence of the crowd, **36**for the mob of the people followed, crying out, "Away with him!"

Paul Speaks to the People

37As Paul was about to be brought into the barracks, he said to the tribune, "May I say something to you?" And he said, "Do you know Greek? **38**Are you not the Egyptian, then, who recently stirred up a revolt and led the four thousand men of the Assassins out into the wilderness?" **39**Paul replied, "I am a Jew, from Tarsus in Cilicia, a citizen of no obscure city. I beg you, permit me to speak to the people." **40**And when he had given him permission, Paul, standing on the steps, motioned with his hand to the people. And when there was a great hush, he addressed them in the Hebrew language,[2] saying:

22 "Brothers and fathers, hear the defense that I now make before you."

2And when they heard that he was addressing them in the Hebrew language, they became even more quiet. And he said:

3"I am a Jew, born in Tarsus in Cilicia, but brought up in this city, educated at the feet of Gamaliel[3] according to the strict manner of the law of our fathers, being zealous for God as all of you are this day. **4**I persecuted this Way to the death, binding and delivering to prison both men and women, **5**as the high priest and the whole council of elders can bear me witness. From them I received letters to the brothers, and I journeyed toward Damascus to take those also who were there and bring them in bonds to Jerusalem to be punished.

6"As I was on my way and drew near to Damascus, about noon a great light from heaven suddenly shone around me. **7**And I fell to the ground and heard a voice saying to me, 'Saul, Saul, why are you persecuting me?' **8**And I answered, 'Who are you, Lord?' And he said to me, 'I am Jesus of Nazareth, whom you are persecuting.' **9**Now those who were with me saw the light but did not understand[4] the voice of the one who was speaking to me. **10**And I said, 'What shall I do, Lord?' And the Lord said to me, 'Rise, and go into Damascus, and there you will be told all that is appointed for you to do.' **11**And since I could not see because of the brightness of that light, I was led by the hand by those who were with me, and came into Damascus.

12"And one Ananias, a devout man according to the law, well spoken of by all the Jews who lived there, **13**came to me, and standing by me said to me, 'Brother Saul, receive your sight.' And at that very hour I received my sight and saw him. **14**And he said, 'The God of our fathers

[1] Some manuscripts omit *and from what has been strangled* [2] Or *the Hebrew dialect (that is, Aramaic)*; also 22:2 [3] Or *city at the feet of Gamaliel, educated* [4] Or *hear with understanding*

appointed you to know his will, to see the Righteous One and to hear a voice from his mouth; [15]for you will be a witness for him to everyone of what you have seen and heard. [16]And now why do you wait? Rise and be baptized and wash away your sins, calling on his name.'

[17]"When I had returned to Jerusalem and was praying in the temple, I fell into a trance [18]and saw him saying to me, 'Make haste and get out of Jerusalem quickly, because they will not accept your testimony about me.' [19]And I said, 'Lord, they themselves know that in one synagogue after another I imprisoned and beat those who believed in you. [20]And when the blood of Stephen your witness was being shed, I myself was standing by and approving and watching over the garments of those who killed him.' [21]And he said to me, 'Go, for I will send you far away to the Gentiles.'"

Paul and the Roman Tribune

[22]Up to this word they listened to him. Then they raised their voices and said, "Away with such a fellow from the earth! For he should not be allowed to live." [23]And as they were shouting and throwing off their cloaks and flinging dust into the air, [24]the tribune ordered him to be brought into the barracks, saying that he should be examined by flogging, to find out why they were shouting against him like this. [25]But when they had stretched him out for the whips,[1] Paul said to the centurion who was standing by, "Is it lawful for you to flog a man who is a Roman citizen and uncondemned?" [26]When the centurion heard this, he went to the tribune and said to him, "What are you about to do? For this man is a Roman citizen." [27]So the tribune came and said to him, "Tell me, are you a Roman citizen?" And he said, "Yes." [28]The tribune answered, "I bought this citizenship for a large sum." Paul said, "But I am a citizen by birth." [29]So those who were about to examine him withdrew from him immediately, and the tribune also was afraid, for he realized that Paul was a Roman citizen and that he had bound him.

Paul Before the Council

[30]But on the next day, desiring to know the real reason why he was being accused by the Jews, he unbound him and commanded the chief priests and all the council to meet, and he brought Paul down and set him before them.

23 And looking intently at the council, Paul said, "Brothers, I have lived my life before God in all good conscience up to this day." [2]And the high priest Ananias commanded those who stood by him to strike him on the mouth. [3]Then Paul said to him, "God is going to strike you, you whitewashed wall! Are you sitting to judge me according to the law, and yet contrary to the law

you order me to be struck?" [4]Those who stood by said, "Would you revile God's high priest?" [5]And Paul said, "I did not know, brothers, that he was the high priest, for it is written, "'You shall not speak evil of a ruler of your people.'"

[6]Now when Paul perceived that one part were Sadducees and the other Pharisees, he cried out in the council, "Brothers, I am a Pharisee, a son of Pharisees. It is with respect to the hope and the resurrection of the dead that I am on trial." [7]And when he had said this, a dissension arose between the Pharisees and the Sadducees, and the assembly was divided. [8]For the Sadducees say that there is no resurrection, nor angel, nor spirit, but the Pharisees acknowledge them all. [9]Then a great clamor arose, and some of the scribes of the Pharisees' party stood up and contended sharply, "We find nothing wrong in this man. What if a spirit or an angel spoke to him?" [10]And when the dissension became violent, the tribune, afraid that Paul would be torn to pieces by them, commanded the soldiers to go down and take him away from among them by force and bring him into the barracks.

[11]The following night the Lord stood by him and said, "Take courage, for as you have testified to the facts about me in Jerusalem, so you must testify also in Rome."

A Plot to Kill Paul

[12]When it was day, the Jews made a plot and bound themselves by an oath neither to eat nor drink till they had killed Paul. [13]There were more than forty who made this conspiracy. [14]They went to the chief priests and elders and said, "We have strictly bound ourselves by an oath to taste no food till we have killed Paul. [15]Now therefore you, along with the council, give notice to the tribune to bring him down to you, as though you were going to determine his case more exactly. And we are ready to kill him before he comes near."

[16]Now the son of Paul's sister heard of their ambush, so he went and entered the barracks and told Paul. [17]Paul called one of the centurions and said, "Take this young man to the tribune, for he has something to tell him." [18]So he took him and brought him to the tribune and said, "Paul the prisoner called me and asked me to bring this young man to you, as he has something to say to you." [19]The tribune took him by the hand, and going aside asked him privately, "What is it that you have to tell me?" [20]And he said, "The Jews have agreed to ask you to bring Paul down to the council tomorrow, as though they were going to inquire somewhat more closely about him. [21]But do not be persuaded by them, for more than forty of their men are lying in ambush for him, who have bound themselves by an oath neither to eat nor drink till

[1] Or when they had tied him up with leather strips   a Ex. 22:28

they have killed him. And now they are ready, waiting for your consent." [22]So the tribune dismissed the young man, charging him, "Tell no one that you have informed me of these things."

Paul Sent to Felix the Governor

[23]Then he called two of the centurions and said, "Get ready two hundred soldiers, with seventy horsemen and two hundred spearmen to go as far as Caesarea at the third hour of the night.[1] [24]Also provide mounts for Paul to ride and bring him safely to Felix the governor." [25]And he wrote a letter to this effect:

[26]"Claudius Lysias, to his Excellency the governor Felix, greetings. [27]This man was seized by the Jews and was about to be killed by them when I came upon them with the soldiers and rescued him, having learned that he was a Roman citizen. [28]And desiring to know the charge for which they were accusing him, I brought him down to their council. [29]I found that he was being accused about questions of their law, but charged with nothing deserving death or imprisonment. [30]And when it was disclosed to me that there would be a plot against the man, I sent him to you at once, ordering his accusers also to state before you what they have against him."

[31]So the soldiers, according to their instructions, took Paul and brought him by night to Antipatris. [32]And on the next day they returned to the barracks, letting the horsemen go on with him. [33]When they had come to Caesarea and delivered the letter to the governor, they presented Paul also before him. [34]On reading the letter, he asked what province he was from. And when he learned that he was from Cilicia, [35]he said, "I will give you a hearing when your accusers arrive." And he commanded him to be guarded in Herod's praetorium.

Paul Before Felix at Caesarea

24 And after five days the high priest Ananias came down with some elders and a spokesman, one Tertullus. They laid before the governor their case against Paul. [2]And when he had been summoned, Tertullus began to accuse him, saying:

"Since through you we enjoy much peace, and since by your foresight, most excellent Felix, reforms are being made for this nation, [3]in every way and everywhere we accept this with all gratitude. [4]But, to detain[2] you no further, I beg you in your kindness to hear us briefly. [5]For we have found this man a plague, one who stirs up riots among all the Jews throughout the world and is a ringleader of the sect of the Nazarenes. [6]He even tried to profane the temple, but we

seized him.[3] [8]By examining him yourself you will be able to find out from him about everything of which we accuse him."

[9]The Jews also joined in the charge, affirming that all these things were so.

[10]And when the governor had nodded to him to speak, Paul replied:

"Knowing that for many years you have been a judge over this nation, I cheerfully make my defense. [11]You can verify that it is not more than twelve days since I went up to worship in Jerusalem, [12]and they did not find me disputing with anyone or stirring up a crowd, either in the temple or in the synagogues or in the city. [13]Neither can they prove to you what they now bring up against me. [14]But this I confess to you, that according to the Way, which they call a sect, I worship the God of our fathers, believing everything laid down by the Law and written in the Prophets, [15]having a hope in God, which these men themselves accept, that there will be a resurrection of both the just and the unjust. [16]So I always take pains to have a clear conscience toward both God and man. [17]Now after several years I came to bring alms to my nation and to present offerings. [18]While I was doing this, they found me purified in the temple, without any crowd or tumult. But some Jews from Asia— [19]they ought to be here before you and to make an accusation, should they have anything against me. [20]Or else let these men themselves say what wrongdoing they found when I stood before the council, [21]other than this one thing that I cried out while standing among them: 'It is with respect to the resurrection of the dead that I am on trial before you this day.'"

Paul Kept in Custody

[22]But Felix, having a rather accurate knowledge of the Way, put them off, saying, "When Lysias the tribune comes down, I will decide your case." [23]Then he gave orders to the centurion that he should be kept in custody but have some liberty, and that none of his friends should be prevented from attending to his needs.

[24]After some days Felix came with his wife Drusilla, who was Jewish, and he sent for Paul and heard him speak about faith in Christ Jesus. [25]And as he reasoned about righteousness and self-control and the coming judgment, Felix was alarmed and said, "Go away for the present. When I get an opportunity I will summon you." [26]At the same time he hoped that money would be given him by Paul. So he sent for him often and conversed with him. [27]When two years had elapsed, Felix was succeeded by Porcius Festus. And desiring to do the Jews a favor, Felix left Paul in prison.

---

[1] That is, 9 P.M. [2] Or weary [3] Some manuscripts add and we would have judged him according to our law. [7]But the chief captain Lysias came and with great violence took him out of our hands, [8]commanding his accusers to come before you.

Paul Appeals to Caesar

25 Now three days after Festus had arrived in the province, he went up to Jerusalem from Caesarea. ²And the chief priests and the principal men of the Jews laid out their case against Paul, and they urged him, ³asking as a favor against Paul[1] that he summon him to Jerusalem—because they were planning an ambush to kill him on the way. ⁴Festus replied that Paul was being kept at Caesarea and that he himself intended to go there shortly. ⁵"So," said he, "let the men of authority among you go down with me, and if there is anything wrong about the man, let them bring charges against him."

⁶After he stayed among them not more than eight or ten days, he went down to Caesarea. And the next day he took his seat on the tribunal and ordered Paul to be brought. ⁷When he had arrived, the Jews who had come down from Jerusalem stood around him, bringing many and serious charges against him that they could not prove. ⁸Paul argued in his defense, "Neither against the law of the Jews, nor against the temple, nor against Caesar have I committed any offense." ⁹But Festus, wishing to do the Jews a favor, said to Paul, "Do you wish to go up to Jerusalem and there be tried on these charges before me?" ¹⁰But Paul said, "I am standing before Caesar's tribunal, where I ought to be tried. To the Jews I have done no wrong, as you yourself know very well. ¹¹If then I am a wrongdoer and have committed anything for which I deserve to die, I do not seek to escape death. But if there is nothing to their charges against me, no one can give me up to them. I appeal to Caesar." ¹²Then Festus, when he had conferred with his council, answered, "To Caesar you have appealed; to Caesar you shall go."

Paul Before Agrippa and Bernice

¹³Now when some days had passed, Agrippa the king and Bernice arrived at Caesarea and greeted Festus. ¹⁴And as they stayed there many days, Festus laid Paul's case before the king, saying, "There is a man left prisoner by Felix, ¹⁵and when I was at Jerusalem, the chief priests and the elders of the Jews laid out their case against him, asking for a sentence of condemnation against him. ¹⁶I answered them that it was not the custom of the Romans to give up anyone before the accused met the accusers face to face and had opportunity to make his defense concerning the charge laid against him. ¹⁷So when they came together here, I made no delay, but on the next day took my seat on the tribunal and ordered the man to be brought. ¹⁸When the accusers stood up, they brought no charge in his case of such evils as I supposed. ¹⁹Rather they had certain points of dispute with him about their own religion and about a certain Jesus, who was dead, but whom Paul asserted to be alive. ²⁰Being at a loss how to investigate these questions, I asked whether he wanted to go to Jerusalem and be tried there regarding them. ²¹But when Paul had appealed to be kept in custody for the decision of the emperor, I ordered him to be held until I could send him to Caesar." ²²Then Agrippa said to Festus, "I would like to hear the man myself." "Tomorrow," said he, "you will hear him."

²³So on the next day Agrippa and Bernice came with great pomp, and they entered the audience hall with the military tribunes and the prominent men of the city. Then, at the command of Festus, Paul was brought in. ²⁴And Festus said, "King Agrippa and all who are present with us, you see this man about whom the whole Jewish people petitioned me, both in Jerusalem and here, shouting that he ought not to live any longer. ²⁵But I found that he had done nothing deserving death. And as he himself appealed to the emperor, I decided to go ahead and send him. ²⁶But I have nothing definite to write to my lord about him. Therefore I have brought him before you all, and especially before you, King Agrippa, so that, after we have examined him, I may have something to write. ²⁷For it seems to me unreasonable, in sending a prisoner, not to indicate the charges against him."

Paul's Defense Before Agrippa

26 So Agrippa said to Paul, "You have permission to speak for yourself." Then Paul stretched out his hand and made his defense:

²"I consider myself fortunate that it is before you, King Agrippa, I am going to make my defense today against all the accusations of the Jews, ³especially because you are familiar with all the customs and controversies of the Jews. Therefore I beg you to listen to me patiently. ⁴"My manner of life from my youth, spent from the beginning among my own nation and in Jerusalem, is known by all the Jews. ⁵They have known for a long time, if they are willing to testify, that according to the strictest party of our religion I have lived as a Pharisee. ⁶And now I stand here on trial because of my hope in the promise made by God to our fathers, ⁷to which our twelve tribes hope to attain, as they earnestly worship night and day. And for this hope I am accused by Jews, O king! ⁸Why is it thought incredible by any of you that God raises the dead?

⁹"I myself was convinced that I ought to do many things in opposing the name of Jesus of Nazareth. ¹⁰And I did so in Jerusalem. I not only locked up many of the saints in prison after receiving authority from the chief priests, but when they were put to death I cast my vote against them. ¹¹And I punished them often in all

[1] Greek him

the synagogues and tried to make them blaspheme, and in raging fury against them I persecuted them even to foreign cities.

Paul Tells of His Conversion

[12]"In this connection I journeyed to Damascus with the authority and commission of the chief priests. [13]At midday, O king, I saw on the way a light from heaven, brighter than the sun, that shone around me and those who journeyed with me. [14]And when we had all fallen to the ground, I heard a voice saying to me in the Hebrew language,[1] 'Saul, Saul, why are you persecuting me? It is hard for you to kick against the goads.' [15]And I said, 'Who are you, Lord?' And the Lord said, 'I am Jesus whom you are persecuting. [16]But rise and stand upon your feet, for I have appeared to you for this purpose, to appoint you as a servant and witness to the things in which you have seen me and to those in which I will appear to you, [17]delivering you from your people and from the Gentiles—to whom I am sending you [18]to open their eyes, so that they may turn from darkness to light and from the power of Satan to God, that they may receive forgiveness of sins and a place among those who are sanctified by faith in me.'

[19]"Therefore, O King Agrippa, I was not disobedient to the heavenly vision, [20]but declared first to those in Damascus, then in Jerusalem and throughout all the region of Judea, and also to the Gentiles, that they should repent and turn to God, performing deeds in keeping with their repentance. [21]For this reason the Jews seized me in the temple and tried to kill me. [22]To this day I have had the help that comes from God, and so I stand here testifying both to small and great, saying nothing but what the prophets and Moses said would come to pass: [23]that the Christ must suffer and that, by being the first to rise from the dead, he would proclaim light both to our people and to the Gentiles."

[24]And as he was saying these things in his defense, Festus said with a loud voice, "Paul, you are out of your mind; your great learning is driving you out of your mind." [25]But Paul said, "I am not out of my mind, most excellent Festus, but I am speaking true and rational words. [26]For the king knows about these things, and to him I speak boldly. For I am persuaded that none of these things has escaped his notice, for this has not been done in a corner. [27]King Agrippa, do you believe the prophets? I know that you believe." [28]And Agrippa said to Paul, "In a short time would you persuade me to be a Christian?"[2] [29]And Paul said, "Whether short or long, I would to God that not only you but also all who hear me this day might become such as I am—except for these chains."

[30]Then the king rose, and the governor and

Bernice and those who were sitting with them. [31]And when they had withdrawn, they said to one another, "This man is doing nothing to deserve death or imprisonment." [32]And Agrippa said to Festus, "This man could have been set free if he had not appealed to Caesar."

Paul Sails for Rome

27 And when it was decided that we should sail for Italy, they delivered Paul and some other prisoners to a centurion of the Augustan Cohort named Julius. [2]And embarking in a ship of Adramyttium, which was about to sail to the ports along the coast of Asia, we put to sea, accompanied by Aristarchus, a Macedonian from Thessalonica. [3]The next day we put in at Sidon. And Julius treated Paul kindly and gave him leave to go to his friends and be cared for. [4]And putting out to sea from there we sailed under the lee of Cyprus, because the winds were against us. [5]And when we had sailed across the open sea along the coast of Cilicia and Pamphylia, we came to Myra in Lycia. [6]There the centurion found a ship of Alexandria sailing for Italy and put us on board. [7]We sailed slowly for a number of days and arrived with difficulty off Cnidus, and as the wind did not allow us to go farther, we sailed under the lee of Crete off Salmone. [8]Coasting along it with difficulty, we came to a place called Fair Havens, near which was the city of Lasea.

[9]Since much time had passed, and the voyage was now dangerous because even the Fast[3] was already over, Paul advised them, [10]saying, "Sirs, I perceive that the voyage will be with injury and much loss, not only of the cargo and the ship, but also of our lives." [11]But the centurion paid more attention to the pilot and to the owner of the ship than to what Paul said. [12]And because the harbor was not suitable to spend the winter in, the majority decided to put out to sea from there, on the chance that somehow they could reach Phoenix, a harbor of Crete, facing both southwest and northwest, and spend the winter there.

The Storm at Sea

[13]Now when the south wind blew gently, supposing that they had obtained their purpose, they weighed anchor and sailed along Crete, close to the shore. [14]But soon a tempestuous wind, called the northeaster, struck down from the land. [15]And when the ship was caught and could not face the wind, we gave way to it and were driven along. [16]Running under the lee of a small island called Cauda,[4] we managed with difficulty to secure the ship's boat. [17]After hoisting it up, they used supports to undergird the ship. Then, fearing that they would run aground on the Syrtis, they lowered the gear,[5] and thus they were driven along. [18]Since we were violently

[1] Or the Hebrew dialect (that is, Aramaic) [2] Or In a short time you would persuade me to act like a Christian! [3] That is, the Day of Atonement [4] Some manuscripts Clauda [5] That is, the sea-anchor (or possibly the mainsail)

storm-tossed, they began the next day to jettison the cargo. **19** And on the third day they threw the ship's tackle overboard with their own hands. **20** When neither sun nor stars appeared for many days, and no small tempest lay on us, all hope of our being saved was at last abandoned.

21 Since they had been without food for a long time, Paul stood up among them and said, "Men, you should have listened to me and not have set sail from Crete and incurred this injury and loss. **22** Yet now I urge you to take heart, for there will be no loss of life among you, but only of the ship. **23** For this very night there stood before me an angel of the God to whom I belong and whom I worship, **24** and he said, 'Do not be afraid, Paul; you must stand before Caesar. And behold, God has granted you all those who sail with you.' **25** So take heart, men, for I have faith in God that it will be exactly as I have been told. **26** But we must run aground on some island."

27 When the fourteenth night had come, as we were being driven across the Adriatic Sea, about midnight the sailors suspected that they were nearing land. **28** So they took a sounding and found twenty fathoms.[1] A little farther on they took a sounding again and found fifteen fathoms.[2] **29** And fearing that we might run on the rocks, they let down four anchors from the stern and prayed for day to come. **30** And as the sailors were seeking to escape from the ship, and had lowered the ship's boat into the sea under pretense of laying out anchors from the bow, **31** Paul said to the centurion and the soldiers, "Unless these men stay in the ship, you cannot be saved." **32** Then the soldiers cut away the ropes of the ship's boat and let it go.

33 As day was about to dawn, Paul urged them all to take some food, saying, "Today is the fourteenth day that you have continued in suspense and without food, having taken nothing. **34** Therefore I urge you to take some food. For it will give you strength, for not a hair is to perish from the head of any of you." **35** And when he had said these things, he took bread, and giving thanks to God in the presence of all he broke it and began to eat. **36** Then they all were encouraged and ate some food themselves. **37** (We were in all 276[3] persons in the ship.) **38** And when they had eaten enough, they lightened the ship, throwing out the wheat into the sea.

The Shipwreck

39 Now when it was day, they did not recognize the land, but they noticed a bay with a beach, on which they planned if possible to run the ship ashore. **40** So they cast off the anchors and left them in the sea, at the same time loosening the ropes that tied the rudders. Then hoisting the foresail to the wind they made for the beach.

41 But striking a reef,[4] they ran the vessel aground. The bow stuck and remained immovable, and the stern was being broken up by the surf. **42** The soldiers' plan was to kill the prisoners, lest any should swim away and escape. **43** But the centurion, wishing to save Paul, kept them from carrying out their plan. He ordered those who could swim to jump overboard first and make for the land, **44** and the rest on planks or on pieces of the ship. And so it was that all were brought safely to land.

Paul on Malta

28 After we were brought safely through, we then learned that the island was called Malta. **2** The native people[5] showed us unusual kindness, for they kindled a fire and welcomed us all, because it had begun to rain and was cold. **3** When Paul had gathered a bundle of sticks and put them on the fire, a viper came out because of the heat and fastened on his hand. **4** When the native people saw the creature hanging from his hand, they said to one another, "No doubt this man is a murderer. Though he has escaped from the sea, Justice[6] has not allowed him to live." **5** He, however, shook off the creature into the fire and suffered no harm. **6** They were waiting for him to swell up or suddenly fall down dead. But when they had waited a long time and saw no misfortune come to him, they changed their minds and said that he was a god.

7 Now in the neighborhood of that place were lands belonging to the chief man of the island, named Publius, who received us and entertained us hospitably for three days. **8** It happened that the father of Publius lay sick with fever and dysentery. And Paul visited him and prayed, and putting his hands on him healed him. **9** And when this had taken place, the rest of the people on the island who had diseases also came and were cured. **10** They also honored us greatly,[7] and when we were about to sail, they put on board whatever we needed.

Paul Arrives at Rome

11 After three months we set sail in a ship that had wintered in the island, a ship of Alexandria, with the twin gods[8] as a figurehead. **12** Putting in at Syracuse, we stayed there for three days. **13** And from there we made a circuit and arrived at Rhegium. And after one day a south wind sprang up, and on the second day we came to Puteoli. **14** There we found brothers[9] and were invited to stay with them for seven days. And so we came to Rome. **15** And the brothers there, when they heard about us, came as far as the Forum of Appius and Three Taverns to meet us. On seeing them, Paul thanked God and took courage. **16** And when we came into Rome, Paul

---

[1] About 120 feet; a fathom (Greek *orguia*) was about 6 feet or 2 meters [2] About 90 feet (see previous note) [3] Some manuscripts *seventy-six,* or *about seventy-six* [4] Or *sandbank,* or *crosscurrent*; Greek *place between two seas* [5] Greek *barbaroi* (that is, non–Greek speakers); also verse 4 [6] Or *justice* [7] Greek *honored us with many honors* [8] That is, the Greek gods Castor and Pollux [9] Or *brothers and sisters*; also verses 15, 21

was allowed to stay by himself, with the soldier that guarded him.

Paul in Rome

17After three days he called together the local leaders of the Jews, and when they had gathered, he said to them, "Brothers, though I had done nothing against our people or the customs of our fathers, yet I was delivered as a prisoner from Jerusalem into the hands of the Romans. **18**When they had examined me, they wished to set me at liberty, because there was no reason for the death penalty in my case. **19**But because the Jews objected, I was compelled to appeal to Caesar—though I had no charge to bring against my nation. **20**For this reason, therefore, I have asked to see you and speak with you, since it is because of the hope of Israel that I am wearing this chain." **21**And they said to him, "We have received no letters from Judea about you, and none of the brothers coming here has reported or spoken any evil about you. **22**But we desire to hear from you what your views are, for with regard to this sect we know that everywhere it is spoken against."

23When they had appointed a day for him, they came to him at his lodging in greater numbers. From morning till evening he expounded to them, testifying to the kingdom of God and trying to convince them about Jesus both from the Law of Moses and from the Prophets. **24**And some were convinced by what he said, but others disbelieved. **25**And disagreeing among themselves, they departed after Paul had made one statement: "The Holy Spirit was right in saying to your fathers through Isaiah the prophet:

26ª "'Go to this people, and say,
You will indeed hear but never understand,
    and you will indeed see but never perceive.
27   For this people's heart has grown dull,
    and with their ears they can barely hear,
    and their eyes they have closed;
lest they should see with their eyes
    and hear with their ears
and understand with their heart
    and turn, and I would heal them.'

28Therefore let it be known to you that this salvation of God has been sent to the Gentiles; they will listen."[1]

30He lived there two whole years at his own expense,[2] and welcomed all who came to him, **31**proclaiming the kingdom of God and teaching about the Lord Jesus Christ with all boldness and without hindrance.

---

[1] Some manuscripts add verse 29: *And when he had said these words, the Jews departed, having much dispute among themselves* [2] Or *in his own hired dwelling* ª Isa. 6:9, 10

ROMANS

Introduction

Romans is the longest and most systematically reasoned of Paul's letters. Paul announces its theme in 1:16-17: the gospel is God's power for salvation, because it shows us that the righteousness of God is through faith for all who believe. Paul explains the need for justification through faith because of sin (1:16–4:25). He then spells out the results of justification by faith in terms of both present experience and future hope (5:1–8:39). In the next three chapters, he expresses his sorrow that many of his fellow Israelites have not embraced the gospel, and he wrestles with the theological implications of this (chs. 9–11). He concludes by describing how the gospel should affect one's everyday life (chs. 12–16). Paul wrote his letter to Rome in about A.D. 57.

Greeting

1 Paul, a servant[1] of Christ Jesus, called to be an apostle, set apart for the gospel of God, ²which he promised beforehand through his prophets in the holy Scriptures, ³concerning his Son, who was descended from David[2] according to the flesh ⁴and was declared to be the Son of God in power according to the Spirit of holiness by his resurrection from the dead, Jesus Christ our Lord, ⁵through whom we have received grace and apostleship to bring about the obedience of faith for the sake of his name among all the nations, ⁶including you who are called to belong to Jesus Christ,

⁷To all those in Rome who are loved by God and called to be saints:

Grace to you and peace from God our Father and the Lord Jesus Christ.

Longing to Go to Rome

⁸First, I thank my God through Jesus Christ for all of you, because your faith is proclaimed in all the world. ⁹For God is my witness, whom I serve with my spirit in the gospel of his Son, that without ceasing I mention you ¹⁰always in my prayers, asking that somehow by God's will I may now at last succeed in coming to you. ¹¹For I long to see you, that I may impart to you some spiritual gift to strengthen you— ¹²that is, that we may be mutually encouraged by each other's faith, both yours and mine. ¹³I want you to know, brothers,[3] that I have often intended to come to you (but thus far have been prevented), in order that I may reap some harvest among you as well as among the rest of the Gentiles. ¹⁴I am under obligation both to Greeks and to barbarians,[4] both to the wise and to the foolish. ¹⁵So I am eager to preach the gospel to you also who are in Rome.

The Righteous Shall Live by Faith

¹⁶For I am not ashamed of the gospel, for it is the power of God for salvation to everyone who believes, to the Jew first and also to the Greek. ¹⁷For in it the righteousness of God is revealed from faith for faith,[5] ªas it is written, "The righteous shall live by faith."[6]

God's Wrath on Unrighteousness

¹⁸For the wrath of God is revealed from heaven against all ungodliness and unrighteousness of men, who by their unrighteousness suppress the truth. ¹⁹For what can be known about God is plain to them, because God has shown it to them. ²⁰For his invisible attributes, namely, his eternal power and divine nature, have been clearly perceived, ever since the creation of the world, in the things that have been made. So they are without excuse. ²¹For although they knew God, they did not honor him as God or give thanks to him, but they became futile in their thinking, and their foolish hearts were darkened. ²²Claiming to be wise, they became fools, ²³and exchanged the glory of the immortal God for images resembling mortal man and birds and animals and creeping things.

²⁴Therefore God gave them up in the lusts of their hearts to impurity, to the dishonoring of their bodies among themselves, ²⁵because they exchanged the truth about God for a lie and worshiped and served the creature rather than the Creator, who is blessed forever! Amen.

²⁶For this reason God gave them up to dishonorable passions. For their women exchanged natural relations for those that are contrary to nature; ²⁷and the men likewise gave up natural relations with women and were consumed with passion for one another, men committing shameless acts with men and receiving in themselves the due penalty for their error.

²⁸And since they did not see fit to acknowledge God, God gave them up to a debased mind to do what ought not to be done. ²⁹They were filled with all manner of unrighteousness, evil, covetousness, malice. They are full of envy,

---

[1] Or slave; Greek bondservant [2] Or who came from the offspring of David [3] Or brothers and sisters. The plural Greek word adelphoi (translated "brothers") refers to siblings in a family. In New Testament usage, depending on the context, adelphoi may refer either to men or to both men and women who are siblings (brothers and sisters) in God's family, the church [4] That is, non-Greeks [5] Or beginning and ending in faith [6] Or The one who by faith is righteous shall live ª Hab. 2:4

murder, strife, deceit, maliciousness. They are gossips, [30]slanderers, haters of God, insolent, haughty, boastful, inventors of evil, disobedient to parents, [31]foolish, faithless, heartless, ruthless. [32]Though they know God's decree that those who practice such things deserve to die, they not only do them but give approval to those who practice them.

God's Righteous Judgment

2 Therefore you have no excuse, O man, every one of you who judges. For in passing judgment on another you condemn yourself, because you, the judge, practice the very same things. [2]We know that the judgment of God rightly falls on those who practice such things. [3]Do you suppose, O man—you who judge those who practice such things and yet do them yourself—that you will escape the judgment of God? [4]Or do you presume on the riches of his kindness and forbearance and patience, not knowing that God's kindness is meant to lead you to repentance? [5]But because of your hard and impenitent heart you are storing up wrath for yourself on the day of wrath when God's righteous judgment will be revealed.

[6]He will render to each one according to his works: [7]to those who by patience in well-doing seek for glory and honor and immortality, he will give eternal life; [8]but for those who are self-seeking[1] and do not obey the truth, but obey unrighteousness, there will be wrath and fury. [9]There will be tribulation and distress for every human being who does evil, the Jew first and also the Greek, [10]but glory and honor and peace for everyone who does good, the Jew first and also the Greek. [11]For God shows no partiality.

God's Judgment and the Law

[12]For all who have sinned without the law will also perish without the law, and all who have sinned under the law will be judged by the law. [13]For it is not the hearers of the law who are righteous before God, but the doers of the law who will be justified. [14]For when Gentiles, who do not have the law, by nature do what the law requires, they are a law to themselves, even though they do not have the law. [15]They show that the work of the law is written on their hearts, while their conscience also bears witness, and their conflicting thoughts accuse or even excuse them [16]on that day when, according to my gospel, God judges the secrets of men by Christ Jesus.

[17]But if you call yourself a Jew and rely on the law and boast in God [18]and know his will and approve what is excellent, because you are instructed from the law; [19]and if you are sure that you yourself are a guide to the blind, a light to those who are in darkness, [20]an instructor of the foolish, a teacher of children, having in the law the embodiment of knowledge and truth— [21]you then who teach others, do you not teach yourself? While you preach against stealing, do you steal? [22]You who say that one must not commit adultery, do you commit adultery? You who abhor idols, do you rob temples? [23]You who boast in the law dishonor God by breaking the law. [24]For, [a]as it is written, "The name of God is blasphemed among the Gentiles because of you."

[25]For circumcision indeed is of value if you obey the law, but if you break the law, your circumcision becomes uncircumcision. [26]So, if a man who is uncircumcised keeps the precepts of the law, will not his uncircumcision be regarded[2] as circumcision? [27]Then he who is physically uncircumcised but keeps the law will condemn you who have the written code[3] and circumcision but break the law. [28]For no one is a Jew who is merely one outwardly, nor is circumcision outward and physical. [29]But a Jew is one inwardly, and circumcision is a matter of the heart, by the Spirit, not by the letter. His praise is not from man but from God.

God's Righteousness Upheld

3 Then what advantage has the Jew? Or what is the value of circumcision? [2]Much in every way. To begin with, the Jews were entrusted with the oracles of God. [3]What if some were unfaithful? Does their faithlessness nullify the faithfulness of God? [4]By no means! Let God be true though every one were a liar, as it is written,

[b]"That you may be justified in your words,
    and prevail when you are judged."

[5]But if our unrighteousness serves to show the righteousness of God, what shall we say? That God is unrighteous to inflict wrath on us? (I speak in a human way.) [6]By no means! For then how could God judge the world? [7]But if through my lie God's truth abounds to his glory, why am I still being condemned as a sinner? [8]And why not do evil that good may come?—as some people slanderously charge us with saying. Their condemnation is just.

No One Is Righteous

[9]What then? Are we Jews[4] any better off?[5] No, not at all. For we have already charged that all, both Jews and Greeks, are under sin, [10]as it is written:

[c]"None is righteous, no, not one;
[11]   no one understands;
    no one seeks for God.
[12]   All have turned aside; together they have
        become worthless;
    no one does good,
    not even one."

---

[1]Or contentious [2]Or counted [3]Or the letter [4]Greek Are we [5]Or at any disadvantage? [a]Isa. 52:5 [b]Ps. 51:4 (Gk.) [c]Ps. 14:1-3; 53:1-3

13 *a*"Their throat is an open grave;
　　they use their tongues to deceive."
　b"The venom of asps is under their lips."
14 *c*"Their mouth is full of curses and bitterness."
15 *d*"Their feet are swift to shed blood;
16 　in their paths are ruin and misery,
17 　and the way of peace they have not known."
18 *e*"There is no fear of God before their eyes."

19 Now we know that whatever the law says it speaks to those who are under the law, so that every mouth may be stopped, and the whole world may be held accountable to God. 20 For by works of the law no human being*1* will be justified in his sight, since through the law comes knowledge of sin.

The Righteousness of God Through Faith

21 But now the righteousness of God has been manifested apart from the law, although the Law and the Prophets bear witness to it— 22 the righteousness of God through faith in Jesus Christ for all who believe. For there is no distinction: 23 for all have sinned and fall short of the glory of God, 24 and are justified by his grace as a gift, through the redemption that is in Christ Jesus, 25 whom God put forward as a propitiation by his blood, to be received by faith. This was to show God's righteousness, because in his divine forbearance he had passed over former sins. 26 It was to show his righteousness at the present time, so that he might be just and the justifier of the one who has faith in Jesus.

27 Then what becomes of our boasting? It is excluded. By what kind of law? By a law of works? No, but by the law of faith. 28 For we hold that one is justified by faith apart from works of the law. 29 Or is God the God of Jews only? Is he not the God of Gentiles also? Yes, of Gentiles also, 30 since God is one—who will justify the circumcised by faith and the uncircumcised through faith. 31 Do we then overthrow the law by this faith? By no means! On the contrary, we uphold the law.

Abraham Justified by Faith

4 What then shall we say was gained by*2* Abraham, our forefather according to the flesh? 2 For if Abraham was justified by works, he has something to boast about, but not before God. 3 For what does the Scripture say? *f*"Abraham believed God, and it was counted to him as righteousness." 4 Now to the one who works, his wages are not counted as a gift but as his due. 5 And to the one who does not work but believes in*3* him who justifies the ungodly, his faith is counted as righteousness, 6 just as David also speaks of the blessing of the one to whom God counts righteousness apart from works:

7 *g*"Blessed are those whose lawless deeds are
　　forgiven,
　　and whose sins are covered;
8 　blessed is the man against whom the Lord
　　will not count his sin."

9 Is this blessing then only for the circumcised, or also for the uncircumcised? We say that faith was counted to Abraham as righteousness. 10 How then was it counted to him? Was it before or after he had been circumcised? It was not after, but before he was circumcised. 11 He received the sign of circumcision as a seal of the righteousness that he had by faith while he was still uncircumcised. The purpose was to make him the father of all who believe without being circumcised, so that righteousness would be counted to them as well, 12 and to make him the father of the circumcised who are not merely circumcised but who also walk in the footsteps of the faith that our father Abraham had before he was circumcised.

The Promise Realized Through Faith

13 For the promise to Abraham and his offspring that he would be heir of the world did not come through the law but through the righteousness of faith. 14 For if it is the adherents of the law who are to be the heirs, faith is null and the promise is void. 15 For the law brings wrath, but where there is no law there is no transgression.

16 That is why it depends on faith, in order that the promise may rest on grace and be guaranteed to all his offspring—not only to the adherent of the law but also to the one who shares the faith of Abraham, who is the father of us all, 17 as it is written, *h*"I have made you the father of many nations"—in the presence of the God in whom he believed, who gives life to the dead and calls into existence the things that do not exist. 18 In hope he believed against hope, that he should become the father of many nations, as he had been told, *i*"So shall your offspring be." 19 He did not weaken in faith when he considered his own body, which was as good as dead (since he was about a hundred years old), or when he considered the barrenness of Sarah's womb. 20 No distrust made him waver concerning the promise of God, but he grew strong in his faith as he gave glory to God, 21 fully convinced that God was able to do what he had promised. 22 That is why his faith was "counted to him as righteousness." 23 But the words "it was counted to him" were not written for his sake alone, 24 but for ours also. It will be counted to us who believe in him who raised from the dead Jesus our Lord, 25 who was delivered up for our trespasses and raised for our justification.

---

1 Greek *flesh* *2* Some manuscripts *say about* *3* Or *but trusts;* compare verse 24 *a* Ps. 5:9 *b* Ps. 140:3 *c* Ps. 10:7 (Gk.) *d* Prov. 1:16; 3:15-17; Isa. 59:7, 8 *e* Ps. 36:1 *f* Gen. 15:6 (Gk.) *g* Ps. 32:1, 2 *h* Gen. 17:5 *i* Gen. 15:5

Peace with God Through Faith

5 Therefore, since we have been justified by faith, we[1] have peace with God through our Lord Jesus Christ. [2]Through him we have also obtained access by faith[2] into this grace in which we stand, and we[3] rejoice[4] in hope of the glory of God. [3]More than that, we rejoice in our sufferings, knowing that suffering produces endurance, [4]and endurance produces character, and character produces hope, [5]and hope does not put us to shame, because God's love has been poured into our hearts through the Holy Spirit who has been given to us.

[6]For while we were still weak, at the right time Christ died for the ungodly. [7]For one will scarcely die for a righteous person—though perhaps for a good person one would dare even to die— [8]but God shows his love for us in that while we were still sinners, Christ died for us. [9]Since, therefore, we have now been justified by his blood, much more shall we be saved by him from the wrath of God. [10]For if while we were enemies we were reconciled to God by the death of his Son, much more, now that we are reconciled, shall we be saved by his life. [11]More than that, we also rejoice in God through our Lord Jesus Christ, through whom we have now received reconciliation.

Death in Adam, Life in Christ

[12]Therefore, just as sin came into the world through one man, and death through sin, and so death spread to all men because all sinned— [13]for sin indeed was in the world before the law was given, but sin is not counted where there is no law. [14]Yet death reigned from Adam to Moses, even over those whose sinning was not like the transgression of Adam, who was a type of the one who was to come.

[15]But the free gift is not like the trespass. For if many died through one man's trespass, much more have the grace of God and the free gift by the grace of that one man Jesus Christ abounded for many. [16]And the free gift is not like the result of that one man's sin. For the judgment following one trespass brought condemnation, but the free gift following many trespasses brought justification. [17]For if, because of one man's trespass, death reigned through that one man, much more will those who receive the abundance of grace and the free gift of righteousness reign in life through the one man Jesus Christ.

[18]Therefore, as one trespass[5] led to condemnation for all men, so one act of righteousness[6] leads to justification and life for all men. [19]For as by the one man's disobedience the many were made sinners, so by the one man's obedience the many will be made righteous. [20]Now the law came in to increase the trespass, but where sin increased, grace abounded all the more, [21]so that, as sin reigned in death, grace also might reign through righteousness leading to eternal life through Jesus Christ our Lord.

Dead to Sin, Alive to God

6 What shall we say then? Are we to continue in sin that grace may abound? [2]By no means! How can we who died to sin still live in it? [3]Do you not know that all of us who have been baptized into Christ Jesus were baptized into his death? [4]We were buried therefore with him by baptism into death, in order that, just as Christ was raised from the dead by the glory of the Father, we too might walk in newness of life.

[5]For if we have been united with him in a death like his, we shall certainly be united with him in a resurrection like his. [6]We know that our old self[7] was crucified with him in order that the body of sin might be brought to nothing, so that we would no longer be enslaved to sin. [7]For one who has died has been set free[8] from sin. [8]Now if we have died with Christ, we believe that we will also live with him. [9]We know that Christ, being raised from the dead, will never die again; death no longer has dominion over him. [10]For the death he died he died to sin, once for all, but the life he lives he lives to God. [11]So you also must consider yourselves dead to sin and alive to God in Christ Jesus.

[12]Let not sin therefore reign in your mortal body, to make you obey its passions. [13]Do not present your members to sin as instruments for unrighteousness, but present yourselves to God as those who have been brought from death to life, and your members to God as instruments for righteousness. [14]For sin will have no dominion over you, since you are not under law but under grace.

Slaves to Righteousness

[15]What then? Are we to sin because we are not under law but under grace? By no means! [16]Do you not know that if you present yourselves to anyone as obedient slaves,[9] you are slaves of the one whom you obey, either of sin, which leads to death, or of obedience, which leads to righteousness? [17]But thanks be to God, that you who were once slaves of sin have become obedient from the heart to the standard of teaching to which you were committed, [18]and, having been set free from sin, have become slaves of righteousness. [19]I am speaking in human terms, because of your natural limitations. For just as you once presented your members as slaves to impurity and to lawlessness leading to more lawlessness, so now present your members as slaves to righteousness leading to sanctification.

[20]For when you were slaves of sin, you were free in regard to righteousness. [21]But what fruit were you getting at that time from the things of

---

[1] Some manuscripts *let us* [2] Some manuscripts omit *by faith* [3] Or *let us*; also verse 3 [4] Or *boast*; also verses 3, 11 [5] Or *the trespass of one* [6] Or *the act of righteousness of one* [7] Greek *man* [8] Greek *has been justified* [9] Greek *bondservants*. Twice in this verse and verse 19; also once in verses 17, 20

which you are now ashamed? For the end of those things is death. ²²But now that you have been set free from sin and have become slaves of God, the fruit you get leads to sanctification and its end, eternal life. ²³For the wages of sin is death, but the free gift of God is eternal life in Christ Jesus our Lord.

Released from the Law

7 Or do you not know, brothers¹—for I am speaking to those who know the law—that the law is binding on a person only as long as he lives? ²For a married woman is bound by law to her husband while he lives, but if her husband dies she is released from the law of marriage.² ³Accordingly, she will be called an adulteress if she lives with another man while her husband is alive. But if her husband dies, she is free from that law, and if she marries another man she is not an adulteress.

⁴Likewise, my brothers, you also have died to the law through the body of Christ, so that you may belong to another, to him who has been raised from the dead, in order that we may bear fruit for God. ⁵For while we were living in the flesh, our sinful passions, aroused by the law, were at work in our members to bear fruit for death. ⁶But now we are released from the law, having died to that which held us captive, so that we serve in the new way of the Spirit and not in the old way of the written code.³

The Law and Sin

⁷What then shall we say? That the law is sin? By no means! Yet if it had not been for the law, I would not have known sin. For I would not have known what it is to covet if ªthe law had not said, "You shall not covet." ⁸But sin, seizing an opportunity through the commandment, produced in me all kinds of covetousness. For apart from the law, sin lies dead. ⁹I was once alive apart from the law, but when the commandment came, sin came alive and I died. ¹⁰The very commandment that promised life proved to be death to me. ¹¹For sin, seizing an opportunity through the commandment, deceived me and through it killed me. ¹²So the law is holy, and the commandment is holy and righteous and good.

¹³Did that which is good, then, bring death to me? By no means! It was sin, producing death in me through what is good, in order that sin might be shown to be sin, and through the commandment might become sinful beyond measure. ¹⁴For we know that the law is spiritual, but I am of the flesh, sold under sin. ¹⁵For I do not understand my own actions. For I do not do what I want, but I do the very thing I hate. ¹⁶Now if I do what I do not want, I agree with the law, that it is good. ¹⁷So now it is no longer I who do it, but

sin that dwells within me. ¹⁸For I know that nothing good dwells in me, that is, in my flesh. For I have the desire to do what is right, but not the ability to carry it out. ¹⁹For I do not do the good I want, but the evil I do not want is what I keep on doing. ²⁰Now if I do what I do not want, it is no longer I who do it, but sin that dwells within me.

²¹So I find it to be a law that when I want to do right, evil lies close at hand. ²²For I delight in the law of God, in my inner being, ²³but I see in my members another law waging war against the law of my mind and making me captive to the law of sin that dwells in my members. ²⁴Wretched man that I am! Who will deliver me from this body of death? ²⁵Thanks be to God through Jesus Christ our Lord! So then, I myself serve the law of God with my mind, but with my flesh I serve the law of sin.

Life in the Spirit

8 There is therefore now no condemnation for those who are in Christ Jesus.⁴ ²For the law of the Spirit of life has set you⁵ free in Christ Jesus from the law of sin and death. ³For God has done what the law, weakened by the flesh, could not do. By sending his own Son in the likeness of sinful flesh and for sin,⁶ he condemned sin in the flesh, ⁴in order that the righteous requirement of the law might be fulfilled in us, who walk not according to the flesh but according to the Spirit. ⁵For those who live according to the flesh set their minds on the things of the flesh, but those who live according to the Spirit set their minds on the things of the Spirit. ⁶For to set the mind on the flesh is death, but to set the mind on the Spirit is life and peace. ⁷For the mind that is set on the flesh is hostile to God, for it does not submit to God's law; indeed, it cannot. ⁸Those who are in the flesh cannot please God.

⁹You, however, are not in the flesh but in the Spirit, if in fact the Spirit of God dwells in you. Anyone who does not have the Spirit of Christ does not belong to him. ¹⁰But if Christ is in you, although the body is dead because of sin, the Spirit is life because of righteousness. ¹¹If the Spirit of him who raised Jesus from the dead dwells in you, he who raised Christ Jesus from the dead will also give life to your mortal bodies through his Spirit who dwells in you.

Heirs with Christ

¹²So then, brothers,⁷ we are debtors, not to the flesh, to live according to the flesh. ¹³For if you live according to the flesh you will die, but if by the Spirit you put to death the deeds of the body, you will live. ¹⁴For all who are led by the Spirit of God are sons⁸ of God. ¹⁵For you did not receive the spirit of slavery to fall back into fear, but you

---

¹ Or *brothers and sisters*; also verse 4 ² Greek *law concerning the husband* ³ Greek *of the letter* ⁴ Some manuscripts add *who walk not according to the flesh (but according to the Spirit)* ⁵ Some manuscripts *me* ⁶ Or *and as a sin offering* ⁷ Or *brothers and sisters*; also verse 29 ⁸ See discussion on "sons" in the preface ª Ex. 20:17; Deut. 5:21

have received the Spirit of adoption as sons, by whom we cry, "Abba! Father!" [16]The Spirit himself bears witness with our spirit that we are children of God, [17]and if children, then heirs—heirs of God and fellow heirs with Christ, provided we suffer with him in order that we may also be glorified with him.

Future Glory

[18]For I consider that the sufferings of this present time are not worth comparing with the glory that is to be revealed to us. [19]For the creation waits with eager longing for the revealing of the sons of God. [20]For the creation was subjected to futility, not willingly, but because of him who subjected it, in hope [21]that the creation itself will be set free from its bondage to corruption and obtain the freedom of the glory of the children of God. [22]For we know that the whole creation has been groaning together in the pains of childbirth until now. [23]And not only the creation, but we ourselves, who have the firstfruits of the Spirit, groan inwardly as we wait eagerly for adoption as sons, the redemption of our bodies. [24]For in this hope we were saved. Now hope that is seen is not hope. For who hopes for what he sees? [25]But if we hope for what we do not see, we wait for it with patience.

[26]Likewise the Spirit helps us in our weakness. For we do not know what to pray for as we ought, but the Spirit himself intercedes for us with groanings too deep for words. [27]And he who searches hearts knows what is the mind of the Spirit, because[j] the Spirit intercedes for the saints according to the will of God. [28]And we know that for those who love God all things work together for good,[2] for those who are called according to his purpose. [29]For those whom he foreknew he also predestined to be conformed to the image of his Son, in order that he might be the firstborn among many brothers. [30]And those whom he predestined he also called, and those whom he called he also justified, and those whom he justified he also glorified.

God's Everlasting Love

[31]What then shall we say to these things? If God is for us, who can be[3] against us? [32]He who did not spare his own Son but gave him up for us all, how will he not also with him graciously give us all things? [33]Who shall bring any charge against God's elect? It is God who justifies. [34]Who is to condemn? Christ Jesus is the one who died—more than that, who was raised—who is at the right hand of God, who indeed is interceding for us.[4] [35]Who shall separate us from the love of Christ? Shall tribulation, or distress, or persecution, or famine, or nakedness, or danger, or sword? [36]As it is written,

[a]"For your sake we are being killed all the day long;
    we are regarded as sheep to be slaughtered."

[37]No, in all these things we are more than conquerors through him who loved us. [38]For I am sure that neither death nor life, nor angels nor rulers, nor things present nor things to come, nor powers, [39]nor height nor depth, nor anything else in all creation, will be able to separate us from the love of God in Christ Jesus our Lord.

God's Sovereign Choice

9 I am speaking the truth in Christ—I am not lying; my conscience bears me witness in the Holy Spirit— [2]that I have great sorrow and unceasing anguish in my heart. [3]For I could wish that I myself were accursed and cut off from Christ for the sake of my brothers,[5] my kinsmen according to the flesh. [4]They are Israelites, and to them belong the adoption, the glory, the covenants, the giving of the law, the worship, and the promises. [5]To them belong the patriarchs, and from their race, according to the flesh, is the Christ who is God over all, blessed forever. Amen.

[6]But it is not as though the word of God has failed. For not all who are descended from Israel belong to Israel, [7]and not all are children of Abraham because they are his offspring, but [b]"Through Isaac shall your offspring be named." [8]This means that it is not the children of the flesh who are the children of God, but the children of the promise are counted as offspring. [9]For this is what the promise said: [c]"About this time next year I will return, and Sarah shall have a son." [10]And not only so, but also when Rebekah had conceived children by one man, our forefather Isaac, [11]though they were not yet born and had done nothing either good or bad—in order that God's purpose of election might continue, not because of works but because of him who calls— [12]she was told, [d]"The older will serve the younger." [13]As it is written, [e]"Jacob I loved, but Esau I hated."

[14]What shall we say then? Is there injustice on God's part? By no means! [15]For he says to Moses, [f]"I will have mercy on whom I have mercy, and I will have compassion on whom I have compassion." [16]So then it depends not on human will or exertion,[6] but on God, who has mercy. [17]For the Scripture says to Pharaoh, [g]"For this very purpose I have raised you up, that I might show my power in you, and that my name might be proclaimed in all the earth." [18]So then he has mercy on whomever he wills, and he hardens whomever he wills.

[19]You will say to me then, "Why does he still find fault? For who can resist his will?" [20]But who are you, O man, to answer back to God?

---

[1] Or that [2] Some manuscripts *God works all things together for good, or God works in all things for the good* [3] Or *who is* [4] Or *Is it Christ Jesus who died . . . for us?* [5] Or *brothers and sisters* [6] Greek *not of him who wills or runs* [a] Ps. 44:22 [b] Gen. 21:12 [c] Gen. 18:10, 14 [d] Gen. 25:23 [e] Mal. 1:2, 3 [f] Ex. 33:19 [g] Ex. 9:16

Will what is molded say to its molder, "Why have you made me like this?" [21]Has the potter no right over the clay, to make out of the same lump one vessel for honorable use and another for dishonorable use? [22]What if God, desiring to show his wrath and to make known his power, has endured with much patience vessels of wrath prepared for destruction, [23]in order to make known the riches of his glory for vessels of mercy, which he has prepared beforehand for glory— [24]even us whom he has called, not from the Jews only but also from the Gentiles? [25]As indeed he says in Hosea,

[a]"Those who were not my people I will call 'my people,'
   and her who was not beloved I will call 'beloved.'"
[26] [b]"And in the very place where it was said to them, 'You are not my people,'
   there they will be called 'sons of the living God.'"

[27]And Isaiah cries out concerning Israel: [c]"Though the number of the sons of Israel[1] be as the sand of the sea, only a remnant of them will be saved, [28]for the Lord will carry out his sentence upon the earth fully and without delay." [29]And as Isaiah predicted,

[d]"If the Lord of hosts had not left us offspring, we would have been like Sodom
   and become like Gomorrah."

Israel's Unbelief

[30]What shall we say, then? That Gentiles who did not pursue righteousness have attained it, that is, a righteousness that is by faith; [31]but that Israel who pursued a law that would lead to righteousness[2] did not succeed in reaching that law. [32]Why? Because they did not pursue it by faith, but as if it were based on works. They have stumbled over the stumbling stone, [33]as it is written,

[e]"Behold, I am laying in Zion a stone of stumbling, and a rock of offense;
   and whoever believes in him will not be put to shame."

10 Brothers,[3] my heart's desire and prayer to God for them is that they may be saved. [2]For I bear them witness that they have a zeal for God, but not according to knowledge. [3]For, being ignorant of the righteousness of God, and seeking to establish their own, they did not submit to God's righteousness. [4]For Christ is the end of the law for righteousness to everyone who believes.[4]

The Message of Salvation to All

[5]For Moses writes about the righteousness that is based on the law, that the person who

does the commandments shall live by them. [6]But the righteousness based on faith says, "Do not say in your heart, 'Who will ascend into heaven?'" (that is, to bring Christ down) [7]or "'Who will descend into the abyss?'" (that is, to bring Christ up from the dead). [8]But what does it say? [f]"The word is near you, in your mouth and in your heart" (that is, the word of faith that we proclaim); [9]because, if you confess with your mouth that Jesus is Lord and believe in your heart that God raised him from the dead, you will be saved. [10]For with the heart one believes and is justified, and with the mouth one confesses and is saved. [11]For the Scripture says, "Everyone who believes in him will not be put to shame." [12]For there is no distinction between Jew and Greek; for the same Lord is Lord of all, bestowing his riches on all who call on him. [13]For [g]"everyone who calls on the name of the Lord will be saved."

[14]How then will they call on him in whom they have not believed? And how are they to believe in him of whom they have never heard?[5] And how are they to hear without someone preaching? [15]And how are they to preach unless they are sent? As it is written, [h]"How beautiful are the feet of those who preach the good news!" [16]But they have not all obeyed the gospel. For Isaiah says, [i]"Lord, who has believed what he has heard from us?" [17]So faith comes from hearing, and hearing through the word of Christ.

[18]But I ask, have they not heard? Indeed they have, for

[j]"Their voice has gone out to all the earth, and their words to the ends of the world."

[19]But I ask, did Israel not understand? First Moses says,

[k]"I will make you jealous of those who are not a nation;
   with a foolish nation I will make you angry."

[20]Then Isaiah is so bold as to say,

[l]"I have been found by those who did not seek me;
   I have shown myself to those who did not ask for me."

[21]But of Israel he says, [m]"All day long I have held out my hands to a disobedient and contrary people."

The Remnant of Israel

11 I ask, then, has God rejected his people? By no means! For I myself am an Israelite, a descendant of Abraham,[6] a member of the tribe of Benjamin. [2]God has not rejected his people whom he foreknew. Do you not know

[1]Or children of Israel [2]Greek a law of righteousness [3]Or Brothers and sisters [4]Or end of the law, that everyone who believes may be justified [5]Or him whom they have never heard [6]Or one of the offspring of Abraham [a]Hos. 2:23 [b]Hos. 1:10 [c]Isa. 10:22, 23 [d]Isa. 1:9 [e]Isa. 28:16 [f]Deut. 30:14 [g]Joel 2:32 [h]Isa. 52:7 [i]Isa. 53:1 [j]Ps. 19:4 [k]Deut. 32:21 [l]Isa. 65:1 [m]Isa. 65:2

what the Scripture says of Elijah, how he appeals to God against Israel? [3]ᵃ"Lord, they have killed your prophets, they have demolished your altars, and I alone am left, and they seek my life." [4]But what is God's reply to him? ᵇ"I have kept for myself seven thousand men who have not bowed the knee to Baal." [5]So too at the present time there is a remnant, chosen by grace. [6]But if it is by grace, it is no longer on the basis of works; otherwise grace would no longer be grace.

[7]What then? Israel failed to obtain what it was seeking. The elect obtained it, but the rest were hardened, [8]as it is written,

"God gave them a spirit of stupor,
    eyes that would not see
    and ears that would not hear,
    down to this very day."

[9]And David says,

ᶜ"Let their table become a snare and a trap,
    a stumbling block and a retribution for
        them;
[10]   let their eyes be darkened so that they cannot
        see,
    and bend their backs forever."

Gentiles Grafted In

[11]So I ask, did they stumble in order that they might fall? By no means! Rather through their trespass salvation has come to the Gentiles, so as to make Israel jealous. [12]Now if their trespass means riches for the world, and if their failure means riches for the Gentiles, how much more will their full inclusion[1] mean!

[13]Now I am speaking to you Gentiles. Inasmuch then as I am an apostle to the Gentiles, I magnify my ministry [14]in order somehow to make my fellow Jews jealous, and thus save some of them. [15]For if their rejection means the reconciliation of the world, what will their acceptance mean but life from the dead? [16]If the dough offered as firstfruits is holy, so is the whole lump, and if the root is holy, so are the branches.

[17]But if some of the branches were broken off, and you, although a wild olive shoot, were grafted in among the others and now share in the nourishing root[2] of the olive tree, [18]do not be arrogant toward the branches. If you are, remember it is not you who support the root, but the root that supports you. [19]Then you will say, "Branches were broken off so that I might be grafted in." [20]That is true. They were broken off because of their unbelief, but you stand fast through faith. So do not become proud, but fear. [21]For if God did not spare the natural branches, neither will he spare you. [22]Note then the kindness and the severity of God: severity toward those who have fallen, but God's kindness to you,

provided you continue in his kindness. Otherwise you too will be cut off. [23]And even they, if they do not continue in their unbelief, will be grafted in, for God has the power to graft them in again. [24]For if you were cut from what is by nature a wild olive tree, and grafted, contrary to nature, into a cultivated olive tree, how much more will these, the natural branches, be grafted back into their own olive tree.

The Mystery of Israel's Salvation

[25]Lest you be wise in your own sight, I want you to understand this mystery, brothers:[3] a partial hardening has come upon Israel, until the fullness of the Gentiles has come in. [26]And in this way all Israel will be saved, as it is written,

ᵈ"The Deliverer will come from Zion,
    he will banish ungodliness from Jacob";
[27]   "and this will be my covenant with them
        when I take away their sins."

[28]As regards the gospel, they are enemies of God for your sake. But as regards election, they are beloved for the sake of their forefathers. [29]For the gifts and the calling of God are irrevocable. [30]For just as you were at one time disobedient to God but now have received mercy because of their disobedience, [31]so they too have now been disobedient in order that by the mercy shown to you they also may now[4] receive mercy. [32]For God has consigned all to disobedience, that he may have mercy on all.

[33]Oh, the depth of the riches and wisdom and knowledge of God! How unsearchable are his judgments and how inscrutable his ways!

[34]   "For who has known the mind of the Lord,
        or who has been his counselor?"
[35]   "Or who has given a gift to him
        that he might be repaid?"

[36]For from him and through him and to him are all things. To him be glory forever. Amen.

A Living Sacrifice

12 I appeal to you therefore, brothers,[5] by the mercies of God, to present your bodies as a living sacrifice, holy and acceptable to God, which is your spiritual worship.[6] [2]Do not be conformed to this world,[7] but be transformed by the renewal of your mind, that by testing you may discern what is the will of God, what is good and acceptable and perfect.[8]

Gifts of Grace

[3]For by the grace given to me I say to everyone among you not to think of himself more highly than he ought to think, but to think with sober judgment, each according to the measure of faith that God has assigned. [4]For as in one body

---

[1] Greek *their fullness* [2] Greek *root of richness*; some manuscripts *richness* [3] Or *brothers and sisters* [4] Some manuscripts omit *now* [5] Or *brothers and sisters* [6] Or *your rational service* [7] Greek *age* [8] Or *what is the good and acceptable and perfect will of God* ᵃ 1 Kgs. 19:10, 14 ᵇ 1 Kgs. 19:18 ᶜ Ps. 69:22, 23 ᵈ Isa. 59:20, 21

we have many members,[1] and the members do not all have the same function, [5]so we, though many, are one body in Christ, and individually members one of another. [6]Having gifts that differ according to the grace given to us, let us use them: if prophecy, in proportion to our faith; [7]if service, in our serving; the one who teaches, in his teaching; [8]the one who exhorts, in his exhortation; the one who contributes, in generosity; the one who leads,[2] with zeal; the one who does acts of mercy, with cheerfulness.

Marks of the True Christian

[9]Let love be genuine. Abhor what is evil; hold fast to what is good. [10]Love one another with brotherly affection. Outdo one another in showing honor. [11]Do not be slothful in zeal, be fervent in spirit,[3] serve the Lord. [12]Rejoice in hope, be patient in tribulation, be constant in prayer. [13]Contribute to the needs of the saints and seek to show hospitality.

[14]Bless those who persecute you; bless and do not curse them. [15]Rejoice with those who rejoice, weep with those who weep. [16]Live in harmony with one another. Do not be haughty, but associate with the lowly.[4] Never be wise in your own sight. [17]Repay no one evil for evil, but give thought to do what is honorable in the sight of all. [18]If possible, so far as it depends on you, live peaceably with all. [19]Beloved, never avenge yourselves, but leave it[5] to the wrath of God, for it is written, [a]"Vengeance is mine, I will repay, says the Lord." [20]To the contrary, [b]"if your enemy is hungry, feed him; if he is thirsty, give him something to drink; for by so doing you will heap burning coals on his head." [21]Do not be overcome by evil, but overcome evil with good.

Submission to the Authorities

13 Let every person be subject to the governing authorities. For there is no authority except from God, and those that exist have been instituted by God. [2]Therefore whoever resists the authorities resists what God has appointed, and those who resist will incur judgment. [3]For rulers are not a terror to good conduct, but to bad. Would you have no fear of the one who is in authority? Then do what is good, and you will receive his approval, [4]for he is God's servant for your good. But if you do wrong, be afraid, for he does not bear the sword in vain. For he is the servant of God, an avenger who carries out God's wrath on the wrongdoer. [5]Therefore one must be in subjection, not only to avoid God's wrath but also for the sake of conscience. [6]For because of this you also pay taxes, for the authorities are ministers of God, attending to this very thing. [7]Pay to all what is owed to them: taxes to whom taxes are owed, revenue to whom reve-

nue is owed, respect to whom respect is owed, honor to whom honor is owed.

Fulfilling the Law Through Love

[8]Owe no one anything, except to love each other, for the one who loves another has fulfilled the law. [9]For the commandments, [c]"You shall not commit adultery, You shall not murder, You shall not steal, You shall not covet," and any other commandment, are summed up in this word: [d]"You shall love your neighbor as yourself." [10]Love does no wrong to a neighbor; therefore love is the fulfilling of the law.

[11]Besides this you know the time, that the hour has come for you to wake from sleep. For salvation is nearer to us now than when we first believed. [12]The night is far gone; the day is at hand. So then let us cast off the works of darkness and put on the armor of light. [13]Let us walk properly as in the daytime, not in orgies and drunkenness, not in sexual immorality and sensuality, not in quarreling and jealousy. [14]But put on the Lord Jesus Christ, and make no provision for the flesh, to gratify its desires.

Do Not Pass Judgment on One Another

14 As for the one who is weak in faith, welcome him, but not to quarrel over opinions. [2]One person believes he may eat anything, while the weak person eats only vegetables. [3]Let not the one who eats despise the one who abstains, and let not the one who abstains pass judgment on the one who eats, for God has welcomed him. [4]Who are you to pass judgment on the servant of another? It is before his own master[6] that he stands or falls. And he will be upheld, for the Lord is able to make him stand.

[5]One person esteems one day as better than another, while another esteems all days alike. Each one should be fully convinced in his own mind. [6]The one who observes the day, observes it in honor of the Lord. The one who eats, eats in honor of the Lord, since he gives thanks to God, while the one who abstains, abstains in honor of the Lord and gives thanks to God. [7]For none of us lives to himself, and none of us dies to himself. [8]For if we live, we live to the Lord, and if we die, we die to the Lord. So then, whether we live or whether we die, we are the Lord's. [9]For to this end Christ died and lived again, that he might be Lord both of the dead and of the living.

[10]Why do you pass judgment on your brother? Or you, why do you despise your brother? For we will all stand before the judgment seat of God; [11]for it is written,

[e]"As I live, says the Lord, every knee shall bow
to me,
and every tongue shall confess[7] to God."

---

[1]Greek *parts; also verse 5* [2]*Or gives aid* [3]*Or fervent in the Spirit* [4]*Or give yourselves to humble tasks* [5]Greek *give place* [6]*Or lord* [7]*Or shall give praise*
[a]Deut. 32:35 [b]Prov. 25:21, 22 [c]Ex. 20:13-17; Deut. 5:17-21 [d]Lev. 19:18 [e]Isa. 45:23

¹²So then each of us will give an account of himself to God.

Do Not Cause Another to Stumble

¹³Therefore let us not pass judgment on one another any longer, but rather decide never to put a stumbling block or hindrance in the way of a brother. ¹⁴I know and am persuaded in the Lord Jesus that nothing is unclean in itself, but it is unclean for anyone who thinks it unclean. ¹⁵For if your brother is grieved by what you eat, you are no longer walking in love. By what you eat, do not destroy the one for whom Christ died. ¹⁶So do not let what you regard as good be spoken of as evil. ¹⁷For the kingdom of God is not a matter of eating and drinking but of righteousness and peace and joy in the Holy Spirit. ¹⁸Whoever thus serves Christ is acceptable to God and approved by men. ¹⁹So then let us pursue what makes for peace and for mutual upbuilding.

²⁰Do not, for the sake of food, destroy the work of God. Everything is indeed clean, but it is wrong for anyone to make another stumble by what he eats. ²¹It is good not to eat meat or drink wine or do anything that causes your brother to stumble.¹ ²²The faith that you have, keep between yourself and God. Blessed is the one who has no reason to pass judgment on himself for what he approves. ²³But whoever has doubts is condemned if he eats, because the eating is not from faith. For whatever does not proceed from faith is sin.²

The Example of Christ

15 We who are strong have an obligation to bear with the failings of the weak, and not to please ourselves. ²Let each of us please his neighbor for his good, to build him up. ³For Christ did not please himself, but as it is written, ᵃ"The reproaches of those who reproached you fell on me." ⁴For whatever was written in former days was written for our instruction, that through endurance and through the encouragement of the Scriptures we might have hope. ⁵May the God of endurance and encouragement grant you to live in such harmony with one another, in accord with Christ Jesus, ⁶that together you may with one voice glorify the God and Father of our Lord Jesus Christ. ⁷Therefore welcome one another as Christ has welcomed you, for the glory of God.

Christ the Hope of Jews and Gentiles

⁸For I tell you that Christ became a servant to the circumcised to show God's truthfulness, in order to confirm the promises given to the patriarchs, ⁹and in order that the Gentiles might glorify God for his mercy. As it is written,

ᵇ"Therefore I will praise you among the Gentiles,
    and sing to your name."

¹⁰And again it is said,

ᶜ"Rejoice, O Gentiles, with his people."

¹¹And again,

ᵈ"Praise the Lord, all you Gentiles,
    and let all the peoples extol him."

¹²And again Isaiah says,

ᵉ"The root of Jesse will come,
    even he who arises to rule the Gentiles;
    in him will the Gentiles hope."

¹³May the God of hope fill you with all joy and peace in believing, so that by the power of the Holy Spirit you may abound in hope.

Paul the Minister to the Gentiles

¹⁴I myself am satisfied about you, my brothers,³ that you yourselves are full of goodness, filled with all knowledge and able to instruct one another. ¹⁵But on some points I have written to you very boldly by way of reminder, because of the grace given me by God ¹⁶to be a minister of Christ Jesus to the Gentiles in the priestly service of the gospel of God, so that the offering of the Gentiles may be acceptable, sanctified by the Holy Spirit. ¹⁷In Christ Jesus, then, I have reason to be proud of my work for God. ¹⁸For I will not venture to speak of anything except what Christ has accomplished through me to bring the Gentiles to obedience—by word and deed, ¹⁹by the power of signs and wonders, by the power of the Spirit of God—so that from Jerusalem and all the way around to Illyricum I have fulfilled the ministry of the gospel of Christ; ²⁰and thus I make it my ambition to preach the gospel, not where Christ has already been named, lest I build on someone else's foundation, ²¹but as it is written,

ᶠ"Those who have never been told of him will see,
    and those who have never heard will understand."

Paul's Plan to Visit Rome

²²This is the reason why I have so often been hindered from coming to you. ²³But now, since I no longer have any room for work in these regions, and since I have longed for many years to come to you, ²⁴I hope to see you in passing as I go to Spain, and to be helped on my journey there by you, once I have enjoyed your company for a while. ²⁵At present, however, I am going to Jerusalem bringing aid to the saints. ²⁶For Macedonia and Achaia have been pleased to make some contribution for the poor among the saints

¹ Some manuscripts add *or be hindered or be weakened* ²Some manuscripts insert here 16:25-27 ³*Or brothers and sisters;* also verse 30 ᵃPs. 69:9 ᵇ2 Sam. 22:50; Ps. 18:49 ᶜDeut. 32:43 ᵈPs. 117:1 ᵉIsa. 11:10 ᶠIsa. 52:15

at Jerusalem. [27] For they were pleased to do it, and indeed they owe it to them. For if the Gentiles have come to share in their spiritual blessings, they ought also to be of service to them in material blessings. [28] When therefore I have completed this and have delivered to them what has been collected,[1] I will leave for Spain by way of you. [29] I know that when I come to you I will come in the fullness of the blessing[2] of Christ.

[30] I appeal to you, brothers, by our Lord Jesus Christ and by the love of the Spirit, to strive together with me in your prayers to God on my behalf, [31] that I may be delivered from the unbelievers in Judea, and that my service for Jerusalem may be acceptable to the saints, [32] so that by God's will I may come to you with joy and be refreshed in your company. [33] May the God of peace be with you all. Amen.

Personal Greetings

16 I commend to you our sister Phoebe, a servant[3] of the church at Cenchreae, [2] that you may welcome her in the Lord in a way worthy of the saints, and help her in whatever she may need from you, for she has been a patron of many and of myself as well.

[3] Greet Prisca and Aquila, my fellow workers in Christ Jesus, [4] who risked their necks for my life, to whom not only I give thanks but all the churches of the Gentiles give thanks as well. [5] Greet also the church in their house. Greet my beloved Epaenetus, who was the first convert[4] to Christ in Asia. [6] Greet Mary, who has worked hard for you. [7] Greet Andronicus and Junia,[5] my kinsmen and my fellow prisoners. They are well known to the apostles,[6] and they were in Christ before me. [8] Greet Ampliatus, my beloved in the Lord. [9] Greet Urbanus, our fellow worker in Christ, and my beloved Stachys. [10] Greet Apelles, who is approved in Christ. Greet those who belong to the family of Aristobulus. [11] Greet my kinsman Herodion. Greet those in the Lord who belong to the family of Narcissus. [12] Greet those

workers in the Lord, Tryphaena and Tryphosa. Greet the beloved Persis, who has worked hard in the Lord. [13] Greet Rufus, chosen in the Lord; also his mother, who has been a mother to me as well. [14] Greet Asyncritus, Phlegon, Hermes, Patrobas, Hermas, and the brothers[7] who are with them. [15] Greet Philologus, Julia, Nereus and his sister, and Olympas, and all the saints who are with them. [16] Greet one another with a holy kiss. All the churches of Christ greet you.

Final Instructions and Greetings

[17] I appeal to you, brothers, to watch out for those who cause divisions and create obstacles contrary to the doctrine that you have been taught; avoid them. [18] For such persons do not serve our Lord Christ, but their own appetites,[8] and by smooth talk and flattery they deceive the hearts of the naive. [19] For your obedience is known to all, so that I rejoice over you, but I want you to be wise as to what is good and innocent as to what is evil. [20] The God of peace will soon crush Satan under your feet. The grace of our Lord Jesus Christ be with you.

[21] Timothy, my fellow worker, greets you; so do Lucius and Jason and Sosipater, my kinsmen.

[22] I Tertius, who wrote this letter, greet you in the Lord.

[23] Gaius, who is host to me and to the whole church, greets you. Erastus, the city treasurer, and our brother Quartus, greet you.[9]

Doxology

[25] Now to him who is able to strengthen you according to my gospel and the preaching of Jesus Christ, according to the revelation of the mystery that was kept secret for long ages [26] but has now been disclosed and through the prophetic writings has been made known to all nations, according to the command of the eternal God, to bring about the obedience of faith— [27] to the only wise God be glory forevermore through Jesus Christ! Amen.

---

[1] Greek *sealed to them this fruit* [2] Some manuscripts insert *of the gospel* [3] Or *deaconess* [4] Greek *firstfruit* [5] Or *Junias* [6] Or *messengers* [7] Or *brothers and sisters;* also verse 17 [8] Greek *their own belly* [9] Some manuscripts insert verse 24: *The grace of our Lord Jesus Christ be with you all. Amen.*

1 CORINTHIANS

Introduction

The city of Corinth was at the heart of an important trade route in the ancient world. Like many cities that thrive on trade, Corinth had a reputation for sexual immorality, religious diversity, and corruption. The church that Paul planted there (Acts 18) floundered under all of these influences and began to divide over various issues. First Corinthians addresses many practical questions dividing the church—questions concerning such things as spiritual gifts, marriage, food offered to idols, and the resurrection. Paul urged the Corinthians to be unified and to give themselves fully to "the work of the Lord" (15:58). Chapter 13 includes a well-known passage on the nature and importance of love. Paul wrote this letter to the Corinthians from Ephesus about A.D. 55.

Greeting

1 Paul, called by the will of God to be an apostle of Christ Jesus, and our brother Sosthenes,

²To the church of God that is in Corinth, to those sanctified in Christ Jesus, called to be saints together with all those who in every place call upon the name of our Lord Jesus Christ, both their Lord and ours:

³Grace to you and peace from God our Father and the Lord Jesus Christ.

Thanksgiving

⁴I give thanks to my God always for you because of the grace of God that was given you in Christ Jesus, ⁵that in every way you were enriched in him in all speech and all knowledge— ⁶even as the testimony about Christ was confirmed among you— ⁷so that you are not lacking in any spiritual gift, as you wait for the revealing of our Lord Jesus Christ, ⁸who will sustain you to the end, guiltless in the day of our Lord Jesus Christ. ⁹God is faithful, by whom you were called into the fellowship of his Son, Jesus Christ our Lord.

Divisions in the Church

¹⁰I appeal to you, brothers,[1] by the name of our Lord Jesus Christ, that all of you agree, and that there be no divisions among you, but that you be united in the same mind and the same judgment. ¹¹For it has been reported to me by Chloe's people that there is quarreling among you, my brothers. ¹²What I mean is that each one of you says, "I follow Paul," or "I follow Apollos," or "I follow Cephas," or "I follow Christ." ¹³Is Christ divided? Was Paul crucified for you? Or were you baptized in the name of Paul? ¹⁴I thank God that I baptized none of you except Crispus and Gaius, ¹⁵so that no one may say that you were baptized in my name. ¹⁶(I did baptize also the household of Stephanas. Beyond that, I do not know whether I baptized anyone else.) ¹⁷For Christ did not send me to baptize but to preach the gospel, and not with words of eloquent wisdom, lest the cross of Christ be emptied of its power.

Christ the Wisdom and Power of God

¹⁸For the word of the cross is folly to those who are perishing, but to us who are being saved it is the power of God. ¹⁹For it is written,

ᵃ"I will destroy the wisdom of the wise,
    and the discernment of the discerning I will
        thwart."

²⁰Where is the one who is wise? Where is the scribe? Where is the debater of this age? Has not God made foolish the wisdom of the world? ²¹For since, in the wisdom of God, the world did not know God through wisdom, it pleased God through the folly of what we preach to save those who believe. ²²For Jews demand signs and Greeks seek wisdom, ²³but we preach Christ crucified, a stumbling block to Jews and folly to Gentiles, ²⁴but to those who are called, both Jews and Greeks, Christ the power of God and the wisdom of God. ²⁵For the foolishness of God is wiser than men, and the weakness of God is stronger than men.

²⁶For consider your calling, brothers: not many of you were wise according to worldly standards,[2] not many were powerful, not many were of noble birth. ²⁷But God chose what is foolish in the world to shame the wise; God chose what is weak in the world to shame the strong; ²⁸God chose what is low and despised in the world, even things that are not, to bring to nothing things that are, ²⁹so that no human being[3] might boast in the presence of God. ³⁰And because of him[4] you are in Christ Jesus, who became to us wisdom from God, righteousness and sanctification and redemption, ³¹so that, as it is written, "Let the one who boasts, boast in the Lord."

---

[1] Or brothers and sisters. The plural Greek word adelphoi (translated "brothers") refers to siblings in a family. In New Testament usage, depending on the context, adelphoi may refer either to men or to both men and women who are siblings (brothers and sisters) in God's family, the church; also verses 11, 26 [2] Greek according to the flesh [3] Greek no flesh [4] Greek And from him ᵃIsa. 29:14

Proclaiming Christ Crucified

2 And I, when I came to you, brothers,[1] did not come proclaiming to you the testimony[2] of God with lofty speech or wisdom. [2]For I decided to know nothing among you except Jesus Christ and him crucified. [3]And I was with you in weakness and in fear and much trembling, [4]and my speech and my message were not in plausible words of wisdom, but in demonstration of the Spirit and of power, [5]that your faith might not rest in the wisdom of men but in the power of God.

Wisdom from the Spirit

[6]Yet among the mature we do impart wisdom, although it is not a wisdom of this age or of the rulers of this age, who are doomed to pass away. [7]But we impart a secret and hidden wisdom of God, which God decreed before the ages for our glory. [8]None of the rulers of this age understood this, for if they had, they would not have crucified the Lord of glory. [9]But, as it is written,

"What no eye has seen, nor ear heard,
    nor the heart of man imagined,
what God has prepared for those who love
    him"—

[10]these things God has revealed to us through the Spirit. For the Spirit searches everything, even the depths of God. [11]For who knows a person's thoughts except the spirit of that person, which is in him? So also no one comprehends the thoughts of God except the Spirit of God. [12]Now we have received not the spirit of the world, but the Spirit who is from God, that we might understand the things freely given us by God. [13]And we impart this in words not taught by human wisdom but taught by the Spirit, interpreting spiritual truths to those who are spiritual.[3]

[14]The natural person does not accept the things of the Spirit of God, for they are folly to him, and he is not able to understand them because they are spiritually discerned. [15]The spiritual person judges all things, but is himself to be judged by no one. [16a]"For who has understood the mind of the Lord so as to instruct him?" But we have the mind of Christ.

Divisions in the Church

3 But I, brothers,[4] could not address you as spiritual people, but as people of the flesh, as infants in Christ. [2]I fed you with milk, not solid food, for you were not ready for it. And even now you are not yet ready, [3]for you are still of the flesh. For while there is jealousy and strife among you, are you not of the flesh and behaving only in a human way? [4]For when one says, "I follow Paul," and another, "I follow Apollos," are you not being merely human?

[5]What then is Apollos? What is Paul? Servants through whom you believed, as the Lord assigned to each. [6]I planted, Apollos watered, but God gave the growth. [7]So neither he who plants nor he who waters is anything, but only God who gives the growth. [8]He who plants and he who waters are one, and each will receive his wages according to his labor. [9]For we are God's fellow workers. You are God's field, God's building.

[10]According to the grace of God given to me, like a skilled master builder I laid a foundation, and someone else is building upon it. Let each one take care how he builds upon it. [11]For no one can lay a foundation other than that which is laid, which is Jesus Christ. [12]Now if anyone builds on the foundation with gold, silver, precious stones, wood, hay, straw— [13]each one's work will become manifest, for the Day will disclose it, because it will be revealed by fire, and the fire will test what sort of work each one has done. [14]If the work that anyone has built on the foundation survives, he will receive a reward. [15]If anyone's work is burned up, he will suffer loss, though he himself will be saved, but only as through fire.

[16]Do you not know that you[5] are God's temple and that God's Spirit dwells in you? [17]If anyone destroys God's temple, God will destroy him. For God's temple is holy, and you are that temple.

[18]Let no one deceive himself. If anyone among you thinks that he is wise in this age, let him become a fool that he may become wise. [19]For the wisdom of this world is folly with God. For it is written, [b]"He catches the wise in their craftiness," [20]and again, [c]"The Lord knows the thoughts of the wise, that they are futile." [21]So let no one boast in men. For all things are yours, [22]whether Paul or Apollos or Cephas or the world or life or death or the present or the future—all are yours, [23]and you are Christ's, and Christ is God's.

The Ministry of Apostles

4 This is how one should regard us, as servants of Christ and stewards of the mysteries of God. [2]Moreover, it is required of stewards that they be found trustworthy. [3]But with me it is a very small thing that I should be judged by you or by any human court. In fact, I do not even judge myself. [4]For I am not aware of anything against myself, but I am not thereby acquitted. It is the Lord who judges me. [5]Therefore do not pronounce judgment before the time, before the Lord comes, who will bring to light the things now hidden in darkness and will disclose the purposes of the heart. Then each one will receive his commendation from God.

[6]I have applied all these things to myself and Apollos for your benefit, brothers,[6] that you may learn by us not to go beyond what is written, that none of you may be puffed up in favor of one against another. [7]For who sees anything differ-

ent in you? What do you have that you did not receive? If then you received it, why do you boast as if you did not receive it?

⁸Already you have all you want! Already you have become rich! Without us you have become kings! And would that you did reign, so that we might share the rule with you! ⁹For I think that God has exhibited us apostles as last of all, like men sentenced to death, because we have become a spectacle to the world, to angels, and to men. ¹⁰We are fools for Christ's sake, but you are wise in Christ. We are weak, but you are strong. You are held in honor, but we in disrepute. ¹¹To the present hour we hunger and thirst, we are poorly dressed and buffeted and homeless, ¹²and we labor, working with our own hands. When reviled, we bless; when persecuted, we endure; ¹³when slandered, we entreat. We have become, and are still, like the scum of the world, the refuse of all things.

¹⁴I do not write these things to make you ashamed, but to admonish you as my beloved children. ¹⁵For though you have countless guides in Christ, you do not have many fathers. For I became your father in Christ Jesus through the gospel. ¹⁶I urge you, then, be imitators of me. ¹⁷That is why I sent¹ you Timothy, my beloved and faithful child in the Lord, to remind you of my ways in Christ,² as I teach them everywhere in every church. ¹⁸Some are arrogant, as though I were not coming to you. ¹⁹But I will come to you soon, if the Lord wills, and I will find out not the talk of these arrogant people but their power. ²⁰For the kingdom of God does not consist in talk but in power. ²¹What do you wish? Shall I come to you with a rod, or with love in a spirit of gentleness?

Sexual Immorality Defiles the Church

5 It is actually reported that there is sexual immorality among you, and of a kind that is not tolerated even among pagans, for a man has his father's wife. ²And you are arrogant! Ought you not rather to mourn? Let him who has done this be removed from among you.

³For though absent in body, I am present in spirit; and as if present, I have already pronounced judgment on the one who did such a thing. ⁴When you are assembled in the name of the Lord Jesus and my spirit is present, with the power of our Lord Jesus, ⁵you are to deliver this man to Satan for the destruction of the flesh, so that his spirit may be saved in the day of the Lord.³

⁶Your boasting is not good. Do you not know that a little leaven leavens the whole lump? ⁷Cleanse out the old leaven that you may be a new lump, as you really are unleavened. For Christ, our Passover lamb, has been sacrificed. ⁸Let us therefore celebrate the festival, not with the old leaven, the leaven of malice and evil, but with the unleavened bread of sincerity and truth.

⁹I wrote to you in my letter not to associate with sexually immoral people— ¹⁰not at all meaning the sexually immoral of this world, or the greedy and swindlers, or idolaters, since then you would need to go out of the world. ¹¹But now I am writing to you not to associate with anyone who bears the name of brother if he is guilty of sexual immorality or greed, or is an idolater, reviler, drunkard, or swindler—not even to eat with such a one. ¹²For what have I to do with judging outsiders? Is it not those inside the church whom you are to judge? ¹³God judges⁴ those outside. "Purge the evil person from among you."

Lawsuits Against Believers

6 When one of you has a grievance against another, does he dare go to law before the unrighteous instead of the saints? ²Or do you not know that the saints will judge the world? And if the world is to be judged by you, are you incompetent to try trivial cases? ³Do you not know that we are to judge angels? How much more, then, matters pertaining to this life! ⁴So if you have such cases, why do you lay them before those who have no standing in the church? ⁵I say this to your shame. Can it be that there is no one among you wise enough to settle a dispute between the brothers, ⁶but brother goes to law against brother, and that before unbelievers? ⁷To have lawsuits at all with one another is already a defeat for you. Why not rather suffer wrong? Why not rather be defrauded? ⁸But you yourselves wrong and defraud—even your own brothers!⁵

⁹Or do you not know that the unrighteous⁶ will not inherit the kingdom of God? Do not be deceived: neither the sexually immoral, nor idolaters, nor adulterers, nor men who practice homosexuality,⁷ ¹⁰nor thieves, nor the greedy, nor drunkards, nor revilers, nor swindlers will inherit the kingdom of God. ¹¹And such were some of you. But you were washed, you were sanctified, you were justified in the name of the Lord Jesus Christ and by the Spirit of our God.

Flee Sexual Immorality

¹²"All things are lawful for me," but not all things are helpful. "All things are lawful for me," but I will not be enslaved by anything. ¹³"Food is meant for the stomach and the stomach for food"—and God will destroy both one and the other. The body is not meant for sexual immorality, but for the Lord, and the Lord for the body. ¹⁴And God raised the Lord and will also raise us up by his power. ¹⁵Do you not know that your bodies are members of Christ? Shall I then take the members of Christ and make them members

---

¹Or am sending ²Some manuscripts add Jesus ³Some manuscripts add Jesus ⁴Or will judge ⁵Or brothers and sisters ⁶Or wrongdoers ⁷The two Greek terms translated by this phrase refer to the passive and active partners in consensual homosexual acts

of a prostitute? Never! [16]Or do you not know that he who is joined[1] to a prostitute becomes one body with her? For, as it is written, a"The two will become one flesh." [17]But he who is joined to the Lord becomes one spirit with him. [18]Flee from sexual immorality. Every other sin[2] a person commits is outside the body, but the sexually immoral person sins against his own body. [19]Or do you not know that your body is a temple of the Holy Spirit within you, whom you have from God? You are not your own, [20]for you were bought with a price. So glorify God in your body.

Principles for Marriage

7 Now concerning the matters about which you wrote: "It is good for a man not to have sexual relations with a woman." [2]But because of the temptation to sexual immorality, each man should have his own wife and each woman her own husband. [3]The husband should give to his wife her conjugal rights, and likewise the wife to her husband. [4]For the wife does not have authority over her own body, but the husband does. Likewise the husband does not have authority over his own body, but the wife does. [5]Do not deprive one another, except perhaps by agreement for a limited time, that you may devote yourselves to prayer; but then come together again, so that Satan may not tempt you because of your lack of self-control.

[6]Now as a concession, not a command, I say this.[3] [7]I wish that all were as I myself am. But each has his own gift from God, one of one kind and one of another.

[8]To the unmarried and the widows I say that it is good for them to remain single as I am. [9]But if they cannot exercise self-control, they should marry. For it is better to marry than to burn with passion.

[10]To the married I give this charge (not I, but the Lord): the wife should not separate from her husband [11](but if she does, she should remain unmarried or else be reconciled to her husband), and the husband should not divorce his wife.

[12]To the rest I say (I, not the Lord) that if any brother has a wife who is an unbeliever, and she consents to live with him, he should not divorce her. [13]If any woman has a husband who is an unbeliever, and he consents to live with her, she should not divorce him. [14]For the unbelieving husband is made holy because of his wife, and the unbelieving wife is made holy because of her husband. Otherwise your children would be unclean, but as it is, they are holy. [15]But if the unbelieving partner separates, let it be so. In such cases the brother or sister is not enslaved. God has called you[4] to peace. [16]For how do you know, wife, whether you will save your husband? Or how do you know, husband, whether you will save your wife?

Live as You Are Called

[17]Only let each person lead the life that the Lord has assigned to him, and to which God has called him. This is my rule in all the churches. [18]Was anyone at the time of his call already circumcised? Let him not seek to remove the marks of circumcision. Was anyone at the time of his call uncircumcised? Let him not seek circumcision. [19]For neither circumcision counts for anything nor uncircumcision, but keeping the commandments of God. [20]Each one should remain in the condition in which he was called. [21]Were you a slave[5] when called? Do not be concerned about it. (But if you can gain your freedom, avail yourself of the opportunity.) [22]For he who was called in the Lord as a slave is a freedman of the Lord. Likewise he who was free when called is a slave of Christ. [23]You were bought with a price; do not become slaves of men. [24]So, brothers,[6] in whatever condition each was called, there let him remain with God.

The Unmarried and the Widowed

[25]Now concerning[7] the betrothed,[8] I have no command from the Lord, but I give my judgment as one who by the Lord's mercy is trustworthy. [26]I think that in view of the present[9] distress it is good for a person to remain as he is. [27]Are you bound to a wife? Do not seek to be free. Are you free from a wife? Do not seek a wife. [28]But if you do marry, you have not sinned, and if a betrothed woman[10] marries, she has not sinned. Yet those who marry will have worldly troubles, and I would spare you that. [29]This is what I mean, brothers: the appointed time has grown very short. From now on, let those who have wives live as though they had none, [30]and those who mourn as though they were not mourning, and those who rejoice as though they were not rejoicing, and those who buy as though they had no goods, [31]and those who deal with the world as though they had no dealings with it. For the present form of this world is passing away.

[32]I want you to be free from anxieties. The unmarried man is anxious about the things of the Lord, how to please the Lord. [33]But the married man is anxious about worldly things, how to please his wife, [34]and his interests are divided. And the unmarried or betrothed woman is anxious about the things of the Lord, how to be holy in body and spirit. But the married woman is anxious about worldly things, how to please her husband. [35]I say this for your own benefit, not to lay any restraint upon you, but to promote good order and to secure your undivided devotion to the Lord.

---

[1]Or who holds fast (compare Genesis 2:24 and Deuteronomy 10:20); also verse 17 [2]Or Every sin [3]Or I say this: [4]Some manuscripts us [5]Greek bondservant; also twice in verse 22 and once in verse 23 (plural) [6]Or brothers and sisters; also verse 29 [7]The expression Now concerning introduces a reply to a question in the Corinthians' letter; see 7:1 [8]Greek virgins [9]Or impending [10]Greek virgin; also verse 34 a Gen. 2:24

36If anyone thinks that he is not behaving properly toward his betrothed,[1] if his[2] passions are strong, and it has to be, let him do as he wishes: let them marry—it is no sin. **37**But whoever is firmly established in his heart, being under no necessity but having his desire under control, and has determined this in his heart, to keep her as his betrothed, he will do well. **38**So then he who marries his betrothed does well, and he who refrains from marriage will do even better.

39A wife is bound to her husband as long as he lives. But if her husband dies, she is free to be married to whom she wishes, only in the Lord. **40**Yet in my judgment she is happier if she remains as she is. And I think that I too have the Spirit of God.

Food Offered to Idols

8 Now concerning[3] food offered to idols: we know that "all of us possess knowledge." This "knowledge" puffs up, but love builds up. **2**If anyone imagines that he knows something, he does not yet know as he ought to know. **3**But if anyone loves God, he is known by God.[4]

4Therefore, as to the eating of food offered to idols, we know that "an idol has no real existence," and that "there is no God but one." **5**For although there may be so-called gods in heaven or on earth—as indeed there are many "gods" and many "lords"— **6**yet for us there is one God, the Father, from whom are all things and for whom we exist, and one Lord, Jesus Christ, through whom are all things and through whom we exist.

7However, not all possess this knowledge. But some, through former association with idols, eat food as really offered to an idol, and their conscience, being weak, is defiled. **8**Food will not commend us to God. We are no worse off if we do not eat, and no better off if we do. **9**But take care that this right of yours does not somehow become a stumbling block to the weak. **10**For if anyone sees you who have knowledge eating[5] in an idol's temple, will he not be encouraged,[6] if his conscience is weak, to eat food offered to idols? **11**And so by your knowledge this weak person is destroyed, the brother for whom Christ died. **12**Thus, sinning against your brothers[7] and wounding their conscience when it is weak, you sin against Christ. **13**Therefore, if food makes my brother stumble, I will never eat meat, lest I make my brother stumble.

Paul Surrenders His Rights

9 Am I not free? Am I not an apostle? Have I not seen Jesus our Lord? Are not you my workmanship in the Lord? **2**If to others I am not an apostle, at least I am to you, for you are the seal of my apostleship in the Lord.

3This is my defense to those who would examine me. **4**Do we not have the right to eat and drink? **5**Do we not have the right to take along a believing wife,[8] as do the other apostles and the brothers of the Lord and Cephas? **6**Or is it only Barnabas and I who have no right to refrain from working for a living? **7**Who serves as a soldier at his own expense? Who plants a vineyard without eating any of its fruit? Or who tends a flock without getting some of the milk?

8Do I say these things on human authority? Does not the Law say the same? **9**For it is written in the Law of Moses, *"You shall not muzzle an ox when it treads out the grain." Is it for oxen that God is concerned? **10**Does he not speak entirely for our sake? It was written for our sake, because the plowman should plow in hope and the thresher thresh in hope of sharing in the crop. **11**If we have sown spiritual things among you, is it too much if we reap material things from you? **12**If others share this rightful claim on you, do not we even more?

Nevertheless, we have not made use of this right, but we endure anything rather than put an obstacle in the way of the gospel of Christ. **13**Do you not know that those who are employed in the temple service get their food from the temple, and those who serve at the altar share in the sacrificial offerings? **14**In the same way, the Lord commanded that those who proclaim the gospel should get their living by the gospel.

15But I have made no use of any of these rights, nor am I writing these things to secure any such provision. For I would rather die than have anyone deprive me of my ground for boasting. **16**For if I preach the gospel, that gives me no ground for boasting. For necessity is laid upon me. Woe to me if I do not preach the gospel! **17**For if I do this of my own will, I have a reward, but if not of my own will, I am still entrusted with a stewardship. **18**What then is my reward? That in my preaching I may present the gospel free of charge, so as not to make full use of my right in the gospel.

19For though I am free from all, I have made myself a servant to all, that I might win more of them. **20**To the Jews I became as a Jew, in order to win Jews. To those under the law I became as one under the law (though not being myself under the law) that I might win those under the law. **21**To those outside the law I became as one outside the law (not being outside the law of God but under the law of Christ) that I might win those outside the law. **22**To the weak I became weak, that I might win the weak. I have become all things to all people, that by all means I might save some. **23**I do it all for the sake of the gospel, that I may share with them in its blessings.

24Do you not know that in a race all the run-

---

[1] Greek *virgin*; also verses 37, 38 [2] Or *her* [3] The expression *Now concerning* introduces a reply to a question in the Corinthians' letter; see 7:1 [4] Greek *him* [5] Greek *reclining at table* [6] Or *fortified*; Greek *built up* [7] Or *brothers and sisters* [8] Greek *a sister as wife* [a] Deut. 25:4

ners run, but only one receives the prize? So run that you may obtain it. [25]Every athlete exercises self-control in all things. They do it to receive a perishable wreath, but we an imperishable. [26]So I do not run aimlessly; I do not box as one beating the air. [27]But I discipline my body and keep it under control,[1] lest after preaching to others I myself should be disqualified.

Warning Against Idolatry

10 For I want you to know, brothers,[2] that our fathers were all under the cloud, and all passed through the sea, [2]and all were baptized into Moses in the cloud and in the sea, [3]and all ate the same spiritual food, [4]and all drank the same spiritual drink. For they drank from the spiritual Rock that followed them, and the Rock was Christ. [5]Nevertheless, with most of them God was not pleased, for they were overthrown in the wilderness.

[6]Now these things took place as examples for us, that we might not desire evil as they did. [7]Do not be idolaters as some of them were; as it is written, [a]"The people sat down to eat and drink and rose up to play." [8]We must not indulge in sexual immorality as some of them did, and twenty-three thousand fell in a single day. [9]We must not put Christ[3] to the test, as some of them did and were destroyed by serpents, [10]nor grumble, as some of them did and were destroyed by the Destroyer. [11]Now these things happened to them as an example, but they were written down for our instruction, on whom the end of the ages has come. [12]Therefore let anyone who thinks that he stands take heed lest he fall. [13]No temptation has overtaken you that is not common to man. God is faithful, and he will not let you be tempted beyond your ability, but with the temptation he will also provide the way of escape, that you may be able to endure it.

[14]Therefore, my beloved, flee from idolatry. [15]I speak as to sensible people; judge for yourselves what I say. [16]The cup of blessing that we bless, is it not a participation in the blood of Christ? The bread that we break, is it not a participation in the body of Christ? [17]Because there is one bread, we who are many are one body, for we all partake of the one bread. [18]Consider the people of Israel:[4] are not those who eat the sacrifices participants in the altar? [19]What do I imply then? That food offered to idols is anything, or that an idol is anything? [20]No, I imply that what pagans sacrifice they offer to demons and not to God. I do not want you to be participants with demons. [21]You cannot drink the cup of the Lord and the cup of demons. You cannot partake of the table of the Lord and the table of demons. [22]Shall we provoke the Lord to jealousy? Are we stronger than he?

Do All to the Glory of God

[23]"All things are lawful," but not all things are helpful. "All things are lawful," but not all things build up. [24]Let no one seek his own good, but the good of his neighbor. [25]Eat whatever is sold in the meat market without raising any question on the ground of conscience. [26]For [b]"the earth is the Lord's, and the fullness thereof." [27]If one of the unbelievers invites you to dinner and you are disposed to go, eat whatever is set before you without raising any question on the ground of conscience. [28]But if someone says to you, "This has been offered in sacrifice," then do not eat it, for the sake of the one who informed you, and for the sake of conscience— [29]I do not mean your conscience, but his. For why should my liberty be determined by someone else's conscience? [30]If I partake with thankfulness, why am I denounced because of that for which I give thanks?

[31]So, whether you eat or drink, or whatever you do, do all to the glory of God. [32]Give no offense to Jews or to Greeks or to the church of God, [33]just as I try to please everyone in everything I do, not seeking my own advantage, but that of many, that they may be saved.

11 Be imitators of me, as I am of Christ.

Head Coverings

[2]Now I commend you because you remember me in everything and maintain the traditions even as I delivered them to you. [3]But I want you to understand that the head of every man is Christ, the head of a wife[5] is her husband, and the head of Christ is God. [4]Every man who prays or prophesies with his head covered dishonors his head, [5]but every wife[6] who prays or prophesies with her head uncovered dishonors her head, since it is the same as if her head were shaven. [6]For if a wife will not cover her head, then she should cut her hair short. But since it is disgraceful for a wife to cut off her hair or shave her head, let her cover her head. [7]For a man ought not to cover his head, since he is the image and glory of God, but woman is the glory of man. [8]For man was not made from woman, but woman from man. [9]Neither was man created for woman, but woman for man. [10]That is why a wife ought to have a symbol of authority on her head, because of the angels.[7] [11]Nevertheless, in the Lord woman is not independent of man nor man of woman; [12]for as woman was made from man, so man is now born of woman. And all things are from God. [13]Judge for yourselves: is it proper for a wife to pray to God with her head uncovered? [14]Does not nature itself teach you that if a man wears long hair it is a disgrace for him, [15]but if a woman has long hair, it is her glory? For her hair is given to her for a covering.

---

[1] Greek *I pummel my body and make it a slave* [2] Or *brothers and sisters* [3] Some manuscripts *the Lord* [4] Greek *Consider Israel according to the flesh* [5] Greek *gunē*. This term may refer to a *woman* or a *wife*, depending on the context [6] In verses 5-13, the Greek word *gunē* is translated *wife* in verses that deal with wearing a veil, a sign of being married in first-century culture [7] Or *messengers*, that is, people sent to observe and report [a] Ex. 32:6 [b] Ps. 24:1

16 If anyone is inclined to be contentious, we have no such practice, nor do the churches of God.

The Lord's Supper

17 But in the following instructions I do not commend you, because when you come together it is not for the better but for the worse. **18** For, in the first place, when you come together as a church, I hear that there are divisions among you. And I believe it in part,[1] **19** for there must be factions among you in order that those who are genuine among you may be recognized. **20** When you come together, it is not the Lord's supper that you eat. **21** For in eating, each one goes ahead with his own meal. One goes hungry, another gets drunk. **22** What! Do you not have houses to eat and drink in? Or do you despise the church of God and humiliate those who have nothing? What shall I say to you? Shall I commend you in this? No, I will not.

23 For I received from the Lord what I also delivered to you, that the Lord Jesus on the night when he was betrayed took bread, **24** and when he had given thanks, he broke it, and said, "This is my body which is for[2] you. Do this in remembrance of me."[3] **25** In the same way also he took the cup, after supper, saying, "This cup is the new covenant in my blood. Do this, as often as you drink it, in remembrance of me." **26** For as often as you eat this bread and drink the cup, you proclaim the Lord's death until he comes.

27 Whoever, therefore, eats the bread or drinks the cup of the Lord in an unworthy manner will be guilty concerning the body and blood of the Lord. **28** Let a person examine himself, then, and so eat of the bread and drink of the cup. **29** For anyone who eats and drinks without discerning the body eats and drinks judgment on himself. **30** That is why many of you are weak and ill, and some have died.[4] **31** But if we judged[5] ourselves truly, we would not be judged. **32** But when we are judged by the Lord, we are disciplined[6] so that we may not be condemned along with the world. **33** So then, my brothers,[7] when you come together to eat, wait for[8] one another— **34** if anyone is hungry, let him eat at home—so that when you come together it will not be for judgment. About the other things I will give directions when I come.

Spiritual Gifts

12 Now concerning[9] spiritual gifts,[10] brothers,[11] I do not want you to be uninformed. **2** You know that when you were pagans you were led astray to mute idols, however you were led. **3** Therefore I want you to understand that no one speaking in the Spirit of God ever says "Jesus is accursed!" and no one can say "Jesus is Lord" except in the Holy Spirit.

4 Now there are varieties of gifts, but the same Spirit; **5** and there are varieties of service, but the same Lord; **6** and there are varieties of activities, but it is the same God who empowers them all in everyone. **7** To each is given the manifestation of the Spirit for the common good. **8** For to one is given through the Spirit the utterance of wisdom, and to another the utterance of knowledge according to the same Spirit, **9** to another faith by the same Spirit, to another gifts of healing by the one Spirit, **10** to another the working of miracles, to another prophecy, to another the ability to distinguish between spirits, to another various kinds of tongues, to another the interpretation of tongues. **11** All these are empowered by one and the same Spirit, who apportions to each one individually as he wills.

One Body with Many Members

12 For just as the body is one and has many members, and all the members of the body, though many, are one body, so it is with Christ. **13** For in one Spirit we were all baptized into one body—Jews or Greeks, slaves[12] or free—and all were made to drink of one Spirit.

14 For the body does not consist of one member but of many. **15** If the foot should say, "Because I am not a hand, I do not belong to the body," that would not make it any less a part of the body. **16** And if the ear should say, "Because I am not an eye, I do not belong to the body," that would not make it any less a part of the body. **17** If the whole body were an eye, where would be the sense of hearing? If the whole body were an ear, where would be the sense of smell? **18** But as it is, God arranged the members in the body, each one of them, as he chose. **19** If all were a single member, where would the body be? **20** As it is, there are many parts,[13] yet one body.

21 The eye cannot say to the hand, "I have no need of you," nor again the head to the feet, "I have no need of you." **22** On the contrary, the parts of the body that seem to be weaker are indispensable, **23** and on those parts of the body that we think less honorable we bestow the greater honor, and our unpresentable parts are treated with greater modesty, **24** which our more presentable parts do not require. But God has so composed the body, giving greater honor to the part that lacked it, **25** that there may be no division in the body, but that the members may have the same care for one another. **26** If one member suffers, all suffer together; if one member is honored, all rejoice together.

27 Now you are the body of Christ and individually members of it. **28** And God has appointed in

---

[1] Or I believe a certain report [2] Some manuscripts broken for [3] Or as my memorial; also verse 25 [4] Greek have fallen asleep (as in 15:6, 20) [5] Or discerned [6] Or when we are judged we are being disciplined by the Lord [7] Or brothers and sisters [8] Or share with [9] The expression Now concerning introduces a reply to a question in the Corinthians' letter; see 7:1 [10] Or spiritual persons [11] Or brothers and sisters [12] Or servants; Greek bondservants [13] Or members; also verse 22

the church first apostles, second prophets, third teachers, then miracles, then gifts of healing, helping, administrating, and various kinds of tongues. ²⁹Are all apostles? Are all prophets? Are all teachers? Do all work miracles? ³⁰Do all possess gifts of healing? Do all speak with tongues? Do all interpret? ³¹But earnestly desire the higher gifts.

And I will show you a still more excellent way.

The Way of Love

13 If I speak in the tongues of men and of angels, but have not love, I am a noisy gong or a clanging cymbal. ²And if I have prophetic powers, and understand all mysteries and all knowledge, and if I have all faith, so as to remove mountains, but have not love, I am nothing. ³If I give away all I have, and if I deliver up my body to be burned,¹ but have not love, I gain nothing.

⁴Love is patient and kind; love does not envy or boast; it is not arrogant ⁵or rude. It does not insist on its own way; it is not irritable or resentful;² ⁶it does not rejoice at wrongdoing, but rejoices with the truth. ⁷Love bears all things, believes all things, hopes all things, endures all things.

⁸Love never ends. As for prophecies, they will pass away; as for tongues, they will cease; as for knowledge, it will pass away. ⁹For we know in part and we prophesy in part, ¹⁰but when the perfect comes, the partial will pass away. ¹¹When I was a child, I spoke like a child, I thought like a child, I reasoned like a child. When I became a man, I gave up childish ways. ¹²For now we see in a mirror dimly, but then face to face. Now I know in part; then I shall know fully, even as I have been fully known.

¹³So now faith, hope, and love abide, these three; but the greatest of these is love.

Prophecy and Tongues

14 Pursue love, and earnestly desire the spiritual gifts, especially that you may prophesy. ²For one who speaks in a tongue speaks not to men but to God; for no one understands him, but he utters mysteries in the Spirit. ³On the other hand, the one who prophesies speaks to people for their upbuilding and encouragement and consolation. ⁴The one who speaks in a tongue builds up himself, but the one who prophesies builds up the church. ⁵Now I want you all to speak in tongues, but even more to prophesy. The one who prophesies is greater than the one who speaks in tongues, unless someone interprets, so that the church may be built up.

⁶Now, brothers,³ if I come to you speaking in tongues, how will I benefit you unless I bring you some revelation or knowledge or prophecy or teaching? ⁷If even lifeless instruments, such as the flute or the harp, do not give distinct notes, how will anyone know what is played? ⁸And if the bugle gives an indistinct sound, who will get ready for battle? ⁹So with yourselves, if with your tongue you utter speech that is not intelligible, how will anyone know what is said? For you will be speaking into the air. ¹⁰There are doubtless many different languages in the world, and none is without meaning, ¹¹but if I do not know the meaning of the language, I will be a foreigner to the speaker and the speaker a foreigner to me. ¹²So with yourselves, since you are eager for manifestations of the Spirit, strive to excel in building up the church.

¹³Therefore, one who speaks in a tongue should pray for the power to interpret. ¹⁴For if I pray in a tongue, my spirit prays but my mind is unfruitful. ¹⁵What am I to do? I will pray with my spirit, but I will pray with my mind also; I will sing praise with my spirit, but I will sing with my mind also. ¹⁶Otherwise, if you give thanks with your spirit, how can anyone in the position of an outsider⁴ say "Amen" to your thanksgiving when he does not know what you are saying? ¹⁷For you may be giving thanks well enough, but the other person is not being built up. ¹⁸I thank God that I speak in tongues more than all of you. ¹⁹Nevertheless, in church I would rather speak five words with my mind in order to instruct others, than ten thousand words in a tongue.

²⁰Brothers, do not be children in your thinking. Be infants in evil, but in your thinking be mature. ²¹In the Law it is written, ᵃ"By people of strange tongues and by the lips of foreigners will I speak to this people, and even then they will not listen to me, says the Lord." ²²Thus tongues are a sign not for believers but for unbelievers, while prophecy is a sign⁵ not for unbelievers but for believers. ²³If, therefore, the whole church comes together and all speak in tongues, and outsiders or unbelievers enter, will they not say that you are out of your minds? ²⁴But if all prophesy, and an unbeliever or outsider enters, he is convicted by all, he is called to account by all, ²⁵the secrets of his heart are disclosed, and so, falling on his face, he will worship God and declare that God is really among you.

Orderly Worship

²⁶What then, brothers? When you come together, each one has a hymn, a lesson, a revelation, a tongue, or an interpretation. Let all things be done for building up. ²⁷If any speak in a tongue, let there be only two or at most three, and each in turn, and let someone interpret. ²⁸But if there is no one to interpret, let each of them keep silent in church and speak to himself and to God. ²⁹Let two or three prophets speak, and let the others weigh what is said. ³⁰If a revelation is made to another sitting there, let the first be silent. ³¹For

¹ Some manuscripts *deliver up my body* [to death] *that I may boast* ² Greek *irritable and does not count up wrongdoing* ³ Or *brothers and sisters;* also verses 20, 26, 39 ⁴ Or *of him that is without gifts* ⁵ Greek lacks *a sign* ᵃ Isa. 28:11, 12

you can all prophesy one by one, so that all may learn and all be encouraged, [32]and the spirits of prophets are subject to prophets. [33]For God is not a God of confusion but of peace.

As in all the churches of the saints, [34]the women should keep silent in the churches. For they are not permitted to speak, but should be in submission, as the Law also says. [35]If there is anything they desire to learn, let them ask their husbands at home. For it is shameful for a woman to speak in church.

[36]Or was it from you that the word of God came? Or are you the only ones it has reached? [37]If anyone thinks that he is a prophet, or spiritual, he should acknowledge that the things I am writing to you are a command of the Lord. [38]If anyone does not recognize this, he is not recognized. [39]So, my brothers, earnestly desire to prophesy, and do not forbid speaking in tongues. [40]But all things should be done decently and in order.

The Resurrection of Christ

15 Now I would remind you, brothers,[1] of the gospel I preached to you, which you received, in which you stand, [2]and by which you are being saved, if you hold fast to the word I preached to you—unless you believed in vain.

[3]For I delivered to you as of first importance what I also received: that Christ died for our sins in accordance with the Scriptures, [4]that he was buried, that he was raised on the third day in accordance with the Scriptures, [5]and that he appeared to Cephas, then to the twelve. [6]Then he appeared to more than five hundred brothers at one time, most of whom are still alive, though some have fallen asleep. [7]Then he appeared to James, then to all the apostles. [8]Last of all, as to one untimely born, he appeared also to me. [9]For I am the least of the apostles, unworthy to be called an apostle, because I persecuted the church of God. [10]But by the grace of God I am what I am, and his grace toward me was not in vain. On the contrary, I worked harder than any of them, though it was not I, but the grace of God that is with me. [11]Whether then it was I or they, so we preach and so you believed.

The Resurrection of the Dead

[12]Now if Christ is proclaimed as raised from the dead, how can some of you say that there is no resurrection of the dead? [13]But if there is no resurrection of the dead, then not even Christ has been raised. [14]And if Christ has not been raised, then our preaching is in vain and your faith is in vain. [15]We are even found to be misrepresenting God, because we testified about God that he raised Christ, whom he did not raise if it is true that the dead are not raised. [16]For if the dead are not raised, not even Christ has been

raised. [17]And if Christ has not been raised, your faith is futile and you are still in your sins. [18]Then those also who have fallen asleep in Christ have perished. [19]If in Christ we have hope[2] in this life only, we are of all people most to be pitied.

[20]But in fact Christ has been raised from the dead, the firstfruits of those who have fallen asleep. [21]For as by a man came death, by a man has come also the resurrection of the dead. [22]For as in Adam all die, so also in Christ shall all be made alive. [23]But each in his own order: Christ the firstfruits, then at his coming those who belong to Christ. [24]Then comes the end, when he delivers the kingdom to God the Father after destroying every rule and every authority and power. [25]For he must reign until he has put all his enemies under his feet. [26]The last enemy to be destroyed is death. [27]For [a]"God[3] has put all things in subjection under his feet." But when it says, "all things are put in subjection," it is plain that he is excepted who put all things in subjection under him. [28]When all things are subjected to him, then the Son himself will also be subjected to him who put all things in subjection under him, that God may be all in all.

[29]Otherwise, what do people mean by being baptized on behalf of the dead? If the dead are not raised at all, why are people baptized on their behalf? [30]Why are we in danger every hour? [31]I protest, brothers, by my pride in you, which I have in Christ Jesus our Lord, I die every day! [32]What do I gain if, humanly speaking, I fought with beasts at Ephesus? If the dead are not raised, [b]"Let us eat and drink, for tomorrow we die." [33]Do not be deceived: "Bad company ruins good morals."[4] [34]Wake up from your drunken stupor, as is right, and do not go on sinning. For some have no knowledge of God. I say this to your shame.

The Resurrection Body

[35]But someone will ask, "How are the dead raised? With what kind of body do they come?" [36]You foolish person! What you sow does not come to life unless it dies. [37]And what you sow is not the body that is to be, but a bare kernel, perhaps of wheat or of some other grain. [38]But God gives it a body as he has chosen, and to each kind of seed its own body. [39]For not all flesh is the same, but there is one kind for humans, another for animals, another for birds, and another for fish. [40]There are heavenly bodies and earthly bodies, but the glory of the heavenly is of one kind, and the glory of the earthly is of another. [41]There is one glory of the sun, and another glory of the moon, and another glory of the stars; for star differs from star in glory.

[42]So is it with the resurrection of the dead. What is sown is perishable; what is raised is imperishable. [43]It is sown in dishonor; it is raised

---

[1]Or brothers and sisters; also verses 6, 31, 50, 58 [2]Or we have hoped [3]Greek he [4]Probably from Menander's comedy Thais [a]Ps. 8:6 [b]Isa. 22:13

in glory. It is sown in weakness; it is raised in power. ⁴⁴It is sown a natural body; it is raised a spiritual body. If there is a natural body, there is also a spiritual body. ⁴⁵Thus it is written, ᵃ"The first man Adam became a living being";ᴵ the last Adam became a life-giving spirit. ⁴⁶But it is not the spiritual that is first but the natural, and then the spiritual. ⁴⁷The first man was from the earth, a man of dust; the second man is from heaven. ⁴⁸As was the man of dust, so also are those who are of the dust, and as is the man of heaven, so also are those who are of heaven. ⁴⁹Just as we have borne the image of the man of dust, we shall² also bear the image of the man of heaven.

Mystery and Victory

⁵⁰I tell you this, brothers: flesh and blood cannot inherit the kingdom of God, nor does the perishable inherit the imperishable. ⁵¹Behold! I tell you a mystery. We shall not all sleep, but we shall all be changed, ⁵²in a moment, in the twinkling of an eye, at the last trumpet. For the trumpet will sound, and the dead will be raised imperishable, and we shall be changed. ⁵³For this perishable body must put on the imperishable, and this mortal body must put on immortality. ⁵⁴When the perishable puts on the imperishable, and the mortal puts on immortality, then shall come to pass the saying that is written:

ᵇ"Death is swallowed up in victory."
⁵⁵ "O death, where is your victory?
    O death, where is your sting?"

⁵⁶The sting of death is sin, and the power of sin is the law. ⁵⁷But thanks be to God, who gives us the victory through our Lord Jesus Christ.

⁵⁸Therefore, my beloved brothers, be steadfast, immovable, always abounding in the work of the Lord, knowing that in the Lord your labor is not in vain.

The Collection for the Saints

16 Now concerning³ the collection for the saints: as I directed the churches of Galatia, so you also are to do. ²On the first day of every week, each of you is to put something aside and store it up, as he may prosper, so that there will be no collecting when I come. ³And when I arrive, I will send those whom you accredit by letter to carry your gift to Jerusalem. ⁴If it seems advisable that I should go also, they will accompany me.

Plans for Travel

⁵I will visit you after passing through Macedonia, for I intend to pass through Macedonia, ⁶and perhaps I will stay with you or even spend the winter, so that you may help me on my journey, wherever I go. ⁷For I do not want to see you now just in passing. I hope to spend some time with you, if the Lord permits. ⁸But I will stay in Ephesus until Pentecost, ⁹for a wide door for effective work has opened to me, and there are many adversaries.

¹⁰When Timothy comes, see that you put him at ease among you, for he is doing the work of the Lord, as I am. ¹¹So let no one despise him. Help him on his way in peace, that he may return to me, for I am expecting him with the brothers.

Final Instructions

¹²Now concerning our brother Apollos, I strongly urged him to visit you with the other brothers, but it was not at all his will⁴ to come now. He will come when he has opportunity. ¹³Be watchful, stand firm in the faith, act like men, be strong. ¹⁴Let all that you do be done in love.

¹⁵Now I urge you, brothers⁵—you know that the household⁶ of Stephanas were the first converts in Achaia, and that they have devoted themselves to the service of the saints— ¹⁶be subject to such as these, and to every fellow worker and laborer. ¹⁷I rejoice at the coming of Stephanas and Fortunatus and Achaicus, because they have made up for your absence, ¹⁸for they refreshed my spirit as well as yours. Give recognition to such men.

Greetings

¹⁹The churches of Asia send you greetings. Aquila and Prisca, together with the church in their house, send you hearty greetings in the Lord. ²⁰All the brothers send you greetings. Greet one another with a holy kiss.

²¹I, Paul, write this greeting with my own hand. ²²If anyone has no love for the Lord, let him be accursed. Our Lord, come!⁷ ²³The grace of the Lord Jesus be with you. ²⁴My love be with you all in Christ Jesus. Amen.

---

¹Greek *a living soul* ²Some manuscripts *let us* ³The expression *Now concerning* introduces a reply to a question in the Corinthians' letter; see 7:1; also verse 12 ⁴Or *God's will for him* ⁵Or *brothers and sisters*; also verse 20 ⁶Greek *house* ⁷Greek *Maranatha* (a transliteration of Aramaic) ᵃGen. 2:7 ᵇIsa. 25:8

2 CORINTHIANS

Introduction

Paul's second letter to the Corinthians discusses some of the things previously addressed but also deals with new issues. While 1 Corinthians called for believers to be unified with each other, in this letter Paul urges the church to be unified with him in his ministry. Paul's opponents were undermining his work, claiming that his suffering (11:24-29) proved he was not a true apostle. Paul responds that his suffering highlights his dependence on Christ, as it points to Christ's strength rather than his own. Second Corinthians includes stirring perspectives on gospel ministry (chs. 2–5), encouragements to holy living (chs. 6–7), and instructions about giving (chs. 8–9). Paul wrote this letter from Macedonia a year after writing 1 Corinthians, about A.D. 56.

Greeting

1 Paul, an apostle of Christ Jesus by the will of God, and Timothy our brother,

To the church of God that is at Corinth, with all the saints who are in the whole of Achaia:

²Grace to you and peace from God our Father and the Lord Jesus Christ.

God of All Comfort

³Blessed be the God and Father of our Lord Jesus Christ, the Father of mercies and God of all comfort, ⁴who comforts us in all our affliction, so that we may be able to comfort those who are in any affliction, with the comfort with which we ourselves are comforted by God. ⁵For as we share abundantly in Christ's sufferings, so through Christ we share abundantly in comfort too.¹ ⁶If we are afflicted, it is for your comfort and salvation; and if we are comforted, it is for your comfort, which you experience when you patiently endure the same sufferings that we suffer. ⁷Our hope for you is unshaken, for we know that as you share in our sufferings, you will also share in our comfort.

⁸For we do not want you to be ignorant, brothers,² of the affliction we experienced in Asia. For we were so utterly burdened beyond our strength that we despaired of life itself. ⁹Indeed, we felt that we had received the sentence of death. But that was to make us rely not on ourselves but on God who raises the dead. ¹⁰He delivered us from such a deadly peril, and he will deliver us. On him we have set our hope that he will deliver us again. ¹¹You also must help us by prayer, so that many will give thanks on our behalf for the blessing granted us through the prayers of many.

Paul's Change of Plans

¹²For our boast is this, the testimony of our conscience, that we behaved in the world with simplicity³ and godly sincerity, not by earthly wisdom but by the grace of God, and supremely so toward you. ¹³For we are not writing to you anything other than what you read and acknowledge⁴ and I hope you will fully acknowledge— ¹⁴just as you did partially acknowledge us—that on the day of our Lord Jesus you will boast of us as we will boast of you.

¹⁵Because I was sure of this, I wanted to come to you first, so that you might have a second experience of grace. ¹⁶I wanted to visit you on my way to Macedonia, and to come back to you from Macedonia and have you send me on my way to Judea. ¹⁷Was I vacillating when I wanted to do this? Do I make my plans according to the flesh, ready to say "Yes, yes" and "No, no" at the same time? ¹⁸As surely as God is faithful, our word to you has not been Yes and No. ¹⁹For the Son of God, Jesus Christ, whom we proclaimed among you, Silvanus and Timothy and I, was not Yes and No, but in him it is always Yes. ²⁰For all the promises of God find their Yes in him. That is why it is through him that we utter our Amen to God for his glory. ²¹And it is God who establishes us with you in Christ, and has anointed us, ²²and who has also put his seal on us and given us his Spirit in our hearts as a guarantee.⁵

²³But I call God to witness against me—it was to spare you that I refrained from coming again to Corinth. ²⁴Not that we lord it over your faith, but we work with you for your joy, for you stand firm in your faith.

2 For I made up my mind not to make another painful visit to you. ²For if I cause you pain, who is there to make me glad but the one whom I have pained? ³And I wrote as I did, so that when I came I might not suffer pain from those who should have made me rejoice, for I felt sure of all of you, that my joy would be the joy of you all. ⁴For I wrote to you out of much affliction and anguish of heart and with many tears, not to cause you pain but to let you know the abundant love that I have for you.

---

¹ Or For as the sufferings of Christ abound for us, so also our comfort abounds through Christ ² Or brothers and sisters. The plural Greek word adelphoi (translated "brothers") refers to siblings in a family. In New Testament usage, depending on the context, adelphoi may refer either to men or to both men and women who are siblings (brothers and sisters) in God's family, the church ³ Some manuscripts holiness ⁴ Or understand; twice in this verse; also verse 14 ⁵ Or down payment

Forgive the Sinner

[5] Now if anyone has caused pain, he has caused it not to me, but in some measure—not to put it too severely—to all of you. [6] For such a one, this punishment by the majority is enough, [7] so you should rather turn to forgive and comfort him, or he may be overwhelmed by excessive sorrow. [8] So I beg you to reaffirm your love for him. [9] For this is why I wrote, that I might test you and know whether you are obedient in everything. [10] Anyone whom you forgive, I also forgive. Indeed, what I have forgiven, if I have forgiven anything, has been for your sake in the presence of Christ, [11] so that we would not be outwitted by Satan; for we are not ignorant of his designs.

Triumph in Christ

[12] When I came to Troas to preach the gospel of Christ, even though a door was opened for me in the Lord, [13] my spirit was not at rest because I did not find my brother Titus there. So I took leave of them and went on to Macedonia.

[14] But thanks be to God, who in Christ always leads us in triumphal procession, and through us spreads the fragrance of the knowledge of him everywhere. [15] For we are the aroma of Christ to God among those who are being saved and among those who are perishing, [16] to one a fragrance from death to death, to the other a fragrance from life to life. Who is sufficient[1] for these things? [17] For we are not, like so many, peddlers of God's word, but as men of sincerity, as commissioned by God, in the sight of God we speak in Christ.

Ministers of the New Covenant

3 Are we beginning to commend ourselves again? Or do we need, as some do, letters of recommendation to you, or from you? [2] You yourselves are our letter of recommendation, written on our[2] hearts, to be known and read by all. [3] And you show that you are a letter from Christ delivered by us, written not with ink but with the Spirit of the living God, not on tablets of stone but on tablets of human hearts.[3]

[4] Such is the confidence that we have through Christ toward God. [5] Not that we are sufficient in ourselves to claim anything as coming from us, but our sufficiency is from God, [6] who has made us competent[4] to be ministers of a new covenant, not of the letter but of the Spirit. For the letter kills, but the Spirit gives life.

[7] Now if the ministry of death, carved in letters on stone, came with such glory that the Israelites could not gaze at Moses' face because of its glory, which was being brought to an end, [8] will not the ministry of the Spirit have even more glory? [9] For if there was glory in the ministry of condemnation, the ministry of righteousness must far exceed it in glory. [10] Indeed, in this case, what once had glory has come to have no glory at all, because of the glory that surpasses it. [11] For if what was being brought to an end came with glory, much more will what is permanent have glory.

[12] Since we have such a hope, we are very bold, [13] not like Moses, who would put a veil over his face so that the Israelites might not gaze at the outcome of what was being brought to an end. [14] But their minds were hardened. For to this day, when they read the old covenant, that same veil remains unlifted, because only through Christ is it taken away. [15] Yes, to this day whenever Moses is read a veil lies over their hearts. [16] But when one[5] turns to the Lord, the veil is removed. [17] Now the Lord[6] is the Spirit, and where the Spirit of the Lord is, there is freedom. [18] And we all, with unveiled face, beholding the glory of the Lord,[7] are being transformed into the same image from one degree of glory to another. For this comes from the Lord who is the Spirit.

The Light of the Gospel

4 Therefore, having this ministry by the mercy of God,[8] we do not lose heart. [2] But we have renounced disgraceful, underhanded ways. We refuse to practice cunning or to tamper with God's word, but by the open statement of the truth we would commend ourselves to everyone's conscience in the sight of God. [3] And even if our gospel is veiled, it is veiled only to those who are perishing. [4] In their case the god of this world has blinded the minds of the unbelievers, to keep them from seeing the light of the gospel of the glory of Christ, who is the image of God. [5] For what we proclaim is not ourselves, but Jesus Christ as Lord, with ourselves as your servants[9] for Jesus' sake. [6] For God, who said, "Let light shine out of darkness," has shone in our hearts to give the light of the knowledge of the glory of God in the face of Jesus Christ.

Treasure in Jars of Clay

[7] But we have this treasure in jars of clay, to show that the surpassing power belongs to God and not to us. [8] We are afflicted in every way, but not crushed; perplexed, but not driven to despair; [9] persecuted, but not forsaken; struck down, but not destroyed; [10] always carrying in the body the death of Jesus, so that the life of Jesus may also be manifested in our bodies. [11] For we who live are always being given over to death for Jesus' sake, so that the life of Jesus also may be manifested in our mortal flesh. [12] So death is at work in us, but life in you.

[13] Since we have the same spirit of faith according to what has been written, [a] "I believed, and so I spoke," we also believe, and so we also speak, [14] knowing that he who raised the Lord Jesus will raise us also with Jesus and bring us with you

---

[1] Or *competent* [2] Some manuscripts *your* [3] Greek *fleshly hearts* [4] Or *sufficient* [5] Greek *he* [6] Or *this Lord* [7] Or *reflecting the glory of the Lord* [8] Greek *as we have received mercy* [9] Greek *bondservants* [a] Ps. 116:10

into his presence. [15]For it is all for your sake, so that as grace extends to more and more people it may increase thanksgiving, to the glory of God.

[16]So we do not lose heart. Though our outer self[1] is wasting away, our inner self is being renewed day by day. [17]For this light momentary affliction is preparing for us an eternal weight of glory beyond all comparison, [18]as we look not to the things that are seen but to the things that are unseen. For the things that are seen are transient, but the things that are unseen are eternal.

Our Heavenly Dwelling

5 For we know that if the tent that is our earthly home is destroyed, we have a building from God, a house not made with hands, eternal in the heavens. [2]For in this tent we groan, longing to put on our heavenly dwelling, [3]if indeed by putting it on[2] we may not be found naked. [4]For while we are still in this tent, we groan, being burdened—not that we would be unclothed, but that we would be further clothed, so that what is mortal may be swallowed up by life. [5]He who has prepared us for this very thing is God, who has given us the Spirit as a guarantee.

[6]So we are always of good courage. We know that while we are at home in the body we are away from the Lord, [7]for we walk by faith, not by sight. [8]Yes, we are of good courage, and we would rather be away from the body and at home with the Lord. [9]So whether we are at home or away, we make it our aim to please him. [10]For we must all appear before the judgment seat of Christ, so that each one may receive what is due for what he has done in the body, whether good or evil.

The Ministry of Reconciliation

[11]Therefore, knowing the fear of the Lord, we persuade others. But what we are is known to God, and I hope it is known also to your conscience. [12]We are not commending ourselves to you again but giving you cause to boast about us, so that you may be able to answer those who boast about outward appearance and not about what is in the heart. [13]For if we are beside ourselves, it is for God; if we are in our right mind, it is for you. [14]For the love of Christ controls us, because we have concluded this: that one has died for all, therefore all have died; [15]and he died for all, that those who live might no longer live for themselves but for him who for their sake died and was raised.

[16]From now on, therefore, we regard no one according to the flesh. Even though we once regarded Christ according to the flesh, we regard him thus no longer. [17]Therefore, if anyone is in Christ, he is a new creation.[3] The old has passed away; behold, the new has come. [18]All this is from God, who through Christ reconciled us to himself and gave us the ministry of reconciliation; [19]that is, in Christ God was reconciling[4] the world to himself, not counting their trespasses against them, and entrusting to us the message of reconciliation. [20]Therefore, we are ambassadors for Christ, God making his appeal through us. We implore you on behalf of Christ, be reconciled to God. [21]For our sake he made him to be sin who knew no sin, so that in him we might become the righteousness of God.

6 Working together with him, then, we appeal to you not to receive the grace of God in vain. [2]For he says,

[a]"In a favorable time I listened to you,
     and in a day of salvation I have helped you."

Behold, now is the favorable time; behold, now is the day of salvation. [3]We put no obstacle in anyone's way, so that no fault may be found with our ministry, [4]but as servants of God we commend ourselves in every way: by great endurance, in afflictions, hardships, calamities, [5]beatings, imprisonments, riots, labors, sleepless nights, hunger; [6]by purity, knowledge, patience, kindness, the Holy Spirit, genuine love; [7]by truthful speech, and the power of God; with the weapons of righteousness for the right hand and for the left; [8]through honor and dishonor, through slander and praise. We are treated as impostors, and yet are true; [9]as unknown, and yet well known; as dying, and behold, we live; as punished, and yet not killed; [10]as sorrowful, yet always rejoicing; as poor, yet making many rich; as having nothing, yet possessing everything.

[11]We have spoken freely to you,[5] Corinthians; our heart is wide open. [12]You are not restricted by us, but you are restricted in your own affections. [13]In return (I speak as to children) widen your hearts also.

The Temple of the Living God

[14]Do not be unequally yoked with unbelievers. For what partnership has righteousness with lawlessness? Or what fellowship has light with darkness? [15]What accord has Christ with Belial?[6] Or what portion does a believer share with an unbeliever? [16]What agreement has the temple of God with idols? For we are the temple of the living God; as God said,

[b]"I will make my dwelling among them and
          walk among them,
     and I will be their God,
     and they shall be my people.
[17]   Therefore [c]go out from their midst,
     and be separate from them, says the Lord,
     and touch no unclean thing;
          then I will welcome you,

---

[1] Greek man [2] Some manuscripts *putting it off* [3] Or *creature* [4] Or *God was in Christ, reconciling* [5] Greek *Our mouth is open to you* [6] Greek *Beliar* [a] Isa. 49:8 [b] Lev. 26:12 [c] Isa. 52:11

[18] and I will be a father to you,
and you shall be sons and daughters to me,
says the Lord Almighty."

7 Since we have these promises, beloved, let us cleanse ourselves from every defilement of body[1] and spirit, bringing holiness to completion in the fear of God.

Paul's Joy

[2]Make room in your hearts[2] for us. We have wronged no one, we have corrupted no one, we have taken advantage of no one. [3]I do not say this to condemn you, for I said before that you are in our hearts, to die together and to live together. [4]I am acting with great boldness toward you; I have great pride in you; I am filled with comfort. In all our affliction, I am overflowing with joy.

[5]For even when we came into Macedonia, our bodies had no rest, but we were afflicted at every turn—fighting without and fear within. [6]But God, who comforts the downcast, comforted us by the coming of Titus, [7]and not only by his coming but also by the comfort with which he was comforted by you, as he told us of your longing, your mourning, your zeal for me, so that I rejoiced still more. [8]For even if I made you grieve with my letter, I do not regret it—though I did regret it, for I see that that letter grieved you, though only for a while. [9]As it is, I rejoice, not because you were grieved, but because you were grieved into repenting. For you felt a godly grief, so that you suffered no loss through us.

[10]For godly grief produces a repentance that leads to salvation without regret, whereas worldly grief produces death. [11]For see what earnestness this godly grief has produced in you, but also what eagerness to clear yourselves, what indignation, what fear, what longing, what zeal, what punishment! At every point you have proved yourselves innocent in the matter. [12]So although I wrote to you, it was not for the sake of the one who did the wrong, nor for the sake of the one who suffered the wrong, but in order that your earnestness for us might be revealed to you in the sight of God. [13]Therefore we are comforted.

And besides our own comfort, we rejoiced still more at the joy of Titus, because his spirit has been refreshed by you all. [14]For whatever boasts I made to him about you, I was not put to shame. But just as everything we said to you was true, so also our boasting before Titus has proved true. [15]And his affection for you is even greater, as he remembers the obedience of you all, how you received him with fear and trembling. [16]I rejoice, because I have perfect confidence in you.

Encouragement to Give Generously

8 We want you to know, brothers,[3] about the grace of God that has been given among the churches of Macedonia, [2]for in a severe test of affliction, their abundance of joy and their extreme poverty have overflowed in a wealth of generosity on their part. [3]For they gave according to their means, as I can testify, and beyond their means, of their own accord, [4]begging us earnestly for the favor[4] of taking part in the relief of the saints— [5]and this, not as we expected, but they gave themselves first to the Lord and then by the will of God to us. [6]Accordingly, we urged Titus that as he had started, so he should complete among you this act of grace. [7]But as you excel in everything—in faith, in speech, in knowledge, in all earnestness, and in our love for you[5]—see that you excel in this act of grace also.

[8]I say this not as a command, but to prove by the earnestness of others that your love also is genuine. [9]For you know the grace of our Lord Jesus Christ, that though he was rich, yet for your sake he became poor, so that you by his poverty might become rich. [10]And in this matter I give my judgment: this benefits you, who a year ago started not only to do this work but also to desire to do it. [11]So now finish doing it as well, so that your readiness in desiring it may be matched by your completing it out of what you have. [12]For if the readiness is there, it is acceptable according to what a person has, not according to what he does not have. [13]For I do not mean that others should be eased and you burdened, but that as a matter of fairness [14]your abundance at the present time should supply their need, so that their abundance may supply your need, that there may be fairness. [15]As it is written, a"Whoever gathered much had nothing left over, and whoever gathered little had no lack."

Commendation of Titus

[16]But thanks be to God, who put into the heart of Titus the same earnest care I have for you. [17]For he not only accepted our appeal, but being himself very earnest he is going[6] to you of his own accord. [18]With him we are sending[7] the brother who is famous among all the churches for his preaching of the gospel. [19]And not only that, but he has been appointed by the churches to travel with us as we carry out this act of grace that is being ministered by us, for the glory of the Lord himself and to show our good will. [20]We take this course so that no one should blame us about this generous gift that is being administered by us, [21]for we aim at what is honorable not only in the Lord's sight but also in the sight of man. [22]And with them we are sending our brother whom we have often tested and found

---

[1] Greek *flesh* [2] Greek lacks *in your hearts* [3] Or *brothers and sisters* [4] The Greek word *charis* can mean *favor* or *grace* or *thanks*, depending on the context
[5] Some manuscripts *in your love for us* [6] Or *he went* [7] Or *we sent*; also verse 22 a Ex. 16:18

earnest in many matters, but who is now more earnest than ever because of his great confidence in you. ²³As for Titus, he is my partner and fellow worker for your benefit. And as for our brothers, they are messengers¹ of the churches, the glory of Christ. ²⁴So give proof before the churches of your love and of our boasting about you to these men.

The Collection for Christians in Jerusalem

9 Now it is superfluous for me to write to you about the ministry for the saints, ²for I know your readiness, of which I boast about you to the people of Macedonia, saying that Achaia has been ready since last year. And your zeal has stirred up most of them. ³But I am sending² the brothers so that our boasting about you may not prove empty in this matter, so that you may be ready, as I said you would be. ⁴Otherwise, if some Macedonians come with me and find that you are not ready, we would be humiliated—to say nothing of you—for being so confident. ⁵So I thought it necessary to urge the brothers to go on ahead to you and arrange in advance for the gift³ you have promised, so that it may be ready as a willing gift, not as an exaction.⁴

The Cheerful Giver

⁶The point is this: whoever sows sparingly will also reap sparingly, and whoever sows bountifully⁵ will also reap bountifully. ⁷Each one must give as he has decided in his heart, not reluctantly or under compulsion, for God loves a cheerful giver. ⁸And God is able to make all grace abound to you, so that having all sufficiency⁶ in all things at all times, you may abound in every good work. ⁹As it is written,

ᵃ"He has distributed freely, he has given to the poor;
    his righteousness endures forever."

¹⁰He who supplies seed to the sower and bread for food will supply and multiply your seed for sowing and increase the harvest of your righteousness. ¹¹You will be enriched in every way to be generous in every way, which through us will produce thanksgiving to God. ¹²For the ministry of this service is not only supplying the needs of the saints but is also overflowing in many thanksgivings to God. ¹³By their approval of this service, they⁷ will glorify God because of your submission flowing from your confession of the gospel of Christ, and the generosity of your contribution for them and for all others, ¹⁴while they long for you and pray for you, because of the surpassing grace of God upon you. ¹⁵Thanks be to God for his inexpressible gift!

Paul Defends His Ministry

10 I, Paul, myself entreat you, by the meekness and gentleness of Christ—I who am humble when face to face with you, but bold toward you when I am away!— ²I beg of you that when I am present I may not have to show boldness with such confidence as I count on showing against some who suspect us of walking according to the flesh. ³For though we walk in the flesh, we are not waging war according to the flesh. ⁴For the weapons of our warfare are not of the flesh but have divine power to destroy strongholds. ⁵We destroy arguments and every lofty opinion raised against the knowledge of God, and take every thought captive to obey Christ, ⁶being ready to punish every disobedience, when your obedience is complete.

⁷Look at what is before your eyes. If anyone is confident that he is Christ's, let him remind himself that just as he is Christ's, so also are we. ⁸For even if I boast a little too much of our authority, which the Lord gave for building you up and not for destroying you, I will not be ashamed. ⁹I do not want to appear to be frightening you with my letters. ¹⁰For they say, "His letters are weighty and strong, but his bodily presence is weak, and his speech of no account." ¹¹Let such a person understand that what we say by letter when absent, we do when present. ¹²Not that we dare to classify or compare ourselves with some of those who are commending themselves. But when they measure themselves by one another and compare themselves with one another, they are without understanding.

¹³But we will not boast beyond limits, but will boast only with regard to the area of influence God assigned to us, to reach even to you. ¹⁴For we are not overextending ourselves, as though we did not reach you. For we were the first to come all the way to you with the gospel of Christ. ¹⁵We do not boast beyond limit in the labors of others. But our hope is that as your faith increases, our area of influence among you may be greatly enlarged, ¹⁶so that we may preach the gospel in lands beyond you, without boasting of work already done in another's area of influence. ¹⁷"Let the one who boasts, boast in the Lord." ¹⁸For it is not the one who commends himself who is approved, but the one whom the Lord commends.

Paul and the False Apostles

11 I wish you would bear with me in a little foolishness. Do bear with me! ²For I feel a divine jealousy for you, since I betrothed you to one husband, to present you as a pure virgin to Christ. ³But I am afraid that as the serpent deceived Eve by his cunning, your thoughts will be led astray from a sincere and pure devotion

---

¹ Greek *apostles* ² Or *I have sent* ³ Greek *blessing*; twice in this verse ⁴ Or *a gift expecting something in return*; Greek *greed* ⁵ Greek *with blessings*; twice in this verse ⁶ Or *all contentment* ⁷ Or *you* ᵃ Ps. 112:9

to Christ. **4**For if someone comes and proclaims another Jesus than the one we proclaimed, or if you receive a different spirit from the one you received, or if you accept a different gospel from the one you accepted, you put up with it readily enough. **5**Indeed, I consider that I am not in the least inferior to these super-apostles. **6**Even if I am unskilled in speaking, I am not so in knowledge; indeed, in every way we have made this plain to you in all things.

7Or did I commit a sin in humbling myself so that you might be exalted, because I preached God's gospel to you free of charge? **8**I robbed other churches by accepting support from them in order to serve you. **9**And when I was with you and was in need, I did not burden anyone, for the brothers who came from Macedonia supplied my need. So I refrained and will refrain from burdening you in any way. **10**As the truth of Christ is in me, this boasting of mine will not be silenced in the regions of Achaia. **11**And why? Because I do not love you? God knows I do!

12And what I do I will continue to do, in order to undermine the claim of those who would like to claim that in their boasted mission they work on the same terms as we do. **13**For such men are false apostles, deceitful workmen, disguising themselves as apostles of Christ. **14**And no wonder, for even Satan disguises himself as an angel of light. **15**So it is no surprise if his servants, also, disguise themselves as servants of righteousness. Their end will correspond to their deeds.

Paul's Sufferings as an Apostle

16I repeat, let no one think me foolish. But even if you do, accept me as a fool, so that I too may boast a little. **17**What I am saying with this boastful confidence, I say not with the Lord's authority but as a fool. **18**Since many boast according to the flesh, I too will boast. **19**For you gladly bear with fools, being wise yourselves! **20**For you bear it if someone makes slaves of you, or devours you, or takes advantage of you, or puts on airs, or strikes you in the face. **21**To my shame, I must say, we were too weak for that!

But whatever anyone else dares to boast of—I am speaking as a fool—I also dare to boast of that. **22**Are they Hebrews? So am I. Are they Israelites? So am I. Are they offspring of Abraham? So am I. **23**Are they servants of Christ? I am a better one—I am talking like a madman—with far greater labors, far more imprisonments, with countless beatings, and often near death. **24**Five times I received at the hands of the Jews the forty lashes less one. **25**Three times I was beaten with rods. Once I was stoned. Three times I was shipwrecked; a night and a day I was adrift at sea; **26**on frequent journeys, in danger from rivers, danger from robbers, danger from my own people, danger from Gentiles, danger in the city,

danger in the wilderness, danger at sea, danger from false brothers; **27**in toil and hardship, through many a sleepless night, in hunger and thirst, often without food,¹ in cold and exposure. **28**And, apart from other things, there is the daily pressure on me of my anxiety for all the churches. **29**Who is weak, and I am not weak? Who is made to fall, and I am not indignant?

30If I must boast, I will boast of the things that show my weakness. **31**The God and Father of the Lord Jesus, he who is blessed forever, knows that I am not lying. **32**At Damascus, the governor under King Aretas was guarding the city of Damascus in order to seize me, **33**but I was let down in a basket through a window in the wall and escaped his hands.

Paul's Visions and His Thorn

12 I must go on boasting. Though there is nothing to be gained by it, I will go on to visions and revelations of the Lord. **2**I know a man in Christ who fourteen years ago was caught up to the third heaven—whether in the body or out of the body I do not know, God knows. **3**And I know that this man was caught up into paradise—whether in the body or out of the body I do not know, God knows— **4**and he heard things that cannot be told, which man may not utter. **5**On behalf of this man I will boast, but on my own behalf I will not boast, except of my weaknesses. **6**Though if I should wish to boast, I would not be a fool, for I would be speaking the truth. But I refrain from it, so that no one may think more of me than he sees in me or hears from me. **7**So to keep me from becoming conceited because of the surpassing greatness of the revelations,² a thorn was given me in the flesh, a messenger of Satan to harass me, to keep me from becoming conceited. **8**Three times I pleaded with the Lord about this, that it should leave me. **9**But he said to me, "My grace is sufficient for you, for my power is made perfect in weakness." Therefore I will boast all the more gladly of my weaknesses, so that the power of Christ may rest upon me. **10**For the sake of Christ, then, I am content with weaknesses, insults, hardships, persecutions, and calamities. For when I am weak, then I am strong.

Concern for the Corinthian Church

11I have been a fool! You forced me to it, for I ought to have been commended by you. For I was not at all inferior to these super-apostles, even though I am nothing. **12**The signs of a true apostle were performed among you with utmost patience, with signs and wonders and mighty works. **13**For in what were you less favored than the rest of the churches, except that I myself did not burden you? Forgive me this wrong!

14Here for the third time I am ready to come to

---

¹ Or often in fasting ² Or hears from me, even because of the surpassing greatness of the revelations. So to keep me from becoming conceited

you. And I will not be a burden, for I seek not what is yours but you. For children are not obligated to save up for their parents, but parents for their children. [15]I will most gladly spend and be spent for your souls. If I love you more, am I to be loved less? [16]But granting that I myself did not burden you, I was crafty, you say, and got the better of you by deceit. [17]Did I take advantage of you through any of those whom I sent to you? [18]I urged Titus to go, and sent the brother with him. Did Titus take advantage of you? Did we not act in the same spirit? Did we not take the same steps?

[19]Have you been thinking all along that we have been defending ourselves to you? It is in the sight of God that we have been speaking in Christ, and all for your upbuilding, beloved. [20]For I fear that perhaps when I come I may find you not as I wish, and that you may find me not as you wish—that perhaps there may be quarreling, jealousy, anger, hostility, slander, gossip, conceit, and disorder. [21]I fear that when I come again my God may humble me before you, and I may have to mourn over many of those who sinned earlier and have not repented of the impurity, sexual immorality, and sensuality that they have practiced.

Final Warnings

13 This is the third time I am coming to you. Every charge must be established by the evidence of two or three witnesses. [2]I warned those who sinned before and all the others, and I warn them now while absent, as I did when present on my second visit, that if I come again I will not spare them— [3]since you seek proof that Christ is speaking in me. He is not weak in dealing with you, but is powerful among you. [4]For he was crucified in weakness, but lives by the power of God. For we also are weak in him, but in dealing with you we will live with him by the power of God.

[5]Examine yourselves, to see whether you are in the faith. Test yourselves. Or do you not realize this about yourselves, that Jesus Christ is in you?—unless indeed you fail to meet the test! [6]I hope you will find out that we have not failed the test. [7]But we pray to God that you may not do wrong—not that we may appear to have met the test, but that you may do what is right, though we may seem to have failed. [8]For we cannot do anything against the truth, but only for the truth. [9]For we are glad when we are weak and you are strong. Your restoration is what we pray for. [10]For this reason I write these things while I am away from you, that when I come I may not have to be severe in my use of the authority that the Lord has given me for building up and not for tearing down.

Final Greetings

[11]Finally, brothers,[1] rejoice. Aim for restoration, comfort one another,[2] agree with one another, live in peace; and the God of love and peace will be with you. [12]Greet one another with a holy kiss. [13]All the saints greet you.

[14]The grace of the Lord Jesus Christ and the love of God and the fellowship of the Holy Spirit be with you all.

---

[1]Or brothers and sisters   [2]Or listen to my appeal

GALATIANS

Introduction

Paul's letter to the Galatians was addressed to a group of churches in Galatia, a region of present-day Turkey. Paul had preached the gospel in these churches. He wrote to counter those who taught that Christians must be circumcised in order to be accepted by God. Paul began with a defense of his apostolic authority (chs. 1–2), then made it clear that all believers, Jew and Gentile alike, enjoy complete salvation in Christ (chs. 3–4). In chapters 5–6 Paul showed how the gospel of grace leads to true freedom and godly living. Perhaps the central message of Galatians is "a person is not justified by works of the law but through faith in Jesus Christ" (2:16). Paul wrote this letter sometime between A.D. 48 and 55.

Greeting

1 Paul, an apostle—not from men nor through man, but through Jesus Christ and God the Father, who raised him from the dead— ²and all the brothers[1] who are with me,

To the churches of Galatia:

³Grace to you and peace from God our Father and the Lord Jesus Christ, ⁴who gave himself for our sins to deliver us from the present evil age, according to the will of our God and Father, ⁵to whom be the glory forever and ever. Amen.

No Other Gospel

⁶I am astonished that you are so quickly deserting him who called you in the grace of Christ and are turning to a different gospel— ⁷not that there is another one, but there are some who trouble you and want to distort the gospel of Christ. ⁸But even if we or an angel from heaven should preach to you a gospel contrary to the one we preached to you, let him be accursed. ⁹As we have said before, so now I say again: If anyone is preaching to you a gospel contrary to the one you received, let him be accursed.

¹⁰For am I now seeking the approval of man, or of God? Or am I trying to please man? If I were still trying to please man, I would not be a servant[2] of Christ.

Paul Called by God

¹¹For I would have you know, brothers, that the gospel that was preached by me is not man's gospel.[3] ¹²For I did not receive it from any man, nor was I taught it, but I received it through a revelation of Jesus Christ. ¹³For you have heard of my former life in Judaism, how I persecuted the church of God violently and tried to destroy it. ¹⁴And I was advancing in Judaism beyond many of my own age among my people, so extremely zealous was I for the traditions of my fathers. ¹⁵But when he who had set me apart before I was born,[4] and who called me by his grace, ¹⁶was pleased to reveal his Son to[5] me, in order that I might preach him among the Gentiles, I did not immediately consult with anyone;[6] ¹⁷nor did I go up to Jerusalem to those who were apostles before me, but I went away into Arabia, and returned again to Damascus.

¹⁸Then after three years I went up to Jerusalem to visit Cephas and remained with him fifteen days. ¹⁹But I saw none of the other apostles except James the Lord's brother. ²⁰(In what I am writing to you, before God, I do not lie!) ²¹Then I went into the regions of Syria and Cilicia. ²²And I was still unknown in person to the churches of Judea that are in Christ. ²³They only were hearing it said, "He who used to persecute us is now preaching the faith he once tried to destroy." ²⁴And they glorified God because of me.

Paul Accepted by the Apostles

2 Then after fourteen years I went up again to Jerusalem with Barnabas, taking Titus along with me. ²I went up because of a revelation and set before them (though privately before those who seemed influential) the gospel that I proclaim among the Gentiles, in order to make sure I was not running or had not run in vain. ³But even Titus, who was with me, was not forced to be circumcised, though he was a Greek. ⁴Yet because of false brothers secretly brought in— who slipped in to spy out our freedom that we have in Christ Jesus, so that they might bring us into slavery— ⁵to them we did not yield in submission even for a moment, so that the truth of the gospel might be preserved for you. ⁶And from those who seemed to be influential (what they were makes no difference to me; God shows no partiality)—those, I say, who seemed influential added nothing to me. ⁷On the contrary, when they saw that I had been entrusted with the gospel to the uncircumcised, just as Peter had been entrusted with the gospel to the circumcised ⁸(for he who worked through Peter for his apostolic ministry to the circumcised worked also through me for mine to the Gentiles), ⁹and when James and Cephas and John, who seemed to be pillars, perceived the grace that was given to me,

---

[1] Or brothers and sisters. The plural Greek word adelphoi (translated "brothers") refers to siblings in a family. In New Testament usage, depending on the context, adelphoi may refer either to men or to both men and women who are siblings (brothers and sisters) in God's family, the church; also verse 11 [2] Or slave; Greek bondservant [3] Greek not according to man [4] Greek set me apart from my mother's womb [5] Greek in [6] Greek with flesh and blood

they gave the right hand of fellowship to Barnabas and me, that we should go to the Gentiles and they to the circumcised. [10]Only, they asked us to remember the poor, the very thing I was eager to do.

Paul Opposes Peter

[11]But when Cephas came to Antioch, I opposed him to his face, because he stood condemned. [12]For before certain men came from James, he was eating with the Gentiles; but when they came he drew back and separated himself, fearing the circumcision party. [13]And the rest of the Jews acted hypocritically along with him, so that even Barnabas was led astray by their hypocrisy. [14]But when I saw that their conduct was not in step with the truth of the gospel, I said to Cephas before them all, "If you, though a Jew, live like a Gentile and not like a Jew, how can you force the Gentiles to live like Jews?"

Justified by Faith

[15]We ourselves are Jews by birth and not Gentile sinners; [16]yet we know that a person is not justified[1] by works of the law but through faith in Jesus Christ, so we also have believed in Christ Jesus, in order to be justified by faith in Christ and not by works of the law, because by works of the law no one will be justified.

[17]But if, in our endeavor to be justified in Christ, we too were found to be sinners, is Christ then a servant of sin? Certainly not! [18]For if I rebuild what I tore down, I prove myself to be a transgressor. [19]For through the law I died to the law, so that I might live to God. [20]I have been crucified with Christ. It is no longer I who live, but Christ who lives in me. And the life I now live in the flesh I live by faith in the Son of God, who loved me and gave himself for me. [21]I do not nullify the grace of God, for if righteousness[2] were through the law, then Christ died for no purpose.

By Faith, or by Works of the Law?

3 O foolish Galatians! Who has bewitched you? It was before your eyes that Jesus Christ was publicly portrayed as crucified. [2]Let me ask you only this: Did you receive the Spirit by works of the law or by hearing with faith? [3]Are you so foolish? Having begun by the Spirit, are you now being perfected by[3] the flesh? [4]Did you suffer[4] so many things in vain—if indeed it was in vain? [5]Does he who supplies the Spirit to you and works miracles among you do so by works of the law, or by hearing with faith— [6]just as *a*Abraham "believed God, and it was counted to him as righteousness"?

[7]Know then that it is those of faith who are the sons of Abraham. [8]And the Scripture, foreseeing that God would justify[5] the Gentiles by faith, preached the gospel beforehand to Abraham, saying, *b*"In you shall all the nations be blessed." [9]So then, those who are of faith are blessed along with Abraham, the man of faith.

The Righteous Shall Live by Faith

[10]For all who rely on works of the law are under a curse; for it is written, *c*"Cursed be everyone who does not abide by all things written in the Book of the Law, and do them." [11]Now it is evident that no one is justified before God by the law, for *d*"The righteous shall live by faith."[6] [12]But the law is not of faith, rather *e*"The one who does them shall live by them." [13]Christ redeemed us from the curse of the law by becoming a curse for us—for it is written, *f*"Cursed is everyone who is hanged on a tree"— [14]so that in Christ Jesus the blessing of Abraham might come to the Gentiles, so that we might receive the promised Spirit[7] through faith.

The Law and the Promise

[15]To give a human example, brothers:[8] even with a man-made covenant, no one annuls it or adds to it once it has been ratified. [16]Now the promises were made to Abraham and to his offspring. It does not say, "And to offsprings," referring to many, but referring to one, "And to your offspring," who is Christ. [17]This is what I mean: the law, which came 430 years afterward, does not annul a covenant previously ratified by God, so as to make the promise void. [18]For if the inheritance comes by the law, it no longer comes by promise; but God gave it to Abraham by a promise.

[19]Why then the law? It was added because of transgressions, until the offspring should come to whom the promise had been made, and it was put in place through angels by an intermediary. [20]Now an intermediary implies more than one, but God is one.

[21]Is the law then contrary to the promises of God? Certainly not! For if a law had been given that could give life, then righteousness would indeed be by the law. [22]But the Scripture imprisoned everything under sin, so that the promise by faith in Jesus Christ might be given to those who believe.

[23]Now before faith came, we were held captive under the law, imprisoned until the coming faith would be revealed. [24]So then, the law was our guardian until Christ came, in order that we might be justified by faith. [25]But now that faith has come, we are no longer under a guardian, [26]for in Christ Jesus you are all sons of God, through faith. [27]For as many of you as were baptized into Christ have put on Christ. [28]There is neither Jew nor Greek, there is neither slave[9] nor

---

[1]Or *counted righteous* (three times in verse 16); also verse 17 [2]Or *justification* [3]Or *now ending with* [4]Or *experience* [5]Or *count righteous*; also verses 11, 24 [6]Or *The one who by faith is righteous will live* [7]Greek *receive the promise of the Spirit* [8]Or *brothers and sisters* [9]Greek *bondservant* *a*Gen. 15:6 *b*Gen. 12:3 *c*Deut. 27:26 *d*Hab. 2:4 *e*Lev. 18:5 *f*Deut. 21:23

free, there is no male and female, for you are all one in Christ Jesus. ²⁹And if you are Christ's, then you are Abraham's offspring, heirs according to promise.

Sons and Heirs

4 I mean that the heir, as long as he is a child, is no different from a slave,¹ though he is the owner of everything, ²but he is under guardians and managers until the date set by his father. ³In the same way we also, when we were children, were enslaved to the elementary principles² of the world. ⁴But when the fullness of time had come, God sent forth his Son, born of woman, born under the law, ⁵to redeem those who were under the law, so that we might receive adoption as sons. ⁶And because you are sons, God has sent the Spirit of his Son into our hearts, crying, "Abba! Father!" ⁷So you are no longer a slave, but a son, and if a son, then an heir through God.

Paul's Concern for the Galatians

⁸Formerly, when you did not know God, you were enslaved to those that by nature are not gods. ⁹But now that you have come to know God, or rather to be known by God, how can you turn back again to the weak and worthless elementary principles of the world, whose slaves you want to be once more? ¹⁰You observe days and months and seasons and years! ¹¹I am afraid I may have labored over you in vain.

¹²Brothers,³ I entreat you, become as I am, for I also have become as you are. You did me no wrong. ¹³You know it was because of a bodily ailment that I preached the gospel to you at first, ¹⁴and though my condition was a trial to you, you did not scorn or despise me, but received me as an angel of God, as Christ Jesus. ¹⁵What then has become of the blessing you felt? For I testify to you that, if possible, you would have gouged out your eyes and given them to me. ¹⁶Have I then become your enemy by telling you the truth?⁴ ¹⁷They make much of you, but for no good purpose. They want to shut you out, that you may make much of them. ¹⁸It is always good to be made much of for a good purpose, and not only when I am present with you, ¹⁹my little children, for whom I am again in the anguish of childbirth until Christ is formed in you! ²⁰I wish I could be present with you now and change my tone, for I am perplexed about you.

Example of Hagar and Sarah

²¹Tell me, you who desire to be under the law, do you not listen to the law? ²²For it is written that Abraham had two sons, one by a slave woman and one by a free woman. ²³But the son of the slave was born according to the flesh, while the son of the free woman was born through promise. ²⁴Now this may be interpreted allegorically: these women are two covenants. One is from Mount Sinai, bearing children for slavery; she is Hagar. ²⁵Now Hagar is Mount Sinai in Arabia;⁵ she corresponds to the present Jerusalem, for she is in slavery with her children. ²⁶But the Jerusalem above is free, and she is our mother. ²⁷For it is written,

> ª"Rejoice, O barren one who does not bear;
>   break forth and cry aloud, you who are not in labor!
> For the children of the desolate one will be more
>   than those of the one who has a husband."

²⁸Now you,⁶ brothers, like Isaac, are children of promise. ²⁹But just as at that time he who was born according to the flesh persecuted him who was born according to the Spirit, so also it is now. ³⁰But what does the Scripture say? ᵇ"Cast out the slave woman and her son, for the son of the slave woman shall not inherit with the son of the free woman." ³¹So, brothers, we are not children of the slave but of the free woman.

Christ Has Set Us Free

5 For freedom Christ has set us free; stand firm therefore, and do not submit again to a yoke of slavery.

²Look: I, Paul, say to you that if you accept circumcision, Christ will be of no advantage to you. ³I testify again to every man who accepts circumcision that he is obligated to keep the whole law. ⁴You are severed from Christ, you who would be justified⁷ by the law; you have fallen away from grace. ⁵For through the Spirit, by faith, we ourselves eagerly wait for the hope of righteousness. ⁶For in Christ Jesus neither circumcision nor uncircumcision counts for anything, but only faith working through love.

⁷You were running well. Who hindered you from obeying the truth? ⁸This persuasion is not from him who calls you. ⁹A little leaven leavens the whole lump. ¹⁰I have confidence in the Lord that you will take no other view than mine, and the one who is troubling you will bear the penalty, whoever he is. ¹¹But if I, brothers,⁸ still preach⁹ circumcision, why am I still being persecuted? In that case the offense of the cross has been removed. ¹²I wish those who unsettle you would emasculate themselves!

¹³For you were called to freedom, brothers. Only do not use your freedom as an opportunity for the flesh, but through love serve one another. ¹⁴For the whole law is fulfilled in one word: ᶜ"You shall love your neighbor as yourself." ¹⁵But if you bite and devour one another, watch out that you are not consumed by one another.

---

¹ Greek *bondservant; also verse 7* ² Or *elemental spirits; also verse 9* ³ Or *Brothers and sisters; also verses 28, 31* ⁴ Or *by dealing truthfully with you* ⁵ Some manuscripts *For Sinai is a mountain in Arabia* ⁶ Some manuscripts *we* ⁷ Or *counted righteous* ⁸ Or *brothers and sisters; also verse 13* ⁹ Greek *proclaim*
ª Isa. 54:1 ᵇ Gen. 21:10 ᶜ Lev. 19:18

Walk by the Spirit

[16]But I say, walk by the Spirit, and you will not gratify the desires of the flesh. [17]For the desires of the flesh are against the Spirit, and the desires of the Spirit are against the flesh, for these are opposed to each other, to keep you from doing the things you want to do. [18]But if you are led by the Spirit, you are not under the law. [19]Now the works of the flesh are evident: sexual immorality, impurity, sensuality, [20]idolatry, sorcery, enmity, strife, jealousy, fits of anger, rivalries, dissensions, divisions, [21]envy,[1] drunkenness, orgies, and things like these. I warn you, as I warned you before, that those who do such things will not inherit the kingdom of God. [22]But the fruit of the Spirit is love, joy, peace, patience, kindness, goodness, faithfulness, [23]gentleness, self-control; against such things there is no law. [24]And those who belong to Christ Jesus have crucified the flesh with its passions and desires.

[25]If we live by the Spirit, let us also walk by the Spirit. [26]Let us not become conceited, provoking one another, envying one another.

Bear One Another's Burdens

6 Brothers,[2] if anyone is caught in any transgression, you who are spiritual should restore him in a spirit of gentleness. Keep watch on yourself, lest you too be tempted. [2]Bear one another's burdens, and so fulfill the law of Christ. [3]For if anyone thinks he is something, when he is nothing, he deceives himself. [4]But let each one test his own work, and then his reason to boast will be in himself alone and not in his neighbor. [5]For each will have to bear his own load.

[6]One who is taught the word must share all good things with the one who teaches. [7]Do not be deceived: God is not mocked, for whatever one sows, that will he also reap. [8]For the one who sows to his own flesh will from the flesh reap corruption, but the one who sows to the Spirit will from the Spirit reap eternal life. [9]And let us not grow weary of doing good, for in due season we will reap, if we do not give up. [10]So then, as we have opportunity, let us do good to everyone, and especially to those who are of the household of faith.

Final Warning and Benediction

[11]See with what large letters I am writing to you with my own hand. [12]It is those who want to make a good showing in the flesh who would force you to be circumcised, and only in order that they may not be persecuted for the cross of Christ. [13]For even those who are circumcised do not themselves keep the law, but they desire to have you circumcised that they may boast in your flesh. [14]But far be it from me to boast except in the cross of our Lord Jesus Christ, by which[3] the world has been crucified to me, and I to the world. [15]For neither circumcision counts for anything, nor uncircumcision, but a new creation. [16]And as for all who walk by this rule, peace and mercy be upon them, and upon the Israel of God.

[17]From now on let no one cause me trouble, for I bear on my body the marks of Jesus. [18]The grace of our Lord Jesus Christ be with your spirit, brothers. Amen.

---

[1]Some manuscripts add *murder* [2]Or *Brothers and sisters*; also verse 18 [3]Or *through whom*

EPHESIANS

Introduction

The apostle Paul wrote Ephesians to the churches around Ephesus (Acts 19) to display the scope of God's eternal plan for all humanity—for Jews and Gentiles alike. This is the mystery of God, hidden for ages but now made known in Jesus Christ. The first three chapters focus on what Christians should believe, unfolding the glorious riches of God's grace in Christ. Dead sinners are made alive and gain eternal salvation "by grace . . . through faith" (2:8). The last three chapters explain the implications of God's grace for the church, for individuals, and for families. This second section comes to a climax with a command to stand with the armor of God against the devil. Paul wrote this letter while in prison, probably in Rome about A.D. 60.

Greeting

1 Paul, an apostle of Christ Jesus by the will of God,

To the saints who are in Ephesus, and are faithful[1] in Christ Jesus:

²Grace to you and peace from God our Father and the Lord Jesus Christ.

Spiritual Blessings in Christ

³Blessed be the God and Father of our Lord Jesus Christ, who has blessed us in Christ with every spiritual blessing in the heavenly places, ⁴even as he chose us in him before the foundation of the world, that we should be holy and blameless before him. In love ⁵he predestined us[2] for adoption as sons through Jesus Christ, according to the purpose of his will, ⁶to the praise of his glorious grace, with which he has blessed us in the Beloved. ⁷In him we have redemption through his blood, the forgiveness of our trespasses, according to the riches of his grace, ⁸which he lavished upon us, in all wisdom and insight ⁹making known[3] to us the mystery of his will, according to his purpose, which he set forth in Christ ¹⁰as a plan for the fullness of time, to unite all things in him, things in heaven and things on earth.

¹¹In him we have obtained an inheritance, having been predestined according to the purpose of him who works all things according to the counsel of his will, ¹²so that we who were the first to hope in Christ might be to the praise of his glory. ¹³In him you also, when you heard the word of truth, the gospel of your salvation, and believed in him, were sealed with the promised Holy Spirit, ¹⁴who is the guarantee[4] of our inheritance until we acquire possession of it,[5] to the praise of his glory.

Thanksgiving and Prayer

¹⁵For this reason, because I have heard of your faith in the Lord Jesus and your love[6] toward all the saints, ¹⁶I do not cease to give thanks for you, remembering you in my prayers, ¹⁷that the God of our Lord Jesus Christ, the Father of glory, may give you a spirit of wisdom and of revelation in the knowledge of him, ¹⁸having the eyes of your hearts enlightened, that you may know what is the hope to which he has called you, what are the riches of his glorious inheritance in the saints, ¹⁹and what is the immeasurable greatness of his power toward us who believe, according to the working of his great might ²⁰that he worked in Christ when he raised him from the dead and seated him at his right hand in the heavenly places, ²¹far above all rule and authority and power and dominion, and above every name that is named, not only in this age but also in the one to come. ²²And he put all things under his feet and gave him as head over all things to the church, ²³which is his body, the fullness of him who fills all in all.

By Grace Through Faith

2 And you were dead in the trespasses and sins ²in which you once walked, following the course of this world, following the prince of the power of the air, the spirit that is now at work in the sons of disobedience— ³among whom we all once lived in the passions of our flesh, carrying out the desires of the body[7] and the mind, and were by nature children of wrath, like the rest of mankind. ⁴But[8] God, being rich in mercy, because of the great love with which he loved us, ⁵even when we were dead in our trespasses, made us alive together with Christ—by grace you have been saved— ⁶and raised us up with him and seated us with him in the heavenly places in Christ Jesus, ⁷so that in the coming ages he might show the immeasurable riches of his grace in kindness toward us in Christ Jesus. ⁸For by grace you have been saved through faith. And this is not your own doing; it is the gift of God, ⁹not a result of works, so that no one may boast. ¹⁰For we are his workmanship, created in Christ Jesus for good works, which God prepared beforehand, that we should walk in them.

---

[1] Some manuscripts *saints who are also faithful* (omitting *in Ephesus*) [2] Or *before him in love, having predestined us* [3] Or *he lavished upon us in all wisdom and insight, making known . . .* [4] Or *down payment* [5] Or *until God redeems his possession* [6] Some manuscripts omit *your love* [7] Greek *flesh* [8] Or *And*

One in Christ

[11]Therefore remember that at one time you Gentiles in the flesh, called "the uncircumcision" by what is called the circumcision, which is made in the flesh by hands— [12]remember that you were at that time separated from Christ, alienated from the commonwealth of Israel and strangers to the covenants of promise, having no hope and without God in the world. [13]But now in Christ Jesus you who once were far off have been brought near by the blood of Christ. [14]For he himself is our peace, who has made us both one and has broken down in his flesh the dividing wall of hostility [15]by abolishing the law of commandments expressed in ordinances, that he might create in himself one new man in place of the two, so making peace, [16]and might reconcile us both to God in one body through the cross, thereby killing the hostility. [17]And he came and preached peace to you who were far off and peace to those who were near. [18]For through him we both have access in one Spirit to the Father. [19]So then you are no longer strangers and aliens,[1] but you are fellow citizens with the saints and members of the household of God, [20]built on the foundation of the apostles and prophets, Christ Jesus himself being the cornerstone, [21]in whom the whole structure, being joined together, grows into a holy temple in the Lord. [22]In him you also are being built together into a dwelling place for God by[2] the Spirit.

The Mystery of the Gospel Revealed

3 For this reason I, Paul, a prisoner for Christ Jesus on behalf of you Gentiles— [2]assuming that you have heard of the stewardship of God's grace that was given to me for you, [3]how the mystery was made known to me by revelation, as I have written briefly. [4]When you read this, you can perceive my insight into the mystery of Christ, [5]which was not made known to the sons of men in other generations as it has now been revealed to his holy apostles and prophets by the Spirit. [6]This mystery is[3] that the Gentiles are fellow heirs, members of the same body, and partakers of the promise in Christ Jesus through the gospel. [7]Of this gospel I was made a minister according to the gift of God's grace, which was given me by the working of his power. [8]To me, though I am the very least of all the saints, this grace was given, to preach to the Gentiles the unsearchable riches of Christ, [9]and to bring to light for everyone what is the plan of the mystery hidden for ages in[4] God who created all things, [10]so that through the church the manifold wisdom of God might now be made known to the rulers and authorities in the heavenly places. [11]This was according to the eternal purpose that he has

realized in Christ Jesus our Lord, [12]in whom we have boldness and access with confidence through our faith in him. [13]So I ask you not to lose heart over what I am suffering for you, which is your glory.

Prayer for Spiritual Strength

[14]For this reason I bow my knees before the Father, [15]from whom every family[5] in heaven and on earth is named, [16]that according to the riches of his glory he may grant you to be strengthened with power through his Spirit in your inner being, [17]so that Christ may dwell in your hearts through faith—that you, being rooted and grounded in love, [18]may have strength to comprehend with all the saints what is the breadth and length and height and depth, [19]and to know the love of Christ that surpasses knowledge, that you may be filled with all the fullness of God.

[20]Now to him who is able to do far more abundantly than all that we ask or think, according to the power at work within us, [21]to him be glory in the church and in Christ Jesus throughout all generations, forever and ever. Amen.

Unity in the Body of Christ

4 I therefore, a prisoner for the Lord, urge you to walk in a manner worthy of the calling to which you have been called, [2]with all humility and gentleness, with patience, bearing with one another in love, [3]eager to maintain the unity of the Spirit in the bond of peace. [4]There is one body and one Spirit—just as you were called to the one hope that belongs to your call— [5]one Lord, one faith, one baptism, [6]one God and Father of all, who is over all and through all and in all. [7]But grace was given to each one of us according to the measure of Christ's gift. [8]Therefore it says,

[a]"When he ascended on high he led a host of captives,
and he gave gifts to men."

[9](In saying, "He ascended," what does it mean but that he had also descended into the lower regions, the earth?[6] [10]He who descended is the one who also ascended far above all the heavens, that he might fill all things.) [11]And he gave the apostles, the prophets, the evangelists, the shepherds[7] and teachers,[8] [12]to equip the saints for the work of ministry, for building up the body of Christ, [13]until we all attain to the unity of the faith and of the knowledge of the Son of God, to mature manhood,[9] to the measure of the stature of the fullness of Christ, [14]so that we may no longer be children, tossed to and fro by the waves and carried about by every wind of doctrine, by human cunning, by craftiness in deceit-

[1] Or *sojourners* [2] Or *in* [3] The words *This mystery is* are inferred from verse 4 [4] Or *by* [5] Or *fatherhood*; the Greek word *patria* is closely related to the word for *Father* in verse 14 [6] Or *the lower parts of the earth?* [7] Or *pastors* [8] Or *the shepherd-teachers* [9] Greek *to a full-grown man* [a] Ps. 68:18

ful schemes. [15]Rather, speaking the truth in love, we are to grow up in every way into him who is the head, into Christ, [16]from whom the whole body, joined and held together by every joint with which it is equipped, when each part is working properly, makes the body grow so that it builds itself up in love.

The New Life

[17]Now this I say and testify in the Lord, that you must no longer walk as the Gentiles do, in the futility of their minds. [18]They are darkened in their understanding, alienated from the life of God because of the ignorance that is in them, due to their hardness of heart. [19]They have become callous and have given themselves up to sensuality, greedy to practice every kind of impurity. [20]But that is not the way you learned Christ!— [21]assuming that you have heard about him and were taught in him, as the truth is in Jesus, [22]to put off your old self,[1] which belongs to your former manner of life and is corrupt through deceitful desires, [23]and to be renewed in the spirit of your minds, [24]and to put on the new self, created after the likeness of God in true righteousness and holiness.

[25]Therefore, having put away falsehood, let each one of you speak the truth with his neighbor, for we are members one of another. [26]Be angry and do not sin; do not let the sun go down on your anger, [27]and give no opportunity to the devil. [28]Let the thief no longer steal, but rather let him labor, doing honest work with his own hands, so that he may have something to share with anyone in need. [29]Let no corrupting talk come out of your mouths, but only such as is good for building up, as fits the occasion, that it may give grace to those who hear. [30]And do not grieve the Holy Spirit of God, by whom you were sealed for the day of redemption. [31]Let all bitterness and wrath and anger and clamor and slander be put away from you, along with all malice. [32]Be kind to one another, tenderhearted, forgiving one another, as God in Christ forgave you.

Walk in Love

5 Therefore be imitators of God, as beloved children. [2]And walk in love, as Christ loved us and gave himself up for us, a fragrant offering and sacrifice to God.

[3]But sexual immorality and all impurity or covetousness must not even be named among you, as is proper among saints. [4]Let there be no filthiness nor foolish talk nor crude joking, which are out of place, but instead let there be thanksgiving. [5]For you may be sure of this, that everyone who is sexually immoral or impure, or who is covetous (that is, an idolater), has no inheritance in the kingdom of Christ and God. [6]Let no one deceive you with empty words, for because

of these things the wrath of God comes upon the sons of disobedience. [7]Therefore do not become partners with them; [8]for at one time you were darkness, but now you are light in the Lord. Walk as children of light [9](for the fruit of light is found in all that is good and right and true), [10]and try to discern what is pleasing to the Lord. [11]Take no part in the unfruitful works of darkness, but instead expose them. [12]For it is shameful even to speak of the things that they do in secret. [13]But when anything is exposed by the light, it becomes visible, [14]for anything that becomes visible is light. Therefore it says,

"Awake, O sleeper,
    and arise from the dead,
    and Christ will shine on you."

[15]Look carefully then how you walk, not as unwise but as wise, [16]making the best use of the time, because the days are evil. [17]Therefore do not be foolish, but understand what the will of the Lord is. [18]And do not get drunk with wine, for that is debauchery, but be filled with the Spirit, [19]addressing one another in psalms and hymns and spiritual songs, singing and making melody to the Lord with your heart, [20]giving thanks always and for everything to God the Father in the name of our Lord Jesus Christ, [21]submitting to one another out of reverence for Christ.

Wives and Husbands

[22]Wives, submit to your own husbands, as to the Lord. [23]For the husband is the head of the wife even as Christ is the head of the church, his body, and is himself its Savior. [24]Now as the church submits to Christ, so also wives should submit in everything to their husbands.

[25]Husbands, love your wives, as Christ loved the church and gave himself up for her, [26]that he might sanctify her, having cleansed her by the washing of water with the word, [27]so that he might present the church to himself in splendor, without spot or wrinkle or any such thing, that she might be holy and without blemish.[2] [28]In the same way husbands should love their wives as their own bodies. He who loves his wife loves himself. [29]For no one ever hated his own flesh, but nourishes and cherishes it, just as Christ does the church, [30]because we are members of his body. [31][a]"Therefore a man shall leave his father and mother and hold fast to his wife, and the two shall become one flesh." [32]This mystery is profound, and I am saying that it refers to Christ and the church. [33]However, let each one of you love his wife as himself, and let the wife see that she respects her husband.

---

[1] Greek _man_; also verse 24 [2] Or _holy and blameless_ [a] Gen. 2:24

Children and Parents

6 Children, obey your parents in the Lord, for this is right. [2a]"Honor your father and mother" (this is the first commandment with a promise), [3]"that it may go well with you and that you may live long in the land." [4]Fathers, do not provoke your children to anger, but bring them up in the discipline and instruction of the Lord.

Slaves and Masters

[5]Slaves,[1] obey your earthly masters[2] with fear and trembling, with a sincere heart, as you would Christ, [6]not by the way of eye-service, as people-pleasers, but as servants[3] of Christ, doing the will of God from the heart, [7]rendering service with a good will as to the Lord and not to man, [8]knowing that whatever good anyone does, this he will receive back from the Lord, whether he is a slave or free. [9]Masters, do the same to them, and stop your threatening, knowing that he who is both their Master[4] and yours is in heaven, and that there is no partiality with him.

The Whole Armor of God

[10]Finally, be strong in the Lord and in the strength of his might. [11]Put on the whole armor of God, that you may be able to stand against the schemes of the devil. [12]For we do not wrestle against flesh and blood, but against the rulers, against the authorities, against the cosmic powers over this present darkness, against the spiritual forces of evil in the heavenly places. [13]Therefore take up the whole armor of God, that you may be able to withstand in the evil day, and having done all, to stand firm. [14]Stand therefore, having fastened on the belt of truth, and having put on the breastplate of righteousness, [15]and, as shoes for your feet, having put on the readiness given by the gospel of peace. [16]In all circumstances take up the shield of faith, with which you can extinguish all the flaming darts of the evil one; [17]and take the helmet of salvation, and the sword of the Spirit, which is the word of God, [18]praying at all times in the Spirit, with all prayer and supplication. To that end keep alert with all perseverance, making supplication for all the saints, [19]and also for me, that words may be given to me in opening my mouth boldly to proclaim the mystery of the gospel, [20]for which I am an ambassador in chains, that I may declare it boldly, as I ought to speak.

Final Greetings

[21]So that you also may know how I am and what I am doing, Tychicus the beloved brother and faithful minister in the Lord will tell you everything. [22]I have sent him to you for this very purpose, that you may know how we are, and that he may encourage your hearts.

[23]Peace be to the brothers,[5] and love with faith, from God the Father and the Lord Jesus Christ. [24]Grace be with all who love our Lord Jesus Christ with love incorruptible.

[1] Or servants; Greek bondservants; similarly verse 8 [2] Or your masters according to the flesh [3] Or slaves; Greek bondservants [4] Greek Lord [5] Or brothers and sisters [a] Ex. 20:12

PHILIPPIANS

Introduction

Philippians overflows with joy and thanksgiving. Paul wrote to the church in Philippi to thank them for a gift. He reported the joyful news that Epaphroditus, who had brought their gift to Paul, had recovered from his illness and was returning to Philippi. Paul said that he had learned the secret of being content in any situation, and he told them about his situation in prison. He expressed joy that more people were hearing about Christ even if some were proclaiming the gospel with bad motives. Wanting the Christians in Philippi to be unified, he challenged them to be servants just as Jesus was when he "made himself nothing" and became a man rather than clinging to the rights of his divine nature (2:1-11). Paul wrote this letter while in prison, probably in Rome about A.D. 60.

Greeting

1 Paul and Timothy, servants[1] of Christ Jesus,
To all the saints in Christ Jesus who are at Philippi, with the overseers[2] and deacons:[3]
²Grace to you and peace from God our Father and the Lord Jesus Christ.

Thanksgiving and Prayer

³I thank my God in all my remembrance of you, ⁴always in every prayer of mine for you all making my prayer with joy, ⁵because of your partnership in the gospel from the first day until now. ⁶And I am sure of this, that he who began a good work in you will bring it to completion at the day of Jesus Christ. ⁷It is right for me to feel this way about you all, because I hold you in my heart, for you are all partakers with me of grace,[4] both in my imprisonment and in the defense and confirmation of the gospel. ⁸For God is my witness, how I yearn for you all with the affection of Christ Jesus. ⁹And it is my prayer that your love may abound more and more, with knowledge and all discernment, ¹⁰so that you may approve what is excellent, and so be pure and blameless for the day of Christ, ¹¹filled with the fruit of righteousness that comes through Jesus Christ, to the glory and praise of God.

The Advance of the Gospel

¹²I want you to know, brothers,[5] that what has happened to me has really served to advance the gospel, ¹³so that it has become known throughout the whole imperial guard[6] and to all the rest that my imprisonment is for Christ. ¹⁴And most of the brothers, having become confident in the Lord by my imprisonment, are much more bold to speak the word[7] without fear.

¹⁵Some indeed preach Christ from envy and rivalry, but others from good will. ¹⁶The latter do it out of love, knowing that I am put here for the defense of the gospel. ¹⁷The former proclaim Christ out of rivalry, not sincerely but thinking to afflict me in my imprisonment. ¹⁸What then? Only that in every way, whether in pretense or in truth, Christ is proclaimed, and in that I rejoice.

To Live Is Christ

Yes, and I will rejoice, ¹⁹for I know that through your prayers and the help of the Spirit of Jesus Christ this will turn out for my deliverance, ²⁰as it is my eager expectation and hope that I will not be at all ashamed, but that with full courage now as always Christ will be honored in my body, whether by life or by death. ²¹For to me to live is Christ, and to die is gain. ²²If I am to live in the flesh, that means fruitful labor for me. Yet which I shall choose I cannot tell. ²³I am hard pressed between the two. My desire is to depart and be with Christ, for that is far better. ²⁴But to remain in the flesh is more necessary on your account. ²⁵Convinced of this, I know that I will remain and continue with you all, for your progress and joy in the faith, ²⁶so that in me you may have ample cause to glory in Christ Jesus, because of my coming to you again.

²⁷Only let your manner of life be worthy[8] of the gospel of Christ, so that whether I come and see you or am absent, I may hear of you that you are standing firm in one spirit, with one mind striving side by side for the faith of the gospel, ²⁸and not frightened in anything by your opponents. This is a clear sign to them of their destruction, but of your salvation, and that from God. ²⁹For it has been granted to you that for the sake of Christ you should not only believe in him but also suffer for his sake, ³⁰engaged in the same conflict that you saw I had and now hear that I still have.

Christ's Example of Humility

2 So if there is any encouragement in Christ, any comfort from love, any participation in the Spirit, any affection and sympathy, ²complete my joy by being of the same mind, having

---

[1] Or slaves; Greek bondservants [2] Or bishops; Greek episkopoi [3] Or servants, or ministers; Greek diakonoi [4] Or you all have fellowship with me in grace [5] Or brothers and sisters. The plural Greek word adelphoi (translated "brothers") refers to siblings in a family. In New Testament usage, depending on the context, adelphoi may refer either to men or to both men and women who are siblings (brothers and sisters) in God's family, the church; also verse 14 [6] Greek in the whole praetorium [7] Some manuscripts add of God [8] Greek Only behave as citizens worthy

the same love, being in full accord and of one mind. ³Do nothing from rivalry or conceit, but in humility count others more significant than yourselves. ⁴Let each of you look not only to his own interests, but also to the interests of others. ⁵Have this mind among yourselves, which is yours in Christ Jesus,¹ ⁶who, though he was in the form of God, did not count equality with God a thing to be grasped, ⁷but made himself nothing, taking the form of a servant,² being born in the likeness of men. ⁸And being found in human form, he humbled himself by becoming obedient to the point of death, even death on a cross. ⁹Therefore God has highly exalted him and bestowed on him the name that is above every name, ¹⁰so that at the name of Jesus every knee should bow, in heaven and on earth and under the earth, ¹¹and every tongue confess that Jesus Christ is Lord, to the glory of God the Father.

Lights in the World

¹²Therefore, my beloved, as you have always obeyed, so now, not only as in my presence but much more in my absence, work out your own salvation with fear and trembling, ¹³for it is God who works in you, both to will and to work for his good pleasure. ¹⁴Do all things without grumbling or questioning, ¹⁵that you may be blameless and innocent, children of God without blemish in the midst of a crooked and twisted generation, among whom you shine as lights in the world, ¹⁶holding fast to the word of life, so that in the day of Christ I may be proud that I did not run in vain or labor in vain. ¹⁷Even if I am to be poured out as a drink offering upon the sacrificial offering of your faith, I am glad and rejoice with you all. ¹⁸Likewise you also should be glad and rejoice with me.

Timothy and Epaphroditus

¹⁹I hope in the Lord Jesus to send Timothy to you soon, so that I too may be cheered by news of you. ²⁰For I have no one like him, who will be genuinely concerned for your welfare. ²¹For they all seek their own interests, not those of Jesus Christ. ²²But you know Timothy's³ proven worth, how as a son⁴ with a father he has served with me in the gospel. ²³I hope therefore to send him just as soon as I see how it will go with me, ²⁴and I trust in the Lord that shortly I myself will come also.

²⁵I have thought it necessary to send to you Epaphroditus my brother and fellow worker and fellow soldier, and your messenger and minister to my need, ²⁶for he has been longing for you all and has been distressed because you heard that he was ill. ²⁷Indeed he was ill, near to death. But God had mercy on him, and not only on him but on me also, lest I should have sorrow upon sorrow. ²⁸I am the more eager to send him, therefore, that you may rejoice at seeing him again, and that I may be less anxious. ²⁹So receive him in the Lord with all joy, and honor such men, ³⁰for he nearly died for the work of Christ, risking his life to complete what was lacking in your service to me.

Righteousness Through Faith in Christ

3 Finally, my brothers,⁵ rejoice in the Lord. To write the same things to you is no trouble to me and is safe for you.

²Look out for the dogs, look out for the evildoers, look out for those who mutilate the flesh. ³For we are the circumcision, who worship by the Spirit of God⁶ and glory in Christ Jesus and put no confidence in the flesh— ⁴though I myself have reason for confidence in the flesh also. If anyone else thinks he has reason for confidence in the flesh, I have more: ⁵circumcised on the eighth day, of the people of Israel, of the tribe of Benjamin, a Hebrew of Hebrews; as to the law, a Pharisee; ⁶as to zeal, a persecutor of the church; as to righteousness under the law,⁷ blameless. ⁷But whatever gain I had, I counted as loss for the sake of Christ. ⁸Indeed, I count everything as loss because of the surpassing worth of knowing Christ Jesus my Lord. For his sake I have suffered the loss of all things and count them as rubbish, in order that I may gain Christ ⁹and be found in him, not having a righteousness of my own that comes from the law, but that which comes through faith in Christ, the righteousness from God that depends on faith— ¹⁰that I may know him and the power of his resurrection, and may share his sufferings, becoming like him in his death, ¹¹that by any means possible I may attain the resurrection from the dead.

Straining Toward the Goal

¹²Not that I have already obtained this or am already perfect, but I press on to make it my own, because Christ Jesus has made me his own. ¹³Brothers, I do not consider that I have made it my own. But one thing I do: forgetting what lies behind and straining forward to what lies ahead, ¹⁴I press on toward the goal for the prize of the upward call of God in Christ Jesus. ¹⁵Let those of us who are mature think this way, and if in anything you think otherwise, God will reveal that also to you. ¹⁶Only let us hold true to what we have attained.

¹⁷Brothers, join in imitating me, and keep your eyes on those who walk according to the example you have in us. ¹⁸For many, of whom I have often told you and now tell you even with tears, walk as enemies of the cross of Christ. ¹⁹Their end is destruction, their god is their belly, and they glory

¹ Or which was also in Christ Jesus ² Greek bondservant ³ Greek his ⁴ Greek child ⁵ Or brothers and sisters; also verses 13, 17 ⁶ Some manuscripts God in spirit ⁷ Greek in the law

in their shame, with minds set on earthly things. ²⁰But our citizenship is in heaven, and from it we await a Savior, the Lord Jesus Christ, ²¹who will transform our lowly body to be like his glorious body, by the power that enables him even to subject all things to himself.

4 Therefore, my brothers,¹ whom I love and long for, my joy and crown, stand firm thus in the Lord, my beloved.

Exhortation, Encouragement, and Prayer

²I entreat Euodia and I entreat Syntyche to agree in the Lord. ³Yes, I ask you also, true companion,² help these women, who have labored side by side with me in the gospel together with Clement and the rest of my fellow workers, whose names are in the book of life.

⁴Rejoice in the Lord always; again I will say, Rejoice. ⁵Let your reasonableness be known to everyone. The Lord is at hand; ⁶do not be anxious about anything, but in everything by prayer and supplication with thanksgiving let your requests be made known to God. ⁷And the peace of God, which surpasses all understanding, will guard your hearts and your minds in Christ Jesus.

⁸Finally, brothers, whatever is true, whatever is honorable, whatever is just, whatever is pure, whatever is lovely, whatever is commendable, if there is any excellence, if there is anything worthy of praise, think about these things. ⁹What you have learned and received and heard and seen in me—practice these things, and the God of peace will be with you.

God's Provision

¹⁰I rejoiced in the Lord greatly that now at length you have revived your concern for me. You were indeed concerned for me, but you had no opportunity. ¹¹Not that I am speaking of being in need, for I have learned in whatever situation I am to be content. ¹²I know how to be brought low, and I know how to abound. In any and every circumstance, I have learned the secret of facing plenty and hunger, abundance and need. ¹³I can do all things through him who strengthens me.

¹⁴Yet it was kind of you to share³ my trouble. ¹⁵And you Philippians yourselves know that in the beginning of the gospel, when I left Macedonia, no church entered into partnership with me in giving and receiving, except you only. ¹⁶Even in Thessalonica you sent me help for my needs once and again. ¹⁷Not that I seek the gift, but I seek the fruit that increases to your credit.⁴ ¹⁸I have received full payment, and more. I am well supplied, having received from Epaphroditus the gifts you sent, a fragrant offering, a sacrifice acceptable and pleasing to God. ¹⁹And my God will supply every need of yours according to his riches in glory in Christ Jesus. ²⁰To our God and Father be glory forever and ever. Amen.

Final Greetings

²¹Greet every saint in Christ Jesus. The brothers who are with me greet you. ²²All the saints greet you, especially those of Caesar's household.

²³The grace of the Lord Jesus Christ be with your spirit.

---

¹Or brothers and sisters; also verses 8, 21 ²Or loyal Syzygus; Greek true yokefellow ³Or have fellowship in ⁴Or I seek the profit that accrues to your account

COLOSSIANS

Introduction

Paul wrote to the church in Colossae to fortify it against false teachers who might try to impose strict rules about eating and drinking and religious festivals. Paul shows the superiority of Christ over all human philosophies and traditions. He writes of Christ's deity ("He is the image of the invisible God, the firstborn of all creation" [1:15]) and of the reconciliation he accomplished with his blood. He explains that the right way of living in this world is to focus on heavenly rather than earthly things. God's chosen people must leave their sinful lives behind and live in a godly way, looking to Christ as the head of the church (1:18). Paul wrote while in prison, probably about the same time as he wrote to the Ephesians.

Greeting

1 Paul, an apostle of Christ Jesus by the will of God, and Timothy our brother,

²To the saints and faithful brothers¹ in Christ at Colossae:

Grace to you and peace from God our Father

Thanksgiving and Prayer

³We always thank God, the Father of our Lord Jesus Christ, when we pray for you, ⁴since we heard of your faith in Christ Jesus and of the love that you have for all the saints, ⁵because of the hope laid up for you in heaven. Of this you have heard before in the word of the truth, the gospel, ⁶which has come to you, as indeed in the whole world it is bearing fruit and growing—as it also does among you, since the day you heard it and understood the grace of God in truth, ⁷just as you learned it from Epaphras our beloved fellow servant.² He is a faithful minister of Christ on your³ behalf ⁸and has made known to us your love in the Spirit.

⁹And so, from the day we heard, we have not ceased to pray for you, asking that you may be filled with the knowledge of his will in all spiritual wisdom and understanding, ¹⁰so as to walk in a manner worthy of the Lord, fully pleasing to him, bearing fruit in every good work and increasing in the knowledge of God. ¹¹May you be strengthened with all power, according to his glorious might, for all endurance and patience with joy, ¹²giving thanks⁴ to the Father, who has qualified you⁵ to share in the inheritance of the saints in light. ¹³He has delivered us from the domain of darkness and transferred us to the kingdom of his beloved Son, ¹⁴in whom we have redemption, the forgiveness of sins.

The Preeminence of Christ

¹⁵He is the image of the invisible God, the firstborn of all creation. ¹⁶For by⁶ him all things were created, in heaven and on earth, visible and invisible, whether thrones or dominions or rulers or authorities—all things were created through

him and for him. ¹⁷And he is before all things, and in him all things hold together. ¹⁸And he is the head of the body, the church. He is the beginning, the firstborn from the dead, that in everything he might be preeminent. ¹⁹For in him all the fullness of God was pleased to dwell, ²⁰and through him to reconcile to himself all things, whether on earth or in heaven, making peace by the blood of his cross.

²¹And you, who once were alienated and hostile in mind, doing evil deeds, ²²he has now reconciled in his body of flesh by his death, in order to present you holy and blameless and above reproach before him, ²³if indeed you continue in the faith, stable and steadfast, not shifting from the hope of the gospel that you heard, which has been proclaimed in all creation⁷ under heaven, and of which I, Paul, became a minister.

Paul's Ministry to the Church

²⁴Now I rejoice in my sufferings for your sake, and in my flesh I am filling up what is lacking in Christ's afflictions for the sake of his body, that is, the church, ²⁵of which I became a minister according to the stewardship from God that was given to me for you, to make the word of God fully known, ²⁶the mystery hidden for ages and generations but now revealed to his saints. ²⁷To them God chose to make known how great among the Gentiles are the riches of the glory of this mystery, which is Christ in you, the hope of glory. ²⁸Him we proclaim, warning everyone and teaching everyone with all wisdom, that we may present everyone mature in Christ. ²⁹For this I toil, struggling with all his energy that he powerfully works within me.

2 For I want you to know how great a struggle I have for you and for those at Laodicea and for all who have not seen me face to face, ²that their hearts may be encouraged, being knit together in love, to reach all the riches of full assurance of understanding and the knowledge of God's mystery, which is Christ, ³in whom are

---

¹ Or brothers and sisters. The plural Greek word adelphoi (translated "brothers") refers to siblings in a family. In New Testament usage, depending on the context, adelphoi may refer either to men or to both men and women who are siblings (brothers and sisters) in God's family, the church ² Greek fellow bondservant ³ Some manuscripts our ⁴ Or patience, with joy giving thanks ⁵ Some manuscripts us ⁶ That is, by means of; or in ⁷ Or to every creature

hidden all the treasures of wisdom and knowledge. [4] I say this in order that no one may delude you with plausible arguments. [5] For though I am absent in body, yet I am with you in spirit, rejoicing to see your good order and the firmness of your faith in Christ.

Alive in Christ

[6] Therefore, as you received Christ Jesus the Lord, so walk in him, [7] rooted and built up in him and established in the faith, just as you were taught, abounding in thanksgiving.

[8] See to it that no one takes you captive by philosophy and empty deceit, according to human tradition, according to the elemental spirits[1] of the world, and not according to Christ. [9] For in him the whole fullness of deity dwells bodily, [10] and you have been filled in him, who is the head of all rule and authority. [11] In him also you were circumcised with a circumcision made without hands, by putting off the body of the flesh, by the circumcision of Christ, [12] having been buried with him in baptism, in which you were also raised with him through faith in the powerful working of God, who raised him from the dead. [13] And you, who were dead in your trespasses and the uncircumcision of your flesh, God made alive together with him, having forgiven us all our trespasses, [14] by canceling the record of debt that stood against us with its legal demands. This he set aside, nailing it to the cross. [15] He disarmed the rulers and authorities[2] and put them to open shame, by triumphing over them in him.[3]

Let No One Disqualify You

[16] Therefore let no one pass judgment on you in questions of food and drink, or with regard to a festival or a new moon or a Sabbath. [17] These are a shadow of the things to come, but the substance belongs to Christ. [18] Let no one disqualify you, insisting on asceticism and worship of angels, going on in detail about visions,[4] puffed up without reason by his sensuous mind, [19] and not holding fast to the Head, from whom the whole body, nourished and knit together through its joints and ligaments, grows with a growth that is from God.

[20] If with Christ you died to the elemental spirits of the world, why, as if you were still alive in the world, do you submit to regulations— [21] "Do not handle, Do not taste, Do not touch" [22] (referring to things that all perish as they are used)— according to human precepts and teachings? [23] These have indeed an appearance of wisdom in promoting self-made religion and asceticism and severity to the body, but they are of no value in stopping the indulgence of the flesh.

Put On the New Self

3 If then you have been raised with Christ, seek the things that are above, where Christ is, seated at the right hand of God. [2] Set your minds on things that are above, not on things that are on earth. [3] For you have died, and your life is hidden with Christ in God. [4] When Christ who is your[5] life appears, then you also will appear with him in glory.

[5] Put to death therefore what is earthly in you:[6] sexual immorality, impurity, passion, evil desire, and covetousness, which is idolatry. [6] On account of these the wrath of God is coming.[7] [7] In these you too once walked, when you were living in them. [8] But now you must put them all away: anger, wrath, malice, slander, and obscene talk from your mouth. [9] Do not lie to one another, seeing that you have put off the old self[8] with its practices [10] and have put on the new self, which is being renewed in knowledge after the image of its creator. [11] Here there is not Greek and Jew, circumcised and uncircumcised, barbarian, Scythian, slave,[9] free; but Christ is all, and in all.

[12] Put on then, as God's chosen ones, holy and beloved, compassionate hearts, kindness, humility, meekness, and patience, [13] bearing with one another and, if one has a complaint against another, forgiving each other; as the Lord has forgiven you, so you also must forgive. [14] And above all these put on love, which binds everything together in perfect harmony. [15] And let the peace of Christ rule in your hearts, to which indeed you were called in one body. And be thankful. [16] Let the word of Christ dwell in you richly, teaching and admonishing one another in all wisdom, singing psalms and hymns and spiritual songs, with thankfulness in your hearts to God. [17] And whatever you do, in word or deed, do everything in the name of the Lord Jesus, giving thanks to God the Father through him.

Rules for Christian Households

[18] Wives, submit to your husbands, as is fitting in the Lord. [19] Husbands, love your wives, and do not be harsh with them. [20] Children, obey your parents in everything, for this pleases the Lord. [21] Fathers, do not provoke your children, lest they become discouraged. [22] Slaves,[10] obey in everything those who are your earthly masters,[11] not by way of eye-service, as people-pleasers, but with sincerity of heart, fearing the Lord. [23] Whatever you do, work heartily, as for the Lord and not for men, [24] knowing that from the Lord you will receive the inheritance as your reward. You are serving the Lord Christ. [25] For the wrongdoer will be paid back for the wrong he has done, and there is no partiality.

4 Masters, treat your slaves[12] justly and fairly, knowing that you also have a Master in heaven.

---

[1] Or elementary principles; also verse 20 [2] Probably demonic rulers and authorities [3] Or in it (that is, the cross) [4] Or about the things he has seen [5] Some manuscripts our [6] Greek therefore your members that are on the earth [7] Some manuscripts add upon the sons of disobedience [8] Greek man; also as supplied in verse 10 [9] Greek bondservant [10] Or Servants; Greek Bondservants [11] Or your masters according to the flesh [12] Or servants; Greek bondservants

Further Instructions

²Continue steadfastly in prayer, being watchful in it with thanksgiving. ³At the same time, pray also for us, that God may open to us a door for the word, to declare the mystery of Christ, on account of which I am in prison— ⁴that I may make it clear, which is how I ought to speak.

⁵Walk in wisdom toward outsiders, making the best use of the time. ⁶Let your speech always be gracious, seasoned with salt, so that you may know how you ought to answer each person.

Final Greetings

⁷Tychicus will tell you all about my activities. He is a beloved brother and faithful minister and fellow servant¹ in the Lord. ⁸I have sent him to you for this very purpose, that you may know how we are and that he may encourage your hearts, ⁹and with him Onesimus, our faithful and beloved brother, who is one of you. They will tell you of everything that has taken place here.

¹⁰Aristarchus my fellow prisoner greets you, and Mark the cousin of Barnabas (concerning whom you have received instructions—if he comes to you, welcome him), ¹¹and Jesus who is called Justus. These are the only men of the circumcision among my fellow workers for the kingdom of God, and they have been a comfort to me. ¹²Epaphras, who is one of you, a servant of Christ Jesus, greets you, always struggling on your behalf in his prayers, that you may stand mature and fully assured in all the will of God. ¹³For I bear him witness that he has worked hard for you and for those in Laodicea and in Hierapolis. ¹⁴Luke the beloved physician greets you, as does Demas. ¹⁵Give my greetings to the brothers² at Laodicea, and to Nympha and the church in her house. ¹⁶And when this letter has been read among you, have it also read in the church of the Laodiceans; and see that you also read the letter from Laodicea. ¹⁷And say to Archippus, "See that you fulfill the ministry that you have received in the Lord."

¹⁸I, Paul, write this greeting with my own hand. Remember my chains. Grace be with you.

¹ Greek *fellow bondservant*; also verse 12 ² Or *brothers and sisters*

1 THESSALONIANS

Introduction

Paul wrote this letter to encourage new believers in their faith, to exhort them to godly living, to give them assurance about the eternal state of believers who had died, and to defend the integrity of his ministry as an apostle. Thessalonica (present-day Thessaloniki, Greece) was the capital of Roman Macedonia. It was on important trade routes. Paul, twice identified as the author (1:1; 2:18), visited Thessalonica on his second missionary journey but was forced to flee because of Jewish opposition. He sent Timothy to work with the largely Gentile church there, and Timothy brought him good news of their faith (3:6). This is one of Paul's first letters, probably written about A.D. 50–51.

Greeting

1 Paul, Silvanus, and Timothy,
To the church of the Thessalonians in God the Father and the Lord Jesus Christ:
Grace to you and peace.

The Thessalonians' Faith and Example

² We give thanks to God always for all of you, constantly¹ mentioning you in our prayers, ³ remembering before our God and Father your work of faith and labor of love and steadfastness of hope in our Lord Jesus Christ. ⁴ For we know, brothers² loved by God, that he has chosen you, ⁵ because our gospel came to you not only in word, but also in power and in the Holy Spirit and with full conviction. You know what kind of men we proved to be among you for your sake. ⁶ And you became imitators of us and of the Lord, for you received the word in much affliction, with the joy of the Holy Spirit, ⁷ so that you became an example to all the believers in Macedonia and in Achaia. ⁸ For not only has the word of the Lord sounded forth from you in Macedonia and Achaia, but your faith in God has gone forth everywhere, so that we need not say anything. ⁹ For they themselves report concerning us the kind of reception we had among you, and how you turned to God from idols to serve the living and true God, ¹⁰ and to wait for his Son from heaven, whom he raised from the dead, Jesus who delivers us from the wrath to come.

Paul's Ministry to the Thessalonians

2 For you yourselves know, brothers,³ that our coming to you was not in vain. ² But though we had already suffered and been shamefully treated at Philippi, as you know, we had boldness in our God to declare to you the gospel of God in the midst of much conflict. ³ For our appeal does not spring from error or impurity or any attempt to deceive, ⁴ but just as we have been approved by God to be entrusted with the gospel, so we speak, not to please man, but to please God who tests our hearts. ⁵ For we never came with words of flattery,⁴ as you know, nor with a pretext for greed—God is witness. ⁶ Nor did we seek glory from people, whether from you or from others, though we could have made demands as apostles of Christ. ⁷ But we were gentle⁵ among you, like a nursing mother taking care of her own children. ⁸ So, being affectionately desirous of you, we were ready to share with you not only the gospel of God but also our own selves, because you had become very dear to us.

⁹ For you remember, brothers, our labor and toil: we worked night and day, that we might not be a burden to any of you, while we proclaimed to you the gospel of God. ¹⁰ You are witnesses, and God also, how holy and righteous and blameless was our conduct toward you believers. ¹¹ For you know how, like a father with his children, ¹² we exhorted each one of you and encouraged you and charged you to walk in a manner worthy of God, who calls you into his own kingdom and glory.

¹³ And we also thank God constantly⁶ for this, that when you received the word of God, which you heard from us, you accepted it not as the word of men but as what it really is, the word of God, which is at work in you believers. ¹⁴ For you, brothers, became imitators of the churches of God in Christ Jesus that are in Judea. For you suffered the same things from your own countrymen as they did from the Jews, ¹⁵ who killed both the Lord Jesus and the prophets, and drove us out, and displease God and oppose all mankind ¹⁶ by hindering us from speaking to the Gentiles that they might be saved—so as always to fill up the measure of their sins. But God's wrath has come upon them at last!⁷

Paul's Longing to See Them Again

¹⁷ But since we were torn away from you, brothers, for a short time, in person not in heart,

---

¹ Or without ceasing ² Or brothers and sisters. The plural Greek word adelphoi (translated "brothers") refers to siblings in a family. In New Testament usage, depending on the context, adelphoi may refer either to men or to both men and women who are siblings (brothers and sisters) in God's family, the church ³ Or brothers and sisters; also verses 9, 14, 17 ⁴ Or with a flattering speech ⁵ Some manuscripts infants ⁶ Or without ceasing ⁷ Or completely, or forever

we endeavored the more eagerly and with great desire to see you face to face, [18]because we wanted to come to you—I, Paul, again and again—but Satan hindered us. [19]For what is our hope or joy or crown of boasting before our Lord Jesus at his coming? Is it not you? [20]For you are our glory and joy.

3 Therefore when we could bear it no longer, we were willing to be left behind at Athens alone, [2]and we sent Timothy, our brother and God's coworker[1] in the gospel of Christ, to establish and exhort you in your faith, [3]that no one be moved by these afflictions. For you yourselves know that we are destined for this. [4]For when we were with you, we kept telling you beforehand that we were to suffer affliction, just as it has come to pass, and just as you know. [5]For this reason, when I could bear it no longer, I sent to learn about your faith, for fear that somehow the tempter had tempted you and our labor would be in vain.

Timothy's Encouraging Report

[6]But now that Timothy has come to us from you, and has brought us the good news of your faith and love and reported that you always remember us kindly and long to see us, as we long to see you— [7]for this reason, brothers,[2] in all our distress and affliction we have been comforted about you through your faith. [8]For now we live, if you are standing fast in the Lord. [9]For what thanksgiving can we return to God for you, for all the joy that we feel for your sake before our God, [10]as we pray most earnestly night and day that we may see you face to face and supply what is lacking in your faith?

[11]Now may our God and Father himself, and our Lord Jesus, direct our way to you, [12]and may the Lord make you increase and abound in love for one another and for all, as we do for you, [13]so that he may establish your hearts blameless in holiness before our God and Father, at the coming of our Lord Jesus with all his saints.

A Life Pleasing to God

4 Finally, then, brothers,[3] we ask and urge you in the Lord Jesus, that as you received from us how you ought to walk and to please God, just as you are doing, that you do so more and more. [2]For you know what instructions we gave you through the Lord Jesus. [3]For this is the will of God, your sanctification:[4] that you abstain from sexual immorality; [4]that each one of you know how to control his own body[5] in holiness and honor, [5]not in the passion of lust like the Gentiles who do not know God; [6]that no one transgress and wrong his brother in this matter, because the Lord is an avenger in all these things, as we told you beforehand and solemnly warned you.

[7]For God has not called us for impurity, but in holiness. [8]Therefore whoever disregards this, disregards not man but God, who gives his Holy Spirit to you.

[9]Now concerning brotherly love you have no need for anyone to write to you, for you yourselves have been taught by God to love one another, [10]for that indeed is what you are doing to all the brothers throughout Macedonia. But we urge you, brothers, to do this more and more, [11]and to aspire to live quietly, and to mind your own affairs, and to work with your hands, as we instructed you, [12]so that you may walk properly before outsiders and be dependent on no one.

The Coming of the Lord

[13]But we do not want you to be uninformed, brothers, about those who are asleep, that you may not grieve as others do who have no hope. [14]For since we believe that Jesus died and rose again, even so, through Jesus, God will bring with him those who have fallen asleep. [15]For this we declare to you by a word from the Lord,[6] that we who are alive, who are left until the coming of the Lord, will not precede those who have fallen asleep. [16]For the Lord himself will descend from heaven with a cry of command, with the voice of an archangel, and with the sound of the trumpet of God. And the dead in Christ will rise first. [17]Then we who are alive, who are left, will be caught up together with them in the clouds to meet the Lord in the air, and so we will always be with the Lord. [18]Therefore encourage one another with these words.

The Day of the Lord

5 Now concerning the times and the seasons, brothers,[7] you have no need to have anything written to you. [2]For you yourselves are fully aware that the day of the Lord will come like a thief in the night. [3]While people are saying, "There is peace and security," then sudden destruction will come upon them as labor pains come upon a pregnant woman, and they will not escape. [4]But you are not in darkness, brothers, for that day to surprise you like a thief. [5]For you are all children[8] of light, children of the day. We are not of the night or of the darkness. [6]So then let us not sleep, as others do, but let us keep awake and be sober. [7]For those who sleep, sleep at night, and those who get drunk, are drunk at night. [8]But since we belong to the day, let us be sober, having put on the breastplate of faith and love, and for a helmet the hope of salvation. [9]For God has not destined us for wrath, but to obtain salvation through our Lord Jesus Christ, [10]who died for us so that whether we are awake or asleep we might live with him. [11]Therefore

---

[1] Some manuscripts *servant* [2] Or *brothers and sisters* [3] Or *brothers and sisters; also verses 10, 13* [4] Or *your holiness* [5] Or *how to take a wife for himself;* Greek *how to possess his own vessel* [6] Or *by the word of the Lord* [7] Or *brothers and sisters; also verses 4, 12, 14, 25, 26, 27* [8] Or *sons;* twice in this verse

encourage one another and build one another up, just as you are doing.

Final Instructions and Benediction

¹²We ask you, brothers, to respect those who labor among you and are over you in the Lord and admonish you, ¹³and to esteem them very highly in love because of their work. Be at peace among yourselves. ¹⁴And we urge you, brothers, admonish the idle,¹ encourage the fainthearted, help the weak, be patient with them all. ¹⁵See that no one repays anyone evil for evil, but always seek to do good to one another and to everyone. ¹⁶Rejoice always, ¹⁷pray without ceasing, ¹⁸give thanks in all circumstances; for this is the will of God in Christ Jesus for you. ¹⁹Do not quench the Spirit. ²⁰Do not despise prophecies, ²¹but test everything; hold fast what is good. ²²Abstain from every form of evil.

²³Now may the God of peace himself sanctify you completely, and may your whole spirit and soul and body be kept blameless at the coming of our Lord Jesus Christ. ²⁴He who calls you is faithful; he will surely do it.

²⁵Brothers, pray for us.

²⁶Greet all the brothers with a holy kiss.

²⁷I put you under oath before the Lord to have this letter read to all the brothers.

²⁸The grace of our Lord Jesus Christ be with you.

---

¹Or *disorderly, or undisciplined*

2 THESSALONIANS

Introduction

This letter from the apostle Paul was probably written shortly after his first letter to the church in Thessalonica. He had been boasting of them to other churches, telling of their faith and their love for each other in the face of persecution. Paul reminded them that God will repay their persecutors. He also addressed two recurring problems in this church. First, they were concerned that the Lord had already returned. Paul urged them not to become "shaken in mind or alarmed," fearing that "the day of the Lord" (2:2) had already come. Second, he admonished them not to be idle, commanding them that, "If anyone is not willing to work, let him not eat" (3:10).

Greeting

1 Paul, Silvanus, and Timothy,
To the church of the Thessalonians in God our Father and the Lord Jesus Christ:

²Grace to you and peace from God our Father and the Lord Jesus Christ.

Thanksgiving

³We ought always to give thanks to God for you, brothers,¹ as is right, because your faith is growing abundantly, and the love of every one of you for one another is increasing. ⁴Therefore we ourselves boast about you in the churches of God for your steadfastness and faith in all your persecutions and in the afflictions that you are enduring.

The Judgment at Christ's Coming

⁵This is evidence of the righteous judgment of God, that you may be considered worthy of the kingdom of God, for which you are also suffering— ⁶since indeed God considers it just to repay with affliction those who afflict you, ⁷and to grant relief to you who are afflicted as well as to us, when the Lord Jesus is revealed from heaven with his mighty angels ⁸in flaming fire, inflicting vengeance on those who do not know God and on those who do not obey the gospel of our Lord Jesus. ⁹They will suffer the punishment of eternal destruction, away from² the presence of the Lord and from the glory of his might, ¹⁰when he comes on that day to be glorified in his saints, and to be marveled at among all who have believed, because our testimony to you was believed. ¹¹To this end we always pray for you, that our God may make you worthy of his calling and may fulfill every resolve for good and every work of faith by his power, ¹²so that the name of our Lord Jesus may be glorified in you, and you in him, according to the grace of our God and the Lord Jesus Christ.

The Man of Lawlessness

2 Now concerning the coming of our Lord Jesus Christ and our being gathered together to him, we ask you, brothers,³ ²not to be quickly shaken in mind or alarmed, either by a spirit or a spoken word, or a letter seeming to be from us, to the effect that the day of the Lord has come. ³Let no one deceive you in any way. For that day will not come, unless the rebellion comes first, and the man of lawlessness⁴ is revealed, the son of destruction,⁵ ⁴who opposes and exalts himself against every so-called god or object of worship, so that he takes his seat in the temple of God, proclaiming himself to be God. ⁵Do you not remember that when I was still with you I told you these things? ⁶And you know what is restraining him now so that he may be revealed in his time. ⁷For the mystery of lawlessness is already at work. Only he who now restrains it will do so until he is out of the way. ⁸And then the lawless one will be revealed, whom the Lord Jesus will kill with the breath of his mouth and bring to nothing by the appearance of his coming. ⁹The coming of the lawless one is by the activity of Satan with all power and false signs and wonders, ¹⁰and with all wicked deception for those who are perishing, because they refused to love the truth and so be saved. ¹¹Therefore God sends them a strong delusion, so that they may believe what is false, ¹²in order that all may be condemned who did not believe the truth but had pleasure in unrighteousness.

Stand Firm

¹³But we ought always to give thanks to God for you, brothers beloved by the Lord, because God chose you as the firstfruits⁶ to be saved, through sanctification by the Spirit and belief in the truth. ¹⁴To this he called you through our gospel, so that you may obtain the glory of our Lord Jesus Christ. ¹⁵So then, brothers, stand firm and hold to the traditions that you were taught by us, either by our spoken word or by our letter.

---

¹ Or brothers and sisters. The plural Greek word adelphoi (translated "brothers") refers to siblings in a family. In New Testament usage, depending on the context, adelphoi may refer either to men or to both men and women who are siblings (brothers and sisters) in God's family, the church ² Or destruction that comes from ³ Or brothers and sisters; also verses 13, 15 ⁴ Some manuscripts sin ⁵ Greek the son of perdition (a Hebrew idiom) ⁶ Some manuscripts chose you from the beginning

[16] Now may our Lord Jesus Christ himself, and God our Father, who loved us and gave us eternal comfort and good hope through grace, [17] comfort your hearts and establish them in every good work and word.

Pray for Us

3 Finally, brothers,[1] pray for us, that the word of the Lord may speed ahead and be honored,[2] as happened among you, [2] and that we may be delivered from wicked and evil men. For not all have faith. [3] But the Lord is faithful. He will establish you and guard you against the evil one.[3] [4] And we have confidence in the Lord about you, that you are doing and will do the things that we command. [5] May the Lord direct your hearts to the love of God and to the steadfastness of Christ.

Warning Against Idleness

[6] Now we command you, brothers, in the name of our Lord Jesus Christ, that you keep away from any brother who is walking in idleness and not in accord with the tradition that you received from us. [7] For you yourselves know how you ought to imitate us, because we were not idle when we were with you, [8] nor did we eat anyone's bread without paying for it, but with toil and labor we worked night and day, that we might not be a burden to any of you. [9] It was not because we do not have that right, but to give you in ourselves an example to imitate. [10] For even when we were with you, we would give you this command: If anyone is not willing to work, let him not eat. [11] For we hear that some among you walk in idleness, not busy at work, but busybodies. [12] Now such persons we command and encourage in the Lord Jesus Christ to do their work quietly and to earn their own living.[4]

[13] As for you, brothers, do not grow weary in doing good. [14] If anyone does not obey what we say in this letter, take note of that person, and have nothing to do with him, that he may be ashamed. [15] Do not regard him as an enemy, but warn him as a brother.

Benediction

[16] Now may the Lord of peace himself give you peace at all times in every way. The Lord be with you all.

[17] I, Paul, write this greeting with my own hand. This is the sign of genuineness in every letter of mine; it is the way I write. [18] The grace of our Lord Jesus Christ be with you all.

---

[1] Or brothers and sisters; also verses 6, 13   [2] Or glorified   [3] Or evil   [4] Greek eat their own bread

1 TIMOTHY

Introduction

First Timothy is one of three pastoral letters (including 2 Timothy and Titus) that the aging apostle Paul sent to those who would continue his work. Timothy was, in every way, Paul's spiritual son. Young but gifted, Timothy had been assigned to lead the church at Ephesus—a church needing order in worship as well as doctrinal correction, plagued as it was by false teachers. Paul's letter, likely written about A.D. 62–66, counseled the young man on matters of church leadership—from proper worship, to qualifications for overseers (elders) and deacons, to advice on confronting false teaching and how to treat various individuals within a congregation. Paul charged Timothy to live a life beyond reproach, giving believers a standard to emulate.

Greeting

1 Paul, an apostle of Christ Jesus by command of God our Savior and of Christ Jesus our hope,

²To Timothy, my true child in the faith:

Grace, mercy, and peace from God the Father and Christ Jesus our Lord.

Warning Against False Teachers

³As I urged you when I was going to Macedonia, remain at Ephesus so that you may charge certain persons not to teach any different doctrine, ⁴nor to devote themselves to myths and endless genealogies, which promote speculations rather than the stewardship¹ from God that is by faith. ⁵The aim of our charge is love that issues from a pure heart and a good conscience and a sincere faith. ⁶Certain persons, by swerving from these, have wandered away into vain discussion, ⁷desiring to be teachers of the law, without understanding either what they are saying or the things about which they make confident assertions.

⁸Now we know that the law is good, if one uses it lawfully, ⁹understanding this, that the law is not laid down for the just but for the lawless and disobedient, for the ungodly and sinners, for the unholy and profane, for those who strike their fathers and mothers, for murderers, ¹⁰the sexually immoral, men who practice homosexuality, enslavers,² liars, perjurers, and whatever else is contrary to sound³ doctrine, ¹¹in accordance with the gospel of the glory of the blessed God with which I have been entrusted.

Christ Jesus Came to Save Sinners

¹²I thank him who has given me strength, Christ Jesus our Lord, because he judged me faithful, appointing me to his service, ¹³though formerly I was a blasphemer, persecutor, and insolent opponent. But I received mercy because I had acted ignorantly in unbelief, ¹⁴and the grace of our Lord overflowed for me with the faith and love that are in Christ Jesus. ¹⁵The say-

ing is trustworthy and deserving of full acceptance, that Christ Jesus came into the world to save sinners, of whom I am the foremost. ¹⁶But I received mercy for this reason, that in me, as the foremost, Jesus Christ might display his perfect patience as an example to those who were to believe in him for eternal life. ¹⁷To the King of ages, immortal, invisible, the only God, be honor and glory forever and ever.⁴ Amen.

¹⁸This charge I entrust to you, Timothy, my child, in accordance with the prophecies previously made about you, that by them you may wage the good warfare, ¹⁹holding faith and a good conscience. By rejecting this, some have made shipwreck of their faith, ²⁰among whom are Hymenaeus and Alexander, whom I have handed over to Satan that they may learn not to blaspheme.

Pray for All People

2 First of all, then, I urge that supplications, prayers, intercessions, and thanksgivings be made for all people, ²for kings and all who are in high positions, that we may lead a peaceful and quiet life, godly and dignified in every way. ³This is good, and it is pleasing in the sight of God our Savior, ⁴who desires all people to be saved and to come to the knowledge of the truth. ⁵For there is one God, and there is one mediator between God and men, the man⁵ Christ Jesus, ⁶who gave himself as a ransom for all, which is the testimony given at the proper time. ⁷For this I was appointed a preacher and an apostle (I am telling the truth, I am not lying), a teacher of the Gentiles in faith and truth.

⁸I desire then that in every place the men should pray, lifting holy hands without anger or quarreling; ⁹likewise also that women should adorn themselves in respectable apparel, with modesty and self-control, not with braided hair and gold or pearls or costly attire, ¹⁰but with what is proper for women who profess godliness—with good works. ¹¹Let a woman learn quietly with all submissiveness. ¹²I do not permit

¹Or good order ²That is, those who take someone captive in order to sell him into slavery ³Or healthy ⁴Greek to the ages of ages ⁵men and man render the same Greek word that is translated people in verses 1 and 4

a woman to teach or to exercise authority over a man; rather, she is to remain quiet. [13]For Adam was formed first, then Eve; [14]and Adam was not deceived, but the woman was deceived and became a transgressor. [15]Yet she will be saved through childbearing—if they continue in faith and love and holiness, with self-control.

Qualifications for Overseers

3 The saying is trustworthy: If anyone aspires to the office of overseer, he desires a noble task. [2]Therefore an overseer[1] must be above reproach, the husband of one wife,[2] sober-minded, self-controlled, respectable, hospitable, able to teach, [3]not a drunkard, not violent but gentle, not quarrelsome, not a lover of money. [4]He must manage his own household well, with all dignity keeping his children submissive, [5]for if someone does not know how to manage his own household, how will he care for God's church? [6]He must not be a recent convert, or he may become puffed up with conceit and fall into the condemnation of the devil. [7]Moreover, he must be well thought of by outsiders, so that he may not fall into disgrace, into a snare of the devil.

Qualifications for Deacons

[8]Deacons likewise must be dignified, not double-tongued,[3] not addicted to much wine, not greedy for dishonest gain. [9]They must hold the mystery of the faith with a clear conscience. [10]And let them also be tested first; then let them serve as deacons if they prove themselves blameless. [11]Their wives likewise must[4] be dignified, not slanderers, but sober-minded, faithful in all things. [12]Let deacons each be the husband of one wife, managing their children and their own households well. [13]For those who serve well as deacons gain a good standing for themselves and also great confidence in the faith that is in Christ Jesus.

The Mystery of Godliness

[14]I hope to come to you soon, but I am writing these things to you so that, [15]if I delay, you may know how one ought to behave in the household of God, which is the church of the living God, a pillar and buttress of the truth. [16]Great indeed, we confess, is the mystery of godliness:

He[5] was manifested in the flesh,
vindicated[6] by the Spirit,[7]
    seen by angels,
proclaimed among the nations,
    believed on in the world,
    taken up in glory.

Some Will Depart from the Faith

4 Now the Spirit expressly says that in later times some will depart from the faith by devoting themselves to deceitful spirits and teachings of demons, [2]through the insincerity of liars whose consciences are seared, [3]who forbid marriage and require abstinence from foods that God created to be received with thanksgiving by those who believe and know the truth. [4]For everything created by God is good, and nothing is to be rejected if it is received with thanksgiving, [5]for it is made holy by the word of God and prayer.

A Good Servant of Christ Jesus

[6]If you put these things before the brothers,[8] you will be a good servant of Christ Jesus, being trained in the words of the faith and of the good doctrine that you have followed. [7]Have nothing to do with irreverent, silly myths. Rather train yourself for godliness; [8]for while bodily training is of some value, godliness is of value in every way, as it holds promise for the present life and also for the life to come. [9]The saying is trustworthy and deserving of full acceptance. [10]For to this end we toil and strive,[9] because we have our hope set on the living God, who is the Savior of all people, especially of those who believe.

[11]Command and teach these things. [12]Let no one despise you for your youth, but set the believers an example in speech, in conduct, in love, in faith, in purity. [13]Until I come, devote yourself to the public reading of Scripture, to exhortation, to teaching. [14]Do not neglect the gift you have, which was given you by prophecy when the council of elders laid their hands on you. [15]Practice these things, immerse yourself in them,[10] so that all may see your progress. [16]Keep a close watch on yourself and on the teaching. Persist in this, for by so doing you will save both yourself and your hearers.

Instructions for the Church

5 Do not rebuke an older man but encourage him as you would a father, younger men as brothers, [2]older women as mothers, younger women as sisters, in all purity.

[3]Honor widows who are truly widows. [4]But if a widow has children or grandchildren, let them first learn to show godliness to their own household and to make some return to their parents, for this is pleasing in the sight of God. [5]She who is truly a widow, left all alone, has set her hope on God and continues in supplications and prayers night and day, [6]but she who is self-indulgent is dead even while she lives. [7]Command these things as well, so that they may be without

---

[1]Or bishop; Greek episkopos; a similar term occurs in verse 1 [2]Or a man of one woman; also verse 12 [3]Or devious in speech [4]Or Wives, likewise, must, or Women, likewise, must [5]Greek Who; some manuscripts God; others Which [6]Or justified [7]Or vindicated in spirit [8]Or brothers and sisters. The plural Greek word adelphoi (translated "brothers") refers to siblings in a family. In New Testament usage, depending on the context, adelphoi may refer either to men or to both men and women who are siblings (brothers and sisters) in God's family, the church [9]Some manuscripts and suffer reproach [10]Greek be in them

reproach. [8]But if anyone does not provide for his relatives, and especially for members of his household, he has denied the faith and is worse than an unbeliever.

[9]Let a widow be enrolled if she is not less than sixty years of age, having been the wife of one husband,[1] [10]and having a reputation for good works: if she has brought up children, has shown hospitality, has washed the feet of the saints, has cared for the afflicted, and has devoted herself to every good work. [11]But refuse to enroll younger widows, for when their passions draw them away from Christ, they desire to marry [12]and so incur condemnation for having abandoned their former faith. [13]Besides that, they learn to be idlers, going about from house to house, and not only idlers, but also gossips and busybodies, saying what they should not. [14]So I would have younger widows marry, bear children, manage their households, and give the adversary no occasion for slander. [15]For some have already strayed after Satan. [16]If any believing woman has relatives who are widows, let her care for them. Let the church not be burdened, so that it may care for those who are truly widows.

[17]Let the elders who rule well be considered worthy of double honor, especially those who labor in preaching and teaching. [18]For the Scripture says, [a]"You shall not muzzle an ox when it treads out the grain," and, "The laborer deserves his wages." [19]Do not admit a charge against an elder except on the evidence of two or three witnesses. [20]As for those who persist in sin, rebuke them in the presence of all, so that the rest may stand in fear. [21]In the presence of God and of Christ Jesus and of the elect angels I charge you to keep these rules without prejudging, doing nothing from partiality. [22]Do not be hasty in the laying on of hands, nor take part in the sins of others; keep yourself pure. [23](No longer drink only water, but use a little wine for the sake of your stomach and your frequent ailments.) [24]The sins of some men are conspicuous, going before them to judgment, but the sins of others appear later. [25]So also good works are conspicuous, and even those that are not cannot remain hidden.

6 Let all who are under a yoke as slaves[2] regard their own masters as worthy of all honor, so that the name of God and the teaching may not be reviled. [2]Those who have believing masters must not be disrespectful on the ground that they are brothers; rather they must serve all the better since those who benefit by their good service are believers and beloved.

False Teachers and True Contentment

Teach and urge these things. [3]If anyone teaches a different doctrine and does not agree with the sound[3] words of our Lord Jesus Christ and the teaching that accords with godliness, [4]he is puffed up with conceit and understands nothing. He has an unhealthy craving for controversy and for quarrels about words, which produce envy, dissension, slander, evil suspicions, [5]and constant friction among people who are depraved in mind and deprived of the truth, imagining that godliness is a means of gain. [6]Now there is great gain in godliness with contentment, [7]for we brought nothing into the world, and[4] we cannot take anything out of the world. [8]But if we have food and clothing, with these we will be content. [9]But those who desire to be rich fall into temptation, into a snare, into many senseless and harmful desires that plunge people into ruin and destruction. [10]For the love of money is a root of all kinds of evils. It is through this craving that some have wandered away from the faith and pierced themselves with many pangs.

Fight the Good Fight of Faith

[11]But as for you, O man of God, flee these things. Pursue righteousness, godliness, faith, love, steadfastness, gentleness. [12]Fight the good fight of the faith. Take hold of the eternal life to which you were called and about which you made the good confession in the presence of many witnesses. [13]I charge you in the presence of God, who gives life to all things, and of Christ Jesus, who in his testimony before[5] Pontius Pilate made the good confession, [14]to keep the commandment unstained and free from reproach until the appearing of our Lord Jesus Christ, [15]which he will display at the proper time—he who is the blessed and only Sovereign, the King of kings and Lord of lords, [16]who alone has immortality, who dwells in unapproachable light, whom no one has ever seen or can see. To him be honor and eternal dominion. Amen.

[17]As for the rich in this present age, charge them not to be haughty, nor to set their hopes on the uncertainty of riches, but on God, who richly provides us with everything to enjoy. [18]They are to do good, to be rich in good works, to be generous and ready to share, [19]thus storing up treasure for themselves as a good foundation for the future, so that they may take hold of that which is truly life.

[20]O Timothy, guard the deposit entrusted to you. Avoid the irreverent babble and contradictions of what is falsely called "knowledge," [21]for by professing it some have swerved from the faith.

Grace be with you.[6]

---

[1] Or *a woman of one man* [2] Greek *bondservants* [3] Or *healthy* [4] Greek *for;* some manuscripts insert [it is] *certain* [that] [5] Or *in the time of* [6] The Greek for *you* is plural [a] Deut. 25:4

2 TIMOTHY

Introduction

Paul wrote this letter as he awaited execution. Despite all that Paul was facing—death, the end of his ministry, abandonment by most of his friends for fear of persecution—he faithfully directed his spiritual son Timothy to the hope that is in Christ. As he exhorted Timothy to boldness, endurance, and faithfulness in the face of false teaching, Paul showed his customary concern for sound doctrine. Scripture, said Paul, is "breathed out by God" and is sufficient in all things pertaining to the faith and practice of Christians (3:16-17). Older believers, therefore, should be eager to pass on their knowledge of Scripture to those who are younger in the faith (2:2). Paul probably wrote from Rome, A.D. 67 or 68.

Greeting

1 Paul, an apostle of Christ Jesus by the will of God according to the promise of the life that is in Christ Jesus,

²To Timothy, my beloved child:

Grace, mercy, and peace from God the Father and Christ Jesus our Lord.

Guard the Deposit Entrusted to You

³I thank God whom I serve, as did my ancestors, with a clear conscience, as I remember you constantly in my prayers night and day. ⁴As I remember your tears, I long to see you, that I may be filled with joy. ⁵I am reminded of your sincere faith, a faith that dwelt first in your grandmother Lois and your mother Eunice and now, I am sure, dwells in you as well. ⁶For this reason I remind you to fan into flame the gift of God, which is in you through the laying on of my hands, ⁷for God gave us a spirit not of fear but of power and love and self-control.

⁸Therefore do not be ashamed of the testimony about our Lord, nor of me his prisoner, but share in suffering for the gospel by the power of God, ⁹who saved us and called us to¹ a holy calling, not because of our works but because of his own purpose and grace, which he gave us in Christ Jesus before the ages began,² ¹⁰and which now has been manifested through the appearing of our Savior Christ Jesus, who abolished death and brought life and immortality to light through the gospel, ¹¹for which I was appointed a preacher and apostle and teacher, ¹²which is why I suffer as I do. But I am not ashamed, for I know whom I have believed, and I am convinced that he is able to guard until that Day what has been entrusted to me.³ ¹³Follow the pattern of the sound⁴ words that you have heard from me, in the faith and love that are in Christ Jesus. ¹⁴By the Holy Spirit who dwells within us, guard the good deposit entrusted to you.

¹⁵You are aware that all who are in Asia turned away from me, among whom are Phygelus and Hermogenes. ¹⁶May the Lord grant mercy to the household of Onesiphorus, for he often refreshed me and was not ashamed of my chains, ¹⁷but when he arrived in Rome he searched for me earnestly and found me— ¹⁸may the Lord grant him to find mercy from the Lord on that Day!—and you well know all the service he rendered at Ephesus.

A Good Soldier of Christ Jesus

2 You then, my child, be strengthened by the grace that is in Christ Jesus, ²and what you have heard from me in the presence of many witnesses entrust to faithful men who will be able to teach others also. ³Share in suffering as a good soldier of Christ Jesus. ⁴No soldier gets entangled in civilian pursuits, since his aim is to please the one who enlisted him. ⁵An athlete is not crowned unless he competes according to the rules. ⁶It is the hard-working farmer who ought to have the first share of the crops. ⁷Think over what I say, for the Lord will give you understanding in everything.

⁸Remember Jesus Christ, risen from the dead, the offspring of David, as preached in my gospel, ⁹for which I am suffering, bound with chains as a criminal. But the word of God is not bound! ¹⁰Therefore I endure everything for the sake of the elect, that they also may obtain the salvation that is in Christ Jesus with eternal glory. ¹¹The saying is trustworthy, for:

> If we have died with him, we will also live with him;
> ¹² if we endure, we will also reign with him;
> if we deny him, he also will deny us;
> ¹³ if we are faithless, he remains faithful—

for he cannot deny himself.

A Worker Approved by God

¹⁴Remind them of these things, and charge them before God⁵ not to quarrel about words, which does no good, but only ruins the hearers. ¹⁵Do your best to present yourself to God as one approved,⁶ a worker who has no need to be ashamed, rightly handling the word of truth. ¹⁶But avoid irreverent babble, for it will lead peo-

¹Or with ²Greek before times eternal ³Or what I have entrusted to him; Greek my deposit ⁴Or healthy ⁵Some manuscripts the Lord ⁶That is, one approved after being tested

ple into more and more ungodliness, ¹⁷and their talk will spread like gangrene. Among them are Hymenaeus and Philetus, ¹⁸who have swerved from the truth, saying that the resurrection has already happened. They are upsetting the faith of some. ¹⁹But God's firm foundation stands, bearing this seal: "The Lord knows those who are his," and, "Let everyone who names the name of the Lord depart from iniquity."

²⁰Now in a great house there are not only vessels of gold and silver but also of wood and clay, some for honorable use, some for dishonorable. ²¹Therefore, if anyone cleanses himself from what is dishonorable,¹ he will be a vessel for honorable use, set apart as holy, useful to the master of the house, ready for every good work.

²²So flee youthful passions and pursue righteousness, faith, love, and peace, along with those who call on the Lord from a pure heart. ²³Have nothing to do with foolish, ignorant controversies; you know that they breed quarrels. ²⁴And the Lord's servant² must not be quarrelsome but kind to everyone, able to teach, patiently enduring evil, ²⁵correcting his opponents with gentleness. God may perhaps grant them repentance leading to a knowledge of the truth, ²⁶and they may come to their senses and escape from the snare of the devil, after being captured by him to do his will.

Godlessness in the Last Days

3 But understand this, that in the last days there will come times of difficulty. ²For people will be lovers of self, lovers of money, proud, arrogant, abusive, disobedient to their parents, ungrateful, unholy, ³heartless, unappeasable, slanderous, without self-control, brutal, not loving good, ⁴treacherous, reckless, swollen with conceit, lovers of pleasure rather than lovers of God, ⁵having the appearance of godliness, but denying its power. Avoid such people. ⁶For among them are those who creep into households and capture weak women, burdened with sins and led astray by various passions, ⁷always learning and never able to arrive at a knowledge of the truth. ⁸Just as Jannes and Jambres opposed Moses, so these men also oppose the truth, men corrupted in mind and disqualified regarding the faith. ⁹But they will not get very far, for their folly will be plain to all, as was that of those two men.

All Scripture Is Breathed Out by God

¹⁰You, however, have followed my teaching, my conduct, my aim in life, my faith, my patience, my love, my steadfastness, ¹¹my persecutions and sufferings that happened to me at Antioch, at Iconium, and at Lystra—which persecutions I endured; yet from them all the Lord rescued me. ¹²Indeed, all who desire to live a godly life in Christ Jesus will be persecuted,

¹³while evil people and impostors will go on from bad to worse, deceiving and being deceived. ¹⁴But as for you, continue in what you have learned and have firmly believed, knowing from whom³ you learned it ¹⁵and how from childhood you have been acquainted with the sacred writings, which are able to make you wise for salvation through faith in Christ Jesus. ¹⁶All Scripture is breathed out by God and profitable for teaching, for reproof, for correction, and for training in righteousness, ¹⁷that the man of God⁴ may be competent, equipped for every good work.

Preach the Word

4 I charge you in the presence of God and of Christ Jesus, who is to judge the living and the dead, and by his appearing and his kingdom: ²preach the word; be ready in season and out of season; reprove, rebuke, and exhort, with complete patience and teaching. ³For the time is coming when people will not endure sound⁵ teaching, but having itching ears they will accumulate for themselves teachers to suit their own passions, ⁴and will turn away from listening to the truth and wander off into myths. ⁵As for you, always be sober-minded, endure suffering, do the work of an evangelist, fulfill your ministry.

⁶For I am already being poured out as a drink offering, and the time of my departure has come. ⁷I have fought the good fight, I have finished the race, I have kept the faith. ⁸Henceforth there is laid up for me the crown of righteousness, which the Lord, the righteous judge, will award to me on that Day, and not only to me but also to all who have loved his appearing.

Personal Instructions

⁹Do your best to come to me soon. ¹⁰For Demas, in love with this present world, has deserted me and gone to Thessalonica. Crescens has gone to Galatia,⁶ Titus to Dalmatia. ¹¹Luke alone is with me. Get Mark and bring him with you, for he is very useful to me for ministry. ¹²Tychicus I have sent to Ephesus. ¹³When you come, bring the cloak that I left with Carpus at Troas, also the books, and above all the parchments. ¹⁴Alexander the coppersmith did me great harm; the Lord will repay him according to his deeds. ¹⁵Beware of him yourself, for he strongly opposed our message. ¹⁶At my first defense no one came to stand by me, but all deserted me. May it not be charged against them! ¹⁷But the Lord stood by me and strengthened me, so that through me the message might be fully proclaimed and all the Gentiles might hear it. So I was rescued from the lion's mouth. ¹⁸The Lord will rescue me from every evil deed and bring

¹ Greek *from these things* ² Greek *bondservant* ³ The Greek for *whom* is plural ⁴ That is, a messenger of God (the phrase echoes a common Old Testament expression) ⁵ Or *healthy* ⁶ Some manuscripts *Gaul*

me safely into his heavenly kingdom. To him be the glory forever and ever. Amen.

Final Greetings

¹⁹Greet Prisca and Aquila, and the household of Onesiphorus. ²⁰Erastus remained at Corinth, and I left Trophimus, who was ill, at Miletus. ²¹Do your best to come before winter. Eubulus sends greetings to you, as do Pudens and Linus and Claudia and all the brothers.[1]

²²The Lord be with your spirit. Grace be with you.[2]

TITUS

Introduction

This pastoral letter from Paul to Titus was intended to offer encouragement and wisdom as Titus endured ongoing opposition from the ungodly and from legalists within his congregations. Paul instructed Titus to complete his assigned job of establishing overseers (elders) for the churches under his care. He described what sort of people these leaders should be, and how all believers should live in relation to each other as well as in their interactions with nonbelievers. Proper Christian behavior is based on the fact that "the grace of God has appeared, bringing salvation for all people," and therefore those who believe in Christ are to "live self-controlled, upright, and godly lives" as they await his return (2:11-13). Paul probably wrote this letter in the 60s A.D.

Greeting

1 Paul, a servant[1] of God and an apostle of Jesus Christ, for the sake of the faith of God's elect and their knowledge of the truth, which accords with godliness, [2]in hope of eternal life, which God, who never lies, promised before the ages began[2] [3]and at the proper time manifested in his word through the preaching with which I have been entrusted by the command of God our Savior;

[4]To Titus, my true child in a common faith:

Grace and peace from God the Father and Christ Jesus our Savior.

Qualifications for Elders

[5]This is why I left you in Crete, so that you might put what remained into order, and appoint elders in every town as I directed you— [6]if anyone is above reproach, the husband of one wife,[3] and his children are believers and not open to the charge of debauchery or insubordination. [7]For an overseer,[4] as God's steward, must be above reproach. He must not be arrogant or quick-tempered or a drunkard or violent or greedy for gain, [8]but hospitable, a lover of good, self-controlled, upright, holy, and disciplined. [9]He must hold firm to the trustworthy word as taught, so that he may be able to give instruction in sound[5] doctrine and also to rebuke those who contradict it.

[10]For there are many who are insubordinate, empty talkers and deceivers, especially those of the circumcision party. [11]They must be silenced, since they are upsetting whole families by teaching for shameful gain what they ought not to teach. [12]One of the Cretans,[6] a prophet of their own, said, "Cretans are always liars, evil beasts, lazy gluttons."[7] [13]This testimony is true. Therefore rebuke them sharply, that they may be sound in the faith, [14]not devoting themselves to Jewish myths and the commands of people who turn away from the truth. [15]To the pure, all things are pure, but to the defiled and unbelieving, nothing is pure; but both their minds and their consciences are defiled. [16]They profess to know God, but they deny him by their works. They are detestable, disobedient, unfit for any good work.

Teach Sound Doctrine

2 But as for you, teach what accords with sound[8] doctrine. [2]Older men are to be sober-minded, dignified, self-controlled, sound in faith, in love, and in steadfastness. [3]Older women likewise are to be reverent in behavior, not slanderers or slaves to much wine. They are to teach what is good, [4]and so train the young women to love their husbands and children, [5]to be self-controlled, pure, working at home, kind, and submissive to their own husbands, that the word of God may not be reviled. [6]Likewise, urge the younger men to be self-controlled. [7]Show yourself in all respects to be a model of good works, and in your teaching show integrity, dignity, [8]and sound speech that cannot be condemned, so that an opponent may be put to shame, having nothing evil to say about us. [9]Slaves[9] are to be submissive to their own masters in everything; they are to be well-pleasing, not argumentative, [10]not pilfering, but showing all good faith, so that in everything they may adorn the doctrine of God our Savior.

[11]For the grace of God has appeared, bringing salvation for all people, [12]training us to renounce ungodliness and worldly passions, and to live self-controlled, upright, and godly lives in the present age, [13]waiting for our blessed hope, the appearing of the glory of our great God and Savior Jesus Christ, [14]who gave himself for us to redeem us from all lawlessness and to purify for himself a people for his own possession who are zealous for good works.

[15]Declare these things; exhort and rebuke with all authority. Let no one disregard you.

Be Ready for Every Good Work

3 Remind them to be submissive to rulers and authorities, to be obedient, to be ready for every good work, [2]to speak evil of no one, to

---

[1] Or slave; Greek bondservant [2] Greek before times eternal [3] Or a man of one woman [4] Or bishop; Greek episkopos [5] Or healthy; also verse 13 [6] Greek One of them [7] Probably from Epimenides of Crete [8] Or healthy; also verses 2, 8 [9] Or servants; Greek bondservants

avoid quarreling, to be gentle, and to show perfect courtesy toward all people. [3]For we ourselves were once foolish, disobedient, led astray, slaves to various passions and pleasures, passing our days in malice and envy, hated by others and hating one another. [4]But when the goodness and loving kindness of God our Savior appeared, [5]he saved us, not because of works done by us in righteousness, but according to his own mercy, by the washing of regeneration and renewal of the Holy Spirit, [6]whom he poured out on us richly through Jesus Christ our Savior, [7]so that being justified by his grace we might become heirs according to the hope of eternal life. [8]The saying is trustworthy, and I want you to insist on these things, so that those who have believed in God may be careful to devote themselves to good works. These things are excellent and profitable for people. [9]But avoid foolish controversies, genealogies, dissensions, and quarrels about the law, for they are unprofitable and worthless. [10]As for a person who stirs up division, after warning him once and then twice, have nothing more to do with him, [11]knowing that such a person is warped and sinful; he is self-condemned.

Final Instructions and Greetings

[12]When I send Artemas or Tychicus to you, do your best to come to me at Nicopolis, for I have decided to spend the winter there. [13]Do your best to speed Zenas the lawyer and Apollos on their way; see that they lack nothing. [14]And let our people learn to devote themselves to good works, so as to help cases of urgent need, and not be unfruitful.

[15]All who are with me send greetings to you. Greet those who love us in the faith.

Grace be with you all.

PHILEMON

Introduction

Philemon is about reconciliation and relationships between Christians. Onesimus (which means "useful") was a slave of a believer named Philemon in Colossae. Apparently Onesimus had stolen from Philemon and fled. At some time while Paul was under arrest, Onesimus met him and became a Christian. Paul apparently wrote this letter at the same time as Colossians and gave it to Onesimus to carry back to Philemon (see Col. 4:9). Paul appealed to Philemon to accept Onesimus back into his household, but as a brother in the Lord rather than a slave. In Paul's estimation, Onesimus was far more "useful" (v. 11) now that he was a Christian. Paul even promised to pay whatever debt Onesimus might owe Philemon.

Greeting

[1]Paul, a prisoner for Christ Jesus, and Timothy our brother,

To Philemon our beloved fellow worker [2]and Apphia our sister and Archippus our fellow soldier, and the church in your house:

[3]Grace to you and peace from God our Father and the Lord Jesus Christ.

Philemon's Love and Faith

[4]I thank my God always when I remember you in my prayers, [5]because I hear of your love and of the faith that you have toward the Lord Jesus and for all the saints, [6]and I pray that the sharing of your faith may become effective for the full knowledge of every good thing that is in us for the sake of Christ.[1] [7]For I have derived much joy and comfort from your love, my brother, because the hearts of the saints have been refreshed through you.

Paul's Plea for Onesimus

[8]Accordingly, though I am bold enough in Christ to command you to do what is required, [9]yet for love's sake I prefer to appeal to you—I, Paul, an old man and now a prisoner also for Christ Jesus— [10]I appeal to you for my child, Onesimus,[2] whose father I became in my imprisonment. [11](Formerly he was useless to you, but now he is indeed useful to you and to me.) [12]I am sending him back to you, sending my very heart.

[13]I would have been glad to keep him with me, in order that he might serve me on your behalf during my imprisonment for the gospel, [14]but I preferred to do nothing without your consent in order that your goodness might not be by compulsion but of your own accord. [15]For this perhaps is why he was parted from you for a while, that you might have him back forever, [16]no longer as a slave[3] but more than a slave, as a beloved brother—especially to me, but how much more to you, both in the flesh and in the Lord.

[17]So if you consider me your partner, receive him as you would receive me. [18]If he has wronged you at all, or owes you anything, charge that to my account. [19]I, Paul, write this with my own hand: I will repay it—to say nothing of your owing me even your own self. [20]Yes, brother, I want some benefit from you in the Lord. Refresh my heart in Christ.

[21]Confident of your obedience, I write to you, knowing that you will do even more than I say. [22]At the same time, prepare a guest room for me, for I am hoping that through your prayers I will be graciously given to you.

Final Greetings

[23]Epaphras, my fellow prisoner in Christ Jesus, sends greetings to you, [24]and so do Mark, Aristarchus, Demas, and Luke, my fellow workers.

[25]The grace of the Lord Jesus Christ be with your spirit.

---

[1] Or for Christ's service [2] Onesimus means useful (see verse 11) or beneficial (see verse 20) [3] Greek bondservant; twice in this verse

HEBREWS

Introduction

The letter to the Hebrews was written to encourage Christians in a time of trial. It does so by focusing on the absolute supremacy and sufficiency of Jesus Christ. While God spoke in the past "many times and in many ways," he has now spoken to us "by his Son," Jesus Christ, who is the "exact imprint" of God's nature and who "upholds the universe by the word of his power" (1:1-3). Jesus accomplished complete salvation for all who trust in him (1:1–10:18). We dare not "neglect such a great salvation" (2:3; 5:12–6:20; 10:19-39). Rather, in our faith and in our everyday living, we should imitate the example of Christ and of those on the honor roll of faith (chs. 11–13). This letter, whose author is unknown, was probably written between A.D. 60 and 70.

The Supremacy of God's Son

1 Long ago, at many times and in many ways, God spoke to our fathers by the prophets, ²but in these last days he has spoken to us by his Son, whom he appointed the heir of all things, through whom also he created the world. ³He is the radiance of the glory of God and the exact imprint of his nature, and he upholds the universe by the word of his power. After making purification for sins, he sat down at the right hand of the Majesty on high, ⁴having become as much superior to angels as the name he has inherited is more excellent than theirs.

⁵For to which of the angels did God ever say,

ᵃ"You are my Son,
today I have begotten you"?

Or again,

ᵇ"I will be to him a father,
and he shall be to me a son"?

⁶And again, when he brings the firstborn into the world, he says,

ᶜ"Let all God's angels worship him."

⁷Of the angels he says,

ᵈ"He makes his angels winds,
and his ministers a flame of fire."

⁸But of the Son he says,

ᵉ"Your throne, O God, is forever and ever,
the scepter of uprightness is the scepter of
your kingdom.
⁹ You have loved righteousness and hated wickedness;
therefore God, your God, has anointed you
with the oil of gladness beyond your companions."

¹⁰And,

ᶠ"You, Lord, laid the foundation of the earth in
the beginning,
and the heavens are the work of your
hands;
¹¹ they will perish, but you remain;
they will all wear out like a garment,
¹² like a robe you will roll them up,
like a garment they will be changed.¹
But you are the same,
and your years will have no end."

¹³And to which of the angels has he ever said,

ᵍ"Sit at my right hand
until I make your enemies a footstool for
your feet"?

¹⁴Are they not all ministering spirits sent out to serve for the sake of those who are to inherit salvation?

Warning Against Neglecting Salvation

2 Therefore we must pay much closer atten- tion to what we have heard, lest we drift away from it. ²For since the message declared by angels proved to be reliable, and every transgres- sion or disobedience received a just retribution, ³how shall we escape if we neglect such a great salvation? It was declared at first by the Lord, and it was attested to us by those who heard, ⁴while God also bore witness by signs and won- ders and various miracles and by gifts of the Holy Spirit distributed according to his will.

The Founder of Salvation

⁵Now it was not to angels that God subjected the world to come, of which we are speaking. ⁶It has been testified somewhere,

ʰ"What is man, that you are mindful of him,
or the son of man, that you care for him?
⁷ You made him for a little while lower than the
angels;

---

¹Some manuscripts omit *like a garment* ᵃPs. 2:7 ᵇ2 Sam. 7:14 ᶜDeut. 32:43 (Gk.) ᵈPs. 104:4 ᵉPs. 45:6, 7 ᶠPs. 102:25-27 ᵍPs. 110:1 ʰPs. 8:4-6

you have crowned him with glory and
honor,[1]

8   putting everything in subjection under his
feet."

Now in putting everything in subjection to him,
he left nothing outside his control. At present, we
do not yet see everything in subjection to him.
[9]But we see him who for a little while was made
lower than the angels, namely Jesus, crowned
with glory and honor because of the suffering of
death, so that by the grace of God he might taste
death for everyone.
[10]For it was fitting that he, for whom and by
whom all things exist, in bringing many sons to
glory, should make the founder of their salvation
perfect through suffering. [11]For he who sanctifies and those who are sanctified all have one
source.[2] That is why he is not ashamed to call
them brothers,[3] [12]saying,

[a]"I will tell of your name to my brothers;
    in the midst of the congregation I will sing
    your praise."

[13]And again,

"I will put my trust in him."

And again,

[b]"Behold, I and the children God has given me."

[14]Since therefore the children share in flesh
and blood, he himself likewise partook of the
same things, that through death he might
destroy the one who has the power of death, that
is, the devil, [15]and deliver all those who through
fear of death were subject to lifelong slavery.
[16]For surely it is not angels that he helps, but he
helps the offspring of Abraham. [17]Therefore he
had to be made like his brothers in every respect,
so that he might become a merciful and faithful
high priest in the service of God, to make propitiation for the sins of the people. [18]For because
he himself has suffered when tempted, he is able
to help those who are being tempted.

Jesus Greater Than Moses

3 Therefore, holy brothers,[4] you who share in
a heavenly calling, consider Jesus, the apostle
and high priest of our confession, [2]who was
faithful to him who appointed him, just as Moses
also was faithful in all God's[5] house. [3]For Jesus
has been counted worthy of more glory than
Moses—as much more glory as the builder of a
house has more honor than the house itself.
[4](For every house is built by someone, but the
builder of all things is God.) [5]Now Moses was
faithful in all God's house as a servant, to testify

to the things that were to be spoken later, [6]but
Christ is faithful over God's house as a son. And
we are his house if indeed we hold fast our confidence and our boasting in our hope.[6]

A Rest for the People of God

[7]Therefore, as the Holy Spirit says,

[c]"Today, if you hear his voice,
8   do not harden your hearts as in the rebellion,
     on the day of testing in the wilderness,
9   where your fathers put me to the test
     and saw my works for forty years.
10   Therefore I was provoked with that genera-
     tion,
     and said, 'They always go astray in their heart;
     they have not known my ways.'
11   As I swore in my wrath,
     'They shall not enter my rest.'"

[12]Take care, brothers, lest there be in any of you
an evil, unbelieving heart, leading you to fall
away from the living God. [13]But exhort one
another every day, as long as it is called "today,"
that none of you may be hardened by the deceitfulness of sin. [14]For we have come to share in
Christ, if indeed we hold our original confidence
firm to the end. [15]As it is said,

[d]"Today, if you hear his voice,
    do not harden your hearts as in the rebellion."

[16]For who were those who heard and yet
rebelled? Was it not all those who left Egypt led
by Moses? [17]And with whom was he provoked
for forty years? Was it not with those who
sinned, whose bodies fell in the wilderness?
[18]And to whom did he swear that they would not
enter his rest, but to those who were disobedient?
[19]So we see that they were unable to enter
because of unbelief.

4 Therefore, while the promise of entering his
rest still stands, let us fear lest any of you
should seem to have failed to reach it. [2]For good
news came to us just as to them, but the message
they heard did not benefit them, because they
were not united by faith with those who listened.[7] [3]For we who have believed enter that rest,
as he has said,

[e]"As I swore in my wrath,
    'They shall not enter my rest,'"

although his works were finished from the foundation of the world. [4]For he has somewhere spoken of the seventh day in this way: [f]"And God
rested on the seventh day from all his works."
[5]And again in this passage he said,

[g]"They shall not enter my rest."

---

[1] Some manuscripts insert *and set him over the works of your hands* [2] Greek *all are of one* [3] Or *brothers and sisters.* The plural Greek word *adelphoi*
(translated "brothers") refers to siblings in a family. In New Testament usage, depending on the context, *adelphoi* may refer either to men or to both
men and women who are siblings (brothers and sisters) in God's family, the church; also verse 12 [4] Or *brothers and sisters;* also verse 12 [5] Greek *his;* also
verses 5, 6 [6] Some manuscripts insert *firm to the end* [7] Some manuscripts *it did not meet with faith in the hearers* [a] Ps. 22:22 [b] Isa. 8:18 [c] Ps. 95:7-11 [d] Ps.
95:7, 8 [e] Ps. 95:11 [f] Gen. 2:2 [g] Ps. 95:11

⁶Since therefore it remains for some to enter it, and those who formerly received the good news failed to enter because of disobedience, ⁷again he appoints a certain day, "Today," saying through David so long afterward, in the words already quoted,

ᵃ"Today, if you hear his voice,
  do not harden your hearts."

⁸For if Joshua had given them rest, God¹ would not have spoken of another day later on. ⁹So then, there remains a Sabbath rest for the people of God, ¹⁰for whoever has entered God's rest has also rested from his works as God did from his. ¹¹Let us therefore strive to enter that rest, so that no one may fall by the same sort of disobedience. ¹²For the word of God is living and active, sharper than any two-edged sword, piercing to the division of soul and of spirit, of joints and of marrow, and discerning the thoughts and intentions of the heart. ¹³And no creature is hidden from his sight, but all are naked and exposed to the eyes of him to whom we must give account.

Jesus the Great High Priest

¹⁴Since then we have a great high priest who has passed through the heavens, Jesus, the Son of God, let us hold fast our confession. ¹⁵For we do not have a high priest who is unable to sympathize with our weaknesses, but one who in every respect has been tempted as we are, yet without sin. ¹⁶Let us then with confidence draw near to the throne of grace, that we may receive mercy and find grace to help in time of need.

5 For every high priest chosen from among men is appointed to act on behalf of men in relation to God, to offer gifts and sacrifices for sins. ²He can deal gently with the ignorant and wayward, since he himself is beset with weakness. ³Because of this he is obligated to offer sacrifice for his own sins just as he does for those of the people. ⁴And no one takes this honor for himself, but only when called by God, just as Aaron was. ⁵So also Christ did not exalt himself to be made a high priest, but was appointed by him who said to him,

ᵇ"You are my Son,
  today I have begotten you";

⁶as he says also in another place,

ᶜ"You are a priest forever,
  after the order of Melchizedek."

⁷In the days of his flesh, Jesus² offered up prayers and supplications, with loud cries and tears, to him who was able to save him from death, and he was heard because of his reverence. ⁸Although he was a son, he learned obedience through what he suffered. ⁹And being made perfect, he became the source of eternal salvation to all who obey him, ¹⁰being designated by God a high priest after the order of Melchizedek.

Warning Against Apostasy

¹¹About this we have much to say, and it is hard to explain, since you have become dull of hearing. ¹²For though by this time you ought to be teachers, you need someone to teach you again the basic principles of the oracles of God. You need milk, not solid food, ¹³for everyone who lives on milk is unskilled in the word of righteousness, since he is a child. ¹⁴But solid food is for the mature, for those who have their powers of discernment trained by constant practice to distinguish good from evil.

6 Therefore let us leave the elementary doctrine of Christ and go on to maturity, not laying again a foundation of repentance from dead works and of faith toward God, ²and of instruction about washings,³ the laying on of hands, the resurrection of the dead, and eternal judgment. ³And this we will do if God permits. ⁴For it is impossible, in the case of those who have once been enlightened, who have tasted the heavenly gift, and have shared in the Holy Spirit, ⁵and have tasted the goodness of the word of God and the powers of the age to come, ⁶and then have fallen away, to restore them again to repentance, since they are crucifying once again the Son of God to their own harm and holding him up to contempt. ⁷For land that has drunk the rain that often falls on it, and produces a crop useful to those for whose sake it is cultivated, receives a blessing from God. ⁸But if it bears thorns and thistles, it is worthless and near to being cursed, and its end is to be burned.

⁹Though we speak in this way, yet in your case, beloved, we feel sure of better things—things that belong to salvation. ¹⁰For God is not unjust so as to overlook your work and the love that you have shown for his name in serving the saints, as you still do. ¹¹And we desire each one of you to show the same earnestness to have the full assurance of hope until the end, ¹²so that you may not be sluggish, but imitators of those who through faith and patience inherit the promises.

The Certainty of God's Promise

¹³For when God made a promise to Abraham, since he had no one greater by whom to swear, he swore by himself, ¹⁴saying, ᵈ"Surely I will bless you and multiply you." ¹⁵And thus Abraham,⁴ having patiently waited, obtained the promise. ¹⁶For people swear by something greater than themselves, and in all their disputes an oath is final for confirmation. ¹⁷So when God desired to show more convincingly to the heirs

---

¹Greek he ²Greek he ³Or baptisms (that is, cleansing rites) ⁴Greek he ᵃPs. 95:7, 8 ᵇPs. 2:7 ᶜPs. 110:4 ᵈGen. 22:17

of the promise the unchangeable character of his purpose, he guaranteed it with an oath, [18]so that by two unchangeable things, in which it is impossible for God to lie, we who have fled for refuge might have strong encouragement to hold fast to the hope set before us. [19]We have this as a sure and steadfast anchor of the soul, a hope that enters into the inner place behind the curtain, [20]where Jesus has gone as a forerunner on our behalf, having become a high priest forever after the order of Melchizedek.

The Priestly Order of Melchizedek

7 For this Melchizedek, king of Salem, priest of the Most High God, met Abraham returning from the slaughter of the kings and blessed him, [2]and to him Abraham apportioned a tenth part of everything. He is first, by translation of his name, king of righteousness, and then he is also king of Salem, that is, king of peace. [3]He is without father or mother or genealogy, having neither beginning of days nor end of life, but resembling the Son of God he continues a priest forever.

[4]See how great this man was to whom Abraham the patriarch gave a tenth of the spoils! [5]And those descendants of Levi who receive the priestly office have a commandment in the law to take tithes from the people, that is, from their brothers,[1] though these also are descended from Abraham. [6]But this man who does not have his descent from them received tithes from Abraham and blessed him who had the promises. [7]It is beyond dispute that the inferior is blessed by the superior. [8]In the one case tithes are received by mortal men, but in the other case, by one of whom it is testified that he lives. [9]One might even say that Levi himself, who receives tithes, paid tithes through Abraham, [10]for he was still in the loins of his ancestor when Melchizedek met him.

Jesus Compared to Melchizedek

[11]Now if perfection had been attainable through the Levitical priesthood (for under it the people received the law), what further need would there have been for another priest to arise after the order of Melchizedek, rather than one named after the order of Aaron? [12]For when there is a change in the priesthood, there is necessarily a change in the law as well. [13]For the one of whom these things are spoken belonged to another tribe, from which no one has ever served at the altar. [14]For it is evident that our Lord was descended from Judah, and in connection with that tribe Moses said nothing about priests.

[15]This becomes even more evident when another priest arises in the likeness of Melchizedek, [16]who has become a priest, not on the basis of a legal requirement concerning bodily descent, but by the power of an indestructible life. [17]For it is witnessed of him,

*[a]"You are a priest forever,
    after the order of Melchizedek."*

[18]For on the one hand, a former commandment is set aside because of its weakness and uselessness [19](for the law made nothing perfect); but on the other hand, a better hope is introduced, through which we draw near to God.

[20]And it was not without an oath. For those who formerly became priests were made such without an oath, [21]but this one was made a priest with an oath by the one who said to him:

*[a]"The Lord has sworn
    and will not change his mind,
'You are a priest forever.'"*

[22]This makes Jesus the guarantor of a better covenant.

[23]The former priests were many in number, because they were prevented by death from continuing in office, [24]but he holds his priesthood permanently, because he continues forever. [25]Consequently, he is able to save to the uttermost[2] those who draw near to God through him, since he always lives to make intercession for them.

[26]For it was indeed fitting that we should have such a high priest, holy, innocent, unstained, separated from sinners, and exalted above the heavens. [27]He has no need, like those high priests, to offer sacrifices daily, first for his own sins and then for those of the people, since he did this once for all when he offered up himself. [28]For the law appoints men in their weakness as high priests, but the word of the oath, which came later than the law, appoints a Son who has been made perfect forever.

Jesus, High Priest of a Better Covenant

8 Now the point in what we are saying is this: we have such a high priest, one who is seated at the right hand of the throne of the Majesty in heaven, [2]a minister in the holy places, in the true tent[3] that the Lord set up, not man. [3]For every high priest is appointed to offer gifts and sacrifices; thus it is necessary for this priest also to have something to offer. [4]Now if he were on earth, he would not be a priest at all, since there are priests who offer gifts according to the law. [5]They serve a copy and shadow of the heavenly things. For when Moses was about to erect the tent, he was instructed by God, saying, [b]"See that you make everything according to the pattern that was shown you on the mountain." [6]But as it is, Christ[4] has obtained a ministry that is as much more excellent than the old as the covenant he mediates is better, since it is enacted on better promises. [7]For if that first covenant had

---

[1]Or *brothers and sisters* [2]That is, completely; or *at all times* [3]Or *tabernacle*; also verse 5 [4]Greek *he* [a]Ps. 110:4 [b]Ex. 25:40

been faultless, there would have been no occasion to look for a second.

[8] For he finds fault with them when he says:[1]

[a]"Behold, the days are coming, declares the Lord,
> when I will establish a new covenant with the house of Israel
> and with the house of Judah,

[9] not like the covenant that I made with their fathers
> on the day when I took them by the hand to bring them out of the land of Egypt.
> For they did not continue in my covenant,
> and so I showed no concern for them, declares the Lord.

[10] For this is the covenant that I will make with the house of Israel
> after those days, declares the Lord:
> I will put my laws into their minds,
> and write them on their hearts,
> and I will be their God,
> and they shall be my people.

[11] And they shall not teach, each one his neighbor
> and each one his brother, saying, 'Know the Lord,'
> for they shall all know me,
> from the least of them to the greatest.

[12] For I will be merciful toward their iniquities,
> and I will remember their sins no more."

[13] In speaking of a new covenant, he makes the first one obsolete. And what is becoming obsolete and growing old is ready to vanish away.

The Earthly Holy Place

9 Now even the first covenant had regulations for worship and an earthly place of holiness. [2] For a tent[2] was prepared, the first section, in which were the lampstand and the table and the bread of the Presence.[3] It is called the Holy Place. [3] Behind the second curtain was a second section[4] called the Most Holy Place, [4] having the golden altar of incense and the ark of the covenant covered on all sides with gold, in which was a golden urn holding the manna, and Aaron's staff that budded, and the tablets of the covenant. [5] Above it were the cherubim of glory overshadowing the mercy seat. Of these things we cannot now speak in detail.

[6] These preparations having thus been made, the priests go regularly into the first section, performing their ritual duties, [7] but into the second only the high priest goes, and he but once a year, and not without taking blood, which he offers for himself and for the unintentional sins of the people. [8] By this the Holy Spirit indicates that the way into the holy places is not yet opened as long

as the first section is still standing [9] (which is symbolic for the present age).[5] According to this arrangement, gifts and sacrifices are offered that cannot perfect the conscience of the worshiper, [10] but deal only with food and drink and various washings, regulations for the body imposed until the time of reformation.

Redemption Through the Blood of Christ

[11] But when Christ appeared as a high priest of the good things that have come,[6] then through the greater and more perfect tent (not made with hands, that is, not of this creation) [12] he entered once for all into the holy places, not by means of the blood of goats and calves but by means of his own blood, thus securing an eternal redemption. [13] For if the blood of goats and bulls, and the sprinkling of defiled persons with the ashes of a heifer, sanctify[7] for the purification of the flesh, [14] how much more will the blood of Christ, who through the eternal Spirit offered himself without blemish to God, purify our[8] conscience from dead works to serve the living God.

[15] Therefore he is the mediator of a new covenant, so that those who are called may receive the promised eternal inheritance, since a death has occurred that redeems them from the transgressions committed under the first covenant.[9] [16] For where a will is involved, the death of the one who made it must be established. [17] For a will takes effect only at death, since it is not in force as long as the one who made it is alive. [18] Therefore not even the first covenant was inaugurated without blood. [19] For when every commandment of the law had been declared by Moses to all the people, he took the blood of calves and goats, with water and scarlet wool and hyssop, and sprinkled both the book itself and all the people, [20] saying, [b]"This is the blood of the covenant that God commanded for you." [21] And in the same way he sprinkled with the blood both the tent and all the vessels used in worship. [22] Indeed, under the law almost everything is purified with blood, and without the shedding of blood there is no forgiveness of sins.

[23] Thus it was necessary for the copies of the heavenly things to be purified with these rites, but the heavenly things themselves with better sacrifices than these. [24] For Christ has entered, not into holy places made with hands, which are copies of the true things, but into heaven itself, now to appear in the presence of God on our behalf. [25] Nor was it to offer himself repeatedly, as the high priest enters the holy places every year with blood not his own, [26] for then he would have had to suffer repeatedly since the foundation of the world. But as it is, he has appeared once for all at the end of the ages to put away sin

---

[1] Some manuscripts *For finding fault with it he says to them* [2] *tabernacle*; also verses 11, 21 [3] Greek *the presentation of the loaves* [4] Greek *tent*; also verses 6, 8 [5] *Or which is symbolic for the age then present* [6] Some manuscripts *good things to come* [7] *Or For if the blood of goats and bulls, and the sprinkling of defiled persons with the ashes of a heifer, sanctifies* [8] Some manuscripts *your* [9] The Greek word means both *covenant* and *will*; also verses 16, 17 [a] Jer. 31:31-34 [b] Ex. 24:8

by the sacrifice of himself. ²⁷And just as it is appointed for man to die once, and after that comes judgment, ²⁸so Christ, having been offered once to bear the sins of many, will appear a second time, not to deal with sin but to save those who are eagerly waiting for him.

Christ's Sacrifice Once for All

10 For since the law has but a shadow of the good things to come instead of the true form of these realities, it can never, by the same sacrifices that are continually offered every year, make perfect those who draw near. ²Otherwise, would they not have ceased to be offered, since the worshipers, having once been cleansed, would no longer have any consciousness of sins? ³But in these sacrifices there is a reminder of sins every year. ⁴For it is impossible for the blood of bulls and goats to take away sins.

⁵Consequently, when Christ¹ came into the world, he said,

ᵃ"Sacrifices and offerings you have not desired,
    but a body have you prepared for me;
⁶ in burnt offerings and sin offerings
    you have taken no pleasure.
⁷ Then I said, 'Behold, I have come to do your will, O God,
    as it is written of me in the scroll of the book.'"

⁸When he said above, "You have neither desired nor taken pleasure in sacrifices and offerings and burnt offerings and sin offerings" (these are offered according to the law), ⁹then he added, "Behold, I have come to do your will." He does away with the first in order to establish the second. ¹⁰And by that will we have been sanctified through the offering of the body of Jesus Christ once for all.

¹¹And every priest stands daily at his service, offering repeatedly the same sacrifices, which can never take away sins. ¹²But when Christ² had offered for all time a single sacrifice for sins, he sat down at the right hand of God, ¹³waiting from that time until his enemies should be made a footstool for his feet. ¹⁴For by a single offering he has perfected for all time those who are being sanctified.

¹⁵And the Holy Spirit also bears witness to us; for after saying,

¹⁶ ᵇ"This is the covenant that I will make with them
    after those days, declares the Lord:
    I will put my laws on their hearts,
    and write them on their minds,"

¹⁷then he adds,

ᶜ"I will remember their sins and their lawless deeds no more."

¹⁸Where there is forgiveness of these, there is no longer any offering for sin.

The Full Assurance of Faith

¹⁹Therefore, brothers,³ since we have confidence to enter the holy places by the blood of Jesus, ²⁰by the new and living way that he opened for us through the curtain, that is, through his flesh, ²¹and since we have a great priest over the house of God, ²²let us draw near with a true heart in full assurance of faith, with our hearts sprinkled clean from an evil conscience and our bodies washed with pure water. ²³Let us hold fast the confession of our hope without wavering, for he who promised is faithful. ²⁴And let us consider how to stir up one another to love and good works, ²⁵not neglecting to meet together, as is the habit of some, but encouraging one another, and all the more as you see the Day drawing near.

²⁶For if we go on sinning deliberately after receiving the knowledge of the truth, there no longer remains a sacrifice for sins, ²⁷but a fearful expectation of judgment, and a fury of fire that will consume the adversaries. ²⁸Anyone who has set aside the law of Moses dies without mercy on the evidence of two or three witnesses. ²⁹How much worse punishment, do you think, will be deserved by the one who has spurned the Son of God, and has profaned the blood of the covenant by which he was sanctified, and has outraged the Spirit of grace? ³⁰For we know him who said, ᵈ"Vengeance is mine; I will repay." And again, ᵉ"The Lord will judge his people." ³¹It is a fearful thing to fall into the hands of the living God.

³²But recall the former days when, after you were enlightened, you endured a hard struggle with sufferings, ³³sometimes being publicly exposed to reproach and affliction, and sometimes being partners with those so treated. ³⁴For you had compassion on those in prison, and you joyfully accepted the plundering of your property, since you knew that you yourselves had a better possession and an abiding one. ³⁵Therefore do not throw away your confidence, which has a great reward. ³⁶For you have need of endurance, so that when you have done the will of God you may receive what is promised. ³⁷For,

"Yet a little while,
    and ᶠthe coming one will come and will not delay;
³⁸ but my righteous one shall live by faith,
    and if he shrinks back,
    my soul has no pleasure in him."

³⁹But we are not of those who shrink back and are destroyed, but of those who have faith and preserve their souls.

---

¹Greek he ²Greek this one ³Or brothers and sisters ᵃPs. 40:6-8 ᵇJer. 31:33 ᶜJer. 31:34 ᵈDeut. 32:35 ᵉDeut. 32:36 ᶠHab. 2:3, 4

By Faith

11 Now faith is the assurance of things hoped for, the conviction of things not seen. ²For by it the people of old received their commendation. ³By faith we understand that the universe was created by the word of God, so that what is seen was not made out of things that are visible.

⁴By faith Abel offered to God a more acceptable sacrifice than Cain, through which he was commended as righteous, God commending him by accepting his gifts. And through his faith, though he died, he still speaks. ⁵By faith Enoch was taken up so that he should not see death, and he was not found, because God had taken him. Now before he was taken he was commended as having pleased God. ⁶And without faith it is impossible to please him, for whoever would draw near to God must believe that he exists and that he rewards those who seek him. ⁷By faith Noah, being warned by God concerning events as yet unseen, in reverent fear constructed an ark for the saving of his household. By this he condemned the world and became an heir of the righteousness that comes by faith.

⁸By faith Abraham obeyed when he was called to go out to a place that he was to receive as an inheritance. And he went out, not knowing where he was going. ⁹By faith he went to live in the land of promise, as in a foreign land, living in tents with Isaac and Jacob, heirs with him of the same promise. ¹⁰For he was looking forward to the city that has foundations, whose designer and builder is God. ¹¹By faith Sarah herself received power to conceive, even when she was past the age, since she considered him faithful who had promised. ¹²Therefore from one man, and him as good as dead, were born descendants as many as the stars of heaven and as many as the innumerable grains of sand by the seashore.

¹³These all died in faith, not having received the things promised, but having seen them and greeted them from afar, and having acknowledged that they were strangers and exiles on the earth. ¹⁴For people who speak thus make it clear that they are seeking a homeland. ¹⁵If they had been thinking of that land from which they had gone out, they would have had opportunity to return. ¹⁶But as it is, they desire a better country, that is, a heavenly one. Therefore God is not ashamed to be called their God, for he has prepared for them a city.

¹⁷By faith Abraham, when he was tested, offered up Isaac, and he who had received the promises was in the act of offering up his only son, ¹⁸of whom it was said, ᵃ"Through Isaac shall your offspring be named." ¹⁹He considered that God was able even to raise him from the dead, from which, figuratively speaking, he did receive

him back. ²⁰By faith Isaac invoked future blessings on Jacob and Esau. ²¹By faith Jacob, when dying, blessed each of the sons of Joseph, bowing in worship over the head of his staff. ²²By faith Joseph, at the end of his life, made mention of the exodus of the Israelites and gave directions concerning his bones.

²³By faith Moses, when he was born, was hidden for three months by his parents, because they saw that the child was beautiful, and they were not afraid of the king's edict. ²⁴By faith Moses, when he was grown up, refused to be called the son of Pharaoh's daughter, ²⁵choosing rather to be mistreated with the people of God than to enjoy the fleeting pleasures of sin. ²⁶He considered the reproach of Christ greater wealth than the treasures of Egypt, for he was looking to the reward. ²⁷By faith he left Egypt, not being afraid of the anger of the king, for he endured as seeing him who is invisible. ²⁸By faith he kept the Passover and sprinkled the blood, so that the Destroyer of the firstborn might not touch them.

²⁹By faith the people crossed the Red Sea as on dry land, but the Egyptians, when they attempted to do the same, were drowned. ³⁰By faith the walls of Jericho fell down after they had been encircled for seven days. ³¹By faith Rahab the prostitute did not perish with those who were disobedient, because she had given a friendly welcome to the spies.

³²And what more shall I say? For time would fail me to tell of Gideon, Barak, Samson, Jephthah, of David and Samuel and the prophets— ³³who through faith conquered kingdoms, enforced justice, obtained promises, stopped the mouths of lions, ³⁴quenched the power of fire, escaped the edge of the sword, were made strong out of weakness, became mighty in war, put foreign armies to flight. ³⁵Women received back their dead by resurrection. Some were tortured, refusing to accept release, so that they might rise again to a better life. ³⁶Others suffered mocking and flogging, and even chains and imprisonment. ³⁷They were stoned, they were sawn in two,¹ they were killed with the sword. They went about in skins of sheep and goats, destitute, afflicted, mistreated— ³⁸of whom the world was not worthy—wandering about in deserts and mountains, and in dens and caves of the earth.

³⁹And all these, though commended through their faith, did not receive what was promised, ⁴⁰since God had provided something better for us, that apart from us they should not be made perfect.

Jesus, Founder and Perfecter of Our Faith

12 Therefore, since we are surrounded by so great a cloud of witnesses, let us also lay aside every weight, and sin which clings so closely, and let us run with endurance the race

¹ Some manuscripts add *they were tempted* ᵃGen. 21:12

that is set before us, ²looking to Jesus, the founder and perfecter of our faith, who for the joy that was set before him endured the cross, despising the shame, and is seated at the right hand of the throne of God.

Do Not Grow Weary

³Consider him who endured from sinners such hostility against himself, so that you may not grow weary or fainthearted. ⁴In your struggle against sin you have not yet resisted to the point of shedding your blood. ⁵And have you forgotten the exhortation that addresses you as sons?

*"My son, do not regard lightly the discipline of the Lord,
    nor be weary when reproved by him.
⁶   For the Lord disciplines the one he loves,
    and chastises every son whom he receives."

⁷It is for discipline that you have to endure. God is treating you as sons. For what son is there whom his father does not discipline? ⁸If you are left without discipline, in which all have participated, then you are illegitimate children and not sons. ⁹Besides this, we have had earthly fathers who disciplined us and we respected them. Shall we not much more be subject to the Father of spirits and live? ¹⁰For they disciplined us for a short time as it seemed best to them, but he disciplines us for our good, that we may share his holiness. ¹¹For the moment all discipline seems painful rather than pleasant, but later it yields the peaceful fruit of righteousness to those who have been trained by it.

¹²Therefore lift your drooping hands and strengthen your weak knees, ¹³and make straight paths for your feet, so that what is lame may not be put out of joint but rather be healed. ¹⁴Strive for peace with everyone, and for the holiness without which no one will see the Lord. ¹⁵See to it that no one fails to obtain the grace of God; that no "root of bitterness" springs up and causes trouble, and by it many become defiled; ¹⁶that no one is sexually immoral or unholy like Esau, who sold his birthright for a single meal. ¹⁷For you know that afterward, when he desired to inherit the blessing, he was rejected, for he found no chance to repent, though he sought it with tears.

A Kingdom That Cannot Be Shaken

¹⁸For you have not come to what may be touched, a blazing fire and darkness and gloom and a tempest ¹⁹and the sound of a trumpet and a voice whose words made the hearers beg that no further messages be spoken to them. ²⁰For they could not endure the order that was given, *"If even a beast touches the mountain, it shall be stoned." ²¹Indeed, so terrifying was the sight that Moses said, "I tremble with fear." ²²But you

have come to Mount Zion and to the city of the living God, the heavenly Jerusalem, and to innumerable angels in festal gathering, ²³and to the assembly¹ of the firstborn who are enrolled in heaven, and to God, the judge of all, and to the spirits of the righteous made perfect, ²⁴and to Jesus, the mediator of a new covenant, and to the sprinkled blood that speaks a better word than the blood of Abel.

²⁵See that you do not refuse him who is speaking. For if they did not escape when they refused him who warned them on earth, much less will we escape if we reject him who warns from heaven. ²⁶At that time his voice shook the earth, but now he has promised, *"Yet once more I will shake not only the earth but also the heavens." ²⁷This phrase, "Yet once more," indicates the removal of things that are shaken—that is, things that have been made—in order that the things that cannot be shaken may remain. ²⁸Therefore let us be grateful for receiving a kingdom that cannot be shaken, and thus let us offer to God acceptable worship, with reverence and awe, ²⁹for our God is a consuming fire.

Sacrifices Pleasing to God

13 Let brotherly love continue. ²Do not neglect to show hospitality to strangers, for thereby some have entertained angels unawares. ³Remember those who are in prison, as though in prison with them, and those who are mistreated, since you also are in the body. ⁴Let marriage be held in honor among all, and let the marriage bed be undefiled, for God will judge the sexually immoral and adulterous. ⁵Keep your life free from love of money, and be content with what you have, for he has said, *"I will never leave you nor forsake you." ⁶So we can confidently say,

*"The Lord is my helper;
    I will not fear;
    what can man do to me?"

⁷Remember your leaders, those who spoke to you the word of God. Consider the outcome of their way of life, and imitate their faith. ⁸Jesus Christ is the same yesterday and today and forever. ⁹Do not be led away by diverse and strange teachings, for it is good for the heart to be strengthened by grace, not by foods, which have not benefited those devoted to them. ¹⁰We have an altar from which those who serve the tent have no right to eat. ¹¹For the bodies of those animals whose blood is brought into the holy places by the high priest as a sacrifice for sin are burned outside the camp. ¹²So Jesus also suffered outside the gate in order to sanctify the people through his own blood. ¹³Therefore let us go to him outside the camp and bear the

¹Or *church* ᵃProv. 3:11, 12 ᵇEx. 19:12, 13 ᶜHag. 2:6 ᵈJosh. 1:5 ᵉPs. 118:6

reproach he endured. [14]For here we have no lasting city, but we seek the city that is to come. [15]Through him then let us continually offer up a sacrifice of praise to God, that is, the fruit of lips that acknowledge his name. [16]Do not neglect to do good and to share what you have, for such sacrifices are pleasing to God.

[17]Obey your leaders and submit to them, for they are keeping watch over your souls, as those who will have to give an account. Let them do this with joy and not with groaning, for that would be of no advantage to you.

[18]Pray for us, for we are sure that we have a clear conscience, desiring to act honorably in all things. [19]I urge you the more earnestly to do this in order that I may be restored to you the sooner.

Benediction

[20]Now may the God of peace who brought again from the dead our Lord Jesus, the great shepherd of the sheep, by the blood of the eternal covenant, [21]equip you with everything good that you may do his will, working in us[1] that which is pleasing in his sight, through Jesus Christ, to whom be glory forever and ever. Amen.

Final Greetings

[22]I appeal to you, brothers,[2] bear with my word of exhortation, for I have written to you briefly. [23]You should know that our brother Timothy has been released, with whom I shall see you if he comes soon. [24]Greet all your leaders and all the saints. Those who come from Italy send you greetings. [25]Grace be with all of you.

---

[1] Some manuscripts you [2] Or brothers and sisters

JAMES

Introduction

Sometimes called "the Proverbs of the New Testament," the book of James practically and faithfully reminds Christians how to live. From perseverance to true faith to controlling one's tongue, submitting to God's will, and having patience, this book aids readers in living authentically and wisely for Christ. Many have claimed that James and the apostle Paul differed on the question of faith versus works, but in reality the spiritual fruit that James talks about simply demonstrates the true faith of which Paul wrote. Their writings are complementary rather than contradictory. Possibly one of the earliest of the New Testament writings (A.D. 40–50), the book is believed to have been written by Jesus' brother James (Gal. 1:19).

Greeting

1 James, a servant[1] of God and of the Lord Jesus Christ,

To the twelve tribes in the Dispersion:

Greetings.

Testing of Your Faith

[2] Count it all joy, my brothers,[2] when you meet trials of various kinds, [3] for you know that the testing of your faith produces steadfastness. [4] And let steadfastness have its full effect, that you may be perfect and complete, lacking in nothing.

[5] If any of you lacks wisdom, let him ask God, who gives generously to all without reproach, and it will be given him. [6] But let him ask in faith, with no doubting, for the one who doubts is like a wave of the sea that is driven and tossed by the wind. [7] For that person must not suppose that he will receive anything from the Lord; [8] he is a double-minded man, unstable in all his ways.

[9] Let the lowly brother boast in his exaltation, [10] and the rich in his humiliation, because like a flower of the grass[3] he will pass away. [11] For the sun rises with its scorching heat and withers the grass; its flower falls, and its beauty perishes. So also will the rich man fade away in the midst of his pursuits.

[12] Blessed is the man who remains steadfast under trial, for when he has stood the test he will receive the crown of life, which God has promised to those who love him. [13] Let no one say when he is tempted, "I am being tempted by God," for God cannot be tempted with evil, and he himself tempts no one. [14] But each person is tempted when he is lured and enticed by his own desire. [15] Then desire when it has conceived gives birth to sin, and sin when it is fully grown brings forth death.

[16] Do not be deceived, my beloved brothers. [17] Every good gift and every perfect gift is from above, coming down from the Father of lights with whom there is no variation or shadow due to change.[4] [18] Of his own will he brought us forth by the word of truth, that we should be a kind of firstfruits of his creatures.

Hearing and Doing the Word

[19] Know this, my beloved brothers: let every person be quick to hear, slow to speak, slow to anger; [20] for the anger of man does not produce the righteousness of God. [21] Therefore put away all filthiness and rampant wickedness and receive with meekness the implanted word, which is able to save your souls.

[22] But be doers of the word, and not hearers only, deceiving yourselves. [23] For if anyone is a hearer of the word and not a doer, he is like a man who looks intently at his natural face in a mirror. [24] For he looks at himself and goes away and at once forgets what he was like. [25] But the one who looks into the perfect law, the law of liberty, and perseveres, being no hearer who forgets but a doer who acts, he will be blessed in his doing.

[26] If anyone thinks he is religious and does not bridle his tongue but deceives his heart, this person's religion is worthless. [27] Religion that is pure and undefiled before God, the Father, is this: to visit orphans and widows in their affliction, and to keep oneself unstained from the world.

The Sin of Partiality

2 My brothers,[5] show no partiality as you hold the faith in our Lord Jesus Christ, the Lord of glory. [2] For if a man wearing a gold ring and fine clothing comes into your assembly, and a poor man in shabby clothing also comes in, [3] and if you pay attention to the one who wears the fine clothing and say, "You sit here in a good place," while you say to the poor man, "You stand over there," or, "Sit down at my feet," [4] have you not then made distinctions among yourselves and become judges with evil thoughts? [5] Listen, my beloved brothers, has not God chosen those who are poor in the world to be rich in faith and heirs of the kingdom, which he has

---

[1] Or *slave*; Greek *bondservant* [2] Or *brothers and sisters*. The plural Greek word *adelphoi* (translated "brothers") refers to siblings in a family. In New Testament usage, depending on the context, *adelphoi* may refer either to men or to both men and women who are siblings (brothers and sisters) in God's family, the church; also verses 16, 19 [3] Or *a wild flower* [4] Some manuscripts *variation due to a shadow of turning* [5] Or *brothers and sisters*; also verses 5, 14

promised to those who love him? [6]But you have dishonored the poor man. Are not the rich the ones who oppress you, and the ones who drag you into court? [7]Are they not the ones who blaspheme the honorable name by which you were called?

[8]If you really fulfill the royal law according to the Scripture, [a]"You shall love your neighbor as yourself," you are doing well. [9]But if you show partiality, you are committing sin and are convicted by the law as transgressors. [10]For whoever keeps the whole law but fails in one point has become accountable for all of it. [11]For he who said, [b]"Do not commit adultery," also said, [c]"Do not murder." If you do not commit adultery but do murder, you have become a transgressor of the law. [12]So speak and so act as those who are to be judged under the law of liberty. [13]For judgment is without mercy to one who has shown no mercy. Mercy triumphs over judgment.

Faith Without Works Is Dead

[14]What good is it, my brothers, if someone says he has faith but does not have works? Can that faith save him? [15]If a brother or sister is poorly clothed and lacking in daily food, [16]and one of you says to them, "Go in peace, be warmed and filled," without giving them the things needed for the body, what good[1] is that? [17]So also faith by itself, if it does not have works, is dead.

[18]But someone will say, "You have faith and I have works." Show me your faith apart from your works, and I will show you my faith by my works. [19]You believe that God is one; you do well. Even the demons believe—and shudder! [20]Do you want to be shown, you foolish person, that faith apart from works is useless? [21]Was not Abraham our father justified by works when he offered up his son Isaac on the altar? [22]You see that faith was active along with his works, and faith was completed by his works; [23]and the Scripture was fulfilled that says, [d]"Abraham believed God, and it was counted to him as righteousness"—and he was called a friend of God. [24]You see that a person is justified by works and not by faith alone. [25]And in the same way was not also Rahab the prostitute justified by works when she received the messengers and sent them out by another way? [26]For as the body apart from the spirit is dead, so also faith apart from works is dead.

Taming the Tongue

3 Not many of you should become teachers, my brothers, for you know that we who teach will be judged with greater strictness. [2]For we all stumble in many ways. And if anyone does not stumble in what he says, he is a perfect man, able also to bridle his whole body. [3]If we put bits into the mouths of horses so that they

obey us, we guide their whole bodies as well. [4]Look at the ships also: though they are so large and are driven by strong winds, they are guided by a very small rudder wherever the will of the pilot directs. [5]So also the tongue is a small member, yet it boasts of great things.

How great a forest is set ablaze by such a small fire! [6]And the tongue is a fire, a world of unrighteousness. The tongue is set among our members, staining the whole body, setting on fire the entire course of life,[2] and set on fire by hell.[3] [7]For every kind of beast and bird, of reptile and sea creature, can be tamed and has been tamed by mankind, [8]but no human being can tame the tongue. It is a restless evil, full of deadly poison. [9]With it we bless our Lord and Father, and with it we curse people who are made in the likeness of God. [10]From the same mouth come blessing and cursing. My brothers,[4] these things ought not to be so. [11]Does a spring pour forth from the same opening both fresh and salt water? [12]Can a fig tree, my brothers, bear olives, or a grapevine produce figs? Neither can a salt pond yield fresh water.

Wisdom from Above

[13]Who is wise and understanding among you? By his good conduct let him show his works in the meekness of wisdom. [14]But if you have bitter jealousy and selfish ambition in your hearts, do not boast and be false to the truth. [15]This is not the wisdom that comes down from above, but is earthly, unspiritual, demonic. [16]For where jealousy and selfish ambition exist, there will be disorder and every vile practice. [17]But the wisdom from above is first pure, then peaceable, gentle, open to reason, full of mercy and good fruits, impartial and sincere. [18]And a harvest of righteousness is sown in peace by those who make peace.

Warning Against Worldliness

4 What causes quarrels and what causes fights among you? Is it not this, that your passions[5] are at war within you? [2]You desire and do not have, so you murder. You covet and cannot obtain, so you fight and quarrel. You do not have, because you do not ask. [3]You ask and do not receive, because you ask wrongly, to spend it on your passions. [4]You adulterous people![7] Do you not know that friendship with the world is enmity with God? Therefore whoever wishes to be a friend of the world makes himself an enemy of God. [5]Or do you suppose it is to no purpose that the Scripture says, "He yearns jealously over the spirit that he has made to dwell in us"? [6]But he gives more grace. Therefore it says, [e]"God opposes the proud, but gives grace to the humble." [7]Submit yourselves therefore to God. Resist the devil, and he will flee from you. [8]Draw near

---

[1]Or benefit [2]Or wheel of birth [3]Greek Gehenna [4]Or brothers and sisters; also verse 12 [5]Greek pleasures; also verse 3 [6]Greek in your members [7]Greek You adulteresses! [a]Lev. 19:18 [b]Ex. 20:14 [c]Ex. 20:13 [d]Gen. 15:6 [e]Prov. 3:34

to God, and he will draw near to you. Cleanse your hands, you sinners, and purify your hearts, you double-minded. ⁹Be wretched and mourn and weep. Let your laughter be turned to mourning and your joy to gloom. ¹⁰Humble yourselves before the Lord, and he will exalt you.

¹¹Do not speak evil against one another, brothers.¹ The one who speaks against a brother or judges his brother, speaks evil against the law and judges the law. But if you judge the law, you are not a doer of the law but a judge. ¹²There is only one lawgiver and judge, he who is able to save and to destroy. But who are you to judge your neighbor?

Boasting About Tomorrow

¹³Come now, you who say, "Today or tomorrow we will go into such and such a town and spend a year there and trade and make a profit"— ¹⁴yet you do not know what tomorrow will bring. What is your life? For you are a mist that appears for a little time and then vanishes. ¹⁵Instead you ought to say, "If the Lord wills, we will live and do this or that." ¹⁶As it is, you boast in your arrogance. All such boasting is evil. ¹⁷So whoever knows the right thing to do and fails to do it, for him it is sin.

Warning to the Rich

5 Come now, you rich, weep and howl for the miseries that are coming upon you. ²Your riches have rotted and your garments are moth-eaten. ³Your gold and silver have corroded, and their corrosion will be evidence against you and will eat your flesh like fire. You have laid up treasure in the last days. ⁴Behold, the wages of the laborers who mowed your fields, which you kept back by fraud, are crying out against you, and the cries of the harvesters have reached the ears of the Lord of hosts. ⁵You have lived on the earth in luxury and in self-indulgence. You have fattened your hearts in a day of slaughter. ⁶You have condemned and murdered the righteous person. He does not resist you.

Patience in Suffering

⁷Be patient, therefore, brothers,² until the coming of the Lord. See how the farmer waits for the precious fruit of the earth, being patient about it, until it receives the early and the late rains. ⁸You also, be patient. Establish your hearts, for the coming of the Lord is at hand. ⁹Do not grumble against one another, brothers, so that you may not be judged; behold, the Judge is standing at the door. ¹⁰As an example of suffering and patience, brothers, take the prophets who spoke in the name of the Lord. ¹¹Behold, we consider those blessed who remained steadfast. You have heard of the steadfastness of Job, and you have seen the purpose of the Lord, how the Lord is compassionate and merciful.

¹²But above all, my brothers, do not swear, either by heaven or by earth or by any other oath, but let your "yes" be yes and your "no" be no, so that you may not fall under condemnation.

The Prayer of Faith

¹³Is anyone among you suffering? Let him pray. Is anyone cheerful? Let him sing praise. ¹⁴Is anyone among you sick? Let him call for the elders of the church, and let them pray over him, anointing him with oil in the name of the Lord. ¹⁵And the prayer of faith will save the one who is sick, and the Lord will raise him up. And if he has committed sins, he will be forgiven. ¹⁶Therefore, confess your sins to one another and pray for one another, that you may be healed. The prayer of a righteous person has great power as it is working.³ ¹⁷Elijah was a man with a nature like ours, and he prayed fervently that it might not rain, and for three years and six months it did not rain on the earth. ¹⁸Then he prayed again, and heaven gave rain, and the earth bore its fruit.

¹⁹My brothers, if anyone among you wanders from the truth and someone brings him back, ²⁰let him know that whoever brings back a sinner from his wandering will save his soul from death and will cover a multitude of sins.

---

¹Or brothers and sisters ²Or brothers and sisters; also verses 9, 10, 12, 19 ³Or The effective prayer of a righteous person has great power

1 PETER

Introduction

The readers of the apostle Peter's letter were confused and discouraged by the persecution they were encountering because of their faith. Peter exhorted them to stand strong, repeatedly reminding them of Christ's example, the riches of their inheritance in him, and the hope of his returning again to take them to heaven. Peter explained how Christians should respond when they suffer because of their beliefs. Called the "apostle of hope," Peter's primary message is to trust the Lord, live obediently no matter what your circumstances, and keep your hope fixed on God's ultimate promise of deliverance. Suffering is to be expected, but it is temporary and yields great blessings for those who remain steadfast. Peter probably wrote this letter in the mid-60s A.D.

Greeting

1 Peter, an apostle of Jesus Christ,
To those who are elect exiles of the dispersion in Pontus, Galatia, Cappadocia, Asia, and Bithynia, [2]according to the foreknowledge of God the Father, in the sanctification of the Spirit, for obedience to Jesus Christ and for sprinkling with his blood:
May grace and peace be multiplied to you.

Born Again to a Living Hope

[3]Blessed be the God and Father of our Lord Jesus Christ! According to his great mercy, he has caused us to be born again to a living hope through the resurrection of Jesus Christ from the dead, [4]to an inheritance that is imperishable, undefiled, and unfading, kept in heaven for you, [5]who by God's power are being guarded through faith for a salvation ready to be revealed in the last time. [6]In this you rejoice, though now for a little while, if necessary, you have been grieved by various trials, [7]so that the tested genuineness of your faith—more precious than gold that perishes though it is tested by fire—may be found to result in praise and glory and honor at the revelation of Jesus Christ. [8]Though you have not seen him, you love him. Though you do not now see him, you believe in him and rejoice with joy that is inexpressible and filled with glory, [9]obtaining the outcome of your faith, the salvation of your souls.
[10]Concerning this salvation, the prophets who prophesied about the grace that was to be yours searched and inquired carefully, [11]inquiring what person or time the Spirit of Christ in them was indicating when he predicted the sufferings of Christ and the subsequent glories. [12]It was revealed to them that they were serving not themselves but you, in the things that have now been announced to you through those who preached the good news to you by the Holy Spirit sent from heaven, things into which angels long to look.

Called to Be Holy

[13]Therefore, preparing your minds for action,[1] and being sober-minded, set your hope fully on the grace that will be brought to you at the revelation of Jesus Christ. [14]As obedient children, do not be conformed to the passions of your former ignorance, [15]but as he who called you is holy, you also be holy in all your conduct, [16]since it is written, [a]"You shall be holy, for I am holy." [17]And if you call on him as Father who judges impartially according to each one's deeds, conduct yourselves with fear throughout the time of your exile, [18]knowing that you were ransomed from the futile ways inherited from your forefathers, not with perishable things such as silver or gold, [19]but with the precious blood of Christ, like that of a lamb without blemish or spot. [20]He was foreknown before the foundation of the world but was made manifest in the last times for the sake of you [21]who through him are believers in God, who raised him from the dead and gave him glory, so that your faith and hope are in God.
[22]Having purified your souls by your obedience to the truth for a sincere brotherly love, love one another earnestly from a pure heart, [23]since you have been born again, not of perishable seed but of imperishable, through the living and abiding word of God; [24]for

[b]"All flesh is like grass
  and all its glory like the flower of grass.
The grass withers,
  and the flower falls,
[25] but the word of the Lord remains forever."

And this word is the good news that was preached to you.

A Living Stone and a Holy People

2 So put away all malice and all deceit and hypocrisy and envy and all slander. [2]Like newborn infants, long for the pure spiritual milk, that by it you may grow up into salvation— [3]if indeed you have tasted that the Lord is good.
[4]As you come to him, a living stone rejected by

---

[1] Greek *girding up the loins of your mind* [a] Lev. 11:44 [b] Isa. 40:6, 8

men but in the sight of God chosen and precious, [5]you yourselves like living stones are being built up as a spiritual house, to be a holy priesthood, to offer spiritual sacrifices acceptable to God through Jesus Christ. [6]For it stands in Scripture:

[a]"Behold, I am laying in Zion a stone,
    a cornerstone chosen and precious,
and whoever believes in him will not be put to
    shame."

[7]So the honor is for you who believe, but for those who do not believe,

[b]"The stone that the builders rejected
    has become the cornerstone,"[1]

[8]and

[c]"A stone of stumbling,
    and a rock of offense."

They stumble because they disobey the word, as they were destined to do.

[9]But you are a chosen race, a royal priesthood, a holy nation, a people for his own possession, that you may proclaim the excellencies of him who called you out of darkness into his marvelous light. [10]Once you were not a people, but now you are God's people; once you had not received mercy, but now you have received mercy.

[11]Beloved, I urge you as sojourners and exiles to abstain from the passions of the flesh, which wage war against your soul. [12]Keep your conduct among the Gentiles honorable, so that when they speak against you as evildoers, they may see your good deeds and glorify God on the day of visitation.

Submission to Authority

[13]Be subject for the Lord's sake to every human institution,[2] whether it be to the emperor[3] as supreme, [14]or to governors as sent by him to punish those who do evil and to praise those who do good. [15]For this is the will of God, that by doing good you should put to silence the ignorance of foolish people. [16]Live as people who are free, not using your freedom as a cover-up for evil, but living as servants[4] of God. [17]Honor everyone. Love the brotherhood. Fear God. Honor the emperor.

[18]Servants, be subject to your masters with all respect, not only to the good and gentle but also to the unjust. [19]For this is a gracious thing, when, mindful of God, one endures sorrows while suffering unjustly. [20]For what credit is it if, when you sin and are beaten for it, you endure? But if when you do good and suffer for it you endure, this is a gracious thing in the sight of God. [21]For to this you have been called, because Christ also suffered for you, leaving you an example, so that you might follow in his steps. [22]He committed no

sin, neither was deceit found in his mouth. [23]When he was reviled, he did not revile in return; when he suffered, he did not threaten, but continued entrusting himself to him who judges justly. [24]He himself bore our sins in his body on the tree, that we might die to sin and live to righteousness. By his wounds you have been healed. [25]For you were straying like sheep, but have now returned to the Shepherd and Overseer of your souls.

Wives and Husbands

3 Likewise, wives, be subject to your own husbands, so that even if some do not obey the word, they may be won without a word by the conduct of their wives, [2]when they see your respectful and pure conduct. [3]Do not let your adorning be external—the braiding of hair and the putting on of gold jewelry, or the clothing you wear— [4]but let your adorning be the hidden person of the heart with the imperishable beauty of a gentle and quiet spirit, which in God's sight is very precious. [5]For this is how the holy women who hoped in God used to adorn themselves, by submitting to their own husbands, [6]as Sarah obeyed Abraham, calling him lord. And you are her children, if you do good and do not fear anything that is frightening.

[7]Likewise, husbands, live with your wives in an understanding way, showing honor to the woman as the weaker vessel, since they are heirs with you[5] of the grace of life, so that your prayers may not be hindered.

Suffering for Righteousness' Sake

[8]Finally, all of you, have unity of mind, sympathy, brotherly love, a tender heart, and a humble mind. [9]Do not repay evil for evil or reviling for reviling, but on the contrary, bless, for to this you were called, that you may obtain a blessing. [10]For

[d]"Whoever desires to love life
    and see good days,
let him keep his tongue from evil
    and his lips from speaking deceit;
[11]   let him turn away from evil and do good;
    let him seek peace and pursue it.
[12]   For the eyes of the Lord are on the righteous,
    and his ears are open to their prayer.
But the face of the Lord is against those who
    do evil."

[13]Now who is there to harm you if you are zealous for what is good? [14]But even if you should suffer for righteousness' sake, you will be blessed. Have no fear of them, nor be troubled, [15]but in your hearts honor Christ the Lord as holy, always being prepared to make a defense to anyone who asks you for a reason for the hope that is in you; yet do it with gentleness and

---

[1]Greek *the head of the corner* [2]Or *every institution ordained for people* [3]Or *king; also verse 17* [4]Greek *bondservants* [5]Some manuscripts *since you are joint heirs* [a]Isa. 28:16 [b]Ps. 118:22 [c]Isa. 8:14 [d]Ps. 34:12-16

respect, [16]having a good conscience, so that, when you are slandered, those who revile your good behavior in Christ may be put to shame. [17]For it is better to suffer for doing good, if that should be God's will, than for doing evil.

[18]For Christ also suffered[1] once for sins, the righteous for the unrighteous, that he might bring us to God, being put to death in the flesh but made alive in the spirit, [19]in which[2] he went and proclaimed[3] to the spirits in prison, [20]because[4] they formerly did not obey, when God's patience waited in the days of Noah, while the ark was being prepared, in which a few, that is, eight persons, were brought safely through water. [21]Baptism, which corresponds to this, now saves you, not as a removal of dirt from the body but as an appeal to God for a good conscience, through the resurrection of Jesus Christ, [22]who has gone into heaven and is at the right hand of God, with angels, authorities, and powers having been subjected to him.

Stewards of God's Grace

4 Since therefore Christ suffered in the flesh,[5] arm yourselves with the same way of thinking, for whoever has suffered in the flesh has ceased from sin, [2]so as to live for the rest of the time in the flesh no longer for human passions but for the will of God. [3]For the time that is past suffices for doing what the Gentiles want to do, living in sensuality, passions, drunkenness, orgies, drinking parties, and lawless idolatry. [4]With respect to this they are surprised when you do not join them in the same flood of debauchery, and they malign you; [5]but they will give account to him who is ready to judge the living and the dead. [6]For this is why the gospel was preached even to those who are dead, that though judged in the flesh the way people are, they might live in the spirit the way God does.

[7]The end of all things is at hand; therefore be self-controlled and sober-minded for the sake of your prayers. [8]Above all, keep loving one another earnestly, since love covers a multitude of sins. [9]Show hospitality to one another without grumbling. [10]As each has received a gift, use it to serve one another, as good stewards of God's varied grace: [11]whoever speaks, as one who speaks oracles of God; whoever serves, as one who serves by the strength that God supplies—in order that in everything God may be glorified through Jesus Christ. To him belong glory and dominion forever and ever. Amen.

Suffering as a Christian

[12]Beloved, do not be surprised at the fiery trial when it comes upon you to test you, as though something strange were happening to you. [13]But rejoice insofar as you share Christ's sufferings, that you may also rejoice and be glad when his glory is revealed. [14]If you are insulted for the name of Christ, you are blessed, because the Spirit of glory[6] and of God rests upon you. [15]But let none of you suffer as a murderer or a thief or an evildoer or as a meddler. [16]Yet if anyone suffers as a Christian, let him not be ashamed, but let him glorify God in that name. [17]For it is time for judgment to begin at the household of God; and if it begins with us, what will be the outcome for those who do not obey the gospel of God? [18]And

"If the righteous is scarcely saved,
    what will become of the ungodly and the
        sinner?"[7]

[19]Therefore let those who suffer according to God's will entrust their souls to a faithful Creator while doing good.

Shepherd the Flock of God

5 So I exhort the elders among you, as a fellow elder and a witness of the sufferings of Christ, as well as a partaker in the glory that is going to be revealed: [2]shepherd the flock of God that is among you, exercising oversight,[8] not under compulsion, but willingly, as God would have you;[9] not for shameful gain, but eagerly; [3]not domineering over those in your charge, but being examples to the flock. [4]And when the chief Shepherd appears, you will receive the unfading crown of glory. [5]Likewise, you who are younger, be subject to the elders. Clothe yourselves, all of you, with humility toward one another, for "God opposes the proud but gives grace to the humble."

[6]Humble yourselves, therefore, under the mighty hand of God so that at the proper time he may exalt you, [7]casting all your anxieties on him, because he cares for you. [8]Be sober-minded; be watchful. Your adversary the devil prowls around like a roaring lion, seeking someone to devour. [9]Resist him, firm in your faith, knowing that the same kinds of suffering are being experienced by your brotherhood throughout the world. [10]And after you have suffered a little while, the God of all grace, who has called you to his eternal glory in Christ, will himself restore, confirm, strengthen, and establish you. [11]To him be the dominion forever and ever. Amen.

Final Greetings

[12]By Silvanus, a faithful brother as I regard him, I have written briefly to you, exhorting and declaring that this is the true grace of God. Stand firm in it. [13]She who is at Babylon, who is likewise chosen, sends you greetings, and so does Mark, my son. [14]Greet one another with the kiss of love.

Peace to all of you who are in Christ.

[1] Some manuscripts *died* [2] Or *the Spirit, in whom* [3] Or *preached* [4] Or *when* [5] Some manuscripts add *for us;* some *for you* [6] Some manuscripts insert *and of power* [7] Greek *where will the ungodly and sinner appear?* [8] Some manuscripts omit *exercising oversight* [9] Some manuscripts omit *as God would have you*

2 PETER

Introduction

In this second letter, Peter describes (ch. 2) some twisted versions of Christian truth being taught. Recalling his experience of Christ's glory at the transfiguration (1:17-18), Peter explains the "more sure" truth of the gospel as an antidote to heresy. The gospel is like "a lamp shining in a dark place" (1:19). In chapter 3 Peter focuses on those who scoff at the idea of Christ's triumphant return and the final judgment. Just as God once destroyed the world with water, he will one day bring his fire to it. In light of this, we should live in "holiness and godliness" as we await his return and the salvation he has promised to all believers. Peter probably wrote this letter about A.D. 67–68, shortly before his death.

Greeting

1 Simeon[1] Peter, a servant[2] and apostle of Jesus Christ,

To those who have obtained a faith of equal standing with ours by the righteousness of our God and Savior Jesus Christ:

[2] May grace and peace be multiplied to you in the knowledge of God and of Jesus our Lord.

Make Your Calling and Election Sure

[3] His divine power has granted to us all things that pertain to life and godliness, through the knowledge of him who called us to[3] his own glory and excellence,[4] [4] by which he has granted to us his precious and very great promises, so that through them you may become partakers of the divine nature, having escaped from the corruption that is in the world because of sinful desire. [5] For this very reason, make every effort to supplement your faith with virtue,[5] and virtue with knowledge, [6] and knowledge with self-control, and self-control with steadfastness, and steadfastness with godliness, [7] and godliness with brotherly affection, and brotherly affection with love. [8] For if these qualities[6] are yours and are increasing, they keep you from being ineffective or unfruitful in the knowledge of our Lord Jesus Christ. [9] For whoever lacks these qualities is so nearsighted that he is blind, having forgotten that he was cleansed from his former sins. [10] Therefore, brothers,[7] be all the more diligent to make your calling and election sure, for if you practice these qualities you will never fall. [11] For in this way there will be richly provided for you an entrance into the eternal kingdom of our Lord and Savior Jesus Christ.

[12] Therefore I intend always to remind you of these qualities, though you know them and are established in the truth that you have. [13] I think it right, as long as I am in this body,[8] to stir you up by way of reminder, [14] since I know that the putting off of my body will be soon, as our Lord Jesus Christ made clear to me. [15] And I will make every effort so that after my departure you may be able at any time to recall these things.

Christ's Glory and the Prophetic Word

[16] For we did not follow cleverly devised myths when we made known to you the power and coming of our Lord Jesus Christ, but we were eyewitnesses of his majesty. [17] For when he received honor and glory from God the Father, and the voice was borne to him by the Majestic Glory, "This is my beloved Son,[9] with whom I am well pleased," [18] we ourselves heard this very voice borne from heaven, for we were with him on the holy mountain. [19] And we have something more sure, the prophetic word, to which you will do well to pay attention as to a lamp shining in a dark place, until the day dawns and the morning star rises in your hearts, [20] knowing this first of all, that no prophecy of Scripture comes from someone's own interpretation. [21] For no prophecy was ever produced by the will of man, but men spoke from God as they were carried along by the Holy Spirit.

False Prophets and Teachers

2 But false prophets also arose among the people, just as there will be false teachers among you, who will secretly bring in destructive heresies, even denying the Master who bought them, bringing upon themselves swift destruction. [2] And many will follow their sensuality, and because of them the way of truth will be blasphemed. [3] And in their greed they will exploit you with false words. Their condemnation from long ago is not idle, and their destruction is not asleep.

[4] For if God did not spare angels when they sinned, but cast them into hell[10] and committed them to chains[11] of gloomy darkness to be kept until the judgment; [5] if he did not spare the ancient world, but preserved Noah, a herald of righteousness, with seven others, when he brought a flood upon the world of the ungodly;

---

[1] Some manuscripts *Simon* [2] Or *slave*; Greek *bondservant* [3] Or *by* [4] Or *virtue* [5] Or *excellence*; twice in this verse [6] Greek *these things*; also verses 9, 10, 12 [7] Or *brothers and sisters*. The plural Greek word *adelphoi* (translated "brothers") refers to siblings in a family. In New Testament usage, depending on the context, *adelphoi* may refer either to men or to both men and women who are siblings (brothers and sisters) in God's family, the church [8] Greek *tent*; also verse 14 [9] Or *my Son, my* (or *the*) *Beloved* [10] Greek *Tartarus* [11] Some manuscripts *pits*

⁶if by turning the cities of Sodom and Gomorrah to ashes he condemned them to extinction, making them an example of what is going to happen to the ungodly;¹ ⁷and if he rescued righteous Lot, greatly distressed by the sensual conduct of the wicked ⁸(for as that righteous man lived among them day after day, he was tormenting his righteous soul over their lawless deeds that he saw and heard); ⁹then the Lord knows how to rescue the godly from trials,² and to keep the unrighteous under punishment until the day of judgment, ¹⁰and especially those who indulge in the lust of defiling passion and despise authority.

Bold and willful, they do not tremble as they blaspheme the glorious ones, ¹¹whereas angels, though greater in might and power, do not pronounce a blasphemous judgment against them before the Lord. ¹²But these, like irrational animals, creatures of instinct, born to be caught and destroyed, blaspheming about matters of which they are ignorant, will also be destroyed in their destruction, ¹³suffering wrong as the wage for their wrongdoing. They count it pleasure to revel in the daytime. They are blots and blemishes, reveling in their deceptions,³ while they feast with you. ¹⁴They have eyes full of adultery, insatiable for sin. They entice unsteady souls. They have hearts trained in greed. Accursed children! ¹⁵Forsaking the right way, they have gone astray. They have followed the way of Balaam, the son of Beor, who loved gain from wrongdoing, ¹⁶but was rebuked for his own transgression; a speechless donkey spoke with human voice and restrained the prophet's madness.

¹⁷These are waterless springs and mists driven by a storm. For them the gloom of utter darkness has been reserved. ¹⁸For, speaking loud boasts of folly, they entice by sensual passions of the flesh those who are barely escaping from those who live in error. ¹⁹They promise them freedom, but they themselves are slaves⁴ of corruption. For whatever overcomes a person, to that he is enslaved. ²⁰For if, after they have escaped the defilements of the world through the knowledge of our Lord and Savior Jesus Christ, they are again entangled in them and overcome, the last state has become worse for them than the first. ²¹For it would have been better for them never to have known the way of righteousness than after knowing it to turn back from the holy commandment delivered to them. ²²What the true proverb says has happened to them: "The dog returns to its own vomit, and the sow, after washing herself, returns to wallow in the mire."

The Day of the Lord Will Come

3 This is now the second letter that I am writing to you, beloved. In both of them I am stirring up your sincere mind by way of reminder, ²that you should remember the predictions of the holy prophets and the commandment of the Lord and Savior through your apostles, ³knowing this first of all, that scoffers will come in the last days with scoffing, following their own sinful desires. ⁴They will say, "Where is the promise of his coming? For ever since the fathers fell asleep, all things are continuing as they were from the beginning of creation." ⁵For they deliberately overlook this fact, that the heavens existed long ago, and the earth was formed out of water and through water by the word of God, ⁶and that by means of these the world that then existed was deluged with water and perished. ⁷But by the same word the heavens and earth that now exist are stored up for fire, being kept until the day of judgment and destruction of the ungodly.

⁸But do not overlook this one fact, beloved, that with the Lord one day is as a thousand years, and a thousand years as one day. ⁹The Lord is not slow to fulfill his promise as some count slowness, but is patient toward you,⁵ not wishing that any should perish, but that all should reach repentance. ¹⁰But the day of the Lord will come like a thief, and then the heavens will pass away with a roar, and the heavenly bodies⁶ will be burned up and dissolved, and the earth and the works that are done on it will be exposed.⁷

¹¹Since all these things are thus to be dissolved, what sort of people ought you to be in lives of holiness and godliness, ¹²waiting for and hastening the coming of the day of God, because of which the heavens will be set on fire and dissolved, and the heavenly bodies will melt as they burn! ¹³But according to his promise we are waiting for new heavens and a new earth in which righteousness dwells.

Final Words

¹⁴Therefore, beloved, since you are waiting for these, be diligent to be found by him without spot or blemish, and at peace. ¹⁵And count the patience of our Lord as salvation, just as our beloved brother Paul also wrote to you according to the wisdom given him, ¹⁶as he does in all his letters when he speaks in them of these matters. There are some things in them that are hard to understand, which the ignorant and unstable twist to their own destruction, as they do the other Scriptures. ¹⁷You therefore, beloved, knowing this beforehand, take care that you are not carried away with the error of lawless people and lose your own stability. ¹⁸But grow in the grace and knowledge of our Lord and Savior Jesus Christ. To him be the glory both now and to the day of eternity. Amen.

---

¹ Some manuscripts *an example to those who were to be ungodly* ² Or *temptations* ³ Some manuscripts *love feasts* ⁴ Greek *bondservants* ⁵ Some manuscripts *on your account* ⁶ Or *elements*; also verse 12 ⁷ Greek *found*; some manuscripts *will be burned up*

1 JOHN

Introduction

This apostolic letter speaks authoritatively about the truth of the incarnation—a message his doubting readers needed after hearing false teachers deny the full divinity and humanity of Christ. It reaffirms the core of Christianity, saying that either we exhibit the sound doctrine, obedience, and love that characterize all Christians, or else we are not true Christians. When all the basics of faith are in operation, we not only know joy but can live a holy life and be assured of salvation (3:19, 24)—even though we are still far from perfect (1:9). This assurance comes especially as we find ourselves learning to "love one another" as brothers and sisters in Christ (4:7-8). This general letter to congregations across Asia Minor (now Turkey) was probably written by the apostle John in the late first century A.D.

The Word of Life

1 That which was from the beginning, which we have heard, which we have seen with our eyes, which we looked upon and have touched with our hands, concerning the word of life— ²the life was made manifest, and we have seen it, and testify to it and proclaim to you the eternal life, which was with the Father and was made manifest to us— ³that which we have seen and heard we proclaim also to you, so that you too may have fellowship with us; and indeed our fellowship is with the Father and with his Son Jesus Christ. ⁴And we are writing these things so that our¹ joy may be complete.

Walking in the Light

⁵This is the message we have heard from him and proclaim to you, that God is light, and in him is no darkness at all. ⁶If we say we have fellowship with him while we walk in darkness, we lie and do not practice the truth. ⁷But if we walk in the light, as he is in the light, we have fellowship with one another, and the blood of Jesus his Son cleanses us from all sin. ⁸If we say we have no sin, we deceive ourselves, and the truth is not in us. ⁹If we confess our sins, he is faithful and just to forgive us our sins and to cleanse us from all unrighteousness. ¹⁰If we say we have not sinned, we make him a liar, and his word is not in us.

Christ Our Advocate

2 My little children, I am writing these things to you so that you may not sin. But if anyone does sin, we have an advocate with the Father, Jesus Christ the righteous. ²He is the propitiation for our sins, and not for ours only but also for the sins of the whole world. ³And by this we know that we have come to know him, if we keep his commandments. ⁴Whoever says "I know him" but does not keep his commandments is a liar, and the truth is not in him, ⁵but whoever keeps his word, in him truly the love of God is perfected. By this we may know that we

are in him: ⁶whoever says he abides in him ought to walk in the same way in which he walked.

The New Commandment

⁷Beloved, I am writing you no new commandment, but an old commandment that you had from the beginning. The old commandment is the word that you have heard. ⁸At the same time, it is a new commandment that I am writing to you, which is true in him and in you, because² the darkness is passing away and the true light is already shining. ⁹Whoever says he is in the light and hates his brother is still in darkness. ¹⁰Whoever loves his brother abides in the light, and in him³ there is no cause for stumbling. ¹¹But whoever hates his brother is in the darkness and walks in the darkness, and does not know where he is going, because the darkness has blinded his eyes.

¹² I am writing to you, little children,
    because your sins are forgiven for his
      name's sake.
¹³ I am writing to you, fathers,
    because you know him who is from the
      beginning.
I am writing to you, young men,
    because you have overcome the evil one.
I write to you, children,
    because you know the Father.
¹⁴ I write to you, fathers,
    because you know him who is from the
      beginning.
I write to you, young men,
    because you are strong,
    and the word of God abides in you,
    and you have overcome the evil one.

Do Not Love the World

¹⁵Do not love the world or the things in the world. If anyone loves the world, the love of the Father is not in him. ¹⁶For all that is in the world—the desires of the flesh and the desires of the eyes and pride in possessions—is not from

---

¹ Some manuscripts your ² Or that ³ Or it

the Father but is from the world. [17]And the world is passing away along with its desires, but whoever does the will of God abides forever.

Warning Concerning Antichrists

[18]Children, it is the last hour, and as you have heard that antichrist is coming, so now many antichrists have come. Therefore we know that it is the last hour. [19]They went out from us, but they were not of us; for if they had been of us, they would have continued with us. But they went out, that it might become plain that they all are not of us. [20]But you have been anointed by the Holy One, and you all have knowledge.[1] [21]I write to you, not because you do not know the truth, but because you know it, and because no lie is of the truth. [22]Who is the liar but he who denies that Jesus is the Christ? This is the antichrist, he who denies the Father and the Son. [23]No one who denies the Son has the Father. Whoever confesses the Son has the Father also. [24]Let what you heard from the beginning abide in you. If what you heard from the beginning abides in you, then you too will abide in the Son and in the Father. [25]And this is the promise that he made to us[2]—eternal life.

[26]I write these things to you about those who are trying to deceive you. [27]But the anointing that you received from him abides in you, and you have no need that anyone should teach you. But as his anointing teaches you about everything, and is true, and is no lie—just as it has taught you, abide in him.

Children of God

[28]And now, little children, abide in him, so that when he appears we may have confidence and not shrink from him in shame at his coming. [29]If you know that he is righteous, you may be sure that everyone who practices righteousness has been born of him.

3 See what kind of love the Father has given to us, that we should be called children of God; and so we are. The reason why the world does not know us is that it did not know him. [2]Beloved, we are God's children now, and what we will be has not yet appeared; but we know that when he appears[3] we shall be like him, because we shall see him as he is. [3]And everyone who thus hopes in him purifies himself as he is pure.

[4]Everyone who makes a practice of sinning also practices lawlessness; sin is lawlessness. [5]You know that he appeared to take away sins, and in him there is no sin. [6]No one who abides in him keeps on sinning; no one who keeps on sinning has either seen him or known him. [7]Little children, let no one deceive you. Whoever practices righteousness is righteous, as he is righteous. [8]Whoever makes a practice of sinning is of the

devil, for the devil has been sinning from the beginning. The reason the Son of God appeared was to destroy the works of the devil. [9]No one born of God makes a practice of sinning, for God's[4] seed abides in him, and he cannot keep on sinning because he has been born of God. [10]By this it is evident who are the children of God, and who are the children of the devil: whoever does not practice righteousness is not of God, nor is the one who does not love his brother.

Love One Another

[11]For this is the message that you have heard from the beginning, that we should love one another. [12]We should not be like Cain, who was of the evil one and murdered his brother. And why did he murder him? Because his own deeds were evil and his brother's righteous. [13]Do not be surprised, brothers,[5] that the world hates you. [14]We know that we have passed out of death into life, because we love the brothers. Whoever does not love abides in death. [15]Everyone who hates his brother is a murderer, and you know that no murderer has eternal life abiding in him.

[16]By this we know love, that he laid down his life for us, and we ought to lay down our lives for the brothers. [17]But if anyone has the world's goods and sees his brother in need, yet closes his heart against him, how does God's love abide in him? [18]Little children, let us not love in word or talk but in deed and in truth.

[19]By this we shall know that we are of the truth and reassure our heart before him; [20]for whenever our heart condemns us, God is greater than our heart, and he knows everything. [21]Beloved, if our heart does not condemn us, we have confidence before God; [22]and whatever we ask we receive from him, because we keep his commandments and do what pleases him. [23]And this is his commandment, that we believe in the name of his Son Jesus Christ and love one another, just as he has commanded us. [24]Whoever keeps his commandments abides in God,[6] and God[7] in him. And by this we know that he abides in us, by the Spirit whom he has given us.

Test the Spirits

4 Beloved, do not believe every spirit, but test the spirits to see whether they are from God, for many false prophets have gone out into the world. [2]By this you know the Spirit of God: every spirit that confesses that Jesus Christ has come in the flesh is from God, [3]and every spirit that does not confess Jesus is not from God. This is the spirit of the antichrist, which you heard was coming and now is in the world already. [4]Little children, you are from God and have overcome them, for he who is in you is greater than he who is in the world. [5]They are from the world; there-

---

[1] Some manuscripts *you know everything* [2] Some manuscripts *you* [3] Or *when it appears* [4] Greek *his* [5] Or *brothers and sisters*. The plural Greek word *adelphoi* (translated "brothers") refers to siblings in a family. In New Testament usage, depending on the context, *adelphoi* may refer either to men or to both men and women who are siblings (brothers and sisters) in God's family, the church; also verses 14, 16 [6] Greek *him* [7] Greek *he*

fore they speak from the world, and the world listens to them. [6]We are from God. Whoever knows God listens to us; whoever is not from God does not listen to us. By this we know the Spirit of truth and the spirit of error.

God Is Love

[7]Beloved, let us love one another, for love is from God, and whoever loves has been born of God and knows God. [8]Anyone who does not love does not know God, because God is love. [9]In this the love of God was made manifest among us, that God sent his only Son into the world, so that we might live through him. [10]In this is love, not that we have loved God but that he loved us and sent his Son to be the propitiation for our sins. [11]Beloved, if God so loved us, we also ought to love one another. [12]No one has ever seen God; if we love one another, God abides in us and his love is perfected in us.

[13]By this we know that we abide in him and he in us, because he has given us of his Spirit. [14]And we have seen and testify that the Father has sent his Son to be the Savior of the world. [15]Whoever confesses that Jesus is the Son of God, God abides in him, and he in God. [16]So we have come to know and to believe the love that God has for us. God is love, and whoever abides in love abides in God, and God abides in him. [17]By this is love perfected with us, so that we may have confidence for the day of judgment, because as he is so also are we in this world. [18]There is no fear in love, but perfect love casts out fear. For fear has to do with punishment, and whoever fears has not been perfected in love. [19]We love because he first loved us. [20]If anyone says, "I love God," and hates his brother, he is a liar; for he who does not love his brother whom he has seen cannot[1] love God whom he has not seen. [21]And this commandment we have from him: whoever loves God must also love his brother.

Overcoming the World

5 Everyone who believes that Jesus is the Christ has been born of God, and everyone who loves the Father loves whoever has been born of him. [2]By this we know that we love the children of God, when we love God and obey his commandments. [3]For this is the love of God, that we keep his commandments. And his commandments are not burdensome. [4]For everyone who has been born of God overcomes the world.

And this is the victory that has overcome the world—our faith. [5]Who is it that overcomes the world except the one who believes that Jesus is the Son of God?

Testimony Concerning the Son of God

[6]This is he who came by water and blood—Jesus Christ; not by the water only but by the water and the blood. And the Spirit is the one who testifies, because the Spirit is the truth. [7]For there are three that testify: [8]the Spirit and the water and the blood; and these three agree. [9]If we receive the testimony of men, the testimony of God is greater, for this is the testimony of God that he has borne concerning his Son. [10]Whoever believes in the Son of God has the testimony in himself. Whoever does not believe God has made him a liar, because he has not believed in the testimony that God has borne concerning his Son. [11]And this is the testimony, that God gave us eternal life, and this life is in his Son. [12]Whoever has the Son has life; whoever does not have the Son of God does not have life.

That You May Know

[13]I write these things to you who believe in the name of the Son of God that you may know that you have eternal life. [14]And this is the confidence that we have toward him, that if we ask anything according to his will he hears us. [15]And if we know that he hears us in whatever we ask, we know that we have the requests that we have asked of him.

[16]If anyone sees his brother committing a sin not leading to death, he shall ask, and God[2] will give him life—to those who commit sins that do not lead to death. There is sin that leads to death; I do not say that one should pray for that. [17]All wrongdoing is sin, but there is sin that does not lead to death.

[18]We know that everyone who has been born of God does not keep on sinning, but he who was born of God protects him, and the evil one does not touch him.

[19]We know that we are from God, and the whole world lies in the power of the evil one.

[20]And we know that the Son of God has come and has given us understanding, so that we may know him who is true; and we are in him who is true, in his Son Jesus Christ. He is the true God and eternal life. [21]Little children, keep yourselves from idols.

---

[1] Some manuscripts *how can he* [2] Greek *he*

2 JOHN

Introduction

Second John warns against the same false teaching mentioned in 1 John. This letter, however, was addressed to "the elect lady and her children" (perhaps a local congregation), and focused on Christian hospitality. False teachers were using the kindness of Christians to gain influence within John's congregations. John's letter spoke of this danger and warned against opening one's home to these destroyers of the faith. While the basic themes of 1 John—holding fast to truth, love, and obedience—are evident, there is the additional focus on what Christian hospitality is all about. Only when you find agreement on sound doctrine will you find meaningful fellowship. The letter was probably written by the apostle John in the late first century A.D.

Greeting

¹The elder to the elect lady and her children, whom I love in truth, and not only I, but also all who know the truth, ²because of the truth that abides in us and will be with us forever:

³Grace, mercy, and peace will be with us, from God the Father and from Jesus Christ the Father's Son, in truth and love.

Walking in Truth and Love

⁴I rejoiced greatly to find some of your children walking in the truth, just as we were commanded by the Father. ⁵And now I ask you, dear lady—not as though I were writing you a new commandment, but the one we have had from the beginning—that we love one another. ⁶And this is love, that we walk according to his commandments; this is the commandment, just as you have heard from the beginning, so that you should walk in it. ⁷For many deceiv-

ers have gone out into the world, those who do not confess the coming of Jesus Christ in the flesh. Such a one is the deceiver and the antichrist. ⁸Watch yourselves, so that you may not lose what we¹ have worked for, but may win a full reward. ⁹Everyone who goes on ahead and does not abide in the teaching of Christ, does not have God. Whoever abides in the teaching has both the Father and the Son. ¹⁰If anyone comes to you and does not bring this teaching, do not receive him into your house or give him any greeting, ¹¹for whoever greets him takes part in his wicked works.

Final Greetings

¹²Though I have much to write to you, I would rather not use paper and ink. Instead I hope to come to you and talk face to face, so that our joy may be complete.

¹³The children of your elect sister greet you.

---

¹ Some manuscripts you

3 JOHN

Introduction

Third John supplements statements on Christian hospitality in 2 John. It applauds a Christian named Gaius for living out the teachings of the apostles—he had welcomed traveling Christian missionaries into his home—while condemning Diotrephes, a selfish church leader who not only refused to help these itinerant, godly teachers but also had slandered and opposed those who disagreed with him. This book demonstrates that pride can divide Christians if they are not living by God's Word. To avoid the dual dangers of false teaching and division within the church, believers should practice the dual virtues of love and discernment. The letter was probably written by the apostle John in the late first century A.D.

Greeting

¹The elder to the beloved Gaius, whom I love in truth.

²Beloved, I pray that all may go well with you and that you may be in good health, as it goes well with your soul. ³For I rejoiced greatly when the brothers¹ came and testified to your truth, as indeed you are walking in the truth. ⁴I have no greater joy than to hear that my children are walking in the truth.

Support and Opposition

⁵Beloved, it is a faithful thing you do in all your efforts for these brothers, strangers as they are, ⁶who testified to your love before the church. You will do well to send them on their journey in a manner worthy of God. ⁷For they have gone out for the sake of the name, accepting nothing from the Gentiles. ⁸Therefore we ought to support people like these, that we may be fellow workers for the truth.

⁹I have written something to the church, but Diotrephes, who likes to put himself first, does not acknowledge our authority. ¹⁰So if I come, I will bring up what he is doing, talking wicked nonsense against us. And not content with that, he refuses to welcome the brothers, and also stops those who want to and puts them out of the church.

¹¹Beloved, do not imitate evil but imitate good. Whoever does good is from God; whoever does evil has not seen God. ¹²Demetrius has received a good testimony from everyone, and from the truth itself. We also add our testimony, and you know that our testimony is true.

Final Greetings

¹³I had much to write to you, but I would rather not write with pen and ink. ¹⁴I hope to see you soon, and we will talk face to face.

¹⁵Peace be to you. The friends greet you. Greet the friends, every one of them.

---

¹ Or brothers and sisters. The plural Greek word adelphoi (translated "brothers") refers to siblings in a family. In New Testament usage, depending on the context, adelphoi may refer either to men or to both men and women who are siblings (brothers and sisters) in God's family, the church; also verses 5, 10

JUDE

Introduction

The letter of Jude warns against those who, having gained admission to the church, were perverting the grace of God, denying "our only Master and Lord, Jesus Christ" (v. 4). Jude used Old Testament examples to warn of these "blemishes" on the church. He wrote multiple denunciations of these ungodly people who "defile the flesh" and "reject authority" (v. 8). He urged Christians to continue in godliness and love toward such people, in some cases reasoning with them, in other cases "snatching them out of the fire" (v. 23). Jude closes with one of the most beautiful doxologies in all of Scripture (vv. 24-25). Jude was the brother of James (probably "James the Lord's brother," Gal. 1:19). He likely wrote sometime between A.D. 65 and 80.

Greeting

¹Jude, a servant¹ of Jesus Christ and brother of James,

To those who are called, beloved in God the Father and kept for² Jesus Christ:

²May mercy, peace, and love be multiplied to you.

Judgment on False Teachers

³Beloved, although I was very eager to write to you about our common salvation, I found it necessary to write appealing to you to contend for the faith that was once for all delivered to the saints. ⁴For certain people have crept in unnoticed who long ago were designated for this condemnation, ungodly people, who pervert the grace of our God into sensuality and deny our only Master and Lord, Jesus Christ.

⁵Now I want to remind you, although you once fully knew it, that Jesus, who saved³ a people out of the land of Egypt, afterward destroyed those who did not believe. ⁶And the angels who did not stay within their own position of authority, but left their proper dwelling, he has kept in eternal chains under gloomy darkness until the judgment of the great day— ⁷just as Sodom and Gomorrah and the surrounding cities, which likewise indulged in sexual immorality and pursued unnatural desire,⁴ serve as an example by undergoing a punishment of eternal fire.

⁸Yet in like manner these people also, relying on their dreams, defile the flesh, reject authority, and blaspheme the glorious ones. ⁹But when the archangel Michael, contending with the devil, was disputing about the body of Moses, he did not presume to pronounce a blasphemous judgment, but said, "The Lord rebuke you." ¹⁰But these people blaspheme all that they do not understand, and they are destroyed by all that they, like unreasoning animals, understand instinctively. ¹¹Woe to them! For they walked in the way of Cain and abandoned themselves for the sake of gain to Balaam's error and perished in Korah's rebellion. ¹²These are hidden reefs⁵ at your love feasts, as they feast with you without fear, shepherds feeding themselves; waterless clouds, swept along by winds; fruitless trees in late autumn, twice dead, uprooted; ¹³wild waves of the sea, casting up the foam of their own shame; wandering stars, for whom the gloom of utter darkness has been reserved forever.

¹⁴It was also about these that Enoch, the seventh from Adam, prophesied, saying, "Behold, the Lord comes with ten thousands of his holy ones, ¹⁵to execute judgment on all and to convict all the ungodly of all their deeds of ungodliness that they have committed in such an ungodly way, and of all the harsh things that ungodly sinners have spoken against him." ¹⁶These are grumblers, malcontents, following their own sinful desires; they are loud-mouthed boasters, showing favoritism to gain advantage.

A Call to Persevere

¹⁷But you must remember, beloved, the predictions of the apostles of our Lord Jesus Christ. ¹⁸They⁶ said to you, "In the last time there will be scoffers, following their own ungodly passions." ¹⁹It is these who cause divisions, worldly people, devoid of the Spirit. ²⁰But you, beloved, building yourselves up in your most holy faith and praying in the Holy Spirit, ²¹keep yourselves in the love of God, waiting for the mercy of our Lord Jesus Christ that leads to eternal life. ²²And have mercy on those who doubt; ²³save others by snatching them out of the fire; to others show mercy with fear, hating even the garment⁷ stained by the flesh.

Doxology

²⁴Now to him who is able to keep you from stumbling and to present you blameless before the presence of his glory with great joy, ²⁵to the only God, our Savior, through Jesus Christ our Lord, be glory, majesty, dominion, and authority, before all time and now and forever. Amen.

---

¹ Or slave; Greek bondservant ²Or by ³Some manuscripts although you fully knew it, that the Lord who once saved ⁴Greek other flesh ⁵Or are blemishes ⁶Or Christ, because they ⁷Greek chiton, a long garment worn under the cloak next to the skin

REVELATION

Introduction

"The revelation of Jesus Christ" (1:1) was probably written by the apostle John while in exile on the island of Patmos, off the coast of present-day Turkey. It was addressed to seven actual churches. Revelation begins with letters from Christ himself to these churches, letters that include commendation, criticism, and comfort. Then comes a long series of visions of judgment on the wicked, all in highly symbolic language. The church is depicted under great distress, but is assured of the final triumph of Jesus as "King of kings and Lord of lords" (19:16), bringing to an end the rebellion of humanity and ushering in "a new heaven and a new earth" (21:1), where God himself will reign forever and ever (11:15). Revelation was probably written A.D. 95–96.

Prologue

1 The revelation of Jesus Christ, which God gave him to show to his servants[1] the things that must soon take place. He made it known by sending his angel to his servant[2] John, ²who bore witness to the word of God and to the testimony of Jesus Christ, even to all that he saw. ³Blessed is the one who reads aloud the words of this prophecy, and blessed are those who hear, and who keep what is written in it, for the time is near.

Greeting to the Seven Churches

⁴John to the seven churches that are in Asia:

Grace to you and peace from him who is and who was and who is to come, and from the seven spirits who are before his throne, ⁵and from Jesus Christ the faithful witness, the firstborn of the dead, and the ruler of kings on earth.

To him who loves us and has freed us from our sins by his blood ⁶and made us a kingdom, priests to his God and Father, to him be glory and dominion forever and ever. Amen. ⁷Behold, he is coming with the clouds, and every eye will see him, even those who pierced him, and all tribes of the earth will wail[3] on account of him. Even so. Amen.

⁸"I am the Alpha and the Omega," says the Lord God, "who is and who was and who is to come, the Almighty."

Vision of the Son of Man

⁹I, John, your brother and partner in the tribulation and the kingdom and the patient endurance that are in Jesus, was on the island called Patmos on account of the word of God and the testimony of Jesus. ¹⁰I was in the Spirit on the Lord's day, and I heard behind me a loud voice like a trumpet ¹¹saying, "Write what you see in a book and send it to the seven churches, to Ephesus and to Smyrna and to Pergamum and to Thyatira and to Sardis and to Philadelphia and to Laodicea."

¹²Then I turned to see the voice that was speaking to me, and on turning I saw seven golden lampstands, ¹³and in the midst of the lampstands one like a son of man, clothed with a long robe and with a golden sash around his chest. ¹⁴The hairs of his head were white, like white wool, like snow. His eyes were like a flame of fire, ¹⁵his feet were like burnished bronze, refined in a furnace, and his voice was like the roar of many waters. ¹⁶In his right hand he held seven stars, from his mouth came a sharp two-edged sword, and his face was like the sun shining in full strength.

¹⁷When I saw him, I fell at his feet as though dead. But he laid his right hand on me, saying, "Fear not, I am the first and the last, ¹⁸and the living one. I died, and behold I am alive forevermore, and I have the keys of Death and Hades. ¹⁹Write therefore the things that you have seen, those that are and those that are to take place after this. ²⁰As for the mystery of the seven stars that you saw in my right hand, and the seven golden lampstands, the seven stars are the angels of the seven churches, and the seven lampstands are the seven churches.

To the Church in Ephesus

2 "To the angel of the church in Ephesus write: 'The words of him who holds the seven stars in his right hand, who walks among the seven golden lampstands.

²"'I know your works, your toil and your patient endurance, and how you cannot bear with those who are evil, but have tested those who call themselves apostles and are not, and found them to be false. ³I know you are enduring patiently and bearing up for my name's sake, and you have not grown weary. ⁴But I have this against you, that you have abandoned the love you had at first. ⁵Remember therefore from where you have fallen; repent, and do the works you did at first. If not, I will come to you and remove your lampstand from its place, unless you repent. ⁶Yet this you have: you hate the works of the Nicolaitans, which I also hate. ⁷He who

---

¹ Greek bondservants ² Greek bondservant ³ Or mourn

has an ear, let him hear what the Spirit says to the churches. To the one who conquers I will grant to eat of the tree of life, which is in the paradise of God.'

To the Church in Smyrna

8"And to the angel of the church in Smyrna write: 'The words of the first and the last, who died and came to life.

9"'I know your tribulation and your poverty (but you are rich) and the slander[1] of those who say that they are Jews and are not, but are a synagogue of Satan. 10Do not fear what you are about to suffer. Behold, the devil is about to throw some of you into prison, that you may be tested, and for ten days you will have tribulation. Be faithful unto death, and I will give you the crown of life. 11He who has an ear, let him hear what the Spirit says to the churches. The one who conquers will not be hurt by the second death.'

To the Church in Pergamum

12"And to the angel of the church in Pergamum write: 'The words of him who has the sharp two-edged sword.

13"'I know where you dwell, where Satan's throne is. Yet you hold fast my name, and you did not deny my faith[2] even in the days of Antipas my faithful witness, who was killed among you, where Satan dwells. 14But I have a few things against you: you have some there who hold the teaching of Balaam, who taught Balak to put a stumbling block before the sons of Israel, so that they might eat food sacrificed to idols and practice sexual immorality. 15So also you have some who hold the teaching of the Nicolaitans. 16Therefore repent. If not, I will come to you soon and war against them with the sword of my mouth. 17He who has an ear, let him hear what the Spirit says to the churches. To the one who conquers I will give some of the hidden manna, and I will give him a white stone, with a new name written on the stone that no one knows except the one who receives it.'

To the Church in Thyatira

18"And to the angel of the church in Thyatira write: 'The words of the Son of God, who has eyes like a flame of fire, and whose feet are like burnished bronze.

19"'I know your works, your love and faith and service and patient endurance, and that your latter works exceed the first. 20But I have this against you, that you tolerate that woman Jezebel, who calls herself a prophetess and is teaching and seducing my servants[3] to practice sexual immorality and to eat food sacrificed to idols. 21I gave her time to repent, but she refuses to repent of her sexual immorality. 22Behold, I will throw her onto a sickbed, and those who commit adultery with her I will throw into great tribulation,

unless they repent of her works, 23and I will strike her children dead. And all the churches will know that I am he who searches mind and heart, and I will give to each of you according to your works. 24But to the rest of you in Thyatira, who do not hold this teaching, who have not learned what some call the deep things of Satan, to you I say, I do not lay on you any other burden 25Only hold fast what you have until I come. 26The one who conquers and who keeps my works until the end, to him I will give authority over the nations, 27and he will rule them with a rod of iron, as when earthen pots are broken in pieces, even as I myself have received authority from my Father. 28And I will give him the morning star. 29He who has an ear, let him hear what the Spirit says to the churches.'

To the Church in Sardis

3 "And to the angel of the church in Sardis write: 'The words of him who has the seven spirits of God and the seven stars.

"'I know your works. You have the reputation of being alive, but you are dead. 2Wake up, and strengthen what remains and is about to die, for I have not found your works complete in the sight of my God. 3Remember, then, what you received and heard. Keep it, and repent. If you will not wake up, I will come like a thief, and you will not know at what hour I will come against you. 4Yet you have still a few names in Sardis, people who have not soiled their garments, and they will walk with me in white, for they are worthy. 5The one who conquers will be clothed thus in white garments, and I will never blot his name out of the book of life. I will confess his name before my Father and before his angels. 6He who has an ear, let him hear what the Spirit says to the churches.'

To the Church in Philadelphia

7"And to the angel of the church in Philadelphia write: 'The words of the holy one, the true one, who has the key of David, who opens and no one will shut, who shuts and no one opens.

8"'I know your works. Behold, I have set before you an open door, which no one is able to shut. I know that you have but little power, and yet you have kept my word and have not denied my name. 9Behold, I will make those of the synagogue of Satan who say that they are Jews and are not, but lie—behold, I will make them come and bow down before your feet and they will learn that I have loved you. 10Because you have kept my word about patient endurance, I will keep you from the hour of trial that is coming on the whole world, to try those who dwell on the earth. 11I am coming soon. Hold fast what you have, so that no one may seize your crown. 12The one who conquers, I will make him a pillar in the

---

[1] Greek *blasphemy* [2] Or *your faith in me* [3] Greek *bondservants*

temple of my God. Never shall he go out of it, and I will write on him the name of my God, and the name of the city of my God, the new Jerusalem, which comes down from my God out of heaven, and my own new name. [13]He who has an ear, let him hear what the Spirit says to the churches.'

To the Church in Laodicea

[14]"And to the angel of the church in Laodicea write: 'The words of the Amen, the faithful and true witness, the beginning of God's creation.

[15]"'I know your works: you are neither cold nor hot. Would that you were either cold or hot! [16]So, because you are lukewarm, and neither hot nor cold, I will spit you out of my mouth. [17]For you say, I am rich, I have prospered, and I need nothing, not realizing that you are wretched, pitiable, poor, blind, and naked. [18]I counsel you to buy from me gold refined by fire, so that you may be rich, and white garments so that you may clothe yourself and the shame of your nakedness may not be seen, and salve to anoint your eyes, so that you may see. [19]Those whom I love, I reprove and discipline, so be zealous and repent. [20]Behold, I stand at the door and knock. If anyone hears my voice and opens the door, I will come in to him and eat with him, and he with me. [21]The one who conquers, I will grant him to sit with me on my throne, as I also conquered and sat down with my Father on his throne. [22]He who has an ear, let him hear what the Spirit says to the churches.'"

The Throne in Heaven

4 After this I looked, and behold, a door standing open in heaven! And the first voice, which I had heard speaking to me like a trumpet, said, "Come up here, and I will show you what must take place after this." [2]At once I was in the Spirit, and behold, a throne stood in heaven, with one seated on the throne. [3]And he who sat there had the appearance of jasper and carnelian, and around the throne was a rainbow that had the appearance of an emerald. [4]Around the throne were twenty-four thrones, and seated on the thrones were twenty-four elders, clothed in white garments, with golden crowns on their heads. [5]From the throne came flashes of lightning, and rumblings[1] and peals of thunder, and before the throne were burning seven torches of fire, which are the seven spirits of God, [6]and before the throne there was as it were a sea of glass, like crystal.

And around the throne, on each side of the throne, are four living creatures, full of eyes in front and behind: [7]the first living creature like a lion, the second living creature like an ox, the third living creature with the face of a man, and the fourth living creature like an eagle in flight. [8]And the four living creatures, each of them with six wings, are full of eyes all around and within, and day and night they never cease to say,

> "Holy, holy, holy, is the Lord God Almighty,
>   who was and is and is to come!"

[9]And whenever the living creatures give glory and honor and thanks to him who is seated on the throne, who lives forever and ever, [10]the twenty-four elders fall down before him who is seated on the throne and worship him who lives forever and ever. They cast their crowns before the throne, saying,

[11] > "Worthy are you, our Lord and God,
>   to receive glory and honor and power,
>   for you created all things,
>   and by your will they existed and were created."

The Scroll and the Lamb

5 Then I saw in the right hand of him who was seated on the throne a scroll written within and on the back, sealed with seven seals. [2]And I saw a strong angel proclaiming with a loud voice, "Who is worthy to open the scroll and break its seals?" [3]And no one in heaven or on earth or under the earth was able to open the scroll or to look into it, [4]and I began to weep loudly because no one was found worthy to open the scroll or to look into it. [5]And one of the elders said to me, "Weep no more; behold, the Lion of the tribe of Judah, the Root of David, has conquered, so that he can open the scroll and its seven seals."

[6]And between the throne and the four living creatures and among the elders I saw a Lamb standing, as though it had been slain, with seven horns and with seven eyes, which are the seven spirits of God sent out into all the earth. [7]And he went and took the scroll from the right hand of him who was seated on the throne. [8]And when he had taken the scroll, the four living creatures and the twenty-four elders fell down before the Lamb, each holding a harp, and golden bowls full of incense, which are the prayers of the saints. [9]And they sang a new song, saying,

> "Worthy are you to take the scroll
>   and to open its seals,
>   for you were slain, and by your blood you ransomed people for God
>   from every tribe and language and people and nation,
[10] >   and you have made them a kingdom and priests to our God,
>   and they shall reign on the earth."

[11]Then I looked, and I heard around the throne and the living creatures and the elders the voice of many angels, numbering myriads of myriads and thousands of thousands, [12]saying with a

---

[1] Or voices, or sounds

loud voice, "Worthy is the Lamb who was slain, to receive power and wealth and wisdom and might and honor and glory and blessing!" ¹³And I heard every creature in heaven and on earth and under the earth and in the sea, and all that is in them, saying, "To him who sits on the throne and to the Lamb be blessing and honor and glory and might forever and ever!" ¹⁴And the four living creatures said, "Amen!" and the elders fell down and worshiped.

The Seven Seals

6 Now I watched when the Lamb opened one of the seven seals, and I heard one of the four living creatures say with a voice like thunder, "Come!" ²And I looked, and behold, a white horse! And its rider had a bow, and a crown was given to him, and he came out conquering, and to conquer.

³When he opened the second seal, I heard the second living creature say, "Come!" ⁴And out came another horse, bright red. Its rider was permitted to take peace from the earth, so that people should slay one another, and he was given a great sword.

⁵When he opened the third seal, I heard the third living creature say, "Come!" And I looked, and behold, a black horse! And its rider had a pair of scales in his hand. ⁶And I heard what seemed to be a voice in the midst of the four living creatures, saying, "A quart¹ of wheat for a denarius,² and three quarts of barley for a denarius, and do not harm the oil and wine!"

⁷When he opened the fourth seal, I heard the voice of the fourth living creature say, "Come!" ⁸And I looked, and behold, a pale horse! And its rider's name was Death, and Hades followed him. And they were given authority over a fourth of the earth, to kill with sword and with famine and with pestilence and by wild beasts of the earth.

⁹When he opened the fifth seal, I saw under the altar the souls of those who had been slain for the word of God and for the witness they had borne. ¹⁰They cried out with a loud voice, "O Sovereign Lord, holy and true, how long before you will judge and avenge our blood on those who dwell on the earth?" ¹¹Then they were each given a white robe and told to rest a little longer, until the number of their fellow servants³ and their brothers⁴ should be complete, who were to be killed as they themselves had been.

¹²When he opened the sixth seal, I looked, and behold, there was a great earthquake, and the sun became black as sackcloth, the full moon became like blood, ¹³and the stars of the sky fell to the earth as the fig tree sheds its winter fruit when shaken by a gale. ¹⁴The sky vanished like a scroll that is being rolled up, and every mountain and island was removed from its place. ¹⁵Then the kings of the earth and the great ones and the generals and the rich and the powerful, and everyone, slave⁵ and free, hid themselves in the caves and among the rocks of the mountains, ¹⁶calling to the mountains and rocks, "Fall on us and hide us from the face of him who is seated on the throne, and from the wrath of the Lamb, ¹⁷for the great day of their wrath has come, and who can stand?"

The 144,000 of Israel Sealed

7 After this I saw four angels standing at the four corners of the earth, holding back the four winds of the earth, that no wind might blow on earth or sea or against any tree. ²Then I saw another angel ascending from the rising of the sun, with the seal of the living God, and he called with a loud voice to the four angels who had been given power to harm earth and sea, ³saying, "Do not harm the earth or the sea or the trees, until we have sealed the servants⁶ of our God on their foreheads." ⁴And I heard the number of the sealed, 144,000, sealed from every tribe of the sons of Israel:

⁵ 12,000 from the tribe of Judah were sealed,
   12,000 from the tribe of Reuben,
   12,000 from the tribe of Gad,
⁶ 12,000 from the tribe of Asher,
   12,000 from the tribe of Naphtali,
   12,000 from the tribe of Manasseh,
⁷ 12,000 from the tribe of Simeon,
   12,000 from the tribe of Levi,
   12,000 from the tribe of Issachar,
⁸ 12,000 from the tribe of Zebulun,
   12,000 from the tribe of Joseph,
   12,000 from the tribe of Benjamin were sealed.

A Great Multitude from Every Nation

⁹After this I looked, and behold, a great multitude that no one could number, from every nation, from all tribes and peoples and languages, standing before the throne and before the Lamb, clothed in white robes, with palm branches in their hands, ¹⁰and crying out with a loud voice, "Salvation belongs to our God who sits on the throne, and to the Lamb!" ¹¹And all the angels were standing around the throne and around the elders and the four living creatures, and they fell on their faces before the throne and worshiped God, ¹²saying, "Amen! Blessing and glory and wisdom and thanksgiving and honor and power and might be to our God forever and ever! Amen."

¹³Then one of the elders addressed me, saying, "Who are these, clothed in white robes, and

---

¹ Greek choinix, a dry measure equal to about a quart ² A denarius was a day's wage for a laborer ³ Greek fellow bondservants ⁴ Or brothers and sisters. The plural Greek word adelphoi (translated "brothers") refers to siblings in a family. In New Testament usage, depending on the context, adelphoi may refer either to men or to both men and women who are siblings (brothers and sisters) in God's family, the church ⁵ Or servant; Greek bondservant ⁶ Greek bondservants

from where have they come?" ¹⁴I said to him, "Sir, you know." And he said to me, "These are the ones coming out of the great tribulation. They have washed their robes and made them white in the blood of the Lamb.

¹⁵ "Therefore they are before the throne of God,
   and serve him day and night in his temple;
   and he who sits on the throne will shelter
      them with his presence.
¹⁶ They shall hunger no more, neither thirst any-
      more;
   the sun shall not strike them,
   nor any scorching heat.
¹⁷ For the Lamb in the midst of the throne will
      be their shepherd,
   and he will guide them to springs of living
      water,
   and God will wipe away every tear from their
      eyes."

The Seventh Seal and the Golden Censer

8 When the Lamb opened the seventh seal, there was silence in heaven for about half an hour. ²Then I saw the seven angels who stand before God, and seven trumpets were given to them. ³And another angel came and stood at the altar with a golden censer, and he was given much incense to offer with the prayers of all the saints on the golden altar before the throne, ⁴and the smoke of the incense, with the prayers of the saints, rose before God from the hand of the angel. ⁵Then the angel took the censer and filled it with fire from the altar and threw it on the earth, and there were peals of thunder, rumblings,¹ flashes of lightning, and an earthquake.

The Seven Trumpets

⁶Now the seven angels who had the seven trumpets prepared to blow them.

⁷The first angel blew his trumpet, and there followed hail and fire, mixed with blood, and these were thrown upon the earth. And a third of the earth was burned up, and a third of the trees were burned up, and all green grass was burned up.

⁸The second angel blew his trumpet, and something like a great mountain, burning with fire, was thrown into the sea, and a third of the sea became blood. ⁹A third of the living creatures in the sea died, and a third of the ships were destroyed.

¹⁰The third angel blew his trumpet, and a great star fell from heaven, blazing like a torch, and it fell on a third of the rivers and on the springs of water. ¹¹The name of the star is Wormwood.² A third of the waters became wormwood, and many people died from the water, because it had been made bitter.

¹²The fourth angel blew his trumpet, and a third of the sun was struck, and a third of the moon, and a third of the stars, so that a third of their light might be darkened, and a third of the day might be kept from shining, and likewise a third of the night.

¹³Then I looked, and I heard an eagle crying with a loud voice as it flew directly overhead, "Woe, woe, woe to those who dwell on the earth, at the blasts of the other trumpets that the three angels are about to blow!"

9 And the fifth angel blew his trumpet, and I saw a star fallen from heaven to earth, and he was given the key to the shaft of the bottomless pit.³ ²He opened the shaft of the bottomless pit, and from the shaft rose smoke like the smoke of a great furnace, and the sun and the air were darkened with the smoke from the shaft. ³Then from the smoke came locusts on the earth, and they were given power like the power of scorpions of the earth. ⁴They were told not to harm the grass of the earth or any green plant or any tree, but only those people who do not have the seal of God on their foreheads. ⁵They were allowed to torment them for five months, but not to kill them, and their torment was like the torment of a scorpion when it stings someone. ⁶And in those days people will seek death and will not find it. They will long to die, but death will flee from them.

⁷In appearance the locusts were like horses prepared for battle: on their heads were what looked like crowns of gold; their faces were like human faces, ⁸their hair like women's hair, and their teeth like lions' teeth; ⁹they had breastplates like breastplates of iron, and the noise of their wings was like the noise of many chariots with horses rushing into battle. ¹⁰They have tails and stings like scorpions, and their power to hurt people for five months is in their tails. ¹¹They have as king over them the angel of the bottomless pit. His name in Hebrew is Abaddon, and in Greek he is called Apollyon.⁴

¹²The first woe has passed; behold, two woes are still to come.

¹³Then the sixth angel blew his trumpet, and I heard a voice from the four horns of the golden altar before God, ¹⁴saying to the sixth angel who had the trumpet, "Release the four angels who are bound at the great river Euphrates." ¹⁵So the four angels, who had been prepared for the hour, the day, the month, and the year, were released to kill a third of mankind. ¹⁶The number of mounted troops was twice ten thousand times ten thousand; I heard their number. ¹⁷And this is how I saw the horses in my vision and those who rode them: they wore breastplates the color of fire and of sapphire⁵ and of sulfur, and the heads of the horses were like lions' heads,

---

¹Or voices, or sounds ²Wormwood is the name of a plant and of the bitter-tasting extract derived from it ³Greek the abyss; also verses 2, 11 ⁴Abaddon means destruction; Apollyon means destroyer ⁵Greek hyacinth

and fire and smoke and sulfur came out of their mouths. [18]By these three plagues a third of mankind was killed, by the fire and smoke and sulfur coming out of their mouths. [19]For the power of the horses is in their mouths and in their tails, for their tails are like serpents with heads, and by means of them they wound.

[20]The rest of mankind, who were not killed by these plagues, did not repent of the works of their hands nor give up worshiping demons and idols of gold and silver and bronze and stone and wood, which cannot see or hear or walk, [21]nor did they repent of their murders or their sorceries or their sexual immorality or their thefts.

The Angel and the Little Scroll

10 Then I saw another mighty angel coming down from heaven, wrapped in a cloud, with a rainbow over his head, and his face was like the sun, and his legs like pillars of fire. [2]He had a little scroll open in his hand. And he set his right foot on the sea, and his left foot on the land, [3]and called out with a loud voice, like a lion roaring. When he called out, the seven thunders sounded. [4]And when the seven thunders had sounded, I was about to write, but I heard a voice from heaven saying, "Seal up what the seven thunders have said, and do not write it down." [5]And the angel whom I saw standing on the sea and on the land raised his right hand to heaven [6]and swore by him who lives forever and ever, who created heaven and what is in it, the earth and what is in it, and the sea and what is in it, that there would be no more delay, [7]but that in the days of the trumpet call to be sounded by the seventh angel, the mystery of God would be fulfilled, just as he announced to his servants[1] the prophets.

[8]Then the voice that I had heard from heaven spoke to me again, saying, "Go, take the scroll that is open in the hand of the angel who is standing on the sea and on the land." [9]So I went to the angel and told him to give me the little scroll. And he said to me, "Take and eat it; it will make your stomach bitter, but in your mouth it will be sweet as honey." [10]And I took the little scroll from the hand of the angel and ate it. It was sweet as honey in my mouth, but when I had eaten it my stomach was made bitter. [11]And I was told, "You must again prophesy about many peoples and nations and languages and kings."

The Two Witnesses

11 Then I was given a measuring rod like a staff, and I was told, "Rise and measure the temple of God and the altar and those who worship there, [2]but do not measure the court outside the temple; leave that out, for it is given over to the nations, and they will trample the holy city for forty-two months. [3]And I will grant

authority to my two witnesses, and they will prophesy for 1,260 days, clothed in sackcloth."

[4]These are the two olive trees and the two lampstands that stand before the Lord of the earth. [5]And if anyone would harm them, fire pours from their mouth and consumes their foes. If anyone would harm them, this is how he is doomed to be killed. [6]They have the power to shut the sky, that no rain may fall during the days of their prophesying, and they have power over the waters to turn them into blood and to strike the earth with every kind of plague, as often as they desire. [7]And when they have finished their testimony, the beast that rises from the bottomless pit[2] will make war on them and conquer them and kill them, [8]and their dead bodies will lie in the street of the great city that symbolically[3] is called Sodom and Egypt, where their Lord was crucified. [9]For three and a half days some from the peoples and tribes and languages and nations will gaze at their dead bodies and refuse to let them be placed in a tomb, [10]and those who dwell on the earth will rejoice over them and make merry and exchange presents, because these two prophets had been a torment to those who dwell on the earth. [11]But after the three and a half days a breath of life from God entered them, and they stood up on their feet, and great fear fell on those who saw them. [12]Then they heard a loud voice from heaven saying to them, "Come up here!" And they went up to heaven in a cloud, and their enemies watched them. [13]And at that hour there was a great earthquake, and a tenth of the city fell. Seven thousand people were killed in the earthquake, and the rest were terrified and gave glory to the God of heaven.

[14]The second woe has passed; behold, the third woe is soon to come.

The Seventh Trumpet

[15]Then the seventh angel blew his trumpet, and there were loud voices in heaven, saying, "The kingdom of the world has become the kingdom of our Lord and of his Christ, and he shall reign forever and ever." [16]And the twenty-four elders who sit on their thrones before God fell on their faces and worshiped God, [17]saying,

"We give thanks to you, Lord God Almighty,
   who is and who was,
for you have taken your great power
   and begun to reign.
[18] The nations raged,
   but your wrath came,
  and the time for the dead to be judged,
and for rewarding your servants,[4] the
    prophets and saints,
  and those who fear your name,
   both small and great,
and for destroying the destroyers of the earth."

---

[1]Greek bondservants [2]Or the abyss [3]Greek spiritually [4]Greek bondservants

[19]Then God's temple in heaven was opened, and the ark of his covenant was seen within his temple. There were flashes of lightning, rumblings,[1] peals of thunder, an earthquake, and heavy hail.

The Woman and the Dragon

12 And a great sign appeared in heaven: a woman clothed with the sun, with the moon under her feet, and on her head a crown of twelve stars. [2]She was pregnant and was crying out in birth pains and the agony of giving birth. [3]And another sign appeared in heaven: behold, a great red dragon, with seven heads and ten horns, and on his heads seven diadems. [4]His tail swept down a third of the stars of heaven and cast them to the earth. And the dragon stood before the woman who was about to give birth, so that when she bore her child he might devour it. [5]She gave birth to a male child, one who is to rule all the nations with a rod of iron, but her child was caught up to God and to his throne, [6]and the woman fled into the wilderness, where she has a place prepared by God, in which she is to be nourished for 1,260 days.

Satan Thrown Down to Earth

[7]Now war arose in heaven, Michael and his angels fighting against the dragon. And the dragon and his angels fought back, [8]but he was defeated, and there was no longer any place for them in heaven. [9]And the great dragon was thrown down, that ancient serpent, who is called the devil and Satan, the deceiver of the whole world—he was thrown down to the earth, and his angels were thrown down with him. [10]And I heard a loud voice in heaven, saying, "Now the salvation and the power and the kingdom of our God and the authority of his Christ have come, for the accuser of our brothers[2] has been thrown down, who accuses them day and night before our God. [11]And they have conquered him by the blood of the Lamb and by the word of their testimony, for they loved not their lives even unto death. [12]Therefore, rejoice, O heavens and you who dwell in them! But woe to you, O earth and sea, for the devil has come down to you in great wrath, because he knows that his time is short!"

[13]And when the dragon saw that he had been thrown down to the earth, he pursued the woman who had given birth to the male child. [14]But the woman was given the two wings of the great eagle so that she might fly from the serpent into the wilderness, to the place where she is to be nourished for a time, and times, and half a time. [15]The serpent poured water like a river out of his mouth after the woman, to sweep her away with a flood. [16]But the earth came to the help of the woman, and the earth opened its mouth and swallowed the river that the dragon

had poured from his mouth. [17]Then the dragon became furious with the woman and went off to make war on the rest of her offspring, on those who keep the commandments of God and hold to the testimony of Jesus. And he stood[3] on the sand of the sea.

The First Beast

13 And I saw a beast rising out of the sea, with ten horns and seven heads, with ten diadems on its horns and blasphemous names on its heads. [2]And the beast that I saw was like a leopard; its feet were like a bear's, and its mouth was like a lion's mouth. And to it the dragon gave his power and his throne and great authority. [3]One of its heads seemed to have a mortal wound, but its mortal wound was healed, and the whole earth marveled as they followed the beast. [4]And they worshiped the dragon, for he had given his authority to the beast, and they worshiped the beast, saying, "Who is like the beast, and who can fight against it?"

[5]And the beast was given a mouth uttering haughty and blasphemous words, and it was allowed to exercise authority for forty-two months. [6]It opened its mouth to utter blasphemies against God, blaspheming his name and his dwelling,[4] that is, those who dwell in heaven. [7]Also it was allowed to make war on the saints and to conquer them.[5] And authority was given it over every tribe and people and language and nation, [8]and all who dwell on earth will worship it, everyone whose name has not been written before the foundation of the world in the book of life of the Lamb who was slain. [9]If anyone has an ear, let him hear:

[10] If anyone is to be taken captive,
  to captivity he goes;
  if anyone is to be slain with the sword,
  with the sword must he be slain.

Here is a call for the endurance and faith of the saints.

The Second Beast

[11]Then I saw another beast rising out of the earth. It had two horns like a lamb and it spoke like a dragon. [12]It exercises all the authority of the first beast in its presence,[6] and makes the earth and its inhabitants worship the first beast, whose mortal wound was healed. [13]It performs great signs, even making fire come down from heaven to earth in front of people, [14]and by the signs that it is allowed to work in the presence of[7] the beast it deceives those who dwell on earth, telling them to make an image for the beast that was wounded by the sword and yet lived. [15]And it was allowed to give breath to the image of the beast, so that the image of the beast

---

[1] Or *voices,* or *sounds* [2] Or *brothers and sisters* [3] Some manuscripts *And I stood,* connecting the sentence with 13:1 [4] Or *tabernacle* [5] Some manuscripts omit this sentence [6] Or *on its behalf* [7] Or *on behalf of*

might even speak and might cause those who would not worship the image of the beast to be slain. [16]Also it causes all, both small and great, both rich and poor, both free and slave,[1] to be marked on the right hand or the forehead, [17]so that no one can buy or sell unless he has the mark, that is, the name of the beast or the number of its name. [18]This calls for wisdom: let the one who has understanding calculate the number of the beast, for it is the number of a man, and his number is 666.[2]

The Lamb and the 144,000

14 Then I looked, and behold, on Mount Zion stood the Lamb, and with him 144,000 who had his name and his Father's name written on their foreheads. [2]And I heard a voice from heaven like the roar of many waters and like the sound of loud thunder. The voice I heard was like the sound of harpists playing on their harps, [3]and they were singing a new song before the throne and before the four living creatures and before the elders. No one could learn that song except the 144,000 who had been redeemed from the earth. [4]It is these who have not defiled themselves with women, for they are virgins. It is these who follow the Lamb wherever he goes. These have been redeemed from mankind as firstfruits for God and the Lamb, [5]and in their mouth no lie was found, for they are blameless.

The Messages of the Three Angels

[6]Then I saw another angel flying directly overhead, with an eternal gospel to proclaim to those who dwell on earth, to every nation and tribe and language and people. [7]And he said with a loud voice, "Fear God and give him glory, because the hour of his judgment has come, and worship him who made heaven and earth, the sea and the springs of water."

[8]Another angel, a second, followed, saying, "Fallen, fallen is Babylon the great, she who made all nations drink the wine of the passion[3] of her sexual immorality."

[9]And another angel, a third, followed them, saying with a loud voice, "If anyone worships the beast and its image and receives a mark on his forehead or on his hand, [10]he also will drink the wine of God's wrath, poured full strength into the cup of his anger, and he will be tormented with fire and sulfur in the presence of the holy angels and in the presence of the Lamb. [11]And the smoke of their torment goes up forever and ever, and they have no rest, day or night, these worshipers of the beast and its image, and whoever receives the mark of its name."

[12]Here is a call for the endurance of the saints, those who keep the commandments of God and their faith in Jesus.[4]

[13]And I heard a voice from heaven saying,

"Write this: Blessed are the dead who die in the Lord from now on." "Blessed indeed," says the Spirit, "that they may rest from their labors, for their deeds follow them!"

The Harvest of the Earth

[14]Then I looked, and behold, a white cloud, and seated on the cloud one like a son of man, with a golden crown on his head, and a sharp sickle in his hand. [15]And another angel came out of the temple, calling with a loud voice to him who sat on the cloud, "Put in your sickle, and reap, for the hour to reap has come, for the harvest of the earth is fully ripe." [16]So he who sat on the cloud swung his sickle across the earth, and the earth was reaped.

[17]Then another angel came out of the temple in heaven, and he too had a sharp sickle. [18]And another angel came out from the altar, the angel who has authority over the fire, and he called with a loud voice to the one who had the sharp sickle, "Put in your sickle and gather the clusters from the vine of the earth, for its grapes are ripe." [19]So the angel swung his sickle across the earth and gathered the grape harvest of the earth and threw it into the great winepress of the wrath of God. [20]And the winepress was trodden outside the city, and blood flowed from the winepress, as high as a horse's bridle, for 1,600 stadia.[5]

The Seven Angels with Seven Plagues

15 Then I saw another sign in heaven, great and amazing, seven angels with seven plagues, which are the last, for with them the wrath of God is finished.

[2]And I saw what appeared to be a sea of glass mingled with fire—and also those who had conquered the beast and its image and the number of its name, standing beside the sea of glass with harps of God in their hands. [3]And they sing the song of Moses, the servant[6] of God, and the song of the Lamb, saying,

> "Great and amazing are your deeds,
>   O Lord God the Almighty!
> Just and true are your ways,
>   O King of the nations![7]
> [4] Who will not fear, O Lord,
>   and glorify your name?
> For you alone are holy.
>   All nations will come
>   and worship you,
> for your righteous acts have been revealed."

[5]After this I looked, and the sanctuary of the tent[8] of witness in heaven was opened, [6]and out of the sanctuary came the seven angels with the seven plagues, clothed in pure, bright linen, with golden sashes around their chests. [7]And one of the four living creatures gave to the seven angels seven golden bowls full of the wrath of God who

---

[1] Greek bondservant [2] Some manuscripts 616 [3] Or wrath [4] Greek and the faith of Jesus [5] About 184 miles; a stadion was about 607 feet or 185 meters [6] Greek bondservant [7] Some manuscripts the ages [8] Or tabernacle

lives forever and ever, **8**and the sanctuary was filled with smoke from the glory of God and from his power, and no one could enter the sanctuary until the seven plagues of the seven angels were finished.

The Seven Bowls of God's Wrath

16 Then I heard a loud voice from the temple telling the seven angels, "Go and pour out on the earth the seven bowls of the wrath of God."

2So the first angel went and poured out his bowl on the earth, and harmful and painful sores came upon the people who bore the mark of the beast and worshiped its image.

3The second angel poured out his bowl into the sea, and it became like the blood of a corpse, and every living thing died that was in the sea.

4The third angel poured out his bowl into the rivers and the springs of water, and they became blood. **5**And I heard the angel in charge of the waters*1* say,

"Just as you, O Holy One, who is and who was,
    for you brought these judgments.
6 For they have shed the blood of saints and prophets,
    and you have given them blood to drink.
It is what they deserve!"

7And I heard the altar saying,

"Yes, Lord God the Almighty,
    true and just are your judgments!"

8The fourth angel poured out his bowl on the sun, and it was allowed to scorch people with fire. **9**They were scorched by the fierce heat, and they cursed*2* the name of God who had power over these plagues. They did not repent and give him glory.

10The fifth angel poured out his bowl on the throne of the beast, and its kingdom was plunged into darkness. People gnawed their tongues in anguish **11**and cursed the God of heaven for their pain and sores. They did not repent of their deeds.

12The sixth angel poured out his bowl on the great river Euphrates, and its water was dried up, to prepare the way for the kings from the east. **13**And I saw, coming out of the mouth of the dragon and out of the mouth of the beast and out of the mouth of the false prophet, three unclean spirits like frogs. **14**For they are demonic spirits, performing signs, who go abroad to the kings of the whole world, to assemble them for battle on the great day of God the Almighty. **15**("Behold, I am coming like a thief! Blessed is the one who stays awake, keeping his garments on, that he may not go about naked and be seen

exposed!") **16**And they assembled them at the place that in Hebrew is called Armageddon.

The Seventh Bowl

17The seventh angel poured out his bowl into the air, and a loud voice came out of the temple, from the throne, saying, "It is done!" **18**And there were flashes of lightning, rumblings,*3* peals of thunder, and a great earthquake such as there had never been since man was on the earth, so great was that earthquake. **19**The great city was split into three parts, and the cities of the nations fell, and God remembered Babylon the great, to make her drain the cup of the wine of the fury of his wrath. **20**And every island fled away, and no mountains were to be found. **21**And great hailstones, about one hundred pounds*4* each, fell from heaven on people; and they cursed God for the plague of the hail, because the plague was so severe.

The Great Prostitute and the Beast

17 Then one of the seven angels who had the seven bowls came and said to me, "Come, I will show you the judgment of the great prostitute who is seated on many waters, **2**with whom the kings of the earth have committed sexual immorality, and with the wine of whose sexual immorality the dwellers on earth have become drunk." **3**And he carried me away in the Spirit into a wilderness, and I saw a woman sitting on a scarlet beast that was full of blasphemous names, and it had seven heads and ten horns. **4**The woman was arrayed in purple and scarlet, and adorned with gold and jewels and pearls, holding in her hand a golden cup full of abominations and the impurities of her sexual immorality. **5**And on her forehead was written a name of mystery: "Babylon the great, mother of prostitutes and of earth's abominations." **6**And I saw the woman, drunk with the blood of the saints, the blood of the martyrs of Jesus.*5*

When I saw her, I marveled greatly. **7**But the angel said to me, "Why do you marvel? I will tell you the mystery of the woman, and of the beast with seven heads and ten horns that carries her. **8**The beast that you saw was, and is not, and is about to rise from the bottomless pit*6* and go to destruction. And the dwellers on earth whose names have not been written in the book of life from the foundation of the world will marvel to see the beast, because it was and is not and is to come. **9**This calls for a mind with wisdom: the seven heads are seven mountains on which the woman is seated; **10**they are also seven kings, five of whom have fallen, one is, the other has not yet come, and when he does come he must remain only a little while. **11**As for the beast that was and is not, it is an eighth but it belongs to the seven, and it goes to destruction. **12**And the ten horns

---

1 Greek *angel of the waters* *2* Greek *blasphemed*; also verses 11, 21 *3* Or *voices, or sounds* *4* Greek *a talent in weight* *5* Greek *the witnesses to Jesus* *6* Greek *the abyss*

that you saw are ten kings who have not yet received royal power, but they are to receive authority as kings for one hour, together with the beast. [13]These are of one mind, and they hand over their power and authority to the beast. [14]They will make war on the Lamb, and the Lamb will conquer them, for he is Lord of lords and King of kings, and those with him are called and chosen and faithful."

[15]And the angel[1] said to me, "The waters that you saw, where the prostitute is seated, are peoples and multitudes and nations and languages. [16]And the ten horns that you saw, they and the beast will hate the prostitute. They will make her desolate and naked, and devour her flesh and burn her up with fire, [17]for God has put it into their hearts to carry out his purpose by being of one mind and handing over their royal power to the beast, until the words of God are fulfilled. [18]And the woman that you saw is the great city that has dominion over the kings of the earth."

The Fall of Babylon

18 After this I saw another angel coming down from heaven, having great authority, and the earth was made bright with his glory. [2]And he called out with a mighty voice,

> "Fallen, fallen is Babylon the great!
>   She has become a dwelling place for
>   demons,
>   a haunt for every unclean spirit,
>   a haunt for every unclean bird,
>   a haunt for every unclean and detestable
>   beast.
> [3] For all nations have drunk[2]
>   the wine of the passion of her sexual immo-
>   rality,
>   and the kings of the earth have committed
>   immorality with her,
>   and the merchants of the earth have grown
>   rich from the power of her luxurious
>   living."

[4]Then I heard another voice from heaven saying,

> "Come out of her, my people,
>   lest you take part in her sins,
> lest you share in her plagues;
> [5] for her sins are heaped high as heaven,
>   and God has remembered her iniquities.
> [6] Pay her back as she herself has paid back
>   others,
>   and repay her double for her deeds;
>   mix a double portion for her in the cup she
>   mixed.
> [7] As she glorified herself and lived in luxury,
>   so give her a like measure of torment and
>   mourning,
> since in her heart she says,
> 'I sit as a queen,

> I am no widow,
>   and mourning I shall never see.'
> [8] For this reason her plagues will come in a sin-
>   gle day,
>   death and mourning and famine,
>   and she will be burned up with fire;
>   for mighty is the Lord God who has judged
>   her."

[9]And the kings of the earth, who committed sexual immorality and lived in luxury with her, will weep and wail over her when they see the smoke of her burning. [10]They will stand far off, in fear of her torment, and say,

> "Alas! Alas! You great city,
>   you mighty city, Babylon!
> For in a single hour your judgment has come."

[11]And the merchants of the earth weep and mourn for her, since no one buys their cargo anymore, [12]cargo of gold, silver, jewels, pearls, fine linen, purple cloth, silk, scarlet cloth, all kinds of scented wood, all kinds of articles of ivory, all kinds of articles of costly wood, bronze, iron and marble, [13]cinnamon, spice, incense, myrrh, frankincense, wine, oil, fine flour, wheat, cattle and sheep, horses and chariots, and slaves, that is, human souls.[3]

> [14] "The fruit for which your soul longed
>   has gone from you,
>   and all your delicacies and your splendors
>   are lost to you,
>   never to be found again!"

[15]The merchants of these wares, who gained wealth from her, will stand far off, in fear of her torment, weeping and mourning aloud,

> [16] "Alas, alas, for the great city
>   that was clothed in fine linen,
>   in purple and scarlet,
>   adorned with gold,
>   with jewels, and with pearls!
> [17] For in a single hour all this wealth has been
>   laid waste."

And all shipmasters and seafaring men, sailors and all whose trade is on the sea, stood far off [18]and cried out as they saw the smoke of her burning,

> "What city was like the great city?"

[19]And they threw dust on their heads as they wept and mourned, crying out,

> "Alas, alas, for the great city
>   where all who had ships at sea
>   grew rich by her wealth!
> For in a single hour she has been laid waste.
> [20] Rejoice over her, O heaven,

---

[1]Greek he [2]Some manuscripts fallen by [3]Or and slaves, and human lives

and you saints and apostles and prophets,
for God has given judgment for you against
her!"

²¹Then a mighty angel took up a stone like a
great millstone and threw it into the sea, saying,

"So will Babylon the great city be thrown
down with violence,
and will be found no more;
²² and the sound of harpists and musicians, of
flute players and trumpeters,
will be heard in you no more,
and a craftsman of any craft
will be found in you no more,
and the sound of the mill
will be heard in you no more,
²³ and the light of a lamp
will shine in you no more,
and the voice of bridegroom and bride
will be heard in you no more,
for your merchants were the great ones of the
earth,
and all nations were deceived by your sorcery.
²⁴ And in her was found the blood of prophets
and of saints,
and of all who have been slain on earth."

Rejoicing in Heaven

19 After this I heard what seemed to be the
loud voice of a great multitude in heaven,
crying out,

"Hallelujah!
Salvation and glory and power belong to our
God,
²   for his judgments are true and just;
for he has judged the great prostitute
who corrupted the earth with her immorality,
and has avenged on her the blood of his servants."¹

³Once more they cried out,

"Hallelujah!
The smoke from her goes up forever and
ever."

⁴And the twenty-four elders and the four living
creatures fell down and worshiped God who was
seated on the throne, saying, "Amen. Hallelujah!"
⁵And from the throne came a voice saying,

"Praise our God,
all you his servants,
you who fear him,
small and great."

The Marriage Supper of the Lamb

⁶Then I heard what seemed to be the voice of a
great multitude, like the roar of many waters

and like the sound of mighty peals of thunder,
crying out,

"Hallelujah!
For the Lord our God
the Almighty reigns.
⁷ Let us rejoice and exult
and give him the glory,
for the marriage of the Lamb has come,
and his Bride has made herself ready;
⁸ it was granted her to clothe herself
with fine linen, bright and pure"—

for the fine linen is the righteous deeds of the
saints.
⁹And the angel said² to me, "Write this: Blessed
are those who are invited to the marriage supper
of the Lamb." And he said to me, "These are the
true words of God." ¹⁰Then I fell down at his feet
to worship him, but he said to me, "You must not
do that! I am a fellow servant³ with you and
your brothers who hold to the testimony of Jesus.
Worship God." For the testimony of Jesus is the
spirit of prophecy.

The Rider on a White Horse

¹¹Then I saw heaven opened, and behold, a
white horse! The one sitting on it is called Faithful and True, and in righteousness he judges
and makes war. ¹²His eyes are like a flame of
fire, and on his head are many diadems, and he
has a name written that no one knows but himself. ¹³He is clothed in a robe dipped in⁴ blood,
and the name by which he is called is The Word
of God. ¹⁴And the armies of heaven, arrayed in
fine linen, white and pure, were following him
on white horses. ¹⁵From his mouth comes a
sharp sword with which to strike down the
nations, and he will rule them with a rod of iron.
He will tread the winepress of the fury of the
wrath of God the Almighty. ¹⁶On his robe and
on his thigh he has a name written, King of
kings and Lord of lords.
¹⁷Then I saw an angel standing in the sun,
and with a loud voice he called to all the birds
that fly directly overhead, "Come, gather for the
great supper of God, ¹⁸to eat the flesh of kings,
the flesh of captains, the flesh of mighty men,
the flesh of horses and their riders, and the flesh
of all men, both free and slave,⁵ both small and
great." ¹⁹And I saw the beast and the kings of the
earth with their armies gathered to make war
against him who was sitting on the horse and
against his army. ²⁰And the beast was captured,
and with it the false prophet who in its presence⁶
had done the signs by which he deceived those
who had received the mark of the beast and
those who worshiped its image. These two were
thrown alive into the lake of fire that burns with
sulfur. ²¹And the rest were slain by the sword
that came from the mouth of him who was sit-

¹Greek bondservants; also verse 5 ²Greek he said ³Greek fellow bondservant ⁴Some manuscripts sprinkled with ⁵Greek bondservant ⁶Or on its behalf

ting on the horse, and all the birds were gorged with their flesh.

The Thousand Years

20 Then I saw an angel coming down from heaven, holding in his hand the key to the bottomless pit[1] and a great chain. 2And he seized the dragon, that ancient serpent, who is the devil and Satan, and bound him for a thousand years, 3and threw him into the pit, and shut it and sealed it over him, so that he might not deceive the nations any longer, until the thousand years were ended. After that he must be released for a little while.

4Then I saw thrones, and seated on them were those to whom the authority to judge was committed. Also I saw the souls of those who had been beheaded for the testimony of Jesus and for the word of God, and those who had not worshiped the beast or its image and had not received its mark on their foreheads or their hands. They came to life and reigned with Christ for a thousand years. 5The rest of the dead did not come to life until the thousand years were ended. This is the first resurrection. 6Blessed and holy is the one who shares in the first resurrection! Over such the second death has no power, but they will be priests of God and of Christ, and they will reign with him for a thousand years.

The Defeat of Satan

7And when the thousand years are ended, Satan will be released from his prison 8and will come out to deceive the nations that are at the four corners of the earth, Gog and Magog, to gather them for battle; their number is like the sand of the sea. 9And they marched up over the broad plain of the earth and surrounded the camp of the saints and the beloved city, but fire came down from heaven[2] and consumed them, 10and the devil who had deceived them was thrown into the lake of fire and sulfur where the beast and the false prophet were, and they will be tormented day and night forever and ever.

Judgment Before the Great White Throne

11Then I saw a great white throne and him who was seated on it. From his presence earth and sky fled away, and no place was found for them. 12And I saw the dead, great and small, standing before the throne, and books were opened. Then another book was opened, which is the book of life. And the dead were judged by what was written in the books, according to what they had done. 13And the sea gave up the dead who were in it, Death and Hades gave up the dead who were in them, and they were judged, each one of them, according to what they had done. 14Then Death and Hades were thrown into the lake of fire. This is the second death, the

lake of fire. 15And if anyone's name was not found written in the book of life, he was thrown into the lake of fire.

The New Heaven and the New Earth

21 Then I saw a new heaven and a new earth, for the first heaven and the first earth had passed away, and the sea was no more. 2And I saw the holy city, new Jerusalem, coming down out of heaven from God, prepared as a bride adorned for her husband. 3And I heard a loud voice from the throne saying, "Behold, the dwelling place[3] of God is with man. He will dwell with them, and they will be his people,[4] and God himself will be with them as their God.[5] 4He will wipe away every tear from their eyes, and death shall be no more, neither shall there be mourning, nor crying, nor pain anymore, for the former things have passed away."

5And he who was seated on the throne said, "Behold, I am making all things new." Also he said, "Write this down, for these words are trustworthy and true." 6And he said to me, "It is done! I am the Alpha and the Omega, the beginning and the end. To the thirsty I will give from the spring of the water of life without payment. 7The one who conquers will have this heritage, and I will be his God and he will be my son. 8But as for the cowardly, the faithless, the detestable, as for murderers, the sexually immoral, sorcerers, idolaters, and all liars, their portion will be in the lake that burns with fire and sulfur, which is the second death."

The New Jerusalem

9Then came one of the seven angels who had the seven bowls full of the seven last plagues and spoke to me, saying, "Come, I will show you the Bride, the wife of the Lamb." 10And he carried me away in the Spirit to a great, high mountain, and showed me the holy city Jerusalem coming down out of heaven from God, 11having the glory of God, its radiance like a most rare jewel, like a jasper, clear as crystal. 12It had a great, high wall, with twelve gates, and at the gates twelve angels, and on the gates the names of the twelve tribes of the sons of Israel were inscribed— 13on the east three gates, on the north three gates, on the south three gates, and on the west three gates. 14And the wall of the city had twelve foundations, and on them were the twelve names of the twelve apostles of the Lamb.

15And the one who spoke with me had a measuring rod of gold to measure the city and its gates and walls. 16The city lies foursquare, its length the same as its width. And he measured the city with his rod, 12,000 stadia.[6] Its length and width and height are equal. 17He also measured its wall, 144 cubits[7] by human measure-

---

[1] Greek the abyss; also verse 3 [2] Some manuscripts from God, out of heaven, or out of heaven from God [3] Or tabernacle [4] Some manuscripts peoples
[5] Some manuscripts omit as their God [6] About 1,380 miles; a stadion was about 607 feet or 185 meters [7] A cubit was about 18 inches or 45 centimeters

ment, which is also an angel's measurement. [18]The wall was built of jasper, while the city was pure gold, clear as glass. [19]The foundations of the wall of the city were adorned with every kind of jewel. The first was jasper, the second sapphire, the third agate, the fourth emerald, [20]the fifth onyx, the sixth carnelian, the seventh chrysolite, the eighth beryl, the ninth topaz, the tenth chrysoprase, the eleventh jacinth, the twelfth amethyst. [21]And the twelve gates were twelve pearls, each of the gates made of a single pearl, and the street of the city was pure gold, transparent as glass.

[22]And I saw no temple in the city, for its temple is the Lord God the Almighty and the Lamb. [23]And the city has no need of sun or moon to shine on it, for the glory of God gives it light, and its lamp is the Lamb. [24]By its light will the nations walk, and the kings of the earth will bring their glory into it, [25]and its gates will never be shut by day—and there will be no night there. [26]They will bring into it the glory and the honor of the nations. [27]But nothing unclean will ever enter it, nor anyone who does what is detestable or false, but only those who are written in the Lamb's book of life.

The River of Life

22 Then the angel[1] showed me the river of the water of life, bright as crystal, flowing from the throne of God and of the Lamb [2]through the middle of the street of the city; also, on either side of the river, the tree of life[2] with its twelve kinds of fruit, yielding its fruit each month. The leaves of the tree were for the healing of the nations. [3]No longer will there be anything accursed, but the throne of God and of the Lamb will be in it, and his servants[3] will worship him. [4]They will see his face, and his name will be on their foreheads. [5]And night will be no more. They will need no light of lamp or sun, for the Lord God will be their light, and they will reign forever and ever.

Jesus Is Coming

[6]And he said to me, "These words are trustworthy and true. And the Lord, the God of the spirits of the prophets, has sent his angel to show his servants what must soon take place."

[7]"And behold, I am coming soon. Blessed is the one who keeps the words of the prophecy of this book."

[8]I, John, am the one who heard and saw these things. And when I heard and saw them, I fell down to worship at the feet of the angel who showed them to me, [9]but he said to me, "You must not do that! I am a fellow servant[4] with you and your brothers the prophets, and with those who keep the words of this book. Worship God."

[10]And he said to me, "Do not seal up the words of the prophecy of this book, for the time is near. [11]Let the evildoer still do evil, and the filthy still be filthy, and the righteous still do right, and the holy still be holy."

[12]"Behold, I am coming soon, bringing my recompense with me, to repay everyone for what he has done. [13]I am the Alpha and the Omega, the first and the last, the beginning and the end."

[14]Blessed are those who wash their robes,[5] so that they may have the right to the tree of life and that they may enter the city by the gates. [15]Outside are the dogs and sorcerers and the sexually immoral and murderers and idolaters, and everyone who loves and practices falsehood.

[16]"I, Jesus, have sent my angel to testify to you about these things for the churches. I am the root and the descendant of David, the bright morning star."

[17]The Spirit and the Bride say, "Come." And let the one who hears say, "Come." And let the one who is thirsty come; let the one who desires take the water of life without price.

[18]I warn everyone who hears the words of the prophecy of this book: if anyone adds to them, God will add to him the plagues described in this book, [19]and if anyone takes away from the words of the book of this prophecy, God will take away his share in the tree of life and in the holy city, which are described in this book.

[20]He who testifies to these things says, "Surely I am coming soon." Amen. Come, Lord Jesus!

[21]The grace of the Lord Jesus be with all.[6] Amen.

---

[1] Greek he [2] Or the Lamb. In the midst of the street of the city, and on either side of the river, was the tree of life [3] Greek bondservants; also verse 6 [4] Greek fellow bondservant [5] Some manuscripts do his commandments [6] Some manuscripts all the saints

GOD'S PLAN TO SAVE YOU

From the first chapters of Genesis through the closing scenes in Revelation, the Bible is the book of God's salvation. From start to finish, its one unifying theme is that of grace and forgiveness for sinners through God's redeeming work in Jesus Christ. Whatever else you gain through the reading of the Bible, it would be tragic if you missed the heart of its message for you—God's gracious provision of Jesus Christ as the atonement for sin.

IN THE BEGINNING

When God created the heavens and the earth, His work was perfect and pure. God looked upon all He had created and judged it to be "very good" (Genesis 1:31). He took great pleasure in what He made, and the culmination of His creation came with Adam and Eve. They were made in the very image of God, which made them capable of having fellowship with God and bringing glory to His name (Genesis 1:27).

In the Garden of Eden, however, through deception and disobedience Adam and Eve sinned against God, causing a break in their relationship with Him. Sin is real, and sin is deadly. The guilt that resulted from their disobedience caused Adam and Eve to hide from God and to attempt to cover their personal shame. Because they had disobeyed God's command, they were now flawed and shameful in God's presence.

Adam deliberately chose a path of self-will and rebellion, which brought sin and death—including spiritual death—into the world. ". . . sin came into the world through one man, and death through sin, and so death spread to all men because all sinned" (Romans 5:12)—the whole human race is affected by Adam's sin.

To cover the shame and nakedness of Adam and Eve, the Lord made coats from an animal's skin for them to wear (Genesis 3:21). God thus made the first sacrifice, and it followed the clear promise of a Redeemer when God pronounced these words of judgment upon the serpent, or Satan: "I will put enmity between you and the woman, and between your offspring and her offspring; he shall bruise your head, and you shall bruise his heel" (Genesis 3:15). This prophetic word speaks of Jesus Christ and His death on the cross of Calvary.

THE STORY OF REDEMPTION

So the story of redemption and sacrifice begins, and it is repeated throughout the Word of God, culminating in the coming of Jesus Christ and His sacrifice on our behalf. We discover through the Bible that a personal relationship with God is not dependent on good works that we do, or on church membership, or even on living a highly moral life. Rather, God's amazing grace is the fountain through which redemption flows to us.

Separated from God by sin and guilt, we all face two primary spiritual needs. First, we need to be restored to fellowship with God. We are truly guilty before God, and somehow we must find forgiveness. We must face the problem of our sin, and there is no answer to this need within ourselves. The only answer is the Lord Jesus Christ.

Second, we need power to change our lives. Our sin reveals the spiritual depravity of our heart—the selfishness, the lust, the greed, the pride, and the anger that are so destructive. "The heart," God says, "is deceitful above all things, and desperately sick" (Jeremiah 17:9). If we are going to be changed, something must be done in our hearts to turn our lives around. Jesus taught that "unless one is born again he cannot see the kingdom of God" (John 3:3). Only the blood of Jesus can take away the guilt of our sin, and only the Holy Spirit can come into our hearts and make us new people.

REDEMPTION THROUGH CHRIST

Redemption often involves the concept of purchasing something back that has been lost, by the payment of a ransom. It can mean a deliverance from some sort of confinement; such is the case with the deliverance of the children of Israel from their bondage to slavery in Egypt (Exodus 14:29-30; 15:2).

There are many passages in the New Testament that represent Christ's sufferings as a ransom or price, and the result secured is a purchase or redemption (Acts 20:28; 1 Corinthians 6:19-20; Galatians 3:13; 4:4-5; Ephesians 1:7; Colossians 1:14; 1 Timothy 2:5-6; Titus 2:14; Hebrews 9:12; 1 Peter 1:18-19; Revelation 5:9). The idea running through all these texts is that of a payment made for our redemption. Jesus paid the penalty for our sin and redeemed us.

The penalty for our sin and rebellion is death; Jesus stepped in and laid down His life and took the penalty we deserve. The debt against us is not viewed as simply cancelled but as fully paid. Both the Old and New Testament proclaim salvation as an accomplished fact. Christ's blood or life, which He surrendered for us, is the "ransom" by which we are freed from sin. "Blood" is mentioned 460 times in the Bible. Fourteen times in the New Testament, Jesus spoke of His own blood. Why? Because by the shedding of His blood on the cross, He accomplished the salvation of everyone who believes.

THE EXTRAORDINARY GOOD NEWS OF ETERNAL LIFE

The Gospel of John tells the redemptive story of what Jesus Christ did on our behalf. Summarizing his Gospel, John says, "these are written so that you may believe that Jesus is the Christ, the Son of God, and that by believing you may have life in his name" (20:31). Read on as we examine what the apostle John has to say in his Gospel about the eternal life we receive through Jesus Christ.

THE SON OF GOD

John wants to show us who Jesus really is: "In the beginning was the Word, and the Word was with God, and the Word was God. . . . And the Word became flesh and dwelt among us" (John 1:1, 14). Jesus, during His life on earth, was God in human form! And just in case John's introduction isn't clear enough, a few sentences later he quotes John the Baptist, who says, "I have seen and have borne witness that this is the Son of God" (1:34). Throughout the book, John gives evidences of Jesus' deity—that Jesus performed many miracles (2:1-11; 4:46-54; 5:1-17; 6:1-13, 16-21; 9:1-7; 11:38-44), and that He fulfilled prophecies written about Him centuries before (2:13-22; 3:14; 5:46; 12:14-16).

GOD'S LOVE

But why would Jesus, who is God, leave heaven to live on earth as a human? Jesus Himself tells us why: "For God so loved the world, that he gave his only Son, that whoever believes in him should not perish but have eternal life. For God did not send his Son into the world to condemn the world, but in order that the world might be saved through him" (John 3:16-17). God saw us as we were, dead in our sin. That's why Jesus came. God is a forgiving God whose love and patience call all to repent of their sins.

WHY DO WE NEED TO BE SAVED?

So why do we need to be saved? Jesus said, "Truly, truly, I say to you, everyone who commits sin is a slave to sin" (John 8:34). If we are honest with ourselves, we cannot deny that from the moment of our birth we have done wrong things—things that make us guilty before God and deserving of His judgment. The Bible calls these wrong things sin, and sin separates us from God. And because we are separated from God, we face the awful prospect of "the wrath of God" (3:36), which is eternal.

JESUS IS THE ONLY WAY

Can anyone save us from God's wrath and assure us of heaven? Some people believe they can get to heaven by doing good works, or by following the teachings of a religion, or even by giving money to churches or charities. But Jesus clearly said that none of these things would save us: "I am the way, and the truth, and the life. No one comes to the Father except through me" (John 14:6). He did not say that He simply knew the way to heaven; *Jesus said He is the only way to heaven.* No human effort can give us eternal life. Christ, and Christ alone, is the one and only Redeemer.

In fact, the only "work" that can save us is the "work" of believing in what Jesus has done to accomplish our salvation: "This is the work of God, that you believe in him whom he has sent" (John 6:29). And to those who so believe, the promise of God stands firm: ". . . to all who did receive him, who believed in his name, he gave the right to become children of God" (1:12).

HOW DOES JESUS SAVE US?

John the Baptist calls Jesus the "Lamb of God, who takes away the sin of the world" (John 1:29). Jesus came into this world knowing what it would cost Him, and He explains that salvation comes through His death on the cross as the perfect and sufficient sacrifice for our sins (3:14-15). He bore in His pure being the fullness of sin, that God might forgive sinners and make them pure. And the price of Christ's bearing those sins was death. The gates of salvation are open wide to all who accept His invitation to enter by faith.

Chapters 18–19 describe Jesus' death, and then chapter 20 describes His glorious triumph over death as He rose from the dead. Jesus' resurrection means that He can give eternal life to all who believe in Him. "I am the resurrection and the life. Whoever believes in me, though he die, yet shall he live, and everyone who lives and believes in me shall never die" (John 11:25-26).

DO YOU BELIEVE?

That last verse (John 11:26) actually ends with Jesus asking, "Do you believe this?" It is a question that every person must answer: Do you believe that Jesus Christ is the Son of God? Is Jesus the object of your faith? Not faith in ritual, not faith in sacrifices, not faith in morals, not faith in yourself. Do you believe that Jesus died on the cross to free you from the guilt and judgment of sin? Do you believe that He rose from the grave, breaking the power of death and making a way for you to have eternal life in heaven? If so, you may express your faith in Him by praying this prayer:

> *Heavenly Father, I believe that Jesus Christ is Your Son, and that He died on the cross to save me from my sin. I believe that He rose again to life, and that He invites me to live forever with Him in heaven as part of Your family. Because of what Jesus has done, I ask You to forgive me of my sin and give me eternal life. I invite You to come into my heart and life. I want to trust Jesus as my Savior and follow Him as my Lord. Help me to live in a way that pleases and honors You. Amen.*

GROWING IN CHRIST

Once you have received the gift of eternal life and have been made a new creation (2 Corinthians 5:17), you will want to grow in your knowledge of Jesus and your obedience to Him. Jesus' teaching about how to live for God can be summed up in three simple instructions.

Read the Bible. Jesus said, "Whoever has my commandments and keeps them, he it is who loves me" (John 14:21). One way to show your love for God is to read the Bible and to live out your new life on the basis of its teaching. Read the Bible daily to learn how to live a life that honors God and gives testimony to others that Jesus has made a difference in your life.

Pray. Communication with God through prayer keeps your focus on eternal things. If you are truly following Jesus, your desires will be for God's glory and for His kingdom, the church. Jesus promised, "If you abide in me, and my words abide in you, ask whatever you wish, and it will be done for you" (John 15:7).

Seek Christian Fellowship. Meeting regularly with Christian brothers and sisters allows you to follow Jesus' example of love and to fulfill His command to "love one another . . . just as I have loved you" (John 13:34). Just as Jesus surrounded Himself daily with His disciples and followers, find a Bible-believing church where you can meet with other Christians. There you will find joy and encouragement in the fellowship of God's people.

ASSURANCE

If you have accepted Christ as your Savior, you may be wondering, *What happens if I sin after I'm saved?* All Christians sin from time to time. But the good news is that Jesus' death paid for all your sin, both past and future. If you humbly admit your sin to God, the Bible promises that God will forgive you and cleanse you from all your sin. Pray for God's help to keep you from falling into sin again. Jesus assures us that "whoever comes to me I will never cast out" (John 6:37). Your salvation is sure because Christ's sacrifice of Himself on the cross is greater than any sin.

You might also wonder, *What happens when I don't feel close to God? Am I still saved?* When a person has accepted the gift of salvation, Jesus describes His relationship with them as being like the relationship between a shepherd and his sheep: "My sheep hear my voice, and I know them, and they follow me. I give them eternal life, and they will never perish, and no one will snatch them out of my hand" (John 10:27-28). Salvation is not based on your feelings but on the fact that God has welcomed you into His family through faith in Jesus. Nothing on earth or in heaven can break that bond—*nothing*.

If you feel far away from God, examine your life to see if there is unconfessed sin standing between you and God. Continue to read the Bible and pray regularly, filling your mind with God's truth and goodness. Talk with other Christians and learn from their experiences. You will grow closer to God as your knowledge and experience of Him grows. Rest assured in the promise that no one can separate you from His love (Romans 8:35-39).

SIX-MONTH
NEW TESTATMENT READING PLAN

The following plan guides you through the entire New Testament over a six-month span. You don't have to wait until January 1; you can start on any day of the year and simply complete one reading each day. The numbers after the book refer to the chapters, which are indicated in each book by a large bold font.

Date	Reading
January 1	Matthew 1–2
January 2	Matthew 3–4
January 3	Matthew 5
January 4	Matthew 6
January 5	Matthew 7
January 6	Matthew 8
January 7	Matthew 9
January 8	Matthew 10
January 9	Matthew 11
January 10	Matthew 12
January 11	Matthew 13
January 12	Matthew 14
January 13	Matthew 15
January 14	Matthew 16–17
January 15	Matthew 18
January 16	Matthew 19
January 17	Matthew 20
January 18	Matthew 21
January 19	Matthew 22
January 20	Matthew 23
January 21	Matthew 24
January 22	Matthew 25
January 23	Matthew 26
January 24	Matthew 27
January 25	Matthew 28—Mark 1
January 26	Mark 2
January 27	Mark 3
January 28	Mark 4
January 29	Mark 5
January 30	Mark 6
January 31	Mark 7
February 1	Mark 8
February 2	Mark 9
February 3	Mark 10
February 4	Mark 11
February 5	Mark 12
February 6	Mark 13
February 7	Mark 14

Date	Reading
February 8	Mark 15
February 9	Mark 16
February 10	Luke 1
February 11	Luke 2
February 12	Luke 3
February 13	Luke 4
February 14	Luke 5
February 15	Luke 6
February 16	Luke 7
February 17	Luke 8
February 18	Luke 9
February 19	Luke 10
February 20	Luke 11
February 21	Luke 12
February 22	Luke 13
February 23	Luke 14
February 24	Luke 15
February 25	Luke 16
February 26	Luke 17
February 27	Luke 18
February 28	Luke 19
March 1	Luke 20
March 2	Luke 21
March 3	Luke 22
March 4	Luke 23
March 5	Luke 24
March 6	John 1
March 7	John 2
March 8	John 3
March 9	John 4
March 10	John 5
March 11	John 6
March 12	John 7
March 13	John 8
March 14	John 9
March 15	John 10
March 16	John 11
March 17	John 12
March 18	John 13
March 19	John 14
March 20	John 15
March 21	John 16
March 22	John 17
March 23	John 18
March 24	John 19
March 25	John 20
March 26	John 21—Acts 1
March 27	Acts 2

Date	Reading
March 28	Acts 3
March 29	Acts 4
March 30	Acts 5
March 31	Acts 6
April 1	Acts 7
April 2	Acts 8
April 3	Acts 9
April 4	Acts 10
April 5	Acts 11
April 6	Acts 12
April 7	Acts 13
April 8	Acts 14
April 9	Acts 15
April 10	Acts 16
April 11	Acts 17
April 12	Acts 18
April 13	Acts 19
April 14	Acts 20
April 15	Acts 21
April 16	Acts 22
April 17	Acts 23
April 18	Acts 24–25
April 19	Acts 26
April 20	Acts 27
April 21	Acts 28
April 22	Romans 1
April 23	Romans 2
April 24	Romans 3–4
April 25	Romans 5–6
April 26	Romans 7
April 27	Romans 8
April 28	Romans 9–10
April 29	Romans 11
April 30	Romans 12–13
May 1	Romans 14–15
May 2	Romans 16—1 Corinthians 1
May 3	1 Corinthians 2–3
May 4	1 Corinthians 4–5
May 5	1 Corinthians 6–7
May 6	1 Corinthians 8–9
May 7	1 Corinthians 10
May 8	1 Corinthians 11
May 9	1 Corinthians 12–13
May 10	1 Corinthians 14
May 11	1 Corinthians 15
May 12	1 Corinthians 16—2 Corinthians 1
May 13	2 Corinthians 2–4
May 14	2 Corinthians 5–6

Date	Reading
May 15	2 Corinthians 7–8
May 16	2 Corinthians 9–10
May 17	2 Corinthians 11–12
May 18	2 Corinthians 13—Galatians 1
May 19	Galatians 2–3
May 20	Galatians 4–5
May 21	Galatians 6—Ephesians 1
May 22	Ephesians 2–3
May 23	Ephesians 4
May 24	Ephesians 5
May 25	Ephesians 6—Philippians 1
May 26	Philippians 2–3
May 27	Philippians 4—Colossians 1
May 28	Colossians 2–3
May 29	Colossians 4—1 Thessalonians 2
May 30	1 Thessalonians 3–4
May 31	1 Thessalonians 5—2 Thessalonians 1
June 1	2 Thessalonians 2–3
June 2	1 Timothy 1–3
June 3	1 Timothy 4–5
June 4	1 Timothy 6—2 Timothy 1
June 5	2 Timothy 2–3
June 6	2 Timothy 4—Titus 2
June 7	Titus 3—Philemon
June 8	Hebrews 1–3
June 9	Hebrews 4–6
June 10	Hebrews 7–8
June 11	Hebrews 9
June 12	Hebrews 10
June 13	Hebrews 11
June 14	Hebrews 12–13
June 15	James 1–2
June 16	James 3–5
June 17	1 Peter 1–2
June 18	1 Peter 3–4
June 19	1 Peter 5—2 Peter 2
June 20	2 Peter 3—1 John 2
June 21	1 John 3–4
June 22	1 John 5—3 John
June 23	Jude 1—Revelation 1
June 24	Revelation 2–3
June 25	Revelation 4–6
June 26	Revelation 7–9
June 27	Revelation 10–12
June 28	Revelation 13–15
June 29	Revelation 16–17
June 30	Revelation 18–20
July 1	Revelation 21–22

ABOUT THE ESV BIBLE

THE BIBLE

"This Book [is] the most valuable thing that this world affords. Here is Wisdom; this is the royal Law; these are the lively Oracles of God." With these words the Moderator of the Church of Scotland hands a Bible to the new monarch in Britain's coronation service. These words echo the King James Bible translators, who wrote in 1611: "God's sacred Word . . . is that inestimable treasure that excelleth all the riches of the earth." This assessment of the Bible is the motivating force behind the publication of the English Standard Version.

TRANSLATION LEGACY

The English Standard Version (ESV) stands in the classic mainstream of English Bible translations over the past half-millennium. The fountainhead of that stream was William Tyndale's New Testament of 1526; marking its course were the King James Version of 1611 (KJV), the English Revised Version of 1885 (RV), the American Standard Version of 1901 (ASV), and the Revised Standard Version of 1952 and 1971 (RSV). In that stream, faithfulness to the text and vigorous pursuit of accuracy were combined with simplicity, beauty, and dignity of expression. Our goal has been to carry forward this legacy for a new century.

To this end each word and phrase in the ESV has been carefully weighed against the original Hebrew, Aramaic, and Greek, to ensure the fullest accuracy and clarity and to avoid under-translating or overlooking any nuance of the original text. The words and phrases themselves grow out of the Tyndale–King James legacy, and most recently out of the RSV, with the 1971 RSV text providing the starting point for our work. Archaic language has been brought to current usage and significant corrections have been made in the translation of key texts. But throughout, our goal has been to retain the depth of meaning and enduring language that have made their indelible mark on the English-speaking world and have defined the life and doctrine of the church over the last four centuries.

TRANSLATION PHILOSOPHY

The ESV is an "essentially literal" translation that seeks as far as possible to capture the precise wording of the original text and the personal style of each Bible writer. As such, its emphasis is on "word-for-word" correspondence, at the same time taking into account differences of grammar, syntax, and idiom between current literary English and the original languages. Thus it seeks to be transparent to the original text, letting the reader see as directly as possible the structure and meaning of the original.

In contrast to the ESV, some Bible versions have followed a "thought-for-thought" rather than "word-for-word" translation philosophy, emphasizing "dynamic equivalence" rather than the "essentially literal" meaning of the original. A "thought-for-thought" translation is of necessity more inclined to reflect the interpretive opinions of the translator and the influences of contemporary culture.

Every translation is at many points a trade-off between literal precision and readability, between "formal equivalence" in expression and "functional equivalence" in communication, and the ESV is no exception. Within this framework we have sought to be "as literal as possible" while maintaining clarity of expression and literary excellence. Therefore, to the extent that plain English permits and the meaning in each case allows, we have sought to use the same English word for important recurring words in the original; and, as far as grammar and syntax allow, we have rendered Old Testament passages cited in the New in ways that show their correspondence. Thus in each of these areas, as well as throughout the Bible as a whole, we have sought to capture the echoes and overtones of meaning that are so abundantly present in the original texts.

As an essentially literal translation, then, the ESV seeks to carry over every possible nuance of meaning in the original words of Scripture into our own language. As such, it is ideally suited for in-depth study of the Bible. Indeed, with its emphasis on literary excellence, the ESV is equally suited for public reading and preaching, for private reading and reflection, for both academic and devotional study, and for Scripture memorization.

TRANSLATION STYLE

The ESV also carries forward classic translation principles in its literary style. Accordingly it retains theological terminology—words such as grace, faith, justification, sanctification, redemption, regeneration, reconciliation, propitiation—because of their central importance for Christian doctrine and also because the underlying Greek words were already becoming key words and technical terms in New Testament times.

The ESV lets the stylistic variety of the biblical writers fully express itself—from the exalted prose that opens Genesis, to the flowing narratives of the historical books, to the rich metaphors and dramatic imagery of the poetic books, to the ringing rhetorical indictments in the prophetic books, to the smooth elegance of Luke, to the profound simplicities of John, and the closely reasoned logic of Paul.

In punctuating, paragraphing, dividing long sentences, and rendering connectives, the ESV follows the path that seems to make the ongoing flow of thought clearest in English. The biblical languages regularly connect sentences by frequent repetition of words such as "and," "but," and "for," in a way that goes beyond the conventions of literary English. Effective translation, however, requires that these links in the original be reproduced so that the flow of the argument will be transparent to the reader. We have therefore normally translated these connectives, though occasionally we have varied the rendering by using alternatives (such as "also," "however," "now," "so," "then," or "thus") when they better capture the sense in specific instances.

In the area of gender language, the goal of the ESV is to render literally what is in the original. For example, "anyone" replaces "any man" where there is no word corresponding to "man" in the original languages, and "people" rather than "men" is regularly used where the original languages refer to both men and women. But the words "man" and "men" are retained where a male meaning component is part of the original Greek or Hebrew. Likewise, the word "man" has been retained where the original text intends to convey a clear contrast between "God" on the one hand and "man" on the other hand, with "man" being used in the collective sense of the whole human race (see Luke 2:52). Similarly, the English word "brothers" (translating the Greek word *adelphoi*) is retained as an important familial form of address between fellow-Jews and fellow-Christians in the first century. A recurring note is included to indicate that the term "brothers" (*adelphoi*) was often used in Greek to refer to both men and women, and to indicate the specific instances in the text where this is the case. In addition, the English word "sons" (translating the Greek word *huioi*) is retained in specific instances because the underlying Greek term usually includes a male meaning component and it was used as a legal term in the adoption and inheritance laws of first-century Rome. As used by the apostle Paul, this term refers to the status of all Christians, both men and women, who, having been adopted into God's family, now enjoy all the privileges, obligations, and inheritance rights of God's children.

The inclusive use of the generic "he" has also regularly been retained, because this is consistent with similar usage in the original languages and because an essentially literal translation would be impossible without it. Similarly, where God and man are compared or contrasted in the original, the ESV retains the generic use of "man" as the clearest way to express the contrast within the framework of essentially literal translation.

In each case the objective has been transparency to the original text, allowing the reader to understand the original on its own terms rather than on the terms of our present-day culture.

THE TRANSLATION OF SPECIALIZED TERMS

In the translation of biblical terms referring to God, the ESV takes great care to convey the specific nuances of meaning of the original Hebrew and Greek terms. First, concerning terms that refer to God in the Old Testament: God, the Maker of heaven and earth, introduced himself to the people of Israel with the special, personal name, whose consonants are YHWH (see Exodus 3:14-15). Scholars call this the "Tetragrammaton," a Greek term referring to the four Hebrew letters YHWH. The exact pronunciation of YHWH is uncertain, because the Jewish people considered the personal name of God to be so holy that it should never be spoken aloud. Instead of reading the word YHWH, they would normally read the Hebrew word *adonai* ("Lord"), and the ancient translations into Greek, Syriac, and Aramaic also followed suit. When the vowels of the word *adonai* are placed with the consonants of YHWH, this results in the familiar word *Jehovah* that was used in some earlier English Bible translations. As is common among English translations today, the ESV usually renders the personal name of God (YHWH) with the word LORD (printed in small capitals). An exception to this is when the Hebrew word *adonai* appears together with YHWH, in which case the two words are rendered together as "the Lord [in lower case] GOD [in small capitals]." In contrast to the personal name for God (YHWH), the more general name for God in Old Testament Hebrew is *'elohim* and its related forms of *'el* or *'eloah*, all of which are normally translated "God" (in lower case letters). The use of these different ways to translate the Hebrew words for God is especially beneficial to the English reader, enabling the reader to see and understand the different ways that the *personal* name and the *general* name for God are both used to refer to the *One True God* of the Old Testament.

Second, in the New Testament, the Greek word *Christos* has been translated consistently as "Christ." Although the term originally meant "anointed," among Jews in New Testament times the term came to designate the Messiah, the great Savior that God had promised to raise up. In other New Testament contexts, however, especially among Gentiles, *Christos* ("Christ") was on its way to becoming a proper name. It is important, therefore, to keep the context in mind in understanding the various ways that *Christos* ("Christ") is used in the New Testament. At the same time, in accord with its "essentially literal" translation philosophy, the ESV has retained consistency and concordance in the translation of *Christos* ("Christ") throughout the New Testament.

A third specialized term, the word "behold," usually has been retained as the most common translation for the Hebrew word *hinneh* and the Greek word *idou*. Both of these words mean something like "Pay careful attention to what follows! This is important!" Other than the word "behold," there is no single word in English that fits well in most contexts. Although "Look!" and "See!" and "Listen!" would be workable in some contexts, in many others these words lack sufficient weight and dignity. Given the principles of "essentially literal" translation, it is important not to leave *hinneh* and *idou* completely untranslated, and so to lose the intended emphasis in the original languages. The older and more formal word "behold" has usually been retained, therefore, as the best available option for conveying the original sense of meaning.

TEXTUAL BASIS

The ESV is based on the Masoretic text of the Hebrew Bible as found in *Biblia Hebraica Stuttgartensia* (2nd ed., 1983), and on the Greek text in the 1993 editions of the *Greek New Testament* (4th corrected ed.), published by the United Bible Societies (UBS), and *Novum Testamentum Graece* (27th ed.), edited by Nestle and Aland. The currently renewed respect among Old Testament scholars for the Masoretic text is reflected in the ESV's attempt, wherever possible, to translate difficult Hebrew passages as they stand in the Masoretic text rather than resorting to emendations or to finding an alternative reading in the ancient versions. In exceptional, difficult cases, the Dead Sea Scrolls, the Septuagint, the Samaritan Pentateuch, the Syriac Peshitta, the Latin Vulgate, and other sources were consulted to shed possible light on the text, or, if necessary, to support a divergence from the Masoretic text. Similarly, in a few difficult cases in the New Testament, the ESV has followed a Greek text different from the text given preference in the UBS/Nestle-Aland 27th edition. In this regard the footnotes that accompany the ESV text are an integral part of the ESV translation, informing the reader of textual variations and difficulties and showing how these have been resolved by the ESV translation team. In addition to this, the footnotes indicate significant alternative readings and occasionally provide an explanation for technical terms or for a difficult reading in the text. Throughout, the translation team has benefited greatly from the massive textual resources that have become readily available recently, from new insights into biblical laws and culture, and from current advances in Hebrew and Greek lexicography and grammatical understanding.

PUBLISHING TEAM

The ESV publishing team includes more than a hundred people. The fourteen-member Translation Oversight Committee has benefited from the work of fifty biblical experts serving as Translation Review Scholars and from the comments of the more than fifty members of the Advisory Council, all of which has been carried out under the auspices of the Good News Publishers Board of Directors. This hundred-member team, which shares a common commitment to the truth of God's Word and to historic Christian orthodoxy, is international in scope and includes leaders in many denominations.

TO GOD'S HONOR AND PRAISE

We know that no Bible translation is perfect or final; but we also know that God uses imperfect and inadequate things to His honor and praise. So to our triune God and to His people we offer what we have done, with our prayers that it may prove useful, with gratitude for much help given, and with ongoing wonder that our God should ever have entrusted to us so momentous a task.

Soli Deo Gloria!—To God alone be the glory!

*The Translation Oversight Committee**

---

*A complete list of the Translation Oversight Committee, the Translation Review Scholars, and the Advisory Council is available upon request from Crossway Bibles, a publishing ministry of Good News Publishers.

FEATURES

This edition of the English Standard Version of the Bible includes a number of additional features to encourage the reading and study of the Bible:

SECTION HEADINGS

Section headings have been included throughout the text. While the headings are not part of the Bible text itself, they have been provided to help identify and locate important themes and topics throughout the Bible.

TEXTUAL FOOTNOTES

Several kinds of footnotes related to the ESV text are provided throughout the ESV Bible. These footnotes appear at the bottom of the page and are indicated in the ESV text by a superscript *number* that *follows* the word or phrase to which the footnote applies (e.g., "Isaac²"). Superscript *letters* that *precede* a word indicate cross-references (see explanation below). The footnotes included in the ESV Bible are an integral part of the text and provide important information concerning the understanding and translation of the text.

CROSS-REFERENCE FOOTNOTES

In addition to the numeric (textual) footnotes, the New Testament includes two kinds of cross-reference notes. These are identified *alphabetically* and follow the numeric notes at the bottom of each page. These include (1) *direct quotations from the Old Testament* (indirect quotations and allusions are not included), and (2) *parallel passages in the four Gospels*. These cross-references are included to help the reader understand the relationship of the New Testament to the Old Testament, and the harmony of the Gospels in the New Testament.

For more information on the ESV Bible
or to purchase a complete edition,
visit your local book store or visit www.esv.org